Lecture Notes in Computer Science $\qquad$ 9752

Commenced Publication in 1973
Founding and Former Series Editors:
Gerhard Goos, Juris Hartmanis, and Jan van Leeuwen

Editorial Board

More information about this series at http://www.springer.com/series/7409

Fiona Fui-Hoon Nah · Chuan-Hoo Tan (Eds.)

HCI in Business, Government, and Organizations: Information Systems

Third International Conference, HCIBGO 2016
Held as Part of HCI International 2016
Toronto, Canada, July 17–22, 2016
Proceedings, Part II

 Springer

Editors
Fiona Fui-Hoon Nah
Missouri University of Science and
  Technology
Rolla, MO
USA

Chuan-Hoo Tan
National University of Singapore
Singapore
Singapore

ISSN 0302-9743   ISSN 1611-3349 (electronic)
Lecture Notes in Computer Science
ISBN 978-3-319-39398-8   ISBN 978-3-319-39399-5 (eBook)
DOI 10.1007/978-3-319-39399-5

Library of Congress Control Number: 2016939936

LNCS Sublibrary: SL3 – Information Systems and Applications, incl. Internet/Web, and HCI

This Springer imprint is published by Springer Nature
The registered company is Springer International Publishing AG Switzerland

Foreword

The 18th International Conference on Human-Computer Interaction, HCI International 2016, was held in Toronto, Canada, during July 17–22, 2016. The event incorporated the 15 conferences/thematic areas listed on the following page.

A total of 4,354 individuals from academia, research institutes, industry, and governmental agencies from 74 countries submitted contributions, and 1,287 papers and 186 posters have been included in the proceedings. These papers address the latest research and development efforts and highlight the human aspects of the design and use of computing systems. The papers thoroughly cover the entire field of human-computer interaction, addressing major advances in knowledge and effective use of computers in a variety of application areas. The volumes constituting the full 27-volume set of the conference proceedings are listed on pages IX and X.

I would like to thank the program board chairs and the members of the program boards of all thematic areas and affiliated conferences for their contribution to the highest scientific quality and the overall success of the HCI International 2016 conference.

This conference would not have been possible without the continuous and unwavering support and advice of the founder, Conference General Chair Emeritus and Conference Scientific Advisor Prof. Gavriel Salvendy. For his outstanding efforts, I would like to express my appreciation to the communications chair and editor of *HCI International News*, Dr. Abbas Moallem.

April 2016   Constantine Stephanidis

HCI International 2016 Thematic Areas and Affiliated Conferences

Thematic areas:

- Human-Computer Interaction (HCI 2016)
- Human Interface and the Management of Information (HIMI 2016)

Affiliated conferences:

- 13th International Conference on Engineering Psychology and Cognitive Ergonomics (EPCE 2016)
- 10th International Conference on Universal Access in Human-Computer Interaction (UAHCI 2016)
- 8th International Conference on Virtual, Augmented and Mixed Reality (VAMR 2016)
- 8th International Conference on Cross-Cultural Design (CCD 2016)
- 8th International Conference on Social Computing and Social Media (SCSM 2016)
- 10th International Conference on Augmented Cognition (AC 2016)
- 7th International Conference on Digital Human Modeling and Applications in Health, Safety, Ergonomics and Risk Management (DHM 2016)
- 5th International Conference on Design, User Experience and Usability (DUXU 2016)
- 4th International Conference on Distributed, Ambient and Pervasive Interactions (DAPI 2016)
- 4th International Conference on Human Aspects of Information Security, Privacy and Trust (HAS 2016)
- Third International Conference on HCI in Business, Government, and Organizations (HCIBGO 2016)
- Third International Conference on Learning and Collaboration Technologies (LCT 2016)
- Second International Conference on Human Aspects of IT for the Aged Population (ITAP 2016)

Conference Proceedings Volumes Full List

1. LNCS 9731, Human-Computer Interaction: Theory, Design, Development and Practice (Part I), edited by Masaaki Kurosu
2. LNCS 9732, Human-Computer Interaction: Interaction Platforms and Techniques (Part II), edited by Masaaki Kurosu
3. LNCS 9733, Human-Computer Interaction: Novel User Experiences (Part III), edited by Masaaki Kurosu
4. LNCS 9734, Human Interface and the Management of Information: Information, Design and Interaction (Part I), edited by Sakae Yamamoto
5. LNCS 9735, Human Interface and the Management of Information: Applications and Services (Part II), edited by Sakae Yamamoto
6. LNAI 9736, Engineering Psychology and Cognitive Ergonomics, edited by Don Harris
7. LNCS 9737, Universal Access in Human-Computer Interaction: Methods, Techniques, and Best Practices (Part I), edited by Margherita Antona and Constantine Stephanidis
8. LNCS 9738, Universal Access in Human-Computer Interaction: Interaction Techniques and Environments (Part II), edited by Margherita Antona and Constantine Stephanidis
9. LNCS 9739, Universal Access in Human-Computer Interaction: Users and Context Diversity (Part III), edited by Margherita Antona and Constantine Stephanidis
10. LNCS 9740, Virtual, Augmented and Mixed Reality, edited by Stephanie Lackey and Randall Shumaker
11. LNCS 9741, Cross-Cultural Design, edited by Pei-Luen Patrick Rau
12. LNCS 9742, Social Computing and Social Media, edited by Gabriele Meiselwitz
13. LNAI 9743, Foundations of Augmented Cognition: Neuroergonomics and Operational Neuroscience (Part I), edited by Dylan D. Schmorrow and Cali M. Fidopiastis
14. LNAI 9744, Foundations of Augmented Cognition: Neuroergonomics and Operational Neuroscience (Part II), edited by Dylan D. Schmorrow and Cali M. Fidopiastis
15. LNCS 9745, Digital Human Modeling and Applications in Health, Safety, Ergonomics and Risk Management, edited by Vincent G. Duffy
16. LNCS 9746, Design, User Experience, and Usability: Design Thinking and Methods (Part I), edited by Aaron Marcus
17. LNCS 9747, Design, User Experience, and Usability: Novel User Experiences (Part II), edited by Aaron Marcus
18. LNCS 9748, Design, User Experience, and Usability: Technological Contexts (Part III), edited by Aaron Marcus
19. LNCS 9749, Distributed, Ambient and Pervasive Interactions, edited by Norbert Streitz and Panos Markopoulos
20. LNCS 9750, Human Aspects of Information Security, Privacy and Trust, edited by Theo Tryfonas

HCI in Business, Government, and Organizations

Program Board Chairs: **Fiona Fui-Hoon Nah, USA, and Chuan-Hoo Tan, Singapore**

- Miguel Aguirre-Urreta, USA
- Andreas Auinger, Austria
- Michel Avital, Denmark
- Ashley Calvert, USA
- Hock Chuan Chan, Singapore
- Patrick Chau, Hong Kong, SAR China
- Benjamin Choi, Australia
- Cecil Chua, New Zealand
- Constantinos K. Coursaris, USA
- Jasbir Dhaliwal, USA
- Soussan Djamasbi, USA
- Brenda Eschenbrenner, USA
- Nobuyuki Fukawa, USA
- Jie Mein Goh, Canada
- Richard Hall, USA
- Khaled Hassanein, Canada
- Milena Head, Canada
- Sue Hessey, UK
- Michael Hilgers, USA
- Netta Iivari, Finland
- Jack Zhenhui Jiang, Singapore
- Qiqi Jiang, P.R. China
- Richard Johnson, USA
- Rajiv Khosla, Australia
- Bart Knijnenburg, USA
- Yi-Cheng Ku, Taiwan
- Young E. (Anna) Lee, USA
- Younghwa "Gabe" Lee, USA
- Roderick Lee, USA
- James Lewis, USA
- Na "Lina" Li, USA
- Honglei Li, UK
- Yan Li, France
- Mei Lu, USA
- Anna McNab, USA
- Gregory Moody, USA
- Robbie Nakatsu, USA
- Chih-Hung Peng, Hong Kong, SAR China
- Rene Riedl, Austria
- Khawaja Saeed, USA
- Norman Shaw, Canada
- Choong Ling Sia, Hong Kong, SAR China
- Austin Silva, USA
- Juliana Sutanto, UK
- Chee Wee Tan, Denmark
- Noam Tractinsky, Israel
- Horst Treiblmaier, Austria
- Ozgur Turetken, Canada
- Nathan Twyman, USA
- Dezhi Wu, USA
- I-Chin Wu, Taiwan
- Dongming Xu, Australia
- Cheng Yi, P.R. China
- Dezhi Yin, USA

The full list with the program board chairs and the members of the program boards of all thematic areas and affiliated conferences is available online at:

http://www.hci.international/2016/

HCI International 2017

The 19th International Conference on Human-Computer Interaction, HCI International 2017, will be held jointly with the affiliated conferences in Vancouver, Canada, at the Vancouver Convention Centre, July 9–14, 2017. It will cover a broad spectrum of themes related to human-computer interaction, including theoretical issues, methods, tools, processes, and case studies in HCI design, as well as novel interaction techniques, interfaces, and applications. The proceedings will be published by Springer. More information will be available on the conference website: http://2017.hci.international/.

General Chair
Prof. Constantine Stephanidis
University of Crete and ICS-FORTH
Heraklion, Crete, Greece
E-mail: general_chair@hcii2017.org

http://2017.hci.international/

Contents – Part II

HCI in the Public Administration and Government

HCI at Work

Mobile Applications and Services

Contents – Part I

Business Analytics and Visualization

Branding, Marketing and Consumer Behaviour

Digital Innovation

Designing Information Systems

User-Centered Requirements Analysis and Design Solutions for Chronic Disease Self-management

Maryam Ariaeinejad, Norm Archer[✉], Michael Stacey,
Ted Rapanos, Fadi Elias, and Faysal Naji

McMaster University, Hamilton, Canada
{ariaeim, archer, rapanost}@mcmaster.ca,
staceymi@hhsc.ca,
{fadi.elias, faysal.naji}@medportal.ca

Abstract. An aging population and the attendant growth in the need to care for people with serious chronic illnesses has created a demand for online support systems that can assist older adults to self-manage their illnesses. This could play a role in relieving some of the load on the healthcare system. Determining user-centered requirements of older adults for such systems is different from usual requirements analysis because older adults have particular needs, depending upon their chronic illnesses, their ability to manage technology, their access to appropriate technologies, and their cognitive abilities. This paper discusses in detail the use of the persona-scenario approach to elicit these needs from outpatients, informal care givers, and physicians. It proposes several suitable interface designs, depending on outpatient ability to deal with the proposed systems.

Keywords: Chronic disease · Self-management · Patient interface · Persona · Scenario · Design

1 Introduction

Due to the growing cost of healthcare, particularly because of the aging population, health self-management technologies may be able to play an important role in empowering patients to be more active in managing their own health and reducing healthcare costs. Internet use for communications, self-monitoring, and accessing online health information has led to a recent surge of interest in online health self-management of chronic illnesses. They are the leading cause of death in western nations (heart disease and cancer account for 48 % of all deaths in the U.S. [1]). Few people are unaffected by chronic conditions. The likelihood of developing a chronic illness and experiencing its resulting impact on quality of life is greatest for the socio-economically deprived, who may also suffer poverty because of disabilities resulting from chronic illness [2].

Interest in chronic disease self-management is considerable for older adults, who tend to develop chronic diseases as they age. Unfortunately they are also less adept

© Springer International Publishing Switzerland 2016
F.F.-H. Nah and C.-H. Tan (Eds.): HCIBGO 2016, Part II, LNCS 9752, pp. 3–15, 2016.
DOI: 10.1007/978-3-319-39399-5_1

with technologies, and their cognitive abilities decline with age, making it more difficult for them to take advantage of such technologies [3]. Chronic illnesses are often caused or exacerbated by lifestyle risk factors, including low levels of physical activity, poor nutrition, obesity, tobacco use, and excessive alcohol consumption [1]. Risks from chronic illness may be reduced if patients improve their lifestyle behaviours [4].

Most recent research in online support for disease self-management has shown some success [5] in improved health outlook. Self-efficacy encourages patient activation (i.e. knowledge, skill, and confidence for managing one's health) of their self-management process, resulting in improved health outcomes [6]. Interventions specifically for outpatients with certain chronic conditions may enhance activation levels even more [7].

Although results from online chronic disease self-management are promising, there are still major underlying gaps: (1) long-term sustainability in terms of patient recruitment, continuation, and operating cost, (2) keeping patient self-management motivation high, and (3) dealing with psychosocial patient characteristics such as social isolation, loneliness, depression, avoidance coping and low self-efficacy. In addition, (4) older adults are likely to have more chronic illnesses than younger people, and are less likely to be able to use technology effectively for health self-management [3]. It may therefore be necessary to provide alternative support mechanisms for these individuals.

1.1 Objective

The objective of this study is to address the gaps noted above through an innovative approach to promote patient adoption and continuing participation in health self-management. An effective self-management system should support outpatients in a manner that fits into one of three categories proposed by Schulman-Green et al. [8] for patients who need to self-manage chronic illnesses: (a) Illness Needs; (b) Activating

Table 1. Self-management supports and categories [8]

Support	Category	Description
1	(a)	Educate patients about chronic illnesses and related comorbidities
2	(a); (c)	Train patients about chronic illness self-management approaches (e.g. monitoring blood pressure, heart rate, weight), problem-solving, coping techniques, and decision support
3	(a); (c)	Modify lifestyles (regularly exercising, smoking cessation, etc.)
4	(b); (c)	Provide links to counseling, advice and other support services
5	(b)	Help personal caregivers, such as spouses, to assist patients in managing their chronic illnesses
6	(b); (c)	Access community health, social resources, family, and friends to combat social isolation and loneliness
7	(a); (b); (c)	Motivate patients to adhere to self-management regimens, using creative mechanisms
8	(a); (b); (c)	Engage patients through effective user-friendly interface designs

Resources; and (c) Living with a Chronic Illness. Eight supports that our system provides appear in Table 1, along with the three equivalent Schulman-Green et al. [8] categories.

1.2 Research Questions Addressed by the Study

1. What are the needs, preferences, and abilities of people with chronic illnesses and their informal caregivers, and can disease self-management meet these requirements?
2. What are the needs and preferences of healthcare providers who work with patients utilizing health self-management solutions?
3. What is the most appropriate design solution to address the outcomes, satisfaction and sustainability of use among end-users?

2 Peripheral Arterial Disease

Because of the diversity in chronic diseases, this paper focuses on one such disease, Peripheral Arterial Disease (PAD), in order to develop a prototype system design that can demonstrate effective self-management of a specific chronic disease. PAD is a condition that involves narrowing and occlusion of non-cerebral and non-coronary arteries distal to the arch of the aorta [9, 10]. It is one of the most common chronic illnesses among people over 50 years old [9] – with an estimated worldwide prevalence of 10 %, growing to 15–20 % in people over 70 years of age [11, 12].

The most important risk factors associated with PAD are age, cigarette smoking (current and former), diabetes mellitus, hypertension, hyperlipidemia, obesity (body-mass index BMI) lack of physical activity, and history of cardiovascular disease [13]. Its strongest risk correlations are with smoking and diabetes, in that order [14].

3 Self-management System Design

For many self-management technologies, usability design is less than satisfactory, resulting in low rates of elective adoption. Three factors can improve adoption rates: (1) suitability and relevance, (2) perceived usability, and (3) anticipated benefits of using it [15]. Traditional information technology (IT) development may ignore specific user needs and preferences, and systems not personalized (as in our case) to an aging patient population [16, 17]. Several methods of interface design, including focus groups [16] and interviews [18] may help to engage users in interface design. Supported by user-centered design (UCD), we identified user healthcare needs and preferences; thus informing user requirements, interface design and implementation decisions.

The method we chose is called a persona-scenario exercise. It has been used extensively to engage users in the design of human-centred interfaces [16, 18, 19]. Our goals were to: (1) understand the preferences and needs of our users – clinicians, patients and their informal caregivers; and (2) to provide a service to meet their requirements.

3.1 Personas and Scenarios

Personas can help to define "hypothetical archetypes of actual users" [20]. This utilizes user information in an ethnographic approach that focuses on users' behavioral characteristics, animating them in the minds of designers, developers, and testers. Each persona involves a fictitious person who plays the role of a group of users who will potentially use the system. These personas are then allowed to play their roles in user scenarios, resulting in use cases and hence test cases for the proposed intervention [21]. A persona-scenario exercise helps to foster support and uptake of the resulting online system design. The persona-scenario approach has been used elsewhere in developing other healthcare applications [17, 22, 23].

4   Study Procedure

Data were collected from six persona-scenario discussion sessions with ten participants (n = 10). This gave enough data to estimate the final outcomes of the exercise fairly accurately. Our study process involved three main steps, as follows:

Step 1. Recruiting participants. The first step in developing a persona is to determine the user groups who should participate in the interviews. For patients who have developed a specific disease such as PAD, with treatment being managed primarily by specialists, the groups most commonly involved in patient support include:

1. Surgeon Specialists (Senior Surgeons and Residents)
2. Outpatients
3. Family Members: Informal Caregivers
4. Family Physicians

In this study, we focused on the first three groups, which were most extensively involved in the self-management process, in order to limit the scope of the work. Family physicians will be brought into a more extended self-management process design later. The relevance to our discussion with each group of participants was:

- Vascular surgeons who work regularly with and are very familiar with the needs of patients with PAD and comorbid illnesses
- Outpatients with PAD who were also potential users of the prototype MyPADMGT disease self-management system that was been in use for almost two years
- Informal caregivers who could help outpatients to perform self-management tasks

Recruiting was carried out through handouts given to outpatients attending regular vascular clinics. We interviewed a group of senior vascular surgeons and residents together, and separately outpatients and informal caregivers, either individually or in groups of two. All interviews took place at the Hamilton General Hospital and each interviewee received 40 dollars and parking expenses for participating. The study was approved by the hospital's Research Ethics Board.

Step 2. Interviewing process – personas and scenarios. Each participant signed an informed consent form and received a copy. Each interview lasted less than 2 h. Each person received a tailored discussion guide, an introduction to the program components, and support from a facilitator (conversations were recorded and transcribed later). To design personas and scenarios, we conducted semi-structured interviews. In the first part, demographic information was gathered on interviewee characteristics, such as age, gender, education, etc. They were also asked to describe personas that represented their authentic needs. The second part focused on how they might deal with a system such as MyPADMGT, based on the persona that had been developed. Each participant or pair generated an experience of the self-management program by their persona with one or two "scenarios" that reflected their attitudes towards available information, measures, the possible frequency of usage, and how they might learn about and use the system. We needed to learn about their skills, what online technology they might be familiar with, wishes and expectations, and finally, in which situations they would use the system. Interviews were semi-structured; the interviewer was able to discuss any interesting topics that came up during the interviews. At the end of each session the patient or patient group had developed a persona and one or more scenarios.

Baseline patient and informal caregiver demographics are shown in Tables 2 and 3. All were 59 years of age or over. All patients had been diagnosed with PAD.

Table 2. Patient Demographics

Characteristics	Information
Gender	5 male
Age	59–77
Smoking status	1 smoker 3 former smokers 1 non-smoker
Duration of PAD	1 less than a year 3 between one to two years 1 three years
Experience of medical intervention	3 yes 2 no
Existence of an informal caregiver at home	2 yes 3 no
Access to the Internet	3 yes 1 yes but not using 1 no

Table 3. Informal Caregiver Demographics

Characteristics	Information
Gender	Female
Age	Between 70 and 80
Smoking status of the patient	Former smoker

(Continued)

Table 3. (*Continued*)

Characteristics	Information
Duration of PAD for the patient	Less than a month
Experience of medical intervention for the patient	Yes
Informal caregiver relationship	Spousal
Access to the Internet	Yes

Step 3. Analyzing the results. Summaries of the persona-scenario exercises were transcribed verbatim and coded for qualitative analysis. Based on themes found from the analysis, a system design was developed, including a design to-do list. It became clear that there were three distinctive groups of users and that we should create three personas. The first persona reflected the perceptions of users and/or caregivers who were comfortable with online technology, and usually own a home computer or smart phone. The second persona was a group of users with/without caregivers who were not comfortable with technology and needed a manual tool. They usually do not own a computer at home or smart phone. The third persona participants were similar to the first persona, but with limited access to the Internet, so they needed an offline manual tool. A fourth persona was developed to represent informal caregivers. Online patient personas and caregiver personas are in Tables 4a and 4b, and the surgeon persona is in Table 5. Due to lack of space only online personas are included.

Table 4a. Online patient persona

Name	Joe	Short introduction
Age	60	Joe is an active independent person, who is interested in learning more about his condition – walking difficulties and pain in his legs – and taking care of himself. He is also interested in participating because he believes it can help others as well. He can learn the application if somebody sits with him and teaches him how to use it so he can use it on his own afterwards. He prefers the online version
Education	High school	
Employment	Construction	
Caregiver	Spouse	
Smoking status	Smoker (trying to quit)	
Medical intervention	Yes	
Duration of PAD	1 year	
Knowledge about the disease	"I searched a little bit. I brought up a picture that shows what the disease does and what doctors do" "Doctors do not give you enough information. They just give you enough to get you by…Nobody really says what it is. It is cut and dried."	
Comfort with technology	"Computers yes! Smart phones, I know nothing about them! I have five computers at home" "I spend 10 to 12 h in a day on computers! I am retired, I have nothing to do…"	

Table 4b. Informal caregiver persona

Name	Rose	Short introduction
Age	77	Rose is an active social women who tries to take care of her husband to the best of her knowledge. If she knows she can do something to improve her husband's health she will do it. Her husband is not as active as she is, and he has different problems like back pain that stop him from being active
Education	High school	
Employment	Financial services	
Relationship to patient	Spousal	She will easily learn to use the online version with a little help for the first steps, and she will probably try to use it regularly. They have a big family, so there is always someone else to help
Patient smoking status	Was smoker	
Patient medical intervention	Yes	
Patient's duration of PAD	1 month	
Knowledge about the disease		"We look things up in the Internet. As I said we liked to know what it is, and have a general idea about what is going on." "I am not aware of the disease impact, characteristics and treatments. But I need to go online and read a little about it."
Comfort with technology		"I use the Internet all the time and my husband has his own iPad. We both use the Internet. But my phone is just a regular phone because I am home all the time. I don't text because by type of the phone I have it would take forever to text. We research on the computer, we use Skype and face time with family."

Table 5. Surgeon persona

Name	John	Short introduction
Age	50	John is an experienced surgeon who is interested in research because he believes he can make a difference. He is involved in several studies and gives a lot of talks as a specialist in his field. After many years of experience, he is pretty comfortable in his job. He believes that there is no real cure for PAD and technology is just a new Band-Aid, but he also believes it can be used for prevention which is the only successful trend in recent years
Education	MD, MSc, FRCS	
Employment	26 years in the hospital system	
Desires	Focused on clinical research and system level approach to patient care	
Attitude	Carefully optimistic – has lost his initial total optimism!	He is really interested in using the reports of the MyPADMGT system, which he believes will make his job much easier and provide patients with required information that they need. He will introduce it to the patients and follow up with them to ensure they use it correctly. He is also extremely busy and overwhelmed with the number of new technologies so it is hard to get his attention, so it is better to begin working with his residents

(Continued)

Table 5. (*Continued*)

Name	John	Short introduction
Hopes and fears about the disease:	"Very conservative after 15 years of seeing a lot of disasters with PAD" "More interested in prevention because it is the only successful trend in these years, rather than tackling the disease after it comes."	
Comfort with technology	"Pretty comfortable with existing and new technology"	

4.1   Design Themes

The results of the persona-scenario interviews were coded into 13 themes and 6 categories (Table 6).

Table 6. Design categories and themes

Categories	Themes
1. Technology	1.1. Patient or informal caregiver comfort in using the technology – prefer the online version of MyPADMGT
	1.2. Patient or informal caregiver discomfort with smartphones – no interest in mobile version of MyPADMGT
	1.3. Patient or informal caregiver discomfort in using the technology – prefer a manual version of MyPADMGT
2. Tool characteristics	2.1. How to introduce the tool
	2.2. Patient expectations
	2.3. Willingness (or not) to use the tool to communicate with other patients
3. Knowledge	3.1. Lack of knowledge about the disease, self-management, and willingness to learn more
4. Willingness	4.1. Patient willingness to improve lifestyle
	4.2. Patient willingness to use the tool
5. Support	5.1. Social communications
	5.2. Existence of informal caregiver at home
6. Barriers	6.1. Comorbidity existence
	6.2. Barriers to self-management

5   Research Outcomes

Following the detailed system design process our research outcomes included: (a) a complete health self-management system, based on the existing online prototype, upgraded through the results of the persona-scenario studies; (b) a comparison of the results from the categories of personas, in terms of their contribution to design quality; and ultimately (not included in this paper) (c) measures of success in end-user engagement and satisfaction, gathered from participant feedback questionnaires.

Three solutions were derived for self-management support systems.

1. Cellphones or smartphones [24] to monitor and record personal data directly through reminders and automatic devices such as weigh scales, heart monitors, cameras, etc. These can significantly improve the usability and effectiveness of a health self-management system through portability and automation of monitored measures. While this is the most effective approach, it is preferred by less than 40 % of older adults. The causes are that many older adults lack technological experience, or they may not have access Internet access or they may not be able to afford it.

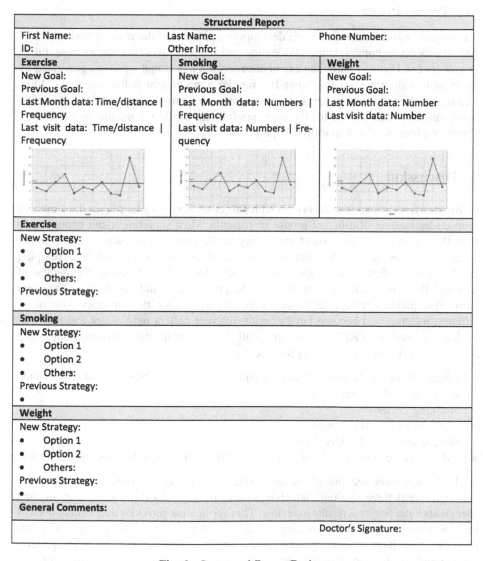

Fig. 1. Structured Report Design

2. Using Interactive Voice Response (IVR) systems to provide services in support of patient health self-management. However, findings consistently show that people in general and particularly older people dislike IVR systems [25].
3. The third method is the use of simplified manual systems that allow outpatients to record important lifestyle data and vital signs weekly or more frequently. The advantages of such systems are that they can operate at minimal cost, providing patient status and details to physicians during each patient visit to the clinic, and they are preferred by a majority of older outpatients.

5.1 Process Design

A flowchart was developed to guide developers and users of the revised MyPADMGT system process, accommodating both online and manual users (not shown here due to lack of space). Figure 1 shows an example structured report that would be generated by the system at the time a patient attends a regular appointment at the outpatient clinic. The report shows patient progress towards goals previously agreed with the patient's physician, and goals agreed for the next appointment (up to six months in the future). These graphics are for demonstration purposes only.

6 Discussion

In this study, we found that interviews with surgeons were very helpful in developing a deep understanding of different groups of patients. Most surgeons spend enough time with their patients to understand them very well. This makes patient segmentation much easier, and helped the interview process to be very productive in developing good solutions. Patient interviews were mostly focused on learning the details of patients' lives and understanding their needs, preferences, and capabilities. Surgeons more than patients were able to see usage patterns, since they interact with many different patients, and become familiar with different patient behaviours and needs.

The revised MyPADMGT system will focus on lifestyle changes, including addressing and monitoring, as appropriate:

- Education about chronic illnesses, so patients understand how to deal with related symptoms and problems
- Smoking cessation
- Walking and exercise programs
- Weight and heart healthy diets
- Taking medications for blood pressure, diabetes, etc., including regular reminders

In the first three sections of the structured report in Fig. 1, goals and strategies are set. In the next three sections (not shown here) of (e.g. blood pressure), patients and specialists have progress results to review. This application provides data to help doctors keep patients on track. In the smoking cessation section, patients have the option to note problems they have in quitting, like stress, family struggles, etc. This helps patients think about any barriers they have encountered while attempting to quit smoking.

6.1 Barriers

A major barrier to patient success with disease self-management is being able to educate patients in the nature of their diseases and how best to deal with related problems. MyPADMGT is designed to provide this type of support. A second barrier is that patients with PAD often have other serious comorbidities that require them to deal with several specialists (e.g. cardiologists and vascular surgeons) as well as their family physicians. Keeping personal patient records of their disease self-management activities and results in MyPADMGT can assist a great deal in guiding specialist care in many such situations.

Apart from a focus on patients with serious chronic illnesses, the lifestyle changes promoted by MyPADMGT also aid in preventive care through life style changes. This provides for a healthier and longer life for everyone who follows this approach, so this should be a consideration for anyone concerned about their health.

7 Conclusions

Our conclusions, based on findings from the patient persona-scenario exercises are as follows. In order to be adopted and used by our target clientele (physicians, outpatients with PAD and other serious chronic illnesses, and patients interested in preventive care) our system must be:

- Inexpensive
- Reliable
- Easy to learn
- Easy to use
- Adaptable to individual requirements
- Able to provide a link between outpatients and their providers as appropriate
- Help outpatients to understand and manage their chronic illness(es)
- Support both online and manual records for monitoring progress

References

1. Centers for Disease Control and Prevention: Chronic diseases and health promotion. Centers for Disease Control: Atlanta, Geogia (2012). http://www.cdc.gov/chronicdisease/overview/index.htm. Accessed 21 July 2015
2. Fang, R., Kmetic, A., Millar, J., Drasic, L.: Disparities in chronic disease among Canada's low-income populations. Prev. Chron. Dis. **6**(4), A115 (2009)
3. Archer, N., Keshavjee, K., Demers, C., Lee, R.: Online self-managment interventions for chronically ill patients: cognitive impairment and technology issues. Int. J. Med. Inform. **83**, 264–272 (2014)
4. Lorig, K., Ritter, P.L., Plant, K., Laurent, D.D., Kelly, P., Rowe, S.: The South Australia health chronic disease self-management Internet trial. Health Educ. Behav. **40**, 67–77 (2013)

5. McDermott, M.S., While, A.E.: Maximizing the healthcare environment: a systematic review exploring the potential of computer technology to promote self-management of chronic illness in healthcare settings. Patient Educ. Couns. **92**, 13–22 (2013)

6. Solomon, M., Wagner, S.I., Goes, J.: Effects of a web-based intervention for adults with chronic conditions on patient activation: online randomized controlled trial. J. Med. Internet Res. **14**(1), e32 (2012)

7. Long, K.R., Ritter, P.L., Laurent, D.D., Plant, K.: Internet-based chronic disease self-management: a randomized trial. Med. Care **44**(11), 964–971 (2006)

8. Schulman-Green, D., Jaser, S., Martin, F., Alonzo, A., Grey, M., McCorkle, R., Redeker, N. S., Reynolds, N., Whittemore, R.: Processes of self-management in chronic illness. J. Nurs. Sch **44**(2), 136–144 (2012)

9. Peach, G., Griffin, M., Jones, K.G., Thompson, M.M., Hinchliffe, R.J.: Diagnosis and management of peripheral arterial disease. BMJ **345**, e5208 (2012)

10. Criqui, M.H.: Progression of peripheral arterial disease predicts cardiovascular disease morbidity and mortality. J. Am. Coll. Cardiol. **52**(21), 1736–1742 (2008)

11. Criqui, M.H., Langer, R.D., Fronek, A., Feigelson, H.S., Klauber, M.R., McCann, T.J.: Mortality over a period of 10 years in patients with peripheral arterial disease. N. Engl. J. Med. **326**, 381–386 (1992)

12. Belch, J.J.F., Topol, E.J., Agnelli, G., Bertrand, M., Califf, R.M., Clement, D.L.: Critical issues in peripheral arterial disease detection and management: a call to action. Arch. Intern. Med. **163**, 884–892 (2003)

13. Fowkes, F.G.R., Rudan, D., Rudan, I., Aboyans, V., Denenberg, J.O., McDermott, M.M., Norman, P.E., Sampson, U.K., Williams, L.J., Mensah, G.A., Criqui, M.H.: Comparison of global estimates of prevalence and risk factors for peripheral arterial disease in 2000 and 2010: a systematic review and analysis. Lancet **382**(9901), 1329–1340 (2013)

14. Murabito, J.M., D'Agostino, R.B., Silbershatz, H., Wilson, W.F.: Intermittent claudication: Incidence in the Framingham Study. Circulation **96**, 44–49 (1997)

15. LeRouge, C., Ma, J., Sneha, S., Tolle, K.: User profiles and personas in the design and development of consumer health technologies. Int. J. Med. Inform. **82**, e251–e268 (2013)

16. Bate, P., Robert, G.: Experience-based design: From redesigning the system around the patient to co-designing services with the patient. Qual. Saf. Health Care **15**, 307–310 (2006)

17. Ellis, R.D., Kurniawan, S.H.: Increasing the usability of online information for older users: a case study in participatory design. Int. J. Human-Comp. Int. **12**(2), 263–276 (2000)

18. Reeder, B., Turner, A.M.: Scenario-based design: a method for connecting information system design with public health operations and emergency management. J. Biomed. Inform. **44**(6), 978–988 (2011)

19. Bredies, K.: Using system analysis and personas for e-health interaction design. In: Undisciplined! Design Research Society Conference 2008. Sheffield Hallam University, Sheffield UK (2009)

20. Cooper, A.: The Inmates Are Running the Asylum: Why High-Tech Products Drive Us Crazy and How to Restore the Sanity, 2nd edn. SAMS, Indianapolis (2009)

21. Pruitt, J., Adlin, T.: The Persona Lifecyle: Keeping People in Mind Throughout Product Design. Morgan Kaufmann, San Francisco (2010)

22. Turner, A.M., Reeder, B., Ramey, J.: Scenarios, personas and user stories: user-centered evidence-based design representations of communicable disease investigations. J. Biomed. Inform. **46**(4), 575–584 (2013)

23. Goldberg, L., Lide, B., Lowry, S., Massett, H.A., O'Connell, T., Preece, J., Quesenbery, W., Shneiderman, B.: Usability and accessibility in consumer health informatics: current trends and future challenges. Am. J. Prev. Med. **40**(552), 5187–5197 (2011)

24. Klasjna, P., Pratt, W.: Healthcare in the pocket: mapping the space of mobile-phone health interventions. J. Biomed. Inform. **45**, 184–198 (2012)
25. Miller, D., Gagnon, M., Talbot, V., Messier, C.: Predictors of successful communication with interactive voice response systems in older people. J. Gerontol. Ser. B. Psychol. Sci. Soc. Sci. **68**(4), 495–503 (2013)

Defective Still Deflective – How Correctness of Decision Support Systems Influences User's Performance in Production Environments

Philipp Brauner[✉], André Calero Valdez, Ralf Philipsen, and Martina Ziefle

Human-Computer Interaction Center (HCIC) Chair of Communication Science,
RWTH Aachen University, Campus-Boulevard 57, 52074 Aachen, Germany
{brauner,calero-valdez,philipsen,ziefle}@comm.rwth-aachen.de

Abstract. The increasing dynamic and complexity of todays global supply chains and the growing amount and complexity of information challenge decision makers in manufacturing companies. Decision Support Systems (DSS) can be a viable solution to address these challenges and increase the overall decision efficiency and effectivity. However, a thought-through design and implementation of these systems is crucial for their efficacy.

This article presents the current state-of-the-art of Decisions Support Systems and highlights their benefits and pitfalls. Also, we present an empirical study in which we compared different levels of decision support and decision automation in a simulated supply chain game environment.

We identify and quantify how human factors influence the decision quality and decision performance in this supply chain scenario. We show that an adequately designed system raises the overall performance. However, insufficiently designed systems have the reverse effect and lead operators to miss severe situations, which can have fatal consequences for manufacturing companies.

Keywords: Decision support systems · Automation · Enterprise resource planning · Supply chain management · Business simulation game · Human factors · Industrial Internet · Industry 4.0 · Integrative Production Technology · Usability

1 Introduction

Strengthening of the competitiveness of manufacturing companies is a constant source for innovation and renewal. Today's emergence of increasing horizontal and vertical interconnectedness of virtually all production and managerial systems of companies is often referred to as the "Industrial Internet" or "Industry 4.0" [1]. We are in the midst of this next industrial revolution. Currently it is neither sufficiently understood how the human factors perspective relates to the increasing wealth in detail, complexity, and amount of information in companies, nor, how human operators can be adequately supported to harness this rich source of information.

In this article we argue that Decision Support Systems (DSS) are a necessity to help human operators to handle the flood of information and that these system positively influence decision speed and accuracy. However, we also argue that these systems have

© Springer International Publishing Switzerland 2016
F.F.-H. Nah and C.-H. Tan (Eds.): HCIBGO 2016, Part II, LNCS 9752, pp. 16–27, 2016.
DOI: 10.1007/978-3-319-39399-5_2

detrimental consequences on decision speed and accuracy, if they suggest wrong or inadequate decisions, as operators are easily deflected by these systems.

The remainder of this article is structured as follows: Sect. 2 outlines related work and the current state of the art of the human factors perspective on decision support systems. Section 3 describes our experimental approach. Section 4 presents the results of the experiment. Section 5 discusses the significance of this study and the recommendations for actions for the design and evaluation of decision support systems. Finally, Sect. 6 touches the limitations of this study and Sect. 7 outlines the future research agenda.

2   Related Work

In order to understand the focus of this research we first outline what our understanding of a decision support system is and what the purpose of such a system it serves. We then elaborate on the human processing of tabular data to provide the quantitative background for our research hypotheses.

2.1   Decision Support System

The term decision support system (DSS) has been coined since the 1970's [2, 3]. The early precursors of modern DSS can be found in research on organizational decision-making and technical work in the 1950's and 1960's. The idea was to integrate the computational and storage power of computers into the complex decision making tasks of workers. In order to do so, it was necessary to encode knowledge, models, and rules into a computable form. Decision support was reached by providing querying systems, reports, and visualizations.

DSSs aid in solving problems by automatizing the programmable part of a decision problem [3]. This part can be routine, repetitive, well structured or easily solved by a computer. The user can then find a suitable decision by integrating the output of the DSS in the non-programmable part of the problem, which is new, novel, ill-structured or difficult to solve. As reasons for avoiding full-automation can be various (e.g., responsibility, ethical, political, and organizational considerations), the user must make the final decision. Typically a DSS provides the user an indicator for the choice to be made or presents an argument for the specific solution.

Modern forms of DSSs are data warehouses [4], OLAP [5], data-mining [6] and web-based DSSs. Data-centric DSS gain importance as the amount of available data increases, while at the same time the amount of data becomes too overwhelming for any user to process. Modern DSSs implement methods from artificial intelligence to help processing the large amount of information and thus provide fuzzy output that needs further interpretation [7]. The success of DSSs has been shown in various fields, in particular in medicine [8] and defense [9].

The need to study the effect of human factors on the use of DSSs has been mentioned in medicine [8, 10] or stock trading [11]. In particular, user factors, such as gender [12], are likely to influence decision accuracy and thereby performance. Moreover, trust and perceived effectiveness play a decisive role regarding the use of DSSs: A possible imbalance between users' evaluations and actual performance of the decision support can lead to a detrimental neglect of such systems [13, 14].

An application of DSS in Industry 4.0 settings would face similar challenges and should therefore be investigated in a similar fashion to understand the benefit and pitfalls of using a Decision Support System. But, where to start?

One way of supporting the user is achieved by providing indicators of tabular data for inventory control, which takes a significant toll on human cognitive processing [15, 16]. These indicators can help, but can also be deceptive in unclear unexpected scenarios (i.e., black-swan effects). In such cases, a DSS can by defective or dysfunctional, as it provides *correct* support for an *incorrect* scenario. Nevertheless, providing support in processing tabular data is in general considered helpful. Yet, the effects of having a defective DSS must be weighed against the benefits of a functional DSS. To quantify this effect, one must first understand the toll of processing tabular data without a DSS.

2.2 Processing of Tabular Data

Speicher et al. investigated the influence of number of lines, number of digits, as well as concreteness of the given information on speed and accuracy in table reading tasks [15]. All factors had a positive influence on performance, whereas accuracy was not affected. The study also revealed that practice had a positive influence on both, performance and accuracy. Furthermore, participants with higher perceptual speed were faster, whereas they did not achieved a higher number of accurate results.

Mittelstädt et al. further considered task complexity and readability while processing tabular data. As in the previous work, all factors influenced performance [16]. Also, the study revealed that people with higher perceptual speed were able to compensate the detrimental influence of lower readability on task performance.

How can we integrate these findings into the usage of a DSS? How do users perform in similar tasks when a DSS is present? Understanding the efficacy of a DSS is crucial when deciding where, when, and how a DSS should be used.

3 Method

To understand the efficacy of decision support systems for manufacturing companies we conducted an experiment and measured the influence of different decision support systems on efficiency and effectivity. We used a simplified business simulation game as a basis for measuring the influence of the system on the efficiency and effectivity of the decisions. The following sections describe (1) the underlying business simulation game, (2) the considered experimental variables, (3) the experimental procedure, and (4) the characteristics of the sample.

3.1 Business Simulation Game

The game is based on Forrester's Beer Distribution Game [17] and our own Quality Intelligence Game [18]. Both resemble decision-making tasks in a supply chain environment. The former addresses communication across the supply chain whereas the latter focuses on multi-criteria decision making, as it also includes investments in quality management. In contrast to the originally turn-based games, we reduced the complexity of the underlying simulation to singular decision tasks for this baseline experiment. Hence, a wrong decision had no influence on the subsequent decisions, whereas poor decisions at the start of the real games had to be compensated later on.

The task of the participants is to read the tabulated stock levels and projected customer demands for a set of products and to decide if enough stocks are present or if new products must be ordered. For reasons of simplicity, only binary answers are requested (i.e., *procurement* if at least one product is out of stock, *no procurement* if enough stocks are present for every product).

3.2 Experimental Procedure and Investigated Variables

The experiment consists of a three different sets (no DSS, correct DSS, defective DSS) with 30 decisions situations within each set (150 trials in total) for each participant. For each situation the participants decide whether new materials need to be procured by pressing one of two distinctly marked buttons on a keyboard (procurement/no procurement) and time and accuracy for each decision is recorded. Feedback on the correctness is given after each trial and the participants take a short break between the sets. The overall experimental procedure is illustrated in Fig. 1.

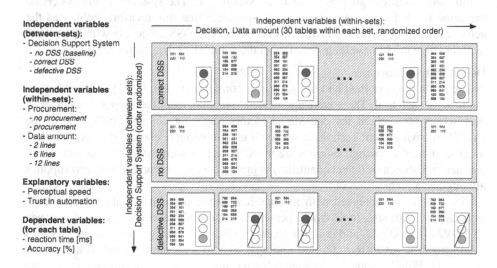

Fig. 1. Schematic representation of the experiment.

Independent variables (between-set):
Decision Support System: Three different types of DSSs are presented: No DSS, a correct DSS, and a defective DSS. If a DSS is available, a traffic light next to the data table suggests a procurement decision. A red light indicates that insufficient stocks are available and that new supplies must be ordered. A green light indicates that enough stocks are present. If a DSS is present, this system is either working correctly or malfunctioning. A malfunctioning system presents the wrong suggestion with a 50 % (sic!) chance. As feedback is given immediately after each table the participant should notice the defective DSS quickly.

Independent variables (within-set):
Procurement: Half of the presented tables contain data that require a procurement decision, as the stock of exactly one good is lower than the demand. Otherwise, no procurement is required.
Data amount: The presented tables differ in length (2, 6, 12 lines of data). The amount of information is varied as previous studies suggest that many flaws in user interfaces can be compensated for easier tasks with less information, but that the difficulties arise only for more complex or information dense tasks [15, 16].

Explanatory variables:
Perceptual speed is measured by the Number Comparison Test [19] as a possible moderator variable. A recent study identified that people with higher perceptual speed can compensate inferior user interfaces better than people with lower perceptual speed [16]. Thus, we assume that higher perceptual speed is also beneficial for compensating the influence of deflective decision support systems.
Trust in Automation: This self-developed scale assesses an individual's trust in automation with questions such as "I trust the system", or "The system will always create the same result for the same input". We speculate that this measure influences the achieved accuracy for the sets with the malfunctioning DSS, as people with lower trust in automation might base their decision on the actual data than on the DSS.

Dependent variables:
The reaction times in [ms] and the accuracy (correct/incorrect, in [%]) is recorded via log files for each trial. These were aggregated to median reaction times and mean accuracy scores for each of the considered factors (decision, length, DSS). Due to the simplified environment each decision could unambiguously classified as correct (i.e., no procurement as enough supplies are in stock, or procurement as at least one supply was not available in sufficient quantities) or incorrect (e.g., procurement of new supplies although enough are in stock).

The results are analyzed with parametrical and non-parametrical methods, using bivariate correlations, single, and repeated uni- and multivariate analyses of variance (ANOVA/MANOVA), and multiple linear regressions. The type I error rate (level of significance) is set to $\alpha = .05$ and findings $.05 < p < .1$ are reported as marginally significant. Pillai's value is considered for the multivariate tests and effect sizes are reported as η^2. If the assumption of sphericity is not met, Grenhouse-Geisser-corrected values are considered (but uncorrected dfs are reported for readability).

3.3 Description of the Sample

20 people aged from 22 to 54 years (avg. 29.6 ± 7.2 years) participated in the experiment (8 female, 12 male). The perceptual speed (PS) score of the participants ranged from 18 to 39 points with an arithmetic mean of 24.7 ± 5.0 points (higher values indicate a higher perceptual speed). The trust in automation (TA) of the sample ranged from 2.5 to 5.2 points (scale from 1 to 6, higher values indicate a higher trust) with an arithmetic mean of 4.0 ± 0.9. The scale has an outstanding internal reliability (Cronbach's $\alpha = .906$, 6 items). A correlation analysis reveals a strong significant relationship between Sex and PS, with women having a higher perceptual speed than men [$\rho_{n=20,2} = .581, p < .01$].

4 Results

The results section is structured as follows. First, the findings for the baseline experiment (i.e., no decision support system) are presented. Then, the influence of a correctly working DSS is shown, followed by the effect if a faulty DSS.

4.1 Baseline (No Decision Support System)

The average median reaction time without DSS is 5.186 ± 1.49 s with an accuracy of 92.6 ± 7.3 %. The fastest participant completed the set without DSS in 2.9 s/table whereas the slowest person took 9.7 s/table. The lowest achieved accuracy score is 77 % compared to 100 % (no errors) as the highest score. Overall, time and accuracy are not related [$\rho_{n=19,2} = .104, p = .673 > .05$], which indicates that the participants took the task seriously and did not rush through the trials at the cost of accuracy.

The average median reaction times were neither influenced by the age [$\rho_{n=18,2} = -.172$, $p = .495 > .05$], the sex [$\rho_{n=19,2} = .097, p = .692 > .05$], the TA [$\rho_{n=19,2} = -.041$, $p = .869 > .05$], nor the PS [$\rho_{n=19,2} = .066, p = .789 > .05$] of the participants. The average accuracy is neither influenced by the age [$\rho_{n=18,2} = .385, p = .114 > .05$], TA [$\rho_{n=19,2} = .135$, $p = .582 > .05$], nor PS [$\rho_{n=19,2} = -.023, p = .927 > .05$], but by Sex [$\rho_{n=19,2} = -.595$, $p = .007 < .01$] with women achieving lower accuracy scores than men.

Despite the small sample size, all investigated within-subject factors and their interaction terms were significant as presented in the following:

Factor Data amount: The number of lines of the tables significantly influences the reaction times and accuracy [$V = .966, F_{4,15} = 100.482, p < .001, \eta^2 = .966$]. As expected, tables with 2 lines were completed significantly faster (M = 2.438 s) than tables with 6 lines (M = 4.683 s), or tables with 12 lines (M = 8.592 s) [$F_{2,36} = 255.97, p < .001, \eta^2 = .934$]. The accuracy of short tables was slightly higher (95.8 %) than for medium (93.2 %), or for long Tables (88.9 %), though this difference is only marginally significant [$F_{2,36} = 2.764$, $p = .092 < .1, \eta^2 = .133$]. Furthermore, reaction times for medium and long tables were strongly correlated [$\rho_{n=19,2} = .795, p < .001$]. Likewise, accuracy for long and medium tables [$\rho_{n=19,2} = .795, p < .001$], as well as long and short tables were strongly correlated [$\rho_{n=19,2} = .795, p < .001$]. Figure 2 (left) illustrates this effect.

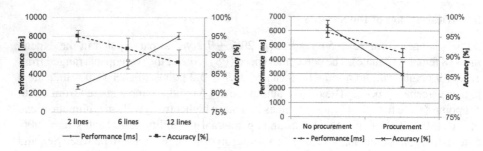

Fig. 2. Effect of <u>data amount</u> and <u>procurement</u> decision on speed and accuracy.

Factor <u>Procurement</u>: The decision (procurement/no procurement) also sig. influences decision time and accuracy [$V = .870$, $F_{2,17} = 56.883$, $p < .001$, $\eta^2 = .870$]. The time for a *procurement* decision is significantly lower than for *no procurement* decision (4.470 ± 2.06 s vs. 5.904 ± 1.73 s) [$F_{1,18} = 22.059$, $p < .001$, $\eta^2 = .551$] and surprisingly the case of a procurement decision is significantly less accurate (86.6 %) than the case of no procurement (97.2 %) [$F_{1,18} = 16.003$, $p < .001$, $\eta^2 = .471$] (see Fig. 2, right).

Interaction <u>Procurement</u> × <u>Data Amount</u>: As Fig. 3 illustrates procurement decision and amount of data show a significant interaction [$V = .635$, $F_{4,15} = 6.525$, $p = .003 < .05$, $\eta^2 = .635$]. The reaction times diverge depending on the procurement decision and order decisions are entered significantly faster than no-orders with increasing data amount [$F_{1,36} = 10.059$, $p < .001$, $\eta^2 = .359$]. However, the accuracy of the procurement decision decrease with increasing data amount, whereas the accuracy of no-procurement decisions seems unaffected [$F_{2,36} = 2.866$, $p = .082 < .1$, $\eta^2 = .137$].

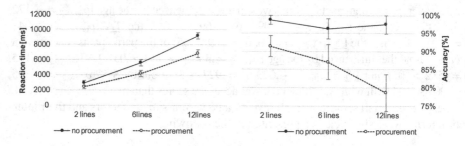

Fig. 3. Sig. interaction between <u>procurement</u> × <u>data amount</u> on reaction time and accuracy.

4.2   Effect of a Decision Support System

The availability of a decision support system (DSS) has a significant influence on both speed and accuracy [$V = .681$, $F_{4,15} = 8.006$, $p < .001$, $\eta^2 = .681$].

Specifically, the average median reaction times with the correct DSS were significantly lower (3.023 ± 1.405 s) than without DSS (4.715 ± 1.486 s). Even the erroneous system reduced the reaction times (4.101 ± 0.931 s) compared to the baseline.

The DSS also significantly influenced the attained accuracy. The correctly working DSS yielded in higher accuracy scores (95.1 ± 9.3 %) than the baseline system (92.6 ± 7.3 %). Yet, the defective system yielded in a reduced accuracy (86.5 ± 9.3 %). Figure 4 and Table 1 illustrate the overall influence of a correctly working and a defective DSS on performance and accuracy.

Table 1. Mean median reaction times and accuracy for different decision support systems.

	No DSS (baseline)		Correct DSS		Defective DSS	
	RT	Accuracy	RT	Accuracy	RT	Accuracy
Overall:	4.715s	92.6%	3.023s	95.1%	4.101s	86.5%
Data amount:						
2 lines	2.438s	95.7%	2.083s	98.4%	2.331s	90.5%
6 lines	4.946s	93.2%	3.529s	93.7%	4.683s	90.0%
12 lines	8.592s	90.0%	5.265s	93.2%	7.696s	79.0%
Procurement decision:						
buy	3.855s	86.6%	3.061s	91.9%	3.467s	80.1%
No buy	6.019s	97.2%	3.658s	98.1%	5.027s	92.0%

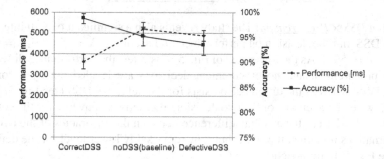

Fig. 4. Influence of no, correct, and defective decision support systems on performance and accuracy.

Interaction DSS × Data amount: There is a significant overall interaction between the DSS type and the length of the tables [$V = .718$, $F_{2,17} = 3.495$, $p < .001$, $\eta^2 = .718$]. As Fig. 5 (upper row) illustrates, the correctly working DSS has a significant positive influence on the reaction times, especially for larger data tables. However, the reaction times for the defective DSS were just a nuance smaller than for the baseline experiment, even for the large data sets (left). On the other side (right), the correctly working DSS had a positive influence on the overall accuracy of the decisions compared to the baseline experiment, again, especially for larger tables. Strikingly, the accuracy for the defective DSS drops compared to the baseline experiment. This effect is observable for all table sizes, but it its particularly strong for large tables.

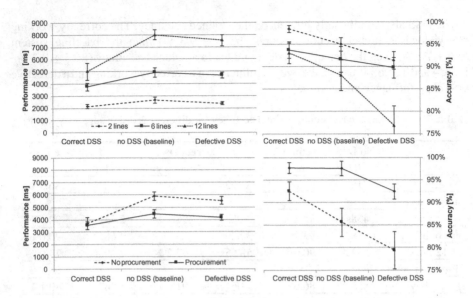

Fig. 5. Effect of no, correct, and defective <u>decision support systems</u> on performance and accuracy depending on <u>data amount</u> (upper row) and <u>procurement decision</u> (lower row).

Interaction DSS × Procurement: The study reveals also a significant overall interaction between DSS and the decision on performance and accuracy [$V = .597$, $F_{4,15} = 5.548$, $p < .001$, $\eta^2 = .597$]. As the lower row of Fig. 5 illustrates, the performance differences between procurement and no procurement decisions are leveled out by a correctly working DSS, whereas the difference persists for the defective DSS (see Fig. 5, lower-left). Likewise, the accuracy of the two decision alternatives converge for the correctly working DSS, whereas the absolute difference between the accuracies of the two decision alternatives remain at the same, but now remarkably lower level for the deflective DSS (see Fig. 5, bottom-right).

5   Discussion

The presented experiment provides valuable insights for the design of Decision Support Systems (DSS) for inventory control, supply chain management, and probably a multitude of other managerial decision tasks.

Although the given task of comparing a set of numbers is exceptionally easy, the participants' accuracy is affected by the amount of information (i.e., length of the tables) and surprisingly, also by the type of the decision (procurement vs. no procurement). The finding that the reaction times increase with increasing information amount is in lines with previous research [15]. Yet, the current study found that the accuracy of the decision decreases when more data has to be considered, which was not found in the previous work.

The evaluation of the influence of the Decision Support Systems on effectivity and efficiency shows that providing decision support to workers in material disposition is possible and that performance and accuracy increases with correctly working systems.

Hence, it is advisable for developers of software for production systems to carefully design such support systems, as they reduce the error rate, increase the performance, and probably also increase job satisfaction of the workers.

However, if the Decisions Support Systems work incorrectly, they seem to deflect operators from performing their tasks correctly. The participants of the experiment received feedback on the correctness of their actions immediately after each decision; hence, they must have noticed the defectiveness of the system. This is also confirmed by the achieved performances for the defective DSS, which is decreased compared to the correct DSS and en par with the baseline. Yet, the lower achieved accuracy (compared to the baseline) indicates that the participants followed the DSS's suggestions, despite knowing about its defectiveness.

The diabolical finding of this article is that these shattering effects are concealed by the simpler tasks of the experiment and only emerge clearly for the longest tables with the highest information density. This underlines that during design and development of any interactive systems, the complexity of the later actual tasks should never be underestimated. Otherwise, the interactive system might work perfectly well in a clean development setup with simplistic dummy data, but will horribly fail if people start using the system for actual work with real data. Especially in the context of manufacturing companies, this might not only lead to a decrease in employee satisfaction, but also to competitive disadvantages through reduced effectivity as shown in the experiment above.

Concluding, the article highlights the rising importance of including the human factors and human-centered design in the development of managerial systems.

6   Limitations

Obviously, the prototypic task of this experiment is easy to automate and implementing a perfectly working DSS for this task is trivial. Nevertheless, this study exemplifies that performance and accuracy of human operators in managerial tasks is influenced by the amount of information and possible support systems.

The current experiment focused on an easy number comparison task. We suspect that the positive influence of a correctly working DSS and the negative influence of a defective system is even stronger for more complicated tasks. Correspondingly, a previous publication suggests that task performance is affected by task complexity and interface usability: Poor interface usability can be compensated in simple tasks (i.e., similar performance), but poor usability in combination with complex tasks yields in significantly lower performance [16]. Furthermore, the presented data was static, but how will the findings shift if the underlying data is unclear or tainted with uncertainty? Consequently, a follow-up must address the influence of different DSSs, complexity, and uncertainty on speed, accuracy, and the participants' perceptions.

The presented findings are based on a sample of 20 participants. Yet, the low p-values and the strong effect sizes suggest that this within-subjects experiment identified various crucial aspects that must be considered when implementing decision support systems. Contrary to previous studies and contrary to our expectations, the considered user-diversity factors (i.e., age, the well-validated number comparison score [19], and trust in automation) did not significantly influence accuracy and performance. We suspect that this is caused by the rather small sample and their homogeneity (university students or graduates) and suggest a validation of this study with a larger and more diverse sample.

Within the limited space of this article, we did not immerse into the analysis of post-hoc tests for the more than n-nary factors, such as the amount of data.

7 Outlook

The present article showed that business simulation games and game-based learning environments are a suitable method to understand human-factors and individual decision making abilities in simulated though complex environments. We also showed that these environments could be used to study the benefits and pitfalls of decision support systems in their respective contexts.

The findings presented above are based on a small and rather young sample. The current shift in the demographic structure of many developed societies demands that future studies address the interrelationship between age and the ability to understand and control complex socio-technical production systems. Future studies must therefore investigate how age and the associated decline in sensomotoric ability and decelerated cognitive control influences efficiency and effectivity in inventory control tasks [20]. Although age is often considered as a barrier for interacting with technology, it can also be speculated that the vaster experience and increased serenity of older employees may yield in less exaggerated decision behavior. This, in turn, may then yield in a reduced variance across the whole supply chain (cf. Forrester's bullwhip effect [21]).

The current findings are based on the simplified supply chain game. To ensure ecological validity further studies will need to quantify the influence of different types of decision support systems in more complex and realistic decision making tasks. A companion study on the before-mentioned Quality-Intelligence Game already identified that properly designed user interfaces in combination with a DSS can significantly increase the overall performance and satisfaction of players [22, 23]. Yet, the influences of defective systems in complex environments have not yet been investigated.

Acknowledgements. We thank all participants of this strenuous experiment and Frederic Speicher and Anaïs Habermann for their support. The German Research Foundation (DFG) founded this project within the Cluster of Excellence "Integrative Production Technology for High-Wage Countries" (EXC 128).

References

1. Lee, J., Bagheri, B., Kao, H.A.: A cyber-physical systems architecture for industry 4.0-based manufacturing systems. Manuf. Lett. **3**, 18–23 (2015)
2. Shim, J.P., Warkentin, M., Courtney, J.F., Power, D.J., Sharda, R., Carlsson, C.: Past, present, and future of decision support technology (2002)

3. Gorry, G.A., Morton, M.S.S.: A framework for management information systems. Sloan Manage. Rev. **13**, 50–70 (1971)
4. Kimball, R., Ross, M.: The Data Warehouse Toolkit: The Complete Guide to Dimensional Modelling. Wiley, New York (1996)
5. Codd, E., Codd, S., Salley, C.: Providing OLAP to user-analysts: an IT mandate (1993)
6. Bra, A., Lungu, I.: Improving decision support systems with data mining techniques. In: Advances in Data Mining Knowledge Discovery and Applications. InTech (2012)
7. Phillips-Wren, G.: Ai tools in decision making support systems: a review. Int. J. Artif. Intell. Tools **21**, 1–13 (2012)
8. Tomaszewski, W.: Computer-based medical decision support system based on guidelines, clinical pathways and decision nodes. Acta Bioeng. Biomech. **14**(1), 107–116 (2012)
9. Wen, W., Wang, W.K., Wang, C.H.: A knowledge-based intelligent decision support system for national defense budget planning. Expert Syst. Appl. **28**, 55–66 (2005)
10. Shibl, R., Lawley, M., Debuse, J.: Factors influencing decision support system acceptance. Decis. Support Syst. **54**, 953–961 (2013)
11. Chen, C.-W., Koufaris, M.: The impact of decision support system features on user overconfidence and risky behavior. Eur. J. Inf. Syst. **24**, 607–623 (2014)
12. Djamasbi, S., Loiacono, E.T.: Do men and women use feedback provided by their decision support systems (DSS) differently? Decis. Support Syst. **44**, 854–869 (2008)
13. Althuizen, N., Reichel, A., Wierenga, B.: Help that is not recognized: harmful neglect of decision support systems. Decis. Support Syst. **54**, 719–728 (2012)
14. Ben-Zvi, T.: Measuring the perceived effectiveness of decision support systems and their impact on performance. Decis. Support Syst. **54**, 248–256 (2012)
15. Ziefle, M., Brauner, P., Speicher, F.: Effects of data presentation and perceptual speed on speed and accuracy in table reading for inventory control. Occup. Ergon. **12**, 119–129 (2015)
16. Mittelstädt, V., Brauner, P., Blum, M., Ziefle, M.: On the visual design of ERP systems – the role of information complexity, presentation and human factors. In: 6th International Conference on Applied Human Factors and Ergonomics (AHFE 2015) and the Affiliated Conferences, AHFE 2015, pp. 270–277 (2015)
17. Sterman, J.D.: Modeling managerial behavior: misperceptions of feedback in a dynamic decision making experiment. Manage. Sci. **35**, 321–339 (1989)
18. Stiller, S., Falk, B., Philipsen, R., Brauner, P., Schmitt, R., Ziefle, M.: A game-based approach to understand human factors in supply chains and quality management. Procedia CIRP **20**, 67–73 (2014)
19. Ekstrom, R.B., French, J.W., Harman, H.H., Dermen, D.: Kit of Factor-Referenced Cognitive Tests. Educational Testing Service, Princeton (1976)
20. Fisk, A.D., Rogers, W.A.: Handbook of Human Factors and the Older Adult. Academic Press, Cambridge (1997)
21. Forrester, J.W.: Industrial Dynamics. MIT Press, Cambridge (1961)
22. Philipsen, R., Brauner, P., Stiller, S., Ziefle, M., Schmitt, R.: Understanding and supporting decision makers in quality management of production networks. In: Advances in the Ergonomics in Manufacturing. Managing the Enterprise of the Future 2014: Proceedings of the 5th International Conference on Applied Human Factors and Ergonomics, AHFE 2014, pp. 94–105. CRC Press, Boca Raton (2014)
23. Philipp, B., Ralf, P., Martina, Z.: Projecting efficacy and use of business simulation games in the production domain using technology acceptance models. In: Proceedings of the Applied Human Factors and Ergonomics Conference, AHFE 2016 (2016, in press)

Building a Classification Model for Physician Recommender Service Based on Needs for Physician Information

Ming-Hsin Chiu[⊠] and Wei-Chung Cheng

Graduate Institute of Library and Information Studies,
National Taiwan Normal University, Taipei, Taiwan
phoebechiu@ntnu.edu.tw,
weichung@ntu.edu.tw

Abstract. This study aimed to analyze the questions asking for recommendations for doctors collected from Health category of Yahoo Answers. Questions of such implicitly describe the physician information needs in situations where choosing a new physician who fits the patients' expectation is a top priority. 400 questions were analyzed qualitatively to induce the attributes of the articulated physician information needs of patients and caregivers of eight medical specialties. The attributes were categorized into physician-related, patient-related, illness and disease-related, and institution and procedural-related. The attributes inform practice in designing systems for context-based classification model for physician recommender service.

Keywords: Physician information · Information needs · Classification model · Physician recommender service

1 Background

Physician information is vital and can make the difference between a positive medical encounter and a negative one when making a physician selection decision. Physician information ranges from general information such as physician's gender, medical specialty, practice location, education background, to experience-based patients' rating and reviews on physicians. The availability of patient-oriented online health information and the development of comprehensive health information portals have profoundly changed the way patients seek health information [1–3]. Past studies have confirmed the benefit of accessing physician information for patients' physician decision-making. Patients can examine the quality reports of health care institutions and patient reviews on physicians prior to the clinical visit [4, 5]. The provision of health care providers' personal information might enable patient access to physicians' personal lives that were previously considered beyond the scope of traditional physician-patient relationship [6, 7]. From the patients and caregivers' perspective, physician information in the form of online physician reviews increase patient empowerment to take proactive actions by supporting useful information on selection of physicians [8, 9]. From the health care providers' perspective, the patient reviews can be considered as a form of quality

F.F.-H. Nah and C.-H. Tan (Eds.): HCIBGO 2016, Part II, LNCS 9752, pp. 28–38, 2016.
DOI: 10.1007/978-3-319-39399-5_3

evaluation, and improvement can be made based on the review results in order to provide better health care services [10].

Physician information on the Internet can be categorized into three types: professional information, such as curriculum vitae, awards, and publications; personal information, such as social network sites, and family and financial information; and physician rating information that is patient-generated and out of an individual physician's direct control [11]. However, problems of physician information retrieval remain in multiple aspects. However, certain characteristics of physician information, such as physicians' bedside manner and personality, are extremely subjective and difficult to describe. In instances when patients and caregivers are looking for information for making decision on physician selection, or when they won't be able to seeing the same physicians and needing to switch physicians due changes to their health coverage or other reasons, the uncertainty of not knowing which physician to contact and consult increases the difficulty of search for physician information. Consequently, many turn to health-related open forums and solicit recommendations for names of physicians who might be fitting the patients' health situation and expectation. For example, "I am 37 years old and live in Virginia but currently taking a job assignment in Rome NY for 3 months. I am 8 weeks pregnant with my first child and it's very difficult to drive back to VA every other week to see my OB at home. I'm so stressed out right now because it's very important that I'm in OB care during my 1st Trimester but I have to be away from home. I am willing to drive to Syracuse and any other surrounding cities for a good OB. I'm also looking for a High Risk specialist or a lab who can do First Trimester screening for me. Please help!!!" Questions of such implicitly describe the physician information needs in situations where choosing a new physician who fits the patients' expectation is a top priority. Investigating questions of physician information needs can advance the development of the patient-centered approach to physician selection.

2 Research Methods

This study analyzed 400 questions asking for recommendations for doctors collected from Health category of Yahoo Answers. Fifty questions of each of the eight medical specialties were purposefully solicited because these medical specialties usually have high demand for physician referral or recommendation. The eight medical specialties are gynecology and obstetrics, oncology, orthopedics and rehabilitation, dentistry, aesthetic medicine, neurology and neurosurgery, otolaryngology, and Chinese medicine. A combination of keywords, including "recommend," "recommending," "doctor (s)," "physician(s)," "recommended doctor(s)/physician(s)," "recommend a doctor/ physician," and "recommendations for doctor(s)/physician(s)" "would you (please) recommend a doctor/physician" were used to search for requests asking for recommendations for doctors. These keywords were typed into the search box of Health category of Yahoo! Answers, and names of the eight medical specialties were also used as keywords to filter and select only questions that met the criteria. The keyword search process was performed repeatedly until fifty questions for each of the eight medical specialties were fully collected.

Each question requesting for recommendations for doctors was numbered and classified into the medical specialty it belonged to, and was reasoned and designated as patients' and caregivers' articulated physician information needs. An Excel spreadsheet for each medical specialty was created and fifty questions for each specialty were recorded into the spreadsheets. For the purpose of this study, a unit of observation was the question requesting for recommended doctors, and a unit of analysis was a text chunk represented a single descriptor that an asker used to describe his or her physician information needs. The questions were analyzed with procedures of Grounded Theory, including open coding, axial coding, and selective coding [12]. With this method, coding categories were derived directly and inductively from the raw data- questions of request for recommended physicians. A classification model of descriptions of physician information needs was established based on the results of qualitative Grounded Theory analysis. Then the classification model was used as the coding schemes for the second stage of data analysis- quantitative content analysis. Similar to the procedures developed by [13], each question was coded for features of information need descriptions, and certain features were further subdivided into additional attributes. Percentage distribution of each attribute was determined as the ratio of the total number of observed frequency divided by the total of 400 questions.

The principal investigator along with two coders then performed constant comparison of Grounded Theory on recurring themes extracted from the questions. In the data analysis process, first, the researchers scanned through all the questions to gain familiarity with the requests. The characteristics found in the literature as well as the concepts derived from our own medical experiences were used as the initial coding schemes. Second, two coders read all the questions line-by-line, and unitized the concepts into themes, that is, when a new concept was mentioned outside of the original coding schemes, a new code was created and added to the existing coding template. For example, the idea of "language spoken" was not in the original coding scheme, it was later added to the coding schemes because it emerged from the data analysis process. Two coders independently coded 240 (60 %) questions, and they achieved high inter-coder reliability (kappa range 0.8–1.0 across codes); thus the principle investigator coded the rest of the questions. Then quantitative analysis was conducted with frequency count and percentage distribution to determine the patterns and characteristics of how patients conceptualized and articulated their physician information needs. In addition to analyzing the characteristics that are exhibited in 400 questions from eight medical specialties, this study also investigated the characteristics that are inherent across medical specialties.

3 Preliminary Findings

After analyzing 400 questions, the physician information needs are classified into four dimensions: "physician-related", "patient-related", "illness and disease-related", and "institution and procedural-related". Each question may at the same time address multiple types of attributes (Table 1).

Table 1. The attributes of four dimensions

Dimension	Attributes	Frequency	Examples (English)
Physician-related	Physician gender	381 (95 %)	Know of a good <u>female obstetrician</u> in Mississauga? Can someone recommend a good doc?
	Physician skills and expertise	160 (40 %)	I live in Texas and I am looking for <u>a dentist who does the most excellent porcelain veneers</u> and is affordable
	Physician reputation	68 (17 %)	Who is <u>the most famous plastic surgeon</u> in Korea? Anyone out there from Korea know?
	Physician bedside manner	58 (15 %)	Every time I go he is yelling at one of the staff. I know <u>he is a good doctor, but I don't think it is professional to berate the staff in direct ear shot of patients</u>. Should I stay or should I find another doctor?
	Physician personality	42 (11 %)	I'm looking for a great dentist in NYC…Any recommendations? I'm looking for a great dentist <u>with the qualifications of patience and understanding</u>
	Physician's practice	36 (9 %)	Has anyone given birth <u>at Johns Hopkins Hospital</u>? How was your experience?
	Physician medical specialty	4 (1 %)	My friend diagnosed with cancer. Pls recommend good <u>oncologist</u> in Malaysia. Also let me have the contact No. & address
	Language spoken	4 (1 %)	Is it ok for me to visit a <u>psychologist who does speak my language</u>? my English is not fluent enough as to explain all my deepest concerns in this language
Patient-related	Experience of treating patient of a particular gender	122 (31 %)	Please recommend a good obstetrician gynecologist in or around Beaverton, Portland.? <u>I am 2- 3 weeks pregnant</u> and I am new to this place

(Continued)

Table 1. (*Continued*)

Dimension	Attributes	Frequency	Examples (English)
	Patient's medical history	109 (27 %)	Need info on prognosis of Glioblastoma tumors. My little sister (age 32) has had brain tumors over the last 14 years with at least 12 surgeries being done for removal of the tumors, two of which cant be removed due to their location
	Patient's location	59 (15 %)	I'm trying to have a baby and it just wont work. Is there a doctor that you recommend? I live in New Hampshire
	Experience of treating patient of a particular age	20 (5 %)	I am 34 years old, work out like anything, but not getting the six pack. Can anybody suggest good liposuction doctor who creates six pack by liposuction?
Illness and disease-related	Illness and disease	257 (64 %)	Is there anyone can recommend a good doctor in the Dallas, Plano, Addison area? I've been having horrible migraines and need to see a physician.
	Symptoms	201 (50 %)	Should I go to The Hospital? You see, I spit up blood. Not cough, spit. And 2 days ago, I passed out. I went to the doctor yesterday and he said my counts weren't low. I also bruise and bleed easily
Institution and procedural-related	Practice location	287 (72 %)	How to find a doctor for my kids? We are looking for a decent family doctor in the Fayetteville, NC area. Any one have any recommendations?
	Medical treatment	253 (63 %)	I would like to find a doctor who will prescribe me with Xanax. If anyone could recommend a doctor. I would greatly appreciate it. Thanks a lot
	Medical cost of caring	36 (9 %)	Can anyone recommend a good cheap dentist abroad?

(*Continued*)

Table 1. (*Continued*)

Dimension	Attributes	Frequency	Examples (English)
	Classification of healthcare facility	33 (8 %)	I just moved here to Aurora, Illinois so I don't really know where I could find a free or sliding scale fee clinics for low income people. Does anyone from the area know?
	Insurance coverage	25 (6 %)	I am currently under my parents' health insurance, I am 20 and a full time college student, will my parents' insurance drop me because I am pregnant?
	Practice hours	7 (2 %)	My mom broke nose but we can't find any clinic open at night. Do you know any clinic open after 9 pm?
	With a particular medical equipment and supplies	7 (2 %)	Are CT scans dangerous? My doctor wants me to go for another CT scan. What do you think? 3 CT in 9 months?

3.1 Physician-Related Dimension

Attributes of Physician-Related Dimension. There are eight attributes in this dimension, which includes the medical specialty (95 %), skills and expertise (40 %), reputation (17 %), personality (15 %), practice (11 %), bedside manner (9 %), language spoken (1 %), and physicians' gender (1 %) (Fig. 1). Most of the questions are about "physician's medical specialty", for instance, *"My friend is diagnosed with cancer. Pls recommend good oncologist in Malaysia. Also let me have the contact No. & address"*. The second highest is "physician skills and expertise". For example, a patient addressed *"I live in Texas and I am looking for a dentist who is excellent in porcelain veneers and is affordable"*. People directly name the medical specialty of the physicians they consider would be a good fit.

Attributes of Physician-Related Dimension by Medical Specialty. Attributes in different medical specialties show diverse characteristics. "Physician's medical specialty" is the most mentioned attributes in all medical specialties, which suggests that when people have need for physician for their health problems, they would describe medical specialty for the physician wanted for their health situations. For instance, *"My friend diagnosed with cancer. Pls recommend good oncologist in Malaysia."* Second, "physician skills and expertise" is also a common question in most of medical specialties except Obstetrics and Gynecology. Third, "language spoken" and "physician gender" are less asked than the other attributes, but they both are shown in Aesthetic medicine and Obstetrics and Gynecology, which means that questions raised by people

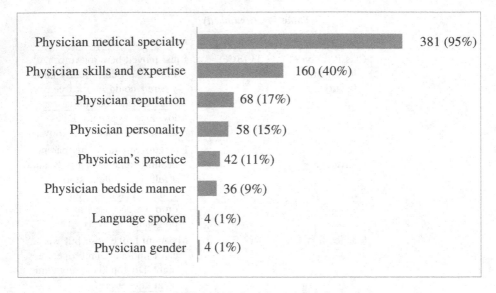

Fig. 1. Attributes of physician-related dimension

who have these kinds of problems might intend to ask for the physician's language spoken ability or mention patient's gender. For example, *"my friend wants to come to Taiwan and has a cosmetic surgery, does anyone recommend doctors who speaks English well in Taipei?"* or *"know of a good female obstetrician in Mississauga?"*

3.2   Patient-Related Dimension

Attributes of Patient-Related Dimension. This dimension includes four attributes centered on patients' gender (31 %), patients' medical history (27 %), patients' loca-tion (15 %), and patients' age (5 %) (Fig. 2). Attributes that account for the highest proportion than the others are gender and medical history. Questions of gender are such as *"I am 2- 3 weeks pregnant and I am new to this place...please share your experience with different doctors here."* On the other hand, questions of the medical history are, for example, *"my little sister (age 32) has had brain tumors over the last 14 years with at least 12 surgeries being done for removal of the tumors, two of which cant be removed due to their location."*

Attributes of Patient-Related Dimension by Medical Specialty. In this dimension, "patient's medical history" and "experience of treating patient of a particular gender" are the two most common attributes in all medical specialties. So it can be understood that "patient's medical history" and "experience of treating patient of a particular gender" are usually discussed. For instance, *"My little sister (age 32) has had brain tumors over the last 14 years with at least 12 surgeries being done for removal of the tumors, two of which can't be removed due to their location."* is a typical question

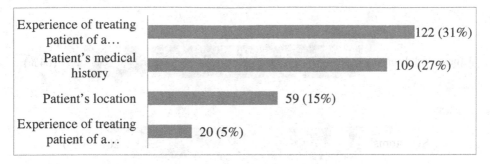

Fig. 2. Attributes of patient-related dimension

represented the attribute of "patient's medical history". And *"my mom broke her bones, please recommend a good doctor near Wanhua."* is the example for attribute of "experience of treating patient of a particular gender." On the other hand, medical specialty with higher instances of "experience of treating patient of a particular age" attribute, such as Dentistry can be classified as everyday special practice which means that the health problem would occur at patient of any age. So people may ask for a doctor who has such experience. For example, *"could you recommend dentist for children in Tucheng? My child is about 1 year old."* It's also obvious that for patients requesting for recommendation of Obstetrics and Gynecology physician, they would need more location information, such as *"I'm trying to have a baby and it just won't work. Is there a doctor that you recommend? I live in New Hampshire."*

3.3 Illness and Disease-Related Dimension

Attributes of Illness And Disease-Related Dimension. There are two attributes in Illness and Disease-related dimension (Fig. 3); these are illness and disease (64 %), and symptoms (50 %). Patients usually name and specify the medical terms in the question. For example, as *"I have been having horrible migraines and need to see a physician."* on attribute of illness and disease (64 %) or explain the situation he/she encounter, like *"I spit up blood. Not cough, spit. And 2 days ago, I passed out"* on attributes of symptoms (50 %).

Attributes of Illness and Disease-Related Dimension by Medical Specialty. Attribute of "illness and disease" is used more than "symptoms" in most of medical specialties except Neurology and Neurosurgeon and Orthopaedics. People raised their question with exact illness terms often, such as *"does anyone know authoritative doctor for Leukemia in Kaohsiung?"* and the later one indicates that there are descriptions for illness in the questions, for example, *"I've got some health issue recently, like dizzy, having head ache, and want to puke. Can anyone suggest a hospital in Taoyuan?"*

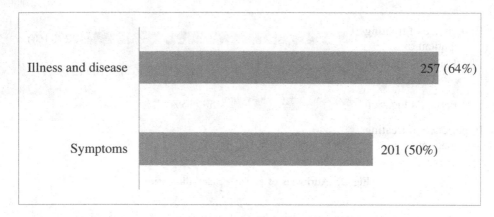

Fig. 3. Attributes of patient-related dimension

3.4 Institution and Procedural-Related Dimension

Attributes of Institution And Procedural-Related Dimension. This dimension contains seven attributes: medical treatment (72 %), practice location (63 %), medical cost of caring (9 %), classification of healthcare facility (8 %), practice hours (6 %), with particular medical equipment and supplies (2 %), and insurance coverage (2 %). The attribute account for highest proportion is medical treatment (72 %). An example of questions of medical treatment is *"I am looking to see a doctor about my anxiety. I would like to find a doctor who will prescribe me <u>with Xanax</u>."* The second most commonly found attribute is practice location, and an example could be *"We are looking for a decent family doctor <u>in the Fayetteville, NC area</u>. Any one has any recommendations?"* (Fig. 4).

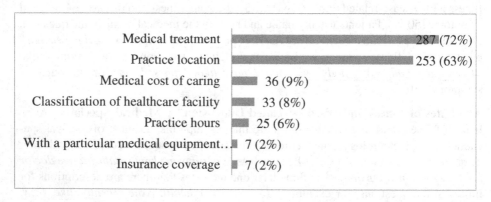

Fig. 4. Attributes of institution and procedural-related dimension

Attributes of Institution and Procedural-Related Dimension by Medical Specialty. In all medical specialties, attributes of "medical treatment" and "practice location" are asked more frequently than the others. People meet problems in Aesthetic medicine, Dentistry and Oncology raised questions with higher proportion of attribute of medical treatment. However, attribute of "practice location" is higher than "medical treatment" in Chinese medicine and Otolaryngological. For example, *"Will anyone recommend a considerate doctor who had done laparotomy surgery?"* represents the characteristic of attributes of medical treatment. So it can be explained that people who have questions for Aesthetic medicine, Dentistry and Oncology, may focus on the medical treatments. On the other hand, people will value the importance of attribute of practice location when they have problems in Chinese medicine and Otolaryngological, such as *"I've got a cold, can anyone recommend a doctor in old town in Tainan?"*

4 Implications of the Study

The major significance of this study differs from past research on patients' information needs of physician selection lies in the contextualized nature of the questions analyzed. This study focuses on uncovering the complexity, uncertainty, and ambiguity of physician information retrieval by analyzing the nature of physician information needs from the users' perspective, and re-examining the alternative attributes of the information organization for physician referral and recommendation systems. The attributes of the articulated of physician information needs derived from data analysis can be considered as the criteria that a patient or caregiver may follow when trying to find a "good" doctor for his health needs. The criteria may inform practice in designing systems for context-based classification model for physician recommender service.

References

1. Fox, S.: The engaged e-patient population. Pew Internet & American Life Project (2008). http://www.pewInternet.org/Reports/2008/The-Engaged-Epatient-Population.aspx
2. Madden, M., Fox, S.: Finding answers online in sickness and in health. Pew Internet & American life project 2 May 2006. http://pewresearch.org/pubs/220/finding-answers-online-in-sickness-and-in-health
3. Murray, E., Lo, B., Pollack, L., et al.: The impact of health information on the Internet on health care and the physician–patient relationship: national U.S. survey among 1.050 U.S. physicians. J. Med. Internet Res. **5**(3), e17 (2003)
4. Bates, D.W., Gawande, A.A.: The impact of the internet on quality measurement. Health Aff. **19**(6), 104–114 (2000)
5. Fanjiang, G., Glahn, T., Chang, H., Rogers, W.H., Safran, D.G.: Providing patients web-based data to inform physician choice: if you build it, will they come? J. Gen. Intern. Med. **22**, 1463–1466 (2007)
6. Gorrindo, T., Groves, J.E.: Web searching for information about physicians. JAMA **300**, 213–215 (2008)
7. Sinnott, J.T., Joseph, J.P.: Web searches about physicians. JAMA **300**, 2249–2250 (2008)

8. Hay, M.C., Strathmann, C., Lieber, E., Wick, K., Giesser, B.: Why patients go online: multiple sclerosis, the internet, and physician-patient communication. Neurologist **14**(6), 374–381 (2008)
9. Sciamanna, C.N., Clark, M.A., Diaz, J.A., Newton, S.: Filling the gaps in physician communication: the role of the Internet among primary care patients. Int. J. Med. Inform. **72**(1), 1–8 (2003)
10. Strech, D.: Ethical principles for physician rating sites. J. Med. Internet Res. **13**(4), e113 (2011)
11. Mostaghimi, A., Crotty, B.H., Landon, B.E.: The availability and nature of physician information on the internet. J. Gen. Intern. Med. **25**(11), 1152–1156 (2010)
12. Glaser, B., Strauss, A.: The Discovery of Grounded Theory. Weidenfeld and Nicholson, London (1967)
13. Lee, J.H.: Analysis of user needs and information features in natural language queries seeking music information. J. Am. Soc. Inf. Sci. Technol. **61**, 1025–1045 (2010)

Flow and the Art of ERP Education

Craig C. Claybaugh[✉]

Missouri University of Science and Technology, Rolla, USA
claybaughc@mst.edu

Abstract. As ERP systems have become a part of most organizations, universities have responded by incorporating these systems into their curriculum. This research looks at how the use of a simulation game can be used to enhance student learning through student engagement and learning intentions. Drawing upon flow literature and expectation-confirmation theory, this study presents an Attitude Change Model of game-based ERP Learning. In particular, this study focuses on how student immersion influences satisfaction and attitude change in ERP learning.

Keywords: Enterprise resource planning (ERP) · Flow · Attitude change

1 Introduction

The adoption and use of ERP systems has become a common way for firms to optimize efficiency [1, 2]. Universities and corporate training programs have realized the importance of ERP systems in the business world and have incorporated such systems (e.g., SAP or Oracle) into their curricula and training [3, 4]. As ERP system implementations normally encompass a substantial redesign of business processes [5, 6], the use of such systems as a learning environment provides an superb chance to allow students to gain understanding into the integration and functionality of business and IT [7].

While there has been an extensive body of ERP research on specific topics such as adoption and implementation [8, 9], assimilation [1], job characteristics and satisfaction [10], and ERP upgrades [11], extant research remains relatively scant in examining flow-based ERP learning. Given the significance of ERP learning this study poses the following research question: how does flow influence satisfaction and attitude change? Using the lens of expectation-confirmation theory (ECT) [12] the proposed study presents an attitude change model of flow based ERP learning. To address this research question a survey of students participating in an ERP simulation game will be used to test the research model.

2 Conceptual Background

The conceptual background in this paper draws on expectation-confirmation theory (ECT) and flow [12, 13]. These two concepts are used to from the research model which seeks to examine how subjects perceive the use of a simulation game to enhance their

© Springer International Publishing Switzerland 2016
F.F.-H. Nah and C.-H. Tan (Eds.): HCIBGO 2016, Part II, LNCS 9752, pp. 39–46, 2016.
DOI: 10.1007/978-3-319-39399-5_4

learning outcomes. The model proposed here looks at how flow immersion influences a student's attitude change and intention to learn material presented to the student through a business simulation.

2.1 Expectation-Confirmation Theory

The expectation-confirmation theory (ECT) is a theory which describes how preconditions to a stimulus are used to measure a pre and post behavioral attitude [14]. The ECT comprises four primary constructs: expectations, perceived performance, confirmation, and satisfaction [3]. The ECT posits that an individual's expectations and perceived performance affect positive or negative disconfirmation after an event takes place (like training). If a service beats expectations (positive disconfirmation) post-procurement satisfaction will be increased. If a service fails to meet initial expectations (negative disconfirmation), the consumer is likely to be dissatisfied. Individuals who had a positive experience will be likely to repurchase a product or service, while, at the same time, an individual who is dissatisfied would be less likely to buy the service again [2, 15]. IS researchers have applied the theory to IT usage [12, 16, 17] and web consumer satisfaction [18]. In the context of this study the theory will be applied to flow based learning.

Research also has demonstrated that ECT has a strong relationship with individual's attitude formation and future behavior intention [19]. In particular, ECT emphasizes external influence and information processing of consumer/users in attitude formation and modification. The aforementioned research streams have distinctive perceptions in examining attitudes. This study is in line with influence focus stream and examines the role of flow in a team based environment and a learners' attitude towards this learning.

2.2 Flow

Flow is a psychological concept of human behavior where one would be completely absorbed and engaged in an activity that nothing else seems to matter [20]. Drawing on past conceptions of flow, Nah et al. [21] characterize common flow characteristics as including the following elements: (1) a challenging activity that requires skills, (2) merging of action and awareness, (3) clear goals and immediate feedback, (4) concentration on the task at hand, (5) a sense of control, (6) loss of self-consciousness, (7) transformation or distorted sense of time, and (8) self-rewarding or autotelic experience. Flow, as a behavioral state, has been found to positively influence learning, attitudes, intentions, and behaviors [13]. A popular extension to flow literature is the impact this state has on game participants. As individuals engage in a game activity they immerse themselves into the context of the game and ignore all other distractions. When a game is used to facilitate ERP learning it provides an ideal context to study flow and how it influences attitude change in individuals.

Learning intention describes a future state of the learner to engage in more learning related activities [9]. The greater the individual feels there to be a benefit to learning the ERP material the greater they should be induced to want to learn the material. This attitude perception of the learning activity (a simulation game in this context) the better they will be inclined to continue to learn about ERP systems.

We rely on ECT to examine the role of flow in satisfaction and attitude change of the ERP simulation game, a tool used to facilitate ERP learning in higher education. The proposed research model can be found in Fig. 1.

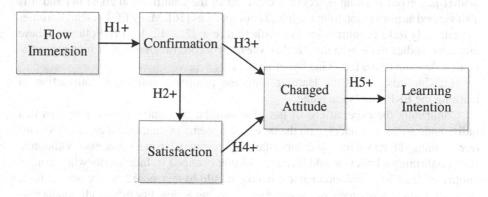

Fig. 1. Research model

2.3 Flow Immersion

Flow immersion is seen as an individual's sense of being in a complete state of concentration and focused attention to the event taking place [13], in this context ERP learning through a simulation game. In the context of this study flow is seen as being the result of two factors: telepresence and focused attention. Telepresence can be thought as a sensation of being a part of the phenomenal environment created by a medium (simulation game here) such that it induces the user of the medium to react directly with the items in the environment as if they were physically present objects [21]. Telepresence can also be referred to as the facilitated perception of an environment or the extent to which one feels present in a mediated situation [21]. Focused attention is achieved when one is focusing attention on the task/environment to the point where other thoughts are removed and distractions are ignored while attending to the task [22]. For flow to occur, the user needs to be immersed into the gaming situation such that complete focus is achieved. This also implies that the task is the focus of attention and the technology used is not that big of a deal. This focused attention will allow individuals to concentrate and achieve their goals in the context of a simulation game.

With this sense of immersion, individuals would focus on the game and its outcome all while performing tasks associated with an ERP system. With this strong sense of flow immersion the individual is motivated to perform tasks well to achieve the goal of winning the game. In the long run, the individual will feel that they learn more about the ERP system. At the same time, confirmation can be positive or negative depending on whether the individual perceived game engagement is above or below initial expectations before participating in the ERP simulation game [17]. This leads us to the following hypothesis:

H1: Flow immersion positively influences confirmation of learning the ERP simulation game.

Confirmation is defined as a learner's awareness of the comparison between the expectations of the ERP simulation game use and perceived learning outcome [12]. The difference between a learner's preliminary expectations of the ERP simulation game and his/her perceived learning outcome is captured in the confirmation construct and it is also viewed as a deviation from the initial anticipations [16]. Many ECT research studies have directly linked confirmation to satisfaction (e.g. [2, 3, 12, 16, 19]. Following these previous studies the expectation is that a learner's confirmation would increase satisfaction, leading to the following hypothesis:

H2: Confirmation of the learning outcome positively influences satisfaction of learning the ERP simulation game.

Confirming the expectations of the ERP simulation game outcome proposes that individuals are able to understand the potential benefits of understanding ERP systems (e.g., gaining IT knowledge and understanding complex business process). Validation (i.e., confirming a belief) would increase attitude change [3]. Individuals who strongly confirmed the ERP simulation game outcome would have a more positive post-attitude than pre-attitude assessment of the game as a learning action. For those individuals who do not experience what they expected they are likely to have a negative attitude toward the ERP simulation compared to their pre-attitude. Hence, we hypothesize:

H3: Confirmation of the learning outcome positively influences changed attitude toward learning the ERP simulation game.

Satisfaction is defined as an individual's affective feelings about the learning achieved through the ERP simulation game [12]. In the context of IT usage multiple studies have found a significant link between the association of satisfaction and attitude towards IT artifacts [3, 14]. Thus an individual's high satisfaction of learning the ERP system would result in increased feelings toward it. Thus, we have the following hypothesis:

H4: Satisfaction of learning the ERP system positively influences changed attitude toward learning the ERP simulation game.

Changed attitude refers to individual learners' altered (increased or decreased) assessment from the experience of the ERP simulation [2, 23]. The purpose of the ERP simulation game is to engage individuals in a learning act in a flow inducing environment with a focus on ERP functionality and business process. These individuals as learners engaged in flow, would increase their appraisal toward the ERP simulation experience and be induced to learn about ERP systems.

H5: Changed attitude toward learning the ERP simulation game experience positively influences intention to learn ERP systems.

3   Method

The proposed research model would be evaluated using a survey of students engaged in an ERP simulation game [4]. Established scales for the constructs are found in the appendix and come from existing literature. The model would be tested using SEM as the data analysis choice.

3.1 Subjects and Procedure

Subjects for this study will be both graduate and undergraduate students at a Midwestern public university in the United States. The students will be enrolled in an ERP class which uses the ERP simulation game as a method to facilitate student learning in the classroom. Students will be assigned to a team of four to run a fake company. Students will be introduced to the game and get an understanding of how the game operates. After the students have finished participating in the game students will be asked to fill out the survey.

3.2 Measures

The potential measures and their sources are shown in the appendix. These measures are consistent with how past studies have measured and analyzed ECT [24]. The measures will use a 7-point Likert-type scale. Items regarding the background and demographics of the students such as gender, academic standing, and prior experience with ERP systems will also be part of the questionnaire.

4 Expected Contributions and Discussion

This study has the potential to validate how individuals enter a state of flow when they participate in a game to enhance student learning. By systematically investigating flow in a team-based learning situation, we will extend the theoretical boundaries of the ECT with a focus on attitude change. This state of flow induces them to participate in the game more thoroughly than the standard lecture approach of instruction. The results will show how attitude changes their approach to learning.

There is no single way for education about ERP systems to be delivered. One of the keys to long term success in education is to change your approach and continuously improve the course content and delivery. This study seeks to support the assumption that inducing students into a state of flow will positively impact their task performance and enhance their learning outcomes. The results are expected to be of value to instructional designers and instructors so that a state of flow can be induced while still engaging students in a playful activity. It should also be pointed out that inducing flow might not enhance learning for all students. Some students might react negatively to the stress associated with being asked to run a simulation game. Other students might not like the team dynamics of the simulation game.

A future study might expand this work and look at how other factors interact with flow and its impact on learning. For example, individual difference (need for cognition or student skill levels) might impact the ability of students to enter a state of flow [22]. Gender might also influence how students perceive the simulated competition or its related stresses [3, 22]. These differences in each student are a part of every course delivery and should be studied to determine which might need to be addressed in course design.

Appendix: Measurement Items

Telepresence - The following items are answered on a 1–7 scale of strongly disagree to strongly agree [13].

I forgot about my immediate surroundings when I was engaged in the ERP simulation game.
When the simulation game ended, I felt like I came back to the "real world" after a journey.
During the simulation game, I forgot that I was in the middle of a course assignment.

Focused attention - The following items are answered on a 1–7 scale of strongly disagree to strongly agree [21].

When going through the simulation game, I am not distracted.
When intruded by someone while going through the simulation game, I am annoyed.
When going through the simulation game, I don't surf the Internet or things like that.
When going through the simulation game, I have a feeling of concentration.
When going through the simulation game, I am unaware of what is going on around me.

Confirmation of learning the simulation game.
Seven-point scales anchored with "strongly disagree" and "strongly agree" [3].

Learning via the SAP simulation game was better than what I had expected.
Overall, most of my learning expectations regarding the learning SAP simulation game were verified.
Overall, most of my learning expectations regarding the learning SAP simulation game were confirmed.

Satisfaction of learning the simulation game [3].
Seven-point semantic scales: How do you feel about your overall experience with the SAP simulation game:

Very dissatisfied/very satisfied.
Very displeased/very pleased.
Very frustrated/very contented.

Attitude toward learning the simulation game [3].
Seven-point semantic scales: For me, learning the SAP simulation game is:

A bad idea/a good idea.
Foolish/beneficial.
Undesirable/desirable.

Intention to learn ERP systems [3].
Seven-point scales anchored with "strongly disagree" and "strongly agree".

I intend to learn about ERP systems.
I predict that I will learn about ERP systems.
I am willing to learn about ERP systems.

References

1. Liang, H., Saraf, N., Hu, Q., Yajiong, X.: Assimilation of enterprise systems: the effect of institutional pressures and the mediating role of top management. MIS Q. **31**(1), 59–87 (2007)
2. Sieber, T., Siau, K., Nah, F., Sieber, M.: SAP implementation at the University of Nebraska. J. Inf. Technol. Cases Appl. **2**(1), 41–72 (2000)
3. Kwak, D.H., Srite, M., Hightower, R., Haseman, W.: How team cohesion leads to attitude change in the context of ERP learning. In: International Conference on Information Systems (2013)
4. Léger, P.-M.: Using a simulation game approach to teach enterprise resource planning concepts. J. Inf. Syst. Educ. **17**, 441–448 (2006)
5. Claybaugh, C.C., Haseman, W.D.: Understanding professional connections in LINKEDIN —a question of trust. J. Comput. Inf. Syst. **54**(1), 94–105 (2013)
6. Robey, D., Ross, J.W., Boudreau, M.: Learning to implement enterprise systems: an exploratory study of the dialectics of change. J. Manag. Inf. Syst. **19**(1), 17–46 (2002)
7. Cronan, T.P., Léger, P.-M., Robert, J., Robert, J., Babin, G., Charland, P.: Comparing objective measures and perceptions of cognitive learning in an ERP simulation game: a research note. Simul. Gaming **43**(4), 461–480 (2012)
8. Holland, C.P., Light, B.: A critical success factor model for ERP implementation. IEEE Softw. **16**(3), 30–36 (1999)
9. Markus, M.L., Tanis, C.: The enterprise system experience—from adoption to success. In: Zmud, R.W. (ed.) Framing the Domains of IT Research: Projecting the Future Through the Past, pp. 173–207. Pinnaflex Educational Resources Inc., Cincinnati (2000)
10. Morris, M.G., Venkatesh, V.: Job characteristics and job satisfaction: understanding the role of enterprise resource planning system implementation. MIS Q. **34**(1), 143–161 (2010)
11. Claybaugh, C.C., Ramamurthy, K., Haseman, W.D.: Assimilation of enterprise technology upgrades: a factor-based study. Enterp. Inf. Syst. pp. 1–34 (2015)
12. Bhattacherjee, A.: Understanding information systems continuance: an expectation-confirmation model. MIS Q. **25**(3), 351–370 (2001)
13. Nah, F.F.-H., Eschenbrenner, B., DeWester, D.: Enhancing brand equity through flow and telepresence: a comparison of 2D and 3D virtual worlds. MIS Q. **35**(3), 731–747 (2011)
14. Bhattacherjee, A., Sanford, C.: Influence processes for information technology acceptance: an elaboration likelihood model. MIS Q. **30**(4), 805–825 (2006)
15. Oliver, R.L.: A cognitive model for the antecedents and consequences of satisfaction. J. Mark. Res. **17**(4), 460–469 (1980)
16. Bhattacherjee, A., Premkumar, G.: Understanding changes in belief and attitude toward information technology usage: a theoretical model and longitudinal test. MIS Q. **28**(2), 229–254 (2004)
17. Spreng, R.A., MacKenzie, S.B., Olshavsky, R.W.: A reexamination of the determinants of consumer satisfaction. J. Mark. **60**, 15–32 (1996)
18. McKinney, V., Yoon, K., Zahedi, F.M.: The measurement of web-customer satisfaction: an expectation and disconfirmation approach. Inf. Syst. Res. **13**(3), 296–315 (2002)
19. Patterson, P.G., Johnson, L.W., Spreng, R.A.: Modeling the determinants of customer satisfaction for business-to-business professional services. J. Acad. Mark. Sci. **25**(1), 4–17 (1997)
20. Csikszentmihalyi, M.: Flow: The Psychology of Optimal Experience. Harper & Row, New York (1990)

21. Nah, F.F.-H., Eschenbrenner, B., Zeng, Q., Telaprolu, V.R., Sepehr, S.: Flow in gaming: literature synthesis and framework development. Int. J. Inf. Syst. Manag. **1**(1–2), 83–124 (2014)
22. Shin, N.: Online learner's 'flow' experience: an empirical study. Br. J. Educ. Technol. **37**(5), 705–720 (2006)
23. Léger, P.-M., Robert, J., Babin, G., Pellerin, R., Wagner, B.: ERPsim, ERPsim Lab. HEC Montréal, Montréal (2007)
24. Venkatesh, V., Goyal, S.: Expectation disconfirmation and technology adoption: polynomial modeling and response surface analysis. MIS Q. **34**(2), 281–303 (2010)

Accessible Learning Experience Design and Implementation

Phillip J. Deaton[(✉)]

Digital Content and Accessibility, Michigan State University, East Lansing, MI, USA
deatonph@msu.edu

Abstract. In order to create equivalent educational experiences in higher education for students with disabilities, a full integration of universal design ideas needs to be implemented into the design of websites and courses. This paper discusses the theory of an Accessible Learning Experience by looking holistically at the objectives of higher education institutions, and seeks to develop and implement strategies to ensure the accessibility of content for an organization's diverse audiences.

Keywords: Higher education · Accessibility · Universal design · Course design · Web design · Disability

1 Introduction

Organizations are increasingly acknowledging the importance of the accessibility of content offerings and systems while also expanding their missions through outreach, research, and instruction. Universities are charged with maintaining a variety of programs and with preparing students for the workforce while maintaining a brand of world-wide engagement. As the roles and goals of higher education institutions evolve [1] and increasingly rely on electronic and information technology (EIT) [2], which includes the web, software, and hardware [3, 4], it is essential to consider the experiences that we craft.

As higher education institutions work to expand their outreach, and to acknowledge and increase the diversity of their students [5], they also work to build their global brands around ideas of diversity and inclusion [6]. The university is no longer a regional source of education and empowerment, but is instead a global identity that participates in global research, service-learning that engages students and communities, and innovation by encouraging students, faculty, and staff to identify needs and to create solutions to them using interdisciplinary teams to innovate and create content that is representative of the work and learning of students and the university. The distance barriers that information once encountered are now gone, and any research that is done now can and should easily be made available to scholars around the world [7].

Due to the various roles of universities in the present day and moving forward, it is important to recognize the different processes that universities use to accomplish their unique but broadening goals. Knowledge is a primary end-product of higher education and information-delivery is frequently done using the web. As university websites hold

© Springer International Publishing Switzerland 2016
F.F.-H. Nah and C.-H. Tan (Eds.): HCIBGO 2016, Part II, LNCS 9752, pp. 47–55, 2016.
DOI: 10.1007/978-3-319-39399-5_5

more and more valuable information, it is important to consider how a university's web presence is used. This web presence creates an experience that is used to offer a service, whether it be to students, employees, or external individuals who are interacting with the website to learn about the university, research, and other objectives of the university. According to Hart-Davidson et al. [8], one of the observations that content strategists are making when working with organizations is that websites are increasingly representative of an organization's overall goals, rather than just a product or one service offering.

Acknowledging the importance of an organization's websites, an accessible website for persons with disabilities is an important aspect of conveying organizational objectives and services. Accessible EIT is EIT that can be broadly used, operated, and understood by individuals with a variety of disabilities [9]. To design an accessible website, course, or piece of content, organizations should consider how individuals with disabilities use their web content, and how their content creation process and environment can work to build accessibility throughout development. For an Accessible Learning Experience to be created for students with disabilities, students need to be able to access materials in an equal amount of time. According to the first page of the Resolution Agreement between the U.S. Department of Education, Office of Civil Rights and the University of Montana:

'Accessible' means that individuals with disabilities are able to independently acquire the same information, engage in the same interactions, and enjoy the same services within the same timeframe as individuals without disabilities, with substantially equivalent ease of use [10].

This definition of accessibility is in line with other Resolution Agreements which endeavor to define the term "accessible" broadly [11–13]. This definition also reflects one of the main barriers that students with disabilities express experiencing, which is the amount of time it takes to access the same assignments and readings, or to perform the same tasks with accommodation [14]. Reacting to students with disabilities and arranging accommodation requires time and is expensive in resources [15], and is impractical and not fully beneficial to students, instructors, or support staff. Accommodation is necessary in some instances, but it is better to be proactive about providing accessibility, so that students do not have to wait for accommodation.

Accessible Learning Experiences are developed through the designing of processes, strategic objectives, and user experiences that use the principles of accessibility, Universal Design, and Universal Design for Learning. Whichever process the designer uses to build experiences, an Accessible Learning Experience is the product of good design strategies and tactics, and a point to aim for when designing new systems and content. Accessible Learning Experience design requires designers to consider functional requirements when creating new content.

2   Accessible Learning Experience Design

An Accessible Learning Experience is a user experience that provides learners with a variety of disabilities (be they students or users) an equivalent experience to learners without disabilities, and in an equivalent amount of time. An Accessible Learning Experience is an end product for an end user that can and should be created by following best practices for accessible design as they evolve. Accessible Learning Experiences are not built solely out of principles of Universal Design, or an equivalent heuristic, but rather are built around the processes that support the development of systems (websites, courses, etc.) and ongoing organizational support.

2.1 Process Development

The support structure to develop these experiences revolves around the creation of and maintenance of processes which reinforce quality user experiences for all. As Lazar, Goldstein, and Taylor discuss on page 179, building a plan for accessibility requires specific goals and looking holistically at organizations, and that "organizational contexts" define how organizations should develop plans [16]. In order to enact ongoing plans, organizations need to build processes into existing teams and consider how to develop organizational awareness for individuals with disabilities and the varying ways that these users access and use technology. Process development for accessibility requires executive buy-in and leadership, clear communication and training, and a culture of awareness for digital accessibility [17]. Processes for building Accessible Learning Experiences vary by the goals of the organization trying to implement these experiences for their students, users, or customers.

For an educational institution, an organization may have the goals as described in the introduction, but for a corporation the goal may be to educate customers on service offerings, or to ensure that information about products can be widely accessed so that more products can be sold online. Developing processes that move towards offering an Accessible Learning Experience requires revising these goals. Providing support for the user's ability to learn a system gives users the tools they need to make informed decisions on purchasing products.

2.2 Ongoing Organizational Support

To consistently provide Accessible Learning Experiences, organizations need to provide support to instructors and developers through training and technical expertise. Technical experts in institutions should work with various teams to provide training and instructional material that is kept up to date, and that evolves with new emerging technologies and technical guidance. Teaching accessibility can be difficult, and while there is some research about effective instructional content for accessibility [18], it can be difficult to maintain effective programs for organizational needs. There is no way to quickly mend the accessibility of an organization, or for organizations to holistically change processes which are used in research, instruction, outreach, and design of digital content without administrative support. Accessibility is a journey along defined processes rather than a destination point. As content representative of organizations is created and distributed daily, it is important to consistently follow and develop processes to protect the rights of students, consumers, and users with disabilities.

3   Functional Requirements of Accessible Learning Experiences

To create Accessible Learning Experiences, a variety of theories and implementation strategies can be followed, but there are several core pieces to an Accessible Learning Experience. Several of these requirements are developed from the settlement language referenced earlier in this paper. An Accessible Learning Experience is an experience wherein a user (whether they are a student or a customer learning how to navigate a website's interface and content) has equal access to EIT content.

Firstly, an Accessible Learning Experience requires that a user with a disability be able to interact with EIT content with the same level of independence. If a "regular" user can navigate, operate, and use robustly a system alone, then a user with a disability should be able to as well. If a user is expected to engage in peer or expert interaction to complete tasks, then a system must allow for a user with a disability to engage their peers or be assisted by an expert similarly. While many users with disabilities may use assistive technologies, certain elements of design and programmatic design will drastically affect the ways in which these technologies work. As Bouck discusses on pages 17–20, assistive technology has an impact on the accessibility of content, but the digital environments that content providers use or create plays a significant role in determining whether or not a user will be able to independently acquire information [19].

In recognizing the importance of assistive technology, it is also important to note that all users with similar disabilities will benefit from or use assistive technology [20]. Design content that can be manipulated independently by the end user, or manipulated by the user's use of assistive technology, but do not design content that presumes the user's use of assistive technology, or that forces the user to use assistive technology that they may or may not be comfortable with using. Just as the designer/content creator should build for an independently accessible experience, the designer should also respect the principle that the user plays a role in building the digital environment by choosing and personalizing the user agent used to access content and by choosing whether or not they choose to use certain assistive technologies in certain situations. In education, this is particularly critical, as the user's personalization of the ubiquitous technologies used to access contextually educational EIT does play a role in personalizing what educators may perceive to be a standardized environment for interacting with ideas [21]. Peter Blanck echoes this idea on page 39, by describing applications and content that are "universal, yet capable of individualized operation" [22].

Secondly, an Accessible Learning Experience requires that a user with a disability have access to the same information when using EIT. Information cannot be segregated, and optional information, if designed to be optionally included in a curricula (or to provide optional information to a user), should optionally be available to users with a disability. Information that is secondary to one user may be primary to another. For example, while one consumer may not need to know that your organization charges an international service fee for transactions, this piece of information may be critical to understanding and decision-making for other users.

Again, in education this is particularly important as users interact with the information they need to arrive at competencies, especially in the increasing popular Flipped Learning classrooms (flipped classrooms), where students prepare themselves for project-based classrooms by interacting with video and written instructional material prior to each face-to-face or online class period [23]. Students have a great deal of ownership over what they perceive as optional/secondary content as they work to scaffold their competencies such that they are prepared for class.

Thirdly, an Accessible Learning Experience means that students with disabilities should be able to access the same types of interactions as students without disabilities. Alternative modes of access may change the learning experience that students receive, as learners with different learning styles may benefit differently from the types of media that they are interacting with. If you are providing multiple types of media for users to interact with, then that each iteration of that information should follow best practices for accessibility. With each redesign of information media, we are crafting separate experiences and need to consider the impact that this information will have on the user. Additionally, the way that information is structured affects how we process and interact with information [24, 25]. Ensuring that students with disabilities should have access to all interactions in courses means that the instructor will not risk the reduction of usefulness of information by changing the media, and also that the instructor will not need to maintain separate learning experiences, but instead curate one that is more beneficial to all students. If an instructor wishes to provide instructional material across multiple media, then it will likely be advantageous to do so, but the instructor should make sure that all of these interactions are as accessible as they can be made to be.

Fourthly, an Accessible Learning Experience requires that students with disabilities be able to acquire information in the same timeframe as individuals without disabilities. Time is a large barrier for students with disabilities who may need to work with University offices and to reformat content themselves in order to interact with it. Ensuring that content can be accessed in a reasonably equivalent amount of time gives students the access that they need to succeed. In the unlikely event that it is unreasonable to expect users with certain interaction strategies to be able to interact with systems in an equivalent timeframe, it is important to remove barriers as you are able and to work towards this point.

Fifth, an Accessible Learning Experience requires that students be able to interact with content in a way that the settlements refer to as "substantially equivalent ease of use". This idea invokes that in order to fairly assess the level of accessibility of content it is necessary to understand the usability of it for persons with disabilities [26]. To measure this in practice, it is necessary to do usability testing and gather user research on both students with disabilities and students without disabilities. In order to understand whether a component of curricular content or a website offers equivalent ease of use, it is important to gather qualitative (and quantitative data, where funding permits) on student experiences. To define an Accessible Learning Experience it is essential to weave this fifth principle into the four mentioned above, and to consider time impact on students with disabilities when designing and developing websites, courses, and curricula. It is important to note that the changes in institutional engagement and the access to global information broadens the users that organizations will receive.

These five functional requirements for an Accessible Learning Experience should inform the processes that organizations design to ensure the accessibility of their EIT. It is important to note that these recommendations for can be applied and used in the

design of interfaces for websites. Usability specialists oftentimes highlight the importance of learnability in interface design [27, 28], either by suggesting that learnability
is part of usability or by suggesting that there is a correlation between learnability and
usability [29]. Accessible Learning Experiences are experiences that are crafted to be
equivalently accessible for users with disabilities who interact with EIT including software, hardware, websites, and media.

4   Implementation

Implementing Accessible Learning Experiences requires institutional knowledge. There
is no prescription to offer administrators and advocates that are looking to increase the
accessibility of their offerings. Considering accessibility requires broadly considering
the goals of an institution, the current processes, and the impact on users. Moving
towards accessibility requires holistic institutional commitment and enough executive
buy-in to be able to reach out to all aspects of the university. One way to think about
accessibility in higher ed is to consider a course development process. The Quality
Matters program has eight general standards that can give institutions a guide for asking
questions about how to build accessibility into institutional policies and workflows:
course overview and introduction, learning objectives (competencies), assessment and
measurement, instructional materials, course activities and learner interaction, course
technology, learner support, and accessibility and usability [30].

An example series of questions to ask about your organization is: do our learning
objectives support diverse interaction strategies? How do we evaluate course technology
for accessibility? Answers to these questions might be: our IT team has an expert staff
of accessibility specialists who provide centralized training and support to faculty and
instructors who are creating course content, and we evaluate the accessibility of EIT that
we purchase.

Other questions may be: How do we convey information about accessibility services
in our syllabi, and how do we ensure that faculty follow best practices for syllabus
creation and course introduction? How do we ensure that our assessments don't discrim-
inate? How do we remediate content that we have on our websites while being innovative
and developing a strategy for creating content moving forward? How do we use diverse
media and pedagogical strategies in an accessible way? How do we measure accessibility
and usability? How do we track progress towards a more accessible university? These
questions can vary, but administrators will notice key areas of overlap and areas where
working groups or focused teams may be needed. Accessible Learning Experience
designers will ask these questions and develop answers by working with students,
faculty, and staff to gather information to meet these functional requirements.

Having teams that focus on the challenges that accessibility of EIT brings in various
areas is a must. It is not enough to task someone with spending a small percentage of
their time on accessibility. All individuals who create content that is representative of
an organization should spend small amounts of time thinking about accessibility and in
being trained in best practices for document design (with these practices including
accessibility). Having a disability services unit as well as a unit in IT that focuses on

accessibility is a start, but it may also be practical to position accessibility advocates in various other units, depending on the organization.

5 Discussion

It is difficult to impossible to provide a practical checklist that can be followed to provide Accessible Learning Experiences to all students at the onset. Therefore the most important thing that organizations can do is to listen to students with disabilities, to invite students with disabilities to participate in committees on accessibility, and to continuously improve the educational experience for all by learning from the necessary accommodation of students with disabilities. The idea of an Accessible Learning Experience is not around to downplay the need for accommodation, and meeting these functional requirements for a large percentage of learners will not eliminate the need for accommodation. In proactively seeking to create Accessible Learning Experiences, designers of websites and instruction will reduce the need to react to accommodation requests that may boost the expense depending on turnaround time, such as for captioning requests. Accessible Learning Experiences always put the student first and also encourages the participation of students with disabilities in designing processes and in understanding training needs.

Prioritization is another key concept of Accessible Learning Experiences. With the wide breadth of content that organizations create, it is important to have a plan for how to prioritize content remediation and training. Theories are useful, but only as useful as the end product for the users with disabilities, and continuing to learn and understand how many people use content and gathering analytics can be useful in informing administrators on focus areas. It is also important to note varying legal obligations when creating prioritization. Additionally, consider how copyright may have an impact on your ability to provide accessible content to students with disabilities in a proactive manner [31].

6 Conclusion

Accessible Learning Experiences are experiences that are the product of process development and of tactical content creation strategies. There is no one right way to infuse accessibility into organizations, organizational awareness will dictate how administrators and advocates implement Accessible Learning Experiences. Accessible Learning Experiences are equivalent such that users with disabilities have equal access and right to information in EIT experiences. There are five key components to Accessible Learning Experiences: ensuring that students with disabilities have equal level of independence, have access to the same information, have access to the same interactions, and can complete tasks through these interactions in the same timeframe with similar usability to users without disabilities. As educators create and distribute educational content, it is increasingly important for universities to acknowledge the institution's role and responsibility in providing equal access to all, regardless of disability.

References

1. Faust, D.G.: The Role of the University in a Changing World. Baccalaureate Commencement at the Royal Irish Academy, Trinity College, Dublin, Ireland (2010)
2. Section 508 of the United States Rehabilitation Act of 1973. 29 U.S.C. §794 (2011)
3. Bennett, S., Bishop, A., Dalgarno, B., Waycott, J., Kennedy, G.: Implementing web 2.0 technologies in higher education: a collective case study. Comput. Educ. **59**(2), 524–534 (2012)
4. Franklin, T., Van Harmelen, M.: Web 2.0 for Content for Learning and Teaching in Higher Education. JISC (2007). www.jisc.acuk/media/documents/programmes/digitalrepositories/web2-contentlearningand-teaching.pdf
5. DeBard, R.: Millennials coming to college. New Dir. Student Serv. **106**, 33–45 (2004)
6. Wæraas, A., Solbakk, M.N.: Defining the essence of a university: lessons from higher education branding. High. Educ. **57**(4), 449–462 (2009)
7. Fitzgerald, H.E., Simon, L.A.K.: The world grant ideal and engagement scholarship. J. High. Educ. Outreach Engagem. **16**(3), 33–56 (2012)
8. Hart-Davidson, W., Bernhardt, G., McLeod, M., Rife, M., Grabill, J.T.: Coming to content management: inventing infrastructure for organizational knowledge work. Tech. Commun. Q. **17**(1), 10–34 (2007)
9. World Wide Web Consortium: Web Content Accessibility Guidelines (WCAG) 2.0 (2008)
10. U.S. Department of Education, Office of Civil Rights: University of Montana, Resolution Agreement (2012). http://www.umt.edu/accessibility/docs/FinalResolutionAgreement.pdf
11. U.S. Department of Education Office of Civil Rights: University of Cincinnati, Resolution Agreement (2014). http://www2.ed.gov/documents/press-releases/university-cincinnati-agreement.pdf
12. U.S. Department of Education Office of Civil Rights, South Carolina Technical College System, Resolution Agreement. http://www2.ed.gov/about/offices/list/ocr/docs/investigations/11116002-b.pdf
13. U.S. Department of Education Office of Civil Rights: Youngstown State University, Resolution Agreement (2014). http://www2.ed.gov/documents/press-releases/youngstown-state-university-agreement.pdf
14. Fuller, M., Healey, M., Bradley, A., Hall, T.: Barriers to learning: a systematic study of the experience of disabled students in one university. Stud. High. Educ. **29**(3), 303–318 (2004)
15. Riddell, S.: Chipping away at the mountain: disabled students' experience of higher education. Int. Stud. Sociol. Educ. **8**(2), 203–222 (1998)
16. Lazar, J., Goldstein, D., Taylor, A.: Ensuring Digital Accessibility Through Process and Policy. Morgan Kaufmann, Waltham (2015)
17. Bocconi, S., Ott, M.: ICT and universal access to education: towards a culture of accessibility. In: Lytras, M.D., Ruan, D., Tennyson, R.D., Ordonez De Pablos, P., García Peñalvo, F.J., Rusu, L. (eds.) WSKS 2011. CCIS, vol. 278, pp. 330–337. Springer, Heidelberg (2013)
18. Keates, S.: A pedagogical example of teaching universal access. Univ. Access Inf. Soc. **14**(1), 97–110 (2015)
19. Bouck, E.C.: Assistive Technology. Sage Publications, Los Angeles (2016)
20. Strangman, N., Dalton, B.: Using technology to support struggling readers: a review of the research. In: Handbook of Special Education Technology Research and Practice, pp. 545–569 (2005)

21. Rodriguez-Ascaso, A., Boticario, J.G., Finat, C., del Campo, E., Saneiro, M., Alcocer, E., Gutiérrez y Restrepo, E., Mazzone, E.: Inclusive scenarios to evaluate an open and standards-based framework that supports accessibility and personalisation at higher education. In: Stephanidis, C. (ed.) Universal Access in HCI, Part IV, HCII 2011. LNCS, vol. 6768, pp. 612–621. Springer, Heidelberg (2011)
22. Blanck, P.: eQuality: The Struggle for Web Accessibility by Persons with Cognitive Disabilities. Cambridge University Press, Cambridge (2014)
23. Tsai, C.W., Shen, P.D., Chiang, Y.C., Lin, C.H.: How to solve students' problems in a flipped classroom: a quasi-experimental approach. Univ. Access Inf. Soc. pp. 1–9 (2016)
24. Mohageg, M.F.: The influence of hypertext linking structures on the efficiency of information retrieval. Hum. Factors J. Hum. Factors Ergon. Soc. **34**(3), 351–367 (1992)
25. Calisir, F., Gurel, Z.: Influence of text structure and prior knowledge of the learner on reading comprehension, browsing and perceived control. Comput. Hum. Behav. **19**(2), 135–145 (2003)
26. Horton, S., Quesenbery, W.: A Web for Everyone. Rosenfeld Media, Brooklyn (2013)
27. Holzinger, A.: Usability engineering methods for software developers. Commun. ACM **48**(1), 71–74 (2005)
28. Bevan, N.: Measuring usability as quality of use. Softw. Qual. J. **4**(2), 115–130 (1995)
29. Borsci, S., Federici, S., Lauriola, M.: On the dimensionality of the system usability scale: a test of alternative measurement models. Cogn. Process. **10**(3), 193–197 (2009)
30. Quality Matters: Higher Ed Program Rubric (2014). https://www.qualitymatters.org/rubric
31. Rekas, A.P.: Access to books: human rights, copyright and accessibility. In: Stephanidis, C., Antona, M. (eds.) UAHCI 2013, Part III. LNCS, vol. 8011, pp. 382–388. Springer, Heidelberg (2013)

Better Patient-Doctor Communication –
A Survey and Focus Group Study

Martin Maguire(✉)

Loughborough Design School, Loughborough University,
Leicestershire LE11 3TU, UK
M.C.Maguire@lboro.ac.uk

Abstract. The study explored barriers to effective communication between doctors and patients, and to encourage patients to be more knowledgeable about their health. A survey was conducted with 128 people who commented on the effectiveness of the process of consulting their doctor and rated a number of alternatives to face-to-face consultations. A focus group explored the topics further and a range of possible solutions to address current barriers were suggested. These include: considering alternative methods for GP consultation, providing new systems to give doctors better overviews of the patient population, devising new methods for patients to record information from consultations, use of diagnostic systems in the surgery and meetings or online forums to promote better informed patients.

Keywords: Health · Patient · Patient experience · Doctor · General practitioner (GP) · Patient communication · Ease of communication · Healthcare information systems

1 Introduction

The demands on healthcare systems worldwide are increasing as populations increase and people live longer. Patient numbers and limitations on doctors' time can restrict the level of in-depth or personalised information that patients can receive. This may relate to different options for treatment or long term management of chronic conditions. Further barriers to successful healthcare are patient's lack of understanding of health conditions, finding out about new treatments, and awareness of on-going support to guide them.

Within the UK, there is a drive for more openness within healthcare, encouraging patient empowerment, integration of medical records and patient-centred care [1]. Issues such as ownership of a person's health records and the ethical procedures of different groups handling medical information are important issues for this development. The rationale for these initiatives is that if patients had more information and understanding of their state of health, they would be able to take better control of their health which would generate better health outcomes, place fewer burdens on health services, and lead to more cost-effective healthcare services. Some authors have discussed how IT can enhance medical provider-patient relationships [2].

© Springer International Publishing Switzerland 2016
F.F.-H. Nah and C.-H. Tan (Eds.): HCIBGO 2016, Part II, LNCS 9752, pp. 56–66, 2016.
DOI: 10.1007/978-3-319-39399-5_6

2 Methods of Study

In order to explore the topic of better patient-doctor communication, two studies were carried out. Firstly, a focus group was carried out with a group of 5 members of the public in their 50 s and 60 s. A number of topics were discussed relating to visiting the doctor. The aim was to obtain their views on and to identify and problems they faced. Secondly, a questionnaire survey was administered to a sample of 128 people. The aims of the questionnaire were to obtain patient opinions of online medical information in general, making appointments to see their doctor, and possible methods of communication with their doctor.

3 Results

3.1 Survey

The survey of 128 respondents included 57 males (44.5 %) and 71 females (55.5 %). The age distribution of the sample was 77 people aged 18–29 (60.2 %), 18 people aged 30–49 (14.1 %) and 33 people aged 50 and over (25.8 %), so the survey was oriented towards younger.

In terms of accessing medical information when experiencing medical symptoms, it was found that 46.9 % of respondents go online to seek information before consulting their doctor, 38.3 % make an appointment first, while others (11.7 %) do both at the same time (Fig. 1). One of the reasons that many people go online to find medical information is the ease and immediacy of accessing information from the Internet. This will be situation dependent and as one person said, *"If the symptoms were serious or painful I would just make an appointment"*.

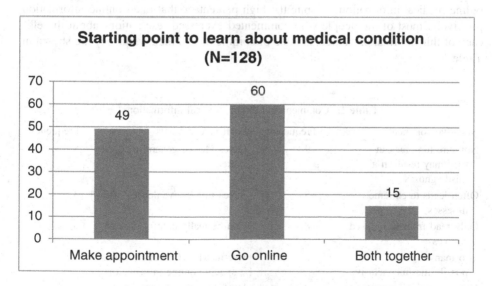

Fig. 1. Survey: starting point to find out about medical condition

Respondents were also asked for their opinion of online medical information and how helpful they found it. Their response was recorded on a Likert rating scale. It was found that 45.4 % of people considered it either 'helpful' or 'very helpful' while 30.5 % felt neutral about it. Others were less confident about online medical assistance, with 11 % rating it either 'unhelpful' or 'very unhelpful' (Fig. 2).

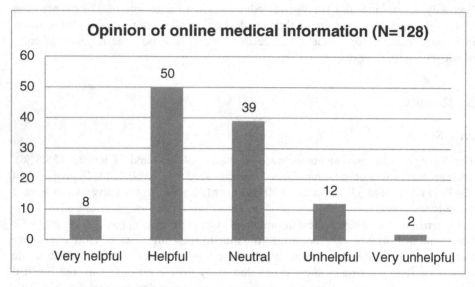

Fig. 2. Survey: helpfulness of online medical information

Comments were also sought from participants on their experience or opinion of online medical information. Despite the high percentage that rated online information positively, most of the people who commented expressed reservations about the efficacy of this information source. A table of comments and their frequency are shown in Table 1.

Table 1. Comments on online medical information

Negative comments	Frequency	Positive comments	Frequency
Not sure how far can trust/may result in a misdiagnoses	19	Gives idea of general medical area	5
Often leads to extreme illnesses	15	Saves time/convenience	3
Only read from recognised sources	8	Can be really helpful or sage	3
Too many possibilities/inconclusive	8	Useful when GP recommends specific online information	1
Not covering all symptoms	3	Useful for the children	1

Some people stated that they wouldn't necessarily take their information from a single source but would review a few different websites to look for consistency of information. There was also a requirement for sites to give more information about medications and their possible effects. In a comparison study of 3 online symptom checkers, usability issues were recorded for all 3 systems including relating symptoms to the options provided, the inflexible nature of the process and assuming knowledge that patients did not necessarily have [3]. Bol et al. provide advice on medical website design for older patients [4].

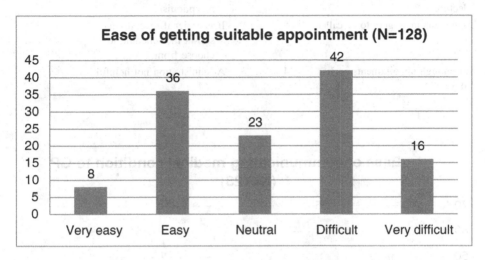

Fig. 3. Survey: ease of getting a suitable appointment

The survey asked about the ease of getting a suitable appointment time to see a doctor at the local GP practice. As Fig. 3 shows, while 34.4 % considered it either 'very easy' or 'easy', 45.3 % rated it as either 'difficult' or 'very difficult' (18 % were neutral). Common problems were: only being able to book an appointment to see a particular doctor several days or weeks in advance, and trying to get in on the day and possibly getting an appointment time that did not fit in well with their working hours. Table 2 lists the problems in booking an appointment and the frequency that they were mentioned:

Respondents were asked how easy patients found it to talk to the doctor and to communicate their medical condition to them. As Fig. 4 shows, 68.8 % of the participants stated that communication was either 'easy' or 'very easy'. 9.4 % of the sample experienced more difficulty and felt that patient-doctor communications was either 'difficult' or 'very difficult' (20.3 % were neutral). A number of comments were made that participants found GPs to be very easy to communicate with. One person stated: *"I have never had any problems and am satisfied with the advice I have received."*

Table 2. Comments on appointment booking

Comments	Frequency	Comments	Frequency
Can only book on day or several weeks in advance e.g. to see a specific GP	17	It's OK if you are flexible	3
Generally can get appointment on day or sometime that week	10	Prefer to book online	3
Difficulty finding appointments that fitting in with work or lectures	8	Online OK but easier to line up and see receptionist	1
Long waits in surgery to be called	5	It is easier if receptionist shows me schedule to choose from	1
Not enough appointments each day	4	Administration not helpful	1

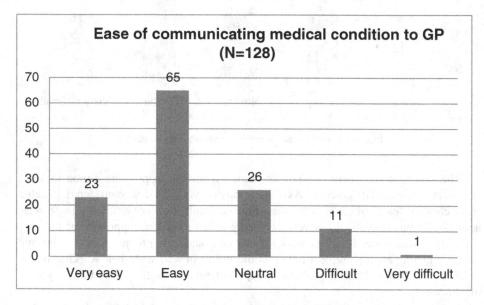

Fig. 4. Survey: ease of communicating with the doctor

However quite a few participants did highlight communication problems, sometimes due to English not being their first language. Interestingly one comment was: *"It is easy to communicate my condition but less easy to receive the advice. I sometimes forget what was said"* and *"Trying to be really clear about how things feel is difficult - sometimes the words don't seem to cover it"*. Regarding listening to the doctor's advice, it was said that: *"There can be a lot to take in with discussion of symptoms, diagnosis, treatment, next steps, contraindications, etc."*, and also: *"It is not easy to understand the terminology from doctor. Sometimes I just lack the necessary medical vocabulary.* " This might indicate that providing some kind of record for the patient to take away might assist them in understanding their condition better and reduce the need for them to return a make another appointment to seek clarification.

Some participants felt that due to the limitation on appointment times, they felt rushed which restricted their ability to ask questions or to be clear about the advice. It was said that: *"The feeling of being rushed and an unclear outcome is also problematic"*, and also: *"I don't think doctors always know what your condition might be or don't want to jump to conclusions too quickly so often tell you to return if symptoms get worse"*.

A further problem was that of seeing different doctors (a possible consequence of limited appointment availability) and having to explain their medical history each time. As one person said, *"Seeing different GPs every time and explaining your medical history and what you've tried before (is a problem)"*, and the difficulty of *"...re-explaining your medical history to a new doctor and showing you have a medical condition"*.

A key part of the survey was to ask participants whether they would be willing to use a range of methods for seeking medical advice as an alternative to traditional face-to-face communication. These included: telephone consultation, email, group session, video-communication and online forum. Figure 5 shows how many of the respondents would consider using each of these methods.

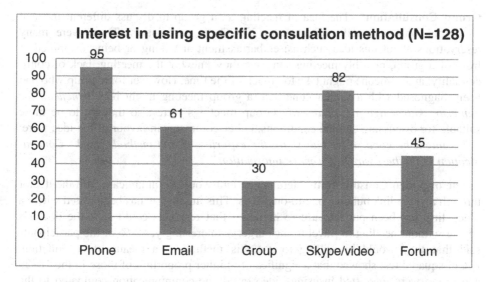

Fig. 5. Survey: interest in alternative methods of patient-GP consultation

Phone: Telephone consultation with the doctor is a well-established method in the UK. 74.2 % of the respondents said that they would use this method of communication with a doctor and a number confirmed that they had already used it and were happy with it. The clear benefit of the method was that it was: *"An easy way to talk to someone professional without having to leave the house"*. Reservations about telephone consultations were: the difficulty of describing some symptoms over the phone and a concern that they may not be expressed properly. Others said that it would be hard to *"Understand what the doctor's saying without a face-to-face chat"*. However it was thought to be less effective for conditions where the doctor should examine you directly. It was said that a telephone call would be a useful mechanism for: a results review, minor ailments and discussing ongoing or recurring issues. Interestingly one person stated that a telephone call could make the experience less intimidating.

Email: There was less support for the idea of emailing the GP although 47.7 % stated that they would consider using it. A positive comment in favour of it was that the person could: *"Think thoroughly about my problem or disease and explain it to them and reply carefully about my answers"*. However it was also said by one person that it was too impersonal while another said that: *"I probably wouldn't trust it as much - might feel that it's automated"*. One person said that they would: *"only use a telephone system with a GP who was known to me and I would very carefully explain my condition to avoid misinterpretation"*. It was also said by one person: *"I might have to wait a while for a response and if ill wouldn't want to keep checking my emails"*. Concern was also expressed that the information might not be confidential. Finally, as for telephone consultations, email would be suitable if: *"No physical examination was necessary but could include images to indicate condition/injuries."* A service for electronic web-based consultation is eVisits. The authors report on an evaluation of its acceptance and its usability [5].

Group Consultation: The idea of meeting as a group to discuss different medical conditions only received support from 23.4 % of participants. There were many reservations about this idea such as: embarrassment at talking or being examined in front of a group, possibly meeting someone they knew at the meeting, lack of confidentiality, and someone might take too much of the time. However for a group who had been diagnosed with a similar condition, a group meeting might be: *"beneficial for gathering knowledge for treatment"*. Group meetings were also thought to be more suitable for discussing chronic conditions. Other comments in favour of the idea were: *"This might be good so we can share the experiences and methods"* and *"Communication is the best way to get more information"*.

Skype or Video Consultation: Here the patient would communicate with the doctor through a video link but on a one-to-one basis. This innovation has been tested where a video link has been put into a care home so that residents could seek the doctor's advice without needing to travel to the surgery. Interestingly, 82 % of the participants said that they would be willing to use this method as a means of consultation. A Chi-squared test showed that a significantly higher proportion of those in the 18–29 age group were interested in using video or Skype communication compared to the other two age groups *(p = 0.001)*. This is not an unexpected result given the familiarity of the 18–29 age groups with online face-to-face communication. The convenience of a video call was recognised by many participants as well as the advantage of instant feedback and face-to-face communication, making the consultation more personal. One respondent had seen a similar system in use on TV which had given them confidence in using such a system.

Forum: An online forum would be organised by the GP practice for its patients with a doctor moderating the discussion. 45 % of respondents stated that they would use such a service. A positive comment in favour was *"I am an online person and surfing a lot to find my answers. This could be a good way to find a solution"*. It was thought that the forum could be most useful for disseminating general information about medical matters but that the forum would need to be carefully moderated. It was also thought that the event could become confusing if forum members had similar symptoms but different illnesses. The method would be more relevant if the medical condition being discussed was on-going rather than for transient ailments. Examples given of possible online forum topics were: nutrition, high blood pressure or diabetes.

3.2   Focus Group Results

The focus group session was conducted with a group of 5 members of the public aged 50 and over. Within the discussion, a number of problems emerged relating to: patient-doctor communication, patient information, diagnosis, decision making, medication and appointments. These are listed in Table 3 alongside some potential solutions. Some of these solutions are related to the different methods of GP consultation studied in the survey:

Table 3. Problems or issues arising from focus group and potential solutions

Problem or issue	Potential solution(s)
Communication: A number of examples of good and poor communication between doctor/GP practice and patient were given. These included: difficulty in communication seriousness of a medical condition, lack of feedback on appointment cancellation, getting blood test results over the phone and being advised that appointment needed	Providing online systems allowing patients to access summary and routine data about themselves would both save on consultation time and lead to more informed patients who could make better choices about their health and treatment. For minor queries like requesting test results, email or telephone communication could save face to face time with a doctor
Complexity of health knowledge: The number of medical conditions and information on treatment that a doctor needs to know about is now so large that it is hard for GPs to keep up to date	Access to medical specialists by video link in the GP practice or to a decision support system that the doctor and patient jointly interact with could promote higher quality patient-doctor interaction and more accurate diagnoses
Conflicting views: Sometimes there is a discrepancy between what the doctor diagnoses and what the patient thinks their condition is (based on knowledge of their own body and medical history). This can cause difficulties if the patient doesn't agree with doctor' diagnosis	The ability to call upon specialist knowledge either via a support system or video link to a specialist may help to resolve these views. The wider provision of scanning devices in more medical centres would also resolve uncertain diagnosis more quickly

(Continued)

Table 3. (*Continued*)

Problem or issue	Potential solution(s)
Choosing services: Patients are being given more choice about treatment but can find it difficult to choose a medical provider or to judge what treatment to have based on limited information and experience. Sometimes a choice of hospital can be refused if a required specialist doesn't practice in that location or if there is a staff shortage. Travelling a long way for a procedure can be problematic	Social media and inspection reviews have allowed quality ratings to be provided to patients to allow them to make selections of hospital or practitioner but it is recognised that these can be misleading. Having the ability to communicate with the department or consultants before choosing a provider can give patients the information and allow them to make a choice more confidently
Patients being proactive in requesting services: Examples were given where referrals was requested by patients to see a specialist (e.g. physiotherapist, dermatologist). One person decided to pay for their own treatment while another persevered with their surgery and was referred. They found the consultation very helpful	A gradual change is taking place where the patient is becoming a more equal partner in their relationship with the medical profession. Also if online systems improve so that they do not always lead to extreme diagnoses, then patients may be accepted by doctors as better informed and be more willing to accept their views. Patients should be more proactive in requesting medical tests which can lead to earlier diagnosis and more effective treatment
Seminars and forums: The idea of a group of local practices organising presentations for patients was well received by the group. It was thought it would be useful to communicate important information to patients e.g. to know whether a child's rash is serious or not and whether they should get medical help. However in the past when a presentation was put on about a medical topic, it wasn't well attended	There is a need to encourage a patient culture of being interested in medical issues even when they are not of immediate concern to them. When events are offered, there is a need for marketing skills to be applied in order to attract interest in the local community. Also going online and being in contact with people who have similar conditions could be helpful in promoting that interest further
Choice of medication: One participant had experience of their normal tablets being swapped for more inexpensive ones but had more side effects resulting in more GP visits about side effects. It was stated that patients need to be assertive and ask for the tablets wanted, rather than change them after a long period of successful use	Possibly IT supported day-to-day recording of a patient's symptoms after taking medications can help determine the most appropriate for them to have
Older people's reluctance to visit the doctor: May result in waiting until very poorly before consulting a doctor	Patient information systems within the surgery can highlight which patients have certain medical conditions and which patients have not been to see their GP for a long time so could be invited for a general check-up

(*Continued*)

Table 3. (*Continued*)

Problem or issue	Potential solution(s)
Emergency appointments: If asked whether an emergency appointment is required, it can be hard for the patient to judge. With long waits to see a particular doctor, patients may take emergency appointments when it is not necessary	Patient education learning about when an emergency appointment is appropriate is helpful. However better communication of information about particular patients in a practice may encourage patients to see another doctor
Regular appointments: Example given of receptionists being helpful in booking follow-up with the GP required/preferred	This useful level of support could be extended to online booking where system highlights future appointments with the same GP
Waiting times: There was an appreciation that appointment may be delayed if person in front has serious problem. Being prepared to wait is the best strategy	Managing people's expectations and informing them of why they have to wait longer than their planned appointment time is also important

While efforts are being made to achieve enhanced patient-doctor partnerships, good communication and transparency of process, the results from the focus group show that further improvements are possible.

4 Discussion

From the results of both studies it can be seen that there is scope to develop new methods to support better patient information and communication with their doctor through a number of different means including:

- Implementing alternative methods of GP contact such as by email or video communication that could fit in better with peoples' preferences, lifestyles and to support those who cannot easily travel to the doctor's surgery.
- Providing IT systems that give doctors a visual or graphical overview of the surgery's patient population may be helpful. Such systems could highlight those with certain medical conditions who should be contacted when new information or a seminar is being offered. Such a system could also show those patients who have not seen a GP for a period of time and should be considered for being invited in for a check-up.
- Offering new ways for patients to access information about themselves such as directly from the patient record. This service will become more common but there may still be barriers, particularly technical ones, to both patients and clinicians engaging with them [6].
- Providing an application or facility that allows patients to come away from a doctor's consultation within updated information about their condition would encourage them to learn more about their health, be able to discuss it with the doctor on a more informed basis and ultimately take more actions to improve it.

- Offering medical forums moderated by a doctor could help people to learn more about their medical condition by posing questions through the forum and improving their knowledge about it.

References

1. First Annual Digital Health Summit and Exhibition: In Collaboration with NHS England and MedeAnalytics, University of Salford, 9 July 2015. http://blogs.salford.ac.uk/onecpd/2015/07/09/round-up-digital-health-summit-exhibition-2015
2. VanOsdol, K.J.: Digital technology to supercharge patient-provider relationships. In: Stephanidis, C., Antona, M. (eds.) UAHCI 2014, Part III. LNCS, vol. 8515, pp. 415–424. Springer, Heidelberg (2014)
3. Hodge, C.: An evaluation of the user experience of online symptom checkers. Design Ergonomics Final Year Dissertation Project, Loughborough School of Design, Loughborough University (2015)
4. Bol, N., Scholz, C., Smets, E.M.A., Loos, E.F., de Haes, H.C.J.M., van Weert, J.C.M.: Senior patients online: which functions should a good patient website offer? In: Stephanidis, C., Antona, M. (eds.) UAHCI 2013, Part II. LNCS, vol. 8010, pp. 32–41. Springer, Heidelberg (2013)
5. Saparova, D., Basic, J., Lu, Y., Kibaru, F., Ma, Y., Yadamsuren, B.: Usability problems in patient- and clinician-oriented health information systems: what are they and how do they differ? In: Duffy, V.G. (ed.) HCII 2013 and DHM 2013, Part I. LNCS, vol. 8025, pp. 276–285. Springer, Heidelberg (2013)
6. Jabour, A., Jones, J.F.: Facilitators and barriers to patients' engagements with personal health records: systematic review. In: Stephanidis, C., Antona, M. (eds.) UAHCI 2013, Part III. LNCS, vol. 8011, pp. 472–481. Springer, Heidelberg (2013)

The Contextual Complexity of Privacy in Smart Homes and Smart Buildings

Faith McCreary[1(✉)], Alexandra Zafiroglu[1], and Heather Patterson[2]

[1] Internet of Things Group, Intel Corporation, Hillsboro, OR 97124, USA
{faith.a.mccreary,alexandra.c.zafiroglu}@intel.com
[2] Intel Labs, Intel Corporation, Santa Clara, CA 95052, USA
heather.m.patterson@intel.com

Abstract. Smart technologies allow unprecedented visibility into activities in homes and buildings, while they enable new services that householders and workers will value. As people become increasingly aware of the magnitude and potentially sensitive nature of the data being collected through these technologies, privacy is emerging as a potential barrier to user adoption. In this paper, we apply leading privacy models to the results of qualitative research in which we solicited ideas for adding intelligence to homes and buildings, paying particular attention to information sensitivity about everyday activities that take place in those settings. We identify locations and activities that are particularly information-sharing sensitive, prioritize the salience of different types of privacy violations for householders and workers, and examine the influence of privacy attitudes on smart device ownership and desired future smart experiences.

Keywords: Internet of things · Privacy · Design · UX strategy · Contextual integrity · Social context · Experience framework · User research

1 Introduction

Smart technologies and analytics make possible new innovative services that people value, but they also enable unprecedented visibility into the mundane–and not so mundane–activities of our daily lives in homes and buildings. With the ever increasing multitude of smart devices that permeate our daily lives, companies (and potentially others) can track and store where we go, what we buy, how much we eat and when, our mood over the course of a day, how many steps we take, how often we maintain our cars, when we go to sleep and wake up, who we talk to, and much more. In this new world, exactly how this data is stored, handled, and protected is of concern to users of services, as well as the companies creating smart technologies and governments looking to protect their citizens. As people are becoming more aware of the magnitude and potentially sensitive nature of the data being collected, the ability – and inability – to regulate where information flows and where it stops ("privacy") is emerging as a potential deterrent to user adoption of new services and experiences.

Addressing user concerns around data collection, storage, handling, use and reuse, will be critical to making smart services broadly appealing. However, designing privacy-mindful experiences is not simple. Successful privacy design involves not only

© Springer International Publishing Switzerland 2016
F.F.-H. Nah and C.-H. Tan (Eds.): HCIBGO 2016, Part II, LNCS 9752, pp. 67–78, 2016.
DOI: 10.1007/978-3-319-39399-5_7

understanding and managing technology-based privacy risks, but also understanding the values, needs and desires of individual users and relevant social groups across a range of settings. Complicating the design challenges of these new technologies is that traditional ways of explaining and managing privacy concerns (e.g., prevalent "notice and choice" model [1]) will be insufficient in a world where smart sensors and technologies are inserted inconspicuously in ordinary objects.

In this paper, we explore the contextual nature of privacy though the application of three leading privacy models and a newly-introduced privacy framework for home activities. Applying these concepts to our research data, we identify combinations of locations and activities that are particularly information-sharing sensitive, prioritize the salience of different types of privacy violations for householders and workers, and the influence of privacy attitudes on current ownership of smart devices and desired future smart home and building experiences.

2   Considering Privacy

A central challenge facing designers is the lack of consensus regarding what privacy means. It has variously been conceived as "the right to be let alone" [2], "the right to be forgotten," [3], or the right of the individual to "control" the acquisition, disclosure, and us of one's personal information [4]. To some, privacy is "a measure of the access that others have to you through information, attention, and physical proximity" [5]; to others it is "the condition under which other people are deprived access to either some information about you or some experience of you" [6]. What issues exactly should designers of smart technologies and services be concerned with?

In this paper, we adopt the perspective of analytic philosopher Nissenbaum that privacy is fundamentally about *appropriate* information sharing [7]. According to Nissenbaum, what people want is not to be guaranteed absolute secrecy, or to have complete control over what is shared about them, but rather to have confidence that when information is shared, it is done so in accordance with generally-understood *context-dependent informational norms*. This perspective is well aligned with the tenets of user-centered design which also suggests that an individual's attitudes will play a significant role in privacy outcomes. Further the broad spectrum of reported privacy concerns (e.g. hacking personal data, location tracking, or disclosure of customer data) suggest that we not treat privacy as a single monolithic entity but instead need to take a more granular approach to understanding privacy concerns.

2.1   Privacy Attitudes

A widely used method for assessing privacy attitudes is Westin's "Privacy Segmentation and Core Privacy Orientation" index [8], which assesses an individual's privacy attitudes based on their level of agreement with the following statements:

1. Consumers have lost all control over how personal information is collected and used by companies.

2. Most businesses handle the personal information they collect about consumers in a proper and confidential way.
3. Existing laws and organizational practices provide a reasonable level of protection for consumer privacy today.

Westin used individuals' responses to classify people as "privacy fundamentalists," who place a high value on privacy and believe strongly in privacy laws and enforcement, "privacy pragmatists," who weigh the value of personal data and potential risks before sharing, or "privacy unconcerned", who do not know what the "privacy fuss" is about and see little need for further legal protections.

2.2   Spectrum of Privacy Concerns

Legal scholar Daniel Solove proposes a taxonomy that organizes privacy issues in terms of harmful or problematic activities that put privacy at risk (see Table 1). We look to the taxonomy for its secondary and unintended use as guide for designers, where each element provides a specific type of concern for designers to focus on.

Table 1. Solove's taxonomy of privacy concerns [9]

Information Collection about an individual or their activities	
Surveillance	Listening, watching, or recording of a person's activities
Interrogation	Questioning or probing for personal information
Information Processing, or how information about an individual is stored and used	
Aggregation	Combining various data about a person
Identification	Linking data to a particular person
Insecurity	No protecting personal data from improper access
Secondary Use	Using data for purposes other than those orginally agreed on
Exclusion	Not providing information about the data collected on a person and/or not allowing them to participate in deciding how it is used
Information Dissemination, or how an individual's data is transferred or shared	
Breach of Confidentiality	Breaking promise to keep personal information confidential
Disclosure	Reveling factual information that impacts one's reputation
Exposure	Revealing a person's nudity, bodily functions, or grief
Increased Accessibility	Making personal data easier to access
Blackmail	Threatening to disclose personal data
Appropriation	Using a person's identify for other's purposes
Distortion	Disseminating false information about someone
Invasion, or intrusions into an individual's private affairs	
Intrusion	Invading without permission into one's personal space or activities
Decisional Interference	Intruding into personal decision-making in private activities

2.3 Contextuality of Privacy

Nissenbaum's contextual model [7] is dependent on social norms. Although not often explicitly articulated, social norms about information flow are tightly bound to our expectations about what type of data is appropriate to share in a given *social context* (e.g., the workplace, home life), about the *subject, sender, and recipient* of that data, and about the "transmission principles" that we expect to be followed in particular situations. Social contexts are complex and dynamic, shot-through with unspoken rules that invite discovery and articulation. As Nissenbaum has noted, "when it comes to the nuts and bolts of privacy law, policy, and design, area experts in respective contexts—education, healthcare, and family and home life—are crucial to understanding roles, functions, and information types. They, not privacy experts, are best equipped to inform processes of norm discovery, articulation and formation." [7]

Recently, Zafiroglu and Patterson applied Nissenbaum's model to home life [10]. This research suggests that a stable set of sub-contexts, or "facets," undergird much of daily life within the home. These facets, such as 'nurturing intimate relationships' and 'keep bodies' (Table 2) are associated with a set of roles, activities, and goals that in turn have strong implications for the conditions under which householders willingly share information. Facets provide guardrails by which designers can gauge the likelihood that data flows introduced by new experiences align with prevailing social norms. When data flows align with existing norms, they are more likely to be accepted by users. When they do not, they may lead to uneasiness or rejection.

Table 2. Overview of home life facets, or sub-contexts, and associated goals

Home life facets	
Nurture intimate relationships	Connecting and coordinating with other householders, knowing where others are and if they are safe and having their needs met
Live with and among others	Avoiding censure, sharing resources, getting assistance when needed, and ensuring the rules are being followed
Consume and engage with media	Enjoying themselves, discovering media quickly and easily, and controlling what others know about consumption habits
Keep bodies	Being clean, looking good, being healthy, and indulging without censure
Keep house	Cleaning, being organized, making the day run smoothly, managing appearances, economizing, and keeping the home supplied
Enjoy and maintain friendships	Building rapport, charming others, not overburdening friends with boring details of home life, and getting help when needed
Maintain, fix, and improve property	Keeping property, sharing info to keep property from harm, improving property, and keeping negative information to themselves
Create and experiment	Goals include mastering new skills, limiting who knows what creating until ready to share, sharing passions with others, and relaxing
Defend your small piece of the world	Securing home, conveniently accessing, monitoring home, obfuscating whether someone is actually home

Although householders have relatively stable sets of expectations and preferences for information boundaries rooted in these facets of home life, their level of sensitivity around sharing a particular data point changes as the data point shifted between facets of home life. What might be very sensitive for a neighbor to know, might be perfectly acceptable for a home insurance company to know. These differences in information sensitivity (and associated preferences) in the home can be categorized according to the transmission principles as: *"secret"*, or what individuals withhold from all but a select few with data expected to never be available outside of the area or context where it was generated; *"shared"*, or what individuals are willing to allow specific others to know when directly necessary and relevant to a provided services or ongoing social relationship; *"traded"*, or what others can share if the individuals receive tangible benefits; and *"tattled"*, or information which if shared individuals fear will harm them.

3 Method

The intent of this research was to solicit ideas for adding intelligence to homes and buildings, paying particular attention to information sensitivity about everyday activities that take place in these locales. The goals were to (1) prioritize potential smart homes and buildings usages based on participants' imagined use of smart technologies in these settings, (2) identify value drivers and barriers to adoption of smart technologies in these contexts, (3) prioritize the salience of different types of privacy violations for householder and workers and (4) understand the influence of privacy attitudes on people's imagined use of smart technologies in these contexts.

The research was conducted using a mobile app loaded on the participants' smart phones, which allowed us to capture their "in-the-moment" thinking about their daily lives and the imagined role of future smart technology in homes and buildings. Participants volunteered for this research with screening done to ensure a representative balance of gender, education levels, and income levels. Further screening was done based on the quality of their initial "in-the-moment" video, whether they owned or rented, housing type, the nature of the buildings that they spent time in, and existing ownership of smart technology.

The research had three stages, with participants completing research tasks for one stage before moving onto the next. We used a mobile app to probe participants on specific topics as they went about their daily routines. This approach let us understand their real-life behaviors and to capture their real-life motivations for smart technology in homes and buildings. The research stages were as follows:

1. *Gather background information,* specifically we asked participants about their employment status, living situation (e.g., solo, with roommates, with children), household income, existing smart home device ownership, home type (e.g. apartment, single-family home), home square footage, and whether they owned or rented. Participants also completed Westin's Privacy Segmentation and Core Privacy Orientation Index [8]. Lastly, we asked about the building where they spent the majority of their time outside the home, along with building type (e.g. office building), number of hours spent there weekly, and building size.

2. *Capture imagined uses of smart,* where we asked participants to create in-situ videos of two items that they would *absolutely love* to have a brain and two items that they would *absolutely hate* to have a brain in their home; we then repeated the process while they were in the non-home building where they spent the most time. Probes were framed in terms of items having a brain, rather than becoming smart, to encourage participants not limiting their thinking to today's smart devices. For each item identified we queried qualitatively about motivations for choosing the item and asked the expected impact of the item having a brain to be rated on 10 point scale from 1 (little or none) to 10 (transforms life).
3. *Identify information sharing sensitivities,* where we asked participants to create in-situ videos of three behaviors that they would be nervous about their home sharing or repeating; we then duplicated the process while they were in the non-home building where they spent the most time. For each identified behavior, we queried qualitatively about their motivations behind the selection, expected impact of sharing, and who already knew about (or could figure out) the behavior.

In all, 264 people met our starting criteria and participated in the research; 54 % of the participants were female with 67 % of the participants having a college degree and 92 % residing in a city or metropolis area. At the start of this research, 40 % of participants owned one or more smart home devices with smart thermostats the most popular at 24 %. 56 % were home owners with over 80 % living in houses with less than 2500 square feet. Over 95 % of the participants reported that they spent time in the building for the purposes of work or schooling, with 52 % of the buildings small or medium sized (<4000 square feet).

4   Results

Participants created 3058 "in-the-moment" snapshots. The snapshots were evenly split between home and buildings, with participants spending the most time outside the home in office buildings (58 %), educational buildings (16 %), retail stores (6 %), restaurants or hotels (6 %). Medical buildings, industrial settings, public buildings, airports, or non-profits comprised the remainder.

The videos and open-ended questions from the studies framed participants' imagined experience of future smart homes and buildings. As with earlier work, we took these narratives as a direct representation of the imagined experience and a critical part of their underlying mental model [11]. The narratives were coded using a mix of structured coding related to the original home life framework and exploratory coding, with the exploratory coding structure iteratively refined as analysis progressed.

4.1   Extending the Facet Framework

The final coding tree represented the participants' over-arching mental model of smart home and building experiences [12] and defined the value propositions they expected smart technologies to deliver. We looked for meta-patterns, or schemas shared by participants as a way of data sense-making. The meta-patterns allowed us to extend the original facet framework to include situations to those in which building occupants willingly share information about their in-building activities, states and conditions in order to achieve a variety of goals. The extended framework details eight sub-contexts, or 'facets' of building life, as shown in Table 3.

The final coding tree also provided new insights into the more granular aspects of the experiences associated with each facet. Specifically, it allowed us to detail with *activities* and specific actions the end-user expected would be supported by smart technologies for each facet goal, areas of *information sensitivity,* and the *motivators,* that were expected value drivers or barriers to adoption of smart technologies.

Table 3. Overview of building life facets, or sub-contexts, and associated goals

Building facets	
Individual doing	Being productive, having autonomy, and being engaged
Keep spaces	Maximizing your comfort, imposing order, and managing your daily routines in your small corner of the larger building
Keep bodies	Being Clean, looking good, being healthy, indulging without censure, and maintaining privacy while sharing facilities
Upkeep and manage structure	Keeping buildings safe and secure, managing costs in a sustainable way, and proactively fixing issues before outages,
Interact and engage with knowledge	Creating and sharing content, discovering information quickly and easily, and sharing their expertise and knowledge
Create and innovate	Creating in peace, mastering new skills, and controlling access and sharing of creation
Grow business	Growing the business, minimizing costs associated with keeping it running, expressing their brand, and staying legal
Partner and act with others	Building rapport with others, working together to achieve share goals, and obfuscating activity to maintain reputation

4.2 The Landscape of Privacy Sensitivity

When participants imagined brainy homes and buildings, they often did not trust what they themselves had imagined (48 % of total concerns raised). Their lack of trust in their future visions was predicated on a mix of different concerns, including worries about reliability of the brainy object to consistently work as expected, how the participant would control of the object and their ability to set boundaries on information the object would generate and potentially share ("privacy").

Privacy concerns had the most negative impact on trust, with both location and facets impacting participant perception of potential privacy risks. Participants called out privacy as a potential risk in their imagined use of smart technologies in buildings nearly 46 % more often than they did in the home, adjusted for total number of snapshots in each setting. Figure 1 shows the distribution of privacy concerns in homes, while Fig. 2 shows the distribution of privacy concerns in buildings.

Bathrooms were areas of concern regardless of building type, but especially if engaged in activities related to "Keep Bodies" (e.g. grooming). Respondents in homes

	Keep Bodies	Consume & Engage with Media	Create & Experiment	Defend your Small Piece of the World	Keep House	Area Total
All Home Spaces (Exact not Specified)	5%	19%	1%	11%	10%	47%
Bathroom	19%	1%	0%	0%	5%	25%
Bedroom	8%	0%	0%	0%	1%	10%
Dining Room	1%	0%	0%	0%	0%	1%
Garage	0%	0%	0%	1%	0%	1%
Indoor-outdoor-transition	0%	0%	0%	7%	0%	7%
Kitchen	1%	0%	0%	0%	6%	7%
Living Room	2%	0%	0%	0%	0%	2%
Office	0%	0%	0%	1%	0%	1%
Shared Space	0%	0%	0%	1%	0%	1%
Facet Total	36%	21%	1%	20%	59%	

Fig. 1. Heatmap of relative percentage of privacy concerns in the home as a function of home facets and home location. Note, facets with less than 1 % of the total privacy concerns were not shown in the interest of table readability.

	Keep Bodies	Keep Spaces	Individual Doing	Upkeep & Manage Structure	Partner & Act with Others	Space Total
All Spaces (Exact Not Specified)	0%	0%	3%	2%	5%	10%
Bathroom	8%	2%	1%	0%	1%	13%
Eating or Dining Area	0%	0%	0%	0%	0%	0%
Classroom or studio	1%	1%	3%	1%	2%	7%
Outdoor-location	0%	0%	0%	0%	1%	2%
Gym or exercise space	1%	0%	0%	0%	0%	1%
Dressing or exam room	0%	0%	0%	1%	0%	4%
Indoor transition space (e.g. hallway)	0%	0%	2%	0%	1%	4%
Indoor-outdoor-transition (e.g. lobby)	1%	0%	6%	2%	5%	14%
Kitchen	1%	1%	0%	0%	0%	2%
Personal Office	9%	5%	8%	0%	11%	33%
Shared spaces	0%	0%	3%	0%	7%	10%
Retail space	0%	0%	1%	0%	0%	2%
Storage Area	0%	0%	0%	0%	1%	1%
Facet Total	21%	8%	29%	6%	33%	

Fig. 2. Heatmap of relative percentage of privacy concerns in buildings as a function of building facets and building location. Note, facets with less than 3 % of the total privacy concerns were not shown in the interest of table readability.

had a high-level of concern about privacy when consuming or engaging with media (e.g. TV shows) regardless of location, while respondents in buildings were most concerned when in their personal offices, especially when engaging with others.

4.3 Categorizing Privacy Concerns

To categorize participants' imagined privacy concerns—that is, the concerns they name when asked to contemplate the hypothetical introduction of intelligence into objects already within their homes and buildings, we used a taxonomy of privacy violations proposed by privacy scholar Daniel Solove [3]. Again, location and facets played a significant role in the nature of privacy locations. The most dramatic differences were between homes and buildings, as shown in Fig. 3. Overall, disclosure, or revealing factual information that impacts one's reputation, was the most frequently mentioned, followed by surveillance.

Home Privacy Concerns

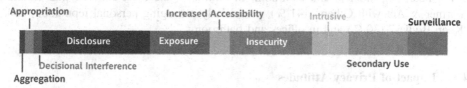

Building Privacy Concerns

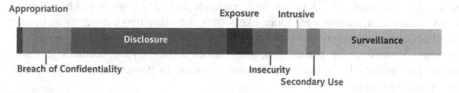

Fig. 3. Relative distribution of types of privacy concerns for home and building life

Respondents in the home were 11 % likely to be concerned with insecurity and 10 % more likely to worry about secondary use, while in buildings they were 20 % more likely to worry about surveillance and 11 % more concerned with breach of confidentiality.

4.4 Shifts in Information Sensitivity

As we examined the data around what behaviors participants would be nervous about their home or building repeating, we recognized differences in information sensitivity in homes and buildings. In the home, participant concerns were motivated primarily by potential embarrassment. In buildings, they were motivated by potential embarrassment, but also by potential consequences, with a shift towards secrecy and tattling. Figure 4 shows the shifts in information sensitivity as participants moved from home to building settings.

Information sensitivity was driven by information type, its recipient, the facet, and the specific location where the activity or behavior takes place. Within the home,

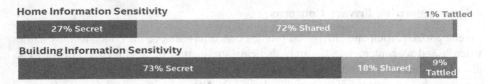

Fig. 4. Relative frequency of different levels of information sensitivity in homes and buildings

participants were most likely to report sharing "secrets" with immediate family, typically a partner or a spouse. In buildings, participants most often shared with a close co-worker or spouse. The contexts with the highest relative frequency of identified secrets were the home facets of "Keep House" (59 %) and "Keep Bodies" (18 %), and in the bedroom, kitchen, and bathroom. In buildings, the most concern was around "Partner & Act with Others" (41 %), particularly managing personal reputation, and "Keep Bodies" (30 %) and in offices and bathrooms.

4.5   Impact of Privacy Attitudes

Westin's Privacy Segmentation and Core Privacy Orientation Index [4] was used to classify participants as Privacy Fundamentalists (25 %), Privacy Pragmatists (28 %), or Privacy Unconcerned (47 %). In our data, respondents that Westin would have labeled as privacy fundamentalists were more likely than the other two categories to be concerned about privacy when they contemplated introducing intelligence into homes and buildings. However, for participants, the influence of privacy attitudes extended beyond just privacy for smart products and services. In particular, privacy attitudes were associated with:

- *Ownership of one or more smart devices*, with privacy pragmatists 10 % less likely to report owning smart devices in the home. Only 32 % reported having such devices in their home, versus 42 % of fundamentalists and 44 % of unconcerned.
- *Desired smart home and building experiences.* Privacy fundamentalists were more likely to imagine security-related uses for smart technologies, which may explain their higher existing ownership of smart devices given today's market focus. They were also most likely to imagine smart as improving their personal productivity. Pragmatists on the other hand saw the most value in intelligence that supported personal care and cleaning. The Unconcerned were the least concerned about security applications of smart, but were the most interested in the social potential of these technologies and often described themselves as oversharers.

5   Discussion

Homes and buildings are complex contextual environments in which information flow expectations differ as a function of multiple factors. By offering a glimpse of the future through eyes of end-users—a future not yet invented but already imagined—our aim is to provide designers of smart homes and buildings with a better understanding of privacy expectations so that they may develop smart home and building usages that resonate with the diverse experiences, roles, concerns, and activities of householders and workers.

First, we found that almost half of imagined home-life privacy concerns were not localized to any particular areas of the home. If one's home truly is one's castle, smart technologies represent a significant threat to our historical, low-tech privacy barriers. It will no longer be sufficient to close the bedroom curtains or ignore knocks at the front door to ensure privacy. Rather, privacy concerns revolve around *activities* that take place within the home: In our data, the most sensitive facets of home life were what Zafiroglu and Patterson call "keep house" and "keep bodies". At first blush this is surprising. Information about cleaning, being organized, making the day run smoothly, managing appearances, economizing and keeping the home supplied may not seem particularly sensitive. However, these activities get to the heart of our ability to present ourselves to others as organized and capable beings who are maintaining parity with our neighbors and friends. They also allow us to feel as though we are living up to the aspirational messages that abound in the modern world.

In the workplace, on the other hand, people reported very few non-localized privacy concerns. In the context of work, we saw that people already assume their daily lives are under scrutiny. Top of mind privacy concerns in this environment included managing our reputations rather than sequestering our physical bodies. Surveillance is a particular worry, with many participants anxious about their ability to hide the details of their daily work lives from co-workers, managers, or others who may judge and perhaps even sanction them for indications of non-work.

Third, we saw that when our research participants imagined others outside the home knowing something about their activities, 72 % of that information was considered *shareable*; only 30 % was considered out of bounds. It is not that people want everyone to know everything about them, but rather that they see the sharing of some information about themselves as acceptable for particular purposes, such as in exchange for a better understanding of their dwelling or household, or in exchange for tangible benefits such as goods or cost savings.

Surprisingly, the opposite pattern materializes for buildings. In these environments, only 18 % of information about activities was considered shareable. Taken together, these two findings seem paradoxical and invite reflection. Why would information collected in private spaces be considered sharable, but information collected in public spaces be considered off-limits? Our data suggests that our research participants have an understanding that activities at work have monetary value for the worker and for the enterprise, rendering it, in both cases, private by default. Where the worker is concerned, scrutiny invites reprobation. Where the company is concerned, the information is not for the worker to share. Within the home, on the other hand, people assume a kind of comfort with and de factor ownership over information—because it is about them, it is theirs to protect, to share selectively, or to distribute widely.

Finally, our work highlights the utility of Solove's taxonomy [3] for mapping privacy concerns related to introducing new technologies. The taxonomy may provide designers with a clearer understanding of privacy, with each class of problems shaping different design solutions. In contexts where *information collection* is of concern, our data suggests that designers should focus on understanding the purpose behind the data being collected, limiting data capture to only the essential, and managing appearances by limiting device capabilities to what is necessary. For *information processing*, they should focus on safeguarding data and limiting its use to those that align with contextual norms. They can reduce *information dissemination* concerns by ensure the data is accurate, openly communicating about how it is being handled, and enabling data management by individuals. Lastly, designers can reduce the perception of *invasion* issues by being useful but not disruptive in the context and enabling people to easily disconnect.

6 Conclusions

We hope that by articulating and implementing innovative privacy design principles, designers can play a pivotal role in building trust and assuaging the public' fears about smart technologies. The facet framework and accompanying approach to exploring the introduction of new technologies provides a tool to help product designers to identify and develop privacy-mindful usages that resonate with the context in which they are deployed.

Acknowledgements. We thank our colleagues for their valuable comments and insights as this work evolved.

References

1. Warner, R., Sloan, R.: Beyond notice and choice: privacy, norms, and consent. J. High Technol. Law (2013)
2. Warren, S., Brandeis, L.: The right to privacy. Harvard Law Rev. **4**(5), 193–220 (1890)
3. Mayer-Schönberger, D.: Delete: The Virtue of Forgetting in the Digital Age. Princeton University Press, Princeton (2009)
4. Kang, J.: Information privacy in cyberspace transactions. Stanford Law Rev. **50**(4), 1193–1294 (1998)
5. Froomkin, A.: The death of privacy? Stanford Law Rev. **52**(5), 1461–1543 (2000)
6. Reiman, J.: Privacy, intimacy, and personhood. Philos. Publ. Aff. **6**(1), 26–44 (1976)
7. Nissenbaum, H.: Privacy in Context: Technology, Policy, and the Integrity of Social Life. Stanford University Press, Palo Alto (2009)
8. Westin, A., Interactive, H.: Privacy On and Off the Internet: What Consumers Want (2002). http://www.ijsselsteijn.nl/slides/Harris.pdf
9. Solove, D.: A taxonomy of privacy. Univ. Pennsylvania Law Rev. **154**(3), 477–560 (2006)
10. Patterson, H., Zafiroglu, A., McCreary, F.: Facets: a framework for developing privacy-minded usages. In: Proceedings of CHI 2016
11. Tuch, A., Trusell, R., Hornbaek, K.: Analyzing users' narratives to understand experience with interactive products. In: Proceedings of CHI 2013, pp. 2079–2088. ACM Press (2013)
12. Young, I.: Mental Models: Aligning Design Strategy with Human Behavior. Rosenfeld Media, Brooklyn (2008)

Investigating HCI Challenges for Designing Smart Environments

Zohreh Pourzolfaghar[✉] and Markus Helfert

School of Computing, Dublin City University, Dublin, Ireland
{zohreh.pourzolfaghar,markus.helfert}@dcu.ie

Abstract. With the advancement of technologies related to 'Internet of Things', we are moving towards environments characterised by full integration and semantics. Various environments are often summarized with terms such as 'Smart City', 'Smart Home', 'Smart Buildings' or 'Smart Commerce'. In the meantime, technologies and standards for interoperability have been developed. However, to realise the full potential one remaining challenge is the design, integration and interoperability of many elements into a smart environment. In order to address this challenge, researchers have proposed concepts for Information Systems Design and Enterprise Architectures. By inspecting interaction challenges -in particular activities in which Humans are involved- during the design process, we endeavour in this paper to identify key challenges for designing smart environments. In order to address the challenges we propose a conversational approach that supports the main design phases and allows professionals to interact during the design phases for smart environments.

Keywords: Design process · Conversational environment · Smart environments · Enterprise architecture

1 Introduction

With the advent of Internet of Things technologies, we inevitably move towards environments recognized by full integration and semantics. Diverse application areas of such technologies are often summarized with terms such as 'Smart City', 'Smart Home', 'Smart Buildings' and lately Smart Commerce (Pan et al. [21]). Smart environments include smart objects, such as houses, buildings, sustainable urban infrastructure, cars, sensor technology and a lot more. Within these environments, through the application of semantic web technologies and intelligent applications, we are able to offer personalized, responsive, and intuitive systems. One prominent example for a smart environment is smart buildings, which include different smart features, analytics, and sensors used to monitor and control the power supply through renewable energy, smart metering technologies, and smart windows (Baetens et al. [3]). As expressed by Zhou et al. [29], in the case of smart buildings most of these smart technologies exploit information about the building design and its operation specifications at a later stage to estimate energy consumptions for industrial or marketing purposes.

Technologies developed over the last years for smart environments are currently summarised as 'Internet of Things'. However, a significant challenge remains to design

© Springer International Publishing Switzerland 2016
F.F.-H. Nah and C.-H. Tan (Eds.): HCIBGO 2016, Part II, LNCS 9752, pp. 79–90, 2016.
DOI: 10.1007/978-3-319-39399-5_8

and maintain the connectivity of smart systems by an integrated information system being able to support business processes and interoperability between the systems. With this paper, we investigate selected design challenges for smart environments and propose an approach to address these. Design processes are typically tacit dominant in which essential knowledge is exchanged between professionals and stakeholders. The knowledge gathered during design is required to be preserved for later design steps, subsequent maintenance, and use.

The paper is structured as follows: After presenting our research approach we review related literature to investigate design problems from an information and knowledge point of view and their impact on design processes. In addition, examining aspects of enterprise architecture, this research summarises the main steps of the Architecture Development Method (ADM) of TOGAF – a common method for enterprise architecture design - to design and implement enterprise architectures (EA). Subsequently, we illustrate design challenges using three examples and discuss the challenges recognised for the design process of smart environments.

2 Research Approach

In order to investigate and attenuate design challenges for smart environments, we argue that applying concepts related to Enterprise Architecture can help. This research is based on conceptual observation and use case descriptions following a qualitative research approach. According to Yin [37], one of the most common methods for data collection in case study is observation. In order to illustrate the design process for smart environments, we will utilise a prominent approach, i.e. TOGAF with its architectural design method (ADM), and a model-driven architecture promulgated by Object Management Group (OMG [38]). ADM defines steps for designing and maintaining enterprise architectures, which initially defines the scope in form of where, what, why, who, and how we design architectures.

The Open Group Architecture Framework (TOGAF) is a framework for enterprise architecture that provides an approach for designing, planning, implementing, and governing enterprise information technology architecture. TOGAF plays an important role in helping to systematise the architecture development process, enabling IT users to build open systems-based solutions to their business needs. According to OMG [38], the ADM is a step-by-step approach to develop enterprise architectures, which caters the business and information technology needs of an organisation. It may be tailored to the organisation's needs and can be then employed to manage the execution of architecture planning activities. TOGAF embraces the concepts and definitions presented in the ANSI/IEEE Standard 1471-2000, specifically the concepts that help guide the development of a view and make the view actionable (Minoli [19]). In order to discuss and investigate the challenges of designing smart environments from an information systems perspective in the following section, we follow the structure of TOGAF and ADM for the purpose of this study.

3 Design Process Problems with Tacit Knowledge Exchange

The design process requires the exchange of domain knowledge or knowledge about systems and artefacts between many stakeholders. As many researchers (e.g. Ibrahim and Paulson [12], Ibrahim and Fay [10]) have stated the design process is tacit dominant. One challenge with tacit knowledge exchange is the human-human interaction due to the fact that professionals attend project meetings and exchange their tacit knowledge. For design processes professionals' interaction happens in a tacit dominant area. Nissen [35] proposed the concept of a knowledge flow life cycle (KFLC). According to the first step of ADM to create business scenario, key challenges of design process are described utilising KFLC theory. For the next step of ADM, a target business process is required to be planned to address challenges arising from knowledge point of view. Further steps are related to information system and application architecture design and implement.

According to Nissen [35] knowledge is created by people, which is typically in the form of tacit knowledge. The knowledge is shared with other individuals in form of tacit knowledge. Then, through the step of 'formalisation', this knowledge is transformed to explicit knowledge, usually stored and maintained in an information and knowledge system. Therefore, professionals are interacting during the design process with each other to exchange knowledge, a fact being confirmed by many researchers. Poursolfaghar [22] pinpointed that the knowledge created by the professionals tends to reside in their minds as tacit knowledge when not explicitly documented during the design phase. Nonetheless, it is invaluable for later use and this is why it should be persevered. In this relation, Ibrahim and Fay [10] expressed that the design professionals are working in dominantly tacit knowledge areas during the planning and conceptual design phase. Indeed, this kind of human-human interactions which strictly depends on tacit knowledge has a high risk of incompletion. Indeed, the knowledge flow might be interrupted with the possibility of knowledge loss. In this regard, Ibrahim and Nissen [11] accentuated that tacitness of the knowledge can augment the probability of knowledge loss. These parts of knowledge, which had been lost prior to the formalisation, are evidences for the knowledge loss phenomena of design processes.

In addition, Kendall and Kendall [14] declared that the basis of human–computer interaction comprises the knowledge about the interplay among the users, tasks, task contexts, Information Technology (IT), and the environments in which the systems are used. Likewise, Bigham et al. [4] illustrated that human-computer interaction has focused on the user's interaction with many different types of information. During the design process, tacit knowledge is exchanged between the experts aiming to apply it for their own planning. However, this knowledge transfer is characterised with high risk of losing tacit knowledge intrinsic to human-human interactions. In other words, challenges in design processes can be related to knowledge transfers, often observed in a human-computer interaction aiming to prevent knowledge loss.

The design of Enterprise Architectures within Information Systems can be seen as a typical design process to design intergraded information systems. As Nakakawa et al. [31] concluded enterprise architecture is an appropriate approach for organising and dealing with inflexibility in business operations, managing organisational changes, mastering organisational complexity, and effectively aligning all the business aspects. Likewise, it is proposed by Ross et al. [32] and ISACA [33] that enterprise architecture is defined as the planning, design, and integration of business, information, and technology infrastructure in order to better achieve enterprise and IT strategies.

The goal of enterprise architecture is to create a unified IT environment across an enterprise or all of the firm's business units, with tight symbiotic links to the business side of the organisation and its strategy. According to Nakakawa et al. [31], although enterprise architecture offers numerous benefits to organisations, reaping them essentially depends on the successful design of the enterprise architecture process. Moreover, they emphasised that during the design of enterprise architectures, it is vital to ensure effective communication between all stakeholders.

Aiming to investigate the challenges to design a comprehensive and integrated information system for smart environments, this study endeavours to review enterprise architecture related design processes utilising TOGAF, and apply EA concepts to the design of smart environments.

4   Design Processes for Smart Environments

The design process of smart environments consists of steps, in which information about elements of the smart environment (e.g. smart technologies, objects etc.) is exchanged between design experts and other stakeholders. Certainly this information is essential for a detailed design, control and commercial usage. Therefore, according to the first step of TOGAF architectural design method, there is a need to take stakeholders' views and concerns into account. Consequently, a target business model is required to be defined to address recognised challenges in terms of making information accessible. During the subsequent 3rd and 4th steps of ADM, information system and required application to overcome existing challenges will be designed.

Al-Hader et al. [30] stated that the concept of design accommodates the major system requirements while implementing the first phase of the development. They hypothesise that developers need to concentrate on encompassing smart environments from the initial planning phase. Recent studies realised that there is a need in smart environments to fully consider the knowledge, experience, and technology of all disciplines and stakeholders (Yin et al. [34]). Hence, going through the next three sections, we will inspect the design process for three examples, namely smart buildings, smart energy, and smart ecommerce from a knowledge point of view. We will investigate existing challenges and benefits of knowledge within a design process. This section is concluded by summarising the challenges for utilising the knowledge in a typical design process for smart environments

4.1   Design Process for Smart Buildings

The design process of smart buildings consists of multidisciplinary interactions, which deal with knowledge from various professions, e.g. green technologies, renewable energy, etc. In this relation, Kuo et al. [16] declared that the modern buildings are equipped with a diverse range of service systems, such as mechanical, electrical, and plumbing works. Investigators continuously attempt to add more sensitive regulatory systems in modern buildings to make the living spaces more convenient. As announced by Cohen [7], green technologies and green energy are two key drivers of smart environments, which are two of six key components of any Smart city. On the other hand, Arain [1] argued that organising this knowledge would be indispensable during the early design process. Therefore, researchers concentrated mostly on the knowledge flow during the early phases of design. In this regard, Ibrahim and Nissen [11] considered that the knowledge, which was exchanged during the building design, could affect their performance. Later, Ibrahim and Paulson [12] underlined the importance of knowledge flow to complete a building project successfully. Likewise, Shumate et al. [25] pinpointed that problems in the construction industry are due to the incomplete flow of knowledge arising from tacit knowledge dominated activities in building projects. Kasimu et al. [13] explained that knowledge is created during the construction stage and if not properly captured, stored, and utilised, it will be lost. In this regard, many other researchers realised that tacit knowledge and its acquisition would have a major impact on organisation and projects' performance. Xiaoyong and Wendi [26] reported that construction depends on knowledge sharing, and, crucially, on tacit knowledge. Later, Lin and Lee [17] proposed a new methodology to capture and formalise construction project knowledge to provide tacit knowledge exchange and a management environment to enable the reuse of domain knowledge and experience in future projects. It is paramount to highlight that they focused on the construction phase as an explicit-dominant area, while this research revolves around the tacit-dominant design phase.

4.2 Design Process for Smart Grid and Smart Energy

Regarding the increased efforts for energy saving and energy cost reduction, utility companies attempt to find new ways to promote more effective ways of energy usage. Toward this, they are required to evaluate energy consumption and estimate energy consumption costs at the one hand. On the other hand, they need to have an accurate estimation about customers' demands. In this relation, demand response management (DRM) has been introduced as one of the main features in smart grids. As Chai et al. [6] expressed, the smart grid is regarded as the next generation power system to fulfil these challenges. Mohsenian-Rad and Leon-Garcia [20] and Zugno et al. [28] explained that DRM refers to routines implemented to control the energy consumption at the customer side and aims to improve energy efficiency and reduce cost. Furthermore, Mohsenian-Rad and Leon-Garcia [20] and Samadi et al. [24] illustrated that the main objective of demand response management is to reduce the peak-to-average ratio and balance both the power supply and demand. According to Yu et al. [27], some innovative techniques including machine learning, data mining, and discovery in database have been successfully applied to building energy consumption. In this regard, Korolija et al. [15] developed regression models to predict the annual heating, cooling, and electrical auxiliary energy consumption of five different types of HVAC systems and two chilled ceiling systems for office buildings in the UK. Regarding EIA [8], the majority of energy consumption in commercial buildings is related to space heating, cooling, and lighting. In this context, Mikučionienė et al. [18] evaluated the influence of each variable on energy consumption by analysing some factors such as insulation of external walls, roof insulation, heating substation and so on. In such a condition, Asadi [2] also expressed that predicting building energy consumption depends on multiple variables such as building characteristics, energy systems characteristics, and the like. In line with precedent researches, Capozzoli et al. [5] stated that it is exceedingly important to have the capability to quickly and reliably estimate the buildings' energy consumption, especially for public authorities and institutions that own and manage large building stocks. Apparently, regarding the studied literature, to estimate or predict the building's energy consumption there is an essential need to have sufficient technological information and knowledge about mechanical, electrical, and ICT installed equipment. While regarding this fact that the design process of buildings is a tacit-dominant area, meaning that professionals exchange their knowledge orally, there is no such possibility for different users to have access to the technical knowledge about the buildings. As a matter of fact, this knowledge just preserves as technical reports for buildings, while it could be only accessed by project parties as booklets.

4.3   Design Process for Smart Commerce

From the other side, many businesses promote their products in smart markets. In this regard, Baetens et al. [3] detailed that awareness of smart components is moderately strong about the commercial market. He performed a survey on what types of smart windows are currently available on the market and their properties and potential for daylight and solar energy control in buildings. There is an essential need for smart markets to have a proper access to today's building characteristics to be able to deal with their needs for smart components due to new regulations for energy saving purposes.

At the same time, many other small businesses may benefit from this information and technical knowledge. Yan and Ghose [36] elucidated that both kinds of retailers could always gain profit from having knowledge about customers' needs and willingness to buy. As such, they concurred that market information is vital for a firm's decision making processes. In addition, Yan et al. [36] laid emphasis on the forecast information accuracy effect on the profit of traditional and online retailers. In this context, He et al. [9] expounded that major retailers such as Marks & Spencer's, A&P grocery stores and Von's Supermarket have made substantial investment in developing tracking information systems and engaging in ongoing marketing research to improve information accuracy. In the light of the studied literature on retailers' activities, it is indispensable for these small business owners to inspect their customers' needs and willingness to buy. For this purpose, they are required to have access to the technical information about buildings' instalments.

By taking into account the aforementioned reasons resulting from a deep literature review, this study is supposed to provide such access for the users from different areas and industries (e.g. utility companies and retailers) by means of developing a comprehensive database for buildings' technological information. In such a condition, utility companies will be able to utilise this knowledge (e.g. building characteristics, mechanical, electrical and ICT equipment's technical information) to have an exact prediction about maximum energy usage for any building. Farther, they may compare these predictions with real usage to inspect overhead usage of any building. As regards the retailers' information needs, they can use this database as a useful reference to identify the future needs of probable tenants of the buildings consistent with the information which is supposed to reside in the proposed database by this research.

4.4   Recognised Design Challenges

In the previous sections, we have illustrated and discussed the challenges of designing smart buildings, smart energy grids, and smart commerce systems. We have emphasised the steps to design the systems and its challenges from a knowledge flow point of view, which are summarised in Table 1.

Table 1. Design phase challenges from knowledge point of view (alongside ADM phases)

ADM phase	ADM aims	Design knowledge challenges
A. Architecture vision	Scope, assumptions and methodologies and evaluation criteria are defined Key stakeholders and their concerns/objectives and the key business requirements are identified Business scenarios are created	– Knowledge from different professions and stakeholders – Gather knowledge for later use e.g. Utilising building knowledge for commercial purpose; importance of accessing building info by public authorities and institution, and small businesses at a later stage
B. Business architecture	Baseline and target Business Architectures using UML or IDEF-0 The relevant viewpoints are too identified	– High risk of knowledge loss phenomena due to tacitness of knowledge (human-human interaction)
C. Information system architectures	Data and application architecture and views on those	– Need to formalise and organising knowledge – High risk of incomplete knowledge flow due to tacitness of knowledge (human-computer interaction)
D. Technology architecture	Develop a technology architecture that will form the basis of the following implementation Identify the relevant Technology Architecture building blocks	– Need to formalise and organising the knowledge during design phase – High risk of incomplete knowledge flow due to tacitness of knowledge (human-computer interaction)

(Continued)

Table 1. (*Continued*)

ADM phase	ADM aims	Design knowledge challenges
E. Opportunities and solutions	Parameters of change, the major phases along the way and the top-level projects to be undertaken in moving from the current environment to the target	– Importance of complete knowledge flow for project success
F. Migration planning	Prioritisation of the projects within the Technology Architecture and costs are estimated for the migration of the various projects	– Importance of complete knowledge flow for project success
G. Implementation governance	For each of the implementation projects, a corresponding implementation organisation is assigned. At the end of this phase the system is fully developed and implemented, compliant to the architecture	– Knowledge from different professions and stakeholders
H. Architecture Change management	The goal of this phase is to manage changes to the architecture in a cohesive and architected way. During this phase, for each change request, the decision is made whether it is necessary to initiate the ADM cycle again, in order to redesign the architecture	– Knowledge from different professions and stakeholders together with preserved knowledge during earlier design phases – High risk of knowledge misinterpretation

Apparently, many researchers have maintained that dominating tacit knowledge during the design phase is the most crucial barrier to make this knowledge accessible by different parties. According to the ADM of TOGAF, the development of architecture views from business to technology is necessary to properly identify the concerns and requirements of the stakeholders (Minoli [19]). Indeed, the recognised challenges for the design process are highlighting different stakeholders' concerns which inhibit their future access to a valuable information resource. To overcome such challenges, we propose a digital environment that can help capture valuable knowledge during the design processes. In this way, one of the recognised challenges for the design process (business process) will be addressed by capturing and formalising tacit knowledge of the experts. Accordingly, some other challenges like knowledge loss and incomplete knowledge flow will be covered. Through the next step of ADM, information system architecture to preserve the captured knowledge is developed. The preserved information would be accessible by authorities, institutions, and small businesses via provided applications and technologies, which are supposed to be designed and developed during the technology architecture step.

4.5 A Digital Conversation Environment

In this section, we will discuss an initial proposal for digital environment that helps to address the listed challenges. Provided solutions to address these challenges could be utilised as a template for designing various information systems for smart environments. Recently, some researchers highlighted the importance of considering knowledge, experience, and technology of all disciplines and stakeholders in smart environments. Therefore, defined patterns for the proposed digital conversation environment can be used for other smart systems.

As a solution, challenges arising from human-human interactions and highly dependent on tacit knowledge of the experts have been converted to a human-computer interaction by means of utilising a pre-defined knowledge exchange environment. Within TOGAF the concept of the Enterprise Continuum has been proposed [38], which provides methods for classifying architecture and solution artefacts within an Architecture Repository. The Enterprise Continuum enables the architect to design enterprise architectures and articulate the broad perspective of what, why, and how the enterprise architecture has been designed. From a Knowledge perspective, Pourzolfaghar et al. [23] have developed a knowledge-based framework for the design phase, which entails the entity of the required architectural, mechanical and electrical knowledge. This allows to transform and to formalise tacit knowledge of the experts to an explicit type. Indeed, this environment will act as an interface between professionals to conform the existing challenges to the design phase.

Developing this framework, the knowledge flow has been combined with design processes. The knowledge aspect of this framework considers architectural, mechanical, electrical and ICT knowledge, which needs to be combined and reviewed. This framework included the entity of the required mechanical and electrical knowledge that has to be considered during the design phase.

The proposed environment helps to provide a condition to make this information accessible by different stakeholders for the control, maintenance, or commercial purposes. As discussed, utility companies use building information to predict or estimate the customers' consumptions to promote effective ways of energy usage, as well as reducing the price. Moreover, small business owners like retailers may benefit from this environment. In this way, they will be able to obtain useful information about all the buildings and their capacities to have an accurate prediction about their energy consumption or future needs for technical equipment. Like so, they will be able to fulfil their estimation, predictions, and demand management. This environment as a comprehensive database for a potential market surrounding the areas around the buildings is supposed to be fed through a conversational environment for the design phase of the smart building project. Additionally, various users (e.g. Utility companies and retailers) can benefit from detailed information and knowledge about technological equipment.

5 Conclusion and Summary

The design process of smart environments is highly tacit dominant in which very essential knowledge is exchanged between the professionals. This valuable knowledge is required to be preserved for later maintenance and use. However, a problem associated with this phase arises from tacitness of knowledge. In this paper we have reviewed design processes and related challenges from an information systems point of view. We have followed the architectural development method proposed within TOGAF to investigate and describe challenges knowledge transfer and formalisation, in particular in regard to human-human and human-computer interaction.

As environments become increasingly connected into smart environments, these challenges hamper increasingly the design of smart environments. Therefore, in order to realise the full potential one remaining challenge is the design, integration and interoperability of many elements into a smart environment. We have proposed a conversational approach that supports the main design phases and allows professionals to interact during the design phases for smart environments. This environment is supposed to be established on an existing knowledge-based framework for the design phase. To develop such an environment, this study makes use of the TOGAF enterprise architecture development method. Accordingly, the recognised challenges are considered as stakeholders' views and target business process is planned to address them. The digital environment helps to address recognised challenges for design process of smart environments in terms of preserving tacit knowledge and making it accessible for various stakeholders. Further research will investigate and confirm the identified challenges in various case studies, such as smart commerce. In addition we aim to refine and evaluate the proposed conversational environment.

Acknowledgement. This work was supported by the Science Foundation Ireland grant "13/RC/2094" and co-funded under the European Regional Development Fund through the Southern & Eastern Regional Operational Programme to Lero - the Irish Software Research Centre (www.lero.ie).

References

1. Arain, F.M.: Strategic management of variation orders for institutional buildings: leveraging on information technology. In: PMI Global Congress Proceedings, Toronto, Canada, pp. 1–17 (2005)
2. Asadi, S., Shams Amiri, S., Mottahed, M.: On the development of multi-linear regression analysis to assess energy consumption in the early stages of building design. Energy Build. **85**, 246–255 (2014)
3. Baetens, R., PetterJelle, B., Gustavsen, A.: Properties, requirements and possibilities of smart windows for dynamic daylight and solar energy control in buildings: a state-of-the-art review. Solar Energy Mater. Solar Cells **94**, 87–105 (2010)
4. Bigham, J.P., Bernstein, M.S., Adar, E.: Human-computer interaction and collective intelligence. In: Malone, T.W., Bernstein, M.S. (eds.) The Collective Intelligence Handbook. MIT Press, Cambridge (2014)
5. Capozzoli, A., Grassi, D., Causone, F.: Estimation models of heating energy consumption in schools for local authorities planning. Energy Build. **105**, 302–313 (2015)
6. Chai, B., Chen, J., Yang, Z., Zhang, Y.: Demand response management with multiple utility companies: a two-level game approach. IEEE Trans. Smart Grid **5**(2), 722–731 (2014)
7. Cohen, B.: What exactly is a smart city? In: Collective Intelligence Handbook (2012). http://www.fastcoexist.com/1680538/what-exactly-is-a-smart-cityIntelligence

8. EIA: Annual Energy Review, DOE/EIA03842010, U.S. Energy Information Administration (2011)
9. He, C., Marklund, J., Vossen, T.: Vertical information sharing in a volatile market. Mark. Sci. **27**(3), 513–530 (2008)
10. Ibrahim, R., Fay, R.: Enhancing cognition by understanding knowledge flow characteristics during design collaboration. ALAM CIPTA, Int. J. Sustain. Trop. Des. Res. Pract. **1**(1), 9–16 (2006)
11. Ibrahim, R., Nissen, M.: Discontinuity in organizations: developing a knowledge-based organizational performance model for discontinuous membership. Int. J. Knowl. Manag. **3**(1), 18–36 (2007)
12. Ibrahim, R., Paulson, B.: Discontinuity in organisations: identifying business environments affecting efficiency of knowledge flows in product lifecycle management. Int. J. Prod. Lifecycle Manag. **3**(1), 21–36 (2008)
13. Kasimu, M.A., Roslan Bin, A., Fadhlin, B.T.A.: Knowledge management models in civil engineering construction firms in Nigeria. Interdiscip. J. Contemp. Res. Bus. **4**(6), 936–950 (2012)
14. Kendall, K.E., Kendall, J.E.: Human-computer interaction/Ch 14. In: Systems Analysis and Design. Pearson/Prentice Hall, Upper Saddle River (2008)
15. Korolija, I., Zhang, Y., Marjanovic-Halburd, L., Hanby, V.I.: Regression models for predicting UK office building energy consumption from heating and cooling demands. Energy Build. **59**, 214–227 (2013)
16. Kuo, C.H., Tsai, M.H., Kang, S.C.: A framework of information visualization for multi-system construction. Autom. Constr. **20**(3), 247–262 (2011)
17. Lin, Y.-C., Lee, H.-Y.: Developing project communities of practice-based knowledge management system in construction. Autom. Constr. **22**, 422–432 (2012)
18. Mikučionienė, R., Martinaitis, V., Keras, E.: Evaluation of energy efficiency measures sustainability by decision tree method. Energy Build. **76**, 64–71 (2014)
19. Minoli, D.: Enterprise Architecture A to Z: Frameworks, Business Process Modelling, SOA, and Infrastructure Technology. CRC Press, Auerbach Publications, Taylor & Francis Group, Hoboken (2008)
20. Mohsenian-Rad, A.H., Leon-Garcia, A.: Optimal residential load control with price prediction in real-time electricity pricing environments. IEEE Trans. Smart Grid **1**(2), 120–133 (2010)
21. Pan, G., Qi, G., Zhang, W., et al.: Trace analysis and mining for smart cities: issues, methods, and applications. IEEE Commun. Mag. **51**(6), 120–126 (2013)
22. Pourzolfaghar, Z.: Improving tacit knowledge capture during conceptual design phase of building projects. UMI thesis, ProQuest LLC Publications, UK (2012)
23. Pourzolfaghar, Z., Ibrahim, R., Abdullah, R., Adam, N.M., Abang, A.A.A.: Improving dynamic knowledge movements with a knowledge-based framework during conceptual design of a green building project. Int. J. Knowl. Manag. **9**(2), 62–79 (2013)
24. Samadi, P., Mohsenian-Rad, A., Schober, R., Wong, V.W.S., Jatskevich, J.: Optimal real-time pricing algorithm based on utility maximization for smart grid. In: Proceedings of IEEE SmartGridComm, pp. 415–420 (2010)
25. Shumate, M., Ibrahim, R., Levitt, R.: Dynamic information retrieval and allocation flows in project teams with discontinuous membership. Eur. J. Int. Manag. **4**(6), 566–575 (2010)
26. Xiaoyong, L., Wendi, Ma.: Knowledge management in construction companies. In: Zhang, Y. (ed.) Future Wireless Networks and Information Systems. LNEE, vol. 144, pp. 313–320. Springer, Heidelberg (2012)
27. Yu, Z., Haghighat, F., Fung, B.C.M., Yoshino, H.: A decision tree method for building energy demand modeling. Energy Build. **42**, 1637–1646 (2010)

28. Zugno, M., Morales, J.M., Pinson, P., Madsen, H.: A bilevel model for electricity retailers' participation in a demand response market environment. Energy Econ. **36**, 182–197 (2013)
29. Zhou, Z., Zhao, F., Wang, J.: Agent-based electricity market simulation with demand response from commercial buildings. IEEE Trans. Smart Grid **2**(4), 580–588 (2011)
30. Al-Hader, M., Rodzi, A., Sharif, A.R., Ahmad, N.: Smart city components architecture. In: Proceeding of International Conference on Computational Intelligence, pp. 93–97 (2009)
31. Nakakawa, A., Van Bommel, P., Erikproper, H.A.: Definition and validation of requirements for collaborative decision-making in enterprise architecture creation. Int. J. Coop. Inf. Syst. **20**(1), 83–136 (2011)
32. Ross, J.W., Weill, P., Robertson, D.C.: Enterprise Architecture as Strategy. Harvard Business School Press, Boston (2006)
33. Information Systems Audit and Control Association (ISACA): COBIT 5. ISACA, Rolling Meadows (2012)
34. Yin, C.T., Xiong, Z., Chen, H., Wang, J.Y., Cooper, D., David, B.: A literature survey on smart cities. Sci. China Inf. Sci. **58**, 1–18 (2015)
35. Nissen, M.E.: Harnessing Knowledge Dynamics: Principled Organizational Knowledge and Learning. IRM Press, Hershey (2006)
36. Yan, R., Ghose, S.: Forecast information and traditional retailer performance in a dual-channel competitive market. J. Bus. Res. **63**, 77–83 (2010)
37. Yin, R.K.: Case study research design and methods, 5th edn. Sage Publications, London (2013). 2013
38. Object Management Group, Inc.: 250 First Ave. Suite 100, Needham, MA 02494, USA, Ph: +1-781-444 0404, Email: info@omg.org, http://www.omg.org

The Influence of Personality on Users' Emotional Reactions

Beverly Resseguier[1(✉)], Pierre-Majorique Léger[2], Sylvain Sénécal[3], Marie-Christine Bastarache-Roberge[4], and François Courtemanche[4]

[1] Department of Psychology, University of Montréal, Vincent-d'Indy Ave, Montréal, Canada
beverly.resseguier@umontreal.ca
[2] Department of Information Technologies, HEC Montréal, Côte-Sainte-Catherine Rd, Montréal, Canada
pml@hec.ca
[3] Department of Marketing, HEC Montréal, Côte-Sainte-Catherine Rd, Montréal, Canada
ss@hec.ca
[4] Tech3lab, HEC Montréal, Louis Colin Blvd, Montréal, Canada
{marie-christine.bastarache-roberge,
francois.courtemanche}@hec.ca

Abstract. In order to develop an accurate and robust neuroadaptive model based on users' idiosyncrasies, the interface needs to use personal information. In this article, we explore the extent to which automatic facial analysis can inform on users' idiosyncrasies. Facial emotion from 88 university students playing an emotionally charged video game was used to explore the relationship between personality trait and facial emotion in human-computer interaction context. We observed multiple statistically significant correlations between users' personality dimensions and their emotions. One personality dimension was mostly related to emotions: emotionality. This paper contributes to the HCI literature by underlining the importance of taking into account users' personality traits in analyzing their emotional reactions to interfaces. Neuroadaptive interfaces using emotional reactions would perform better by also controlling for personality traits of their users and enhance user experience.

Keywords: Personality · Facial expression · Emotion · Idiosyncrasies · User experience

1 Introduction

Recent research has shown the importance of individual idiosyncrasies, such as personality traits, in different human computer interaction contexts such as entertainment [1], mobile application usage [2], games [3] and even abusive use of information technologies [4]. While the value of individual characteristics is considered in models such as the task-technology fit (TTF) model [5], most attempts at operationalizing this part of the model have focused on self-perceived assessments.

© Springer International Publishing Switzerland 2016
F.F.-H. Nah and C.-H. Tan (Eds.): HCIBGO 2016, Part II, LNCS 9752, pp. 91–98, 2016.
DOI: 10.1007/978-3-319-39399-5_9

Research is calling for unobtrusive and non-invasive approaches to capture users' idiosyncrasies in order to better infer cognitive and emotional states [6, 7]. The ultimate goal of neuroadaptive interfaces is to provide users with the right content at the right time [8]. In order to achieve this goal, the interface needs to use some personal information like past behavior or the user's current mental state. According to Parasuraman [9], neuroadaptive interfaces (i.e., based on the users' current mental state) lead to a better synergy between technology and users, therefore ensuring a better user experience. These types of interfaces monitor physiological signals of the user to infer mental states in order to adapt automatically to that state, with the goal of improving the interaction. To successfully implement neuroadaptive interfaces, reliable assessment of a user's mental states during the interaction process is necessary.

In this article, we explore the extent to which automatic facial information can inform on users' idiosyncrasies such as personality traits. We use facial emotion from players in an emotionally charged video game to explore the relationship between the emotion detected during the game and their personality traits. Our results contribute to the development of a neuroadaptive model by outlining a simple and effective way of modelling users' idiosyncrasies that can be used by physiological inference models [7].

2   Literature Review

It is generally agreed that basic human emotions can be associated with specific patterns of facial expressions. Each primary emotion has its own set of facial muscle contractions leading to a unique facial expression [10]. Facial expressions can be produced by pure emotional experiences as well as by many other events, and are caused by simultaneous temporary (between 250 ms and 5 s) contractions of different muscles such as eyelids, lips and mouth [11]. The temporal dimension and intensity of a contraction are crucial to infer a person's emotional state with good accuracy. For example, Fridlund and Izard [12] found a correlation between the zygomatic muscle (a group of muscles near the mouth used for smiling) and positive emotions, and between the corrugator muscle (a group of muscles near the eyes used for frowning) and negative emotions.

There are two methods that can be used to measure facial expressions: electromyography and the use of automatic facial analysis Electromyography (EMG) consists in the recording of electrical activity induced by muscular contraction and relaxation [13–15]. EMG has been used in HCI to measure users' emotional valence in a gaming context [16].

The second method used to measure facial expressions is the Automatic Facial Analysis (AFA), which seeks to infer human's emotions by using a chosen specialized software such as Facereader[1] [17] and Affdex[2]. It is crucial to use an accurate and reliable model of AFA in the field of HCI since it greatly relies on emotional intelligence [18]. The chosen software should detect facial features and associate them with specific facial expressions [19]. Given the disparity of biological features and environmental settings,

---

[1] http://www.noldus.com/human-behavior-research/products/facereader.
[2] http://www.affectiva.com/solutions/affdex/.

this type of analysis requires consideration of many variables [11]. When analyzing facial expressions with a computer-based program, some difficulties may occur such as lighting (the face needs to be lit adequately), face orientation (the face needs to be facing the camera) and the expressions themselves (even emotionally induced, expressions differ between individuals due to physiological differences) [20].

Difficulties like face orientation can be avoided by using programs like Facereader (Noldus, The Netherlands). Such programs use the Active Template Method to associate the user's face to a generic face template. The Active Appearance Model is used to help recognized variations related to all issues listed earlier [20]. Facial expressions can be classified in different physiological, cognitive, and emotional states by using facial actions called action units. A set of action units can be associated with multiple facial action possibilities like raising eyebrows or pinching the lips. Valstar and Pantic [21] explained that different action units, which are individually or collectively associated with physiological, cognitive, or emotional states, can be detected by a computer program or a trained observer. See Riedl and Léger [22] for a review of the measurement of facial emotions.

Prior research has explored the relationship between personality trait and facial emotions. Based on Tomkins's ideo-affective structures [23] and Izard's affective-cognitive structures [24], one's repetitive emotional experiences lead to structural changes that are consolidated in his personality [25]. An experiment investigating physicians' ability to express emotions (happy, sad, anger, and surprise) compared to their personality traits has shown results linking those two concepts [26]. They found that the ability to express sadness was linked with a sadness personality trait and the ability to express anger was linked with a dominance personality trait. Another study conducted by Malatesta-Magai et al. [27] compared Type A and Type B personalities on facial expression of anxiety, depression, anger, and aggression. They found a significant difference in hostile emotional behavior, more specifically suppression of anger facial expression for Type A individuals.

Moreover, Ekman and Rosenberg [10] found a relationship between the Extraversion trait of the Eysenck Personality Questionnaire-Revised [28] and facial responses. They classified the extraversion trait in three categories: introverts, ambiverts and extraverts. For enjoyment displays, the facial response was higher for extraverts than for introverts and ambiverts.

Literature on personality in the field of HCI also shows the importance and usefulness of adding personality variables to interfaces in order to better understand users' behavior [2]. Recent work from Bastarache-Roberge et al. [3] proposes a model to predict flow states of players in a multiplayer game, which shows better accuracy once personality variables are taken into account. Another framework presented by Bostan [1] claims that behavior is affected by situational and personal factors. This extensive knowledge of participants' characteristics, such as personality, was added to improve a prediction model of players and agent behavior in computer games.

3 Methodology

3.1 Methodological Strategy and Participants

For this experiment, we chose to observe users' emotional reactions while they were playing an emotionally charged video game called Team Fortress 2 (Valve Corporation, Bellevue). This first-person shooter game was chosen based on the possibility of manipulating the game's levels of difficulty and extracting players' actions. 88 university students participated in this study (51 male, 31 female).

Players had to alternate between playing the game and watching the other players play on their screen through a spectator mode. Successful and missed shots, as well as game results (win or lose) were extracted from the game logs with an additional plug-in Supstats2 (by F2).

Players were all in the same room, around a hexagonal table, but were not facing each other. They each had their own headset (headphones and microphone) in order to communicate, therefore simulating an online environment.

After a practice game, only two players played the next game, alternating for each game. A total of 7 games were played by session. Teams were also randomly assigned to various difficulty level combinations (easy, normal, and hard). Data from 120 games were collected for this study.

3.2 Measures

Videos of the participant's faces were recorded with webcams using MediaRecorder 2 (Noldus, The Netherlands) and then processed with Facereader 6 (Noldus, The Netherlands) in order to extract six basic emotions: happy, sad, scared, disgusted, surprised, and angry. Emotions were inferred for the whole gameplay and averaged for each participant, leading to six variables.

All participants had to fill in the HEXACO Personality Inventory [29]. It was used to assess personality based on six dimensions: honesty-humility, emotionality, extraversion, agreeableness, conscientiousness and openness to experience.

Based on Lee and Ashton [29], each dimension of the measurement scale is briefly summarized below.

- Honesty-humility dimension is used to describe someone who will not use others for personal profit (material or social), or will not be tempted to break the rules. If the score on this dimension is low, then it describes someone who would do those things and more in order to get what they want.
- The emotionality dimension describes a person who feels strong emotions and needs emotional support from peers. Some of the most common feelings are fear, anxiety, empathy and attachment. If a score is low on this dimension, it describes someone who is not close to his emotions, nor feels the need to share them with others.
- For extraversion, people with high scores are positive and social. They are confident, enthusiastic and energetic. On the contrary, people with low scores on this dimension are uncomfortable under a lot of attention and do not particularly enjoy social activities.

- Agreeableness is used to describe an individual who is forgiving, non-judgmental, cooperative and who has good abilities at controlling their temper. On the contrary, an individual with a low score is more stubborn, critical, and angry when facing mistreatment.
- Someone organized, disciplined, and perfectionist will have a high score on the conscientiousness dimension, and someone unconcerned, impulsive and who is not bothered by work containing mistakes will have a low score.
- The openness to experience dimension describes someone imaginative and curious about nature and other domains of knowledge. A low score describes someone who isn't curious nor creative and who does not appreciate radical or unconventional ideas.

4   Results

To explore the relationship between personality dimensions and discrete emotions of users, a correlation analysis was performed. Table 1 summarizes the results. First, we observe multiple statistically significant correlations (2-tailed) between users' personality dimensions and their emotions during the game sessions, supporting our general contention that personality influences emotional reactions. Second, not all personality dimensions had an influence on emotional reactions (e.g., openness to experience) and some dimensions had influence over a greater number of emotions than others (e.g., emotionality and conscientiousness). Third, the personality dimension mostly related to emotions, emotionality is the one correlated with the greatest number of emotions. We found four significant correlations with disgust ($p = 0.0262$), happiness ($p = 0.0091$), angriness ($p = 0.0001$) and sadness ($p < 0.0001$). It suggests that users' high on emotionality are more expressive than others when interacting with an interface. Fourth,

Table 1. Correlation analysis between personality traits and facial emotions.

	Disgusted	Happy	Surprised	Angry	Scared	Sad
Honesty-humility	−0.013	−0.049	−0.061	0.030	0.109	0.205
p-value	0.839	0.451	0.342	0.644	0.092	0.001**
Emotionality	0.143	0.167	0.109	−0.246	−0.003	0.262
p-value	0.026*	0.009**	0.089	0.000**	0.968	<.000**
eXtraversion	0.130	−0.003	0.046	0.052	−0.089	0.043
p-value	0.043*	0.964	0.479	0.420	0.170	0.506
Agreeableness	0.061	0.011	0.093	−0.230	0.041	0.092
p-value	0.345	0.862	0.151	0.000**	0.528	0.152
Conscientiousness	0.086	0.200	−0.133	−0.009	−0.107	0.186
p-value	0.182	0.002**	0.038*	0.887	0.096	0.004**
Openness to experience	−0.003	−0.11	0.019	−0.033	0.067	0.062
p-value	0.965	0.089	0.771	0.609	0.296	0.337

N = 88, * meaning p < .05 level (2-tailed) and ** meaning p < .01 level (2-tailed).

interestingly two emotions (angry and surprise) had negative correlations with personality dimensions (emotionality and conscientiousness). Based on these results, it seems that a high score on emotionality and agreeableness dimensions is related with lower angriness. This result may suggest that users do not want to show their angriness in social situations. In addition, the more users scored high on the conscientiousness dimension, the less they express their surprise, suggesting that their need for control may inhibit their surprise expression.

5   Discussion and Concluding Comments

The results support our general hypothesis that personality influences emotional reactions. It contributes to the HCI literature by underlining the importance of taking into account users' personality traits in analyzing their emotional reactions to interfaces.

Our results suggest that neuroadaptive interfaces using emotional reactions would perform better by taking into account users' personality traits. Since those two concepts seem to have a relationship, we suggest that personality and emotions are variables that should be taken into account while developing adaptive interfaces in order to improve their accuracy and robustness.

Since the experiment was conducted is a social context (online environment), our results cannot be generalized to an individual context. Alone in a room, users may express themselves differently. This would allow a more intimate relationship between personality traits and emotions, rather than a relationship lowered to a social context, where facial expression is a part of communication and can be influenced by the presence of others. We suggest that this experiment should be replicated in an individual setting, in order to prime different personality dimensions. Another interesting possibility would be to replicate this experiment with other types of interfaces, and observe different emotional reactions.

Because personality traits influence individual emotional reactions, neuroadaptive systems based on users' emotional reactions need to take into account personality traits to optimize the systems' physiological inference.

References

1. Bostan, B.: A motivational framework for analyzing player and virtual agent behavior. Entertainment Comput. **1**(3), 139–146 (2010)
2. Noë, N., et al.: Birds of a feather locate together? Foursquare checkins and personality homophily. Comput. Hum. Behav. **58**, 343–353 (2016)
3. Bastarache-Roberge, M.-C., et al.: Measuring flow using psychophysiological data in a multiplayer gaming context. In: Davis, F.D., Riedl, R., vorn Brocke, J., Léger, P.-M., Randolph, A.B. (eds.) Information Systems and Neuroscience, pp. 187–191. Springer, Heidelberg (2015)
4. Montag, C., Reuter, M.: Internet Addiction: Neuroscientific Approaches and Therapeutical Interventions. Springer, Heidelberg (2015)
5. Goodhue, D.L., Thompson, R.L.: Task-technology fit and individual performance. MIS Q. **19**, 213–236 (1995)

6. Dumont, L., et al.: Using a cognitive analysis grid to inform information systems design. In: Davis, F.D., Riedl, R., vorn Brocke, J., Léger, P.-M., Randolph, A.B. (eds.) Information Systems and Neuroscience, pp. 193–199. Springer, Heidelberg (2015)
7. Courtemanche, F., et al.: Addressing subject-dependency for affective signal processing: modeling subjects' idiosyncracies. In: International Conference on Physiological Computing Systems, Angers, France (2015)
8. Tam, K.Y., Ho, S.Y.: Understanding the impact of web personalization on user information processing and decision outcomes. MIS Q. **30**, 865–890 (2006)
9. Parasuraman, R.: Neuroergonomics brain, cognition, and performance at work. Curr. Dir. Psychol. Sci. **20**(3), 181–186 (2011)
10. Ekman, P., Rosenberg, E.L.: What the Face Reveals: Basic and Applied Studies of Spontaneous Expression Using the Facial Action Coding System (FACS). Oxford University Press, USA (1997)
11. Fasel, B., Luettin, J.: Automatic facial expression analysis: a survey. Pattern Recogn. **36**(1), 259–275 (2003)
12. Fridlund, A., Izard, C.E.: Electromyographic studies of facial expressions of emotions and patterns of emotions. Social psychophysiology: A sourcebook, pp. 243–286 (1983)
13. Clancy, E., Morin, E.L., Merletti, R.: Sampling, noise-reduction and amplitude estimation issues in surface electromyography. J. Electromyogr. Kinesiol. **12**(1), 1–16 (2002)
14. Drewes, C., Electromyography: recording electrical signals from human muscle. Tested studies for laboratory teaching. Association for Biology Laboratory Education (ABLE), vol. 21, pp. 248–270 (2000)
15. Van Nes, F.: Space, colour and typography on visual display terminals. Behav. Inf. Technol. **5**(2), 99–118 (1986)
16. Nacke, L., Lindley, C.A.: Flow and immersion in first-person shooters: measuring the player's gameplay experience. In: Proceedings of the 2008 Conference on Future Play: Research, Play, Share. ACM (2008)
17. Zaman, B., Shrimpton-Smith, T.: The FaceReader: Measuring instant fun of use. In: Proceedings of the 4th Nordic Conference on Human-Computer Interaction: Changing Roles. ACM (2006)
18. Pantic, M., Rothkrantz, L.J.: Toward an affect-sensitive multimodal human-computer interaction. Proc. IEEE **91**(9), 1370–1390 (2003)
19. Cohn, J.F., De la Torre, F.: Automated face analysis for affective. In: The Oxford Handbook of Affective Computing, p. 131. Oxford University Press, Oxford (2014)
20. Den Uyl, M., Van Kuilenburg, H.: The FaceReader: online facial expression recognition. In: Proceedings of Measuring Behavior (2005, Citeseer)
21. Valstar, M., Pantic, M.: Fully automatic facial action unit detection and temporal analysis. In: 2006 Conference on Computer Vision and Pattern Recognition Workshop, CVPRW 2006. IEEE (2006)
22. Riedl, R., Léger, P.-M.: Fundamentals of NeuroIS: Information Systems and the Brain. Springer, Heidelberg (2016)
23. Tomkins, S.S.: Affect, Imagery, Consciousness: Volume I. The Positive Affects. Springer, Heidelberg (1962)
24. Izard, C.E.: The Face of Emotion. Appleton-Century-Crofts, Englewood Cliffs (1971)
25. Matsumoto, D., et al.: Facial Expressions of Emotion. In: Handbook of emotions, vol. 3, pp. 211–234 (2008)
26. DiMatteo, M.R., et al.: Predicting patient satisfaction from physicians' nonverbal communication skills. Med. Care **18**, 376–387 (1980)

27. Malatesta-Magai, C., et al.: Type A behavior pattern and emotion expression in younger and older adults. Psychol. Aging **7**(4), 551 (1992)
28. Eysenck, S.B., Eysenck, H.J., Barrett, P.: A revised version of the psychoticism scale. Pers. Individ. Differ. **6**(1), 21–29 (1985)
29. Lee, K., Ashton, M.C.: Psychometric properties of the HEXACO personality inventory. Multivar. Behav. Res. **39**(2), 329–358 (2004)

Colour Arousal Effect on Users' Decision-Making Processes in the Warning Message Context

Mario Silic[1](✉) and Dianne Cyr[2]

[1] Institute of Information Management (IWI),
University of St. Gallen, St. Gallen, Switzerland
mario.silic@unisg.ch
[2] Beedie School of Business,
Simon Fraser University, Burnaby, Canada
cyr@sfu.ca

Abstract. This research is aimed at understanding how colour affects users' decision-making processes in the context of warning banner messages. So far, little research has examined this complex psychological and cognitive process wherein the psychology of colour can play an important role in the relationship between the warning message and the user's decision-making process. We closed the existing research gap by understanding how different colour applications (black, blue, yellow, red, green, white) influence users' decision-making processes. We built our work on the theory of psychological reversals to colour, supported by the Cognitive-Affective model of communication. We conducted an online experiment measuring actual users' behaviour of 217 participants. We found that the colour application has different arousal effects. Overall, we advance understanding of the psychological process that precedes a decision – with a focus on the importance of colour.

Keywords: Psychology of colour · Warning banner message · User compliance

1 Introduction

Decision-making process is result of trust [1] and different risk factors [2–4] which will ultimately help or hinder the entire process [5] where the colour inputs play an important role. Drivers will stop at traffic red lights as red suggests that there is danger ahead. Colour affects our cognitive systems [6, 7], human perceptions, psychological and emotional reactions and ultimately, our behavioural intentions [8, 9]. The relationship between colour and cognitive functioning has mostly been studied in the field of Psychology. For instance, red was found to be linked to performance attainment [10], which suggests a strong relationship with the emotions whereby diverse psychological reactions can be observed, such as anxiety or pleasure [8]. One such example, wherein first impressions play an important role, is the online context, in which the majority of studies have focused on the impact of colours on website design [11–13], seeking to understand the behaviours of internet shoppers [14, 15]. Overall, past studies have tried to

F.F.-H. Nah and C.-H. Tan (Eds.): HCIBGO 2016, Part II, LNCS 9752, pp. 99–109, 2016.
DOI: 10.1007/978-3-319-39399-5_10

understand how to better capture the user's attention through more appealing website content. In the computer digital world, a warning message on the computer represents communication designed to prevent users from hurting themselves or others [16, 17]. In general, warnings have been found to be quite efficient in preventing hazards and reducing negative outcomes [18–20]. However, and similar to the real-life situation, in the computer context, digital warnings are quite often ignored. Several different explanations have been provided to explain users' non-compliant behaviour, such as: (1) users are habituated to warning messages and consequently, do not read them [21]; and (2) users ignore warnings due to their content [22, 23]. Warning standards and guidelines, such as those put forth by the ANSI – American National Standards Institute – recommend that warnings should be composed of the terms Danger, Warning or Caution combined with a specific colour – red, orange and yellow and an alert symbol [24]. Consequently, the majority of software makers have adopted these guidelines with red being used as a predominant colour. For instance, the latest versions of the Chrome and Internet Explorer web browsers use a red background to inform the user about the potential risk that the user may experience if he/she decides to continue with his/her action.

Past research has concluded that red warnings yield higher adherence rates than black or green warnings in the alcoholic beverage containers context [25]. However, only few studies have tried to understand whether red is really the most efficient colour for computer warning messages when it comes to drawing the user's attention. A study done by Egelman and Schechter [26] investigated the way in which the choice of the background colour (red vs white) in the warning affects the user's decision to comply with the warning. Overall, the number of studies that have investigated the relationship between the colour and the user's cognitive decision-making process is still relatively low. Another challenge with past studies is that they have been poorly supported by the theory. They have mostly used findings from other fields, such as the tobacco industry, in order to implement the same results in the computer warning context. This has resulted in seemingly contradictory and often inconclusive results when it comes to the efficiency of the computer warning message.

Also, the way in which colour affects the user's decision-making process over time has not been addressed by past research. In other words, an understanding of how different colours may affect the user's conscious decisions when the user is confronted by the warning message for the first time, but also during all the consecutive event occurrences, is still lacking. For instance, if the warning message colour is black, instead of red, it could be that the user, upon the third of fourth time of seeing the warning message, would be more careful and attentive to the hazard.

Overall, with this research study we aim to close the existing research gap by studying the effects of colour on the user's decision-making process. We build our work on the theory of psychological reversals to colour [27] to understand how users behave when confronted with the computer warning message.

In the following sections we will present the theoretical background and develop our research model. Then, we will describe the approach and context chosen to empirically test our model, and report our findings. The paper concludes with a discussion on the results, implications and limitations of our study.

2 Theoretical Framework

2.1 Cognitive-Affective Model of Communication

According to the cognitive-affective model of communication suggested by Te'eni [28], there are three factors that affect the communication process: "(1) inputs to the communication process (task, sender-receiver distance, and values and norms of communication with a particular emphasis on inter-cultural communication); (2) a cognitive affective process of communication; and (3) the communication impact on action and relationship". The model suggests that the communication medium and the form of the message will shape the receiver's behaviour. In our context, the communication medium is the warning message itself and the message form corresponds to the colour application. During the communication process, the warning message in combination with the colour application will potentially influence the user's decision-making process in such a way that the user will either react positively to the communication medium content or will not have any affective reaction. Overall, the model suggests that a relationship has to be established between the user and the communication medium (i.e. warning) before the user's behaviour will lead to an action. Hence, there is a balance between relationship and action, between cognition and affect, and between message and medium [28]. Another dimension that is important for the cognitive-affective model of communication is the cultural aspect. As communication action is bounded by social norms and values, users may have different expectations of how the message should be represented.

2.2 Theory of Psychological Reversals

The theory of psychological reversals [27] suggests two levels of preferred felt arousal: one high and one low. Although switching ("reversals") from high to low is possible, either a high or low level will be preferred at a certain point in time. There is a strong association between arousal preference and colour preference, whereby users will be excited and aroused by certain colours and relaxed by others. For instance, warm colours will generally provoke "active feelings" while cool colours are "much less likely to cause extreme reactions" [29]. Similarly, Gerard [30] found that when a red light was projected on a diffusing screen, an increased arousal was observed in the subjects. Clearly, long-wavelength colours (e.g. red, orange) are more stimulating compared to short-wavelength colours (e.g. blue, violet), which are more relaxing [27]. In the online shopping context, it was found that cool tones such as blue are preferred over warm tones such as red [11]. We expect, then, to see different levels of appeal to users who are expected to behave differently when presented with warm or cool tones. As the cognitive-affective model of communication suggests that cognition and affect will be impacted by the communication medium (i.e. warning message), in such circumstances it is likely that the user will feel either high or low arousal. Consequently, there will be a possibility that the user may switch from a high to a low level if he/she is confronted with a different colour application. This could be even more pronounced in a different cultural aspect.

3 Hypothesis Development

The effects of colour on human preferences have received considerable attention from psychologists [31]. Their relevance is not just related to aesthetics. In western cultures, for instance, red means "mistake" (e.g. teachers use red to correct mistakes), stop (e.g. red traffic lights) or danger (e.g. warning message). But it is also associated with love and sexuality (e.g. Amsterdam red light district). When it comes to gender separation, pink is usually attributed to girls and blue to boys [32]. White usually means immaculacy and black corresponds to tragic situations (e.g. death). Overall, different colour applications may have different impacts on the user's decision-making process. However, current research suggests that red is the colour that commonly represents danger, as it denotes risk and danger on warning labels, traffic signals, and many other systems used to inform about the threat (e.g. anti-virus software). However, as can be seen from previous studies, red can provide different levels of arousal. While we expect to find red to be the most efficient colour in transmitting risk in the computer warning message context, the lack of empirical findings related to colour and user decision making suggests that the relationship between colour application and the warning message needs to be better analysed. Consequently, it could be that other colours will have stronger secondary (i.e. second and all consecutive warning message displays) arousal effects on the user's attention. For instance, humans are so habituated to seeing the colour red in everyday life (e.g. traffic signs) that in the computer context the user may pay less attention (i.e. not read the warning itself) and, consequently, may skip over and ignore the message. It could be interesting to see what would happen, for instance, if the computer warning message had a constantly changing background, with the objective of decreasing the user's habituation to seeing the colour red. On the one hand, the user could be confused by this constant colour change, but on the other hand, the user might pay more attention as he/she would not become habituated to always seeing the red background. Overall, we argue that different colour applications will have high or low psychological arousal effects on the user. Hence, we hypothesize:

Hypothesis 1: Different colour applications will have different levels of psychological arousal effects on the user's actual behaviour when confronted by the computer warning message.

4 Research Design

4.1 Participants, Measures and Procedures

In order to test our research hypothesis, we conducted a non-controlled online experiment involving participants from US and India. Institutional Review Board (IRB) approval was given to collect data and human-subject protocols were followed. In addition, every participant had to provide his or her consent for being part of a research study. The participants were informed that the study's objective was to get their view on the photoproduct they like the most. Hence, we used deception to increase realism of the results. We recruited participants from US and India by using Amazon Mechanical Turk.

Our study uses the experiment method to explore and measure the progression, frequency, and duration (i.e. time) of user behaviour when confronted with the warning banner message through different colour applications. Users were provided with a web link, which led them to a website, where they were asked to complete a task. The task consisted of choosing the product image they prefer. After clicking on the task 'start' button, they were presented with the warning banner message (Fig. 1). In order to test the frequency (i.e. the repeated effect) we displayed the warning banner message to the same participants twice – first after the second photoproduct evaluation and second after the fourth evaluation. We limited the number of warning appearances to two in order not to raise any suspicions from the participant's side. The warning message is based on the latest Google Chrome web browser malware warning, which we modified (Fig. 1) slightly (instead of using the word 'malware' we used the word 'safe' for simplicity and comprehension reasons). The background colours were randomly displayed (the random function is used in the web application to control the display), and could be red, blue, green, black, yellow or white. As red is the default colour for warning message in the majority of the web browsers (e.g. Google Chrome, Internet Explore and Firefox) we use red as the control group. Further, the choice for other colours is based on the colour-culture chart as suggested by Russo and Boor [33], but also on past studies [e.g. 11], which found these colours to have a high risk component or to transmit some strong emotions and feelings.

Fig. 1. Warning message displayed (adapted from Google Chrome version 46)

In order to measure users' actual behaviour we use a categorical variable ("decision") which can take two values. When users click on 'Continue' or 'EXIT', the binary decision is registered on a remote SQL server (0 for continue and 1 for Exit) together with several other data such as: browser version, time spent deciding (time is measured in milliseconds and corresponds to the time from when the user clicked on the start button until the user clicks on continue or exit).

4.2 Method for Analysis

To analyse the effects we used the survival techniques such as the Kaplan-Meier Survival Curve, which is an estimator used to estimate survival time from lifetime data. The Kaplan-Meier method is a nonparametric method used to estimate the probability of survival past given time points (i.e. it calculates a survival distribution) [34]. Time to event represents an event course duration, which has a beginning and an end for each user.

In this type of analysis, every participant is characterized by three variables: (1) the duration, (2) the status at the end of the event (exit or continue) and (3) the colour application. Furthermore, to test the effect of the warning message on the duration (repeated use) we use Cox's proportional-hazard regression model, which allows for investigations of the relationships between the survival of the event and independent measures of interest [35].

5   Results

We received 435 events (both first and second occurrence) from 217 participants (one participant second warning event was not registered as participant closed web browser). Detailed demographics are presented in Table 1.

Table 1. Participant demographics

Country	# of users	Gender		Average age
		M	F	
United States	106	59	47	33.4
India	111	66	45	31.8

Further, in order to understand how the warning message impacts user behaviour in presence of a different colour application we analyze the survival time before the hazard occurs (i.e. user clicks on continue button in the warning banner message). As we cannot simply compare the average hazard durations, due to the right skewed distribution of the survival time, we use survival and event history analysis techniques. Event history analysis is a statistical method that deals with timing and duration until the occurrence of an event. The method examines the hazard rate that calculates conditional probability that an event occurs at a particular time interval. In other words, how long it takes the event to occur. To start with, Table 2 provides an overview of the case summary. We can see that total number of events is equally assigned for each colour (except for the blue colour, which has a slightly lower representation compared to the others). Censored means that the event has occurred (i.e. user clicked on continue button). Results indicate that, for instance, in presence of the black colour 39.5 % of participants clicked on continue, while only 23.5 % for yellow colour. Red, white, blue and green colours received very similar results.

Next, we proceed by examining the cumulative survival functions for different intervention groups (i.e. colour types). This is a plot of the cumulative survival proportions against time for each colour type. When the group survival curve appears "above" another colour group's survival curve on the graph (see Fig. 2), it is considered to be demonstrating a beneficial/advantageous effect. However, in our context if a survival curve is above another one, it indicates that it has lower impact on user's behaviors'. For instance, on Fig. 2, black colour is above the yellow colour, which indicates that black colour has lower impact on the user's compliance as its survival curve shows black warning message significantly prolongs the time taken until

Table 2. Case Processing Summary

Colour Type	Total N	N of events	Censored	
			N	Percent
BLACK	76	46	30	39.5 %
RED	80	54	26	32.5 %
WHITE	80	55	25	31.3 %
YELLOW	68	52	16	23.5 %
BLUE	59	40	19	32.2 %
GREEN	72	50	22	30.6 %
Overall	435	297	138	31.7 %

participants chose exit option. Overall, survival graph is a first indication of the colour effects that needs to be further analyzed to understand if it is statistically significant.

In order to understand the typical time until participants experience the event (choose exit action), we need to analyse the means and medians for survival time table. Table 3 presents the mean and median survival time for each of the colour types. As the mean has far less importance than the median as a measure of central tendency, we focus on interpreting the median values and their 95 % confidence intervals.

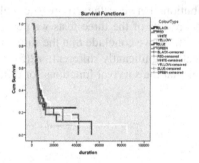

Fig. 2. Survival functions for each colour type (Color figure online)

We can see, for instance, that the median survival time for black colour was 6076 ms with 95 % confidence interval from 4517 ms to 7634 ms. The results from Table 3 indicate that yellow (median value of 3635), green (4707) and red (4902), were the most successful colours at keeping participants from continuing with their non-compliant action (click on continue). Other colours: black (6076), white (6065) and blue (5691) were less successful in keeping participants from being non-compliant.

Further, in order to understand if there were differences in the survival distribution for the different colour types, there are three statistical tests that can be used to test whether the survival functions are equal. These are the log rank test [36], Breslow test [37] and the Tarone-Ware test [38]. Usually all three tests provide very similar results. For instance, the log rank test is testing the null hypothesis that there is no difference in

Table 3. Means and Medians for Survival Time

Colour type	Median			
	Estimate	Std. error	95 % confidence interval	
			Lower bound	Upper bound
RED	4902.000	278.550	4356.042	5447.958
BLACK	6076.000	795.073	4517.658	7634.342
WHITE	6065.000	1171.784	3768.303	8361.697
YELLOW	3635.000	357.149	2934.987	4335.013
BLUE	5691.000	572.842	4568.229	6813.771
GREEN	4707.000	440.012	3844.576	5569.424
Overall	4938.000	170.864	4603.107	5272.893

Table 4. Test of equality of survival distributions for the different levels of colour type.

	Chi-square	df	Sig.
Log Rank (Mantel-Cox)	12.015	5	.035
Breslow (Generalized Wilcoxon)	12.257	5	.031
Tarone-Ware	12.948	5	.024

the overall survival distributions between the groups (i.e. colour types) in the population. Table 4 displays the results of the three tests we performed.

As p < 0.05 for all three tests, we conclude that the survival distribution for the five colour types were statistically significantly different, $\chi2(5) = 12.015$, $p < .05$ for the log rank test. This indicates that the survival functions for different colour applications are statistically different.

6 Discussion

Colour seems to play an important role in this communication process occurring between the communication medium (i.e. the warning message) and the receiver (i.e. the user). We found that colour has an important role in the Cognitive-affective model of communication as it helps to establish a better relationship between the user and the communication medium. This supports the balance between relationship and action, between cognition and affect, and between message and medium [28]. In other words, our study results confirm that users may have different expectations when it comes to the way the message is presented to them. Some colours, such as blue, will have less effect on user's attention, while others (e.g. red) will provoke an increased arousal. This is in line with past studies which found blue to have "calming" effect [27] and red, projected onto a diffusing screen, to produce increased users' arousal [30]. Further, we provide evidence that arousal effect can be high or low, or that users can even switch from high to low arousal effect during different event occurrences. This is supported by the theory of psychological reversals [27]. Our finding suggests that users' will have higher or lower levels of the arousal effect, which will depend on how they feel about the colour that is displayed. While this finding was also supported by others [e.g. 11, 39], this is the first investigation that validated different colour applications in the warning context. This confirms a strong link between arousal and colour preference. Indeed, it was found that warm colours (e.g. red) will create more arousal and attention than cool colours (e.g. blue) [40]. Also, cool colours will elicit greater relaxation and pleasure than warm colours [41]. This effect seems to be valid also in the warning context arousal is linked to the colour application. Moreover, the importance of the communication medium is even more pronounced as cognition and affect will have high or low arousal effect on user's behaviour.

Our study has some practical implications. First, we found that different colour applications (black, blue, yellow, red, green, white) have different psychological arousal effects on the user. As expected, we found red to have a high arousal effect. However, we also found that yellow and green are as powerful as red to prevent users from committing a potentially harmful action. Alternately, black, white and blue were less successful to keep participants from being non-compliant. This finding provides important insight for practice as it gives clear evidence that other colours, such as yellow and green, can have high arousal effect on user's attention. It could be that these colours increase comprehension. Past studies found that when contrasting colours in health warnings on tobacco products, such as black letters on a white background, leads to easier reading process, which, consequently increases comprehension [42, 43]. This suggests that warning designers could think of using other colour applications when displaying warning message to the user.

We believe that future research should further seek to understand colour effects on user's compliance by incorporating additional event occurrences. Indeed, some colours could have a greater secondary effect during successive event occurrences. For instance, in the fifth occurrence red could be simply ignored. The fact that we considered only two cultures is a limitation of our study. Hence, future studies could extend this cultural exploration by adding other cultures to further understand the colour impact in various cultural settings. Another limitation of our study is that, as we used experimental setting and deception approach, we could not collect some background information about our participants, which could be very useful to better understanding of different study's findings.

7   Conclusion

This research aimed at understanding how colour affects users' decision-making processes in the context of warning banner messages. We found that colour plays an important role in the user's decision-making process when confronted with a warning message. Different user arousal effects are observed not only in different cultural settings, but also depending on the event occurrence. Overall, we advance understanding of the psychological process that precedes a decision – with a focus on the importance of colour.

References

1. Silic, M., Back, A.: Information security and open source dual use security software: trust paradox. In: Petrinja, E., Succi, G., El Ioini, N., Sillitti, A. (eds.) OSS 2013. IFIP AICT, vol. 404, pp. 194–206. Springer, Heidelberg (2013)
2. Silic, M., Back, A.: Identification and importance of the technological risks of open source software in the enterprise adoption context. In: Thomas, O., Teuteberg, F. (Hrsg.) 12th International Conference on Wirtschaftsinformatik, pp. 1163–1176 (2015)
3. Silic, M., Back, A.: The influence of risk factors in decision-making process for open source software adoption. Int. J. Inf. Technol. Decis. Mak. **15**, 1–35 (2015)
4. Silic, M., Back, A., Silic, D.: Taxonomy of technological risks of open source software in the enterprise adoption context. Inf. Comput. Secur. **23**, 570–583 (2015)
5. Silic, M.: Dual-use open source security software in organizations – Dilemma: help or hinder? Comput. Secur. Part B **39**, 386–395 (2013)
6. Elliot, A.J., Maier, M.A.: Color and psychological functioning. Curr. Dir. Psychol. Sci. **16**, 250–254 (2007)
7. Kaya, N., Epps, H.H.: Relationship between color and emotion: a study of college students. Coll. Stud. J. **38**, 396 (2004)
8. Valdez, P., Mehrabian, A.: Effects of color on emotions. J. Exp. Psychol. Gen. **123**, 394 (1994)
9. Silic, M.: Understanding colour impact on warning messages: evidence from US and India. In: CHI 2014 Extended Abstracts on Human Factors in Computing Systems. ACM (2016)
10. Elliot, A.J., Maier, M.A., Moller, A.C., Friedman, R., Meinhardt, J.: Color and psychological functioning: the effect of red on performance attainment. J. Exp. Psychol. Gen. **136**, 154 (2007)
11. Cyr, D., Head, M., Larios, H.: Colour appeal in website design within and across cultures: a multi-method evaluation. Int. J. Hum.-Comput. Stud. **68**, 1–21 (2010)
12. Cyr, D., Head, M.: Website design in an international context: the role of gender in masculine versus feminine oriented countries. Comput. Hum. Behav. **29**, 1358–1367 (2013)
13. Cyr, D., Trevor-Smith, H.: Localization of web design: an empirical comparison of German, Japanese, and United States web site characteristics. J. Am. Soc. Inf. Sci. Technol. **55**, 1199–1208 (2004)
14. Menon, S., Kahn, B.: Cross-category effects of induced arousal and pleasure on the Internet shopping experience. J. Retail. **78**, 31–40 (2002)
15. Bhatnagar, A., Misra, S., Rao, H.R.: On risk, convenience, and Internet shopping behavior. Commun. ACM **43**, 98–105 (2000)
16. Wogalter, M.S.: Purposes and scope of warnings. In: Handbook of Warnings, pp. 3–9. Lawrence Erlbaum Associates, Mahwah (2006)
17. Silic, M., Barlow, J., Ormond, D.: Warning! A comprehensive model of the effects of digital information security warning messages. In: The 2015 Dewald Roode Workshop on Information Systems Security Research, IFIP, pp. 1–32. IFIP, Dewald (2015)
18. Coleman, S.: The Minnesota income tax compliance experiment: replication of the social norms experiment. Available at SSRN 1393292 (2007)
19. Goldstein, N.J., Cialdini, R.B., Griskevicius, V.: A room with a viewpoint: using social norms to motivate environmental conservation in hotels. J. Consum. Res. **35**, 472–482 (2008)
20. Schultz, P., Tabanico, J.J.: Criminal beware: a social norms perspective on posting public warning signs*. Criminology **47**, 1201–1222 (2009)
21. Egilman, D., Bohme, S.: A brief history of warnings. In: Handbook of Warnings, pp. 35–48. Lawrence Erlbaum Associates, Mahwah (2006)

22. Akhawe, D., Felt, A.P.: Alice in warningland: a large-scale field study of browser security warning effectiveness. In: Usenix Security, pp. 257–272 (2013)
23. Sunshine, J., Egelman, S., Almuhimedi, H., Atri, N., Cranor, L.F.: Crying wolf: an empirical study of SSL warning effectiveness. In: USENIX Security Symposium, pp. 399–416 (2009)
24. Nema. http://www.nema.org/Standards/z535/Pages/default.aspx. Accessed Jan. 2016
25. Laughery, K.R., Young, S.L., Vaubel, K.P., Brelsford Jr., J.W.: The noticeability of warnings on alcoholic beverage containers. Journal of Public Policy & Marketing **12**, 38–56 (1993)
26. Egelman, S., Schechter, S.: The importance of being earnest [in security warnings]. In: Sadeghi, A.-R. (ed.) FC 2013. LNCS, vol. 7859, pp. 52–59. Springer, Heidelberg (2013)
27. Walters, J., Apter, M.J., Svebak, S.: Color preference, arousal, and the theory of psychological reversals. Motiv. Emot. **6**, 193–215 (1982)
28. Te'eni, D.: Review: a cognitive-affective model of organizational communication for designing IT. MIS Q. **25**, 251–312 (2001)
29. Levy, B.I.: Research into the psychological meaning of color. Am. J. Art Ther. **19**, 87–91 (1984)
30. Gerard, R.M.: Color and emotional arousal. In: American Psychologist, pp. 340–340. Amer Psychological Assoc 750 First St NE, Washington, DC 20002-4242 (1958)
31. Goldberg, J.H., Stimson, M.J., Lewenstein, M., Scott, N., Wichansky, A.M.: Eye tracking in web search tasks: design implications. In: Proceedings of the 2002 Symposium on Eye Tracking Research and Applications, pp. 51–58. ACM (2002)
32. Chiu, S.W., Gervan, S., Fairbrother, C., Johnson, L.L., Owen-Anderson, A.F., Bradley, S.J., Zucker, K.J.: Sex-dimorphic color preference in children with gender identity disorder: a comparison to clinical and community controls. Sex Roles **55**, 385–395 (2006)
33. Russo, P., Boor, S.: How fluent is your interface?: designing for international users. In: Proceedings of the INTERACT 1993 and CHI 1993 Conference on Human Factors in Computing Systems, pp. 342–347. ACM (1993)
34. Kaplan, E.L., Meier, P.: Nonparametric estimation from incomplete observations. J. Am. Stat. Assoc. **53**, 457–481 (1958)
35. Box-Steffensmeier, J.M., Jones, B.S.: Event History Modeling: A Guide for Social Scientists. Cambridge University Press, Cambridge (2004)
36. Mantel, N.: Evaluation of survival data and two new rank order statistics arising in its consideration. Cancer Chemother. Rep. Part 1 **50**, 163–170 (1966)
37. Breslow, N.: A generalized Kruskal-Wallis test for comparing K samples subject to unequal patterns of censorship. Biometrika **57**, 579–594 (1970)
38. Tarone, R.E., Ware, J.: On distribution-free tests for equality of survival distributions. Biometrika **64**, 156–160 (1977)
39. Bonnardel, N., Piolat, A., Le Bigot, L.: The impact of colour on Website appeal and users' cognitive processes. Displays **32**, 69–80 (2011)
40. Birren, F.: Color and Human Response: Aspects of Light and Color Bearing on the Reactions of Living Things and the Welfare of Human Beings. Van Nostrand Reinhold Company, New York (1978)
41. Guilford, J.P.: The affective value of color as a function of hue, tint, and chroma. J. Exp. Psychol. **17**, 342 (1934)
42. Nilsson, T.: Legibility of tobacco health messages with respect to distance. A report to the Tobacco Products Division of the Health Protection Branch of Health and Welfare Canada (1991)
43. Hammond, D.: Health warning messages on tobacco products: a review. Tobacco control tc. 2010.037630 (2011)

HCI Testing in Laboratory or Field Settings

Chuan-Hoo Tan[1(✉)], Austin Silva[2], Rich Lee[3], Kanliang Wang[4],
and Fiona Fui-Hoon Nah[5]

[1] Department of Information Systems, National University of Singapore, Singapore, Singapore
tancho@comp.nus.edu.sg
[2] Sandia National Laboratories, Albuquerque, NM, USA
aussilv@sandia.gov
[3] IBM, Taipei, Taiwan
richchihlee@gmail.com
[4] Department of Management Science and Engineering, Renmin University, Beijing, China
kanliang.wang@gmail.com
[5] Missouri University of Science and Technology, Rolla, MO, USA
nahf@mst.edu

Abstract. This paper presents perspectives from both academia and practice on how an HCI testing is to be conducted and the deliberations that go into the testing. HCI testing can be conducted in closed-door laboratory or in a field setting. While there is an increased interest in field testing of an HCI artifact, there is always an enduring concern over how to administer a field testing given that the testers will have less control over the course of testing. In this paper, we cover HCI testing deliberation as well as the operational issues of field testing, and conclude the paper with an exemplary case of a large-scale field testing conducted in Taiwan.

Keywords: HCI testing · Laboratory · Field

1 Introduction

HCI testing is an integral part of an HCI design and development process. By having human subjects to physically test and use the artifact, HCI designers are able to validate the usability of an artifact and identify opportunities for further design improvements. Among many considerations, two prominent testing choices that a designer faces are (1) closed-door laboratory testing, or (2) field testing which is carried out in a setting that is more open [1]. While closed-door laboratory testing enables testers to have greater control over the course of testing, field testing narrows the gap between the intended usage of the artifact and its actual usage. Through the latter (i.e., actual usage), the HCI designers are able to better understand how an HCI artifact is utilized and valued by the target audience.

Whether to conduct a testing in laboratory or field setting is often based on the nature of the artifact itself. For example, it is viewed that a laboratory is suitable for testing a user interface and assessing an artifact's usability [2] while field is an appropriate setting for evaluating the acceptance of the artifact and its associated functionalities [3]. Two other considerations include (1) whether the artifact is revolutionary/disruptive in nature

© Springer International Publishing Switzerland 2016
F.F.-H. Nah and C.-H. Tan (Eds.): HCIBGO 2016, Part II, LNCS 9752, pp. 110–116, 2016.
DOI: 10.1007/978-3-319-39399-5_11

and (2) company culture and propensity toward opening up the artifact for early field-testing, among others.

This panel takes a slightly different perspective by starting with the proposition that field testing is preferred due to the ability to more realistically test an HCI design. Building on this proposition, we ask: what are the operational considerations for field testing?

In the following sections, we will document the different perspectives taken by the panel members, which covers both the perspectives of academicians and practitioners on HCI testing. We conclude the paper with a large-scale field test conducted in Taiwan.

2   An Academic Perspective of HCI Testing

HCI testing often occurs at a later stage of HCI design and development. Hence, how to go about performing testing can be a delayed deliberation task. Fortunately, we are seeing more contemporary approaches such as agile development [4] and the design thinking principle [5], which further advocates the importance of pushing forward testing early in the artifact development. By having experience in conducting empirical studies in laboratory and field settings for research purposes, we are also able to see the challenges and issues confronting the setting to conduct HCI testing.

The first consideration factor for academicians to conduct field testing is the availability of the venue and the facilitating conditions. For example, a prototype that is still fairly distant from completion (i.e., far from ready to be commercialized) will be very difficult to test in the field setting as it could arouse emotional displeasure by the target audience. Also seeking companies' buy-in and facilitation will be challenging too. Thus, academicians often have to revert back to laboratory testing or conduct testing within the university boundary.

The second consideration factor is how "clean" the data is for us to attribute the causal relationship between an HCI artifact and user behavior. The laboratory setting restricts users from extraneous influences that could adversely affect his/her response to a given artifact. However, the field setting allows HCI testers to be vulnerable to environmental and situational conditions that may change during the course of testing. Thus, the research criterion of validity may be challenged.

The third consideration factor is whether the researchers are able to replicate or reconduct the testing with additional parameters should such needs arise. This is an enduring concern in the academic field due to the nature of the journal review cycle. In our discipline, papers could be in the review process for two to three years or even longer. During the review cycle, it is very plausible that reviewers would give comments and suggestions on how testing should have been conducted. In some cases, the researchers have to conduct another round of testing by taking the reviewers' suggestions into consideration, which raises the issue of whether, and to what extent, a field test could be conducted again. If the field testing involves industry partners, conducting additional rounds of testing may not be feasible.

Our view on HCI testing is: the decision to have the testing conducted in the laboratory or field setting may go beyond the artifact itself, as it could be a forced choice in light of the constraints that academia may face. The next section covers a more detailed discussion on the operational issues relating to field testing.

3   A Practitioner Perspective of HCI Testing

HCI testing deliberations involve the understanding of whether the artifact is ready for testing, the operational considerations, the experimental design, and the analysis and interpretation of the data collected.

Is your artifact ready for field-testing?   There is an increased recognition to launch products into the market quickly, i.e., the benefits of short time to market and first-mover advantage. Furthermore, it is always exciting to see new technologies enter the market. However, doing so requires the artifacts to be tested extensively in the laboratory before escalating to field testing. As a rule of thumb, when they are being tested in the field, it is ideal to first have a field pilot to ensure that the system is working as expected and the data is as clean as possible, since the cleanest data that one can ever hope to achieve is typically gathered in a highly controlled laboratory setting. If the technologies do not perform well in the laboratory testing, it is expected that things can only become worse in the field during live testing. You may not be able to assess or know in advance how well the data will be in the field.

How to conduct the testing?   To truly understand the strengths and limitations of your developed system or procedure, it may be necessary to observe and assess users as they interact with the system in the actual environment that they would naturally perform. Unfortunately, it is nearly impossible to collect that data seamlessly and without noise. The big question becomes: What are you willing to trade in for the realism of the task in order to get the data you want? First, the researcher must understand the task and if there are elements that could be best computerized and simulated. If there are tasks that get automated from physical and observable tasks, the experiment may drift further away from the true environment. But if the subjects were to perform in the actual environment with the normal ambient distractions and interactions, it may be relevant to the overall hypothesis and only give up some fidelity for the sake of clean data.

How to design the testing?   To help assess the importance in needing to go into the field for data collection, one must first decide what the main objective is. If the main objective is feedback on an interface, it may not need to be conducted in the field. However, if the key objective is to measure cognitive load via eye tracking while performing tasks in the operational environment, then there may arise a need to conduct the experiment in the field. Sometimes, researchers will add capabilities and tools on top of an existing study to try to collect more data in order to answer a secondary hypothesis. A study that measures behavioral performance could have an eye-tracking component added to it, but the data may be noisy if it was not designed to be an eye tracking study (i.e., the subject is required by the primary task to move around a lot where the eye tracker may not be able to focus on the subject). The field presents numerous potentials for sources of noise in the data if relying on biometric data such as eye tracking or EEG devices. However, we also caution that creating lab-like mitigations of these sources of noise (like chinrests) can create even more distractions and complications for the users.

Can you handle the data collected? While field studies may hold more promise for operational validity, there may be an introduction of additional noises. With the introduction of noises, one may now have to collect more data than needed in the laboratory. With this new requirement, you now can start to run into big data problems in which you are potentially collecting gigabytes of data across hundreds of subjects. In order to be able to handle this inflow of data after collection, it is important to develop a well-documented data analysis procedure across the team on how the data will be stored, accessed, and updated. If a researcher wants to test something that could affect the policy and practice of an organization, it is important to ensure that the large dataset can be analyzed and validated with ease. However, if the study is a review of usability of new technology where the study involved only a few subjects, it may not present a big data problem. When out in the field, we suggest performing quick data checks on the new data to ensure that the data is being properly collected, or else the remainder of the data collection may need to be postponed. It would also be helpful to thoroughly inspect the data after the first few experimental sessions before continuing with the rest of the sessions.

Can you manage your team? There are opportunities for a research team to specialize in or master one of the domains – lab or field. With a larger team, you can appoint a master and apprentice model in which one team member is the main operator supported by a secondary operator who is approximately equal in terms of knowledge in case the main person is unavailable or cannot conduct the experiment. When conducting testing in the field, it is imperative that the person collecting the data is not only knowledgeable in the data collection process, software, and objectives, but is also aware of the technical aspects of the equipment in case something needs to be modified in the software or hardware. If a problem arises and the data collection proctor is not familiar with the system, it could result in having to cancel the remaining session to return back to the lab for changes. Such cases could result in a total loss of data or collection of the wrong data.

4 A Field Testing Example

To understand HCI testing, it is best to understand the complexity of conducting HCI testing in the field. In what follows, I present an example of how a large-scale field testing was conducted in Taiwan. The methodology is the scenario-driven testing approach [6], which is applied to a complicated and heavy-stressed service system — the Taipei Massive Rapid Transit (Subway) [see Fig. 1]. The testing objective is to validate the quality of design and the potential weakest links of the service disruption to determine if the service systems will meet the users' expectations.

Fig. 1. Taipei mass rapid transit

Several key successful factors are:

1. The explicit functionalities, such as sensing the Smart Cards, debiting the toll, etc.;
2. The implicit expectations, such as the response time of the sensing devices, the time period for the sensing device to take the next customer;
3. The reliability, the Mean Time between Failure (MTBF) and the Mean Time to Repair (MTTR) from the Fatigue Analysis report; and
4. The exceptional procedures (in case of service failure), the seamless manual process or the compensating procedures.

It is essential to establish a clearly defined Quality Function Diagram (QFD) created by the stakeholders and the design team (Fig. 2) before beginning the validation process.

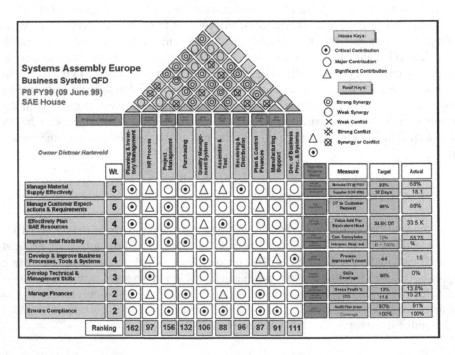

Fig. 2. An example of QFD for transportation

The diagram presents the specific criterion related to the testing details, and serves as the basis for the Work Breakdown Structures (WBS) in the testing project planning.

The testing plan includes:

1. The Integration Testing—this can be done in the lab to record the results of the performance; a service modeling and simulation tool (Fig. 3) will be helpful to find the potential weakest links of the service system through the Stress Impact Analysis (Fig. 4) according to the performance result records;
2. The Field Testing—this is synonymous to Trial Run, based on the predefined scenarios, choosing few test sites, having the actors physically experiencing the system and observing how various payloads impact on it; and
3. The Sustaining Testing—keep monitoring and re-coding the performance results against the stimuli from the real service sites (Fig. 5), a Quality Attribute perspective, use these data as the evidence of continuous improvement.

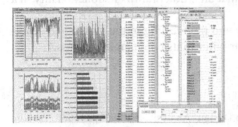

Fig. 3. An example of service modeling & simulation tool

Fig. 4. An example of service system stress impact analysis

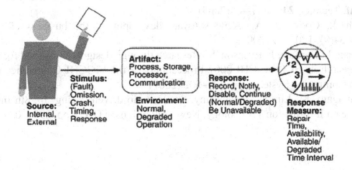

Fig. 5. Fundamental quality attribute model

Based on the aforementioned background information, the suggested panel outlines will also cover the following topics and the associated issues:

1. Service Scenario Design,
2. Service Reliability,
3. Service Testing Types and Procedures,
4. Service System Design,

5. Testing Project Management,
6. Testing Environment, and
7. Simulation and Dynamic Analysis.

5 Concluding Comments

HCI testing continues to remain an integral part of the technology design and development process. We hope through this article and the panel discussion, we are able to generate more insightful and novel ideas of how to go about planning and conducting an HCI testing expedition. There are trade-offs in conducting laboratory and field testing, and both are essential before rolling out a commercial product. The developers or technology-based firms may utilize laboratory testing at earlier stages of product development and conduct more field testing at the later stages. Various iterations of laboratory and field testing may be necessary to ensure that an artifact fulfills its functionality in a realistic setting.

Recognizing the value of both laboratory and field testing in the design and development process of a technology is a key contributor to its commercial success.

References

1. Gerber, A.S., Green, D.P.: Field Experiments: Design, Analysis, and Interpretation, 1st edn. W.W. Norton & Company, New York (2012)
2. Hallahan, K.: Improving public relations web sites through usability research. Public Relat. Rev. 27(2), 223–239 (2001)
3. Kaasinen, E.: User Acceptance of location-aware mobile guides based on seven field studies. Behav. Inf. Technol. 24(1), 37–49 (2005)
4. Highsmith, J., Cockburn, A.: Agile software development: the business of innovation. Computer 34(9), 120–127 (2001)
5. Zimmerman, J., Forlizzi, J., Evenson, S.: Research through design as a method for interaction design research in HCI. In: CHI 2007 Proceedings of the SIGCHI Conference on Human Factors in Computing Systems, pp. 493–502 (2007)
6. Sivashanmugam, K., Lin, D., Palanisamy, S.: Scenario driven testing. In: 8th International Conference on Information Technology: New Generations (ITNG), pp. 299–303 (2011)

A Structure-Behavior Coalescence Method for Human-Computer Interaction System Requirements Specification

Yu-Chen Yang[1(✉)], Yi-Ling Lin[1], and William S. Chao[2]

[1] Department of Information Management, National Sun Yat-Sen University, Kaohsiung, Taiwan
{ycyang,yllin}@mis.nsysu.edu.tw
[2] Association of Chinese Enterprise Architects, Taipei, Taiwan
architectchao@gmail.com

Abstract. For a system requirements method to specify a system as an integrated whole of that system's multiple views, it must be able to integrate the system structure and system behavior when specifying a system.

Current system requirements methods such as data-oriented, function-oriented, control-oriented and object-oriented, more or less, fail to specify a system as an integrated whole of that system's multiple views because they are not able to integrate the system structure and system behavior when specifying a system.

In this paper, we present a structure-behavior coalescence (SBC) method for human-computer interaction (HCI) system requirements specification (SyRS). Structure-behavior coalescence method includes three fundamental diagrams: (a) architecture hierarchy diagram, (b) component operation diagram and (c) interaction flow diagram. SBC method provides a sophisticated way to integrate the system structure and system behavior when used for HCI system requirements specifications.

Keywords: Structure-behavior coalescence method · System requirements specification · Human-Computer interaction

1 Introduction

A system is complex that it consists of multiple views such as structure view, behavior view, function view, data view, etc. The system requirements method specifies the multiple views of a system possibly using two different approaches. The first one is the non-integration approach and the second one is the integration approach.

The non-integration approach respectively picks a model for each view as shown in Fig. 1, the structure view has the structure model; the behavior view has the behavior model; the function view has the function model; the data view has the data model. These multiple models are heterogeneous and unrelated of each other, thus there is no way to put them into a conformity model [11, 17].

© Springer International Publishing Switzerland 2016
F.F.-H. Nah and C.-H. Tan (Eds.): HCIBGO 2016, Part II, LNCS 9752, pp. 117–127, 2016.
DOI: 10.1007/978-3-319-39399-5_12

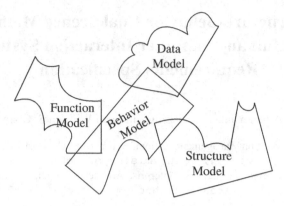

Fig. 1. The Non-integration approach

The integration approach, instead of picking many heterogeneous and unrelated models, will use only one single integration model as shown in Fig. 2. The structure, behavior, function and data views are all integrated in this one single integration model which represents an integrated whole of that system's multiple views [5–8].

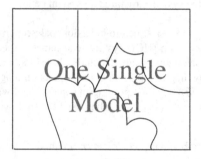

Fig. 2. The integration approach

Among those multiple views, the structure view focuses on the system structure which is described by components and their composition while the behavior view concentrates on the system behavior which involves interactions among external environment's actors and components. Since structure and behavior views are the two most distinguished ones among multiple views, integrating the structure and behavior views becomes the most appropriate method for integrating multiple views of a system as shown in Fig. 3.

For requirements being able to describe a system as an integrated whole of that system's multiple views, an ideal method for human-computer interaction (HCI) [18] system requirements specification should be based on a set of interacting components forming an integrated system structure and system behavior. The purpose of this paper is to explore this principle in depth. The whole paper is organized as follows. Section 1 is the introduction. Current methods such as data-oriented, function-oriented, control-oriented and object-oriented for requirements failing to describe a system as an

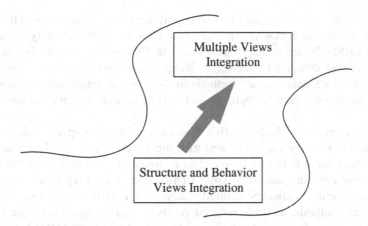

Fig. 3. Structure and behavior views integration facilitates multiple views integration

integrated whole of that system's multiple views are discussed in Sect. 2. Section 3 examines in detail the structure-behavior coalescence (SBC) method which integrates the system structure and system behavior of a system. Advantages of using structure-behavior coalescence as a method for HCI system requirements specification are delineated in Sect. 4. Section 5 is a summary.

2 Related Works

In general, current system requirements methods for HCI system requirement specification fall into three general categories: data, function, control and objects [14, 15], as shown in Fig. 4. Each of these methods, more or less, fails to describe a system as an integrated whole of that system's multiple views.

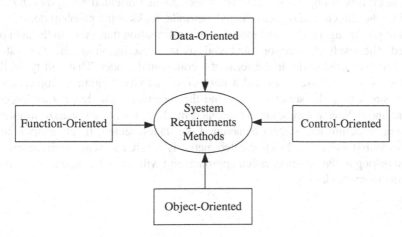

Fig. 4. Current system requirements methods

Data-oriented methods for HCI system requirements specification stress the system state as a data structure. Jackson System Development (JSD) [4] and Entity Relationship Modeling (ERM) [9] are primarily data-oriented. Data-oriented methods concentrate only on data and completely neglect to integrate the system structure and system behavior. Therefore, data-oriented methods for HCI system requirements specification belong to the non-integration approach and will never become an ideal requirement method.

Function-oriented methods for HCI system requirements specification take the primary view of the way a system transforms input data into output data. Each transformation from input data into output data demonstrates a function of the system. A system may contain many such kinds of functions which represent the function view of the system. Classical Structured Analysis (SA) [10] fits into the category of process-based methods, as do Structured Analysis and Design Technique (SADT) [19] and Structured Systems Analysis and Design Method (SSADM) [1]. Process-based methods concentrate only on the function view and completely neglect to integrate the system structure and system behavior. Just like data-oriented methods, function-oriented methods for HCI system requirements specification belong to the non-integration approach and will never become an ideal system requirements method.

Control-oriented methods for HCI system requirements specification emphasize synchronization, deadlock, exclusion, concurrency, and process activation of a system. Petri Net [22] and Flowcharting [2] are primarily control-oriented. Control-oriented methods concentrate only on the control view and completely neglect an integrated structure and behavior views which grasps the essential properties of a system. Just like data-oriented and function-oriented methods, control-oriented methods for HCI system requirements specification belong to the non-integration approach should not and will never become an ideal requirement method.

Object-oriented methods for HCI system requirements specification describe the system as classes of objects and their behaviors. Object-oriented Analysis (OOA) [3], fitting into the category of object-oriented methods, looks at the problem domain, with the aim of producing a conceptual model of the information that exists in the area being analyzed. The result of object-oriented analysis is a description of what the system is behaviorally required to do, in the form of a conceptual model. That will typically be presented as a set of use cases and a number of activity diagrams. Object-oriented methods stress both the structure view and the behavior view, but not an integrated structure and behavior views. Object-oriented methods do not emphasize to integrate the system structure and system behavior. Like data-oriented, function-oriented and control-oriented methods, object-oriented methods for HCI system requirements specification belong to the non-integration approach and will never become an ideal system requirements method.

3   The Approach

Structure-behavior coalescence (SBC) method for HCI system requirement specification uses three fundamental diagrams to accomplish the HCI system requirements specification. These diagrams are: (a) architecture hierarchy diagram, (b) component operation diagram, and (c) interaction flow diagram.

3.1   Architecture Hierarchy Diagram

Structure-behavior coalescence (SBC) method for HCI system requirement specification uses an architecture hierarchy diagram (AHD) to specify the multi-level (hierarchical) decomposition and composition of a human-computer interaction system.

   As an example, Fig. 5 shows that Multimedia KTV is composed of Song_Selection and Songs; Songs is composed of Song_1 and Song_2. Among them, Multimedia KTV and Songs are aggregated systems while Song_Selection, Song_1 and Song_2 are non-aggregated systems.

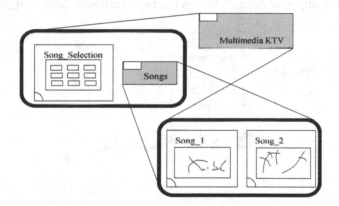

Fig. 5. AHD of the multimedia KTV

3.2   Component Operation Diagram

Structure-behavior coalescence (SBC) method uses a component operation diagram (COD) to specify all components' operations in a human-computer interaction system.

   An operation provided by each component represents a method of that component [3]. Figure 6 shows a COD of the Multimedia KTV. In the figure, component Song_Selection has two operations: Select_Song_1 and Select_Song_2; component Song_1 has two operations: Broadcast_Song_1 and Sing_Song_1; component Song_Selection has two operations: Broadcast_Song_2 and Sing_Song_2.

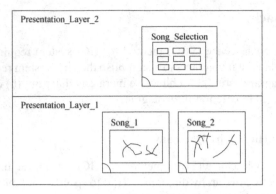

Fig. 6. FD of the multimedia KTV

For a human-computer interaction system, we use a component operation diagram (COD) to design all components' operations. Figure 7 shows a COD of the Multimedia KTV. In the figure, component Song_Selection has two operations: Select_Song_1 and Select_Song_2; component Song_1 has two operations: Broadcast_Song_1 and Sing_Song_1; component Song_Selection has two operations: Broadcast_Song_2 and Sing_Song_2.

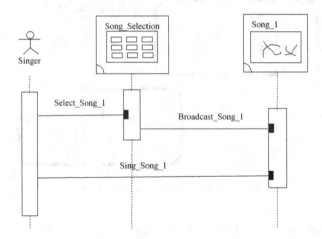

Fig. 7. IFD of the "KalaOK_Song_1" behavior

3.3 Interaction Flow Diagram

Structure-behavior coalescence method uses interaction flow diagram (IFD) to define all individual behavior of a human-computer interaction system. In a human-computer interaction system, if the components, and among them and the external environment's actors to interact, these interactions will lead to the system behavior. That is, "interaction" plays an important factor in integrating the systems structure and systems behavior for a human-computer interaction system.

The overall behavior of a human-computer interaction system consists of many individual behaviors. They tend to be executed concurrently [16, 20, 21]. Each individual behavior represents an execution path. We use an interaction flow diagram (IFD) to define this individual behavior. For example, the overall Multimedia KTV's behavior includes two behaviors: KalaOK_Song_1 and KalaOK_Song_2.

Figure 7 shows the IFD of the KalaOK_Song_1 behavior. First, actor Singer interacts with the Song_Selection component through the Select_Song_1 operation call interaction. Next, component Song_Selection interacts with the Song_1 component through the Broadcast_Song_1 operation call interaction. Finally, actor Singer interacts with the Song_1 component through the Sing_Song_1 operation call interaction.

Figure 8 shows the IFD of the KalaOK_Song_2 behavior. First, actor Singer interacts with the Song_Selection component through the Select_Song_2 operation call interaction. Next, component Song_Selection interacts with the Song_2 component through the Broadcast_Song_2 operation call interaction. Finally, actor Singer interacts with the Song_2 component through the Sing_Song_2 operation call interaction.

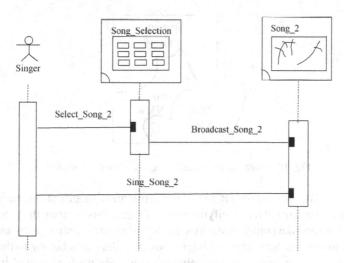

Fig. 8. IFD of the "KalaOK_Song_2" behavior

4   Result and Discussions

In the SBC method for HCI system requirement specification, an operation formula includes (a) operation name, (b) input parameters, and (c) output parameters. Since input/output parameters represent the data view and an operation represents the function view, so data and function views are well integrated in the SBC method for HCI system requirement specification as shown in Fig. 9.

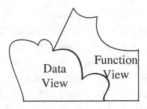

Fig. 9. Data and function views integration

In the SBC method for HCI system requirement specification, a component operation diagram specifies all components' operations in a system. These all components' operations represent the function view of the system. Since components' operations belong to the function view and components belong to the structure view, so data, function and structure views are well integrated in the SBC method for HCI system requirement specification as shown in Fig. 10.

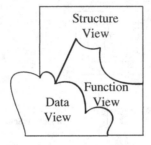

Fig. 10. Data, function and structure views integration

Also in the SBC method for HCI system requirement specification, an interaction flow diagram is constructed by specifying those "interactions" among the external environment's actors and the components. Since external environment's actors and components belong to the structure view and interaction flow diagrams belong to the behavior view, so data, function, structure and behavior views are well integrated in the SBC method for HCI system requirement specification as shown in Fig. 11.

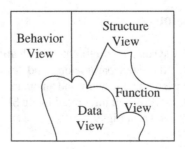

Fig. 11. Data, function, structure and behavior views integration

Let us compare the data-oriented method with the SBC method. As shown in Fig. 12, the data-oriented method for HCI system requirement specification concentrate only on the data view and the SBC method for HCI system requirement specification has the data, function, structure and behavior views all integrated.

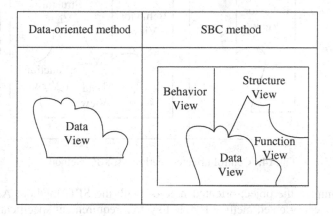

Fig. 12. Data-oriented method vs. SBC method

Let us compare the function-oriented method with the SBC method. As shown in Fig. 13, the function-oriented method for HCI system requirement specification concentrate only on the data and function views and the SBC method for HCI system requirement specification has the function, structure and behavior views all integrated.

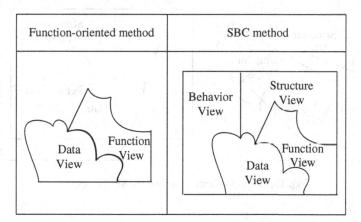

Fig. 13. Function-oriented method vs. SBC method

Let us compare the control-oriented method with the SBC method. As shown in Fig. 14, the control-oriented method for HCI system requirement specification concentrate only on the behavior view and the SBC method for HCI system requirement specification has the function, structure and behavior views all integrated.

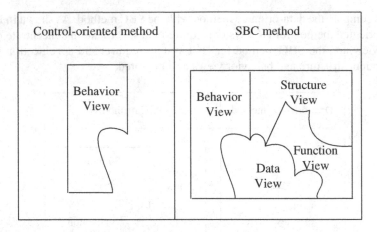

Fig. 14. Control-oriented method vs. SBC method

Let us compare the object-oriented method with the SBC method. As shown in Fig. 15, the object-oriented method for HCI system requirement specification has the structure and behavior views unrelated and the SBC method for HCI system requirement specification has the function, structure and behavior views all integrated.

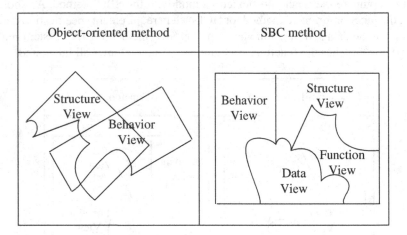

Fig. 15. Object-oriented method vs. SBC method

5   Conclusions

For a system requirements method to specify a human-computer interaction system as an integrated whole of that system's multiple views, it must be able to integrate the system structure and system behavior when specifying a system.

Current human-computer interaction system requirements methods such as process-based, behavioral and object-oriented, more or less, fail to specify a human-computer interaction system as an integrated whole of that system's multiple views because they are not able to integrate the system structure and system behavior when specifying a human-computer interaction system.

The characteristics of the SBC method for HCI system requirement specification lie in its integrating the structure and behavior views hence it is able to integrate the multiple views of a human-computer interaction system. Therefore, for HCI system requirements specification, SBC method is more advanced than the process-based, behavioral and object-oriented methods.

References

1. Ashworth, C.: SSADM: A Practical Approach, 1st edn. McGraw-Hill Book Company Ltd., London (1990)
2. Bashe, C.: IBM's Early Computers. The MIT Press, Cambridge (1986)
3. Booch, G.: Object-oriented Analysis and Design with Applications, 3rd edn. Addison-Wesley, Boston (2007)
4. Cameron, J.R.: The Jackson Approach to Software Development. IEEE Computer Society Press, Silver Spring (1989)
5. Chao, W.S., General Systems Theory 2.0: General Architectural Theory Using the SBC Architecture. CreateSpace Independent Publishing (2014)
6. Chao, W.S.: Systems Thinking 2.0: Architectural Thinking Using the SBC Architecture Description Language. CreateSpace Independent Publishing (2014)
7. Chao, W.S.: A Process Algebra For Systems Architecture: The Structure-Behavior Coalescence Approach. CreateSpace Independent Publishing Platform (2015)
8. Chao, W.S.: An Observation Congruence Model For Systems Architecture: The Structure-Behavior Coalescence Approach. CreateSpace Independent Publishing Platform (2015)
9. Chen, P., et al.: The Entity-Relationship Model - Toward a Unified View of Data. ACM Transactions on Database Systems 1(1), 9–36 (1976)
10. DeMarco, T.: Structured Analysis and System Specification. Prentice Hall, Upper Saddle River (1979)
11. Dennis, A., et al.: Systems Analysis and Design, 4th edn. Wiley, New York (2008)
12. Date, C.J.: An Introduction to Database Systems, 8th edn. Addison Wesley, Boston (2003)
13. Elmasri, R.: Fundamentals of Database Systems, 6th edn. Addison Wesley, Boston (2010)
14. Grady, J.O.: System Requirements Analysis, 2nd edn. Elsevier, Amsterdam (2013)
15. Hatley, D.J., et al.: Process for System Architecture and Requirements Engineering, 1st edn. Addison-Wesley, New York (2000)
16. Hoare, C.A.R.: Communicating Sequential Processes. Prentice-Hall, Upper Saddle River (1985)
17. Kendall, K., et al.: Systems Analysis and Design, 8th edn. Prentice Hall, Boston (2010)
18. MacKenzie, I.S.: Human-Computer Interaction: An Empirical Research Perspective. Morgan Kaufmann, San Francisco (2013)
19. Marca, D.A., et al.: SADT: Structured Analysis and Design Technique. McGraw-Hill, New York (1988)
20. Milner, R.: Communication and Concurrency. Prentice-Hall, Upper Saddle River (1989)
21. Milner, R.: Communicating and Mobile Systems: the π-Calculus, 1st edn. Cambridge University Press, New York (1999)
22. Reisig, W.: A Primer in Petri Net Design. Springer, Heidelberg (1992)

HCI in the Public Administration and Government

Collaboration Between Cognitive Science and Business Management to Benefit the Government Sector

Glory Emmanuel Aviña[✉]

Sandia National Laboratories, Livermore, CA, USA
gremman@sandia.gov

Abstract. Cognitive science is an interdisciplinary science which studies the human dimension, drawing from academic disciplines such as psychology, linguistics, philosophy, and computer modeling. Business management is controlling, leading, monitoring, organizing, and planning critical information to bring useful resources and capabilities to a viable market. Finally, the government sector has many roles, but one primary goal is to bring innovative solutions to maintain and enhance national security. There currently is a gap in the government sector between applied research and solutions applicable to the national security field. This is a deep problem since a critical element to many national security issues is the human dimension and requires cognitive science approaches. One major cause to this gap is the separation between business management and cognitive science: scientific research is either not being tailored to the mission need or deployed at a time when it can best be absorbed by national security concerns. This paper addresses three major themes: (1) how cognitive science and business management benefits the government sector, (2) the current gaps that exist between cognitive science and business management, and (3) how cognitive science and business management may work to address government sector, national security needs.

Keywords: Cognitive science · Business management · Mission impact · Applied research

1 Introduction

When I first started my career at Sandia National Laboratories (Sandia) in 2006, I was a business analyst in the partnerships development organization. My role was to identify internal and external opportunities and enable management to connect the research capabilities in their area to other collaborators. I worked alongside researchers, engineers, and management to identify opportunities in the government sector addressing evolving capabilities of national security needs. Although partnerships occurred and research deliverables were made, the impact Sandia's capabilities had for meeting the needs of the government sector was not always maximized. There were reasons for this, which will be discussed in this paper.

Five years later, I started my career as an experimental psychologist and joined Sandia's cognitive science program. My role was now to design and execute human-subjects studies in order to examine areas of national security concern, focusing on the

© Springer International Publishing Switzerland 2016
F.F.-H. Nah and C.-H. Tan (Eds.): HCIBGO 2016, Part II, LNCS 9752, pp. 131–139, 2016.
DOI: 10.1007/978-3-319-39399-5_13

human-in-the-loop and enhancing high-consequence decision-making. I could see the national security concerns at a high level and use quantitative research to examine these concerns [1], for example, quantifying cyber expertise to help train computer security incident response teams as cybersecurity threats arise. [2] But the research my colleagues and I were involved with was not reaching the front lines to improve policy and practices.

Through these two career experiences I have witnessed the disconnect between business management and research, specifically in studying the human element through cognitive science. I have also witnessed the great potential that exists if these two worlds synchronously work together, especially for the greater good of the government sector and national security.

The purpose of this paper is to discuss three major themes in order to not only highlight the potential between cognitive science and business but also encourage the reader to consider both areas when working in the government sector. First, I will discuss how cognitive science and business management benefits the government sector; then, the current gaps that exist between cognitive science and business management, and finally, how cognitive science and business management may work to address government sector, national security needs.

2   Cognitive Science, Business Management, and the Government Sector

The benefits of cognitive science for the government sector are largely under-recognized. As reported by the Wall Street Journal, the greatest threats to national security in 2015 are human-based: cyberattacks, fragmentation of states, massive waves of migration, global economic strains, and enduring human development problems. [3] For cyberattacks, countries are using cyber hacking and warfare to attack one another, as demonstrated by Russia's invasion of Ukraine. The fragmentation of states includes the unrest and power struggles between territories in the Middle East and Africa. Global economic strains continue as trust and collaboration erodes between major economic players such as China, Japan, the US, and the European Union. Finally, the enduring human development problems such as education and poverty are large challenges to be considered when formulating foreign policy. These threats always have a human-in-the-loop and therefore cognitive science is needed to inform potential solutions.

The benefits of business management for government sector are also an area that is underappreciated. The business development process at Sandia helps technical staff, managers, and program developers to understand the business landscape, especially in the government sector, prioritize areas of opportunity, develop capture plans, strength/weakness/opportunity/threat (SWOT) analyses, and strategic maps, execute these plans, and manage customer relationships. The overall goal is to bring well-developed capabilities and solutions to the forefront of application in the government sector. However, quality research and solutions still fall into the "chasm" [4] and do not have the impact desired and required for national security needs.

To emphasize the maximized impact the government sector is missing out on, we need to define national security. One powerful way to define national security is, "the measurable state of the capability of a nation to overcome the multi-dimensional threats to the apparent well-being of its people and its survival as a nation-state at any given time, by balancing all instruments of state policy through governance, that can be indexed by computation, empirically or otherwise, and is extendable to global security by variables external to it." [5] If research, especially cognitive science research which addresses the human elements to national threats, and business development are not working hand in hand, the potential for probable solutions to be integrated into the government sector will not reach full potential.

3   The Intersection Between Cognitive Science and Business Management

Multiparty, deliberative processes have become a popular way to increase public participation in public policy choices. Their legitimacy depends on participants' ability to understand the issues facing them, and to form and express their own positions on those issues. These tasks pose significant cognitive and emotional challenges. This paper argues that decision analysis, informed by behavioral decision research, offers procedures and standards for creating responsible deliberative processes. These involve (a) formal analysis of decisions, identifying the kernel of most relevant information, (b) communication procedures, recognizing the strengths and weaknesses of lay understanding, and (c) interactive elicitation methods, helping individuals to articulate the implications of their values for specific settings. A construct validity criterion assesses the extent to which the resulting valuations are properly sensitive to decision features. Feasible extensions of traditional decision analysis create opportunities to formalize the aspirations of participants and ensure the intellectual content of deliberative processes is worthy of the political hopes vested in them [6].

4   Gaps that Business Development Cares About, but Cognitive Science Addresses

Business development focuses on strengths, weakness, opportunities, and threats that are available in the market to gauge where research capabilities can be most successful. "Crossing the Chasm," a business phrase Fig. 1 to describe the Adoption Life Cycle [7], has helped researchers and business analysts understand how to navigate technology adoption. In order to penetrate the market with new technologies and solutions, the Adoption Life Cycle informs who to target and how to prime the market for adoption. However, identifying who are early adopters versus late majority, for example, is a time consuming process and difficult to navigate, especially for cutting-edge research. There are three mechanisms within cognitive science, specifically the cognitive science program at Sandia National Laboratories that can help business developers better examine and engage the market:

1. quantitative, efficient methodologies for market research
2. centralizing the human element to bridge the gap between research and market

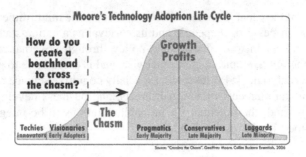

Fig. 1. Moore's Adoption Life Cycle

3. change approaches using personality and communication "types" to dynamic, behavioral models.

4.1 Quantitative, Efficient Methodologies

A business analyst must spend large amounts of time examining and filtering large amounts of documentation and usually uses what is available on the open web as a resource. It is impossible to filter through, synthesize, and process all of the data, especially when there is a limited amount of time to make important decisions. An analyst also faces a number of cognitive hindrances which can limit the quality of market analyses, such as biases, inconsistencies, and limited technical knowledge.

Intelligent web crawling and text analytics together are one methodology that enhances the market research process. Intelligent web crawling works by taking a document or documents that represents a topic of interest. From the document(s), multiple signatures and topic models are quantitatively derived using text algorithms. Using the document signatures and topic models, a web crawler can then be released into the open domain and calculate the relevance a web page has to the source topic of interest using a suite of text algorithms that address multi-dimensional search parameters. A rapid and parallel web crawler can sift through millions of webpages and analyze them for relevancy. From there, only the webpages with some level of relevance are downloaded so that out of millions of webpages, only a small set are brought to the analysts' attention. Analysts can then make determinations about what is relevant using quantitative metrics of relevancy. A web crawler is also able to highlight and visually represent the information it has determined to be of relevance to the analyst so analysts do not have to sift through pages of text. This enables analysts to rapidly decide which webpages have actual relevancy to the source topic. Using a graphical user interface (GUI), analysts can flag relevant content and then automatically generate a report that only pulls the data deemed to be important for decision-making.

Business analysts do not always have the technical depth, time, or resources needed to locate opportunities in the government sector. A white paper, publication, and/or other documentation describing a new technology or capability could be used to seed a web crawler to locate other similar technologies in the market as well as new opportunities. This could inform capability marketing and differentiation. Overall, methodologies that are being used in the cognitive science realm, such as web crawling and text analytics to imitate and enhance human analysts, could be applied to benefit business development activities.

4.2   Centralize the Human Element

Business development analysts lead a number of activities to support internal capability development. Strategic planning, SWOT analyses, website creation, partnerships development, and project plans are a few of these activities. Historically, these activities focus on matching capability potential to market need. Market need is defined through potential collaborators' investment plans, expertise gaps, and strategic plans. Academic articles on strategic planning tend to focus the process on securing funding, defining milestones and benchmarks, and developing 5- and 10-year goals for technology and research advancements [8].

In these activities, fundamentals of human behavior are not addressed. The psychology of planning in research discusses relevant cognitive operations in the strategic planning process. For example, how one communicates their idea to potential customers is a critical piece of technology adoption. Emotion regulation and cognitive construal are dynamics studied within psychology and can benefit how research ideas and technologies are presented to potential stakeholders. Theory in emotion regulation and cognitive construal informs researchers and decision-makers how an idea can be communicated or a situation reframed to suppress negative or inflated emotion to influence positive reactions.

One major gap in connecting the government sector to research solutions is that the technical work is not absorbed by program managers and decision-makers. Researchers' response is typically to add more technical depth, but this does not help managers and stakeholders visualize overall impact and benefit. Osburne, Hatcher, and Zongrone discuss the benefits of cognitive restructuring, which is being flexible with one's decisions and plans as new data comes in. [9] As researchers envision the use of their idea and capabilities, business developers can help to update strategy and communication as data gathering reveals new opportunities and market growth. If a strategy and market analyses are static and researchers do not take the time to update their research plan, researchers may communicate in the technology adoption "chasm" and not be able to help managers and decision-makers address their needs.

Overall, dynamics found in cognitive science theory influence business development activities by connecting each step of the development and adoption cycle to basic human need [10] and human behavior.

4.3   Dynamic, Behavioral Models

An ongoing debate in empirical psychology literature is whether personality can be categorized as "type" (a category that an individual is labeled with, such as "Type A" personality) or should be expressed as "traits" (a spectrum to describe personality: more introverted than extroverted). The business world has traditionally adopted that personality can be categorized into types. Many employees are given the Myers' Briggs Type Indicator (MBTI) and/or Social Styles questionnaires to determine what their category of personality. The MBTI [11] is a type-based personality assessment because it informs an individual, for example, that they are an INTJ, or Introvert, iNtuitive, Thinker, and Judger. Similarly, Social Styles categorizes individuals into Driver, Analytical, Amiable, or Expressive. [12] Personality type questionnaires are beneficial because they provide a framework for work colleagues to discuss dynamics in human behavior. They can be used for team building, to generate innovative thinking, and create cohesion across staff and management levels. However, business practices have adopted these personality theories as a way to predict potential customers' and stakeholders' personality and communication methods.

Empirical literature argues that personality is a multifaceted construct, which points to "trait"-based personality theory. [13, 14] One well-structured definition is that personality is a "stable, organized collection of psychological traits and mechanisms in the human being that influences his or her interactions with and modifications to the psychological, social, and physical environment surrounding them." [15] Business development currently uses type-based personality to teach researchers how to anticipate the communication style of potential customers and fit themselves to others' personality type mold. While this approach can have some benefits, it is more profitable to focus on the environment and provide positive and negative reinforcements to elicit the behaviors desired, such as adoption of innovative technologies. Focusing on individual's personality traits and using the interaction as an opportunity to connect also provides more depth to the conversation instead of mimicking someone's tone and mannerisms.

Ultimately, business development has great intentions for understanding and influencing human behavior. Instead of drawing from famed, type-based personality theories, empirical literature on trait-personality and behavioral reinforcements can provide a more solid foundation for creating an atmosphere for technology adoption.

5   Gaps that Cognitive Science Cares About, but Business Addresses

We have just discussed how cognitive science can serve business development activities. The converse is also true: there are ways that business development practices can serve in gaps that cognitive scientists experience.

5.1   The Research Narrative

Many have heard the phrase, "death by PowerPoint." It is a heartfelt, sorrowful phrase that victims use to describe the experience of sitting with glazed-eyes at a presenter droning through too much information in a short amount of time. [16] The government sector knows this experience well, both as victims as well as perpetrators. In the research, development, and engineering parts of the government sector, this is particularly a frequent crime. Whether presenting to a potential or an existing customer, researchers passionately tell the deep details about their work and expertise but lose their audience in the process. In emerging fields, such as cognitive science, where audiences may not see the relevance or connection to national security, the need to captures the audience is even more crucial. The art of presentation is part of business academia and training.

Business professionals keep the presentation focused on the message (content of presentation) to communicate the overall message of the presentation. [17] They use the "OABC" approach (which stands for the Opening, Agenda, Body, Closing) to frame memorable presentations. [18] Although this stems from psychology's empirical work on memory and repetition, business analysts are better practitioners of this information.

Another strategy cognitive science can draw from business development is the "research narrative." Research narratives are used to outline the storyline from hypothesis to methodology to analyses to findings and implication. They also serve as tools for logical thinking. A research project whose narrative does not hang together is in danger of Wolfgang Pauli's criticism: "What you said was so confused that one could not tell whether it was nonsense or not." [19] Research narratives are important at the end of a research project, when a paper is being written for the scientific community and posterity. Lavoisier, for example, didn't "discover" the role of oxygen in combustion until he began to piece together the research narrative associated with his experiments. [20] They are also important at the beginning of a research project. A coarse storyboard is composed of title, abstract, figures, and key references of the anticipated outcome of a research project. This forces many of the research aspects to be clarified, including those that have been hypothesized to be critical sub-components of creativity, such as originality, perceived utility, and surprisingness. [21] Business planners are very good at this level of organization. Cognitive science, especially as an emerging field, can benefit from these principles.

Many popular theories and concepts in cognitive science are either decompositional or prototype theories. [22] The field of cognitive science is also vast as it crosses and overlaps between academic disciplines. The future of cognitive science will be aimed at situated agents, brain-inspired computing, predictive behavioral modeling [23], dynamic training, etc. There is great depth and breadth in research possibilities. But possibility must be joined with opportunity and needs to address national security concerns in the government sector. Business development continues to be a strong navigator to help bridge the gap between possibility and necessity. While strategic plans, market plans, and other business activities can be informed through cognitive science theory and technologies, navigating cognitive science research opportunities can be educated through business development activities.

6   Benefits to the Government Sector

Ultimately, there are national security needs in the government sector that are not being adequately addressed due to the pace of business (both rapid and slow). In addition, decisions are being made with limited information yet high consequences. National security threats will continue to evolve and decision-makers must be equipped with empirical-based solutions. Research must be informative, logical, and easily integrate to resolve complex problems. A critical element to many national security issues is the human dimension and requires cognitive science approaches. However, scientific research is either not being tailored to the mission need or deployed at a time when it can best be absorbed by national security concerns. Cognitive science and business development can work together by using their areas of expertise to address gaps their counterpart faces. Human-based technology development, empirical research in human behavior, and centralizing the human element make business development more accurate and informative to researchers and potential partners. Business development can help cognitive scientists to communicate effectively and target meaningful research in the government sector. As shown in Fig. 2, the collaboration between these two areas will help to bring solutions to national security concerns at a more efficient pace and will overall serve the government sector.

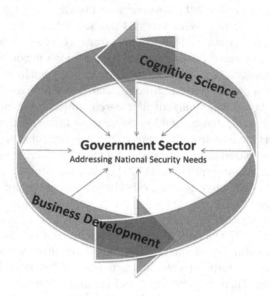

Fig. 2. Collaboration between cognitive science and business development for national security concerns in the government sector.

Acknowledgements. Sandia National Laboratories is a multi-program laboratory managed and operated by Sandia Corporation, a wholly owned subsidiary of Lockheed Martin Corporation, for the U.S. Department of Energy's National Nuclear Security Administration under contract DE-AC04-94AL85000, Sandia Report SAND2016-1668C. Approved for public release; further dissemination unlimited. This research was funded in part or whole by an Interagency Agreement between the Transportation Security Administration and the Department of Energy.

References

1. The White House: President Obama. The Comprehensive National Cybersecurity Initiative. https://www.whitehouse.gov/issues/foreign-policy/cybersecurity/national-initiative. Accessed 23 Feb 2016
2. Silva, A., Emmanuel, G., McClain, J.T., Matzen, L., Forsythe, C.: Measuring expert and novice performance within computer security incident response teams. In: Schmorrow, D.D., Fidopiastis, C.M. (eds.) AC 2015. LNCS, vol. 9183, pp. 144–152. Springer, Heidelberg (2015)

3. Katulis, B.: Five national security issues to watch in 2015. The Wall Street Journal (2014). http://blogs.wsj.com/washwire/2014/12/31/5-national-security-issues-to-watch-in-2015/
4. Moore, G.A.: Crossing the Chasm: Marketing and Selling Technology Products to Mainstream Customers. HarperBusiness, New York (2002)
5. Paleri, P.: National Security: Imperatives and Challenges, p. 521. Tata McGraw-Hill, New Delhi (2008)
6. Gregory, R., Fischhoff, B., McDaniels, T.: Acceptable input: using decision analysis to guide public policy deliberations. Decis. Anal. **2**(1), 4–16 (2005)
7. Moore, G.A.: To succeed in the long-term, focus on the middle-term. Harvard Bus. Rev. **85**(7–8), 84–90 (2006)
8. Winckler, G.: Excellence in strategic planning. In: Tayeb, O., Zahed, A., Ritzen, J. (eds.) Becoming a World-Class University, pp. 105–116. Springer International Publishing, Berlin (2016)
9. Osburn, H.K., Hatcher, J.M., Zongrone, B.M.: Training and development for organizational planning skills. In: The Psychology of Planning in Organizations: Research and Applications, p. 334 (2015)
10. Mumford, M.D., Frese, M. (eds.): The Psychology of Planning in Organizations: Research and Applications. Routledge, New York, NY (2015)
11. Quenk, N.L., Hammer, A.L.: MBTI Manual: A Guide to the Development and Use of the Myers-Briggs Type Indicator, vol. 3. Consulting Psychologists Press, Palo Alto (1998)
12. TRACOM Group: The Social Intelligence Company. Social style: the world's leading interpersonal effectiveness model (2016). http://www.tracomcorp.com/solutions/by-element/social-style/model/
13. Bess, T.L., Harvey, R.J.: Bimodal score distributions and the Myers-Briggs type indicator: Fact or artifact? J. Pers. Assess. **78**(1), 176–186 (2002)
14. Furnham, A.: The development of single trait personality theories. Pers. Individ. Differ. **11**(9), 923–929 (1990)
15. Larsen, R.J., Buss, D.M.: Personality Psychology. Naklada Slap, Jastrebarsko (2008)
16. DuFrene, D.D., Lehman, C.M.: Concept, content, construction, and contingencies: getting the horse before the PowerPoint cart. Bus. Commun. Q. **67**(1), 84–89 (2004)
17. Stowe, K., Schwartz, L., Parent, J., Sendall, P.: Are business school students prepared to present? The pedagogy of presentation skills in business schools. J. Acad. Bus. Educ. **11**, 1–22 (2010)
18. Baker, W.H., Thompson, M.P.: Teaching presentation skills. Bus. Commun. Q. **67**(2), 216–220 (2004)
19. Peierls, R.: Wolfgang Ernst Pauli. 1900–1958. Biographical Mem. Fellows R. Soc. **5**, 174–192 (1960)
20. Cole, S.: Making Science: Between Nature and Society. Harvard University Press, Cambridge (1992)
21. Gottschall, J.: The Storytelling Animal: How Stories Make us Human. Houghton Mifflin Harcourt, Boston (2012)
22. Fodor, J.A.: Concepts: Where Cognitive Science Went Wrong. Clarendon Press, Oxford (1998)
23. Clark, A.: Whatever next? Predictive brains, situated agents, and the future of cognitive science. Behav. Brain Sci. **36**(03), 181–204 (2013)

Gamification Aspects in the Context of Electronic Government and Education: A Case Study

Fernando Timoteo Fernandes[1](✉)
and Plinio Thomaz Aquino Junior[1,2]

[1] IPT - Instituto de Pesquisas Tecnológicas do Estado de São Paulo,
Av. Prof. Almeida Prado, 532, Butantã, São Paulo, SP 05508-901, Brazil
fernando.fernandes@fundacentro.gov.br,
plinio.aquino@fei.edu.br
[2] Centro Universitário da FEI, Av. Humberto de Alencar Castelo Branco, 3972,
Assunção, São Bernardo do Campo, SP 09850-901, Brazil

Abstract. The user experience, product quality and confidence in the institution are critical success factors in the use of services in e-government. The usability evaluation and analysis of user interaction in e-government, usually occurs in a timely manner and limited to few users. One way to provide the user immediate feedback and get usage statistics of a continuously service is using the technique known as gamification. The objective of this study is to propose a method to select and apply electronic game elements as motivational factors in access to information produced by the government and then test the impact of these elements. Thus, this research focuses on scenarios where e-government services have an emphasis on providing information to citizens and enabling a two-way interaction. It is intended to identify gamification mechanisms such as points, badges, levels, rankings and others and apply them to the application's tasks and user's different motivations when they are immersed on a virtual environment. The purpose of this work is to develop an experiment gamification technique in the stages known as improved information services and transactional services of e-government which allow two-way interaction with citizens. This article presents ways to motivate the user and improve citizens feedback. The results demonstrate the successful use of gamification technique in e-government scenarios that provide educational services to citizens.

Keywords: Gamification · User motivation · e-government

1 Introduction

Nowadays, e-government is already spread all over the world, including Asia, Europe, North America and South America, and is implemented on different stages and maturity levels [1, 2]. In Brazil, 25 % of e-government users search for educational services [3]. However, a great part of total internet users, 63 % of citizens, do not access e-government services complaining about the difficulty to find desired services and lack of responses from the government side when requesting a service. In this scenario, raises

© Springer International Publishing Switzerland 2016
F.F.-H. Nah and C.-H. Tan (Eds.): HCIBGO 2016, Part II, LNCS 9752, pp. 140–150, 2016.
DOI: 10.1007/978-3-319-39399-5_14

the question on how to achieve a large number of users and engage them in using e-government services, and provide immediate feedback and an assessment mechanism of an e-government service. Usage of rewarding systems on industry [4] and scenarios like education [5, 6] and enterprise services [7] is considered a way to increase productivity, encourage learning and engage users on using continuously an application. In the e-government context, the research by Bista et al. [8] proposes a model that uses game mechanisms like points and badges as rewards to increase citizen participation and contribution in a virtual community.

This paper aims to extend this model, including new game elements and defines a method to implement and select these elements to new projects. We'll start by defining some key concepts on e-government and its stages, and then we will discuss gamification, user motivation and then explain the proposed gamification method, concluding with the use case and its results.

2   E-Government

E-government could be defined as the "use of information and communication technologies to deliver government information and services to citizen" [9]. There are some authors that categorize e-government on four stages [24, 25]. The usability issues are highlighted as relevant in several works in e-government scenario, focusing on the user profile, user behavior [26] or interfaces evaluation procedures [10, 11]. The United Nations model [9] also defines a four stage model, where the first stage is called Emerging Information Services, when the e-government service is provided in a one-way direction, so the citizen only gets the information and do not send information to the governmental agency. The second stage is called Enhanced Information Services when there are means that citizen can communicate with the governmental agency, and request some service, e.g. through online forms. In this stage, there is a simple two-way communication between citizens and the governmental agency. The third stage is called Transactional Services, when the government agency receives input on government policies, regulations, etc. It could also exist some financial transactions on a secure network to the government. The last stage, called Connected Services, involves agencies cooperating and providing services using interactive tools such as Web 2.0 through integrated applications.

This research intends to explore the use of gamification on stages 2 and 3 exploring the two-way communication with citizens in order to engage users on e-government services. The next section explores what drives user motivation.

3   User Motivation

To understand user experience and motivation when interacting with a product or interface, it's necessary to understand user emotions, what the product represents to the user, his relations with the product and how the user understands the operation of the product [12]. To Hassenzahl [13], the user experience is composed by two perspectives, one being what the product provides to the user so he can achieve his objectives, and the other perspective being what the product provides to satisfy the user needs during his interaction time with the interface. User experience also relates with how the user feels when performing a task, what are his needs and intrinsic motivations like self-affirmation, autonomy, competency when executing the task, comparing positions to other users or enlarge his social network.

For some authors, to understand user motivation, it's necessary to understand the motives that lead a user to perform some task, like the works by Fadel et al. [14] and Zichermann and Cunningham [15] that divide user motivation on two categories, intrinsic motivation and extrinsic motivation. Intrinsic motivation is when the user performs a task by his own, because the activity is pleasurable, challenging or offers the opportunity to learn something new or develop new skills [14]. Extrinsic Motivation relates to the context in which the user is inserted, where the user has the need of an external reward, like social recognition, material rewards or virtual rewards that gives the user status among other users. In this context, we use in this research gamification elements as an approach to reward the user when completing a task, exploring the effects of extrinsic motivation.

4 Gamification

According to Deterding et al. [16], gamification is defined as "the use of game design elements in non-game contexts". The use of game elements as badges and points to reward users tends to create positive experiences [17]. Although, Hamari and Sarsa [18] cites that there should be caution when implement those elements, in order to avoid excess of competition, requiring a good design interface project.

The research made by Borges et al. [19] finds out that a large number of gamification papers focus on engaging users on executing tasks, improve learning experience, improve user skills and there are some papers that propose solutions on how to use gamification. In the next subsections, we will explore the gamification components and mechanics and propose a method to apply gamification based on related works.

4.1 Gamification Elements

Schell [20] defines the elements that compose a game as: mechanics, history, aesthetics and technology. The mechanics are the rules that describe the game objectives, how the players can achieve those objectives and what happens when they achieve them. The history drives the user actions, while aesthetics acts on user feelings and technology is whatever resource that enables the game experience. To Zichermann and Cunningham [15] the games are composed by Dynamics, which focuses on user interaction with another element, Mechanics which are the rules of the game and Aesthetics which are the result of the mechanics and dynamics that acts on user sensations during system interaction. These components are known by the acronym MDA. Next we will explore which mechanics exists to use in our proposed method.

4.2 Gamification Mechanics

The basic gamification mechanics are known as points [15], which enable other game mechanics, such as badges and levels. The Table 1 shows some mechanics used on the case study based on the studies of [15, 21, 22].

Table 1. Gamification mechanics

Mechanic	Description
Points	Numeric value given when executing an action or series of actions
Badges	Visual elements to reward user when performing a task and grant user status among other users. E.g. Reader badge
Levels	Users are Rewarded in a growing order when accumulating points getting new titles or status. E.g. Master, Rookie, etc.
Ranking	Players classification based on user punctuation
Achievements	Usually are capabilities that are locked and are unlocked when certain activities are executed or when user get a determined number of points or level
Quests	Journey or series of tasks that user or a group of users must complete

Such mechanics described on Table 1 are presented on our case study and were selected according to user needs based on the profiles described on virtual environments [22]. The profiles are described in the next section.

4.3 User Profiles on Gamified Environments

The analysis made by Bartle [22] on the different kinds of players on virtual environments like Multi User Dungeons (MUD), which was a real-time virtual world based on text, defined four types of players, describing their characteristics and goals on the MUD environment. Based on those players, some authors defined personality characteristic of each player and game elements that best suits each personality [21].

Using Bartle's player definition, we selected the mechanics defined in [21] that best suits each player to be part of our proposed method. The Table 2 shows such game mechanics.

Table 2. Player types and gamification mechanics

Player	Personality	Game mechanics
Killer	Agressive, dominance	Points, achievements, combos, progress, ranking
Achiever	Perfectionism	Badges, bonuses, combos, levels, progress, reward schedule
Socializer	Extroversion	Quests, customization
Explorer	Independence	Quests, reward schedule

With the player types, personality and game mechanics defined, we researched methods to apply gamification mechanics on new projects. Next section, we describe our findings.

4.4 Gamification Method

This section is a brief overview on the literature to discuss solutions for applying gamification on new projects. The work of Fadel et al. [14] uses concepts of the heuristics of Nielsen [23] to propose a framework called GAMINQ in order to gamify educational applications. The work bases on the theory of learning through a series of questionnaires, where the user is responsible for his own learning progress. The author also shows some prototypes, however, it is not clear the steps to apply the gamification framework.

The work of Bista et al. [8] proposes a model to be used on online communities on e-government, composed by seven elements, and define steps to apply gamification mechanics on new applications. First the designer identifies the members of a community (M), then identify which actions (A) they can perform in the context (C) of the application. For each combination of member, action and context, like John Doe (M) posts (A) on forum (C), are defined rules to obtain points (Rp). The user that accumulates a determined number of points (P) can be rewarded by a badge (B) according to rules defined to obtain those badges (Rb). This research had considered some e-gov aspects like anonymous users and so proposed a few gamification mechanics. However it serves as a base to define contexts and actions that could be gamified.

In an attempt to define a method to apply gamification and select gamification mechanics, we used a subset of the model proposed by Bista et al. [8] and combined with the selection of mechanics proposed by Ferro et al. [21]. The following table lists the steps used to apply gamification on our experiment.

Table 3. Gamification contexts and mechanics selection method

Step	Description
1	Identify contexts (C) and actions (A) that can be gamified on your application. E.g. User comments (A) on a forum (C). User evaluate (A) other users's comment on a forum (C)
2	Select gamification mechanics based on user's expectations. Select at least one gamification mechanic so all kinds of players are addressed

The first step defined in our gamification method is extracted from the Bista et al. model [8]. It provides an identification of what tasks and contexts to gamify an application. The second step identifies which elements to apply based on user profiles [21]. Using the steps from Table 3, we designed an experiment to apply gamification on an educational scenario, where it is possible to distribute content from government to students and there were no e-gov restrictions like user data confidentiality regarding their progress and posts.

5   Project and Experiment Design

The research made by Borges et al. [19] approaches several experiments using gami-fication and concludes that on the most studies there's a subjective description of the results. The author suggests defining control groups with similar expectations and contexts to focus on the results on the gamification itself. Based on this study, we designed an experiment with two groups of students of professional formation schools.

Then, we developed two different versions of a mobile application composed by a series of questionnaires, so users could learn while using the application, as pointed out by Fadel et al. [14]. One developed application was gamified and other not. This way, we could compare results from both applications to validate gamification effectiveness. To design the applications, we followed the steps proposed by our method presented on Table 3. First we identified the actions and contexts as following the first step on Table 3. The results are shown on Table 4.

Table 4. Contexts and actions

ID	Context	Action(s)
1	Registration	Register on application
2	Questionnaires	Answer single questionnaire, conclude lesson, conclude theme
3	Comments	Post comment, evaluate other users comments

Then, following the second step proposed by our method, we selected gamification mechanics that suit each context inside the application. The results could be found on Table 5.

After the context and actions defined as well as the gamification mechanisms selected, we developed the mobile applications so we could use on the experiment. We used as comparison variables, the number of executed tasks like questionnaires answered, lessons completed, and frequency of access on each application.

The variables were selected because they were common to both gamified and non-gamified versions of the applications and could show a perspective of the user's interaction with the product.

The total number of volunteers for the experiment was 26 students divided on two groups. Each group was composed by students registered on the same course but on

Table 5. Gamification mechanics per Action

Context ID	Action	Gamification mechanics	Description	Players approached
1	Register on the application	Points, levels	Grant 100 points for registration and show rookie badge, so the user knows that exists gamification elements	Killer, achiever

(Continued)

Table 5. (*Continued*)

Context ID	Action	Gamification mechanics	Description	Players approached
2	Answer a single questionnaire	Points	Grant 50 points for each correct answer	Killer, achiever
2	Conclude lesson	Points, levels, ranking, quest	Display total points by lesson. Display badges unlocked. View ranking by points. Each lesson concluded, unlock other lessons, as a quest to finish the theme.	Killer, achiever, explorer, socializer
2	Conclude theme	Badges	Grant bronze, silver or gold medals based on user's performance.	Explorer
3	Post comment	Points, badges	Grant 100 points for each comment. Grant Mentor badge for 2 comments with positive evaluation by other users	Killer, achiever
3	Evaluate other users comments	Points, badges	Grant 20 points for evaluation. Grant Moderator badge for 2 evaluations	Achiever killer

two different schools. Each group had 15 days to use the application, and all the tasks performed were logged in a database so we could compare the results from each group.

To illustrate the experiment applications, next are shown a few prints of the mobile applications and the basic differences between them.

The Fig. 1 shows the main differences between both applications. The image on the left shows the non-gamified application, while the figure on right shows the gamified application.

The figure also shows the gamified application including gamification mechanics such as badges and ranking on the bottom menu.

Next we show the core activity screen that included responding to a series of questionnaires (Fig. 2).

The main differences between them are the visual elements representing the gamification mechanic of points and the visual representation of attempts that user had when responding a question. Also, in the gamified version, it was possible to use points acquired and trade them for tips on the actual question through a help button.

After development, we selected two professional schools and for each school, we separated two groups, where in one group we delivered the gamified application, and in the other group we delivered the non-gamified version. The users were guided on the basic tasks of each application, and were instructed on how to use the application and the two-week trial period. The results are shown in the next section.

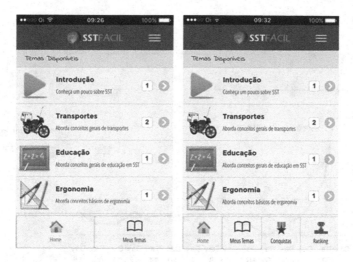

Fig. 1. Developed applications - initial Screens

Fig. 2. Questionnaire screens

6 Results

After 15 days of experiment, we could analyze the results of 26 volunteers, being 15 on the gamified application and 11 on the non-gamified application. The Fig. 3 shows the frequency of access of each group.

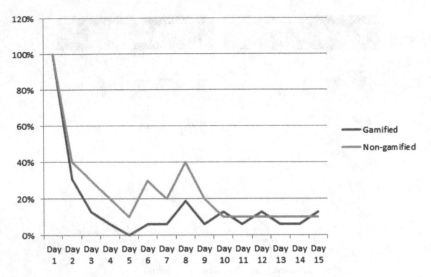

Fig. 3. Frequency of access (Color figure online)

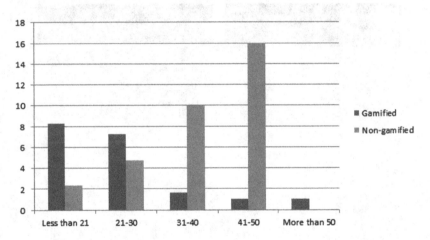

Fig. 4. Average of lessons completed (Color figure online)

As the graph shows, the non-gamified version started with a better frequency of access on the 10 first days, and then in the middle of the experiment the frequency of the gamified version was similar to the non-gamified version.

In order to investigate the impact of gamification on e-gov applications, we then analyzed the average of lessons concluded on each version to understand which age group responded better to gamification mechanics and determine which group have a better performance. The results are shown on Fig. 4.

The results show the number of lessons concluded for younger users were greater than the number of lessons responded by older users. Although the results could not be considered statistically due to reduced number of volunteers, it gives an overview of what could be achieved on large experiments. Unfortunately, there were no comments in the experiment period to compare the results. Next, we show some discussion about the results.

7 Conclusion

The results show an overview of the impact of using gamification mechanics on e-gov on educational contexts. It appears that gamification elements like points, badges and ranking are more efficient to engage younger user rather than older users.

The gamification method proposed on this paper can be used to gamify other e-gov applications on different e-gov and educational scenarios. Due to the chosen e-gov scenario with younger audience and educational context that did not require user confidentiality, we could select mechanics such as points, ranking and badges that enabled comparison among other users.

Further analysis with more users need to be made to statistically compare the effectiveness of gamification mechanics on e-gov. However, the proposed gamification method proved to be viable to be implemented on new e-gov applications. The method could also be applied on different e-government scenarios and stages such as the first and forth stages. Although, the gamification mechanics should be selected and implemented respecting the context of the e-gov agency and its restrictions and confidentiality aspects respected.

References

1. Campos, R., Marques, C.G.: The evolution and the future of the e-government. In: Euro American Conference on Telematics and Information Systems (2007)
2. Lee, S., Tan, X., Trimi, S.: Current practices of leading e-government countries. Commun. ACM **48**, 6 (2005)
3. Brasil. TIC Domicílios e Empresas. São Paulo: Comitê Gestor da Internet no Brasil, p. 662 (2014)
4. Korn, O.: Industrial playgrounds: how gamification helps to enrich work for elderly or impaired persons in production, p. 4. ACM (2012)
5. Erenli, K. The impact of gamification: a recommendation of scenarios for education. In: 15th International Conference on Interactive Collaborative Learning (ICL), p. 8 (2012)
6. Dubois, D.J., Tamburrelli, G.: Understanding gamification mechanisms for software development. In: 9th Joint Meeting on Foundations of Software Engineering - ESEC/FSE 2013. ACM Press, Saint Petersburg, Russia (2013)
7. Rodrigues, L.F., Costa, C.J., Oliveira, A.: The adoption of gamification in e-banking. In: International Conference on Information Systems and Design of Communication - ISDOC 2013, p. 47 (2013)
8. Bista, S.K. et al.: Using gamification in an online community In: 8th International Conference on Collaborative Computing: Networking, Applications and Worksharing, Pittsburgh (2012)
9. UN. e-government Survey, p. 160. United Nations, New York (2012)

10. Filgueiras, L., Aquino Jr., P., Sakai, R., Filho, A.G., Torres, C., Barbarian, I.: Personas como modelo de usuários de serviços de governo eletrônico. In: Proceedings of the 2005 Latin American conference on Human-computer interaction, p. 319–324, Cuernavaca, Mexico, 23–26 October 2005. doi:10.1145/1111360.1111395
11. Filgueiras, L., Aquino Jr., P., Tokairim, V., Torres, C., Barbarian, I.: Usability evaluation as quality assurance of e-government services: the e-poupatempo case. In: IFIP: Building the e-Service Society: e-Commerce, e-Business, and e-Government, pp. 77–87. Kluwer, Boston (2004)
12. Tokkonen, H.: How user experience is understood. In: Science and Information Conference (2013)
13. Hassenzahl, M.: User experience (UX): towards an experiential perspective on product quality, p. 11–15 (2008)
14. Fadel, L.M., et al.: Gamificação na educação, pp. 1–302. Pimenta Cultural, São Paulo (2014)
15. Zichermann, G., Cunningham, C.: Gamification by Design. O'Reilly, Sebastopol (2011)
16. Deterding, S. et al.: From Game Design Elements to Gamefulness : Defining "Gamification", p. 7. ACM (2011)
17. Alves, F.P., Maciel, C., Anacleto, J.C.: Investigando a percepção dos usuários sobre os mecanismos de gamificação da rede social Foursquare. In: IHC 2012 Companion (2012)
18. Hamari, J., Sarsa, H.: Does gamification work ? — a literature review of empirical studies on gamification. In: 47th Hawaii International Conference on System Science. IEEE (2014)
19. Borges, S. et al.: A systematic mapping on gamification applied to education, p. 7. ACM (2014)
20. Schell, J.: The Art of Game Design a Book of Lenses. Elsevier/Morgan Kaufmann, p. 489 (2008)
21. Ferro, L.S., Walz, S.P., Greuter, S.: Towards personalised, gamified systems: an investigation into game design, personality and player typologies, p. 6. ACM (2013)
22. Bartle, R.: Hearts, Clubs, Diamonds, Spades: Players Who Suit MUDs. http://mud.co.uk/richard/hcds.htm
23. Nielsen, J.: Usability Engineering. Academic Press, New York (1993)
24. Layne, K., Lee, J.: Developing fully functional e-government: a four stage model. Gov. Inf. Q. 18(2), 14 (2001)
25. Lau, T.Y., et al.: Adoption of e-government in three Latin American countries: Argentina, Brazil and Mexico. Telecommun. Policy 32(2), 88–100 (2008)
26. Aquino Jr., P.T.: PICaP: padrões e personas para expressão da diversidade de usuários no projeto de interação. In: Tese (Doutorado) - Escola Politécnica da Universidade de S. Paulo, p. 224. São Paulo (2008)

Aligning Public Administrators and Citizens on and Around Open Data: An Activity Theory Approach

Jonathan Groff[✉], Michael Baker, and Françoise Détienne

I3 (Institut Interdisciplinaire de l'Innovation), Centre National de la Recherche Scientifique, Telecom-ParisTech, Université Paris-Saclay, 46 rue Barrault, 75013 Paris, France
{jonathan.groff,michael.baker,
francoise.detienne}@telecom-paristech.fr

Abstract. Open data have recently become key vectors of the implementation of open government in terms of the notion of transparency. The present study is precisely part of an EU-funded project whose aim is to develop a European platform devoted to the collective exploitation of open data. It aims to understand the processes of production and use of open data by, respectively, public administrators-(PAs) and citizen groups. On the basis of an Activity Theory analysis of focus groups involving these two sets of social actors, potential internal and external tensions are identified, with respect to objects, rules and instruments of activity. Main results showed that PAs practice a "strategically opaque transparency" policy by selecting data to open with the aim of preserving politico-economical interests, thereby limiting their reuse. We propose that interactions with citizens on the ROUTE-TA-PA platform could support PAs in publishing relevant data for users, whilst respecting these interests.

Keywords: Open data · Public administrations · Transparency · Activity theory · Tensions · Social platform

1 Introduction

Over the past ten years, open data initiatives have become decisive factors in the policy of *transparency* in governments, and the use of Information and Communication Technologies has been proposed an effective way for promoting it [1]. The research described here is being carried out within the EU-funded project "ROUTE-TO-PA" (www.routetopa.eu), whose aim is to improve the transparency of Public Administrations (PAs) by enabling and improving dialogue between them and citizens, on and around open data produced by such administrations. This is being done by developing two related tools, in collaboration with the administrations of several European cities (Dublin, Den Haag, Groningen, Issy-les-Moulineaux, Prato): (1) a Social Platform for Open Data (SPOD), enabling social interactions involving open data citizen-users and administrator-producers; (2) a visualisation toolset (Transparency-Enhancing-Toolset or TET), integrated with major Open Data Platforms (such as CKAN). The overall design, implementation and evaluation approach is based on agile methods in order to quickly implement, test and improve different versions of the

© Springer International Publishing Switzerland 2016
F.F.-H. Nah and C.-H. Tan (Eds.): HCIBGO 2016, Part II, LNCS 9752, pp. 151–158, 2016.
DOI: 10.1007/978-3-319-39399-5_15

SPOD-TET platform. Since what is to be developed is not only a technical system, but rather a socio-technical system, a participatory design approach is being adopted.

This paper is focused on the first step of this participatory design approach, aiming to understand citizens' and civil servants' goals as well as their motivations for engaging in the production and use of Open Data, and to develop epistemic communities of practice around them. In the framework of Activity Theory [2], this means identifying the distinct activity systems of both potential users and of producers of open data, and the tensions that may emerge within and between them. Within this aim, we organised two focus groups, with PAs and with a specific group of citizens. The first focus group was carried out with seven public administrators in the Paris region; the second involved eight young entrepreneurs who were in the process of creating a company, as well as people who had created their company less than two years ago.

Analysis of the focus group data (verbal interactions) showed that these two groups share respective objects of activity, but are faced with internal tensions, principally due to contradictions between their rules and their goals, as well as external tensions, due to mismatches between users' needs and PAs' rules. We discuss these results and their implications in terms of the design of the socio-technical system.

2   Background: Open Data and Activity Theory

The concept of open data is defined as "the idea that some data should be freely available to everyone to use and republish as they wish, without restrictions from copyright, patents or other mechanisms of control" [3]. In other words, giving citizens access to public data is a means to engage them in their own governance and thereby to involve them in political decision-making. In this way, citizens are not only observers in the process of governance but are also able to contribute to it.

Such participation implies that citizens visualize data but also use and transform it in order to propose collective solutions to public issues. This practice is only possible if datasets are completely accessible and available, and if they can interoperate with others datasets.

Yet, the use of public data, as currently released, is restricted to specific software, due to the various transformative processes that they undergo before publication.

The aim of the present work is precisely to study the effects of these access constraints on the reuse of open data and on their collective exploitation. We will study how this technical limit could impact the relationships between users' and producers' activity systems.

The digital portals that encourage open data reuse are generally focused on the potential applications of data rather than on the mode of data production and storage. As such, data are commonly considered as "naturally" "raw" and in no sense as political or normative agents [4]. However, data, whatever they are, must be produced before being rendered open and/or analysed.

In public administrations, the process of producing open data involves several steps, described by Denis and Goëta [5, 6] as "identification" (finding the services that collect public data), "extraction" (identifying data availability and collecting it) and "rawification" (making data visible and readable by the most common tools handled by developers). This series of sociotechnical manipulations calls into question the concept of *transparency*. Indeed, transparency is defined as "the process through which public authorities make decisions should be understandable and open....... the information on which the decisions are based should be available to the public" [7]. However, the different steps of the open data "fabrication" process are not "open" for citizens, who do not have access to the mechanisms which transform professional data into generic data, adapted to private users (e.g. citizens, IT developers, companies). There is therefore a gap between the officially declared aim of "opening up data" — *sharing information initially reserved to PAs in order to promote a participatory democracy* — and the constraints relating to the open data production process — *proposing restricted content in a specific format.*

Our study addresses the effect of a specific rule related to the PA's activity system on this production process: the protection of citizens' interests. We analyse how this politico-social commitment could lead to internal and external tensions with users' activity systems. According to Activity Theory [2, 8], human activity is articulated by dynamic and reciprocal interrelation of different entities. An activity system is represented by a systemic model that involves: the subject who carries out the action, the instrument-mediator, the object towards which activity is oriented, the division of labour, the community and its rules.

In the present study, we used this framework to analyse and compare activity systems of open data producers and open data users. Our goal is to identify the different components, the possible tensions and double binds implied within and between open data users' and producers' activity systems. In this way, we aim to develop the theoretical and methodological foundations for designing a socio-technical system devoted to collective exploitation of open data.

3   Focus Groups: Implementation and Analysis

We organised two focus groups, one with Public administrators ("PAs") and a second with start-up company chief executive officers (or, "young entrepreneurs"). The first focus group was carried out with seven public administrators in the Paris region. Public administrators are representatives of public affairs. They apply, supervise and coordinate the policy programmes of governments at local and regional levels. The second involved eight young entrepreneurs. (By "young entrepreneurs" we mean people who are in the process of creating a company and people who have created their company less than two years ago).

These two particular groups (PAs and start-up CEOs) were chosen because they both seek to foster the development of an economic environment around the transformation of open data into new applications and services, by creating companies that promote job creation. Young entrepreneurs wish to create sustainable enterprises by using open data. PAs want not only to restore public trust, but also to improve communication between local communities and private companies in order to find a converging model of development that boosts employment.

Each focus group session lasted 2 h 30 min. Participants were interviewed on the usefulness of a community platform devoted to publication, sharing and exploitation of open data. Each participant was asked firstly to answer individually then all participants were invited to complete their answers by interacting together. Following this, participants were asked to verbalize their needs in terms of information, exchanges and functionalities on the basis of a usage scenario which describes a (ficticious) young entrepreneur ("Annie"), who wants to develop applications by using open data. Participants had to exchange and to define collectively their expectations concerning the nature of data, the type of interaction and the tools that they need if they were a start-up CEO such as Annie.

Participants' answers were categorized according to a coding scheme based on dialogic function (e.g. question, assertion, request) and epistemic content [9].

4 Results

Using the conceptual framework of Activity Theory [2, 8], we analysed the activity system of PAs and Young entrepreneurs, i.e. the relations between instrument, subjects and objects. We also identified tensions that could arise within and between these activity systems. We first present each activity system then describe the potential tensions between them.

4.1 PAs' Activity System

Subjects. Open data producers were represented by: Public Administrators in charge of technical services (e.g. information management) and business activities in the Paris Region.

Objects. In accordance with policy commitments, PAs generate public access to policies and financial information with the aim of restoring public trust and thus facilitate dialogue between electors and local governments. They want to make government processes and decisions open. Intrinsically, they share open data in order to drive economic growth in their Region by encouraging companies to design applications using them. They seek to create a business network, gathering entrepreneurs and local governments, focused on open data.

Instruments. PAs consider a collaborative platform devoted to open data as a means: (i) to identify the most relevant data to publish (with the aim of promoting the development of digital applications) and (ii) to identify data which should give entrepreneurs answers to typical initial difficulties associated with creating businesses (e.g. taxation, human resources, watching out for competitors, etc.).

Rules. Public Administrators are required to implement political commitments undertaken by governments. For this reason, they are reticent to publish data that might have a negative effect on the attractiveness of the city in terms of economy, ecology or safety, or else data that would allow local pressure groups to criticise them (or at least oblige them to engage in time-consuming discussions).

Tensions. The main tension is between the PAs' objective of "serving the public and involving citizens in political decision-making" and the rules of their community requiring them to "preserve economical and political interests". These rules lead to processes of selecting which data should be published or not (e.g. PAs are reticent to publish data — such as on air pollution — that might have a negative economic effect on the attractiveness of the city, or data — such as specific subsidies — that would allow local pressure groups to criticise the PA).

So, on one hand PAs intend to involve citizens in political decision-making to restore public trust and to improve accountability of policy makers (European E-Government Action Plan 2011–2015), whilst, on the other hand, they do not provide full access to public data. In sum, they adopt what we term *strategically opaque transparency*, restricting the available data, or else spreading information across disparate data-sets, which renders understanding more arduous. This calls into question the nature of their collaboration with citizens, and thus disrupts the elaboration of collective solutions to societal problems.

Figure 1 shows the activity system of PAs, with potential tensions within it (thick grey double arrows).

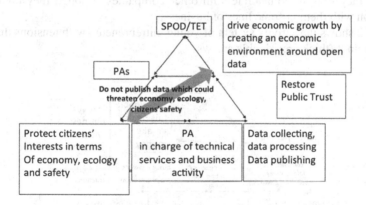

Fig. 1. Activity system of public administrators

4.2   Users/Citizens' Activity System

Subjects. Open data users were represented by: start-up entrepreneurs who develop innovative systems, principally in Information and Communication Technologies (ICT).

Objects. Start-up CEOs want to build sustainable enterprises around open data. They are also interested in participating in a network of private and public organizations with the aim of developing their companies.

Instruments. From the entrepreneurs' points of view, the platform is seen as a tool which gives them possibilities to be informed about public politics in their domain, to share knowledge, experiences and of course to give them the opportunity to create applications and services.

Rules. Start-up CEOs develop innovative products in a highly competitive sector: ICT. So they have to respect privacy policies. These refer to information about design process of new products, financial and economical data, business strategies and organisational frameworks.

Tensions. The most important ones are as follows: (1) entrepreneurs need to interact around updated data in a synchronous way, in order to co-design products within a short time period, but the current tools do not enable them to do so; (2) they need to collaborate with other companies but they do not wish to disclose confidential information with potential competitors.

Firstly, entrepreneurs want to obtain quick answers to their questions. Yet, collective exploitation of open data on a social network is a long process that involves asynchronous interactions.

Secondly, entrepreneurs do not wish to disclose confidential information. At the same time they need personalized answers adapted to their individual problems. In summary, they seek to collaborate with other companies although they could be in competition with them in some lines of business.

Figure 2 shows the activity system of young entrepreneurs with tensions that could appear within it (thick grey double arrows).

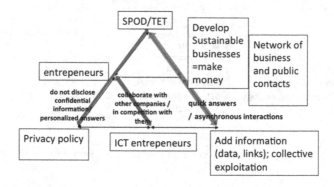

Fig. 2. Activity system of young entrepreneurs

4.3 Tensions Between PAs' and Users' Activity Systems

Our analysis revealed tensions between the two activity systems. They are mainly generated by: (i) the data production mechanism, which involves several tasks among different actors in the division of labour (ii) and the selective publication process, with its underlying the rules relating to the mission of PAs.

(i) PAs have the aim of boosting employment by encouraging the development of sustainable enterprises. Notwithstanding this aim, Open data undergo several stages of "formatting and normalization" before publication [5, 6], involving different services that transform and standardise data. This may slow down the development of start-ups, because they have to recruit persons having specific competency profiles who are able to analyse these standardized formats, which could restrict open data reuse to a limited number of companies.

(ii) Furthermore, PAs have to respect rules related to the implementation of government policy on the ground level. So, even though PAs wish to generate new businesses and stimulate growth by transforming open data into new applications and services, the selective publication process, making some data confidential, does not allow companies to create all the useful and operable tools that they could. In this way, we can see a reduction in the scope of an economic environment, involving business and public actors, developed around the transformation of open data into solutions for all citizens.

Figure 3 shows the external tensions between the two activity systems. The 'lightning bolts' represent tensions.

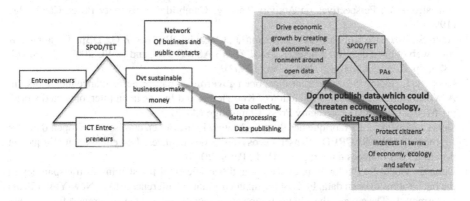

Fig. 3. Tensions between users' and producers' activity systems

5   Conclusion

The tensions within and between public administrations' and young entrepreneurs' activity systems that we have identified would need to be taken into account in the specification of a socio-technical system oriented towards the productive exploitation of open data. The main barrier to transparent publication of open data by Pas, and its productive economic use, resides in PAs' attempt to preserve environmental and economic interests of their municipalities, together with their communication strategies with a political orientation. We propose that in order to address these tensions, they could either be 'relaxed', or else circumnavigated. The internal tensions of the entrepreneurs' activity system could be partially relaxed by interaction in real time around open data visualisations, using the SPOD-TET platform, including the use of private or public discussion spaces. However, deeper relaxing of tensions between the two activity systems would need to rely on changes in the socio-political environment itself. For this project, we propose to navigate around these tensions, in particular those related to the "selective publication process", by developing scenarios around open data which are not "economically or politically sensitive". This last issue calls into question the notion of "transparency" as the straightforward provision and transmission of information, and leads to a more strategic vision of communication between the social actors concerned by open data.

Acknowledgements. This research was carried out within the EU-funded H2020 project "ROUTE-TO-PA" (route-to-pa.eu), contract number 645860. We would like to thank Issy-Média for their cooperation in this research.

References

1. Bertot, J.C., Jaeger, P.T., Grimes, J.M.: Using ICTs to create a culture of transparency: e-government and social media as openness and anti-corruption tools for societies. Gov. Inf. Q. **27**, 264–271 (2010)
2. Engeström, Y.: Perspectives on Activity Theory. Cambridge University Press, Cambridge (1999)
3. Auer, S., Bizer, C., Kobilarov, G., Lehmann, J., Cyganiak, R., Ives, Z.G.: DBpedia: a nucleus for a web of open data. In: Aberer, K., et al. (eds.) ASWC 2007 and ISWC 2007. LNCS, vol. 4825, pp. 722–735. Springer, Heidelberg (2007)
4. Ruppert, E.: Doing the transparent state: open government data as performance indicators. In: A World of Indicators: The Production of Knowledge and Justice in an Interconnected world, pp. 51–78. Cambridge University Press, Cambridge (2013)
5. Denis J., Goëta S.: La fabrique des donnees brutes. Le travail en coulisses de l'open data. In: Journee d'etudes SACRED «Penser l'ecosysteme des donnees. Les enjeux scientifiques et politiques des donnees numeriques». HAL, Paris (2013)
6. Denis J., Goëta S.: Exploration, extraction and 'rawification' the shaping of transparency in the back rooms of open data. In: Neil Postman Graduate Conference. HAL, New-York (2014)
7. Soderman, J.: The citizen, the administration and community law. General report for the 1998 Fide Congress (1998)
8. Engeström, Y.: Learning by Expanding: An Activity-Theoretical Approach to Developmental Research. Cambridge University Press, Helsinki (1987)
9. Grosz, B., Candace, S.: Attention, intentions, and the structure of discourse. Comput. Linguist. **12**(3), 175–204 (1986)

Touchscreen Voting Interface Design for Persons with Dexterity Impairments: Insights from Usability Evaluation of Mobile Voting Prototype

Jennifer Ismirle[1(✉)], Ian O'Bara[1], James E. Jackson[2], and Sarah J. Swierenga[1]

[1] Usability/Accessibility Research and Consulting, Michigan State University,
East Lansing, MI, USA
{ismirlej,obaraian,sswieren}@msu.edu
[2] MSU Information Technology, Michigan State University, East Lansing, MI, USA
jamesedj@msu.edu

Abstract. To address the need for a universal and accessible voting solution, our research team designed and created a mobile voting user interface prototype for individuals with disabilities using specifications gathered from previous research focused on mobile and/or accessible design. We evaluated the usability of our prototype with individuals with moderate dexterity impairments and with no disabilities, and the majority of participants had a positive reaction and experience using this system. Our study generally confirmed previous research, and we discovered further considerations for mobile voting interface design for users with moderate dexterity impairments, involving buttons that are repeatedly pressed, button placement options, interpretations of inputs or touches, and adjustable support that provides various angle and height options.

Keywords: Accessible voting · Dexterity impairments · Disability · Mobile voting · Universal design · Usability

1 Introduction

In the United States, there are at least 34 million voting-age adults with disabilities [1], and this number is likely to increase with the aging of the population. Approximately 19.9 million people in the U.S. have a dexterity impairment that involves difficulty lifting and grasping (e.g., trouble lifting an object or grasping a pencil) [2]. To address the accessibility of voting in the U.S., the Help America Vote Act of 2002 was passed, requiring polling places to be physically accessible and have at least one accessible voting system to be provided for voters with disabilities [3].

Current stations and systems for voting, however, do not adequately address concerns with accessibility [4, 5], and many individuals with disabilities are unable to vote independently, privately, and/or successfully. For example, after the November 2012 election, 30.1 % of voters with disabilities reported difficulties when voting at a polling place in-person versus 8.4 % of voters without disabilities, and the voter turnout rate for individuals with disabilities was 5.7 % less than those without

© Springer International Publishing Switzerland 2016
F.F.-H. Nah and C.-H. Tan (Eds.): HCIBGO 2016, Part II, LNCS 9752, pp. 159–170, 2016.
DOI: 10.1007/978-3-319-39399-5_16

disabilities (i.e., approximately 3 million more persons with disabilities would have voted if these voting rates had been the same) [6].

With the rise of tablet computers and mobile devices, coupled with aging voting machines that will soon need replacing [7], an opportunity to increase the accessibility of voting technology has arisen. For example, mobile usage is becoming widespread as a Pew Research Center Survey found that 42 % of American adults own a tablet computer and 58 % own a smartphone [8].

Mobile voting solutions created with accessibility and universal design in mind provide an opportunity for voters with and without disabilities to use familiar technology, as well as providing a means for those less familiar with the technology or with little technology experience to vote successfully. An accessible mobile voting option at a polling place also addresses the requirement of the U.S. Election Assistance Commission's Voluntary Voting System Guidelines (VVSG) 1.0 that voters with disabilities should be provided with support that is built into voting equipment without requiring the use of personal assistive technology to vote successfully [9]. Prior research has shown that individuals with dexterity or motor impairments have found mobile touchscreen devices to be empowering; however, accessibility issues that limit the extent to which these devices meet the needs of individuals with these types of impairments need to be addressed [10–12].

1.1 Accessible Mobile Voting System User Interface Prototype Design

Our research team designed and created a mobile voting user interface for individuals with disabilities using specifications gathered from previous relevant research, with a primary focus on dexterity and visual impairments [13]. Prior research has examined various touchscreen design elements, but these studies looked at elements in isolation, whereas our touchscreen user interface design incorporated guidance from previous research to create a universal design solution intended to accommodate individuals with limited dexterity, visual impairments, and dyslexia, as well as voters who have limited or no experience with mobile technologies.

When creating the prototype, we referred to research on appropriate button size [14, 15], button spacing [15, 16], and touchscreen gestures and button position [11, 17]. In our mobile voting user interface design, buttons are located near the edges of the screen and the active region of each button is at least 20 mm in length and width (although the visual size may appear smaller), with at least 6.35 mm of spacing between active regions. Where buttons are touching, the minimum button size was increased to provide additional spacing.

All functionality is accessed via tap, which is the preferred and most effective gesture for individuals with motor skill impairments [11]; all other input functions are disabled by default, with the exception of drag, which can only be used in the slider area of the custom scroll bar. Selections are made by touching checkboxes (instead of an entire row) to avoid accidental inputs. Unselected checkboxes are disabled when the maximum number of selections have been made to prevent over-voting.

The size of the ballot text conforms to the National Association for the Visually Handicapped large print standards [18] (modified for bold text using the ratio presented in the Web Content Accessibility Guidelines 2.0 [19]): A minimum of 16 typographic points (5.6 mm or 56px) for normal text and 12.5 typographic points (4.4 mm or 44px) for bold text, as measured by the em-square. In our mobile voting prototype, the size of the bolded contest names and button names is 12.5 typographic points and the size of the body text (i.e., the candidate and party names, etc.) is 16 typographic points. Spacing and separator lines are also included between options for clear layout of lists.

The design is optimized for medium- and large-sized tablets and devices with similar display sizes, as smartphones and small tablets do not provide enough screen area to accommodate a usable and accessible voting system for a wide range of users. The vertical (portrait) device orientation was used for this study, and the screen was locked in this orientation, as changing the display to landscape orientation would have necessitated a redesigned user interface to ensure appropriate usability and accessibility.

2   Methodology

For this first iteration of our accessible mobile voting study, we focused on testing the design with individuals with moderate dexterity impairments and those without disabilities. We analyzed audio and video recordings as well as participant feedback from one-on-one usability evaluation sessions in which participants used the mobile voting prototype on a tablet to cast a sample ballot for a mock election.

2.1   Materials and Procedures

Mobile Testing Configuration. Participants used a Samsung Galaxy Tab 4 with 10.1 inch screen size while seated at an adjustable drafting table with height and angle options (Fig. 1), allowing for customizable angle and position to accommodate individuals whose reach or height differs (including those in wheelchairs of differing heights). The tablet rested on the surface of the table to avoid any strain caused by holding the device, and the table was angled to reduce glare [13]. In addition, the adjustable table was used to provide necessary support for those with dexterity impairments to assist with accuracy of button presses and reduce unintended inputs [20].

During the participant sessions, the tabletop was set at an angle of approximately 26 degrees as the default, with the base of the incline at a height of 71 cm and the peak at a height of 102 cm. The default settings for the table were used for 15 of the 16 participants, and after being asked one participant opted to have the height or angle adjusted. A non-slip matting was also placed on the table to keep the tablet from sliding, and participants could move the position of the tablet within an approximately 40 × 40 cm area that was taped off. Overhead fluorescent lights were turned off, and a lamp with a 60 W lightbulb was placed next to the table, which was adjusted to eliminate glare for each participant.

National Institute of Standards and Technology (NIST) Test Ballot. The NIST Test Ballot [21], which has been used in conformance testing associated with the VVSG 1.0 [9], was used in this study. The ballot uses realistic but fictional names and contests,

Fig. 1. Mobile voting testing configuration

with colors for party names. The ballot used for this study included separate pages for 12 contests (9 single candidate selections, e.g., vote for one; 3 multiple candidate selections, e.g. vote for five), 2 judge retention contests (Yes/No), 4 constitutional amendments (For/Against), and 2 ballot measures (For/Against), as well as View All/Review, Submission, and Confirmation pages. Write-ins are also supported in the prototype; however, it did not include Straight Party voting.

Procedure and Mobile Voting Interface. Participants used the provided tablet to vote the NIST Test Ballot using our mobile voting interface prototype (Fig. 2). Participants were given instructions on which selections to make in each contest, but they were not specifically instructed on how to go about voting using the prototype. An overview of the system was provided in the Help & Options section, which participants could read if they chose to go to this section, and they could view different options that could be adjusted (e.g., font size, contrast, etc.), but these options were not active for this study in order to test the default settings of the system across participants.

During the voting task, participants made selections for twenty contests (as mentioned above). For two of the contests they were asked to complete the write-in option (for one candidate and for two candidates), and at two points in the voting process they were asked to go back and change a previous selection. After completing voting, they then submitted the ballot.

Each contest page had the following button options on the screen: checkboxes for each possible selection on the left side, custom scroll controls along the right side (with options to Screen Up/Screen Down, Scroll Up/Down one item, or use the scroll bar to tap and drag), and navigation and option buttons along the bottom (Prior Contest, Help & Options, View All/Review, and Next Contest).

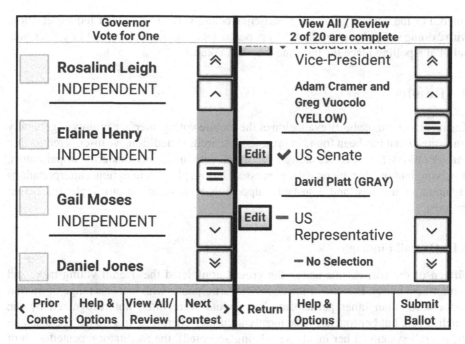

Fig. 2. Example screens of mobile voting prototype: Governor (single candidate) contest screen (left) and View/All Review screen (right).

Key usability measures included voting time, accuracy, and user satisfaction. After completing the ballot, participants were given the System Usability Scale (SUS) questionnaire and rated their level of agreement to ten statements. The SUS is an industry standard used as a quick and reliable tool for measuring usability for a wide range of interfaces, systems, and technologies; the SUS has been proven to be accurate for small sample sizes of 8–14 [22]. Researchers also conducted a brief interview to gather further feedback and satisfaction data.

2.2 Participants

Sixteen participants, including 10 women and 6 men, took part in this study. Half of the participants had moderate dexterity impairments, and half did not have a disability (i.e., control group). Physical limitations for the dexterity group included weakness in arms and hands (which led to fatigue at times), moderate range of motion or control limitations, and/or difficulty walking (use of walkers, crutches, etc.). One participant also mentioned hand/eye coordination and visual tracking issues. Ages for the dexterity group ranged from 18–61, and ages for the control group ranged from 21–63. Six participants from the dexterity group and 4 from the control group were right-handed. All participants were familiar with smartphone or tablet technology and all had experience using the Internet.

Of the 6 participants from the dexterity group who had prior voting experience in a U.S. state or federal election, all had done so via absentee ballot the last time they had voted. For the control group, all 8 participants had voted in a state or federal election, with 2 doing so by absentee ballot, 5 by paper ballot at a polling place, and 1 by electronic ballot at a polling place the last time they had voted.

3   Results

The results of our usability evaluation of the mobile voting interface prototype generally confirmed what has been found in previous research. In addition, we discovered further considerations for interface design for users with moderate dexterity impairments, involving buttons that are repeatedly pressed, button placement options, interpretations of inputs or touches, and adjustable support that provides various angle and height options.

3.1   Overall Findings

Fifteen of the participants across the groups completed the overall voting tasks and submitted a ballot. For one of the dexterity participants, who had less range of motion and control than other participants, her inputs were often not recognized by the touchscreen, but her touches were mostly accurate. Therefore, to gain her feedback on the overall system (if her inputs were being accepted), the facilitator repeated each of her touches.

Across the groups, the majority of participants completed voting and submitted the ballot in approximately 5–15 min. Two of the dexterity participants had longer completion times (between 30–45 min), and they in particular encountered difficulties with unintended inputs and unrecognized touches, and confusion regarding functionality of the scroll options and submitting the ballot. Twelve of the participants had SUS scores in the acceptable range (above 70), while 4 dexterity participants had scores below 70 (Table 1).

Table 1. Results averages for moderate dexterity and control groups

	Dexterity	Control	All
Average time to vote and submit Ballot (mins:secs)	16:16	8:33	12:25
Average system usability score	65.3	88.8	77

The majority of participants had a positive reaction to voting using the mobile voting prototype. When asked whether they would vote with the mobile voting system if it were available in the next election, 13 of the 16 participants answered "yes" (and 3 dexterity answered "no" or "not sure"). Four dexterity participants expressed they have difficulty physically writing and therefore found this system easier to use than an absentee ballot. Ten participants (5 from each group) would prefer to use the mobile voting system from home (or another convenient location) to avoid the pressure and anxiety they feel at a polling place and to allow for as much time as they need.

Although more traditional or native functionality was constrained, the majority expressed that the mobile voting system was easy to use and intuitive (e.g., to figure out after initial confusion about how to scroll using the provided options, and how to choose an option by selecting a checkbox and not by pressing a name). However, some participants wanted an optional, brief overview or tutorial that would explain the functionality and voting process for the interface and the available options that can be adjusted (such as text size and contrast, enabling swiping, location of scroll bar, keyboard options, etc.) at the beginning and throughout the voting process. Additional functionality could also be implemented to anticipate when instructions are needed by users, such as when changing a vote. The overall text size and bolding was useful and accepted, although most control participants desired options to alter the text size at the beginning and during voting to view more options at once on the screen.

The size and placement of the buttons were also well received, along with the simple and clear layout of the ballot and the variety of scrolling options, which allow participants to switch between these options as needed by contest type or rate of reading preference (i.e., most dexterity participants only used the arrow options, but most control participants switched between all of the scrolling options). While using the double arrows (or Page Down) option to scroll, 2 control and 2 dexterity participants (including 1 with visual tracking issues) found it difficult to track how far the double arrows shifted through the options.

Participants appreciated having the list view and Edit options available on the View All/Review page, and after figuring out how to change a vote after a couple presses most also expressed that this feature would help prevent error, and that the ability to edit would be very useful in voting. However, it was unclear to some in each group that the View All/Review screen could be used to navigate the ballot, and that they needed to reach this screen in order to submit their ballot.

3.2   Dexterity-Specific Findings

Repeated-Press Buttons Require Additional Spacing and Support/Reach Considerations. Throughout the voting process, the dexterity participants tended to use the custom scroll buttons (e.g., single or double arrows), and not the scroll bar, to scroll down and up through the selections for each contest. Using these controls required repeated presses for most of the contests. The Next Contest button, which participants had to press each time they finished choosing a selection for a contest, was located directly below the custom scroll options on the right side of the screen. Although the amount of spacing included between these buttons and the placement of the buttons along the edges of the screen was based on previous research, we observed that this spacing proved insufficient, especially for 2 dexterity participants who tended to experience drifting while repeatedly pressing buttons. This proximity of repeated-press buttons led to accidental presses of the Next Contest button when these participants were pressing the options to scroll down, which then required each participant to go back to the previous screen and start scrolling from the top of the list again (i.e., a serious and detrimental consequence, especially for users with dexterity limitations). After completing the ballot, 2 dexterity participants also mentioned wanting a longer scroll bar that extended to the bottom of the screen to help avoid this issue.

In addition, we observed that the placement of the options to scroll down led participants to hover over the screen at times while they pressed these buttons, which then did not allow them to use the support of the table by resting their hand alongside the tablet while pressing a button. Participants who preferred to use their left hand to press buttons also had to move their hand a further distance to reach the custom scroll options and required them to hover over the screen versus those who used their right hand. This hovering, along with the mentioned spacing issues between critical buttons, led to diminished accuracy and accidental inputs for buttons that required repeated presses.

Button Placement Options May be Required to Accommodate Various Hand/ Finger Usage. While using the mobile voting prototype, the majority of the participants used a finger on one preferred hand to press buttons on the screen, and at times used both hands (one finger on each) to type the names of write-in candidates using the provided on-screen keyboard. Most used an index finger to touch buttons on the screen, although usage varied more for the dexterity participants (e.g., use of different fingers or a thumb).

During the sessions, it became apparent that hand preference was an important factor for the ease of use of the interface, as those who preferred to use their left hand had to reach across the screen to use the fixed scroll options on the right side, which led to loss of support for their hand and the screen being blocked by their left hand. Seven participants (4 control and 3 dexterity) used their left hand to press buttons and experienced difficulties and accidental inputs at times for buttons they repeatedly pressed. Of these participants, 3 dexterity and 1 control mentioned their desire for an option to choose the location of the scroll bar to facilitate ease of use and accuracy, and also thereby allow for "switching" of hand usage (e.g., 1 dexterity participant switched to using her left hand because her right hand became fatigued). Therefore, although it has been demonstrated that locating buttons along edges of a screen can lead to greater accuracy for users with motor impairments, users should also not be forced to move far from their arm support in order to press a button.

Inputs or Touches may be Misinterpreted by Commercial Touchscreens. Throughout the voting process, we observed how the touchscreen and operating system of the commercial tablet (Samsung Galaxy Tab 4) used to display our interface during the study interpreted the inputs of users. Specifically, the inputs or touches of 4 dexterity participants were not always recognized and/or the system recognized an input as a double press (e.g., selecting and deselecting a checkbox during a single interaction), and these input issues occurred especially for 2 of these participants. For one of these participants, who also has visual tracking issues, the touchscreen system did not accept his inputs at times when he was pressing checkboxes, and especially when using the provided on-screen keyboard. The second participant could reach and touch all the buttons in the interface usually with a high degree of accuracy, but the system accepted almost none of her inputs, most likely because of particularly long dwell times. However, this participant often experienced accepted inputs for buttons that were closer to her (e.g., Next Contest button) versus buttons that required her to reach or hover over the screen with her right hand (e.g., checkboxes) which may have led to her longer dwell times to compensate for support (e.g., pressing down and then pushing off of the screen for buttons that required more reaching).

Adjustable Support is Useful and Essential. Nearly all of the participants expressed that using the tablet on an angled table was useful for viewing ease and for support if needed; however, one dexterity participant would prefer the table itself to be flat for comfortable support with the tablet propped at an angle to facilitate viewing and a mouse available to use for inputs (e.g., to avoid having to hold her hand up and over the tablet). Participants slid or slightly rotated the tablet within the middle of the table as needed for viewing or ease of interaction, and 6 dexterity and 5 control rested their hand(s) on the table at times or throughout the entire voting process. Specifically, 1 dexterity participant mentioned that the angled table would be essential for him to use the tablet because he could rest his hands along the side of the tablet and then move his fingers to press the on-screen buttons (versus needing to hover or reach), although he would also like to have the option to use a mouse for inputs.

One dexterity participant had more limited range of motion and control than the other participants and her inputs were often not accepted when using the mobile voting proto-type; she experienced less successful inputs when she was required to reach or hover to press a button (e.g., she had more success for the buttons at the bottom of the screen, such as the Next Contest button, while resting her hand near the bottom of the tablet). As mentioned previously, due to the loss of support when reaching for a button, this participant had particularly long dwell times and seemed to use the tablet as support by pushing off the screen when moving her hand away from the tablet.

4 Discussion

From observing and analyzing the usage of our mobile voting prototype by individuals with moderate dexterity impairments and without impairments, we discovered consid-erations that are critical for a universally designed voting system.

Specifically for individuals with moderate dexterity impairments, additional spacing is required between repeated-press buttons (versus what has been found in previous research for touchscreen buttons in general) to compensate for drifting and possible support or hovering issues, and to avoid accidental inputs for these types of buttons. A tablet with a larger screen size could help facilitate enhancements that cannot be sufficiently accommodated on a tablet with a 10.1 in. screen size (e.g., extension of the scroll bar and options to the bottom of the screen with the other buttons near the bottom shifted to the left with their current size maintained) in order to avoid unintended inputs for repeated-press buttons.

The placement of the buttons along the edges of the screen was useful for most participants as they could rest their hands on the table for support along the sides and bottom of the tablet as needed. However, usage varied more amongst the dexterity participants for hand and finger usage (e.g., switching between hands or using not only an index finger) and they may have been limited to the use of only one hand. In addition, due to varying ranges of motion, control, and strength, participants may or may not have rested their hand(s) or arm(s) on the table near the tablet (e.g., usage ranges, preference, or comfort differences may have dictated whether they desired to or were able to rest on the table for support versus hovering above the screen). Therefore, further considerations are needed beyond placing buttons along the edges, such as the option to choose the location of repeated-press options (e.g., scroll options) for left hand usage. The option to rotate the ballot may also be necessary as a landscape-oriented ballot could potentially alleviate reach and support issues (e.g., for buttons near the top of the screen).

Additionally, how touchscreen devices interpret the intentions of users with dexterity disabilities requires further investigation, as well as whether additional considerations may be needed to facilitate support and reduce reaching or hovering. Specifically, users with this type of disability have been shown to press touchscreen buttons for a longer duration (dwell time) with more total force for that time (i.e., greater impulse) than users without disabilities [12, 16]. Because of these specific differences, touchscreen devices calibrated to interpret user intentions based on the specific touch characteristics of users without disabilities may have difficulty correctly interpreting the intentions of users with dexterity-related disabilities, as we found in our study. A calibration setup feature may be necessary to assess the touches of a user (e.g., differences in dwell time and force) and adapt the system as necessary [23, 24] to ensure their inputs are recognized throughout the voting process. A landscape-oriented ballot could also potentially reduce reaching or hovering, which could decrease the amount of unrecognized inputs.

Overall, this study demonstrated that flexibility or adjustability is critical for a universal mobile voting system. The default setting for this mobile voting system was usable for the majority of participants, but options for adjustment will facilitate further ease of use, such as the option to choose the location of the scroll bar, to adjust the text size if and when needed, to calibrate the system based on the user's touches, and so on. In addition, a tablet that is not fully attached to a surface also allows a user the option to hold the tablet if desired, or re-position the tablet on the table as needed. An adjustable surface, allowing for varying height and angle options, also is needed to meet the varying needs of users for ease of viewing and support. Additional input devices should also be available (e.g., styluses of varying sizes, mouse options, external keyboard, etc.) and the option to connect personal input or assistive technology to further facilitate ease of use of the digital ballot [25].

5   Conclusion

To further the development of a universally accessible touchscreen voting interface, we used prior research to design and create a mobile voting prototype. We evaluated the usability of our prototype with individuals with moderate dexterity impairments and with no disabilities. Results of our study can inform user interface designers, election officials, voting system manufacturers, and the general public on the specific needs of different user groups, and considerations that are necessary for a universally designed system. Further research is being conducted with low vision and dyslexia participants, and additional research will investigate the ease of use of the audio features of the mobile voting system with relevant disability groups, including blind and aging participants.

Acknowledgements. The design specifications and prototype development were funded through a research grant from the National Institute of Standards and Technology to Michigan State University: Enhancement of Accessible Mobile Voting System Standards (Grant #70NANB13H150). Principal Investigator: Dr. Sarah J. Swierenga, Michigan State University. We would also like to thank the Michigan Protection & Advocacy Service for their assistance in recruiting participants and for providing space at their facility for conducting some of the usability sessions.

References

1. U.S. Census Bureau: American Community Survey. Disability Characteristics, 2009–2013 American Community Survey 5-year Estimates (2013). http://factfinder.census.gov/
2. Brault, M.W.: Americans with Disabilities: 2010. U.S. Census Bureau, Washington, DC (2012). https://www.census.gov/prod/2012pubs/p70-131.pdf
3. Help America Vote Act of 2002, Pub. L. No. 107-252, 116 Stat. 1666-1730, codified at 42 U.S.C. §§15301–15545 (2002)
4. Bovbjerg, B.: Voters with Disabilities: Challenges to Voting Accessibility. U.S. Government Accountability Office, Washington, D.C. (2013)
5. Swierenga, S.J., Pierce, G.L.: Testing usability performance of accessible voting systems: final report. Technical report, Michigan State University, Usability/Accessibility Research and Consulting, East Lansing, MI (2012)
6. Schur, L., Adya, M., Kruse, D.: Disability, voter turnout, and voting difficulties in the 2012 elections. Report to U.S. EAC and RAAV (2013)
7. Norden, L., Famighetti, C.: America's Voting Machines at Risk. Brennan Center for Justice at New York University School of Law, New York, 11 September 2015
8. Pew Research Center: Pew Research Internet Project: Mobile Technology Fact Sheet (2014). http://www.pewinternet.org/fact-sheets/mobile-technology-fact-sheet/
9. U.S. Election Assistance Commission: Voluntary Voting System Guidelines 1.0. U.S. EAC, Washington, D.C (2005)
10. Anthony, L., Kim, Y., Findlater, L.: Analyzing user-generated youtube videos to understand touchscreen use by people with motor impairments. In: SIGCHI Conference on Human Factors in Computing Systems, pp. 1223–1232. ACM, New York (2013)
11. Guerreiro, T., Nicolau, H., Jorge, J., Gonçalves, D.: Towards accessible touch interfaces. In: Proceedings of the 12th International ACM SIGACCESS Conference on Computers and Accessibility, pp. 19–26. ACM, New York (2010)
12. Irwin, C.B., Sesto, M.E.: Performance and touch characteristics of disabled and non-disabled participants during a reciprocal tapping task using touch screen technology. Appl. Ergon. **43**, 1038–1043 (2012)
13. Pierce, G.L., Jackson, J.E., Swierenga, S.J.: Enhanced user interface and interaction design standards for accessible mobile voting systems. Technical report, Michigan State University, Usability/Accessibility Research and Consulting, East Lansing, MI (2014)
14. Duff, S.N., Irwin, C.B., Skye, J.L., Sesto, M.E., Wiegmann, D.A.: The effect of disability and approach on touch screen performance during a number entry task. Proc. Hum. Factors Ergon. Soc. Annu. Meet. **54**(6), 566–570 (2010)

15. Jin, Z.X., Plocher, T., Kiff, L.: Touch screen user interfaces for older adults: button size and spacing. In: Stephanidis, C. (ed.) HCI 2007. LNCS, vol. 4554, pp. 933–941. Springer, Heidelberg (2007)
16. Sesto, M.E., Irwin, C.B., Chen, K.B., Chourasia, A.O., Wiegmann, D.A.: Effect of touch screen button size and spacing on touch characteristics of users with and without disabilities. Hum. Factors: J. Hum. Factors Ergon. Soc. **54**(3), 425–436 (2012)
17. Nicolau, H., Guerreiro, T., Jorge, J., Gonçalves, D.: Mobile touchscreen user interfaces: bridging the gap between motor-impaired and able-bodied users. Univ. Access Inf. Soc. **13**, 303–313 (2014)
18. National Association for the Visually Handicapped: NAVH Standards & Criteria for Large Print Publications (2006). www.sfgov2.org/ftp/uploadedfiles/mod/programmatic/NAVH06.pdf
19. World Wide Web Consortium: Web Content Accessibility Guidelines (WCAG) 2.0 (2008). http://www.w3.org/TR/WCAG20/
20. Jackson, J.E., Ismirle, J., Swierenga, S.J., Blosser, S.R., Pierce, G.L.: Joystick interaction strategies of individuals with dexterity impairments: observations from the smart voting joystick usability evaluation. In: Antona, M., Stephanidis, C. (eds.) UAHCI 2015. LNCS, vol. 9178, pp. 192–203. Springer, Heidelberg (2015)
21. National Institute of Standards and Technology, U.S. Department of Commerce. NIST Medium Complexity Test Ballot Specification. http://www.nist.gov/itl/vote/accessible voting/upload/NIST_test-ballot-specification.pdf
22. Tullis, T.S., Stetson, J.N.: A comparison of questionnaires for assessing website usability. In: Usability Professionals Association Annual Conference Presentation, Minneapolis (2004)
23. Kurschl, W., Augstein, M., Stitz, H., Heumader, P., Pointner, C.: A user modelling wizard for people with motor impairments. In: Proceedings of 11th International Conference on Advances in Mobile Computing & Multimedia, p. 541. ACM, New York (2013)
24. Wobbrock, J.O., Kane, S.K., Gajos, K.Z., Harada, S., Froehlich, J.: Ability-based design concept principles and examples. ACM Trans. Accessible Comput. **3**(3), 9 (2011)
25. Swierenga, S.J., Zantjer, R.S., Jackson, J.E., Ismirle, J., Blosser, S.R., Pierce, G.L.: Security implications for personal assistive technology in voting. In: Tryfonas, T., Askoxylakis, I. (eds.) HAS 2015. LNCS, vol. 9190, pp. 582–591. Springer, Heidelberg (2015)

As Simple as Possible and as Complex as Necessary

A Communication Kit for Geothermal Energy Projects

Johanna Kluge[(✉)] and Martina Ziefle

Chair of Communication Science/Human Computer Interaction Center, RWTH Aachen,
Campusboulevard 57, 52074 Aachen, Germany
{Kluge,Ziefle}@comm.rwth-aachen.de

Abstract. The successful implementation of renewable energy projects – such as deep geothermal power plants – depends on the acceptance of the local public. Therefore an adequate communication strategy is needed. We conducted three empirical studies to get an empirical basis for a communication strategy. Based on that we created a toolkit for the communication of deep geothermal energy. It consists of several hierarchical arranged tools consisting of empirical based advices for a communication strategy. Basically, to reach acceptance communication should create knowledge, trust and transparency. Cornerstones to achieve this are information and participation.

Keywords: Information strategy · Geothermal energy · Communication kit · Project communication · Information guideline · Renewable energies

1 Introduction

Facing the climate change and its consequences, it is time for a change in energy policy. The finite nature of fossil fuels and their negative impacts on the whole environment show there is no choice other than to turn to renewables. To promote an energy transition its indispensable to support and implement renewable energy forms. Deep geothermal energy is one possible renewable energy form that could assist the changeover from fossil fuels to more renewable energy forms [1].

The implementation of renewables – as every other large-scale technology – is depending on social acceptance [2]. In general we see that the acceptance of renewable energy is overall high. But in Germany we could observe that people often start to oppose to concrete projects in their neighborhood [3, 4]. This is often caused by a bad or hardly existent communication between project managers and the local population. As a consequence an atmosphere of distrust and negative emotions like fear and anger occurs. This is supported by the unfamiliarity of a technology such as geothermal energy. We know from other contexts, such as for example the ICT context, that relatively unknown technologies lead to a higher risk perception and thus fear [5, 6].

Following that, an adequate communication strategy is needed to support the successful implementation and thus acceptance of innovative renewable energy technologies – in this case geothermal energy [1, 7–9]. In the past there was just few

© Springer International Publishing Switzerland 2016
F.F.-H. Nah and C.-H. Tan (Eds.): HCIBGO 2016, Part II, LNCS 9752, pp. 171–182, 2016.
DOI: 10.1007/978-3-319-39399-5_17

(empirical) research on the topic of communication of geothermal energy [7, 9–12]. In this paper we present results from several studies that focus on the understanding of main factors of the acceptance of geothermal energy. The main focus was to examine what a good communication and information strategy should be like when its purpose is to involve, inform and educate people adequately about this relatively unknown technology. The aim is to create a bridge between the knowledge of professionals and the emotions of the non-experts that leads to an equal communication base level between all stakeholders.

2   Theoretical Background

As known from several studies social acceptance of renewable energies is a complex issue [1, 2, 6, 8, 12]. Social Acceptance is a product out of several influencing factors, such as user diversity (in terms of domain knowledge, gender or age) [13–16], but also the type of technology or usage context [17, 18]. Thus, every technical context has individual acceptance patterns. Geothermal energy thus has its own determinants of acceptance. There are several studies that focus on social acceptance of geothermal energy, but most of them stay superficial and provide no concrete specifications for an information strategy. Wüstenhagen et al. for example, emphasizes the need of social acceptance and constructed the so called triangle-model which consists of three dimensions *socio-political-, community-* and *market acceptance* [2]. Studies from Japan, Italy and Australia conclude that especially a lack of knowledge and a high risk perception affect the acceptance of geothermal energy in particular. Moreover, these studies show, that the general public misses common knowledge about geothermal energy in general is low. As a consequence distrust and risk perception in relation to geothermal power plants are rather high [19, 20]. Related results come from studies from Germany, which indicate little understanding in the broader public about geothermal energy production and highlight several concerns especially regarding seismic activity and water pollution [21].

There are also studies comparing social acceptance patterns of geothermal energy between different countries. Reith et al. identified four main issues of rejection of geothermal energy in Germany, France and Italy. These main issues were identified as environmental issues, financial issues, missing involvement issues and NIMBY issues (not in my backyard phenomenon) [22].

Wallquist and Holenstein follow a practical approach. They propose a community engagement process. This includes an analysis of the social site, an intense stakeholder dialog as well as a dialog with the general public. While this procedure is principal transferrable to other geothermal energy projects, there are no concrete recommendations for general communication guidelines provided [7].

Altogether the study of social acceptance and the resulting communication need in the geothermal energy context lacks of a concrete information and communication guideline with the purpose to enable the public to understand geothermal energy production, to engage in dialogue with stakeholders and thus prevent distrust and fear about risks and disadvantages associated with a geothermal energy project.

3   Methodological Approach/Empirical Background

In order to develop a communication kit, a solid empirical basis is necessary. Overall, in a three-tiered approach we conducted several studies to examine the public opinion about geothermal energy. Using different qualitative and quantitative methods, we looked at prevailing fears, perceived benefits as well as seen risks. Possible ways and points in time for communication were also examined. Several questions were addressed:

- What should be the main goal of a communication strategy?
- What aspects should be mainly integrated into a communication concept?
- What topics have to be integrated?
- Which factor has the most influence on the acceptance?

The benefit of a mixed-method approach is to prevent blind spots that may appear depending on a specific method. By including different methods we can triangulate results and thus get deeper insights into our topic. Altogether, 698 participants volunteered to take part in these three studies. Each study had a different thematic focus, so that every needed facet for a communication strategy could be captured. In the following, we present the findings in the respective studies, with a focus on the third study, which will be presented in greater detail in comparison to the first two studies.

3.1   Interview Study: Mental Representation of Geothermal Energy

In the interview study we focused on the examination of the mental representation of geothermal energy in the public. For a deeper understanding of the general publics communication need, knowledge about the underlying cognitive attitudes towards the technology is important. $N = 170$ participants took part in the interview study. We assessed the acceptance-relevant cognitions by an open answer format. This has the advantage that people can freely associate what comes into their mind und thus we can examine the mental representation. Especially in the context of relatively unfamiliar topics, a study design with a given answer format would shape answers in a concrete direction. In the interview important topics were perceived benefits, perceived risks and the question what a transparent communication should be like. Additionally, we asked by which communication channel people prefer to get their information. More detailed results can be found in [11].

Main results of the study are:

- Transparent communication means to the people mainly the disclosure of expert opinions, involvement of the local population, and timely information.
- Perceived benefits of geothermal energy are mainly the ecological benefits of renewables in general and economical benefits such as local energy supply and it's cost saving capacity.
- Perceived disadvantages were above all: unknown risks, earthquakes, and (unexpected) costs.

- The most often named source to get information about geothermal energy is direct mail to households.

3.2   Questionnaire: Identification and Quantification of Perceived Benefits and Barriers

The questionnaire focused on the influence of psychological factors on the acceptance of deep geothermal energy. On the users' side, we included factors that may impact the overall acceptance, as the individual level of environmental awareness, technical self-efficacy as well as attitudes toward renewable energies in general, but also the attitudes toward geothermal energy in specific. Additionally, arguments for and against geothermal energy were integrated as well as the question if people informed themselves about geothermal energy before. Items were formed on the base of the interview study. Overall n = 360 participants took part in this study. Based on the theory of planned behavior [23] a structure equation model was used to analyze the influence of psychological factors on the acceptance of geothermal energy. Additionally the participants were split in an informed and a not informed group to control the influence of knowledge on the acceptance. In Fig. 1, the constructed structure equation model is depicted [12].

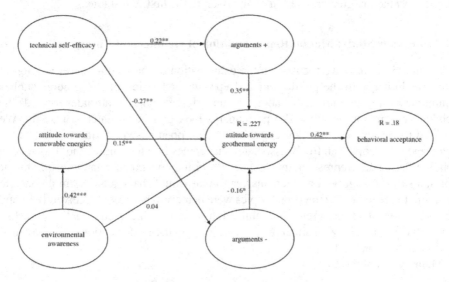

Fig. 1. Structure equation model of the acceptance-relevant factors for the overall behavioral acceptance of geothermal energy (from [12])

Summing up, the main results of this study are:

- General attitudes towards renewable energies as well as environmental awareness do not lead to higher acceptance of geothermal energy.
- Information plays an important role in the acceptance of geothermal energy, because informed people show higher acceptance values.

- Informed people distrust the economical benefit.
- The arguments for geothermal energy influence the attitude towards geothermal energy more than the arguments against geothermal energy.

3.3 Conjoint-Analysis: Preference Simulation with Respect to an Appropriate Communication Strategy

Conjoint-analysis is a method to measure the weighing of several factors in relation to each other. In contrast to traditional questionnaires in which participants answer single factors separately from each other, conjoint analyses simulate real-world user decisions in which users weigh several potential benefits against perceived barriers. Therefore, a choice-based conjoint analysis approach was selected. It mimics the complex decision processes in real world scenarios in which users have to evaluate more than one attribute that influences the final decision [24]. In the context here, we analyzed the communication strategy users prefer by looking at different attributes which were formed to different scenarios. Methodologically, the given decision scenarios and tradeoffs consist of multiple attributes and differ from each other in the attribute levels. As a result, the relative importance of attributes deliver information about which attribute influences the respondents' choice the most. Each attribute had five or six levels:

- **Person that provides information**
  Levels: external experts, independent journalist, politician, spokesman of operating company, director of operating company
- **Point in time and frequency of information during the project process**
  Levels: in operation, strike, begin of bore, permission of seismology, preliminary planning
- **Source of information**
  Levels: app, unofficial media, poster, article in daily newspaper, flyer/information brochure, website
- **Form of participation**
  Levels: telephone service for the public, open house day, tours to other geothermal systems, roundtable discussion with project managers, information event

To examine if people think it is more important to get insights into expert opinions or participation in the project process, people were additionally asked to chose a combination of levels belonging to these attributes. Before participants started to choose possible information packages, they were asked for their wanted frequency of information.

Overall n = 144 participants with an age range from 16–85 years of age took part in this study. 41 % were female and 59 % were male.

Main results of the conjoint analysis and the included questions are:

- **The most trusted person to provide information is the external expert.**
  Figure 2 answers the question who should provide information to the local public. It becomes obvious that the external expert reaches an utility value of 45.8 which is much more than the independent journalists score of 10.2. A political person, or persons connected to the operating company were rejected as trustful information

givers, presumably because participants distrust the independency and objectivity of the information and possible strategic alliances. Thus, for a communication strategy, a person to provide information should be independent from the operating company, neutral and well-informed.

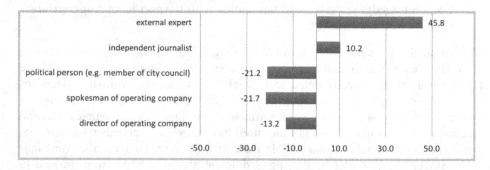

Fig. 2. Utility values for persons providing information

- **Citizens want to be informed as early as possible.**

    A closer look at the results (depicted in Fig. 3) shows that people wish to have information about a regional geothermal energy project as early as possible. As we see in Fig. 3, the preliminary planning has the strongest utility value of 50.4. Second possible point in time for information is the permission of seismology, still with a positive but considerably lower utility score of 20.7 later than that, the point in time even gets to negative utility values, what means that these possibilities are disliked and lead to rejection. Thus it is extraordinarily important for the citizens to get information about a local geothermal energy project at a very early point in time.

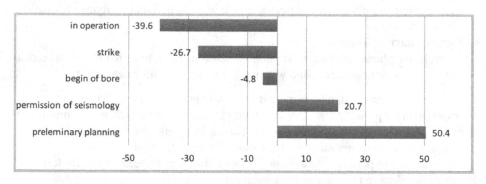

Fig. 3. Utility values for point in time of information

- **Crucial for the decision of one of the presented information combinations is the point in time.**

    As we see in Fig. 4 the kind of information is the least decisive attribute in contrast to the person who provides information and the point in time. Thus, the essential point for a communication concept is first of all the point in time when starting to inform the local public.

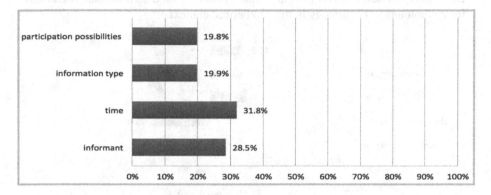

Fig. 4. What attribute is crucial for the decision of one combination?

- **People prefer a regular process of information.**

  Being asked in which time interval information about a local geothermal power plant project should be provided, people decided predominantly for the option weekly (29.20 %) or monthly (39.60 %), as shown in Fig. 5.

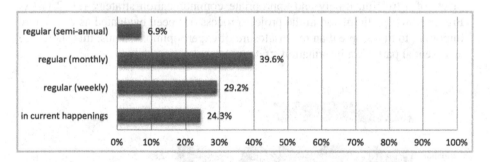

Fig. 5. Preferred frequency of information about a local geothermal project

- **Local newspaper, direct mail to all household and websites are the preferred information channels.**

  Several possible information channels were included in the conjoint-analysis. As Fig. 6 shows, articles in the daily news paper were evaluated with the highest utility values (approx. 21) and thus represent the most important source of information and media. This might be due to the fact that newspapers are coming in each day and are read, in contrast to extra flyers or brochure (8.7) or information delivered on the website (5.5), which are also acceptable but less welcome. However, there were also

media and information channels hat received negative scores. Apps (−11.8), unofficial media (−10.7) or posters (−12.5) were disliked by the participants. Thus, especially the local newspaper, direct mail and websites should be information channels
for a communication strategy in the geothermal context.

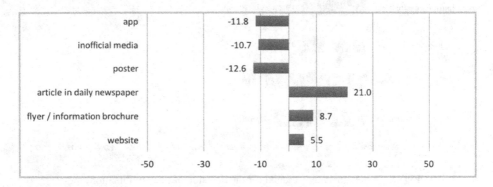

Fig. 6. Utility values for the preferred information channel

- **Participation and disclosure of expert opinions are both important to the people.
  Participation, however, is even more important.**

  As our studies clearly showed, participation and disclosure are very important
  facets of a trustful, timely and appropriate communication strategy (cf. 2.1). As
  Fig. 7 shows, participation in the project process has been evaluated as even more
  important to the people than the disclosure of expert opinions. Thus, this should be
  an essential part of an information strategy.

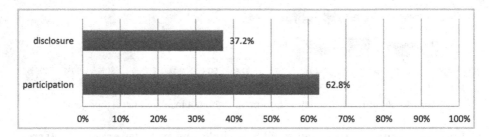

Fig. 7. Relevance of disclosure in contrast to participation

4   Communication Kit

All results of our studies are joining to a broad base for communication and information
recommendations. For an easy handling of this complex resource of results and information also for practitioners, we developed a communication kit, in form of a tool kit.
It consists of the empirical results, results from literature study and contains the essential
conclusions.

This toolkit should be easy to understand and at the same time include all relevant information. Thus we built the kit as a construct with all relevant components that are needed for basic communication demands in a geothermal energy project process. Figure 8 shows the base version of the kit. The overall aim of a good communication and information strategy should be public acceptance. Moreover the creation and development of public knowledge, trust in persons and actions involved, as well as transparency of information, actions and processes [11, 12] are subject to social acceptance. People fear unknown risks in the context of geothermal energy. These fears are a consequence of a low level of information (leaving space for negative feelings, concerns and distrust) and thus have detrimental effects on the acceptance [5, 6, 11, 12]. This is closely intertwined with the need for trust and transparency. As other studies could show, transparency is crucial for a good communication between stakeholders of a geothermal project [1–3, 7]. In our examination we could see that transparent communication is directly linked to trust in the project managers. This arises from the strong wish for the disclosure of expert opinions as an expression of the wish for control. This in turn is caused by the distrust against the operating company and connected representatives.

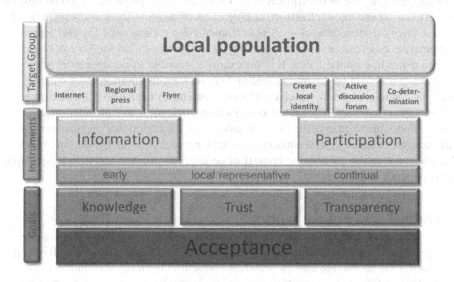

Fig. 8. Communication toolkit

The basic modules (acceptance, knowledge, trust and transparency) can be achieved by a continual and timely communication, as well as by a person that is trusted in.

As our conjoint-study showed, communication from an early point in time is crucial for the people. Also continual communication is essentially for an adequate communication strategy.

The instruments to reach these goals are mainly information and participation.

Information is an essential part of a communication strategy that provides knowledge for the broader public, especially as we know that knowledge about geothermal energy is very low in the general public and is – as we saw in the questionnaire study – essential for the acceptance [5, cf. 2.2].

Ways to provide information in an adequate way are the local newspaper, internet and direct mail, as our studies showed (cf. 2.1).

The second cornerstone for communication is participation. As our empirical base showed, the involvement into the project process is crucial for the public. Participation creates a feeling of trust because people have the feeling of getting insights into the project and the people behind in contrast to an anonymous operating company that often is perceived as not caring for the local requirements.

Ways for participation are to provide a local identity, discussion groups and co-determination. To provide a local identity a proper way is e.g. to order local craftsmen for the power plant construction. Discussion groups may be advisably to inform people on the one hand, and discuss their issues around the project fairly and thus educate and inform the people and additionally create an atmosphere of trust and acceptance on the other hand.

This grounded version of our communication toolkit can be seen as fundamental communication advice in the context of geothermal energy projects, but could also be transferred to other energy infrastructure projects, such as local district heating networks [25], electricity storage technology [26] or transmission technology [27]. Our empirical base provides much more information. Thus, the communication toolkit can be differentiated depending on the focus. It is for example possible to get deeper insights into the topics that should be communicated or find answers to questions like which topic should be communicated by which communication channel and which are negative and positive topics that have to be included into a communication and information strategy. Also, it is possible to change the focus depending on the region that one is interested in (rural area vs. urban area). The communication kit provides a solid foundation of knowledge about communication in the context of geothermal projects and is in this version just as complex as absolutely necessary.

5   Outlook and Future Works

Deep geothermal energy is an innovative and relatively unknown technology. It has high potential for the renewable energy sector. As we know from other technical contexts, the implementation of technologies, unfamiliar to the broader public is difficult and needs acceptance. Without acceptance action groups may build and in the worst case stop a project, which has economical and ecological consequences for all stakeholders. To prevent this communication that educates and informs the local public and enables them to build their own opinion is indispensable.

The here presented communication toolkit for deep geothermal energy is the result of a broad empirical base. It is a version kept as simple as possible. Thus the recommendations for communication are easy to understand and easy to put into practice. The empirical base provides much more information than included here. Next steps will be to include more information and conduct more complex versions. Also we have to examine if this toolkit is transferrable to other large-scale-technology contexts.

Another focus of our future work will be the special communication needs of protest groups. Those groups are an important player in large-scale projects and they have to be included in thoughts about communication strategies.

Acknowledgements. This research project (TIGER) is funded by the German Federal Ministry for Industry and Energy (BMWi, no. FKZ 0325413A). Thanks to Sylvia Kowalewski for excellent project work. The research team owes gratitude to the ministry project coordinator Sarah Wurth for her helpful support in organizational as well as research issues.

References

1. Cataldi, R.: Social acceptance of geothermal projects: problems and costs. In: Proceedings of the European Summer School on Geothermal Energy Applications, pp. 343–351. Oradea/RO (2001)
2. Wüstenhagen, R., Wolsink, M., Bürer, M.J.: Social acceptance of renewable energy innovation: an introduction to the concept. Energy Policy 35(5), 2683–2691 (2007)
3. Vittes, M.E., Pollock III, P.H., Lilie, S.A.: Factors contributing to NIMBY attitudes. Waste Manag. 13(2), 125–129 (1993)
4. Groothuis, P.A., Groothuis, J.D., Whitehead, J.C.: Green vs. green: measuring the compensation required to site electrical generation windmills in a viewshed. Energy Policy 36(4), 1545–1550 (2008)
5. Zaunbrecher, B.S., Kowalewski, S., Ziefle, M.: The willingness to adopt technologies: a cross-sectional study on the influence of technical self-efficacy on acceptance. In: Kurosu, M. (ed.) HCI 2014, Part III. LNCS, vol. 8512, pp. 764–775. Springer, Heidelberg (2014)
6. Zaunbrecher, B., Ziefle, M.: Social acceptance and its role for planning technology infrastructure. A position paper, taking wind power plants as an example. In: 4th International Conference on Smart Cities and Green ICT Systems (SMARTGREENS 2015), pp. 60–65. SCITEPRESS (Science and Technology Publications, Lda) (2015)
7. Wallquist, L., Holenstein, M.: Engaging the public on geothermal energy. In: World Geothermal Congress, pp. 19–25. Melbourne (2015)
8. Möller, A. (ed.): Akzeptanz von Technik und Infrastrukturen: Anmerkungen zu einem aktuellen gesellschaftlichen Problem. Acatech-Deutsche Akademie der Technikwissenschaften. Springer, Heidelberg (2011)
9. Reimer, E., Jakobs, E.M., Borg, A., Trevisan, B.: New ways to develop professional communication concepts. In: IEEE International Professional Communication Conference, pp. 1–7. IEEE (2015)
10. Wirtz-Bruckner, S., Jakobs, E.M., Kowalewski, S., Kluge, J., Ziefle, M.: The potential of Facebook® for communicating complex technologies using the example of deep geothermal energy. In: 2015 IEEE International Professional Communication Conference (IPCC), pp. 1–10. Heidelberg (2011)
11. Kluge, J., Kowalewski, S., Ziefle, M.: Inside the user's mind – perception of risks and benefits of unknown technologies, exemplified by geothermal energy. In: Duffy, V.G. (ed.) DHM 2015. LNCS, vol. 9184, pp. 324–334. Springer, Heidelberg (2015)
12. Kowalewski, S., Borg, A., Kluge, J., Himmel, S., Trevisan, B., Eraßme, D., Jakobs, E.M.: Modelling the influence of human factors on the perception of renewable energies. Taking geothermics as an example. In: Advances in Human Factors, Software and System Engineering, pp. 155–162 (2014)

13. Ziefle, M., Schaar, A.: Gender differences in acceptance and attitudes towards an invasive medical stent. Electron. J. Health Inform. **6**(2), 1–18 (2011)
14. Wilkowska, W., Ziefle, M.: User diversity as a challenge for the integration of medical technology into future home environments. In: Ziefle, M., Röcker, C. (eds.) Human-Centred Design of eHealth Technologies Concepts Methods and Applications, pp. 95–126. IGI Global, Hershey (2011)
15. Ziefle, M., Schaar, A.K.: Technical expertise and its influence on the acceptance of future medical technologies: what is influencing what to which extent? In: Leitner, G., Hitz, M., Holzinger, A. (eds.) USAB 2010. LNCS, vol. 6389, pp. 513–529. Springer, Heidelberg (2010)
16. Busch, T.: Gender differences in self efficacy and attitudes toward computers. J. Educ. Comput. Res. **12**, 147–158 (1995)
17. Arning, K., Ziefle, M.: Different perspectives on technology acceptance: the role of technology type and age. In: Holzinger, A., Miesenberger, K. (eds.) USAB 2009. LNCS, vol. 5889, pp. 20–41. Springer, Heidelberg (2009)
18. Kluge, J., Ziefle, M.: Health is silver, beauty is golden? In: Marinos, L., Askoxylakis, I. (eds.) HAS 2013. LNCS, vol. 8030, pp. 110–118. Springer, Heidelberg (2013)
19. Dowd, A.-M., Boughen, N., Ashworth, P., Carr-Cornish, S.: Geothermal technology in Australia: investigating social acceptance. Energy Policy **39**(10), 6301–6307 (2011)
20. Kubota, H., Hondo, H., Hienuki, S., Kaieda, H.: Determining barriers to developing geothermal power generation in Japan: societal acceptance by stakeholders involved in hot springs. Energy Policy **61**, 1079–1087 (2013)
21. Brian, M.: Vertrauensbildung durch zielgerichtete Kommunikation. In: bbr – Sonderheft Geothermie 2013, pp. 72–74 (2013)
22. Reith, S., Kölbel, T., Schlagermann, P., Pellizzone, A., Allansdottir, A.: Public acceptance of geothermal electricity production. In: GEOELEC: Deliverable, vol. 44 (2013)
23. Ajzen, I.: The theory of planned behavior. Organ. Behav. Hum. Decis. Process. **50**(2), 179–211 (1991)
24. Luce, R.D., Tukey, J.W.: Simultaneous conjoint measurement: a new type of fundamental measurement. J. Math. Psychol. **1**, 1–27 (1964)
25. Zaunbrecher, B., Arning, K., Falke, T., Ziefle, M.: No pipes in my backyard? Preferences for local district heating network design in Germany. In: Energy Research & Social Science, pp. 90–101 (2016)
26. Zaunbrecher, B., Bexten, T., Wirsum, M., Ziefle, M.: What is stored, why and how? Mental models and acceptance of electricity storage technologies. In: 10th International Renewable Energy Storage Conference (IRES 2016) (2016)
27. Zaunbrecher, B., Stieneker, M., De Doncker, R.W., Ziefle, M.: Does transmission technology influence acceptance of overhead power lines? An empirical study. In: 5th International Conference on Smart Cities and Green ICT Systems (Smartgreens 2016) (2016)

Planning Effective HCI Courseware Design to Enhance Online Education and Training

Elspeth McKay[1(✉)] and John Izard[2]

[1] School of Business Information Technology and Logistics, RMIT University,
Melbourne, Australia
elspeth.mckay@rmit.edu.au
[2] School of Education, RMIT University, Melbourne, Australia
john.izard@rmit.edu.au

Abstract. To maintain knowledgeable, well skilled employees and sustain their competitive advantage, Government agencies and the corporate sector adopt online courseware designed for education and training. The instructional design of resulting human-computer interaction (HCI), which occurs during a training session, is left as an afterthought. No attention is given to the emergent socialized work-place where on the job training often involves collaborative partnerships. There are no measurable accounts of the effectiveness of sharing such knowledge and expertise with new employees. To this end, an experimental research study was designed to investigate the interactive effect of instructional strategies augmented with either a digital instructional assistant or a traditional class-room tutor, and participants' preference for training-mode on the acquisition of introductory ethics knowledge. Participants were given the Object-Spatial Imagery and Verbal Questionnaire (OSIVQ) to establish their cognitive style [1]. The QUEST Interactive Test Analysis System provided the cognitive performance measuring tool [2], to define the learning analytics and to ensure there were no measurement errors in the introductory ethics knowledge testing instruments. Therefore, reliability of the testing tools was secured through the QUEST calibration techniques, thereby safeguarding the predictability of the research design. The methodology embraced by this experimental research links HCI with the disciplines of instructional science, cognitive psychology and objective measurement to authenticate valuable mechanisms for adoption by the education, training and skills development sectors.

Keywords: Effective HCI courseware design · ePedagogy · Information communications technology (ICT) tools · Information systems (IS)-design · Online training · Web-designer

1 Introduction

To sustain their competitive advantage, the business sector and Government agencies are always keen to maintain well skilled and knowledgeable employees. A review of current government training practice reveals that key to achieving this desirable result is to adopt smarter use of our digital technologies. It is understandable that courseware

© Springer International Publishing Switzerland 2016
F.F.-H. Nah and C.-H. Tan (Eds.): HCIBGO 2016, Part II, LNCS 9752, pp. 183–195, 2016.
DOI: 10.1007/978-3-319-39399-5_18

designers mirror this continual quest for work-place education/training reform. It would seem from a review of current online training courseware offerings, that top of the Web-designer's list is the notion that virtual reality technologies may bring about optimal learning outcomes; regardless of whether the training is meant for new workers entering the work-force (novice learners), or the longer-term (experienced) workers who are simply wanting to refresh their skill profiles. In order to cater for such a diverse training audience, it is important to first differentiate what an individual knows, from what they do not. Yet knowing how to accurately measure people's understanding and skill remains a training dilemma, given the plethora of information communications technology (ICT) tools that are available for such expertise testing. The resulting outcome from this rather spurious skills pigeonholing technique is to expect employees to translate what they have learned during their training session into immediate (expert level) knowledge and skills in their work-place. To relieve these dilemmas, an HCI courseware design model is suggested as an online design benchmark to encourage corporate sector Web-designers to construct online courseware that will enable employees to remain engaged with their training materials.

The main aim of this paper is to describe the ramifications for effective human-computer interaction (HCI) courseware design arising from a funded research project conducted in Australia, differentiating what people do and do not know [3]. Referring to the model (see Fig. 10) which has been adapted from [4]; the main HCI factors remain as critical today as they were two decades ago. To make sense of the broad-reaching HCI design landscape, it is helpful to divide these factors into two aspects: human-dimension/machine-dimension [5]. These factors primarily relate to the users, highlighting awareness of the need to consider comfort and health, or work-place issues, or the technology deployed. The project described in this paper was primarily concerned with the interactive effects of individual's media preferences on their training outcomes. The human-dimensional factors therefore under consideration were: the user (cognitive processes and capabilities, experience level); user interface (easy/complex, novel, task allocation, repetitive, monitoring, skills components). While the machine-dimensional factors involved: constraints (costs, timescales, budgets, staff, and equipment); system functionality (hardware, software, application); and productivity factors (increases in: output, quality, creative and innovative ideas leading to new products; decreases in: costs, errors, labour requirements, production time). However, to set the context for the reader and before presenting the HCI implications of this project, it is necessary to provide a brief project overview. This project has been published elsewhere in more detail in a number of peer reviewed outlets, namely [3, 6, 7].

2   Project Overview

Due to the requirement from the Government sector to rely on continual employee reskilling, this project set out to facilitate cost effective eLearning, using advanced ICT tools to enhance work-place training with assured predictable training outcomes. The project deliverables involved: installing an 'electronic trainer/professional assistant' to an existing courseware shell; customised online knowledge navigation; and devising efficient and effective eLearning models of best practice in Government training. The initial work was commissioned by a government skill development agency to design and develop a training courseware management information system (CMIS), to enable government agencies to learn how to construct their own training/learning management systems. In 2008 the author was awarded an Australian Research Council (ARC) linkage project grant to add an 'intelligent-AGENT' to the CMIS as a virtual reality avatar or personal eTraining assistant.

Two new features were added to the original CMIS; an electronic personal assistant or avatar (Fig. 1), and a customising pedagogical feature offering online instructional preferences (Fig. 2). At the time, this was considered cutting edge ICT tool development. Technological avatars/digital-agents as they apply to Computer Science, are pieces of software that run without human control or constant supervision to accomplish an individual's training-goals. These agents will typically collect, filter, and process information during each employee's training session, thus playing an important role in balancing exploitation with exploration in knowledge discovery in corporate online training systems [8].

Fig. 1. System AGENT as virtual reality avatar   **Fig. 2.** System schematic model

The second innovation involved the adaptive/flexible eLearning/training tools that were embedded within the CMIS. At the time, these training tools were not prevalent in the government sector. Figure 2 shows how each trainee could determine their own knowledge/skill development path. For instance, novice trainees were given the full step-by-step skill development path; while a more experienced trainee could choose to only refresh certain aspects of their training. Clearly, understanding the online learners' instructional preferences, background knowledge levels, and concerns should enhance the usability and educational-IS design practice resulting in more effective Web-site training courseware [9].

3   Research Design and Methodology

The research question addressed in this project involved an investigation of the interactive effect of learning preference and instructional mode on participants' learning outcomes. A quasi-experimental 3 × 3 research design was employed to carry out the work. The independent variables were identified as learning preference (training mode, experience with eLearning, and work mode training expectation - see Fig. 3) and training strategy (online, face-to-face, and blended online/face-to-face, see Fig. 4).

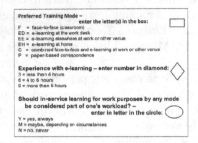

Instructional Strategies	Basic Ethics Knowledge		
	Pre-Test score	Post-Test Score	Performance Improvement
Face-to-Face	A	B	B-A
Blended	X	Y	Y-X
Computerised	C	D	D-C

Fig. 3. Preferred instructional/learning mode   **Fig. 4.** Change in intro to ethics knowledge

3.1   Research Instruments

Test instruments were prepared for a Pilot Study [3] and a Main Experiment to evaluate attainment status with respect to knowledge of 'introductory ethics,' and the extent to which this knowledge can be interpreted in specific contexts. The intention was to prepare a range of items to evaluate multiple levels of knowledge, in accord with research [10] that showed a rectangular distribution of item difficulty over an extended range of achievement was the most effective in detecting achievement status. Without effective measurement of achievement status, one would have difficulty in measuring changes in achievement status as a consequence of a learning intervention [11]. The skill assessment instruments involved only open-ended test-items, as it was judged that a constructed response was the appropriate indication of (ethics) knowledge. Table 1 shows the content-skills coverage of the tests used in the Main Study.

The matrix of scored person responses to each of the test-items was subject to quality control procedures using item response modeling with the 'QUEST interactive test analysis system' [2]. Central to QUEST is a measurement model developed in 1960 by the Danish statistician Rasch [12]. The initial analysis of the pre-test with QUEST used an iterative procedure to describe the uni-dimensional scale with equal intervals along the vertical axis, to represent individual performance (case achievement) and test-item difficulty on the same scale. The estimation procedure investigated the probability of an individual with a particular level of achievement making particular responses to a range of test-items. The diagram showing the pattern of cases (persons) and test-items is known as a variable map (see Fig. 5). Test-items in common with the post-test were fixed (anchored) at the difficulty established for the pre-test so that any changes in achievement as a consequence of the intervention could be evaluated accurately.

3.2   Participants

Overall there were 40 Government workers and 33 vocational students involved in the experiments. Invitations were sent to Government workers through a non-government training consultant (for the Focus Groups and a Pilot Study); while a vocational training

Table 1. Pre-post testing instrument design

Summary of content and context	Main Pre-Test	Main Post-Test
State the key idea of accountability	1 (1)	1 (1)
Name an essential quality of an ethical person	2 (1)	2 (1)
Case Study A: Describes an event where a friend needs urgent medical attention and the issues arising from actions taken to meet that need.		
Case Study A: Note a behaviour adopted for personal-responsibility reasons	3 (1)	3 (1)
Case Study A: Note a behaviour adopted for ethical reasons	4 (1)	4 (1)
Case Study A: Note a decision not precisely covered by protocol but sufficiently similar to be made through judgment		5 (1)
Case Study A: Note a decision that illustrates improper use of status		6 (1)
Case Study B: Provides a protocol on bullying and describes its implementation by a manager with responsibility for doing so.		
Case Study B: Note a decision that complies with the protocol	5 (1)	
Case Study B: Note a decision not precisely covered by protocol but sufficiently similar for an experienced officer to deal with it using discretion	6 (1)	
Case Study B: Note a decision that illustrates improper use of status	7 (1)	
Case Study B: State the most important ethical problem needing to be addressed	8 (1)	7 (1)
Case Study B: Note four distinct stakeholders	9 (4)	8 (4)
Case Study B: Consider all possible alternative ethical solutions and state the best	10 (1)	9 (1)
Case Study B: State why your solution is best	11 (1)	10 (1)
Case Study C: Describes a situation where a private purchase may be discounted because the provider is aware of your potentially influential work role in purchasing.		
Case Study C: State the ethical dilemma	12 (1)	11 (1)
Case Study C: Name a stakeholder and state the stakeholder's interest	13 (2)	12 (2)
Case Study C: Name a second stakeholder with different interests and state the second stakeholder's interest	14 (2)	13 (2)
Case Study C: What would be the right thing to do?	15 (1)	14 (1)
Case Study C: Why is this the right thing to do?	16 (1)	15 (1)
Case Study B: State the ethical dilemma		
Case Study D: Describes a similar situation to Case Study C but where a private purchase by your boss is discounted because the provider is aware of your boss's potentially influential work role in purchasing, leading to a breach of ethics.		
Case Study D: State the ethical dilemma		16 (1)
Case Study D: Who are the stakeholders?		17 (6)
Case Study D: Given your awareness of ethics policy, what is your next step?		18 (1)
Case Study D: If you did not comply, how would you explain this?		19 (1)

Note: The order of item numbers for each test is shown. The numeral in parentheses shows the maximum score for that item.

institute invited students (for the Main Experiment). The researchers were informed that many of these participants had no previous experience with an ethics training course.

4 Data Analysis

The eLearning outcomes were evaluated in terms of the magnitude of change in participant proficiency magnitude of effect size as defined by Cohen's statistical power analysis [13]. The QUEST instigated Rasch analysis [14] generated a set of hypotheses regarding the interactive dynamics of skill development with and without ICT-tools as training mediation techniques. QUEST allows for improved analyses of an individual's performance relative to other participants [15], and relative to the test-item difficulty of introductory ethics knowledge levels. See an example of this in Fig. 5, where each participant or 'case' is depicted by an 'x,' and test-items are shown on the right-side of the map. The Rasch Item Response Theory (IRT) estimates the probability of an individual making a certain response to a test-item. The pre- and post-test results were analysed with a test-item matrix that had each individual's responses for every test-item recorded. Common test-items (identically worded questions) were 'anchored' so that scale scores on the pre-test were comparable with scale scores on the post-test. The difference between pre-test and post-test scaled scores indicated whether learning occurred, whether no learning occurred, or whether the instructional strategy resulted in reduced achievement (see Fig. 8).

Figure 5 shows an annotated QUEST variable map revealing that participants **X11**, **X12**, and **X18** achieved the same level of knowledge at a scale score of −0.80. The colour of the numeral indicates the treatment group (black is face-to-face T1, **green is blended T2**, and **red is computerised T3**). Participants X07, **X15**, and **X30** achieved the same level of knowledge at a scale score of 1.10 close to the average difficulty of the pre-test (0.0), and this level was higher than participants **X11, X12**, and **X18**. This annotated variable map also shows that scoring a 1 on item-5 is more difficult than scoring a 1 on item-12. Getting item-19 correct is easier than scoring 2 or more on either item-16 or item-18. Scoring 4 on item-17 is easier that scoring 2 or more on either item-16 or item-18. Scoring a 2 on item-5.2 is the most difficult achievement. The probability basis of the model is illustrated by the position of participants **X05, X08**, and X32 at an achievement level of 1.56. These participants are more likely than not to score 1 on items-15, -16, and -18 and 3 on item-17.

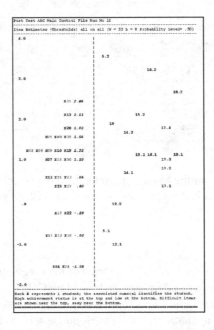

Fig. 5. Annotated QUEST variable map - Post-test (Color figure online)

As reported by Adams and Khoo (1996), the QUEST software package provides item fit statistics. The mean square fit statistics provide a useful way of judging the compatibility of the model and the data. An item to the right of the right-hand dotted line in the diagram (see Fig. 6 for item-13 in this example) shows more variation from the model than expected. As such items are removed from the test. Items to the left of the left-hand dotted line in the diagram indicate less variation than expected (see Fig. 7).

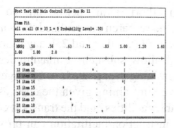

Fig. 6. QUEST fit map misfitting item-13   **Fig. 7.** QUEST fit map - item-13 removed

Learning outcomes were evaluated in terms of the magnitude of change in participant proficiency (magnitude of effect size as defined by Izard's adaptation [11] of Cohen's statistical power analysis [13].

5 Findings

We show the gains in knowledge of introductory ethics achievement for three training treatment groups; face-to-face, computerised and a blend of both. Having access to our individual virtual learning space is critical; this project places Australia at the centre of training through a pseudo virtual reality environment.

As reported in [7], there are three directly parallel sets of data: one set (traditional classroom facilitator-led, T1) for the training sessions not using computer mediation at all or to any significant degree for the whole training period, one set (T2) that comprising a blended training approach that implements both traditional face-to-face and electronic instructional tools, and the third set (T3) for the training environments using the eLearning strategies as a central instructional tool for a whole training period. These data-sets are comparable because they involve the same training facilitators (whose knowledge of the business process and technical competence in eLearning has been identified as of an equally high standard to their general work-place/industry sector training competence), and working with various government employees/trainees in the same locations for each training session. It has been possible to identify paradigmatic differences between the levels of government practice, and demographic variations (time of service, gender and previous education) that may affect the training dynamics and training outcomes across and within the three training environments. Learning outcomes were illustrated by combining the achievement status measures from the Pre-Test with the anchored achievement status measures from the Post-Test, as shown in the following diagram (Fig. 8).

It is important to note that while many participants made progress (shown ▲), some participants in each treatment failed to make progress (shown ▼). It is also necessary to note that many of the changes are of a substantial magnitude, even though the effectiveness of the respective learning interventions (whether online only, a mixture of face-to-face and online, or face-to-face only) was being judged with the same test. Averaging the results shows that T1 group improved by 1.63, T2 group by 1.74, and the T3 group by 1.41.

Despite the expectation of substantial gains with a short training period (around 2 h) is unrealistic for these instructional treatments [7]; the research has realised the anticipated results. Future investigations should include a 1-day, 2-day and 2 + day training sessions to infer the duration of training that will allow substantive magnitudes of learning to be detected. Similarly, the size of each training group needs to be larger: it is difficult to justify such small groups being involved in training given the costs associated with providing trainers, the provision of suitable facilities, and the transport costs for both presenters and participants. Face-to-face instruction/facilitation can provide more opportunities for timely feedback to participants. Moreover further feedback can add opportunities to the eLearning training strategy so that there is greater control of the magnitude of feedback which may be an alternative explanation of differential learning. Secondly, limiting the learning area to a single content area (such as 'an introduction to ethics') would provide no evidence of the extent to which the information obtained generalizes to other online-learning/training content areas. Additional instructional (content) areas therefore need to be added, with sufficient time allowed for the research team and the industry partners to generate appropriate eLearning content, and the assessments (the pre- and post-tests).

In the Pilot Study, the ethics pre-test showed an internal consistency of 0.61 without deleting or adding test-items. This value needed to be improved by using the analysis to modify some test-items, and perhaps to move some test-items from the post-test to the pre-test so both tests are of comparable internal consistency and accuracy [16]. In the Pilot Study, the 'ethics post-test' showed an internal consistency of 0.77 without deleting any test-items. Refinement of this test by deleting some test-items that failed to detect any differences between participants with knowledge and participants lacking knowledge on the dimension of interest (applied knowledge of ethics), would serve to improve the evaluation of post-training knowledge. The complexity of the 'ethics' case studies used in the face-to-face group may well be affecting the post-test evidence of achievement. This shows when participants identify stakeholders (for example), but do not choose the best solution or explain why that is so. Providers of eLearning materials must be able to demonstrate the extent to which learning has occurred. In this case it was made known that some participants did not learn about ethics. Consequently this

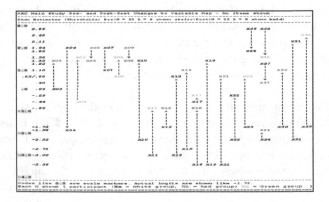

Fig. 8. Learning outcomes

result is worthy of further investigation. However, it was demonstrated that overall learning was positive for the group.

6 Discussion

As mentioned earlier, the research was especially examining the interactive effects of individual's media preferences on their training outcomes. Therefore to unpick the far-reaching HCI design landscape, this project has been helpful in dividing the HCI-design factors of the training courseware management information system (CMIS) into two aspects: human-dimension/machine-dimension [5]. A key project motivation was to adopt a user-centric focus, highlighting awareness of the need to consider comfort and health, or work-place issues, or the technology deployed. So doing, the human-dimensional factors that were under consideration were: the user (cognitive processes and capabilities, experience level); user interface (easy/complex, novel, task allocation, repetitive, monitoring, skills components). So far as the user-HCI factor the participants' cognitive processes were identified in a Object-Spatial Imagery and Verbal Questionnaire (OSIVQ) devised by [1] as a self-report questionnaire for locating the participants' preferences for adopting mental imagery versus verbal representations. The capabilities and experience levels were captured in the pre- and post-tests; while the user interface underwent considerable work prior to the experimentation which closely followed the Merrill Principles of Instruction [17]. Consequently, the following ePedagogical strategies (Fig. 9) were provided in the opening screens of the training courseware management information system (CMIS):

RULES: Just the Facts. Here is where you will be given all the facts about each new topic. To enable you to reach each new LEARNINING OUTCOME. Some people call this part of your training, the FACT LESSON.
EXAMPLES: It's like this. Here are some ways to highlight the concept you are currently working with. While you experience these ones it may be a good idea to think of some other ones that you know about. Perhaps write them down – on a note pad that you may keep beside your computer while you are training.
NON-EXAMPLES: It's never like this. It is very important to also show you things that do not fit into the topic/task or activity – just so that you can think about the types of things that DO NOT REPRESENT THE REAL CONCEPT.
KINDS-of-LESSON: It's kind of like this. Identifying a new object, doing a new activity, or trying out a new process (like filing in a FORM to borrow a book from a library).
PARTS-of-LESSON: It's part of this. Knowing the parts of something or the location of something within the bigger picture; this is really good when you need to learn about new terminology; locations; and the controls of a device.
TRY ME: Have a go. Most people like to try doing something new first. Here is where you can let yourself go; so relax and participate in the exercises to give you some idea of whether you can achieve the required LEARNING OUTCOME.
SHOW ME: Here is the final testing of your performance. If you pass this task – you will be informed by eMail (when the system is functioning in a real training environment). However, if you do not pass – you need to review the earlier RULES – and repeat the learning module again.

Fig. 9. ePedagogical strategies (adapted from Merrill 2002)

While it has been easier to determine that the project's main focus was on the user-centred (human-dimension) aspects of the HCI, the machine-dimension factors were brought to light through interpretation of the findings. The machine-dimensional HCI-factors involved: constraints (costs, timescales, budgets, staff, and equipment); system functionality (hardware, software, application); and productivity factors (increases in: output, quality, creative and innovative ideas leading to new products; decreases in: costs, errors, labour requirements, production time). So far as the machine-dimension the ramifications for effective HCI courseware design arising from this project, differentiate what people do and do not know [3]. The project described herein will facilitate cost effective eLearning practice using advanced ICT tools to enhance work-place training with assured predictable outcomes. The most desirable training approach is to personalise an employee's knowledge development through flexible online learning. Improved IT governance serves to motivate disinterested trainees and energise frustrated management. However, within this digital training realm multi-disciplined specialists are required to resolve the factional dilemmas of corporate IT resource ownership. The timeliness of our project will highlight desirable change management issues to improve efficiencies and effectiveness of existing IT training resources (see Fig. 10). It is proposed that this project has unearthed evidence to support the extension of the earlier mentioned HCI model as proposed by [2]. This project has highlighted the diversity of government participant/trainee characteristics and how these diverse attributes affect their instructional outcomes.

Fig. 10. Human diversity of human-computer interaction dimensions

6.1 Human-Dimension - Trainee Interactions

When considering the Government factors involved within the human-dimensions of HCI it is worth considering that in many places around the world Web 2.0 continues to be promoted as the new incarnation of the Internet because of the social networking aspects afforded by the supporting technologies. This general acceptance may be due to the evolutionary nature of the whole Internet environment per se. As a result, there are many ways to view the term Web 2.0, in the sense that it represents both a range of ICT tools that enable the business sector to profit by, as well as the meme-like characteristics that imply a certain agreement or states of mind [18]. It is the latter definition that sets the broader context for this paper to expand the discussion beyond the popular generation of Web applications and sites that enable openness, interaction and new communities to flourish [19]. As far as the CMIS reflects the capacity to deal with 'group diversity factors,' because the popular notions of the Web 2.0 as we know today, extend beyond the more traditional view of Web 2.0 to mean any type of Web-based (user) collaborative behaviours that occur when people are learning new skills. This link was made when the first concepts of online or Web-based learning were developed in the 1960s at the University of Illinois through the creation of a computer-based education environment called PLATO (Programmed Logic for Automatic Teaching Operations), designed for delivery to university students. As such, PLATO paved the way for online communities

[20] to include: Web application development tools, discussion forums, message boards, interactive testing, e-mail, chat rooms, picture languages, instant messaging, remote screen sharing, and multi-player gaming [21]. There seemed no end to the rise of the Web 2.0 possibilities until the dotcom bubble burst; encouraging the pessimists to await the demise of eCommerce. Despite their warnings the Web survived and since then we have witnessed a resurgence of the Internet according to ref [22].

6.2 Machine-Dimension - System Functionality

It is anticipated that more concentrated research on the design and development of flexible embedded eMentoring strategies will encourage people wanting to update their skills and to access Web-mediated programmes in a just-in-time or on-demand basis. To this end, the project team is committed to provide the instructional/training tools to other business partner units. Moreover, when the newly created Web-based knowledge-navigational/learning aids are further developed and replicated (or customised by other government departments and industry sector organisations), it is anticipated they will find the knowledge navigation tools to be practical and easily adaptable to include other instructional/learning streams. Furthermore, the innovative instructional package is designed to be uploaded to a corporate Intranet. This project has therefore succeeded in its initial endeavour to champion a research that involves an investigation of sound instructional strategies that underpin a CMIS with the capability of providing a Web-mediated (self-guided) eMentoring service for government employees while engaging in their online training. Based on previous work identified within this paper, it is suggested that these strategies add to the previous body of work and may in time contribute to the theoretical understanding of how to evaluate Web-mediated learning reinforcement.

The paper has discussed the project results through the lens of the above model. It is further suggested here that the human-dimensions of HCI can be defined as the social networking that offers the strategic Web 2.0 glue for successful adaptive online training which is often lacking [5]. However, the human-dimensions of HCI are but one piece of the complicated computer-usability or techno-puzzle because it involves two distinct contexts. One relates to the human-dimension or social context of computing, while the other relates to the machine-side, with people's perspectives being shaped by the performance of the technical computing components. Until very recently, the literature has dealt more often with the latter. It is only in recent times that a voice has been given to computer-usability issues that involve the human-dimensions (or the social networking aspects).

Acknowledgements. This research project was funded by the Australian Research Council (ARC), involving industry partners: RMIT University, School of Business Information Technology and Logistics, Government Skills Australia and NetEffective Media Inc.

References

1. Blazhenkova, O., Kozhevnikov, M.: The new object-spatial-verbal cognitive style model: theory and measurement. Appl. Cogn. Psychol. **23**(5), 638–663 (2009)
2. Adams, R.J., Khoo, S.-T.: QUEST: The Interactive Test Analysis System. Australian Council for Educational Research, Melbourne (1996)
3. McKay, E., Izard, J. F.: Online training design: workforce reskilling in government agencies. In: IC3e 2014 IEEE Conference on eLearning, eManagement and Services, Swinburne University, Melbourne, pp. 70–75. IEEE (2014)
4. Preece, J., Rogers, Y., Sharp, H.: Interaction Design: Beyond Human-Computer Interaction. Addison-Wesley, Harlow (2002)
5. McKay, E.: The Human-Dimensions of Human-Computer Interaction: Balancing the HCI Equation. IOS Press, Amsterdam (2008)
6. McKay, E., Izard, J.: Seamless web-mediated training courseware design model: innovating adaptive educational-learning systems. In: Peña-Ayala, A. (ed.) Intelligent and Adaptive ELS. SIST, vol. 17, pp. 417–441. Springer, Heidelberg (2013)
7. McKay, E., Izard, J.F.: Evaluate online training effectiveness: differentiate what they do and do not know. In: 8th International Conference on ICT, Society and Human Beings 2015 (Multi conference on computer science and information systems - MCCSIS). Las Palmas de Gran Canaria, Spain, MCCSIS (2015)
8. Murthy, V.K.: Contextual knowledge management in peer to peer computing: applications to mobile-multiplayer games and robotics. Int. J. Knowl.-Based Intell. Eng. Syst. **9**(4), 303–314 (2005). IOS Press, Amsterdam
9. Lawrence, D., Tavakol, S.: Balanced Website Design Optimising Aesthetics, Usability and Purpose. Springer, London (2007)
10. Izard, J.F.: Quality assurance: asking the right questions. In: 32nd Annual Conference of the International Association Assessment, Singapore, 21–26 May 2006
11. Izard, J.: Gathering evidence for learning. In: Jeffrey, P.L. (ed.) Paper presented at the Australian Association for Research Education (AARE 2004). positioning education research, held Melbourne (2004). http://www.aare.edu.au/data/publications/2004/iza04877.pdf
12. Rasch, G.: Probabilistic Models for Some Intelligence and Attainment Tests. Nielsen & Lydiche, Copenhagen (1960)
13. Cohen, J.: Statistical Power Analysis for the Behavioral Sciences. Academic Press, New York (1977)
14. Bond, T.G., Fox, C.M.: Applying the Rasch Model: Fundamental Measurement in the Human Sciences. Lawrence Erlbaum, New Jersey (2007)
15. McKay, E.: Measurement of cognitive performance in computer programming concept acquisition: interactive effects of visual metaphors and the cognitive style construct. J. Appl. Measur. **1**(3), 257–286 (2000)
16. Izard, J.F.: Best practice in assessment for learning. In: Third Conference of the Association of Commonwealth Examinations and Accreditation Bodies on Redefining the Roles of Educational Assessment. Nadi, Fiji South Pacific Board for Educational Assessment, March 2004
17. Merrill, M.D.: First principles of instruction. ETR&D **50**(3), 43–59 (2002). http://www.indiana.edu/~tedfrick/aect2002/firstprinciplesbymerrill.pdf
18. Allen, C.: Creating shared language and shared artifacts, Life with Alacrity. Life with Alacrity (2009)

19. Millard, D.E., Ross, M.: Web 2.0: hypertext by any other name? In: 17th ACM Conference on Hypertext and Hypermedia, pp. 27–30. ACM Press, Odense, Denmark (2005)
20. Woolley, D.R.: PLATO: The Emergence of Online Community (1994). http://thinkofit.com/plato/dwplato.htm 23-20-15
21. O'Reiley, T.: Web 3.0? Maybe When We Get There (2006). http://radar.oreilly.com/2006/11/web-30-maybe-when-we-get-there.html 24-10-15
22. McCormack, D.A.: Web 2.0: The Future of the Internet and Technology Economy and How Entrepreneurs, Investors, Executives and Consumers Can Take Advantage, ExeceNablers (2002)

"Core" Components in HCI Syllabi: Based on the Practice of CS and LIS Schools in North America

Lei Pei[1($\boxtimes$)] and Qiping Zhang[2]

[1] School of Information Management, Nanjing University, Nanjing, China
plei@nju.edu.cn
[2] Palmer School of Library and Information Science,
Long Island University, Brookville, USA
Qiping.Zhang@liu.edu

Abstract. The "core" of HCI education remains debatable because of its multidiscipline nature. This paper developed an integrated HCI classification schema of teaching topics. A content analysis with 104 HCI syllabi from 28 computer science and 23 library and information science programs in North America revealed no significant differences between two programs. The social network analysis of co-occurrence 2280 teaching topics in courses identified 9 HCI core course components and 4 topic clusters. Three teaching styles emerged in social network analysis of university co-occurrence network. In conclusion, it is suggested that HCI educators should design syllabi or curricula according to their own contexts.

Keywords: HCI education · Syllabi map · Content analysis · Social network analysis

1 Introduction

Human Computer Interaction (HCI) has ever been defined as sub-discipline, multi-disciplinary or interdisciplinary field since late 1960s (Gasen 1996). When computer human interface design (CHI) was first introduced into higher education system, it was a sub-discipline of computer graphics, studying mainly on CAD/CAM, ergonomics and some separated disciplines. But in late 1970s, scholars recognized the multidiscipline nature of HCI, and tried to combine independent areas to create a new discipline. Based on previous research (Denning et al. 1988), HCI has already evolved into one of the nine core areas of Computer Science in 1980s. When an authoritative report ("Lime Green Report") was issued by ACM SIGCHI in 1992, HCI was clearly defined as: "*a discipline concerned with the design, evaluation and implementation of interactive computing systems for human use and with the study of major phenomena surrounding them.*"(Hewett et al. 1992), which manifested the coming of HCI multi-discipline paradigm. Currently, HCI is also viewed as one of the eleven elective courses in IS field (Topi et al. 2010).

Although HCI education has been greatly developed, the knowledge structure of this "emerging" discipline remains unclear. The first survey of HCI education

© Springer International Publishing Switzerland 2016
F.F.-H. Nah and C.-H. Tan (Eds.): HCIBGO 2016, Part II, LNCS 9752, pp. 196–208, 2016.
DOI: 10.1007/978-3-319-39399-5_19

(Mantel and Smelcer 1984) confirmed the emergence of systematical HCI education by scholars in computer graphics, human factor, and industrial psychology, but had no report on the knowledge structure of HCI courses.

To identify the core of HCI education, Gary Perlman and Jean Gasen have been conducting a systematic survey on HCI education since fall 1992 following ACM SIGCHI's curricular program (Gasen 1994a, b, 1994c, 1995a, b 1996, 1997). According to Gasen's report (Gasen 1994a), there were already 67 programs, 160 faculty and 137 courses included in 1993, but they found "HCl Education still on the fringes", lacking "awareness, support and demand", need more supports in further development.

During 2000–2005, there were nearly half of published HCI education papers proposed recognition or further integration (Edwards 2006). Educators worried about the failure of HCI education, argued "the characteristics of a living HCI curriculum" (Lazar et al. 2002). Some researchers complained that educators had little understanding of HCI's multidisciplinary context (Carroll 2003), for lacking of updated data and tools for unstructured data analysis in HCI.

Current researches noticed the diffusion of global consensus as well as localized application in HCI education (Churchill et al. 2013; Boscarioli et al. 2013; Oestreicher 2013), but educators still questioned the core and methodologies in HCI education in terms of multidisciplinary rigor, pedagogical transitions, and new paradigms (Grandhi 2015). A 2011–2014 SIGCHI Project on IICI Education highlighted that the shared understanding of the HCI curriculum is challenged by the competing tensions of standardized vs. flexible curricula, breadth vs. depth of interdisciplinary theories and methods covered, need for technical vs. nontechnical skills, and other conflicts (Churchill 2014).

How can educators adapt to HCI evolvements? In this paper, a content analysis of HCI syllabi is to reveal the most frequent topics, and a social network analysis of teaching topics is to excavate the relationships of topics and the knowledge structure of HCI courses.

2   Related Work

In order to develop a coding schema for HCI syllabi topics, related HCI classification systems, HCI curriculum and research frameworks are reviewed in the following.

2.1   Classification Systems in HCI

Classification systems are not only covering all the terms occurred in this area, but also well-organized by hierarchy or ontology. ACM issued many hierarchy classification systems to organize and control published papers in computer science since 1964, and the latest edition is released in 2012. In 1982, "Computer Graphics", "Computer-communication networks", "Human factors" were first introduced in the system. In 1998, "H.5 INFORMATION INTERFACES AND PRESENTATION (e.g., HCI)" was created as an independent category with 5 sub-categories and 41 items (Coulter et al. 1998). In 2012, the category occurred as first level (Human-centered computing) and broadened to 6 sub-categories and 112 items (CCS2012). But the granularity of this classification is challenged with rapid growing HCI publications.

2.2 Curriculum and Research Frameworks in HCI

Curriculum framework, covering the main topics and major themes occurred in teaching, is quite suitable for syllabi tagging as organization tools. There are two important HCI curriculum frameworks.

The first one was proposed by ACM SIGCHI Curriculum Development Group. The first edition was released in 1984, merely focused on the curriculum structure and tried to select the major themes to "inventory the current state of results in the field of human-computer interaction". In 1992, Hewett etc. issued a framework (NUHCD-P) with 5 aspects content structure of 16 groups, covering almost all the topics that were known and worth teaching (Hewett et al. 1992). This is the most cited framework in HCI education structure research, although 20 years passed.

The second one was proposed by the Joint Task Force on Computing Curricula ACM. They issued curriculum guidelines every five or ten years since 1968. The latest curricular volumes was released in 2013 (CS2013) (Sahami et al. 2013). In Sahami's report, HCI was listed as one core "knowledge body" and covered 10 domains and 86 items.

In addition, (Zhang and Galletta 2006) proposed a HCI research framework covering major HCI research issues.

3 Method

3.1 HCI Syllabi Collection in North America

While most HCI programs reside in CS (computer science) departments (64 %) (Gasen 1994a), many LIS (library and information science) schools also host HCI courses/programs. Thus HCI syllabi were collected from both CS and LIS programs for this study. The weekly topics and course schedule were extracted from HCI syllabi for the analysis of knowledge structure of HCI education.

Collecting Syllabi Data in CS. A random sampling of 28 CS programs was chosen from hundreds of computer science programs all around North America (see Table 1). Then 35 syllabi of HCI and related courses were collected from above program websites. Finally HCI topics (682 records and 917 items) are extracted from syllabi.

Collecting Syllabi Data in LIS. According to LIS courses database (Self-built, updated in September 2015, and tagged by ALISE Classification Schema, data collected from the curriculum of LIS school), there are more than 150 courses classified into HCI, and 118 of them located in North American, affiliating to 43 LIS programs (73 % of all LIS schools). Among 43 organizations and 118 courses, 69 syllabi of 23 LIS program (see Table 1) are publically available. For HCI topics, 970 records and 1400 items are extracted.

Table 1. List of CS and LIS programs for HCI syllabi of this study

CS programs	LIS programs
1. Worcester Polytechnic Institute	1. Wayne State University
2. Vanderbilt University	2. University of Pittsburgh
3. University of Wisconsin–Madison	3. University of Western Ontario
4. University of Stanford	4. University of Washington
5. University of Maryland, Baltimore County	5. University of Texas at Austin
6. University of Manitoba	6. University of Tennessee
7. University of Maine	7. University of Syracus
8. University of Iowa	8. University of Pittsburgh
9. University of Hawaii	9. University of North Texas
10. University of Florida	10. University of North Carolina, Chapel Hill
11. University of Cornell	11. University of Michigan
12. University of California, San Diego	12. University of Maryland
13. Tufts University	13. University of Illinois
14. The University of the West Indies	14. University of Hawaii
15. The University of Texas at El Paso	15. University of Alberta
16. The Pennsylvania State University	16. University of California at Berkeley
17. SUNY Buffalo	17. Rutgers, The State University of New Jersey
18. Nova Southeastern University	18. Queens College/CUNY
19. Northeastern University	19. Pratt Institute
20. North Carolina State University	20. North Carolina Central University
21. Mississippi State University	21. Long Island University
22. Loyola University	22. Indiana University
23. Georgia Institute of Technology	23. Drexel University
24. Dalhousie University	
25. Carnegie Mellon University	
26. Carleton University	
27. Arizona State University	
28. Stevens Institute of Technology	

3.2   Procedure

Step 1: *Topic extraction*. Focused on pure theories and terms mentioned in course schedule, coders extracted terms from the description of "course chapter" or "week chapter" in raw data separately, an initial consistency between two coders reached 82.5 %, 1927 terms in common among a total 2336 terms. After group discussion, 56 terms were deleted, remaining 2280 terms.

Step 2: *Development of an integrated HCI classification schema*. A classification schema was initially developed based on previous related work reviewed in Sect. 2 of this paper. Then all 2280 terms from Step 1 were coded by two coders. In order to keep our classification schema being exhaustive and inclusive for the sampled syllabi, domain (level 1) and category (level 2) codes were revised, merged, reorganized through iterative discussions and coding comparisons.

Table 2 showed our integrated HCI classification schema as a result of this iterative process. Inter-coder reliability as measured by Cohen Kappa was 0.96 for the domain coding, and 0.77 for the category coding.

Table 2. An integrated HCI classification schema

Domain	Category
Foundations/nature of HCI	General introduction
	Theoretic foundations/models
	Research methods/topics
Human aspects of HCI	Human characteristics
	User experience and behavior
	Group & communities
Computing aspects of HCI	Computer
	Web technology
	Ubiquitous and mobile computing
	Systems and application
	System & engineering skills & tools
Interaction of HCI	Interaction devices/technology
	Information interaction
	Designing interaction/interface
	Interactive behavior
Development process	Design process\approaches and methods
	System analysis & requirements
	Conception design
	Prototyping
	Programming and implementation
	Tutorial, demo & running
	Testing & evaluation
	Example systems and case studies
Application & context	Context analysis
	Collaborative & social computing
	Mixed, augmented and virtual reality
	Copyright and security
	Other application
Teaching issues	Lecture
	Capstone/project
	Team work
	Guest lecture
	Report
	Review
	Exam
	Presentation

4 Data Analyses

4.1 Descriptive Analysis of Teaching Topics Distribution

Level 1 - Domain Distribution in CS and LIS Schools. Choosing domain as topic descriptor, there is no difference between CS and LIS schools. The similarity is as big as 99.5 %, which is calculated by correlations of domain counts' distribution, and 98.5 % of domain frequency distribution. There is only a little difference in the domain of "Computing Factors of HCI", with the total frequency of 8 % in CS versus 4.6 % in LIS (See Fig. 1).

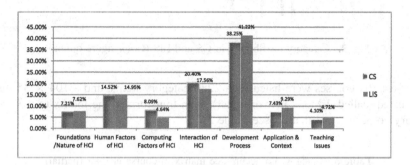

Fig. 1. Domain distribution in CS and LIS (Color figure online)

According to domain counts, the "core" of HCI teaching measured by the top 3 highest frequent domains are: "Development Process", "Interaction of HCI" and "Human Aspects of HCI".

Level 2 - Category Distribution in CS and LIS Schools. Choosing category as topic descriptor, there is still no significant difference between CS and LIS schools, concerning the similarity of 85.3 % calculated by the correlations of counts distribution (See Fig. 2).

Taking a TFIDF-like method, which created a characteristic index (CI) calculated by the count frequency in LIS group dividing the count frequency in CS group, we can find some particular topics in each group (CI > 2). In CS schools, their characteristic categories are: "Copyright and Security", "Example Systems and Case Studies", "Tutorial, Demo & Running", "Interaction Devices/Technology", "System & Engineering Skills & Tools" and "Computer". In LIS schools, characteristic categories are: "Information Interaction", "Context" and "User Experience and Behavior".

4.2 Social Networks Analysis of Course Co-occurrence Network

4.2.1 Construction of Co-occurrence Network

Teaching category co-occurrence relationship is defined as two categories which occurring in the same course. When constructing category co-occurrence relationship

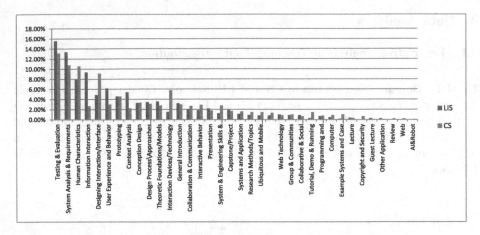

Fig. 2. Category distribution in CS and LIS (Color figure online)

in courses, 104 courses were listed with 2280 category items, and a 104 × 35 matrix was created (called 2-Mode network later), then transformed the matrix to a 35 × 35 category co-occurrence matrix (see Table 3).

Table 3. Category co-occurrence matrix in course chapter (partial)

	Capstone/project	Collaboration & communication	Collaborative & social computing	Computer	Conception design	Context	Copyright and security
Capstone/project	41	9	4	5	19	16	1
Collaboration & communication	9	53	11	7	9	18	3
Collaborative & social computing	4	11	18	1	4	9	1
Computer	5	7	1	14	7	6	1
Conception design	19	9	4	7	75	16	2
Context	16	18	9	6	16	94	4
Copyright and security	1	3	1	1	2	4	7

Centrality Analysis

The centrality of network indicates the "necessary" or popular topics in course design according to existing practices. Figure 3 shows the collapse of "core" in co-occurrence network: when frequency of co-occurrence increased from 20 to 40, the core clusters' size decreased from 17 to 9 (when choose 50 as parameter, the number of points comes down to 3), thus these 9 points could be named as the "necessary" or basic teaching sets, which are: General Introduction, Human Characteristics, Design Process\Methods \Approaches, System Analysis & Requirements, Conception Design, Prototyping, Design Interaction\Interface, Testing & Evaluation, User Experience and Behavior.

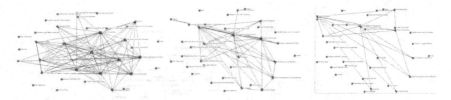

Fig. 3. Collapse of "core" in category co-occurrence network

4.2.2 Cluster Analysis

Transform the 2-Mode network into category-category relationship network, and using two-dimensional MDS analysis by dissimilarity. Figure 4 shows the categories' clusters map, categories co-occurred frequently would be placed near each other in the map. The clusters of teaching topics show that categories can be classified into four distinct fields: Information Aspects, Technical Aspects, Behavioral Aspects and System Design.

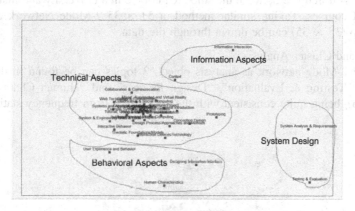

Fig. 4. Multidimensional scaling analysis of HCI categories by course title

4.2.3 Similarity Analysis

Besides that, these categories have weak relationship evaluated by the similarity of distribution among courses, and this relationship may indicate the style of teaching. Figure 5 shows the relationship of categories (similarity > 0.2), and 3 points formed the core "components", which are "Interaction Devices/Technology", "Designing Interaction/Interface" and "System Analysis & Requirements"(See Fig. 5). When choosing closeness as centrality judgment, "Interaction Devices/Technology", "System & Engineering Skills & Tools" and "Designing Interaction/Interface" are in the center.

The experimental result demonstrates that system design and technical analysis is the consensus of foundation in HCI teaching.

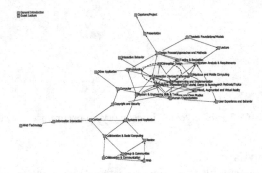

Fig. 5. Categories centrality in category co-occurrence network

4.3   Social Networks Analysis of University Co-occurrence Network

According to heterogeneous distribution of HCI courses in different institutes, we take university as container in the co-occurrence network construction. In this case, there would be less difference between the solo HCI course in a university and that one of a set of HCI courses. Taking similar method, a 51 × 35 2-Mode Network and topic cluster map (35 × 35) can be drawn through the data.

Centrality and Cluster Analysis
Taking the 2-Mode network as analysis object, 3 topics can be found in the center, which are "Testing & Evaluation", "Design Process" and "Human Characteristics" (See Fig. 6), being quite consistent with the conclusion from frequency statistics.

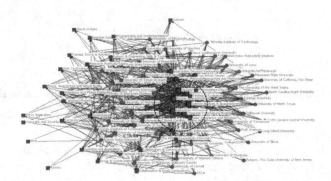

Fig. 6. Centered categories in university_Topic 2-mode network

Compared with Fig. 4, only 3 classes were extracted in the cluster map (See Fig. 7), which means information issues in HCI and behavioral aspects can be merged in university-category co-occurrence scale.

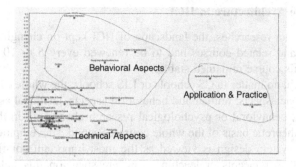

Fig. 7. Multidimensional scaling analysis of HCI categories by university

4.4 Teaching Styles in Category-University Network

Besides that, a university similarity matrix can also be deducted from the co-occurrence matrix. According to Fig. 8, universities can be divided into 3 groups: iSchools, Multidisciplinary Schools and Traditional CS/LIS Schools. Teaching topics in iSchools are quite dissimilar with others (The data of University of Washington is not complete, thus it located in Multidisciplinary Schools), covering behavioral, technical and information aspects of HCI topics. The multidisciplinary schools seem to cover two aspects in behavioral and technical area, and traditional LIS schools and CS schools may only emphasize one aspect. Surprisingly, the course structure between traditional LIS schools and CS schools reached a high consistency.

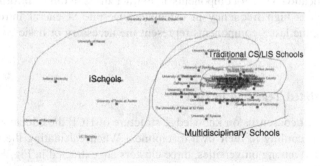

Fig. 8. Multidimensional scaling analysis of university similarity

5 Discussion and Conclusion

What is the core of HCI teaching? As mentioned above, the discussion of "core" in HCI education is argued for years (Gasen et al. 1994b, 1996b; Sears et al. 1997; Churchill et al. 2014), former researchers may "feel" or be aware of the "core" of HCI education, and create some framework or core components lists, while this study calculated and identified the "core" of HCI education in practice.

5.1 Knowledge Architecture in HCI

According to former researches, the landscape of HCI kept on changing and the curriculum of HCI and related courses had to be renewed every 5 or 10 years, but the architecture of this course remained stable.

In our research, no matter in CS schools or LIS schools, the whole construct of HCI contains three basic aspects: human and behavioral aspects, technical aspects, practice and design. First, behavioral or psychological research always put in the front of the syllabi to be the theoretic basis of the whole course. Second, "development process" or HCI thinking in system design is viewed as the most important contribution of this course, nearly 40 % concepts or teaching time are spent on this field. Third, HCI courses tend to be practice oriented, thus presentation and practice play an important role in the course teaching. Fourth, although computing and relative basic techniques tend to be important in semantic structure of HCI, these techniques are always pre-taught or occurred in other courses.

5.2 Core Components in HCI

In our study, the HCI courses do have a boundary-clear core. There seems to be some difference between CS and LIS schools, more behavioral contents ("Information Interaction" and "User Experience and Behavior") in LIS and more programming practice in CS, but data in Figs. 1 and 2 clearly indicate that design and "development process" of interactive system is the most popular topic in HCI teaching, especially user requirements analysis, prototype design and usability test. In Fig. 3, a structural core set of HCI education with 9-components is extracted, excluding "Information Interaction" which has high frequency in calculates. Despite "General Introduction" as teaching issues, the last 8 components represent the necessary or basic content in HCI teaching.

5.3 Differentiated Teaching in HCI

Although they get consensus on knowledge structure of HCI, the educators emphasize different areas according to their own disciplines. When calculating the similarity of topics distribution among universities, three clusters are extracted in Fig. 8, and named "iSchools", "Multidisciplinary Schools" and "Traditional CS/LIS Schools" approximately. The research demonstrates a serious phenomenon ignored before, that the coursed in traditional LIS schools have quite similar structure and contents with those in CS schools, which means the HCI education in traditional LIS schools did not adapt to its own context successfully. On contrary, iSchools tend to be quite dissimilar with others, carrying out differentiated teaching in HCI.

In summary, HCI educators in North America may get consensus on a 9-components core in HCI teaching, but different institutes do have differentiated teaching styles. The HCI educators should design syllabi or curricula according to own contexts, instead of "copy" or strictly based on one authoritative agenda.

References

ACM/IEEE-CS Joint Interim Review Task Force: Computer Science Curriculum 2008: An Interim Revision of CS 2001, Report from the Interim Review Task Force (2008). http://www.acm.org/education/curricula/ComputerScience2008.pdf

ACM/IEEE-CS Joint Task Force for Computer Curricula: Computing Curricula 2005: An Overview Report (2005). http://www.acm.org/education/curric_vols/CC2005-March06Final.pdf

ACM/IEEE-CS Joint Task Force on Computing Curricula: ACM/IEEE Computing Curricula 2001 Final Report (2001). http://www.acm.org/sigcse/cc2001

Boscarioli, C., Bim, S.A., Silveira, M.S., Prates, R.O., Barbosa, S.D.J.: HCI education in Brazil: challenges and opportunities. In: Kurosu, M. (ed.) HCII/HCI 2013, Part I. LNCS, vol. 8004, pp. 3–12. Springer, Heidelberg (2013)

Carroll, J.M. (ed.): HCI Models, Theories, and Frameworks: Toward a Multidisciplinary Science. Morgan Kaufmann, Burlington (2003)

Churchill, E.F., Bowser, A., Preece, J.: Teaching and learning human-computer interaction: past, present, and future. Interactions 20(2), 44–53 (2013)

Churchill, E., Preece, J., Bowser, A.: Developing a living HCI curriculum to support a global community. In: CHI 2014 Extended Abstracts on Human Factors in Computing Systems, pp. 135–138. ACM, April 2014

Coulter, N., French, J., Glinert, E., Horton, T., Mead, N., Rada, R., Ralston, A., Rodkin, C., Rous, B., Tucker, A., Wegner, P.: Computing classification system 1998: current status and future maintenance. Report of the CCS update committee. Comput. Rev. 39(1), 1–2 (1998)

Denning, P., Comer, D.E., Gries, D., Mulder, M.C., Tucker, A.B., Turner, A.J., Young, P.R.: Computing as a discipline: preliminary report of the ACM task force on the core of computer science. ACM SIGCSE Bull. 20(1), 41 (1988)

Edwards, A., Wright, P., Petrie, H.: HCI education: we are failing–why. In: Proceedings of HCI Educators Workshop 2006 (2006)

Churchill, E.F., Bowser, A., Preece, J.: Teaching and learning human-computer interaction: past, present, and future. Interactions 20(2) March–April 2013. doi:10.1145/2427076.2427086

Faiola, A.: The design enterprise: rethinking the HCI education paradigm. Des. Issues 23(3), 30–45 (2007)

Foley, J., Beaudouin-Lafon, M., Grudin, J., Hollan, J., Hudson, S., Olson, J., Verplank, B.: Graduate education in human-computer interaction. In: CHI 2005 Extended Abstracts on Human Factors in Computing Systems, pp. 2113–2114. ACM, April 2005

Gasen, J.: Getting to the "core" of the matter: HCI in higher education. ACM SIGCHI Bull. 26(4), 10–11 (1994)

Gasen, J.B.: Support for HCI educators: a view from the trenches. In: BCS HCI, pp. 15–20 (1995a)

Gasen, J.B.: Looking for footprints: evaluation issues in HCI education. ACM SIGCHI Bull. 27(4), 20–22 (1995)

Gasen, J.B.: HCI education: past, present and future? ACM SIGCHI Bull. 28(1), 25–27 (1996)

Gasen, J.B., Preece, J.: What shapes the face of human-computer interaction in higher education? A framework of the influences. J. Comput. High. Educ. 8(1), 97–123 (1996)

Gasen, J.B., Perlman, G., Attaya-Kelo, M.: Update on the HCI education survey. ACM SIGCHI Bull. 26(2), 8–11 (1994)

Grandhi, S.: Educating ourselves on HCI education. Interactions 22(6), 69–71 (2015)

Hewett, T.T., Baecker, R., Card, S., Carey, T., Gasen, J., Mantei, M., Perlman, G., Strong, G., Verplank, W.: ACM SIGCHI Curricula for Human-Computer Interaction. ACM (1992)

Lazar, J., Preece, J., Gasen, J., Winograd, T.: New issues in teaching HCI: pinning a tail on a moving donkey. In: CHI 2002 Extended Abstracts on Human Factors in Computing Systems, pp. 696–697. ACM, April 2002

Löwgren, J., Quinn, C.N., Gasen, J., Gorny, P.: Designing the teaching of HCI: a CHI 1994 workshop. ACM SIGCHI Bull. 26(4), 28–31 (1994)

Mantel, M., Smelcer, J.B.: Guidelines for reading the human-computer interaction survey results. ACM SIGCHI Bull. 16(2), 9–43 (1984)

Oestreicher, L., Silva, P.A.: Challenges from the future: bridging the gaps through HCI education. In: INTERACT 2013, Cape Town, South Africa, pp. 779–779. Springer, Heidelberg, 2–6 September 2013

Sahami, M., Roach, S., Cuadros-Vargas, E., LeBlanc, R.: ACM/IEEE-CS computer science curriculum 2013: reviewing the ironman report. In: Proceeding of 44th ACM Technical Symposium on Computer Science Education, pp. 13–14. ACM, March 2013

Sears, A., Williams, M.G., Gasen, J.B., Hewett, T., Karat, J., McLaughlin, G.: None of the above: what's really essential in HCI education? In: CHI 1997 Extended Abstracts on Human Factors in Computing Systems, pp. 109–110. ACM, March 1997

Topi, H., Valacich, J.S., Wright, R.T., Kaiser, K.M., Nunamaker, Jr., J.F., Sipior, J.C., De Vreede, G.J.: Curriculum guidelines for undergraduate degree programs in information systems. In: ACM/AIS Task Force, p. 26 (2010)

Zhang, P., Galletta, D.: Foundations of human-computer interaction in management information systems. In: Zhang, P., Galletta, D. (eds.) HCI and MIS: Foundations, Series of Advances in Management Information Systems. vol. 4. M.E. Sharpe publisher (2006)

Identification of Future Human-Computer System Needs in Army Aviation

Kathryn A. Salomon[1,2(✉),P] and David Boudreaux[1(✉)]

[1] U.S. Army Aeromedical Research Laboratory, Fort Rucker, AL, USA
{kathryn.a.salomon2.ctr,
david.a.boudreaux9.mil}@mail.mil
[2] Oak Ridge Institute for Science and Education, Oak Ridge, TN, USA

Abstract. The Army has begun to develop the next generation of rotary-wing aircraft, which will incorporate advanced automated systems. Military operations place a number of cognitive demands on pilots in addition to those seen in commercial aviation. This paper reviews the essential issues in the design of adaptive automation systems for military aircraft and discusses how adaptive automation can utilize psychophysiological feedback to enhance safety and performance.

Keywords: Military · Army · Aviation · Adaptive automation · Pilot-machine interface

1 Introduction

As Army aviation begins to look towards the challenges of the next 30 to 40 years, it is apparent that an increased reliance on technology will play a pivotal role. As the nature of missions change from conflicts between nation states to isolated, independent non-state actors, large-scale ground campaigns shift to smaller, tactical units, the Warfighter of the future will need to be capable of independently handling multiple, complex tasks.

In the civilian aviation sector, human-computer automation capabilities are ubiquitous. Nearly every function in the planning and execution of air travel can be accomplished through the use of sophisticated computer systems. Aviation in the U.S. Army, which predominantly uses rotary-wing aircraft, has not yet incorporated the same level of automation as the civilian sector, partially due to the unique situations in which military pilots conduct operations. However, the Army is moving toward a leaner, more capable adaptive force that increasingly requires multifunctional capabilities to accomplish multiple goals with fewer personnel or resources. For aviators, this will entail additional tasks to meet operational goals that will subsequently increase cognitive demands. This paper will outline the complex nature of operating Army aircraft and identify the need for future incorporation of new automated technology in

© US Government (outside the US) 2016
F.F.-H. Nah and C.-H. Tan (Eds.): HCIBGO 2016, Part II, LNCS 9752, pp. 209–220, 2016.
DOI: 10.1007/978-3-319-39399-5_20

keeping with the Army's goal of preserving military superiority. The paper will also highlight and discuss future research needs and directions to assist in meeting that goal.

2   Impact of Workload on Pilot Performance

Operating an Army aircraft in a deployed environment is a complex and highly stressful task. The multifaceted nature of the tasks required places a high demand on the pilot's attention abilities and cognitive resources. Here, cognitive resources may be thought of as pools of energy that can be utilized for receiving, interpreting, and/or processing information for the purpose of achieving a task [1]. Throughout the duration of a flight, the pilot remains oriented with regard to the aircraft's location in space, surveys the functioning of various systems within the aircraft, is aware of weather conditions, communicates with others on board and on the ground, engages in airspace surveillance for other aircraft and terrain, and keeps track of time-to-mission objectives. The successful completion of a mission, such as bringing Soldiers to a specific location or picking up injured Soldiers, requires the pilot to maintain constant awareness of these aspects throughout the flight operation.

2.1   Factors Affecting Workload

The variety of information the pilot keeps within memory and awareness throughout the flight is used to ensure adequate situation awareness (SA) [1]. The most widely accepted definition of SA is that of Endsley [2], where SA is defined as "the perception of the elements in the environment within a volume of time and space, the comprehension of their meaning, and the projection of their status in the near future" (p. 5). The maintenance of SA throughout a flight ensures that the pilot is able to meet mission objectives, as well as make timely and accurate responses to malfunctions or unexpected events. However, engaging in these tasks throughout the flight can increase the workload experienced by the pilot, particularly during key portions of the flight, such as takeoff and landing. While no agreed-upon definition of mental workload currently exists, it can be broadly defined as a combination of task demands and the operator's ability to respond to them [3].

In general, monitoring the systems and the directional cues of the flight is a relatively low workload task for the experienced pilot, requiring few resources, and the pilot is able to easily maintain SA. In situations where the pilot's workload is low and SA is adequately maintained, the pilot has little to no problem responding to additional, unexpected tasks, such as a change in flight path, by recruiting residual resources to address the task. However, the level of workload experienced is influenced by a multitude of factors throughout a flight. For instance, the pilot may be required to fly in what is known as a degraded visual environment (DVE), which occurs when vision outside the aircraft is degraded due to factors such as weather, nightfall, or dust clouds. Flying in DVE conditions increases workload by requiring continuous monitoring of instrument displays to maintain flight path due to the inability to use outside visual cues. This can create a dangerous situation during critical periods of the flight such as taking off or landing the aircraft [4]. Pilots relying solely on information obtained from instruments place high demands on their visual processing resources and can cause them to engage in cognitive tunneling where they over-focus on certain information while neglecting other information that may be pertinent to the flight [5]. Accidents related to cognitive overload in DVE conditions have resulted in losses of over $100 million a year and a total of 600 lives between 2002 and 2012 [6].

Army pilots are further susceptible to performance decrements due to various additional stressors resulting from operating in a deployed environment that are not typically seen within civilian aviation populations, such as those related to the complexity of the mission (e.g., mission planning, mission characteristics, mission uncertainty) [7]. Furthermore, the majority of Army aviation combat missions occur overnight. This increases the likelihood that a pilot will experience fatigue, which plays an influential role in affecting cognitive state and available resources [8, 9]. Missions occurring overnight cause the pilot to operate in opposition to his or her circadian cycle, resulting in loss of sleep, greater fatigue, and an increased likelihood for errors [10, 11]. Increased fatigue is also related to degraded working memory [12], which may contribute to the loss of SA. To better characterize the performance effects of engaging in multiple, concurrent tasks during flight, the multiple resource model [13] is frequently used to describe the effects of the various task demands on performance.

2.2 Multiple Resource Model

The multiple resource model is based on Wickens' multiple resource theory, which postulates that when an individual is engaged in two or more tasks at one time, performance on the tasks is dependent upon the extent to which the tasks elicit the use of different resources across four dimensions (for an in depth review see [1, 13, 14]). The multiple resource model of attention is based on the postulation of four dichotomous dimensions of information processing that occur when engaged in tasks that require attention. These dimensions include the "stages of processing," "codes of processing," "perceptual modalities," and "visual channels." The model asserts performance is dictated by the amount of overlap of resources nested within these dimensions, such that tasks with little overlap will have little negative influence on performance but tasks with greater overlap will have greater negative influence on performance.

Determining methods for reducing the negative effects of workload on pilots' performance has been at the forefront of many research efforts [15, 16]. Much of the research has pointed to the incorporation of automated technology within the cockpit as a means to reduce workload by removing some of the tasks that the pilot must be responsible for during flight. However, much of the incorporation of automated technology in the cockpit has occurred within commercial aviation settings, with a much lesser extent into military aviation. As Army aviation moves forward, the incorporation of more complex automated technology into the cockpit will be necessary to ensure appropriate distribution of workload for the pilot.

3 Automation

The introduction of automation into commercial aircraft contributed to reducing accidents until the end of the 1990's when the numbers began to level off [17]. While automation assisted in the reduction of total number of mishaps, human error continues to be the primary causal factor in accidents [18, 19]. This trend may indicate a tipping point where the automation has become so complex it is potentially causing as much hindrance as it is assistance. Early automation consisted of static automation that could be turned on when needed and performed simple tasks such as maintaining heading and altitude. As computational power increased, computers began to take on increasingly complex functions previously reserved for the pilot. As the number of accidents began to reduce, a change in the type of error also began to emerge.

3.1 Drawbacks of Automation

In modern commercial aircraft, the computer system is capable of conducting most of the flight operations with the appropriate inputs from the pilot. For instance, Olson [19] noted that pilots typically only assume control of the plane during take-off and landing, the two most cognitively demanding tasks, while allowing the automated system to perform the majority of the flight operations. This has led to the transition of the pilot's role from direct control of the aircraft to what has been called supervisory control [19]. Essentially, the pilot is primarily responsible for monitoring the computer system controlling the aircraft by providing input and ensuring the system is performing as expected. However, as pilots have assumed supervisory control, the number of errors where the pilot neglects to act or adjust the computer system has subsequently increased [20]. Once the operator offloads the responsibility of constantly monitoring system performance, the operator's ability to detect anomalies or potential errors decreases with time, and this leads to underload, complacency, and reduced vigilance of system status [21–23]. Previous research has shown this can become a critical problem because pilots may begin to adopt an "expectations-based" monitoring approach where they begin to limit monitoring of the system to expected indicators at the exclusion of other important information [24].

Underload is of particular concern for future pilots as automation systems are being created in a way to reduce the tasks in which the pilot is actively engaged in. Studies have shown this can create problems in roles such as controlling an aircraft where prolonged low workload conditions make it difficult for the pilot to transition to high workload such as in situations where automation fails or unexpected events arise [25]. The low level of engagement contributes to the pilot having a diminished mental model of how the computer system is controlling the aircraft. A mental model is the pilot's internal accounting of the state of the aircrafts instruments and current mode of all systems. However, there is some debate if underload is a distinct state that can be identified or if it is a reflection of other problems related to supervisory control [3]. Given the relatively small amount of research on this topic, additional studies will need to be done to understand better the impact of underload. Determining if and how we can measure underload will have a significant impact on the future design of automation systems. If evidence does support the existence of underload, it will become important to identify the optimal workload range for the operator of a system. Automation may also be used to increase workload, rather than just reducing it, in order to maintain safe levels of engagement for the operator.

A recurring theme amongst issues with automation is the lack of communication or miscommunication between the human operator and the computer system. If the aircraft is being flown through supervisory control, it is crucial to be aware of the aircraft's mode (i.e., take off, landing, go around, etc.). Research has shown that automation can lead to instances where the pilot is unaware of the mode of the aircraft leading to serious consequences when the pilot attempts to intervene with the system [26, 27]. This problem, referred to as mode error, can have numerous causes such as faulty operator input to the system or switching modes due to issues unknown to the pilot. Another negative outcome of extensive automation use is inert knowledge. According to Woods et al. [28], this is when a pilot is unable to instruct the automated system how to perform a maneuver or process, despite the pilot having the knowledge to do so. This again highlights the need for designing a system that retains the human at its center by ensuring timely and accurate communication between the pilot and computer.

Another product of increased automation capabilities is the additional information that must be made available to the pilot to monitor and process. Since pilots still need the ability to monitor the performance of the aircraft, any information presented on the state of the automation system is additional data that must be observed and processed. This can lead to the problem of information overload whereby the operator is unable to identify problems or unable to recognize when the system is indicating errors because of too much input taxing one sensory modality [19, 29]. The goal should be to find a proper balance between providing the required information and displaying it in a way that the pilot can easily access it when needed.

Collectively, the examples in this section underscore what could be considered a workload reduction fallacy. Though not exhaustive, these issues shed light on a potential causal factor for why safety improvement statistics have stagnated. Despite the goal of automation being to reduce workload on the operator, a point exists where the automation becomes so complex and overwhelming that it may no longer reduce workload and instead create new cognitive demands on the pilot [26, 30]. Some research has even led to the belief that some systems produce "clumsy automation" by engaging or reducing automation at the moments it will have a negative impact on pilot performance [28]. This may indicate a need for automation to flexibly include the operator in the decision making process. Ideally, the automation system should be responsive to the needs of the operator and provide feedback in a continuous fashion so automation can be adjusted accordingly. Adaptive automation has been identified as a more flexible means of using automated technology and has the potential to be feasibly incorporated into aircraft technology.

3.2 Adaptive Automation

Adaptive automation has been defined as the "technological component of joint human-machine systems that can change their behavior to meet the changing needs of their users, often without explicit instructions from their users" [31, p. 1008]. Adaptive automation is able to adjust the behavior of the system through feedback received from the user, the current task, and the environment in which it is operating in. The ability of adaptive automation to assist in reducing operator workload was demonstrated in a study by Wilson and Russell [32], where psychophysiological data was collected while subjects engaged in an unmanned aerial vehicle task and an artificial neural network was used to detect periods of high and low workload. When periods of high workload were detected, the automation engaged, and it was found that performance significantly improved. To ensure the optimal success of the incorporation of adaptive automation within the Army aviation environment, several key aspects of automated technology must be taken into consideration.

As demonstrated by Wilson and Russell [32], one proposed method of informing adaptive automation systems is through psychophysiological feedback from the operator of the system. Psychophysiological feedback could be used to identify when the operator is experiencing conditions that would benefit from increasing automation such as high workload or reducing automation to prevent underload based on current physiological and cognitive state levels throughout a flight. Although some reports have been published, research applying real-time psychophysiological feedback within the context of adaptive automation is still in its infancy stage. The following section briefly outlines established indices of workload, as well as implications for their incorporation into adaptive automation systems.

4 Psychophysiological Indices of Workload

Some of the more commonly used psychophysiological measurements of workload include neuroimaging (e.g., electroencephalogram [EEG] [33]), transcranial Doppler sonography [34], eye tracking [35], cardiovascular measures (e.g., heart rate, heart rate variability, blood pressure [36]), and to a lesser extent, respiration [37], and electrodermal activity [38]. Such measures are able to provide indications of the mental engagement of the individual that correspond to changes in task demands. Psychophysiological measures of workload are appealing to incorporate into adaptive automation systems given the ease of real-time data collection within operational settings the majority of them provide [3].

While each of the previously mentioned measures is known to often provide relatively reliable feedback and assessment regarding an individual's cognitive state, several problems associated with their use remains. One current problem is that the use of multiple psychophysiological measurements can occasionally produce differing results in regards to the workload experienced. A recent example of this is a study by Matthews and colleagues [39] where they compared the sensitivity of various psychophysiological indices (heart rate variability, EEG, cerebral hemodynamics, eye tracking) to differing cognitive demands. They found that while the majority of the measures used demonstrated sensitivity to task demands, the measures tended to be sensitive to either the task type or dual tasking workload manipulation but not to both. The authors asserted that this finding may suggest differential diagnosticity of the various psychophysiological indices used. It may be the case that different psychophysiological indices indicate high workload for different types of tasks, which could assist in determining how to employ automation to reduce the overload. For example, one study found that different indices provided different information regarding performance changes [40]. Specifically, it was found that heart rate measures were linked to overall task demands, whereas the EEG measures were linked to increased demand during mental calculations.

Another concern for the incorporation of psychophysiological indices as a means to inform automated systems is that of individual differences in psychophysiological responses. Individual differences remain a concern for comparisons of psychophysiological measures, with several researchers developing methodologies to compensate for these differences [41]. However, further work is required to determine whether techniques used to compensate for individual differences can be transferred into the algorithms that would be required for adaptive automation systems [42]. Additionally, the role of emotion in influencing several psychophysiological measures should be taken into consideration [43], as well as the effects experience has on psychophysiological measures [33].

In order for human-computer interfaces to take the next step into use in the operational setting, computer systems will require the ability to monitor the cognitive state of the operator in real time. The use of psychophysiological feedback is an appealing choice since it has the ability to noninvasively and continuously monitor the operator's cognitive and physiological state. An intricate understanding of how these psychophysiological indices apply to a pilot operating an aircraft could be the key to the integration of adaptive automation in the cockpit.

5 Future Application of HCI to Army Aviation

The current fleet of Army aircraft has been in service for nearly 30 years. Advances in engineering and technology have led to the development of a new generation of rotary-wing aircraft under a program called Future Vertical Lift (FVL) [44]. In addition to the increased capabilities from these innovative designs, the incorporation of human-computer interface technologies is a near certainty. Automation has not been widely used in the Army's aircraft thus its implementation will require a substantial amount of research to ensure these airframes meet military standards for use in an operational environment.

As outlined in the previous section, adaptive automation can be an invaluable tool for managing workload conditions in a complex work environment such as a cockpit. By selectively initiating computer control of tasks based on the needs of the operator, many of the shortfalls with static automation can be avoided. The majority of Army pilots currently utilize manual controls to fly and manage their aircraft for a number of reasons. One of the most important reasons is the unique and unpredictable environment military aviators must operate in. Maintaining SA is a top priority for these individuals and the prospect of being "out of the loop" is not an option appealing to many pilots. Design of adaptive automation systems for military aircraft should center on establishing what criteria dictates when control of the aircraft resides with the human or the automation.

In order to maintain a human-centered aircraft, the adaptive automation should be a fluid system that systematically isolates individual aviation tasks that can be shifted to computer control to reduce the cognitive burden on a pilot. This would allow for a sharing of tasks with the computer so that the pilot can maintain an accurate mental model of the aircraft. This allows the pilot to maintain SA by understanding what the aircraft is doing and how it is being affected by variables such as fuel, altitude, or airspeed. Inherent within such a scheme is the question of how to remove and return control to the pilot. There is the potential for military aviators delaying, or not utilizing, automation even when available. This could result for two different reasons. Military pilots, may falsely believe they have the skills to navigate out of a bad situation as was the case in a crash off the coast of Florida in 2015 [45]. Second, in conditions where pilots lose SA, they may be unaware that incorrect control inputs or faulty systems will lead to an aviation mishap (i.e., unrecognized spatial disorientation). Given the incredibly short window during which mishaps can occur, an essential feature of an adaptive automation system would require the computer to take control of a high risk task to ensure safe operation. This highlights an important feature of using psychophysiological indices as an input for an adaptive automation system. These measures are obtained without effort or influence from the pilot, which allows the system to address both of these issues by engaging when the pilot is unable to recognize the situation at hand due to excessively high workload or loss of SA. The design of such a system should be based on data indicating the operator is able to maintain SA of the aircraft functions to prevent problems such as mode error. Given the high level of cognitive demand, particularly in the visual and auditory dimensions, considerable effort will need to be made in determining the most efficient way to facilitate communication between the operator and computer.

Perhaps trickier than the question of when to initiate automation is the reverse role of returning the responsibility for the task to the human operator. Assuming the automation will only be initiated during high workload periods or when a number of unexpected events occur, consideration needs to be given to how the pilot will be informed of what functions were transferred to automation. If the pilot is unaware that the adaptive automation is engaged, he or she may divert unnecessary resources to managing the task being automated when there are few resources available. It is conceivable that a specific order of tasks could be diverted in all situations, but this likely would be troublesome because different situations would likely tax different cognitive domains. An alternative may be that a continuous dialogue between the pilot and computer be used as workload increases so that the operator can input which functions the computer should select for automation. This has the advantage of keeping the pilot informed of which tasks are under computer control until the workload subsides. However, this scenario does not account for unexpected and sudden situations where a pilot becomes overloaded or disoriented.

As discussed previously in the paper, there is an abundant body of research linking psychophysiological measures to workload (e.g., [33–36]). Research specific to aviation maneuvers is sparse, particularly rotary-wing aircraft used in the Army, which will require identifying performance measures for specific tasks and compiling evidence to link those performance measures to the operator's cognitive state. A key step in this process will be to isolate specific aviation task/maneuvers and identify specific psychophysiological measures that can detect changes in workload for each of those tasks. Building on the concepts from the multiple resource model, it is likely that some aviation tasks can be performed in conjunction without an appreciable drop in performance whereas others will have significant interference leading to performance decrements. Since many of these tasks will draw on multiple cognitive dimensions, it is important to determine the level of change in each psychophysiological measure for each individual task. If psychophysiological measures will be used to quantify workload in initiating automation, it will require establishing a baseline for each aviation task for future use in a decision matrix that decides whether or not a computer assumes control. For example, eye-tracking can be used to identify a pilot's reduced attention on the altitude indicator due to a greater focus on other visual cues (i.e., the navigation system) compared with the programmed and actual altitude. This could be one of the variables that determine if the pilot is experiencing high workload and a loss of SA which would trigger adaptive automation. Using an absolute value for altitude may not be beneficial for automation in such a scenario because pilot experience also plays a role. For instance, younger pilots focus on maintaining an exact altitude whereas experienced pilots tend to allow for greater variation within an acceptable range without constant monitoring. This example demonstrates why it will be essential to ascertain baselines for isolated tasks through multiple psychophysiological and instrumental inputs.

Since most tasks will consume cognitive resources from multiple dimensions of the model, it will need to be experimentally determined which task pairings lead to excessive workload. This type of data can be used to generate algorithms for designing adaptive automation systems based on the psychophysiological indices and aviation instruments. These algorithms would serve two main purposes. First, the criteria for the determination of when adaptive automation should engage will need to be developed. Given the variety of tasks that occur during flight, the aviator will most likely be performing multiple functions when high workload conditions arise. In order to meet the objective of automation reducing, rather than redistributing, the workload, it may be necessary to establish which tasks the computer will control and which will remain in the pilot's control. In a military setting, there may be specific functions a pilot is unwilling to relinquish control to a computer system. This work may need to include military pilots during the design process to ensure the automation system is designed to maintain operational effectiveness rather than distracting the pilot in an already stressful event.

5.1 Conclusion

The FVL program will be responsible for the most significant changes to Army aviation in decades. Current and emerging technological advances will provide capabilities the majority of pilots have not seen before. Given the relatively infrequent use of automation that currently exists in the Army, it will be critical to ensure any FVL human-computer system design keeps the pilot as the central focus. The following are a series of questions that will need to be addressed through research to ensure successful implementation of automation in future Army aircraft:

- What criteria should be used to determine when adaptive automation engages? Does it need to be individualized?
- What are the most effective, reliable psychophysiological indices for measuring workload and to which cognitive dimensions do they correspond?
- What psychophysiological indices of workload correspond to specific aviation maneuvers? What criteria will be used to determine which maneuvers will be transferred to the computer?
- Should the computer or the human decide when automation takes control? How should this be communicated to the pilot?
- How will the system detect and avoid differing workload levels that are detrimental to performance, including "underload" conditions?
- What psychophysiological indices correlate with reduced performance? What combinations of pilot stressors alter the indices (e.g., fatigue, disorientation, etc.)?

The above list is by no means exhaustive of all the topics that will need to be addressed. As research progresses, new questions and new methods will inevitably arise. The collaboration between the research community and the military will need to remain fluid in order to benefit from the innovative efforts that will come.

References

1. Wickens, C.D.: Situation awareness and workload in aviation. Curr. Dir. Psychol. Sci. **11**, 128–133 (2002)
2. Endsley, M.R.: Theoretical underpinnings of situation awareness: a critical review. In: Situation Awareness Analysis and Measurement. Lawrence Erlbaum Associates, Mahwah (2000)
3. Young, M.S., Brookhuis, K.A., Wickens, C.D., Hancock, P.A.: State of science: mental workload in ergonomics. Ergonomics **58**, 1–17 (2015)
4. Jasion, G., Shrimpton, J.: Prediction of Brownout inception beneath a full-scale helicopter downwash. J. Am. Helicopter Soc. **57**, 1–13 (2012)
5. Allan, K., White, T., Jones, L., Merlo, J., Haas, E., Zets, G., Rupert, A.H.: Getting the buzz: what's next for tactile information delivery? Proc. Hum. Factors Ergon. Soc. Annu. Meet. **2010**, 1331–1334 (2010)
6. Whittle, R.: Army Seeks Brownout Fixes for Helo Pilots, Afghan Tests Loom (2012). http://www.breakingdefense.com/2012/03/army-seeks-brownout-fixes-for-helo-pilots-afghan-tests-loom/
7. Stetz, T.A., Stetz, M.C., Turner, D.D.: Mission, physical, and war stressors' impact on aircrew psychological strain. Aviat. Space Environ. Med. **85**, 568–572 (2014)
8. Caldwell, J.L., Chandler, J.F., Hartzler, B.M.: Battling fatigue in aviation: recent advancements in research and practice. J. Med. Sci. **32**, 47–56 (2012)
9. Rabinowitz, Y.G., Breitbach, J.E., Warner, C.H.: Managing aviator fatigue in a deployed environment: the relationship between fatigue and neurocognitive functioning. Mil. Med. **174**, 358–362 (2009)
10. Caldwell, J.: Work and sleep hours of U.S. Army aviation personnel working reverse cycle. Mil. Med. **166**, 159–166 (2001)
11. Caldwell, J.A.: Fatigue in aviation. Travel Med. Infect. Dis. **3**, 85–96 (2004)

12. Drummond, S.P.A., Anderson, D.E., Straus, L.D., Vogel, E.K., Perez, V.B.: The effects of two types of sleep deprivation on visual working memory capacity and filtering efficiency. PLoS ONE **7**, e35653 (2012)
13. Wickens, C.D.: Processing resources in attention, dual task performance, and workload assessment. Technical report, Office of Naval Research (1980)
14. Wickens, C.D.: Multiple resources and mental workload. Hum. Factors **50**, 449–455 (2008)
15. Liu, D., Guarino, S.L., Roth, E., Harper, K., Vincenzi, D.: Effect of novel adaptive displays on pilot performance and workload. Int. J. Aviat. Psychol. **22**, 242–265 (2012)
16. Raby, M., Wickens, C.D.: Strategic workload management and decision biases in aviation. Int. J. Aviat. Psychol. **4**, 211–240 (1994)
17. Griffin, G.: Human error is biggest obstacle to 100 percent flight safety (2010). http://www.denverpost.com/ci_14398562
18. Shappell, S., Detwiler, C., Holcomb, K., Hackworth, C., Boquet, A., Wiegmann, D.A.: Human error and commercial aviation accidents: an analysis using the human factors analysis and classification system. Hum. Factors **49**, 227–242 (2007)
19. Olson, W.A.: Identifying and mitigating the risks of cockpit automation. Air Command and Staff College Wright Flyer Paper No. 14 (2001)
20. Sarter, N.B., Woods, D.D.: Team play with a powerful and independent agent: a corpus of operational experiences and automation surprises on the airbus A-320. Hum. Factors **39**, 553–569 (1997)
21. Langan-Fox, J., Sankey, M.J., Canty, J.M.: Human factors measurement for future air traffic control systems. Hum. Factors **51**, 595–637 (2009)
22. Mouloua, M., Parasuraman, R.: Human Performance in Automated Systems: Current Research and Trends. Hillsdale (1994)
23. Parasuraman, R., Riley, V.: Humans and automation: use, misuse, disuse, abuse. Hum. Factors **39**, 250–253 (1997)
24. Sarter, N.B., Woods, D.D.: Team play with a powerful and independent agent: a full-mission simulation study. Hum. Factors **42**, 390–402 (2000)
25. Boyer, M., Cummings, M.L., Spence, L.B., Solovey, E.T.: Investigating mental workload changes in a long duration supervisory control task. Interact. Comput. **27**, 512–520 (2015)
26. Johannesen, L., Sarter, N., Cook, R., Dekker, S., Woods, D.D.: Behind Human Error. Ashgate Publishing, Aldershot (2012)
27. Miller, C.A., Parasuraman, R.: Designing for flexible interaction between humans and automation: delegation interfaces for supervisory control. Hum. Factors **49**, 57–75 (2007)
28. Woods, D.D., Johannesen, L.J., Cook, R.I., Sarter, N.B.: Behind human error: cognitive systems, computers and hindsight. Technical report, Crew System Ergonomic Information Analysis Center (1994)
29. Kaber, D.B., Wright, M.C., Sheik-Nainar, M.A.: Investigation of multi-modal interface features for adaptive automation of a human–robot system. Int. J. Hum.-Comput. Stud. **64**, 527–540 (2006)
30. Wiener, E.L.: Human factors of advanced technology (glass cockpit) transport aircraft. Technical report, NASA Ames Research Center (1989)
31. Feigh, K.M., Dorneich, M.C., Hayes, C.C.: Toward a characterization of adaptive systems: a framework for researchers and system designers. Hum. Factors **54**, 1008–1024 (2012)
32. Wilson, G.F., Russell, C.A.: Performance enhancement in an uninhabited air vehicle task using psychophysiologically determined adaptive aiding. Hum. Factors **49**, 1005–1018 (2007)
33. Borghini, G., Astolfi, L., Vecchiato, G., Mattia, D., Babiloni, F.: Measuring neurophysiological signals in aircraft pilots and car drivers for the assessment of mental workload, fatigue, and drowsiness. Neurosci. Biobehav. Rev. **44**, 58–75 (2014)

34. Shaw, T., Finomore, V., Warm, J., Matthews, G.: Effects of regular or irregular event schedules on cerebral hemovelocity during a sustained attention task. J. Clin. Exp. Neuropsychol. **34**, 57–66 (2012)
35. Wickens, C.D., Hollands, J.G.: Engineering Psychology and Human Performance. Pearson Education, Upper Saddle River (2000)
36. Stuiver, A., Brookhuis, K.A., de Waard, D., Mulder, B.: Short-term cardiovascular measures for driver support: increasing sensitivity for detecting changes in mental workload. Int. J. Psychophysiol. **92**, 35–41 (2014)
37. Veltman, J.A., Gaillard, A.W.K.: Physiological indices of workload in a simulated flight task. Biol. Psychol. **42**, 323–342 (1996)
38. Wilson, G.F.: An analysis of mental workload in pilots during flight using multiple psychophysiological measures. Int. J. Aviat. Psychol. **12**, 3–18 (2002)
39. Matthews, G., Reinerman-Jones, L.E., Barber, D.J., Abich, J.: The psychometrics of mental workload: multiple measures are sensitive but divergent. Hum. Factors **57**, 125–143 (2015)
40. Hankins, T.C., Wilson, G.F.: A comparison of heart rate, eye activity, EEG and subjective measures of pilot mental workload during flight. Aviat. Space Environ. Med. **69**, 360–367 (1998)
41. Johannes, B., Gaillard, A.W.K.: A methodology to compensate for individual differences in psychophysiological assessment. Biol. Psychol. **96**, 77–85 (2014)
42. Ting, C.H., Mahfouf, M., Nassef, A., Linkens, D.A., Panoutsos, G., Nickel, P., Roberts, A.C., Hockey, R.J.: Real-time adaptive automation system based on identification of operator functional state in simulated process control operations. IEEE Trans. Syst. Man Cybern. Part A: Syst. Hum. **40**, 251–262 (2010)
43. Bradley, M.M., Lang, P.J.: Emotion and motivation. In: Cacioppo, J.T., Tassinary, L.G., Berntson, G.G. (eds.) Handbook of Psychophysiology, pp. 581–607. Cambridge University Press, New York (2007)
44. Tadjdeh, Y.: Future Vertical Lift Could be Shot in the Arm for Industry (2015). http://www.nationaldefensemagazine.org/archive/2015/October/Pages/FutureVerticalLiftCouldBeShotintheArmforIndustry.aspx
45. Lamothe, D.: How a dangerous night helicopter operation killed 11 Marines and Guardsmen (2015). https://www.washingtonpost.com/news/checkpoint/wp/2015/06/03/how-a-dangerous-night-helicopter-operation-killed-11-marines-and-guardsmen

Bringing Service Design Thinking into the Public Sector to Create Proactive and User-Friendly Public Services

Regina Sirendi[✉] and Kuldar Taveter

Tallinn University of Technology, Akadeemia tee 15a, Tallinn, Estonia
regina.sirendi@ttu.ee

Abstract. Multiple stakeholders need to be taken into consideration when designing and implementing public sector services and processes. It will be asked in this article whether agent-oriented modeling could be beneficial to understand the interactions between these stakeholders and to support the design of proactive, user-friendly, and usable services of e-government. We propose a methodology for service design that can help to design better and more proactive services and hereby promote service design thinking in the public sector. For this on-going research, we take a look into how the family benefits service works in Estonia. To aid this task, structured interviews were conducted with the officials of the Social Insurance Board. The current article makes a contribution to a new way of approaching the design and development of public electronic services.

Keywords: E-governance · User-centric public services · Service design · Agent-oriented modeling · Proactivity

1 Introduction

User centricity is generally acknowledged as a key concept in service design (Stickdorn and Schneider 2011). However, the term "user" has been overemployed and is also misleading because it implies all service users being very much alike each other. As this is not the case, it makes more sense to discuss stakeholders of services rather than just users. Indeed, each service comes with at least two kinds of stakeholders: service consumers and service providers. Stakeholders take on different roles. Broadly speaking, three kinds of roles can be distinguished among service consumers: citizen, public servant, and representative of an organization, such as company or non-governmental organization (NGO). Citizens in turn can be divided into groups depending on the roles they take in the society (Mead 1934).

Multiple stakeholders need to be taken into account when designing and developing public sector services and administrative processes supporting them. The nature of these stakeholders contributes to an increasingly complex system of services and processes. We need verifiable, justifiable and repeatable concepts and methods for dealing with that complexity. This article claims that by efficiently modeling stakeholders' roles, goals, interactions, and knowledge, better public services can be designed and the efficiency and productivity in the public sector can be increased. We use as our methodology for service design Agent-Oriented Modeling (AOM),

© Springer International Publishing Switzerland 2016
F.F.-H. Nah and C.-H. Tan (Eds.): HCIBGO 2016, Part II, LNCS 9752, pp. 221–230, 2016.
DOI: 10.1007/978-3-319-39399-5_21

as proposed by Taveter and Sterling (2009). AOM has been successfully used for designing artifacts that consider the interests of various relevant stakeholders (Miller et al. 2014). In this article, AOM has been adopted to designing and developing public sector services and processes, notably including the users of the services to be designed performing their respective roles. Moreover, AOM also lends itself to fast prototyping of services to be designed and simulation of potential service scenarios in their social context. This article is confined to addressing the usage of AOM models of one particular kind – goal models – for facilitating discussions between different stakeholders.

On the other hand, the increasing complexity and growing capacity of technology and its use in the public sector has now created a situation where the computational power that we possess should be harnessed to truly serve the citizens and pre-empt their needs. However, all stakeholders do not have the same needs and levels of satisfaction (Hamilton et al. 2011). The goals, needs, and levels of satisfaction associated with different services may depend on the role citizens are taking, be it in a public sector, private sector or NGO, or looked at as an individual citizen. In this article we argue that designing proactive services of e-governance should be seen as the next stage in service design for e-governance. In our opinion, proactive public electronic services should be designed in a way that supports the automation and intelligent processing of already available information to reflect the purpose of meeting the needs of different stakeholders yet maintaining a people-first policy. For designing proactive services, AOM is again instrumental because as *agent*-oriented, it intrinsically supports the notion of proactivity, which is one of the main characteristics of agents or active entities, in addition to reactivity and social nature (Taveter and Sterling 2009).

Finally, it is proposed in this article that governments should introduce and implement the concept of service design thinking in the public sector in order to create public electronic services that would truly and purposefully meet the needs of citizens, businesses and NGOs. We claim that adopting service design thinking in the public sector can be facilitated by AOM. By modeling stakeholders' goals, and through different service design methods, such as ethnography, creating personas, stakeholder maps and expectation maps among others (Stickdorn and Schneider 2011), it would be possible meet the needs of the stakeholders in order to provide high quality customer experience.

It has become increasingly important to understand how to design and provide ICT-driven public services efficiently. We plan to obtain that understanding by combining sociological qualitative research, interdisciplinary case study methods, and software engineering approaches in the research on service design thinking in the public sector. The overall research method used by us is Action Design Research (Maung et al. 2011). This article seeks to address the aims of service design and proactivity and service automation through the example of the family benefits system in Estonia.

The current article is structured as follows: literature review is followed by a short overview of the research methodology and the description of a case study on the current status of family benefits service in Estonia. The article illustrates the case of service design thinking and its relevance in the context of e-governance. The methodology of AOM is proving to be a valuable tool for approaching the design of proactive public services.

2   Literature Review

The role of the state is constantly changing and the functions of a government accumulate as increasingly more services are expected to be delivered in a more efficient manner (Sirendi 2012). Consequently, electronic government, a concept that initially emerged in the public administration of industrial countries (Schuppan 2009), developed as a reaction to these expectations. E-governance has become increasingly prevailing in delivering services and public value efficiently and in a timely manner.

The last couple of decades have brought along significant changes in how public sector organizations are run (Bode 2012), what technologies are implemented, and what management styles are relevant. Information is the catalyst and ICT impacts the way the world connects and knowledge is networked (Frasheri 2003). Countries have never been connected to one another to this magnitude before (Sirendi 2012).

A number of authors (Layne and Lee 2001; Reddick 2004; Andersen and Henriksen 2006; Lee 2010) address and describe the perceived phases of government. These models, describing the development of (e-)governance, allow us to make some subjective generalizations, by dividing the development into four general categories: cataloguing – governments focusing on establishing their online presence; transactions, where a government's focus is on connecting "the internal government system to online interfaces and allowing citizens to transact with government electronically" (Layne and Lee 2001), vertical integration, which refers to the connectedness on a local, state, and federal level; and horizontal integration, where integration takes place across and between different functions and services (Layne and Lee 2001). Although these models may explain e-governance development in many countries and may cover the basic features of e-governance growth, these do not explain the potential phases conclusively.

Constant and strong pressure on public expenditure sets a demand to keep on finding ways to increase productivity, while at the same time addressing the needs of the citizens (Karwan and Markland 2006). There is an increasing demand on countries to make use of the allocated resources in a progressively efficient manner (Lindgren and Jansson 2013). The importance of service design in the public sector has arisen. Many service managers must design and re-design services in order to keep their offerings competitive, fresh, and desirable for customers. After each re-design, staff must re-learn to use a modified service system to deliver a high-quality customer experience (Heim and Ketzenberg 2011). Effective service design requires careful attention on different factors such as costs, service levels, efficiency, sales, profits (Narasimhan et al. 2005), and human aspects.

The recent couple of decades have brought insight into the changing concept of service design (Shostack 1982, Shostack 1984; Scheuing and Johnson 1989; Gummesson 1990; Hollins 1993; Kimbell 2011). Now a closer look into service design in the public sector will be taken (Karwan and Markland 2006). Service design uses techniques and research methods of different fields: ethnography, interaction design, and information science (Stickdorn and Schneider 2011), to name a few. The field seeks to understand and design methodologies for both the front and back office of an organization in order to create better, more user-friendly, more usable, and appropriate services (Smith and Fischbacher 2002). Effective service design involves developing a service concept that appeals to end-users while reflecting on operational limitations (Dixon and Verma 2013). The notion of a "service concept" as initially described by (Sasser et al. 1978) in (Karwan and Markland 2006) could be described as a "bundle of goods and services sold to the customer and the relative importance of each component to the consumer" (p. 14).

Unlike a product, service components are often not physical entities, but rather a combination of processes, skills, and resources, that must be integrated properly in order to result in the planned and designed services (Goldstein et al. 2002). When (re-)designing services, managers, designers, community members, and other stakeholders must make decisions about each component of the service (Goldstein et al. 2002). This way numerous decisions are made even for the simplest services as the involved processes are continuously on-going (Goldstein et al. 2002). The variety of stakeholders and their changing missions leave public agencies unable to conclusively achieve efficiency in their operations (Karwan and Markland 2006).

However, there is a growing focus reflected by an extensive amount of literature on the needs of users and growing interest in user-centric services even though little attention is paid to understanding users' preferences (Venkatesh et al. 2012). The design of user-centric e-governance services will continue to be a challenging task, as citizens' demands and needs change (Venkatesh et al. 2012).

As one of the most recent developments, Linders et al. (2015) showcase three illustrative case studies that support that proactive e-governance will be the future for the public sector.

The methodology chosen by us, AOM, has been successfully used in requirements modeling to engage diverse stakeholders (Miller et al. 2011, 2014). AOM enables to capture functional requirements in the form of functional goals for the service to be designed, which are arranged into a hierarchy. In the hierarchy of functional goals, non-functional requirements are represented as quality goals attached to the corresponding functional goals. Moreover, when attempting to understand human issues in service design, a range of consumer emotions need to be considered from the extremes of "customer delight" to "customer outrage" (Cook et al. 2002). Agent-oriented modeling can also be used to address these issues in the form of emotional goals attached to the relevant functional goals (Miller et al. n.d.). It is argued here that by using agent-oriented modeling in the service design context, it would be possible to address more precisely human aspect and gain a better understanding of the existing issues in public electronic services.

3   Research Methodology

It has become increasingly important to understand how to design and provide ICT-driven public services efficiently. We plan to obtain that understanding by combining sociological qualitative research, interdisciplinary case study methods, and software engineering approaches in the research on service design thinking in the public sector. The overall research method used by us is Action Design Research (Maung et al. 2011). We have chosen Action Design Research (ADR) because ADR is a research method for generating prescriptive design knowledge through building and evaluating interrelated ICT artifacts in an organizational setting. In our project this has a specific meaning of working out a repeatable method for designing proactive e-governance services in collaboration with their stakeholders. The ADR method consists of four stages. At Stage 1 the problem is identified and described in collaboration between researchers and stakeholders. At Stage 2 an artifact, which in our case is a prototypical implementation of the proactive family benefits service, is iteratively built and evaluated by stakeholders. At Stage 3 the artifact is rebuilt based on the results to apply to a broader class of problems. At Stage 4 the outcome is further generalized to design principles of proactive services of e-governance. This section describes Stage 1 of the case study in the research project undertaken by us. In our case study Stage 1 consisted of the following steps:

1. Interviewing stakeholders in Estonia's family benefit area.
2. Analyzing interviews by means of qualitative research (structured interviews).
3. Modeling the hierarchy of goals with the associated roles of stakeholders and quality goals and emotional goals by AOM to describe the "ideal" service of family benefits.
4. Using the resulting goal model for facilitating further discussions with stakeholders and obtaining feedback from them.

For accomplishing Step 1, we have carried out three structured interviews with four stakeholders in Estonia's family benefit area to investigate the perceptions of the interviewees about the potential areas of development for the family benefits service. The interviews were designed to understand the access points for increased effectiveness in providing the family benefits service to eligible persons and improving the service. The interviews were conducted with the employees of the Estonian Social Insurance Board. They were questioned regarding the involved stakeholders, potential improvements in efficiency, and the current situation with family benefits. As the debate on proactivity in the public sector is currently under way in Estonia, the interviewees were also questioned about the possibility of providing family benefits service proactively, as initiated by the Estonian Social Insurance Board. Future stages and iteration of the case study research will also include other stakeholders, such as citizens, in the discussion.

4   Family Benefits Service in Estonia

As was described in the previous section, the Estonian National Social Insurance Board was chosen as an example for this article on the current research by us. Estonia has developed into a novel example of a state able to implement practices in e-governance and other information technology solutions was done without in a short period of time. This having any substantial information infrastructure support (Sirendi 2012). Now, Estonia ranks among the first twenty countries in the world in e-governance development (United Nations 2010, 2012, 2014).

In Estonia, currently more than 170 databases are offering services via X-Road, the architectural backbone of e-Estonia – a data exchange layer that was launched in 2002 – which allows the nation's different e-services' databases, both public and private, to function in an interoperable fashion. Through that, estimably over 2000 services are available for use over X-Road (E-Estonia 2016).

However, only a fraction of these services are truly proactive, most notably the service of e-taxation. There is little to nothing written about proactive services in the public sector. Taking into consideration the ever-evolving nature of information technology that is embedded in the domain, it is becoming increasingly important to address proactivity in the public sector, and especially in the context of public services (Püüa 2008; Taveter 2014; Tallo 2015). This parallels with an increasing demand on countries to make use of the allocated resources in an efficient manner (Lindgren and Jansson 2013).

This article seeks to address the aim of proactivity through the example of the family benefits system in Estonia. The case study was chosen because it is a widely used service in Estonia. Family benefits are provided by the Social Insurance Board (Social Insurance Board 2016a) and are available to permanent residents and foreigners who have a temporary residence permit or the right for residence (Social Insurance Board 2016b).

The list of family benefits includes the following social benefits: childbirth allowance; adoption allowance; child allowance; childcare allowance; single parent's child allowance, conscript's child allowance or child allowance of a person in alternative service, foster care allowance, allowance for a start in independent life for person with no parental care, and allowance for big families with seven or more children (Social Insurance Board 2016b). An additional, needs-based family benefit is granted and paid by the local municipality (State Gazette 2016).

The application process is available through different channels both online and offline. The standard process of applying for family benefits includes submitting the applicant's passport or ID card and residence permit, if applicable. Depending on the type of allowance, one or more documents of the following types may be necessary: a certificate of employment, a Certification by the Defense Forces or the Defense Resources Agency, a document regarding the declaration of a parent to be a fugitive, a judgment on the establishment of guardianship or foster care contract, or a certificate by social welfare institutions or by a school for children with special needs (Social Insurance Board 2016b).

The interviews were designed to address the following list of topics: the stakeholders involved in the family benefits service, the efficiency of the service (both online and offline); potential points where an increase in efficiency is possible; the preference in the use of a channel by service users; and the potential weaknesses and constraints of the family benefits service.

The interviewees identified a diverse range of stakeholders, such as those covering support functions, procedural activities, e-service hosting on the state portal eesti.ee, and different registries on the architectural backbone for Estonia – X-Road. A number of stakeholders are involved whether in the application procedure or covering the support functions: the Social Insurance Board, the Ministry of Social Affair, the Estonian Information Systems' Authority, different registries, service developers, and different officials at the Social Insurance Board, who are working on the procedural aspects of the service.

The interviews revealed that increasing the efficiency of the service, both online and offline, would involve moving from an e-service (which currently enables submitting an application by electronic means) to an automated e-service (allowing to gather information from different registries and databases). Also, the offline service would benefit from switching from a service-specific application to a unified application, where the user of the service would be able to apply for a number of services at once to save time on doubling the provided by him/her application data.

Although the e-service is available on the state portal, it turned out from the interviews that only an average of 40 % of the service users are currently opting for that. The numbers vary from city to city, reaching up to 50 % in bigger cities (Tallinn and Tartu), whereas only around 10 % of families are currently using the e-service in the North-Eastern part of the country. The interviewees pointed out that a stronger focus on promoting the service and delivering clarifications in different languages would be beneficial.

The interviews showed that the current situation, where the necessary data is available in the registries, allows the application process to be relatively seamless and quick, taking from 15 to 20 days to process an application. However, should the applicant have been previously working or living abroad, the process would be longer, as each situation would usually be looked at in a case-by-case way.

Currently, the use of the family benefits service requires an individual to show initiative and apply for the benefit. According to the interviewees, proactivity in the provision of family benefits service may be hindered by the fact that different stakeholders may be eligible for the same benefit (e.g. both parents may apply for the childcare allowance). However, a proactive proposal could anyway be made to both.

Figure 1 represents an *initial* goal model describing the "ideal" proactive service of family benefits that was designed for further discussions with stakeholders. The figure represents the main goal of the family benefits service – ensure the well-being of the

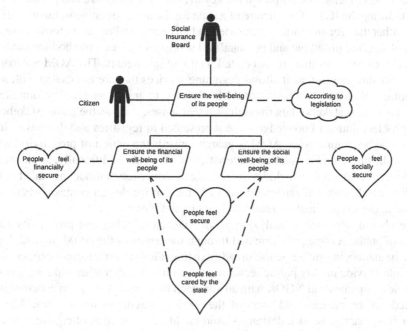

Fig. 1. The first draft of the AOM goal model, affiliated with Stage 3 of the ADR method

people living in a country – with its two sub-goals, representing the financial and social aspects of ensuring the well-being. Attached to the goals are the quality goals and emotional goals, applying to the corresponding goals. Figure 1 also shows the two stakeholder roles Citizen and Social Insurance Board.

5   Conclusions and Future Research

It has become increasingly important to understand how to design and provide ICT-driven public services efficiently. The authors have planned to obtain that understanding by combining sociological qualitative research, interdisciplinary case study methods, and software engineering approaches in the research on service design thinking in the public sector. The overall research method used by us is Action Design Research.

Technological advancements have opened up new possibilities for developing public services, e.g. personalized government services (Pieterson et al. 2007), which bases its core thesis on designing services around citizens' needs, rather than around the needs of the service providers. However, the author believes that the technological environment and current computational capacities would make it possible to take personalization of public services to a next, "proactive", level. Currently, the most relevant discussion regarding proactive public services and proactive government has been initiated regarding the Taiwan's fourth e-governance policy (Linders et al. 2015), which claims that instead of the current "pull" approach of traditional e-governance, where citizens must seek services provided by government, a "push" approach should be implemented where government proactively and seamlessly delivers timely, customized, and relevant services to its citizens. In our opinion the key to achieving proactive and public services lies in tailoring the ICT infrastructure of a state for the needs of citizens, businesses and NGOs rather than for supporting ministries and governmental organizations *per se*. The design of targeted proactive and personalized services requires a method for modeling sociotechnical systems that are associated with multiple agents. The AOM approach is suitable for this purpose, as it allows designing services that are associated with many different stakeholders. Moreover, AOM lends itself to analyzing problem domains of services and their stakeholders through different lenses, such as the goals, stakeholder roles, problem domain knowledge to be represented in registries and databases, interactions, and behaviors. Also, AOM is geared towards the notion of proactivity, which is one of the three fundamental characteristics of an agent. Additionally, as showcased in Miller et al. (n.d.), AOM includes the emotional dimension of modeling stakeholders' attitudes, which makes it especially useful in the service design context, where user-centered approach predicates greatly on emotional dimension.

The chosen approach – analyzing service design thinking and proactivity in the context of public service provision and through the lenses of the AOM methodology – allows the authors to synthesize the already existing information into a conceptual model that would provide mainly public sector organizations, but also other stakeholders such as private companies and NGOs, with an approach that would help them concentrate on the needs of the citizens and users of the service, playing different roles. The new approach – proactive service design – would facilitate automation of e-governance and enable maximum usage of information that is already stored in different registries and information systems run by government. Future research will seek to define how AOM and service design thinking could be the solution for building greater proactivity into the public sector.

References

Aagesen, G.: Citizen-centric process views for government service provisioning (n.d.). www.detgarbra.no/publish/last-ned/802

Andersen, K., Henriksen, H.: E-government maturity models: extension of the Layne and Lee model. Gov. Inf. Q. **23**, 236–248 (2006)

Bode, I.: Processing institutional change in public service provision: the case of the German hospital sector. Public Organ. Rev. **13**, 323–339 (2012)

Cook, L.S., Bowen, D.E., Chase, R.B., Dasu, S., Stewart, D.M., Tansik, D.A.: Human issues in service design. J. Oper. Manag. **20**, 159–174 (2002)

Dixon, M., Verma, R.: Sequence effects in service bundles: implications for service design and scheduling. J. Oper. Manag. **31**, 138–152 (2013)

E-Estonia: X-Road (2016). https://e-estonia.com/component/x-road/

Frasheri, N.: Critical view of e-government challenges for developing countries. In: Krishna, S., Madon, S. (eds.) The Digital Challenge: Information Technology in the Development Context, pp. 183–201. Ashgate, Farnham (2003)

Goldstein, S.M., Johnston, R., Duffy, J.A., Rao, J.: The service concept: the missing link in service design research? J. Oper. Manag. **20**, 121–134 (2002)

Gummesson, E.: Service design. In: Total Quality Management, pp. 97–101, April 1990

Hamilton, F., Pavan, P., McHale, K.: Designing usable e-government services for the citizen – success within the user centred design. Int. J. Public Inf. Syst. **3**, 159–167 (2011)

Heim, G.R., Ketzenberg, M.E.: Learning and relearning effects with innovative service designs: an empirical analysis of top golf courses. J. Oper. Manag. **29**, 449–461 (2011)

Hollins, W.: Design in the service sector. In: Managing Service Quality, pp. 33–37, March 1993

Karwan, K.R., Markland, R.E.: Integrating service design principles and information technology to improve delivery and productivity in public sector operations: the case of the South Carolina DMV. J. Oper. Manag. **24**, 347–362 (2006)

Kimbell, L.: Designing for service as one way of designing services. Int. J. Des. **5**(2), 41–52 (2011)

Layne, K., Lee, J.: Developing fully functional e-government: a four stage model. Gov. Inf. Q. **18**, 122–136 (2001)

Lee, J.: 10 year retrospect on stage models of e-government: a qualitative meta-synthesis. G. Inf. Q. **27**, 220–230 (2010)

Linders, D., Liao, C.Z.-P., Wang, C.-M.: Proactive e-governance: flipping the service delivery model from pull to push in Taiwan. Gov. Inf. Q. (2015)

Lindgren, I., Jansson, G.: Electronic services in the public sector: a conceptual framework. Gov. Inf. Q. **30**, 163–172 (2013)

Maung, K.S., Henfridsson, O., Purao, S., Rossi, M., Lindgren, R.: Action design research. MIS Q. **35**(1), 37–56 (2011)

Mead, G.H.: Mind, Self and Society. In: Morris, C.W. (ed.). University of Chicago Press (1934)

Miller, T., Lu, B., Sterling, L., Beydoun, G., Taveter, K.: Requirements elicitation and specification using the agent paradigm: the case study of an aircraft turnaround simulator. IEEE Trans. Softw. Eng. **40**(10), 1007–1024 (2014)

Miller, T., Pedell, S., Lopez-Lorca, A.A., Mendoza, A., Sterling, L., Keirnand, A.: Emotionally-driven models for people-oriented requirements engineering: the case study of emergency systems (n.d.). http://people.eng.unimelb.edu.au/tmiller/pubs/emotional-goals.pdf

Miller, T., Pedell, S., Sterling, L., Lu, B.: Engaging stakeholders with agent-oriented requirements modelling. In: Weyns, D., Gleizes, M.-P. (eds.) AOSE 2010. LNCS, vol. 6788, pp. 62–78. Springer, Heidelberg (2011)

Narasimhan, R., Talluri, S., Sarkis, J., Ross, A.: Efficient service location design in government services: a decision support system framework. J. Oper. Manag. **23**, 163–178 (2005)

Pieterson, W., Ebbers, W., Van Dijk, J.: Personalization in the public sector: an inventory of organizational and user obstacles towards personalization of electronic services in the public sector. Gov. Inf. Q. **24**(1), 148–164 (2007)

Püüa, M.: E-services need a revolution. (In Estonian) E-teenused Vajavad Revolutsiooni (2008). http://www.delfi.ee/archive/margus-puua-e-teenused-vajavad-revolutsiooni?id=19074613

Reddick, C.G.: A two-stage model of e-government growth: theories and empirical evidence for U.S cities. Gov. Inf. Q. **21**, 51–64 (2004)

Sasser, W.E., Olsen, P., Wychoff, D.D.: Designing the service firm organization. In: Management of Service Operations. Allyn & Bacon, Boston (1978)

Scheuing, E., Johnson, E.: Proposed model for new service development. J. Serv. Mark. **3**(2), 25–35 (1989)

Schuppan, T.: E-government in developing countries: experiences from sub-Saharan Africa. Gov. Inf. Q. **26**, 118–127 (2009)

Shostack, G.L.: How to design a service in European. J. Mark. **16**(1), 49–63 (1982)

Shostack, G. L.: Designing services that deliver. In: Harvard Bus. Rev. pp. 133–139 (1984)

Sirendi, R.: The development of Estonia's e-government. Master's thesis, University of Edinburgh, pp. 1–50 (2012)

Smith, A.M., Fischbacher, M.: Service design in the NHS: collaboration or conflict? J. Mark. Manag. **18**, 923–951 (2002)

Social Insurance Board: Estonian National Social Insurance Board (2016a). http://www.sotsiaalkindlustusamet.ee/?lang=en

Social Insurance Board: Family benefits (2016b). http://www.sotsiaalkindlustusamet.ee/family-benefits/

State Gazette: State Family Benefits Act (2016). https://www.riigiteataja.ee/en/eli/514012014002/consolide

Stickdorn, M., Schneider, J.: This is Service Design Thinking. BIS Publishers, Amsterdam (2011)

Tallo, I.: The developer of e-government condemns resting on the laurels. In: Estonian E-riigi edendaja taunib loorberitel puhkamist (2015). http://pluss.postimees.ee/3115409/e-riigi-edendaja-taunib-loorberitel-puhkamist

Taveter, K.: Estonian e-residency and e-government: how to go forward? In: Estonian Eesti e-residentsus ja e-riik: kuidas edasi? (2014). http://arvamus.postimees.ee/2840205/kuldar-taveter-eesti-e-residentsus-ja-e-riik-kuidas-edasi

Taveter, K., Sterling, L.: The Art of Agent-Oriented Modeling. MIT Press, Cambridge (2009)

United Nations: UN E-Government Survey 2010 (2010). http://unpan3.un.org/egovkb/Portals/egovkb/Documents/un/2010-Survey/Complete-survey.pdf

United Nations: UN E-Government Survey 2012 (2012). http://unpan3.un.org/egovkb/Portals/egovkb/Documents/un/2012-Survey/Complete-Survey.pdf

United Nations: UN E-Government Survey 2014 (2014). http://unpan3.un.org/egovkb/Portals/egovkb/Documents/un/2014-Survey/E-Gov_Complete_Survey-2014.pdf

Venkatesh, V., Chan, F.K.Y., Thong, J.Y.L.: Designing e-government services: key service attributes and citizens' preference structures. J. Oper. Manag. **30**, 116–133 (2012)

The City as an Interface Between Citizens and Public Administrations

Valentina Volpi[1,2(✉)], Antonio Opromolla[1,2], and Carlo Maria Medaglia[1]

[1] Link Campus University, Rome, Italy
{v.volpi,a.opromolla,c.medaglia}@unilink.it
[2] ISIA Roma Design, Rome, Italy

Abstract. The widespread of ICTs has been transforming the physical city. This process has been definitely influencing people's experiences within the urban environment creating new public spaces of interaction, affecting the physical and social urban structures. So, the city can be considered as an interface embedding different relational systems. In this perspective, Public Administration may benefit from the emergence of new interaction patterns for reinforcing the relationship with citizens. In effect, as the success of any public initiative appears to be strongly influenced by human aspects, Public Administrations should use the city interface to facilitate the communication and the collaboration with citizens. This paper aims to reflect on the interactive systems connecting citizens and Public Administration within the public sphere, and on the emergence of new perspectives and relations among people and urban places, in order to suppose new types of public touchpoints and interfaces supporting a sustainable city development.

Keywords: Interaction patterns · Interface · Touchpoints · Urban public space · Citizen engagement · Relational systems

1 Introduction

The Merriam-Webster Dictionary [1] defines an interface as "a. the place or area at which different things meet and communicate with or affect each other; b. a system that is used for operating a computer: a system that controls the way information is shown to a computer user and the way the user is able to work with the computer; c. an area or system through which one machine is connected to another machine".

Referring to the first meaning of the word "interface", the city itself can be considered as the main effective interface between Public Administrations (hereafter PAs) and citizens. In fact, the physical and digital structures of the city influence and shape the interactions between them. At the same time, the repeated use by people of these structures transforms the overall look and behaviour of the city.

An analogy can be also formulated with the second and third meanings by considering the city as the system used to show information to the citizens and letting them interact with the PAs or connecting different PAs. In addition, the pervasiveness of ICTs

© Springer International Publishing Switzerland 2016
F.F.-H. Nah and C.-H. Tan (Eds.): HCIBGO 2016, Part II, LNCS 9752, pp. 231–240, 2016.
DOI: 10.1007/978-3-319-39399-5_22

has been disseminating within the city various types of interfaces that could engage citizens within the city context [2–4].

Furthermore, even HCI field has moved beyond the early paradigm of graphic user interface, based on the desktop metaphor, towards a broader spectrum of user interfaces and new areas of possible interactive systems, not limited to technologies, in so far as they enhance human activity and experience. All this is a consequence of the arise of a more complex and varied environment made of a huge amount of information, new paradigms and mechanisms for collective activity, and a continual diversification of computing devices and contexts of implementation [5]. According to Tuters and de Lange [6], as technology becomes context-aware, "we would thus move from the graphic user interface as desktop, to new metaphors as rooms, streets, cities and even the planet as a whole".

In the same way, and especially in respect of the new capabilities allowed by the ICTs, during the years nature and modes of interaction between PAs and citizens have been multiplied and expanded in context by arising the interest of civic society towards policies and interventions affecting the common sphere. This more active behaviour of citizens towards activities of public interest has led to an openness of PA towards the involvement of citizens into the definition of the policies, fostering at the same time a wider spread of the principles of transparency, collaboration, and participation [7, 8]. Citizens are seen as crucial actors in the design and delivery of public services and city administrators are more and more seen as facilitators of the interaction between the different stakeholders of the city, rather than top-down decision maker and controller. Moreover, the emergence of collaborative service design processes involving citizens and PA (which will benefit from them and other creative citizens initiatives, such as community gardens, food swapping groups, etc.) is bringing a fundamental innovation in society and it is encouraging new forms of co-responsibility in dealing with social, economic, and environmental problems [9, 10].

So, citizens and PAs interact with each other by various ways and through a lots of different systems. Some of them use city patterns and structures or other urban elements to facilitate the interactions. For example, the grassroots initiatives on the territory aiming to the regeneration of shared urban spaces while promoting civic values and sustainability are also appealing to the PA for a better satisfaction of the main needs felt by citizens.

In this paper the authors discuss the possibility to use interactive public space elements as interfaces for attracting different city experiences and for supporting sustainable relationships between citizens and PAs. In detail, in the next section the authors present some related works about the influence of ICTs on the social relations within the city. In the third section the authors focus on the systems that allow building a sustainable relationship between citizens and PA. Then in the fourth section the systems supporting the emergence of sustainable process of change are identified. In the last section the conclusion is presented, pointing out the possibility of a redesign of the urban street furniture to enhance the relation between citizens and PA.

2   The City as Space of Interaction Among People: The Complex System Created by ICTs

A long-time, wide-spreading, and notable literature has been studying the social and relational systems within the city as influenced by its physical structure. Especially the field of urban sociology focuses on the social consequences that result from the physical urban environment, such as the ways people experience themselves and the others, interact, and organize their lives [11]. The arrangement of the urban environment, especially of public spaces, influences the social behaviours of its inhabitants, potentially shaping their relationships with the urban communities, the PA, and the city itself. Moreover, it contributes to build civic awareness. According to Amin [12], "public space, if organized properly, offers the potential for social communion by allowing us to lift our gaze from the daily grind, and as a result, increase our disposition towards the other", although the effective outcome is not predictable.

In the last decades, the academic interest towards the interaction among people and structures within the urban environment has been expanding by the increasing relevance and influence of ICTs on urban spaces, as the pervasiveness of ICTs become a key factor in people's everyday lives and city development [8, 13–15]. The so called ubiquitous technologies have been promising several advantages by releasing people from some troublesome activities and by sustaining the delivery of efficient services. At the same time they have been reinforcing the risk of social control by monitoring and tracking such activities as well. This extreme vision may be opposed by focusing and working on the potentiality of ICTs for "creating social bonds, increasing cultural understanding and making sense of our technologically sophisticated world" [15], "working with the life-supporting role of the urban infrastructure" [12], and offering "a unique opportunity to evaluate the 'relational' as flows, intensities and transductions that mobilize socio-technical assemblages" [14]. In effect, the introduction of ICTs within the urban space has had a revolutionary impact on people, by offering new possibilities of interaction and relation. Castells [16] found a "condition of structural schizophrenia" originated by the different spatial and temporal logics experienced by people: the virtual space of flows that shape the society and the space of places, the physical world where people live. Leaving aside the reflection on identity that Castell brings forth by this condition, the mutual influence between city and society is made evident and conditioned by ICTs. However, ICTs, far from replacing urban life, are a complementary tool that often modifies or is modified by the social or physical urban environments in qualitative new ways [13]. According to de Waal [17], ICTs, or those he called urban media (i.e. "media technologies that in one way or another can influence the experience of a physical location"), play a fundamental role in the urban life. Some of them mainly support efficiency and personalization in city dwellers lives, reducing the possibilities for mutual involvement, but others may combine efficiency and personalization with the aspects of citizenship and social connection, increasing the possibility of achieve more benefits for the city development. In all these cases de Waal, also highlights the importance of the organization, use and experience of the urban public sphere (i.e. "the collection of places in a city that serve as meeting places for city dwellers from various backgrounds") as it is strictly connected to urban communities development. Nowadays, urban media may intrinsically intervene on the experience of the urban public sphere, so that the urban public space can not be considered as a purely physical construct, but it is better addressed as an interface supporting and influencing many types of relationships on the basis of the elements it is made of (in detail de Waal considered five related aspects: platform, programme, protocol, filter, and agency). Ultimately, "the physical city is an 'interface' where collective practices take shape, and when these collective practices change, the shape and meaning of the physical environment change with them" [17].

In this sense the city can be considered a mean of communication and relation between citizens and city administrators, i.e. PAs, and urban technologies along with urban physical structures can be considered the interface elements designers have to properly arrange to support this relationship. For example, according to Schroeter [18], the use of digital and civic technologies directly accessible within the physical space could enhance the citizen's experience of that space and contribute to remove the hierarchical relations between "those who build the city and those who use it".

Since the presentation of the related work has been coming to characterize the city as made of social and physical structures and human interactions also supported by digital interactive systems continually influencing each other, the city can be considered as a complex system able to react and adapt itself to transformational events. Through this process, the city creates the possibilities for new relational opportunities to emerge and encourage the exploitation of sustainable social, economic, and environmental solutions. So, the increasing interconnection among urban levels and domains requires an organic approach, open to contamination, in order to properly deal with social, economic, and environmental challenges.

At the urban level, an organic approach has been elaborated by Alexander et al. [19] by identifying a common pattern language shared by all the people in society that shapes buildings and towns. It was a practical language for building and planning cities according to specific problems occurring in the environment. However, since it does not give predetermined solutions, but rather shows the essential field of relationship needed to solve a problem, different systems of interaction may occurring into a certain space. This approach deeply complies with the urban transformations produced by processes of emergence [20] occurring into a city and it offers a way for trying to bring them into the (urban) design practice.

3   Reflecting on Interactive Urban Systems for Building Sustainable Relationships Between Citizens and Public Administrations

The pervasive use of smartphones, along with other smart devices integrated into the environment, has generated blended spaces of interaction where physical and digital systems are strictly connected and urban life and ICTs mutually modify one another [6]. In effect, when the citizen moves from the app on his/her smartphone, to the physical space surrounding him/her, such as when he/she calculates the route to do in order to reach a specific place, he/she is moving from digital to physical channels and places. Regarding this, a work of the Nielsen Norman Group [21] shows that switching channels, both physical and digital enhances the whole user experience. In effect, in pursuing a certain activity the user sees the possible related touchpoint with the organization as one of the many interactions that contribute to create his/her overall relationship with that organization. For that reason, a seamless user experience is a fundamental condition to guarantee the perception of continuity through the entire user journey. Also in the use of public and urban services the continuity of experience is a crucial aspect that the PA should consider in building a substantial relationship with its citizens. However, rather than focus on public services intended as punctual activities, the PA might going further by investing in developing a less linear (but deeper) process of engagement with the citizens through non-conventional awareness systems. This type of intervention requires a comprehensive reflection on the modes by which the citizens are interconnected with the PA, approaching the city as interface.

Resmini and Rosati [22] show how into the city context the information flow, i.e. an essential element on which the relations between citizens and PAs are founded, follows two patterns: top-down and bottom-up. For example, the city signage is a top-down information flow, while the so called desire paths are bottom-up. Focusing on the relational aspect, often these one-way information flows remain unremarked and unheeded, as closed system. They do not trigger diffuse processes of development or exchange on the territory. On the contrary, when the system standing at the top (i.e. PA) is disposed to get a feedback from the system standing at the bottom (i.e. citizens) a bidirectional information flows occurs. Moreover, if the PA is open to really listen to the citizens' needs, a partnership and active engagement between them may occur. Visually, the top-down flow is represented as a straight arrow pointing up, while the bottom-up flow is represented as a straight arrow pointing down. The bidirectional flow derived from getting feedback from one part to another is represented as two straight arrows put side by side, one pointing up and one down. Finally, the bidirectional flow originated from the active participation of citizens is represented as a single straight arrow pointing both up and down. These representations show the nature and direction of the relationship between two subjects. The OECD [23] classified the relationship between government and citizens according to these patterns. In detail, it indicated the production and delivery of information as a one-way relationship between the government and "passive" citizens, the consultation as a two-way relationship still managed by the government, and the active participation as a two-way relationship that acknowledge an equal standing for citizens, although the final resolution rests with government.

Currently, the openness of government or PA, the growth of participatory democracy and civic engagement, along with the spread of ICTs, have been generating different collaborative approaches and initiatives. As a consequence, new systems of relationship between citizens and PAs, that may be represented with different and various patterns, has been originated. This is the case of sharing services, such as car sharing or carpooling. Since they need to be diffused on the territory and among people in order to be effective, the relationship that is established is not simply bottom-up or top-down. Instead, it might be seen as a wave, since there are a horizontal propagation of the relation among ideally the wider number of people. The PA, by creating the conditions for these services, can be considered as the trigger of the relationship. Differently, co-design processes establish a rounded, involving, and prolonged relationship that theoretically acknowledge an equal standing for citizens and PA. So the relation may take the shape of a spiral.

Giving a representation to the relation between citizens and PAs means reflecting on the exceptional variety of new relationships generated by the transformation of the urban public sphere. Thinking about these relationships helps in designing more effective interactive systems supporting an organic city development and fostering emergent and healthy processes of change. As said, these relational processes become especially noticeable in the public space, where the arrangement of the different urban structures and networks reflects the use made of it by people, in some cases showing their needs and habits. In detail, within the city the interactions between citizens and PA may occur in well-defined and designed spaces or in non-defined spaces. According to Cupers and Miessen [20], the first are the product of architectural plans and of a huge use of resources, while the second ones have no projects and are defined by the temporary and everyday people interventions and use. Moreover, the margins of public spaces are characterized by the continual emergence of elements that escape the restraints imposed by the hierarchical organization of public space and time. This multiplicity observable in public spaces generates openness and unpredictability, two characteristics that maintain the continual (lively) process of transformation of the city.

4   Identifying Interactive Systems Supporting the Emergence of Sustainable Process of Change

Nowadays the touchpoints between citizens and PAs are significantly increased. It is a consequence of the combination of physical and digital channels. In detail, the digitalization of a large number of public services due to the increasing improvement of the open government processes has placed beside the traditional public buildings other spaces of interaction diffused in the urban area. So, since open government is expected to have wide margin of growth, we can suppose an increasing in more interactive and effective points of contact between citizens and PAs on the territory, too.

Beyond the kind of relation between citizens and PA (direct, i.e. addressed to a short-term punctual goal, or indirect, i.e. addressed to a long-term evolving goal), different general contexts of interaction between citizens and PA can be identified on the basis of a combination of ICTs and public spaces. Following, the main contexts of interaction, seen as touchpoints between citizens and PA, are detailed.

First of all, the interaction may occur in spaces commonly related to the PA (e.g. public offices), possibly supported by interactive technologies and devices (e.g. interactive kiosks, smartphones, etc.) or completely set offline. Because of the widespread of e-government, nowadays the in-person interaction in a public office might be the final step of a process started online with the retrieve of information or the download of forms. In this case, the design of accessible and usable spaces has a central role in building the relation with the citizen. A similar situation occurs when the interaction is completely set online on the PA websites or mobile applications. In this case the user interacts with a proper interface which is expected to facilitate the interaction by providing more efficient, cost and time saving services. So the web and mobile interfaces have a crucial role into the definition of a good relationship between citizens and PA.

Indeed, both in physical and digital environments, the user is acting and interacting in a space directly connected to the activities of the PA.

Conversely, the presence of the PA may not be clearly perceived when the interaction occurs through the use of public services, as they are diffused within the whole city and they involve different structural elements. In the last years, the delivery of the city public services has been largely acknowledged as an essential part of the city development and the citizen experience. As a consequence, the public service design has been increasingly based on a citizen-centered approach in order to properly meet citizens' needs.

Another kind of interaction that might show the presence of the PA is the citizen experience diffused on the territory supported by the so called civic technologies accessed through physical fixed devices or mobile devices connected to the Internet. This kind of interactions typically includes the interactive systems based on crowd-sourcing and mapping, e.g. the reporting apps on city disservices.

Civic technologies, along with social networks and other online channels, also might support the organization of workgroups and communities of citizens aimed to the real-ization of offline activities to enhance the city quality of life or ideally retake the control of the city. They include the neighbourhood and community organizing platforms. The workgroups and communities of citizens could be seen as structured processes arisen by emergent people's needs. The interaction that springs typically sets a direct relation among the different stakeholders.

All these kinds of interactive systems imply an active involvement of citizens in the relation with the PAs. But this relation could also be built through an indirect interaction. In fact, in the event that there is not a clear objective to achieve in the near future, the PA should stimulate the emergence of a sustainable involvement of citizens in the city development process, not necessarily actively engaging them, but positively predispose them to possible changes coming to be. In this way, the risk of detachment between the citizens and the urban public sphere may be avoided. This kind of interventions may have direct and indirect effects on the definition of shared city spaces, services, and common practices. In fact, the city can be designed as an interface between citizens and PAs for supporting the emergence of new perspectives and connections among people and places within the city itself. In this sense, public spaces where people meet and carry on doing their own activities and where there is a latent presence of the PA, e.g. parks, squares, etc., might be the ideal set to imagine new interactive systems diffused on the territory, attracting the emergent needs and expectancies of citizens. In detail, the public spaces where the citizens bump into while conduct their activities or using the services offered by the city mainly are: squares, streets, gardens or parks, bus and train stops or platforms, and crossroads. These public spaces are fundamental for building a relation-ship between citizens and PAs. Particularly, the urban street furniture (e.g. bus shelters, street lamps, benches, waste receptacles) may be considered as a touchpoint and an interface between citizens and PAs, as it already is part of the overall user experience of the city. Moreover, in order to enhance the citizens' urban experience, the urban street furniture could integrate different digital devices. They sometimes already are present in the public spaces, but mostly as functional elements lacking in the relational aspect.

On the contrary, as the use of technology should be adequate to the usual activities of citizens, the interactive systems integrated into the urban street furniture, should be a system of attraction and multiplication of relational opportunities occurring into a specific space of the city (even the whole). It should offer new perspectives and inter-pretations about the city, through a process of awareness and consciousness raising. In fact, the experience of public space "supports building awareness of the commons" [12]. In the end, as the conditions for the new interactive systems are created by the PA, the perception of its effective presence might be diffused into several city places, reinforcing the relationship with the citizens.

So, it is important to give attention to the design of the overall interaction model defined by these interactive systems, being aware that a space of indefiniteness and multiplicity has to be saved. In effect, well-defined space of interaction may result unproductive as they tend to stop the emergence of innovative actions or ways to live, communicate, and think. On the contrary, undefined spaces let experience the encounters and confrontations between people [20] and do not impose any type of relation or engagement, as they are developed differently by people, "mediated as they are by sharp differences in social experience, expectations and conduct" [12]. According to de Lange and de Waal [24], "there is a lack of space for spontaneous encounters and public life, and a general lack of involvement with the immediate environment". So, it is funda-mental that the PA looks after the interactive systems supporting people creativity and awareness since, as Low [25] sustained, urban public spaces provide "a place for everyone to relax, learn and recreate, and open so that we have places where interper-sonal and intergroup cooperation and conflict can be worked out in a safe and public forum".

5 Conclusion

The results of this work have to be seen in the light of some limitations. First of all, the whole paper focuses on the abstract concept of the interface between citizens and PA and not on the description of a design or evaluation process concerning real products. In fact, its aim was to define a set of elements to take into account for a future application of what the authors sustain.

Secondly, as the authors focus on an interaction taking place into the physical urban environment and being enhanced by ICTs, there is not a focus on the interaction with all the type of online platforms related to e-government and open democracy, neither on that with the smart city services. Indeed, it would have been difficult to identify all the specific characteristics of each one.

Lastly, the PA has been considered as a subject separated from citizens, even if the authors acknowledged that the PA itself is constituted by citizens and city dwellers demanding for more sustainable process of innovation and relation.

Despite these limitations, the authors offer a useful point of view about the relational systems between citizens and PAs, bringing the assumption that the pervasiveness of the information into digital and physical spaces combined with collaborative processes has been generating different interaction patterns. Furthermore, as a facilitator of the sustainable development of the urban environment, PA should define effective and pleasant interfaces to communicate and collaborate with citizens, as they are fundamental actors in the definition of the city development. So, the authors propose a redesign of the urban street furniture for encouraging citizens' involvement within the city processes. Then, new types of interactive systems might arise in the public spaces of a city as trigger and carrier of the emergent processes occurring into the city.

In conclusion, touchpoints connected to the delivery of a clear public service, such as public offices, e-government services, etc. put a direct and very visible connection between citizens and PAs and they are easily acknowledged by citizens. However, they quite easily risk to attract complaints and anti-collaborative habits from citizens when something in the service delivery process goes wrong. On the contrary latent technologies situated in public spaces and supporting civic awareness are less visible (especially when the benefits produced affect the whole system and not the single citizen), but also less subject to temporary troubles.

So, the future steps of the research will concern first of all the design of an interactive system to support the emergence of sustainable processes of change. It will be a system integrated into the urban street furniture and connecting people with different places and "worlds" within the city, in order to enhance their civic awareness by collecting the traces of the different relationships existing among citizens, communities and PAs left by activities, projects, and transformations of the urban environment. This ideal system of attraction has to capture the spontaneous emergence of "new spatial combinations and new rhythms of usage" [12] in order to foster future processes of change and to give continuity to the user's urban experience, by simultaneously connecting different and distant places of the city.

References

1. Merriam-Webster. http://www.merriam-webster.com
2. Mattern, S.: Interfacing Urban Intelligence. Places J. (2014). https://placesjournal.org/article/interfacing-urban-intelligence/
3. Chang, M., Jungnickel, K., Orloff, C., Shklovski, I.: Engaging the city: public interfaces as civic intermediary. In: Proceeding of CHI 2005 Extended Abstracts on Human Factors in Computing Systems, pp. 2109–2110. ACM, New York (2005)
4. Tomitsch, M., McArthur, I., Haeusler, M.H., Foth, M.: The role of digital screens in urban life: new opportunities for placemaking. In: Foth, M., Brynskov, M., Ojala, T. (eds.) Citizen's Right to the Digital City: Urban Interfaces, Activism, and Placemaking, pp. 37–54. Springer, Singapore (2015)
5. Carroll, J.M.: Human computer interaction - brief intro. In: Soegaard, M., Dam, R.F. (eds.) The Encyclopedia of Human-Computer Interaction, 2nd edn. Interaction Design Foundation, Aarhus, Denmark (2012)
6. Tuters, M., de Lange, M.: Executable urbanisms: messing with ubicomp's singular future. In: Buschauer, R., Willis, K.S. (eds.) Locative Media: Multidisciplinary Perspectives on Media and Locality, pp. 49–70, Transcript, Bielefeld (2013)
7. Chun, S.A., Shulman, S., Sandoval, R., Hovy, E.: Government 2.0: making connections between citizens, data and government. Inf. Polity 15(1–2), 1–9 (2010)

8. Schaffers, H., Komninos, N., Pallot, M., Trousse, B., Nilsson, M., Oliveira, A.: Smart cities and the Future Internet: towards cooperation frameworks for open innovation. In: Domingue, J., et al. (eds.) The Future Internet. LNCS, vol. 6656, pp. 431–446. Springer, Berlin (2011)

9. Houk, M., Koutsomarkou, J., Moulin, E., Scantamburlo, M., Tosics, I. (eds.): Sustainable Regeneration in Urban Areas, URBACT II Capitalisation, April 2015. URBACT Report (2015)

10. Adams, E., Koutsomarkou, J., Moulin, E., Scantamburlo, M. (eds.): Social Innovation in Cities, URBACT II Capitalisation, April 2015. URBACT Report (2015)

11. Flanagan, W.G.: Urban Sociology: Images and Structure, 5th edn. Rowman & Littlefield, Plymouth, UK (2010)

12. Amin, A.: Collective culture and urban public space. City 12(1), 5–24 (2008)

13. Graham, S.: The Cybercities Reader. Routledge, London and New York (2004)

14. Galloway, A.: Intimations of everyday life: ubiquitous computing and the city. Cult. Stud. 18(2–3), 384–408 (2004)

15. Anttiroiko, A.-V.: U-cities reshaping our future: reflections on ubiquitous infrastructure as an enabler of smart urban development. AI Soc. 28(4), 491–507 (2013)

16. Castells, M.: The space of flows. In: The Rise of the Network Society: With a New Preface, Volume I, Second Edition with a New Preface. Wiley-Blackwell, Oxford, UK (2009)

17. de Waal, M.: The City as Interface. How New Media Are Changing the City. nai010, Rotterdam (2014)

18. Schroeter, R.: Engaging new digital locals with interactive urban screens to collaboratively improve the city. In: Proceedings of the ACM 2012 Conference on Computer Supported Cooperative Work, pp. 227–236. ACM, New York (2012)

19. Alexander, C., Ishikawa, S., Silverstein, M.: A Pattern Language: Towns, Buildings, Construction. The Oxford University Press, New York (1977)

20. Cupers, K., Miessen, M.: Spaces of Uncertainty. Verlag Müller + Busmann, Wuppertal (2002)

21. Nielsen Norman Group. https://www.nngroup.com/articles/seamless-cross-channel

22. Resmini, A., Rosati, L.: Pervasive Information Architecture: Designing Cross-Channel User Experiences. Morgan Kaufmann Publishers, San Francisco (2011)

23. OECD: Citizens as Partners: OECD Handbook on Information, Consultation and Public Participation in Policy-Making. OECD Publishing, Paris (2001)

24. de Lange, M., de Waal, M.: Owning the city: new media and citizen engagement in urban design. First Monday 18(11) (2013). http://firstmonday.org/ojs/index.php/fm/article/view/4954/3786

25. Low, S.: The erosion of public space and the public realm: paranoia, surveillance and privatization in New York City. City Soc. 18(1), 43–49 (2006)

Exploring Human-Technology Interaction
in Layered Security Military Applications

Amanda Wachtel$^{(\boxtimes)}$, Matthew Hoffman, Craig Lawton,
Ann Speed, John Gauthier, and Robert Kittinger

Sandia National Laboratories, Albuquerque, USA
{awachte,mjhoffm,crlawto,aespeed,jhgauth,
rskitti}@sandia.gov

Abstract. System-of-systems modeling has traditionally focused on physical systems rather than humans, but recent events have proved the necessity of considering the human in the loop. As technology becomes more complex and layered security continues to increase in importance, capturing humans and their interactions with technologies within the system-of-systems will be increasingly necessary. After an extensive job-task analysis, a novel type of system-of-systems simulation model has been created to capture the human-technology interactions on an extra-small forward operating base to better understand performance, key security drivers, and the robustness of the base. In addition to the model, an innovative framework for using detection theory to calculate d' for individual elements of the layered security system, and for the entire security system as a whole, is under development.

Keywords: System-of-systems · Layered security · Human-technology interaction · Human performance factors · Modeling and simulation · Detection theory

1 Introduction

Historically, systems of systems (SoS) modeling efforts have focused on depicting physical systems and the connections (whether physical connections or communications related) between them. Man-made systems are modeled in detail, while humans mainly play a supportive role when their inclusion is absolutely necessary. For example, the human may be included in the model to provide maintenance to a system. Yet the maintenance time is based on a specified distribution or even a static number, giving little consideration to variation in individuals or circumstances. Due to this idyllic treatment of humans in SoS modeling, many failures seen in real life are missed in the modeling realm.

The danger of failing to include the human in the loop becomes apparent when looking at historical cases. Take for example the security breach at NNSA's Y-12 National Security Complex, which arose in part from distractions, improper technology use, false alarm fatigue, and poor assumptions [1]. Unknown outsiders with unclear intentions can also pose a threat as seen at Patrol Base Bushmaster when an outsider charged the base with a vehicle outfitted with a 2,000 lb vehicle-borne improvised

© Springer International Publishing Switzerland 2016
F.F.-H. Nah and C.-H. Tan (Eds.): HCIBGO 2016, Part II, LNCS 9752, pp. 241–250, 2016.
DOI: 10.1007/978-3-319-39399-5_23

explosive device (VBIED) that killed and injured many of the soldiers [2]. Other examples of human failures in security systems abound. In fact, Jarret Lafleur et al. performed an analysis of 23 heists and found that "A common thread of all defeat methods is that they attack segments of the security system in which humans are in the loop..." [3]. Whether looking at the recent failure of the layered security system at Y-12, successful heists, or the devastating bomb attack on Patrol Base Bushmaster, the conclusion is that the opportunity for a major breakdown in SoS safety or security is due in large part to the human in the loop.

2 Motivation

Since humans account for the majority of uncertainty in an SoS and in layered security, the role of human-technology interaction must be understood. As technology becomes increasingly sophisticated, uncertainties around human performance will grow dramatically. In addition, human inefficiency can lead to high costs, increased logistics, and increased vulnerability. We are focusing our modeling efforts on a first attempt at understanding the effects of human-technology interactions on SoS level performance. From there, this understanding will be incorporated into SoS engineering processes using empirical, data-driven methods. Only when the impact of humans and their interactions with the physical systems present in an SoS framework is fully accounted for will we be able to predict, assess, and improve performance and human efficiency in SoS models and be able to accurately evaluate the effects of potential organizational, doctrinal, or system changes.

3 Use Case

Our first step in beginning to capture human-technology interaction in an SoS was to define a representative use case to focus on. For the initial modeling effort, the use case focused on a patrol base (now classified as an extra-small forward operating base) in the Middle East and the threat posed by vehicle-borne improvised explosive devices (VBIEDs) as motivated by the attack on Patrol Base Bushmaster. The research team is comprised of individuals with expertise in the fields of SoS modeling and industrial-organizational psychology. To develop a conceptual model, all human entities, tasks, and the corresponding systems most relevant to the use case were identified. From there work was done to qualitatively characterize interdependencies between both systems and also humans and systems.

It was also key to identify variables relevant to the performance of the tasks. In simulated deployment environments such as the Navy SEAL's Hell Week, factors such as fatigue and environmental, physical, and psychological stressors were shown to degrade human performance to a greater degree than that caused by intoxication, sedatives, or hypoglycemia [4]. Variables were included in the SoS model to capture factors that impact the ability of human-technology couplings to perform tasks. Such variables include, but are not limited to, the number of tasks a human is required to perform, fatigue, stress, distractions, and environmental conditions.

4 Data Collection

To validate the SoS modeling approach we are engaging with subject matter experts (SMEs) who have experience in layered security on military bases. Focusing on key aspects of an extra-small forward operating base (FOB) such as vehicle checkpoints and the tactical operations center (TOC), a detailed task analysis was conducted. The SMEs filled in details such as the duration of each task, how many humans are needed for each task, what types of technology are used for the task, and task interdependencies. They have also given critical input as to which human and external variables may affect specific instances of human-technology interaction.

4.1 Job-Task Analysis

To begin to analyze the tasks humans perform on FOBs, duties were broken down into guard duties and duties performed within the Tactical Operations Center (TOC) on the base. The guard duties were further broken down to include tasks performed by guards outside of base (i.e. at a checkpoint), at the base gate, and inside the base near critical infrastructure. To model these tasks in an SoS model, tasks are considered to be associated with a location on, or outside of, the FOB. The external guards perform their tasks at a roadblock, the gate guards at the base gate, the internal guards near a target of value, and the surveillance, command, and control tasks are performed inside the TOC. Examples of tasks that would occur at the base gate are checking the driver's identification and checking the vehicle for contraband items and VBIEDs. These examples will be revisited below to help explain the more complex metrics included in the job-task analysis. Each location's tasks were vetted with the SMEs.

Each task listed includes multiple dimensions of data used in the model. Basic metrics include the frequency of the task, how long the task takes to complete, the number of people required to complete the task, and any technologies/equipment used to carry out the task. The nature of the task, whether physical, mental, or both, is also included to begin to capture the human element. Many variables will ultimately be included in the model that act upon the human's ability to successfully complete the task. These include (among many others) factors such as heat, fatigue, time of day, physical injury, dehydration, length of shift, and hunger. Some factors have a greater impact to human performance when the task is more physical in nature, such as not being able to use a complicated, hand-held user interface in extreme cold, while other factors have a greater impact on primarily mental tasks, such as not being able to accurately identify an ID as fake when working long shifts for months on end with little sleep. Which factors impact which tasks was determined primarily through SME input.

In addition to factors that impact human performance, SMEs also helped determine factors that would impact technology functionality. Depending on the technology or equipment in question, these factors could include heat, humidity, rain, lightning, cold, and high wind/sandstorms. It is conceivable that these factors could at times cause the technology to malfunction or become unusable to the humans relying on that technology to complete a task. For example, a sandstorm could prevent a guard at a roadblock from using binoculars to see a vehicle approaching at a distance, while lightning could temporarily disable the communications network and prevent a guard from relaying a threat to the TOC.

While some conditions affect only the human or only the technology, it is clear that many important effects are interactive; i.e., they only occur when a person is using a particular kind of equipment under certain physical and mental conditions. These can range from the cognitively and technologically banal (such as gloves reducing dexterity in cold weather) to the complex (such as a soldier having difficulty using a weapon technology's complex interface during a cognitively demanding combat situation). When including humans in the SoS model, it was of primary importance to capture every time a human is interacting with technology and every way that interaction can be changed by affecting the human, the technology, or both.

4.2   Business Rule Data Elicitation

In addition to the data-driven approach to the job-task analysis outlined above, work is being done to capture the business rules needed for the model by interviewing SMEs about life on base. The data elicitation helps clarify the chain of events from the time a threat is detected to the time when a response team is sent. It also allows the team to understand which tasks and/or technologies pose the greatest difficulty to personnel and how the chain-of-command plays out both daily and in heightened-security situations. A few examples of questions used for business rule elicitation include:

- What are the hardest things for new people to come up to speed with? What are the most common mistakes?
- What equipment do you find most frustrating to use?
- Under what situations do you feel particularly stressed or confused? Bored?
- How often and in what environments do you train? How relevant do you feel the training is to the actual job?
- How many people are on a shift? Are teams usually the same people?
- How is information passed during changes in personnel?
- How much sleep do you get each night? How often do you go between sleep? How often is your sleep disrupted?
- How long does it take for a response team to get there after being dispatched?

Note that the same question may be asked multiple times in various ways to try to be able to work around topics that may elicit strong reactions when worded a certain way. For example, someone who has been on a FOB may not want to admit to having had difficulty using a certain technology, but when asked which technologies new recruits have the most problems with, they are free to respond without commenting on their own personal capabilities.

5   System-of-Systems Model

An SoS model to capture these human-technology interactions is now in the intermediate stages of development. The model is built in FlexSim [5], an off-the-shelf discrete event simulation software traditionally used to build manufacturing models, but which offers flexibility through custom scripting and can thus handle a wide array of models and logic. The simulation is portioned off into a series of tasks, each requiring a specified number of people using given technologies to complete the tasks as discussed in the previous section. Various threats such as malicious outsiders (or insiders), contraband objects, suspicious activity outside the fence, and VBIEDs are randomly generated as the simulation progresses. The model tracks how many times the humans and layered security system are able to correctly detect, assess, and respond to these threats (Fig. 1).

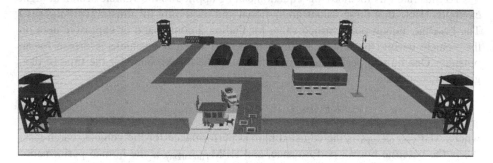

Fig. 1. FlexSim model of extra-small forward operating base

5.1   Human-Technology Performance

Each soldier has a probability distribution associated with their ability to successfully complete the task(s) to which they are assigned. These performance factors are largely based on existing studies and SME input. The factors not only capture a soldier performing a task, they capture them performing the task *using a certain technology*. This means that the likelihood of completing a task can be impacted by changes to the soldier, changes to the technology, or both.

The factors impacting performance may be external, such as a dust storm, or inherent to the system, such as a soldier suffering from extreme fatigue. In either case, the human may or may not have control over the changing situation, yet their performance may be impacted. Factors such as fatigue are obvious culprits but there are seemingly innocuous factors that have an equally large influence. Take for example a soldier using a mirror on a stick and a flashlight to search underneath a vehicle for IEDs. Once the sun sets, the soldier is actually able to better use the technology since the light from the flashlight is now concentrated on the mirror and bounces up onto the undercarriage of the vehicle. Whereas daylight created additional shadows and glare, night has created ideal conditions for this specific task.

To capture the impacts of external and inherent factors on performance, the baseline performance metrics are scaled up or down based on whether the factor is expected to degrade or improve performance. Using Wincek and Haight's human error rate formulas [6] as a mathematical basis for our framework, we have modified the human error rate equation to create the following calculation for human performance.

$$AHP = BHP * HPM_1 * HPM_2 * \cdots * HPM_n \tag{1}$$

where AHP is the adjusted human performance, BHP is the baseline human performance, and HPM is the human performance modifier. HPM is greater than one when the factor increases human performance and less than one when the factor decreases human performance. Each factor that impacts performance on the task in question would be represented by a unique HPM factor. An HPM factor may capture an effect to the human performing the task, to their technology, or to the combination.

To illustrate this method, this equation can be applied to the vehicle search at night example. (Note that these values are notional and used only for illustrative purposes.) The baseline human performance value for finding a contraband or explosive item on the vehicle during the day is assumed to be 0.8 when the vehicle is driven by an outsider. One human performance modifier is applied to account for the time of day, giving the equation

$$AHP_{VehicleSearch} = 0.8 * HPM_{TimeofDay} \tag{2}$$

where $AHP_{VehicleSearch}$ is the adjusted human performance for the vehicle search task, 0.8 is the baseline human performance, and $HPM_{TimeofDay}$ is the human performance modifier based on time of day. If the search takes place during daylight hours, the human performance modifier is 1 to maintain the baseline human performance. However if the search occurs at night, a scale factor of 1.1 is used to increase the performance on the task by ten percent. This methodology is applied to all human-technology performance factors for the external and inherent impacts of interest. Each technology also has inherent reliability data such as how many hours it can be used before needing new batteries, and how long its average lifespan is, resulting in multiple failure modes for each technology in the model. More sophisticated performance adjustment methods could be considered and used within the framework if warranted (and supported by data); however, given the data available, using the product of HPM factors is sufficient to allow exploration of interesting conditional and interactive model behaviors.

5.2   Communications

Additionally, each task is linked into the communications network which can also experience various types of failures. The communications network is primarily used to relay detected threats, assess the situation, and take action to nullify the threat. Each guard task defined in the job-task analysis is capable of communicating with the TOC to report a threat. Communications in the model are handled according to the following communications hierarchy (Fig. 2).

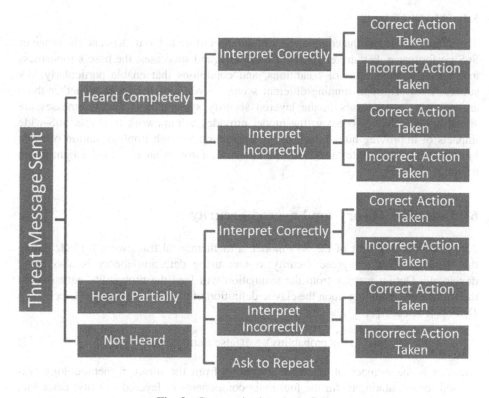

Fig. 2. Communications logic flow

For every threat message that is radioed in to the TOC, the message can be heard completely, heard partially, or not heard at all. Messages that are heard can either be interpreted correctly or incorrectly with the additional option of asking the sender to repeat the message if only part of the message is heard. If the message was never received by the TOC, the sender tries again after a defined time interval. Whether the message is interpreted correctly or incorrectly, the TOC personnel can still take either the correct or the incorrect action. Imagine the scenario where the soldier in the TOC has been trained for a different task or has simply received inadequate training for the TOC. A threat is radioed in and they understand the message, but due to lack of training they inadvertently activate the wrong response. Similarly, a message could be heard incorrectly and the correct action could still be taken by dumb luck. Of course these scenarios are less likely to occur, which are reflected in their probabilities relative to the other scenarios. Each item in the communications logic flow is assigned a probability in the model and the model automatically chooses the communication path when a threat message is sent based on those allocations.

5.3 Model Outputs

The intention is to use the completed extra-small FOB model to understand the range of SoS performance, key drivers in security failures and successes, the base's robustness to unusual combinations of conditions, and conditions that enable particularly low success rates. Through running different scenarios we hope to identify whether there are recurring weaknesses in the layered security system or if the weaknesses are situation-dependent. Moreover, the model provides a framework to assess SoS-wide impacts of improving human-technology interaction through implementation of more intuitive technology interfaces and operations, or through an increased emphasis on training.

6 Detection Theory for Layered Security

Alongside development of the SoS model, a mathematical framework for calculating the "goodness" of a layered security system using detection theory is also being developed. Output metrics from the simulation will feed the probability equations in the framework. Building upon the classic definition of d' in Macmillan and Creelman's *Detection Theory* [7]

$$d' = z(\text{hit probability}) - z(\text{false alarm probability}), \tag{3}$$

where z is the number of standard deviations from the mean, a methodology was created for calculating d' for the four main components of layered security: detection, delay, communications, and response. Each of the four security-area-specific d' values will then be rolled-up into a d' representative of the layered security system as a whole.

The area-specific d's vary based on the domain-specific terms that define what constitutes the hit probability and the false alarm probability. Tables 1, 2, 3 and 4 are given below to help the reader understand what is meant by a hit and a false alarm in each instance.

Table 1. Terminology for detection d'

	Response		
Attack	Detected	Undetected	# Trials
Yes	Hit	Miss (false neg)	n
No	False alarm (false pos)	Correct rejection	m

Table 2. Terminology for delay d'

	Response		
Incident	Delayed	Insufficient delay	# Trials
Adversary	Hit	Miss (false neg)	n
Friendly	False alarm (false pos)	Correct rejection	m

Table 3. Terminology for communications d'

	Response		
Attack	Communicated	Not communicated	# Trials
Yes	Hit	Miss (false neg)	n
No	False alarm (false pos)	Correct rejection	m

Table 4. Terminology for response d'

	Response		
Attack	Adequate	Insufficient	# Trials
Yes	Hit	Miss (false neg)	n
No	False alarm (false pos)	Correct rejection	m

Once the terminology for hits and false alarms has been specified for each area, probabilities for events happening in serial and parallel can also be defined. For detection, delay, communications, and response the events are considered to be sensors, barriers, messages, and responses, respectively. For example the probability of a hit for sensors in parallel can be defined as

$$P_{hit} = \min\left(P_{hit,s1}, P_{hit,s2}\right) \text{OR} \frac{P_{hit,s1} + P_{hit,s2}}{2}, \tag{4}$$

where $P_{hit,s1}$ is the hit probability of the first sensor and $P_{hit,s2}$ is the hit probability of the second sensor. The minimum would be used to calculate the "worst case" hit probability while the average would be used to calculate the "average case" hit probability. The probability of a false alarm for sensors in parallel can be defined as

$$P_{FA} = 1 - (1 - P_{FA,S1})(1 - P_{FA,S2}), \tag{5}$$

where $P_{FA,S1}$ is the probability of a false alarm for sensor one and $P_{FA,S2}$ is the probability of a false alarm for sensor two.

Similar equations have been derived for events in series for multiple sensors, and in series and parallel for the other three areas. As mentioned, the d' values for the individual areas are then combined into a base level d' to measure the effectiveness of the layered security system. The individual d' are aggregated statistically according to the event path through the security system. The result is a single measure of the sensitivity—the ability to respond appropriately to a stimulus—of the physical security system.

7   Future Work

While the methodology employed to capture humans within a systems-of-systems model has shown great potential, many data gaps still exist that must be addressed. The human performance factors used in the model have been obtained from studies with situations as close as possible to those of the tasks being performed in the base camp, but the existing studies may or may not accurately capture the intricacies of using the specific military technologies in question. Ideally, more studies involving military personnel in deployment scenarios would be needed to further refine and validate the model.

Acknowledgements. Sandia National Laboratories is a multi-program laboratory managed and operated by Sandia Corporation, a wholly owned subsidiary of Lockheed Martin Corporation, for the U.S. Department of Energy's National Nuclear Security Administration under contract DE-AC04-94AL85000 (SAND2016-1471 C).

References

1. U.S. Department of Energy Office of Inspector General: Inquiry into the Security Breach at the National Nuclear Security Administration's Y-12 National Security Complex. Special report DOE/IG-0868, DOE (2012)
2. Stars and Stripes. http://www.stripes.com/news/a-moment-that-changed-everything-1.88432
3. Lafleur, J.M., Purvis, L.K., Roesler, A.W.: The Perfect Heist: Recipes from Around the World. SAND2014-1790, Sandia National Laboratories (2014)
4. Lieberman, H.R., Bathalon, G.P., Falco, C.M., Morgan III, C.A., Niro, P.J., Tharion, W.J.: The fog of war: decrements in cognitive performance and mood associated with combat-like stress. Aviat. Space Environ. Med. **76**(7), Section II (2005)
5. FlexSim. https://www.flexsim.com
6. Wincek, J.C., Haight, J.M.: Realistic human error rates for process hazard analyses. Process Saf. Prog. **26**(2), 95–100 (2007). American Institute of Chemical Engineers
7. Macmillan, N.A., Creelman, C.D.: Detection Theory: A User's Guide. Psychology Press, Abingdon (2004)

An Agent-Based Study on the Relationship Between Tiao-kuai Structure and Fragmentation Phenomenon of Crisis Governance

Yun-Feng Wang[✉]

School of Economics and Management, Tongji University, Shanghai, China
tjuwyf@tongji.edu.cn

Abstract. The relationship between fragmentation phenomenon and Tiao-kuai structure is a basic problem of Chinese crisis governance. An agent-based model is developed which has two actors, namely local government and internal bureaucracy agency. It sets capability utilization mode according to the relative bargaining power in urgent environment. After events randomly fall into their respective responsibility field, actor deals with events within ability field. Then the completion rate of utility filed events is calculated to evaluate the fragmentation degree. With exogenous capability allocation and utilization mode, Monte Carlo simulation experiments show that: (1) the fragmentation could be generated by the simplest Tiao-kuai structure; (2) the fragmentation seems inevitable in most cases; (3) local government should pay more attention on capacity allocation instead of utilization mode, but internal agency should keep eyes on both of them; (4) The best choice is equal distribution of capability no matter under which kind of utilization mode.

Keywords: Fragmentation · Tiao-kuai structure · Crisis governance · Agent-based computational organization

1 Introduction

Fragmentation of crisis governance has become a serious problem in China for many years. A huge amount of public sectors' capacity, such as resources, information, efforts, etc., has not appeared at the right time, with a right amount or in the right place. Given the size and urgency of the fragmentation issue, there have been considerable speculations about its causes. Influencing factors include government's power and function setting, operating methods, the way of stimulating and restricting government acts and so on [1, 2]. However, the organizational causations, especially Tiao-kuai structure, are very likely to be the underlying cause of this phenomenon [3].

The Chinese government system is a five-level hierarchy of dyadic nested structure. Two radically different structural approaches was used by national government: (1) the decentralization of economic and political decision making to local governments; (2) the partial centralization of a number of key bureaucracies in order to regulate and discipline local government agents. This governance structure is not a temporary

© Springer International Publishing Switzerland 2016
F.F.-H. Nah and C.-H. Tan (Eds.): HCIBGO 2016, Part II, LNCS 9752, pp. 251–258, 2016.
DOI: 10.1007/978-3-319-39399-5_24

measure. And then the local government which consists of agencies of bureaucracy has to face the fundamental structural problems. Typically individual offices within these bureaucracies are no longer under the supervision of local governments (Kuai); rather, they are directly controlled by their functional administrative superiors (Tiao) [4].

Under such a structure design, the local governments' behaviors, to a large extent, are the equilibrium of a multi-player game of the government system. From top to bottom, the local governments' degree of freedom is shrinking and is imposed increasing rules by the inter-organizational network. The allocation and utilization method of capability could be regarded as an exogenous variable of local government.

Unfortunately, in the existing literature, organizational structure factor is often blended with other factors, which impairs the credibility of conclusions. For example, the role that Tiao-kuai structure plays in the creation of fragmentation is still not clear. And it is not sure whether the best game equilibrium that minimizes the fragmentation exists.

Therefore, this study attempts to address the above shortcomings and further explore the issue by experimentally investigating the following basic questions:

(1) Does the fragmentation phenomenon of crisis governance really come from the Tiao-kuai structure? In other words, can fragmentation phenomenon be produced by a system which only has the simplest Tiao-kuai structure?
(2) Are there any combinations of capability allocation and the rules of capability utilization that would satisfy both the local government and internal agency? That indicates improving or even eliminating fragmentation on both sides simultaneously.

2   Model

The conventional Tiao-kuai structure can be modeled as follows. Event set $\Theta = \{\Phi_1, \Phi_2\}$ should be dealt by actor set $E = \{e_1, e_2\}$, where e_1 is the internal agency, and e_2 is the local government. Actor e_i has the ability to handle with Φ_i, the ability field, where $\Phi_1 = \{\theta_1, \theta_2\}$ and $\Phi_2 = \{\theta_3, \theta_4\}$. Actor e_i has the capability $R(e_i) \rightarrow [0, 1]$, and if it attempts to handle event θ_j completely, it has to lose capability $C(\theta_j) \rightarrow [0, 1]$. In order to balance demand and supply, the total amount of capability of actors is supposed to be equal to the total amount needed to finish Θ,

$$\sum_i R(e_i) = \sum_j C(\theta_j) \tag{1}$$

Let b_{ji} be the ability that e_i decides to use on θ_j, where $\sum_j b_{ji} \leq R(e_i)$, $i \in \{1, 2\}$ and $j \in \{1, 2, 3, 4\}$. Therefore, when e_i chooses to spend b_{ji} on θ_j, we have

$$R'(e_i) = \begin{cases} R(e_i) - b_{ji} & \text{if } b_{ji} \leq C(\theta_j) \\ R(e_i) - C(\theta_j) & \text{if } b_{ji} > C(\theta_j) \end{cases} \tag{2}$$

and

$$C'(\theta_j) = \begin{cases} C(\theta_j) - b_{ji} & \text{if } b_{ji} < C(\theta_j) \\ 0 & \text{if } b_{ji} \geq C(\theta_j) \end{cases} \tag{3}$$

where $R'(e_i)$ is the remaining capability of e_i, and $C'(\theta_j)$ is the amount of capability still needed to finish θ_j.

The actors have their respective responsibility fields for events listed in Table 1. Here θ_j in different positions represents the actor in row has the ability to finish it and the actor in column has responsibility to finish it.

Table 1. Ability and responsibility fields of actors

	Responsibility field of actor e_1	Responsibility field of actor e_2
Ability field of actor e_1	θ_1	θ_2
Ability field of actor e_2	θ_3	θ_4

According to the roles of actors, actor e_i has utility field Ψ_i, where $\Psi_1 = \{\theta_1, \theta_3\}$, $\Psi_2 = \Theta$. That means the internal agency is just required to finish the events among its responsibility field. But the local government should take care of the whole event set Θ.

Formula 1 indicates that if actors could sincerely cooperate with each other, all events could be finished. In that sense, the fragmentation can be evaluated by the completion rate of utility field. For actor e_1, namely the internal agency, the fragmentation index is

$$F_1 = \frac{C'(\theta_1) + C'(\theta_3)}{C(\theta_1) + C(\theta_3)} \tag{4}$$

For actor e_2, namely the local government, the index is

$$F_2 = \frac{\sum_j C'(\theta_j)}{\sum_j C(\theta_j)} \tag{5}$$

Typically, the ability filed, responsibility field and utility filed are discrepant for each actor. There is only one exception where e_1's responsibility field are the same with its utility filed.

In an urgent situation, actors are limited on their choices. Firstly, actors do not have complete information on Θ. Generally they follow the development of situation, and make choices after the event types are certain. The distribution of types among events should be regard as a random process:

$$p(\theta_j) = \begin{cases} \frac{1}{4} & \text{if } j \in \{1, 2, 3, 4\} \\ 0 & \text{otherwise} \end{cases} \tag{6}$$

Secondly, they do not have control on the amount of ability they own. They just spend what they have. Here used the rate of capability to describe the capability allocation between actors:

$$\text{capability rate} = \frac{R(e_1)}{R(e_1) + R(e_2)} \quad (7)$$

Thirdly, in the vast majority of situations they cannot accurately predict the demand of capability, $C(\theta_j)$, and have to decide on the event to be first dealt with. Table 2 lists three strategies are summarized to represent actors' decision process. In strategy 1 and 3, e_1 and e_2's preference is in priority respectively, while in strategy 2, priority is given to actors' own preference.

Table 2. Strategy types given preference of actors

Strategy	Priority of e_1	Priority of e_2
1	$\theta_1 \succ \theta_2$	$\theta_3 \succ \theta_4$
2	$\theta_1 \succ \theta_2$	$\theta_3 \prec \theta_4$
3	$\theta_1 \prec \theta_2$	$\theta_3 \prec \theta_4$

Note that the responsibility field also has an impact on actors' preference. The actor should prefer θ_j that comes from its own responsibility field. For example, if two θ_j both make contributions to improve actor e_i's fragmentation rate, e_i will prefer the one comes from its own responsibility field.

3   Method

3.1   Instantiation of Model

Agent-based simulation system is used to instantiate the theory model. The advantage of this kind of system is that the actors' preference could be expressed exactly by the behavior of agents.

The total amount of capability owned by actors is 10 units. The capability is distributed to internal agency and local government according to the capability rate which is preset.

$$\text{capability of internal agency} = 10 \times \text{capability rate} \quad (8)$$

$$\text{capability of local government} = 10 \times (1 - \text{capability rate}) \quad (9)$$

Given the capability, the actors will deal with the events according to the strategy set. As the actors could only deal with events among their own ability field, the action sequence is not important.

Table 3 presents four types of events corresponding to Table 1 with new terms for convenience. The first and second letters denote the ability field and the responsibility field respectively, namely, A for internal agency and G for local government. The total number of events is 10 which corresponds to the total amount of capability.

Table 3. Four types of events from combinations of ability field and responsibility field

	Internal agency responsibility field	Local government responsibility field
Internal agency ability field	A-A	A-G
Local government ability field	G-A	G-G

According to Table 2, three types of strategy are designed to guide the actors' behavior. Actors are supposed to complete the prior type of event and then the other one if they still have capability. The one with more bargaining power can mobilize capability to its responsibility field, but in a close game, actor can only use its own capability (Table 4).

Table 4. Strategy types given the priority

Type	Strategy	Priority of internal agency	Priority of local government
1	Strong internal agency	A-A	G-A
2	Equal power	A-A	G-G
3	Strong local government	A-G	G-G

Fragmentation index is calculated to evaluate the performance of actors for each run. Actors have their respective index. For internal agency,

$$F_a = \frac{Amount\ of\ A-A\ Done + Amount\ of\ G-A\ Done}{Amount\ of\ A-A + Amount\ of\ G-A} \tag{10}$$

If the total number of A-A and G-A type events is 0, the fragmentation rate is 1. For local government,

$$F_g = \frac{Amount\ of\ Events\ Done}{10} \tag{11}$$

3.2 Experiment Design

In order to answer the two questions mentioned in the introduction, A Monte Carlo simulation experiment is used to test: (1) Is the fragmentation phenomenon really created by the simulation system? (2) How does the phenomenon be affected by the combination of strategy type and capability rate?

In each run, simulation system is given a different combination of strategy type and capability rate, and a randomly distributed event group. The actors decide how to cope with events under constrains of the combination. The fragmentation rate is calculated and recorded after actors make decisions. CRN (Common Random Numbers) is used to reduce the variance of samples, which means each combination is tested by same event groups where each group is randomly created.

4 Disscussion

Each combination of strategy type and capability rate has been made 1000 independent replications. The boxplots of fragmentation rate of internal agency (F_a) and local government (F_g) are shown in Figs. 1 and 2, respectively. Here boxplot is used to illustrate the distribution of fragmentation rate given different strategy types and capability rates. Outliers are also marked as dots.

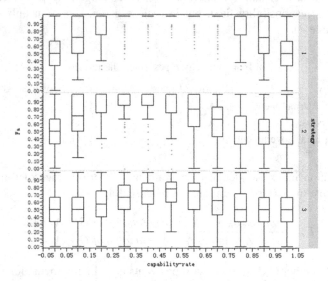

Fig. 1. Comparisons of fragmentation rate of internal agency (F_a)

Obviously the fragmentation phenomenon happens in all cases. Even in the best case F_a or F_g could not reach 1 in a statistical sense. That is F_a under strong internal agency strategy with capability rate from 0.3 to 0.7. The fragmentation seems almost to be eliminated for F_a. However, the F_g in this case looks far away from 1.

Thus a stronger conclusion could be drawn from the experiments: there is no combination could eliminate fragmentation at the same time for both sides. Both F_a and F_g do reach 1 simultaneously in some samples. But note the actors have no idea about what would happen next, thus a combination could reach a perfect state by accident does not indicate that it could perform well in other situations.

Another finding is that local government could ignore the bargaining power but pay more attention on the allocation of capability. The performance of F_g among different strategies appears the same in Fig. 2. Exactly it could be proved that F_g only can be affected by capability rate and is not responding to strategy. This is because the strategy can only affect the order of events being handled with, and all kinds of events in the

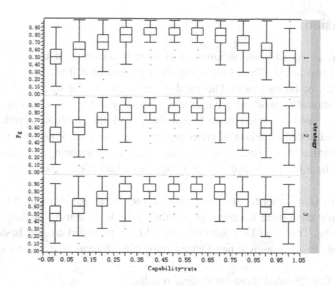

Fig. 2. Comparisons of fragmentation rate of local government (F_g)

utility field of local government, namely the events accomplishment rate or F_g, can only get the same result given the capability allocation.

This study also finds out the best choices for both sides under each strategy. Table 5 compares the mean and 95 % confidence interval of different combinations of strategy type and capability rate. There are several capability rates that could bring better performance of F_a or F_g under given strategy types. Fortunately, there are overlaps of the capability under each strategy. It is very interesting that no matter what the strategy is, the best capability rate seems always to be 0.5, except in strategy 2 where the 0.4 is a better choice to internal agency.

Table 5. Mean and 95 % confidence interval of different combinations of strategy type and capability rate

Strategy type	Capability rate	F_a	F_g	Best choice
1	0.3	0.9449 ± 0.0068	–	
	0.4	0.9834 ± 0.0035	0.8541 ± 0.0072	
	0.5	0.9943 ± 0.0019	0.8743 ± 0.0061	*
	0.6	0.9861 ± 0.0033	0.8483 ± 0.0072	
	0.7	0.9499 ± 0.0065	–	
2	0.2	0.8590 ± 0.0109	–	
	0.3	0.9300 ± 0.0077	–	
	0.4	0.9270 ± 0.0091	0.8541 ± 0.0072	*
	0.5	0.8547 ± 0.0136	0.8743 ± 0.0061	*
	0.6	–	0.8483 ± 0.0072	
3	0.4	0.7088 ± 0.0153	0.8541 ± 0.0072	
	0.5	0.7304 ± 0.0147	0.8743 ± 0.0061	*
	0.6	0.6866 ± 0.0158	0.8483 ± 0.0072	

5   Conclusion

In this paper, an agent-based simulation system is constructed to model local government with two actors. One actor is the local government itself, and the other is the internal agency of bureaucracy. The local government is just one node of the whole inter-organizational network of government. Not only the whole network but also the node's structure and operation mode follow the Tiao-kuai structure. In order to discuss the fragmentation phenomenon of crisis governance, the random events set is used to test the performance of local government. And the capability allocation and the capability utilization mode are set as exogenous variables to exclude interference factors.

The simulation experiments showed that the local government with Tiao-kuai structure inside can create fragment of capability by itself during dealing with unpredictable events. The Tiao-kuai structure should be regarded as the basic source of fragmentation, even though other factors may play important roles to make things worse.

The samples revealed three interesting results:

(1) With Tiao-kuai structure, even with enough capability, there is no way to eliminate fragmentation phenomenon of internal agency and local department at the same time. In fact, only the former could achieve if it is strong enough and does not occupy too much or too little capability.
(2) Local government and internal agency should pay attention on different aspects. For local government only the capability allocation is important, but for internal agency both allocation and utilization are of vital importance to perform better.
(3) Even not optimistic, there is still one way to get better performance in terms of fragmentation. No matter what bargaining power the actors have, the capability of crisis governance would be equally split between local government and internal agency. This rule is effective in all kinds of utilization mode.

References

1. Bin, W.: Transboundary public crisis governance: fragmentation of function and holistic governance (in Chinese). Acad. Forum **5**, 69–71 (2014)
2. Sheng, T.-X.: Problem, root and governance path of government fragmentation (in Chinese). J. Beijing Adm. Coll. **5**, 52–56 (2014)
3. Guo, X.-S., Zhu, Z.-W.: Study on the issues of organization and coordination in terms of transboundary crisis governance: from the perspective of interorganizational network (in Chinese). J. Public Manage. **4**(50–60), 124–125 (2011)
4. Mertha, A.C.: China's "soft" centralization: shifting Tiao/kuai authority relations. China Q. **184**, 791–810 (2005)

A Toolkit for Prototype Implementation of E-Governance Service System Readiness Assessment Framework

Ashraf Ali Waseem[1(✉)], Zubair Ahmed Shaikh[2],
and Aqeel ur Rehman[1]

[1] Hamdard University, Karachi, Pakistan
ashrafaliwaseem@yahoo.com, aqeel.rehman@hamdard.edu
[2] Mohammad Ali Jinnah University, Karachi, Pakistan
zubair.shaikh@jinnah.edu

Abstract. Increasing importance of Open government, E-Participation and Cross-organizational coherence today has clearly shifted the focus towards building and managing, integrated and coordinated government services. This shall not only satisfy citizens' need but also improve governance issues automatically.

In reality, the level of integration, openness and participatory initiatives which are fundamental characteristics of good governance are still in their early stages of development, especially in developing nations. There is much debate among scholars about what constitutes E-Governance success, what methods are best for measuring it, and which variables best describe it.

This research paper presents an E-Governance Readiness Assessment Toolkit as a prototype implementation. The toolkit evaluates each procurement practice of Procuring Agencies for transparency and accountability. The solution is for an indigenous and ongoing case study dealing with the Public Procurement Management System for one of the province of Pakistan. The user bases of the system include people with strong diversity in literacy, poverty indexes, and deteriorating governance. The toolkit is acting as government and public awareness system to check the violation of government policies, rules and regulations pertaining to massive mis-procurements amounting millions of dollars.

Keywords: Human centered design and user centered design · Maturity models in HCI · Service design · Service engineering · Citizen involvement · E-Government · Evaluation methods and techniques · Qualitative and quantitative measurement and evaluation · User experience

1 Introduction

Improving governance and public participation has become a priority for sustainable economy and socio-technical development. Governments are increasing their capacities to achieve these goals. They are trying to transform all public administrations from isolated techno-bureaucratic institutions to a more engaging and accountable citizen centric institutions making them more transparent, responsive, effective and, trusted.

© Springer International Publishing Switzerland 2016
F.F.-H. Nah and C.-H. Tan (Eds.): HCIBGO 2016, Part II, LNCS 9752, pp. 259–270, 2016.
DOI: 10.1007/978-3-319-39399-5_25

E-Governance has been emerged as a research area that involves use of Information and Communication Technologies (ICT) to reconcile and transform the relations among citizens and governments by enhancing citizens' participation in public decision-making [4, 31]. Recent proliferation in digital media offers a variety of novel characteristics related to interactivity, ubiquitous connectivity, and inclusiveness in social networking enabling new forms of society-wide collaboration with a potential impact on democratic participation [30].

To increase positive development outcomes, it is necessary to understand how E-Governance works in different spheres – political, legal-judicial, administrative, economic and socio-environmental [5]. However, despite the widespread efforts to implement E-Governance through research programs, new technologies and projects, the exhaustive studies on the achieved outcomes reveal that it has not yet been successfully incorporated in institutional policy, politics, and governments' readiness [24, 30]. Governments and public administrations hardly use E-Participation during decision-making and policy execution phases [30]. Hence, E-Participation is primarily understood from the legitimacy standpoint rather than as an effective input to influence institutional policy and politics [24, 30]. There is also a generalized trust deficit in representative democracy. According to the latest Euro Barometer Survey [6], the average level of trust in national governments is approximately 27 %.

Thus it is a challenge to come up with a new framework for assessing E-Governance service system readiness given the complexity and controversy involving the subject. This paper suggests that the cornerstone for successfully implementing E-Governance framework in public institutions, as a sustainable added-value activity, involves Human Centered design automation, embodying the principles of E-Participation, Open and Connected-Government.

Following these considerations, this research stands to contribute by proposing a readiness assessment toolkit which is typically needed for the evaluation of all public Procuring Agencies (PAs) for an ongoing pilot project called Procurement Performance Management System (PPMS) of Sindh Public Procurement Regulatory Authority (SPPRA)-a public organization of the Province of Sindh, Pakistan. Weak governance in public procurement hinders market competition and raises the price paid by the administration for goods and services, direct impacting public expenditures and therefore taxpayers' resources [7]. The prototype implementation of E-Governance service, checks the violation of government policies, rules and regulations pertaining to massive mis-procurements amounting millions of dollars.

E-Participation sustainability is heavily dependent on organizational planning and adaptation of open and connected governments thus demanding a holistic engineering approach [10, 14, 17]. Consequently, this research problem consists in endorsing a prototype implementation of E-Governance Service System Readiness Assessment framework that reflects the E-Participation concepts in the structure, operations and policy-making value chain of governments and public administration.

2 Relevance and Importance

The problem of E-Governance is not only related to Management Information Systems (MIS) but now it also emerges as Human Computer Interaction (HCI) and as a Complex, Large-scale, Interconnected, Open, and Socio-technical (CLIOS) system. HCI and Human Intensive Systems (HIS) modeling can effectively be used to design and develop Citizen participatory service systems. It further requires a good understanding and management towards cross disciplinary crowd working and related socio-technical issues.

The latest edition of the United Nations E-Government Survey (2014) [29] assesses the E-Participation status of the 193 United Nations Member States as E-Participation Index (EPI-2014), as depicted in the Fig. 1. The report acknowledges that careful strategies are needed to further improve an enabling environment for E-Participation.

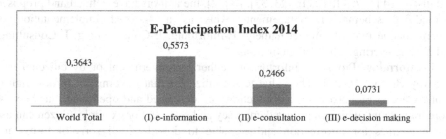

Fig. 1. Shows the average scores of three stages of E-Participation Index (EPI) – 2014 individually and an overall average score of World Total [29].

According to UN the three stages of E-Participation are: e-information, e-consultation, and e-decision making. Interestingly, the overall average score of World Total does not reflect the actual picture of average participations up to the stage 3 (See Fig. 1). This shows that the potential for online participation is still in its early stages of development.

Nevertheless, E-Participation has been witnessed to be a major performance indicator for E-Governance [8, 25–29], many challenges still remaining, including, among others, the inadequacy of institutional change processes and the lack of innovative E-Government leadership [29]. The developed countries, those are good in E-Governance initiatives also performing well in E-Participation maturity levels [15].

Whereas, the implementation of E-Participation maturity levels require an understanding of a multitude of interdependent key dimensions, including openness, backend automation, stakeholders' trust, subjective norms, tools and technologies, rules of engagement, duration and sustainability, accessibility, promotion of HCI and online social networking [12]. These are the critical success factors for implementing true E-Participation, besides others discussed above.

The previous studies supported that citizens with a high level of trust in the government and increasing subjective norms are more motivated to actively participate in government initiated E-Participation tools [2].

The authors, in [9, 13], highlighted that online social networking allowed for the fast mobilization of citizens and the transfer of immediate information. Further, [9, 19] highlighted that how HCI increases with the emergence of web 2.0 technologies and technical tools that enhance support, convenience and understanding in government-citizen communications on a daily basis.

The Stakeholders are primarily called Initiatives Actors with an active role in processes, such as target citizens, subject-matter experts and decision-makers. The two primary groups of interactive stakeholders that can be distinguished in E-Governance concepts are itself Government (G), and Citizens (C), so that the E-Governance readiness assessment plan can be efficiently assessed by their all possible 4-staged group interactions as: G2C, C2G, G2G, and C2C.

Whereas the levels of engagement determine the extent to which the participants take part in the decision-making process and can comprise different levels of involvement. Various topologies of E-Participation engagement levels are introduced and discussed [1, 7, 11, 12, 16, 23, 33]. In [32], the authors have defined and proposed a modified schema of engagement levels as a 4-staged implementation of E-Participation maturity model namely: E-Informing, E-Collaborating, E-Consulting, and E-Empowering. They are defined as:

E-Informing. Providing information (either by government or by citizens) in a one-way channel {G2C}. The value to the citizen is that government information is publicly accessible; processes and functions are described and open; and thus become more transparent, which improves democracy and service. For example, citizen can use search engines for information and are able to download all sorts of forms and documents.

E-Collaborating. Allowing stakeholders (citizens and government) to collaborate their opinions on specific issues of official initiatives in a limited two way channel without online transactions {G2C, C2G}. For example, citizen can ask questions via e-mails.

E-Consulting. The responsibility of final decision is on the government side but the stakeholders play an active role in proposing and shaping policy in an advanced two-way channel consultation {G2C, C2G, G2G}. Complete online transactions can be done without going to an office. Internal and back-end automation of processes have to be redesigned for vertical integrations to provide good services.

E-Empowering. Facilitates the transfer of influence, control, and policy making to the citizen, so the final decision becomes in the public hands {G2C, C2G, G2G, C2C}. All information systems are horizontally integrated and the citizen can get services at one counter. One single point of contact for all services is the ultimate goal.

If we superimpose this E-Participation maturity model on E-Governance 4-staged group interactions, we will get a 4 quadrant matrix as shown in Fig. 2:

Waseem, et al. in [32], suggested that the HCI's Computer Supported Cooperative Work (CSCW) time/space groupware matrix is an effective approach for expressing 4-stages of E-Participation maturity model against the time and space limits of participatory work to support human ICT-mediated interaction, consequently, approaching an E-Governance Service System Readiness Assessment Framework.

Stage 3	Stage 4
{G2C, C2G, G2G}	{G2C, C2G, G2G, C2C}
E-Consulting	E-Empowering
Stage 1	Stage 2
{G2C}	{G2C, C2G}
E-Informing	E-Collaborating

Fig. 2. Superimposition of E-Participation maturity model on E-Governance 4-staged group interactions as 4 quadrant matrix.

2.1 Outcome of a Research Field Survey

In support of our study, the authors here give reference of a research field survey which was conducted by [32] in a local context from 30 government agencies of Pakistan. The survey was conducted to test the online participatory services, offered to the public, in the government department's website(s) for E-Governance Service System Readiness initiatives as per the implementation stages of E-Participation maturity model. The survey concluded that the E-Participation facilities up to the stages 3 and 4 are not available in most of the departments of Pakistan. This proves that the potential for online Participation is still in its early stages of development especially in nations with weak governance.

Following the recent trends and outcomes, it is found that the maturity of stages of E-Participation is essential for E-Governance readiness assessment model. Fortunately, the social extension seeks to optimize processes by enhancing collaboration among stakeholders through the use of Web 2.0 and social media [18]. This increases the motivations for creating socially enabled processes and engaging a broader community in the generation of awareness on the process outcome [3].

3 Choosing SPPRA as a Case Study

The Sindh Public Procurement Regulatory Authority (SPPRA) is a body corporate responsible for prescribing regulations and procedures for the public procurements procured by public sector organizations of Sindh Government.

The SPPRA become fully functional in October 2008. Procurement Legislation introduced in May 2009 with enactment of SPPRA Act 2009. A new set of Rules i.e. Sindh Public Procurement Rules-2010 notified on 8th March 2010 [20].

The ideology of the authority is centered at improving governance, management, transparency, accountability and quality of public procurements of goods, works and services; including consultancy and public-private partnership.

Presently SPPRA has a massive task of coordinating and evaluating the procurement activities of around 730 Procuring Agencies (PAs) – any department or office of Government; or District Government who is registered to procure. This number is expected to rise in coming days. Therefore, SPPRA requires a readiness assessment toolkit that not only facilitates all PAs and the Authority about the procurement processes but also provides an assessment scorecard of each PA for their procurement performances evaluating in terms of compliance of regulations, efficient governance, transparency and decision making.

4 Implementation of E-Participation Maturity Model

The authors suppose that the presented E-Participation maturity model can be implemented on any type of participatory processes workflows that may contain some sort of maturity levels to accomplish a task or a service. To demonstrate this implementation, the authors consider the case study of SPPRA as an example.

As such, if we divide the flowcharts of Basic Procurement Process and Complaint Redressal Mechanism of SPPRA [21] and [22] into four modules related to the 4-stages of E-Participation maturity model, we get Figs. 3 and 4 illustrated below:

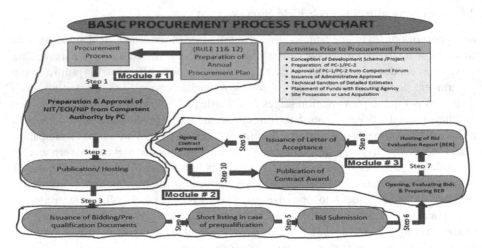

Fig. 3. Division of processes into 1st, 2nd, 3rd modules mapping E-Participation maturity model

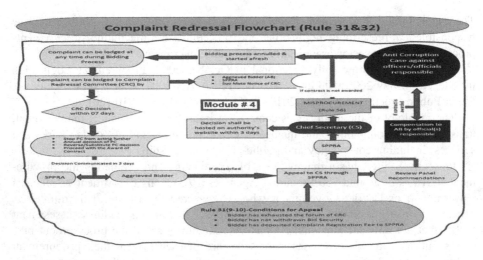

Fig. 4. Selecting all processes into 4th module mapping with E-Participation maturity model

Then if we synchronize the processes of highlighted modules altogether of both figures with the 4-stages of E-Participation maturity model, we can get Table 1 as:

Table 1. Mapping of 4 Modules with the 4-stages of E-Participation maturity model

Stages	E-Participation Stages	Modules	Processes
I	E-Informing {G2C}	1	Procurement Plan; Approval by PC; Advertisement/Hosting of NIT/NIP/EOI
II	E-Collaborating {G2C, C2G}	2	Issuance of Bidding/Prequalifying/RFP Documents; Submission of Prequalification; Short-listing; Bid Submission
III	E-Consulting {G2C, C2G, G2G}	3	Bid Opening & Evaluation; Bid Evaluation Report (BER); Contract Award/Execution; Contract Close/Completion
IV	E-Empowering {G2C, C2G, G2G, C2C}	4	Complaint Redressal Mechanism

Table 1 shows that how the workflows of SPPRA are efficiently correlated with the 4-stages of E-Participation maturity model.

5   Design of the Procurement Process Readiness Assessment Toolkit

The Toolkit is designed to assess readiness of procuring agencies by using the score they get in the compliance of rules and regulations under Sindh Public Procurement Rules-2010 during their procurement practices. This toolkit facilitates all types of procurements like goods, works, services, consultancy services and public private partnership projects, carried out by all procuring agencies. It proceeds and evaluates each prescribed rule while the workflow advances up to the last stage of procurement process as seen in Table 2 below. The stages of procurements are mapped with the 4-stages of E-Participation maturity model as discussed above. The procurement stages are mapped according to their relevance.

For evaluating each PA's procurement practices, the scorecard shall be measured on some prescribed scale. It shall be measured on the basis of the compliance or not compliance of the rules that are to be encountered during procurement processes and business rules. The scale of the score varies depending on the nature of the rules. It may be any numerical range of values or a Boolean value. Each procurement stage contains a set of key rules appropriate for evaluation of a particular procurement type.

Table 2. Procurement Process Readiness Assessment Toolkit under Sindh Public Procurement Rules-2010 [20] for the Procuring Agencies of SPPRA

			Procurement Process Readiness Assessment Toolkit for PAs of SPPRA									
Stage	E-Participation Stages	Procurement Stages	Goods	Score	Works	Score	Services	Score	Consultancy	Score	PPP Projects	Score
I	E-Informing (G2C)	Procurement Plan (R11-12)	R16 R14 Procurement Committee (PC) R7 R8		R16 R14 Procurement Committee (PC) R7 R8		R16 R14 Procurement Committee (PC) R7 R8		R14 Consultant Selection Committee (CSC) R67 R68 R70 R71		R14 Technical & Financial Eva Committee (TFEC) R81 (3) R82 (2)	
		Publication/Advertisement Hosting	R6 R17 R18 R19 R46 R47 Notice Inviting tender (NIT) R15		R6 R17 R18 R19 R46 R47 Notice Inviting tender (NIT) R15		R6 R17 R18 R19 R46 R47 Notice Inviting Prequalification (NIP) R15 R27 R28 R73		R6 R17 R18 R19 R46 R47 Inviting Expression of Interest (EOI) R62 R63 R65 R73		R6 R17 R18 R19 R46 R47 Notice Inviting Prequalification (NIP) R15 R27 R28 R73	
II	E-Collaborating (G2C, C2G)	Short listing/ Issuance of Documents					Short listing Criteria(PQR) of Consultants R74		Submission of Prequalification by Consultants R72 Short listing Criteria(PQR) of Consultants R74		Short listing Criteria(PQR) of Consultants R74	
			Issuance of Tender Documents R20 R21 R22 R23 R29 R44		Issuance of Tender Documents R20 R21 R22 R23 R29 R44		Issuance of Prequalifying Documents R20 R21 R22 R23 R29 R44		Issuance of RFP Documents R20 R75 R22 R23 R29 R44		Issuance of Bidding/RFP Documents R20 R21 R22 R23 R29 R44 R82 (5) R82 (6) R82 (7)	
		Bid Submission	R25 R26 R37 R38		R25 R26 R37 R38		R25 R26 R37 R38		R25 R26 R37 R38		R25 R26 R37 R38	
III	E-Consulting (G2C, C2G, G2G)	Bid Opening & Evaluation	R30 R41 R42 R43 R48 R52 R53		R30 R41 R42 R43 R48 R52 R53		R30 R41 R42 R43 R48 R52 R53		R30 R41 R42 R43 R48 R52 R53 Open Technical R75(2) Evaluation R76 Open Financial R75(2)		R30 R41 R42 R43 R48 R52 R53 R84	
			Bid Evaluation Report (BER) R45		Bid Evaluation Report (BER) R45		Bid Evaluation Report (BER) R45		Bid Evaluation Report (BER) R45		Bid Evaluation Report (BER) R45	
		Contract Award/Execution	R39 R49 R50 R55 R89		R39 R49 R50 R55 R89		R39 R49 R50 R55 R89		R39 R49 R50 R55 R89		R39 R49 R50 R55 R89	
		Contract Close/Completion	R57		R57		R57		R57		R57	
IV	E-Empowering (G2C, C2G, G2G, C2C)	Complaint Redressal	R31 (2) R31 (3) R31 (4) R31 (5) R31 (8) R31 (9-10) R31 (11-13) R31 (15) R56		R31 (2) R31 (3) R31 (4) R31 (5) R31 (8) R31 (9-10) R31 (11-13) R31 (15) R56		R31 (2) R31 (3) R31 (4) R31 (5) R31 (8) R31 (9-10) R31 (11-13) R31 (15) R56		R31 (2) R31 (3) R31 (4) R31 (5) R31 (8) R31 (9-10) R31 (11-13) R31 (15) R56		R31 (2) R31 (3) R31 (4) R31 (5) R31 (8) R31 (9-10) R31 (11-13) R31 (15) R56	
		Total		0		0		0		0		0

All such rules could not be defined here because of the insufficient space. Some of them are listed below as an example.

R11 & R12 (Activities prior to Procurement process):
- Conception of development Scheme/Project
- Preparation of PC I/ PC II
- Approval of PC I/ PC II from competent authority
- Issuance of Administrative approval
- Technical sanction of detailed estimate
- Placement of funds with executing Agency
- Site possession or land acquisition

R15 (Type of Bidding): Open Competitive Bidding
1) International Competitive Bidding (ICB)
  - Open to local and international parties
  - Default method is for >= US $ 10 M
2) National Competitive Bidding (NCB)
  - Open to local but international parties may participate
  - Default method is for < US $ 10 M

R17 (Advertisement):
- If >100,000 to <=1,000,000 SPPRA+ P.A website
- If >1,000,000 SPPRA+ P.A website + 3 widely circulated newspapers (EUS)

R18 (Response Time):
- NCB >= 15 days
- ICB >= 45 days
From 1st publication

R21 (Contents of Bidding Documents):

(a) Letter of invitation for bid;
(b) Data sheet containing information about the assignment;
(c) Instructions for preparing bids;
(d) Amount and manner of payment of bid security and performance guarantee (where applicable);
(e) Manner and place, date and time for submission of bidding documents;
(f) Manner, place, date and time of opening of bids;
(g) Method of procurement used;
(h) A detailed and unambiguous evaluation criteria;
(i) Terms and conditions of the contract agreements, as far as already known by the procuring agency;
(j) Terms of Reference and technical specifications of goods, works or services to be procured, subject to Rule 13;
(k) Manner in which tender price is to be assessed and computed, including information about tax liability;
(l) Currency in which tender price is to be formulated and expressed;
(m) Bid validity period;
(n) A copy of integrity pact to be signed by the parties (where applicable).

R89 (Integrity Pact):
- If procurement is > Rs 10 m for goods and works, and > Rs 2.5 m for services shall be subject to an integrity pact.

The complete details of rules and regulations used in this toolkit under Sindh Public Procurement Rules-2010 can be seen on the SPPRA's official website [20].

The Procurement Process Readiness Assessment Toolkit is necessary to keep an eye on the track record of all procuring agencies for corruption control, transparency, openness, and for any mis-procurement. A precise decision can be made easily on the bases of such evaluation.

6 Future Directions

For efficient implementation of the proposed readiness assessment toolkit, a balanced scorecard is necessary for measuring precise score of each regulation of procurement process. Therefore, it would be designed as our future work.

On the basis of such scorecard a procurement process readiness assessment ranking of all procuring agencies can be established.

7 Conclusion

The problem of E-Governance is not only related to Management Information Systems (MIS) but now it also emerges as Human Computer Interaction (HCI) and as a Complex, Large-scale, Interconnected, Open, and Socio-technical (CLIOS) system. The present research is also suggested that the cornerstone for successfully implementing E-Governance in public institutions, as a sustainable added-value activity, is a systematic organizational planning and automation, embodying the principles of E-Participation, Open and Connected-Government. HCI and Human Intensive Systems (HIS) modeling can effectively be used to design and develop such systems. It further requires a good understanding and management towards cross disciplinary crowd working and related socio-technical, political, and environmental issues.

This research stands to contribute in increasing the performance of Government on corruption control and on participatory governance by proposing a readiness assessment toolkit for an ongoing and indigenous case study related to public procurements of public sector organizations in a province of Pakistan.

This toolkit can assess readiness of procuring agencies using the score they get in the compliance of rules and regulations under Sindh Public Procurement Rules-2010 of SPPRA during their procurement practices. The use of this toolkit will be the test of quality of governance in the State. While doing so, the Government must accord highest importance to transparency and fairness in data collection, analysis and in decision making. The toolkit is practically and efficiently superimposed on the 4 stages of E-Participation maturity model. Hence it shall be a prototype implementation of E-Governance service system readiness assessment framework, proposed in [32].

Acknowledgment. We acknowledge SPPRA's team for their contributions in providing support for understanding their business environment, business regulations, procurement procedures, workflows and challenges pertaining to efficient governance and stakeholders' participations.

References

1. Ahmed, N.: An overview of e-participation models. UN Department of Economic and Social Affairs (UNDESA) (2006). http://unpan1.un.org/intradoc/groups/public/documents/un/unpan023622.pdfAccessed 5 May 2011
2. Alharbi, A., Kang, K., Hawryszkiewycz, I.: The influence of trust and subjective norms on citizens' intentions to engage in E-participation on E-government Websites. In: Australasian Conference on Information Systems, ACIS 2015, Adelaide (2015)
3. Brambilla, M., Fraternali, P., Vaca Ruiz, C. K. : Combining Social Web and BPM for Improving Enterprise Performances: the BPM4People Approach to Social BPM. In: Proceedings of the 21st International Conference Companion on World Wide Web pp. 223–226. ACM April 2012
4. Chadwick, A.: Web 2.0: new challenges for the study of E-Democracy in an era of informational exuberance. J. Law Policy Inf. Soc. 5(1), 45–75 (2012)
5. De Jesus Rosa, P. A. V. :E-participation: promoting dialogue and deliberation between institutions and civil society (2008)
6. European Commission. Standard Euro barometer: Public Opinion in the European Union vol. (81) (2014)
7. Gramberger, M. : Citizens as Partners: OECD Handbook on Information, Consultation and Public Participation in Policy-making (2001)
8. Holzer, M., Kim, S. T.: Digital Governance in Municipalities Worldwide (2007): A Longitudinal Assessment of Municipal Websites throughout the World. RUTGERS University, Joint Publishing Section, USA and United Nations (2007)
9. Lacigova, o, Maizite, A., Cave, B.: E-Participation and social media: a symbiotic relationship? Eur. J. E-pract. 16, 71–76 (2012)
10. Linders, D.: From e-government to we-government: defining a typology for citizen coproduction in the age of social media. Gov. Inf. Q. 29(4), 446–454 (2012)
11. Lukensmeyer, C.J., Torres, L.H.: Public Deliberation: A Manager's Guide to Citizen Engagement. IBM Center for the Business of Government, Washington (2006)

12. Macintosh, A.: Characterizing E-participation in policy-making. In: 37th Hawaii International Conference on System Sciences (HICSS 2004) vol. 00, pp. 1–10. HICSS (2004)
13. McGrath, K., Elbanna, A., Hercheui, M., Panagiotopoulos, P., Saad, E.: Exploring the democratic potential of online social networking: the scope and limitations of E-participation. In: Association for Information Systems (2012)
14. Medimorec, D., Parycek, P., Schossböck, J.: Vitalizing Democracy through E-Participation and Open Government: An Austrian and Eastern European Perspective. Bertelsmann. Accessed 5 May 2011 (2010) http://www.bertelsmann-stiftung.de/cps/rde/xbcr/SID-4B6B2682-20BE4653/bst/Daniel%20Medimorec.pdf
15. Phang, C., Kankanhalli, A.: A framework of ICT exploitation for E-participation initiatives. Commun. ACM 51(12), 128–132 (2008)
16. Al-Dalou, R., Abu-Shanab, E.: E-participation levels and technologies. In: The 6th International Conference on Information Technology, ICIT 2013
17. Scherer, S., Wimmer, M.A.: Reference framework for E-participation projects. In: Tambouris, E., Macintosh, A., de Bruijn, H. (eds.) Electronic Participation. Lecture Notes in Computer Science, vol. 6847, pp. 145–156. Springer, Heidelberg (2011)
18. Shelton, T.: Business Models for the Social Mobile Cloud: Transform Your Business Using Social Media, Mobile Internet, and Cloud Computing. John Wiley & Sons, Hoboken (2013)
19. Soon, C., Soh, Y.D.: Engagement@Web 2.0 between the government and citizens in Singapore: dialogic communication on facebook? Asian J. Commun. 24(1), 42–59 (2014)
20. SPPRA: Sindh Public Procurement Rules-2010, March 2010. http://www.pprasindh.gov.pk/downloads/files/FINALSPPRARULES08022010.pdf
21. SPPRA: procurement process flowchart. http://www.pprasindh.gov.pk/downloads/files/ProcurementProcessFlowWG.JPG
22. SPPRA: Complaint Redressal Mechanism. http://www.pprasindh.gov.pk/downloads/files/ComplaintRedressalFolw.JPG
23. Tambouris, E., Liotas, N., Tarabanis, K.: A Framework for assessing E-participation projects and tools. In: 40th Annual Hawaii International Conference on System Sciences, HICSS 2007. (pp. 90–90). IEEE January 2007
24. Tambouris, E., Macintosh, A., Dalakiouridou, E., Smith, S., Panopoulou, E., Tarabanis, K., Millard, J., E-participation in Europe: current state and practical recommendations In: E-Government Success around the World Cases, Empirical Studies, and Practical Recommendations p. 341 (2013)
25. UNDESA United Nations E-Government Survey 2008, From e-Government to Connected Governance, U.N. Publishing Section, New York (2008a)
26. UNDESA World Public Sector Report 2008, People Matter: Civic Engagement in Public Governance, United Nations, U.N. Publishing Section, New York (2008b)
27. UNDESA United Nations E-Government Survey 2010: Leveraging E-government at a Time of Financial and Economic Crisis. U.N. Publishing Section, New York (2010)
28. UNDESA United Nations E-Government Survey 2012: E-Government for the People. U.N. Publishing Section, New York (2012). http://www.unpan.org/egovkb/global_reports
29. UNDESA United Nations E-Government Survey 2014: E-Government for the Future We Want. U.N. Publishing Section, New York (2014). http://www.unpan.org/e-government
30. Van Dijk, J.: Digital democracy: vision and reality. In: Snellen, I., van de Donk, W. (eds.) Public Administration in the Information Age: Revisited, pp. 30–70. IOS- Press, Amsterdam (2013)
31. Vedel, T.: The idea of electronic democracy: origins. Vis. Questions. Parliamentary Aff. 59 (2), 226–235 (2006)

32. Waseem, A. A., Shaikh, Z. A., Aqeel-ur-Rehman.: E-Governance Service System Readiness Assessment Framework, Int J. Hum.-Comput. Stud., Elsevier B.V., (2016, submitted and under review)
33. Wimmer, M.A.: Ontology for an e-participation virtual resource centre. In: 1st International Conference on Theory and Practice of Electronic Governance- ICEGOV 2007, vol. 10, pp. 89–98 (2007)

HCI at Work

Prevalence of Mobile Phone Interaction in Workplace Meetings

Robert Bajko[1(✉)] and Deborah I. Fels[2]

[1] School of Professional Communication, Toronto, Canada
rbajko@ryerson.ca
[2] Ted Rogers School of Information Technology Management,
Ryerson University, Toronto, Canada
dfels@ryerson.ca

Abstract. In the past few years we have seen a shift in the use of smartphones from a social setting to a corporate setting. Smartphones have been around for the past decade and there appears to have been an increase in their use in meetings and other collocated settings. Since this is a relatively new phenomenon, there is a lack of research in this area. The current paper presents the results of an online survey that was conducted in 2012 about smartphone use in meetings and the attitudes and behaviour of meeting participants. The major findings from the survey revealed that the majority of meeting participants used their smartphones during meetings for work related emergencies and other work tasks such as communicating. Meeting participants also tend to text more often when co-workers were present compared to visitors and superiors. The survey also revealed that meeting participants were three times more likely to make a work phone call compared to a personal phone in a meeting that they were not required to participate.

Keywords: Mobile devices · Smartphones · Computer-supported cooperative work · Meetings

1 Introduction

Mobile device use has been steadily increasing for the better part of 20 years, today, smartphones more so than feature phones. According to Theoharidou et al. [18] a smartphone is defined as a cell phone with advanced capabilities, which executes an identifiable operating system allowing users to extend its functionality with third party applications that are available from an application repository. According to this definition, smartphones must include sophisticated hardware with: (a) advanced processing capabilities, (b) multiple and fast connectivity capabilities, and (optionally) (c) a larger screen than feature phones. As of third quarter of 2015, 68 % of US mobile subscribers owned a smartphone compared to a feature phone up from 35 % in 2011 [3]. In Canada it is estimated that smartphone penetration will reach 68 % by year-end 2015, up from 55 % at year-end 2014 [19], and forecasted to be 80 % by the end of 2016 [11]. While the tablet market penetration is still low, it has seen exponential growth as well. A current survey by eMarketer [12] research group stated that the tablet market in Canada

© Her Majesty the Queen in Right of Canada 2016
F.F.-H. Nah and C.-H. Tan (Eds.): HCIBGO 2016, Part II, LNCS 9752, pp. 273–280, 2016.
DOI: 10.1007/978-3-319-39399-5_26

increased from 34 % in 2013 to 42 % in 2015, with an anticipated penetration rate of 49.5 % by 2019. With the increase in "bring your own technology (BYOT)" policies to work, it has been stated that more than 64 % of workers are using personal and mobile computing systems as of 2014 [8, 9].

One result of BYOT policies is that these personal devices are appearing in meetings and are potentially being used for personal and business purposes simultaneously. The impact of these practices on behaviour, productivity, and work satisfaction has yet to be investigated.

Technology use in meetings is not new. For the past three decades researchers in the field of Computer Supported Cooperative Work (CSCW), or the understanding of the nature and characteristics of cooperative work with the objective of designing adequate computer-based technologies, have investigated how groups use technology, and the advantages and disadvantages it contributes [5, 8, 20]. Positive findings from CSCW research are that groups using technology tend to: (1) improve group task performance; (2) overcome time and space constraints on collaborative efforts; (3) increase the range and speed of access to information; and (4) facilitate conflict resolution [7, 16].

Negative findings tend to relate to distractions caused by technology in meetings. Just as meeting participants in the past had the opportunity to doodle on paper and potentially be distracted; technology might provide the same opportunity. Newman and Cairns [15] postulate that the use of a pen and paper or a laptop in a meeting contributes to distraction and disengagement from the meeting topic at hand. Meeting participants who are distracted with a pen and paper will reengage with the meeting topic within ten seconds. However, individuals who use a laptop will reengage with a brief glance every eight to ten seconds, followed by a return to the ongoing laptop task. Users of paper are much more likely to reengage fully [14]. In much of the earlier research, the technology belonged to the organization and was used almost exclusively for computer-based work related tasks including meetings. In a BYOT environment, mobile technology is personal and used as much for personal activities as it is for work.

Further investigation is needed to determine if the use of mobile devices will be accepted or rejected in meetings. In this paper we report on a follow up survey to our initial survey. The initial survey was conducted in the third quarter of 2010 (see [4] for details), and the second one was conducted in the second quarter of 2012.

2   Method

The second survey was deployed two years after the first one to again assess meeting participant's perceptions and attitudes of mobile technology use during meetings. As technology has changed in the intervening time, a new survey may shed new light on people's attitudes. For the purpose of this paper only the quantitative data are presented and discussed.

Research Questions. The following are the two research questions for the project: (1) What are the attitudes towards having smart mobile technologies in face-to-face meeting settings in organizations? (2) How is smart mobile technology being employed and adopted for use in meetings?

Survey Instrument. The online survey was developed and distributed on an international information systems listserve. In the survey, demographic information, and information on types of technology used during meetings, and perception of technology use in business meetings was gathered. The online survey was made available on the Internet from May 1, 2012 till July 31, 2012.

The survey was composed of 29 questions organized into five sections. The first section contained eight questions to collect demographic information such as age, sex, and employment status. The second section contained 12 questions and asked participants about their technology use (e.g., how often they used a computer and for what activities). The third section contained 11 questions related to one specific meeting that the participant recently attended (e.g., type of meeting, length of meeting and number of people attending). The fourth section contained seven questions that collected data about participant's attitudes towards technology use during meetings. Questions regarding when it was appropriate to use various technologies such as laptops and smartphones in meetings, as well as the different functionality of these devices were included in the survey (e.g., texting and making calls). The last section asked two questions about company attitudes and policies toward technology use.

Participants. Two hundred and fifty-five participants (118 males, 134 females, three unanswered) completed the survey. There were 10 % of participants in the age range of 18–29 years, 49 % in the 30–39 years, 22 % in the 40–49 years, 14 % in the 50–59 years, and 5 % in the 60+ age range.

Twenty three percent of the participants claimed to work in the public sector, 17.8 % in service, 9.5 % in high technology, 5.9 % in manufacturing, 3.6 % in retail, and 40.2 % in "other" as in the combination of two or more of the categories listed above. The majority (47.8 %) were employed in large organization with more than 750 employees, 28.5 % in small organization (2–99 employees), and 23.7 % in medium (100–749 employees). The majority of participants (85.7 %) were employed as full time employees, 8.7 % as part-time employees, while 5.6 % classified themselves as "other" (e.g. contract, seasonal, and volunteer). Over one third (35 %) of participants worked three or fewer years in their current company, 20 % of participants between four and six years, 14 % of participants between seven and nine years, 11 % of participants between 10–12 years, 7 % of participants between 13–15 years, and 13 % of participants were with their current company more than 16+ years.

The majority (57 %) were in management roles (e.g. supervisor (4 %), manager (21 %), director (16 %), vice-president (8 %), and president (8 %)) with the remaining being non-management. Eleven percent of participants worked in the research & development department, 10 % in operations, 10 % in sales/marketing, 3 % in human resources, 1 % in accounting or legal, and 64 % in other such information technology or logistics. Twenty two percent attended face-to-face meeting infrequently, 22 % percent attended once per week, 24 % attended 2–4 times a week, 15 % attended 5–8 times per week, and 17 % attended 9 or more times per week. The majority of participants (71 %) considered themselves as advanced cell phone users (someone who uses a cell phone 5 times or more per day with a combination of phone calls, text messages, mobile Internet surfing, and the use of mobile applications on the phone), 4 % beginner cell phone user (someone who uses a cell phone once or twice per week making phone calls only), 23 % intermediate, and 2 % did not own a cell phone. Ninety seven percent reported using a computer daily. The most common applications used on respondents were email and Office productivity such as using word processing or spreadsheets. To carry out crosstabs some demographic categories were not used due to low numbers (see Sect. 3).

3   Results and Discussion

This paper examines the attitude and behaviour of meeting participants that use mobile devices, particularly smartphones, during meetings. A chi-square analysis was conducted on questions related to: (1) when was it appropriate to use different mobile devices in meetings using 5-point Likert where 1 was always and 5 was never: (2) making personal and work voice calls during a meeting, using 5-point Likert where 1 was "I make/accept phone calls all the time" and 5 was "I never make/accept phone calls"; and (3) sending personal and work related text messages during meetings, using 5-point Likert where 1 was "I text message all the time", and 5 was "I never text message." Significant results are reported to a type 1 error probability of $p < 0.05$ (see Table 1). There were four degrees of freedom in all significant results reported.

Table 1. Chi-square value, mean, and standard deviation of questions related to appropriateness of mobile device use in meetings.

Question	$\chi2$ value	M	SD
Laptop	259.15	2.10	1.09
Blackberry	142.70	2.92	1.31
iPads	114.45	2.57	1.34
iPhone	110.47	3.09	1.33
Work voice calls during meeting	355.26	4.29	1.03
Personal voice calls during meeting	526.19	4.77	0.74
Work texting during meeting	171.89	3.98	1.13
Personal texting during meeting	374.08	4.40	1.06

SmartPhone Use in Meetings. When participants were asked about their smartphones use in meetings, 43 % (110 participants out of 255) stated it was to keep track of time, 38 % (96 participants out of 255) for work related emergencies, 35 % (90 participants out of 255) communication such as email or chat through text messaging, 34 % (86 participants out of 255) for work related activities, 29 % (73 participants out of 255) for personal emergencies, 8 % (20 participants out of 255) for surfing the internet, 2 % (6 participants out of 255) activities not related to work, and 4 % (11 participants out of 255) said other. It seems that the majority of individuals tend to use their smartphone in meetings for work related emergencies and other work tasks such as communicating by email or chat through text messaging but considerably less so for personal use unless it is an emergency. We can theorize that when meeting participants do use their smartphone, that it is related to the meeting tasks at hand, however, which tasks remains to be determined. Further research should address this question.

Text Messaging in Meetings. There was a surprising use of texting in meetings depending on who was present in the room. Fifteen percent (16 out of 109 participants) stated that they would text personal related information when their superior was present. However, if a visitor was present, 18 % (20 out of 109 participants) would text personal related message. If the meeting room only had co-workers, 21 % (34 out of 160 participants) would text personal related information. This change in behaviour based on the presence of certain individuals can be explained by Ajzen's Theory of Planned Behavior [1, 2]. It stated that one of the indicators that determine an individual's behaviour was the individual's perception of whether people important to him thought the behaviour should be performed. According to our data and the Theory of Planned Behavior, individuals tended to text personal related messages more when individuals around were considered to be less influential by the meeting participants.

When asked about personal and work related texting during meetings, 47 % (120 out of 255 participants) reported that they did not text message work related information and 52.9 % (135 out of 255 participants) did not text for personal reasons. However, when we asked participants what they text messaged about during meetings, 43 % (109 out of 255 participants) stated "work tasks that cannot wait" and 31 % (78 out of 255 participants) stated they would text "personal tasks that cannot wait."

It seems that text messaging is becoming increasingly acceptable in meetings particularly for work related text messages. The types of work related text messages were not gathered in this survey, however, we postulate that meeting participants are using their smartphones to collect meeting related answers that cannot be found within the meeting as suggested by Spee and Jarzabkowski [17]. They found that smartphones and instant messaging can be considered strategy tools that allow meeting participants to span intra and interorganizational boundaries through discussion. No longer are meeting attendees limited to communicating only within the formal meeting boundaries, but they can also engage, either on task or not, with resources outside the formal meeting.

Voice Calls in Meetings. While texting during meetings seems to be a more acceptable practice, we also wanted to determine whether this attitude also transferred to voice calls. Seven percent (5 out of 70 participants) stated they would make a phone call if a superior was present. As for visitors and co-workers present, 9 % (6 out of 66 participants) and 10 % (10 out of 98 participants) respectively, would make a personal voice calls during the meeting.

More than a quarter (66 out of 246 participants) stated they would accept or make work related voice calls during a meeting only when they had important work to do that could not wait. The survey also revealed that people were three times more likely to accept or make a work phone call in a meeting that they were not needed compared with 2 % for accepting or making personal voice calls. Only 2 % (6 out of 246 participants) stated that they would accept or make a non-important personal and work phone call during a meeting. A survey conducted by Campbell [6] and others [10, 13] on college students and the use of mobile phones in classrooms found that the phones were considered as a serious source of distraction in the classroom. Collectively, participants reported strong perceptions of ringing as a problem. Since the function of a classroom setting was similar to a meeting room, we posit that individuals view making or accepting voice calls was more disruptive and obtrusive compared with text messaging.

Comparison with Demographic Data. A crosstab analysis was used to determine whether there were correlations between the (1) demographic information (e.g. age, size of company, position within the company, and department the participant works in); and (2) the acceptability of making and accepting personal and work calls during meetings; and (3) the acceptability of texting personal and work messages during meetings. Participants rated the acceptability on a 5-point Likert scale where 1 was always and 5 was never. Significant results are reported to a type 1 error probability of $p < 0.05$ with four degrees of freedom. The results of Cramer's v are reported in Table 2.

Table 2. Cramer's V value for voice calls and text messaging during meetings. Moderately strong relationship shown in bold.

Question	Cramer's v value			
	Age	Company size	Position	Department
Attitude towards work calls	0.11	0.08	**0.22**	0.15
Attitude towards personal calls	0.11	0.08	**0.22**	0.18
Attitude towards work texting	0.10	0.11	**0.21**	**0.24**
Attitude towards personal texting	0.14	0.11	0.19	0.18

Due to the low number of participants in the supervisor position category, the 60+ age category and the accounting and legal option in participant's department this data were removed from the analysis. We found a moderately strong relationship between the department in which the participant worked and attitudes towards texting work related messages during meetings. Individuals who worked in research and development tended to rate texting during meetings in which they are not needed as acceptable ($M = 6.40$, $SD = 1.54$). Individuals who work in operations tended to rate texting important work related messages during meetings as acceptable compared with individuals employed in any other departments ($M = 5.93$, $SD = 1.80$).

We also found a moderately strong relationship between the participant's position within the company and making and accepting voice calls. The data revealed that individuals who were supervisors (44 %), managers (26 %), directors (39 %), and vice presidents (37 %) tended to think that making important work related calls during meetings was acceptable. We found a weak relationship in the ratings among non-management (21 %) towards making work related phone calls during meetings.

Limitations. Even though there were 255 participants who completed the survey, there was still an uneven distribution particularly for the department in which the participant works, age and position in the company. There was only 1 participant (0.5 %) from accounting and 2 (1 %) from legal departments. For the 60+ age demographic there were only 13 participants or (5 %). For the supervisor position demographic there were only 11 participants (4.8 %). In order to better determine attitudes from all of the demographic categories, more participants from these groups must be recruited. Lastly, the data presented here is only a snapshot in time and attitudes towards mobile device use in meetings will likely change over time.

This paper only presents a limited, univariate treatment and analysis of the data to gain a sense of trends that are occurring. Further multivariate analyses are required in order to determine whether there are multiple factors that are correlated. Future papers will report on this aspect of the analysis.

As this was a broadly distributed survey, there was no opportunity to gather any data on details contained in text messages or voice calls or why participants found some mobile device behaviours more acceptable than others. Future research should investigate what type of information participant's text and talk about on their smartphones during meetings and why this behavior is acceptable in the workplace.

4 Conclusion

This paper reported on a 2012 survey conducted into the attitudes and behaviour of meeting participants when smartphones are used during meetings. The data revealed that over two thirds of meeting participants used their smartphones during meetings for work related emergencies and other work tasks such as communicating by email or chat through text messaging. Meeting participants also tended to text more often when co-workers were present compared to visitors or superiors. Participants texted the least amount when superiors where present in the room. The survey also revealed that meeting participants were three times more likely to make a work phone call compared to a personal phone in a meeting in which they were not needed. Furthermore, individuals who work in research and development tended to text message more during meetings in which they were not really needed compared to individuals in other departments. Individuals who worked in operations tended to rate texting important work related messages during meetings as acceptable compared with individuals from other departments.

Future research into why some factors are acceptable and others are not as well as details such length, content and frequency of text messages and phone calls may help to better understand the attitudes and behaviour of smartphone users in the workplace. It may also assist in developing new standards of conduct and work policies around smartphone use in the workplace, specifically during business meetings.

Acknowledgments. We thank all the participants who completed the survey and GRAND National Centre for Excellence for financial support.

References

1. Ajzen, I.: From intentions to actions: A theory of planned behavior. In: Kuhl, J., Beckmann, J. (eds.) Springer series in social psychology, pp. 11–39. Springer, Berlin (1985)
2. Ajzen, I.: The theory of planned behavior. Organ. Behav. Hum. Decis. Process. **50**(2), 179–211 (1991)
3. Anderson, M.: Technology Device Ownership (2015). http://www.pewinternet.org/2015/10/29/technology-device-ownership-2015/

4. Bajko, R.: Mobile telephone usage, attitude, and behavior during group meetings. J. Inf. Syst. Appl. Res. **5**(2), 4 (2012)
5. Bannon, L.J., Schmidt, K.: CSCW: Four characters in search of a context. In: Proceedings of the European Community Conference on Computer Supported Work (EC-CSCW), pp. 358–372, London, September 1989
6. Campbell, S.W.: Perceptions of mobile phones in college classrooms: Ringing, cheating, and classroom policies. Commun. Educ. **55**(3), 280–294 (2006)
7. Cherouana, A., Aouine, A., Khadraoui, A., Mahdaoui, L.: Towards a generic approach for the management and the assessment of cooperative work. In: Morzy, T., Valduriez, P., Bellatreche, L. (eds.) ADBIS 2015. CCIS, vol. 539, pp. 127–134. Springer, Heidelberg (2015)
8. Gill, T.: Adopting enterprise mobility: Advancing the discussion from theoretical to implementable. Corp. Real Estate J. **2**(2), 127–134 (2012)
9. Janssen, K.C., Phillipson, S.: Are we ready for BYOD? A systematic review of the implementation and communication of BYOD pograms in Australian schools. Aust. Educ. Comput. **30**(2) (2015)
10. Kuznekoff, J.H., Titsworth, S.: The impact of mobile phone usage on student learning. Commun. Educ. **62**(3), 233–252 (2013)
11. LaSalle, L.: Smartphone Use: Canadians Calling Less, Using Their Device Like A Mobile Computer (2012). http://www.huffingtonpost.ca/2012/12/20/cellphone-smartphone-use-canada_n_2338011.html
12. Majority of Canada's Internet Users to Use Tablets This Year (2015). http://www.emarketer.com/Article/Majority-of-Canadas-Internet-Users-Use-Tablets-This-Year/1012452
13. McCoy, B.: Digital distractions in the classroom: Student classroom use of digital devices for non-class related purposes (2013)
14. Newman, W.: Must electronic gadgets disrupt our face-to-face conversations? Interactions **13**(6), 18–19 (2006)
15. Newman, W., Cairns, P.: Towards the non-disruptive laptop: modeling the impact of mobile computer usage on meetings (2007)
16. Raisinghani, M.S., Ramarapu, N.K., Simkin, M.G.: The impact of technology on cooperative work groups. Inf. Syst. Manage. **15**(3), 1–7 (1998)
17. Spee, A.P., Jarzabkowski, P.: Strategy tools as boundary objects. Strateg. Organ. **7**(2), 223–232 (2009)
18. Theoharidou, M., Mylonas, A., Gritzalis, D.: A risk assessment method for smartphones. In: Gritzalis, D., Furnell, S., Theoharidou, M. (eds.) SEC 2012. IFIP AICT, vol. 376, pp. 443–456. Springer, Heidelberg (2012)
19. With Growth Comes Change: The Evolving Mobile Landscape in 2015 (2014). http://catalyst.ca/2015-canadian-smartphone-market/
20. Zhu, H., Zhou, M., Hou, M.: Support' collaboration with roles. In: Contemporary Issues in Systems Science and Engineering, pp. 575–598 (2015)

Data Glasses for Picking Workplaces

Impact on Physical Workloads

Daniel Friemert[1,2(✉)], Rolf Ellegast[1,2], and Ulrich Hartmann[2]

[1] Institute for Occupational Safety and Health of the German Social Accident Insurance,
St. Augustin, Germany
ellegast@dguv.de
[2] Department of Mathematics and Technology, University of Applied Sciences Koblenz,
Remagen, Germany
{friemert,hartmann}@hs-koblenz.de

Abstract. In the field of logistics the interest in wearable computing devices is constantly growing. In earlier studies it has been shown that data glasses can be a powerful tool for optimising warehouse management processes. However, those studies exclusively dealt with the impact of smart glasses on the efficiency of labour whereas our approach focuses on investigating the influence of data glasses on physical workloads. For this purpose we have designed a simplified picking workplace that enables us to carry out motion analyses and the concurrent assessment of physiological parameters under lab conditions. In this article we present the key features of our picking machine and the tailor-made measurement protocols together with the adequate evaluation methods that are used to quantify the effects of smart glasses on the physical workloads imposed on the study subjects.

Keywords: Data glasses · Physical workload · Posture · Picking workplace

1 Introduction

Research on the utilisation of data or smart glasses in the field of logistics started some years ago [1, 2]. Meanwhile smart glasses have been tested under real working conditions [3, 4]. These pilot studies have shown that in the near future smart glasses can become a powerful tool to improve warehouse management processes. The logistics personnel of a German car manufacturer for instance used these glasses for order picking. The objective was to improve process security in production. All glass users automatically received all the necessary information such as storage locations or part numbers directly in their field of vision. According to the authors of this study it turned out that one of the main benefits of using smart glasses for picking tasks is that the users have both their hands free while they are working. The camera in the glasses is also used to detect picking errors by reading the product barcodes. Another pilot project to investigate the usefulness of smart glasses has been carried out by a German logistics company in cooperation with a warehouse in the Netherlands and an expert for wearable computing solutions. Here, the technology was used to implement 'vision picking' in warehousing operations. The company's staff was guided through the warehouse by

© Springer International Publishing Switzerland 2016
F.F.-H. Nah and C.-H. Tan (Eds.): HCIBGO 2016, Part II, LNCS 9752, pp. 281–289, 2016.
DOI: 10.1007/978-3-319-39399-5_27

graphics displayed on the smart glass to speed up the picking process and to reduce errors. Both studies have proven that logistics can profit from the tools of augmented reality resulting in a significant efficiency increase during the picking process. However, these pilot studies exclusively dealt with the impact of smart glasses on the *efficiency* of labour. There are few studies that investigated the impact of smart glasses on physical workloads' and they focus mainly on assembly workplaces [5] and not on picking workplaces. Consequently, our approach is to design a realistic model of a picking workplace, where picking tasks can be performed with and without data glasses. Our laboratory mock-up workplace (see Fig. 1) enables us to measure biomechanical and physiological parameters on subjects performing typical consignment tasks. In the following section we focus on the design requirements that are to be imposed on a laboratory mock-up for the assessment of physical workloads at a commissioning workplace.

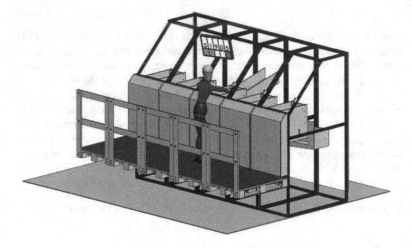

Fig. 1. CAD model of our picking workplace

2   A Picking Workplace Model

Figure 1 depicts the CAD model of our picking machine mock-up. Our laboratory workplace is based on a real industrial machine for fast commissioning. It has the same dimensions as the original but is simplified with respect to the product sorting mechanics and the objects that have to be picked. Our key requirement is to design the workplace interface for the subjects in such a way that it is as close as possible to the working environment of the real machine. In order to standardize the picking tasks we have chosen balls of different weight, diameter and color as picking objects instead of real products. The parameters of our fake products (i.e. the balls) have been derived from the original products. A single picking task is defined as follows: Our machine delivers an incoming box with a certain number of a certain product type to our subject. According to the information on the monitor (see Fig. 2) that is mounted on the rack of the mock-up the products have to be correctly sorted into four boxes (two to the left and two to the right of the incoming central box). For our study a comparative analysis of displaying picking instructions either on the display of a PC monitor or by smart glasses is planned. After having finished all picking tasks for one outgoing box the subject has to push a button thus indicating that this box is ready to be sent away. In our mock-up workplace this step is realised by mechanically removing all the balls from the completed box. But before the balls are fed back into the sorting and distributing mechanism of our machine an error analysis is performed. This task is realised by automated image processing. An image of the balls in the outgoing box is taken by a small webcam. The number and the properties of the balls are then automatically detected and instantly compared to those defined in the picking task displayed on the monitor. All errors are saved in a log file. By analysing the performance of real workers we have estimated that our picking machine has to contain several hundred balls in total. The balls having been processed by the picking subject are lifted to the mechanical sorting system by a fully automatic conveyor belt. This way, the picking objects are permanently circulating without human intervention. The methods for measuring the biomechanical and physiological parameters of the subjects performing picking tasks at our lab workplace and for assessing the corresponding workload are described in the following section.

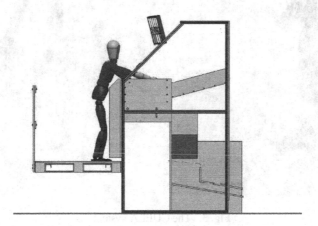

Fig. 2. Lateral view: typical working posture when looking at the monitor

3 Workload Assessment

3.1 Introduction

Our workplace-in-the-lab enables us to completely control the factors (i.e. the independent variables) that influence the outcome of our study. Environmental factors such as light and noise will be held constant in the laboratory workplace. As our machine is designed to deliver pre-defined and exactly repeatable picking tasks for each subject the complexity of the assigned tasks will also be kept constant. This allows us to evaluate the statistical significance of a single factor under the premise that all other factors are unchanged. If we alter for instance the way the information "where to put what" is delivered to the subjects (i.e. PC monitor vs. data glasses) we will be able to quantify the effects of these conditions on the physical workload that our participants are exposed to. This leads to the question how the dependent variable "physical workload" can be operationalised. The first part of the answer to this question can be given by making use of the following toolbox of methods and measurements:

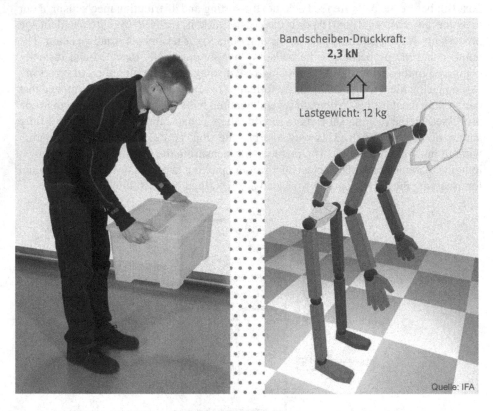

Fig. 3. The CUELA system

3.2 Kinematics

Body postures and movements are recorded in the laboratory study by means of the CUELA system [6]. This ambulatory measuring system is based on the IMU (inertial measurement unit) technology and includes a miniature data storage unit with a flash memory card, which can be attached to the subject's clothing. Figure 3 (left picture) shows the attachment of the measuring system on the subjects. From the measured signals, the following body/joint angles and positions and their corresponding degrees of freedom will be calculated.

- Head: sagittal and lateral inclination
- Upper limb: shoulder joint and elbow (flexion/extension), hand position
- Cervical spine: flexion/extension

- Thoracic spine: sagittal and lateral inclination at Th3
- Lumbar spine: sagittal and lateral inclination at L5
- Thigh right/left: spatial position
- Lower leg right/left: spatial position

The trunk inclination angle will be calculated from the averaged Th3 and L5 sagittal inclination angles. The trunk flexion angle is defined as the angular difference between the Th3 and L5 sagittal inclination. The trunk lateral flexion angle is defined as the angular difference between the Th3 and L5 lateral inclination.

The data logger of the CUELA measuring system permits synchronous recording of all measured data together with physiological parameters, at a sampling rate of 50 Hz. The CUELA software enables these data to be displayed together with the digitized video recording of the workplace situation and a 3D animated figure.

Besides investigating human motion with IMU devices expensive and accurate optical marker based systems have been the state of the art until very recently. However, markerless low-cost systems have always been a desideratum in the field of biomechanics and sports science. Due to increasing computer chip power and the progress in image processing techniques the realization of such a system has become feasible. With the advent of the Microsoft Kinect sensor in 2010 a flexible low-cost tool has entered the computer game market enabling markerless tracking of human motion [7]. In 2014 an improved Kinect 2.0 version with higher tracking accuracy and reduced sensor noise has been launched. Our first pre-tests show that the 3D tracking abilities of the Kinect 2.0 are appropriate to analyze the posture of the upper body of a subject performing a picking task. Hence, for our application the Kinect will be used as an additional calibration tool in order to ameliorate the outcome of the CUELA measurements.

3.3 External Forces

The synchronous registration of ground reaction forces is realized using foot pressure sensitive insoles. Each insole consists of 24 piezo-resistive hydro cells. Based on the ground reaction forces, it is possible to detect the handled load weights by using a biomechanical model.

3.4 Muscle Activity

Electromyography (EMG) is a well-established tool in the field of physiology. EMG with surface electrodes (sEMG) is widely used as a diagnosis instrument for the assessment of electrical activity of skeletal muscles. Though it is difficult to find a simple relationship between EMG signal amplitudes and muscle force production it is generally accepted that a shift of the EMG signal frequencies is an indicator for muscle fatigue. For our main target (i.e. the analysis of the change in posture caused by the use of smart glasses for picking workplaces) sEMG is applied for monitoring the activity of the neck and trapezius muscles. Here, four differential pre-amplified (gain: 1000, band-pass filter: 5e1000 Hz) active Ag/AgCl surface electrodes (Ambu_ Blue Sensor, Denmark) will be used to measure EMG activity. The signals are converted from analog to digital (12-bit) at a sampling frequency of 1024 Hz and stored on flash memory cards in the mobile CUELA EMG signal processor for long-term analysis.

The electrodes will be placed in accordance with the SENIAM recommendations [8]. For assessment of the EMG signals, the root mean square (RMS) values will be calculated from the raw EMG data over consecutive time windows (0.3 s). The RMS values are normalized by the performance of maximum reference activities at the beginning of each measurement; all muscle activities are therefore relative to a maximum voluntary contraction (% MVC).

We suspect that the movement patterns during picking using a conventional PC monitor are an unfavorable combination of flexion and extension, lateral bending and rotation of the head to the left and the right. These complex head movement patterns are accompanied by a high activity of the arms. We use sEMG electrodes attached to all the relevant muscles that move the head during picking to quantify the corresponding muscle activity and possible fatigue.

3.5 Physiological and Psychological Aspects

Additional emotion-related physiological parameters such as heart rate, skin temperature and conductivity are recorded using wearable computer systems. Robust wearable computer systems are available that are designed for users who want to gather information on the emotional state of their subjects without being forced to take care of measurement artefacts, filter chains, or the irritating effects of wires imposing restrictions on the on the subject's mobility [9, 10]. The emotion-related parameters add a psychological component to our dependent variable that we originally introduced as physical workload. The psychological aspect of the workload concept is further extended by using a standardized questionnaire to elicit subjective viewpoints of the study participants after having finished their "picking shift". The Nordic Questionnaire [11] lets the subjects rank the musculoskeletal discomfort experienced during the task as well as the wearing comfort of the computer devices.

3.6 Defining Physical Workload

The second part of the answer to the question of how to measure and quantify the variable "physical workload" is the interpretation and integration of all the data collected with the modalities described above. As a first step existing guidelines for the classification of body postures are taken into account. The software tool WIDAAN that is part of the CUELA system uses the ISO 11226 norm to automatically classify posture angles according to the lights of a traffic signal (see Fig. 4).

After measurement it is possible to mark any actions or situations to highlight certain work activities and have them evaluated. The CUELA software automatically issues a series of statistical evaluations to give a quick impression of the quantified risk factors. Body angles and postures are analyzed with reference to the literature and some relevant standards:

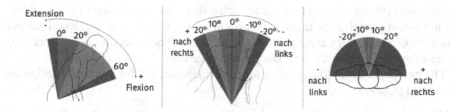

Fig. 4. Classification of upper body postures

- Extreme body angle positions, asymmetrical posture patterns [12]
- Static postures (assessed in accordance with European standards)
- Repetitive movements according to [13, 14]

For each measurement, it is possible to have an OWAS (Ovako Working Posture Analysing System [15] ergonomic analysis carried out. The software automatically identifies work postures classified in accordance with OWAS in connection with the handled weights and evaluates them statistically. As a result, the user receives a list of priorities that distinguishes between four risk classes (action category/class of measures). For the biomechanical assessment of manual load handling and to estimate the associated load on the spine, the measured data can be entered as input data into biomechanical human models [16]. Apart from the measured body/joint movements and forces, the model also requires the subject's data, e.g. body height, length of limbs and body weight, as input variables. From this, force and torque vectors are calculated at the model's joints. For estimation of the loading on the lumbar spine, an interface to the biomechanical model "The Dortmunder" [17] exists.

Finally it is planned to carry out a field study at the real picking workplace of our partner company in order to validate the results achieved under lab conditions.

4   Study Design, Hypotheses and Statistics

As mentioned earlier it is our main goal to quantify the effects of using smart glasses during picking tasks on the physical workloads of the subject. A first study capable of yielding the desired result should have the following general design. Two groups of subjects are chosen randomly out of a huge pool of possible subjects. In our case the population is defined by all the students of our campus (>2.500 persons). Two unbiased samples of this population are then drawn by using a random matriculation number generator. Students that have been selected by this random process are motivated to take part in the study by offering them a financial compensation. The size of the groups is determined by a statistical power analysis. Each subject is assigned an identical set of picking tasks although the order of the tasks will be randomised. Members of the first group (i.e. the control group) receive their picking information on the conventional PC monitor whilst the members of the other group use smart glasses. After having tested several smart glasses available on the market (e.g. Epson, Google) we have decided to choose the Vuzix smart glasses because it turned out that the Vuzix offers a good compromise between wearing comfort and reliability. The first version of Google Glass was not robust enough to be taken into account for our study. However, a new version of Google Glass has been announced. As soon as it will be available on the market we will test the usefulness of the new Google Glass version for our application.

The null hypothesis H0 and its undirected alternative H1 for this study design are formulated as follows:

- H0: The use of smart glasses during picking tasks has **no** effect on the physical workloads imposed on the subjects.
- H1: The use of smart glasses during picking tasks has **an** effect (positive or negative) on the physical workloads imposed on the subjects.

Statistical hypotheses testing methods are then applied to answer the question whether H0 can be rejected (and if H1 can be accepted).

5   Expectations and Outlook

Currently, our laboratory workplace is under construction. The set of sensors listed above is at our disposal. A set of pre-studies has already been designed in order to quantify external factors such as aspects of software ergonomics, the influence of the subject's psychological status and the distortion of the results caused by working with a full body sensor suit. The mock-up is expected to run by the end of May 2016. A first pilot study becomes feasible in May/June 2016. Preliminary results of this pilot study could then be presented at the conference in July 2016.

In the near future, smart glasses will become a popular tool in many working environments. So far, the impact on working efficiency has been the main focus of current research. However, smart technology might as well be beneficial for the health of working people as it improves posture and likewise reduces the risk of work-induced degeneration of muscles and joints. Smart technology will then assist in establishing "physiological movement patterns" at the workplace and help to reduce costs for the health care system. However, in order to test this hypothesis it is crucial to first setup an artificial test environment and to quantify the effects. Thus, monitoring the change of movement patterns caused by introducing smart glasses using sophisticated sensor technology is a key factor for predicting long term work-related health issues.

References

1. Schwerdtfeger, B., Reif, R., Günthner, W., Klinker, G.: Pick-by-Vision: there is something to pick at the end of the augmented tunnel. Virtual Reality **15**, 213–223 (2011)
2. Reif, R., Walch, D.: Augmented & Virtual Reality applications in the field of logistics. Vis. Comput. Int. J. Comput. Graph. **24**, 987–994 (2008)
3. DHL Report about the use of Augmented Reality devices. http://www.delivering-tomorrow.de/wp-content/uploads/2015/08/dhl-report-augmented-reality-2014.pdf
4. Information on the Volkswagen Webpage about a project using data glasses in logistics. http://www.volkswagenag.com/content/vwcorp/info_center/en/news/2015/11/3D_smart_glasses.html

5. Theis, S., Pfendler, C., Alexander, T., Mertens, A., Brandl, C., Schlick, M.: Head-Mounted Displays - Bedingungen des sicheren und beanspruchungsoptimalen Einsatzes. Physische Beanspruchung beim Einsatz von HMDs. Bundesanstalt für Arbeitsschutz und Arbeitsmedizin (2015). ISBN: 978-3-88261-162-5
6. Ellegast, R., Hermanns, I., Schiefer, C.: Workload assessment in field using the ambulatory CUELA system. In: Duffy, V.G. (ed.) ICDHM 2009. LNCS, vol. 5620, pp. 221–226. Springer, Heidelberg (2009)
7. Shum, H.P., Ho, E.S., Jiang, Y., Takagi, S.: Real-time posture reconstruction for Microsoft Kinect. IEEE Trans. Cybern. **43**(5), 1357–1369 (2013)
8. Hermens, H.J., Freriks, B.: The state of the art on sensors and sensor placement procedures for surface electromyography: a proposal for sensor placement procedures. Roessingh Research and Development, Enschede, The Netherlands (1997). www.seniam.org
9. Peter, C., Ebert, E., Beikirch, H.: A wearable multi-sensor system for mobile acquisition of emotion-related physiological data. In: Tao, J., Tan, T., Picard, R.W. (eds.) ACII 2005. LNCS, vol. 3784, pp. 691–698. Springer, Heidelberg (2005)
10. Pantelopoulos, A., Bourbakis, N.G.: A survey on wearable sensor-based systems for health monitoring and prognosis. Syst. Man Cybern. Part C: IEEE Trans. Appl. Rev. **40**(1), 1–12 (2010)
11. Kuorinka, I., Jonsson, B., Kilbom, A.: Standardized Nordic questionnaires for the analysis of musculoskeletal symptoms. Appl. Ergon. **18**, 233–237 (1987)
12. Drury, C.G.: A biomechanical evaluation of the repetitive motion injury potential of industrial jobs. Semin. Occup. Med. **2**, 41–49 (1987)
13. McAtamney, L., Corlett, E.N.: RULA: a survey method for the investigations of work-related upper limb disorders. Appl. Ergon. **24**, 91–99 (1993)
14. Hoehne-Hückstädt, U., Herda, C., Ellegast, R., Hermanns, I., Hamburger, R., Ditchen, D.: Muskel-Skelett-Erkrankungen der oberen Extremität und berufliche Tätigkeit. BGIA-Report 2/2007, Sankt Augustin: HVBG (2007)
15. Karhu, O., Kansi, P., Kuorinka, I.: Correcting working postures in industry: A practical method for analysis. Appl. Ergon. **8**, 199–201 (1977)
16. Ellegast, R.: Personengebundenes Messsystem zur automatisierten Erfassung von Wirbelsäulenbelastungen bei beruflichen Tätigkeiten. BIA-Report 5/98, Sankt Augustin: HVBG (1998). http://www.dguv.de/bgia/de/pub/rep/rep02/biar0598/index.jsp
17. Jäger, M., Luttmann, A., Göllner, R., Laurig, W.: Der Dortmunder - Biomechanische Modellbildung zur Bestimmung und Beurteilung der Belastung der Lendenwirbelsäule bei Lastenhandhabungen. In: Radandt, S., Grieshaber R., Schneider, W. (eds.) Prävention von arbeitsbedingten Gesundheitsgefahren und Erkrankungen, pp. 105–124 (2000)

Degradations and Consequences of ICT in Occupational Prevention Terms as Illustrated by the Transport and Logistics Sector

Virginie Govaere[✉] and Liên Wioland

Working Life Department, INRS, Vandoeuvre, France
{Virginie.govaere,Lien.wioland}@inrs.fr

Abstract. Information and Communications Technologies (ICT) are designed to fluidify and secure information flows and to strengthen workforces. They have permeated companies irrespective of their business sector and the jobs performed by their workers. They evolve rapidly and are composed of hardware, applications and services. Various research studies agree on the fact that these technologies are creating changes in the world of work. INRS has conducted research on these transformations, which may affect both working conditions and operator health. Our inquiry addresses two issues: Are these changes specific to certain ICTs? Does abolition of work boundaries result in propagation of effects to other work situations? Our aim is to provide elements of an answer to these two questions and to identify therefrom possible prevention approaches.

Keywords: ICT · Occupational prevention · Propagation

1   Introduction

Companies implement Information and Communications Technologies (ICTs) to fluidify information flows, to secure these flows and their related transactions, to strengthen workforces and to increase productivity, to promote process standardisation and to ensure traceability among other functions. They permeate companies irrespective of their business sector and the jobs performed by their workers. They evolve rapidly and assume various forms in that they may be composed of hardware (e-phone, tablet, computers, connected glasses, etc.), applications (messaging software, geo-tracking systems, ERP, etc.) and/or services (e-application, social networks, etc.).

Scientific communities focusing on these "objects" are diverse in view of the plurality and ubiquitous nature of ICT. While their mission may be human, social or technical, they have often opted for a "benevolent" or progressive attitude to these technologies, which offer user mobility, socialisation through development of multiple networks, elimination of certain repetitive tasks or enhancement of human (mainly physical) capacities. Yet, for several years, an ever greater number of research studies have addressed the user-related cost and paradoxes of at least the ICTs that are implemented in a work framework, although these studies have never called into question the capacities permitted by these technologies. The studies conducted also agree on the fact

© Springer International Publishing Switzerland 2016
F.F.-H. Nah and C.-H. Tan (Eds.): HCIBGO 2016, Part II, LNCS 9752, pp. 290–301, 2016.
DOI: 10.1007/978-3-319-39399-5_28

that these technologies are creating a change in the world of work; they abolish conventional work boundaries (man-machine combination, work teams, company) and they accelerate time by dictating a work tempo of immediacy [1]. From the literature, we can generally identify five factors governing degradation of working conditions: work intensification, weakening of relations between workers/workforces, blurring of boundaries, information overload and greater activity control [2]. Frequently however, identification focuses primarily on the use of communication tools (email/messaging software, collaborating space, etc.) [3, 4]. Moreover, it often targets a single work situation, while abolition of conventional boundaries is a basic characteristic of ICTs.

Against this background, INRS has conducted research on ICT-induced work transformations, which may affect both working conditions and operator health. Our present inquiry addresses the following two issues: Are the five factors identified from the literature specific to certain ICTs? Does abolition of conventional frontiers result in propagation of degraded conditions to other work situations? Our aim is to provide elements of an answer to these two questions and to identify therefrom possible prevention approaches.

The transport and logistics sector is well suited to investigating various ICT usages (communication, management and production tools). This sector is structured by a complex network of companies, into which different ICTs have been integrated to reduce not only goods reception and market demand processing times, but also work cycle times through task optimisation and rationalisation and generalisation of simultaneous performance of necessary operations independently of space or company area. This is a sector in which goods transit from the producer to the final customer, flowing from one department to another and from one company to another (production site, transporter, storage platform, distribution hub, etc.). This flow of goods is accompanied by a continuous flow of data supported by ICTs.

2 Method

Six transport or logistics companies took part in this study, in which we adopted an ergonomic approach. Each company taking part was followed for three weeks based on the same observation and interview protocol covering all departments within these companies (production and operations).

2.1 Observations

Observations were collected in the form of video and audio recordings. Video recordings were made cameras, which monitored employees performing a usual operation during their work shift. Observations were recorded from the start to the end of the work shift during full days. They were formalised based on a code denoting not only the activity (enabling us to quantify the time and frequency of the operations performed), but also use of various tools, the communications implemented, the purpose of these communications, the speakers, etc. Depending on the principal activity of the company involved, the observed situations concerned:

- Transport operations department personnel and goods transport drivers
- Order preparers, forklift drivers, reception and shipping supervisors, loading bay operatives, procurement and customer managers at logistics platforms.

2.2 Interviews

At all sites, INRS representatives conducted interviews of at least one person from each company work team: senior management, human resources, accounting, operations, drivers, managers… an interview assessment grid was developed and systematically implemented. This comprised topics relating to the interviewed employee, description of the activity performed, changes in the employee's activity in the last 5 and 10 years, changes in the tools used and their usages, operators external to the site or company and activity volume.

3 Results

The ICTs used at the six companies studied included:

- Communication tools: email/messaging software, Electronic Data Interchanges (EDI), smartphones and/or cell phones, Internet
- Production tools: Voice Picking, radio frequency terminal or Radio Frequency Identification (RFID) reader, geo-tracking system, on-board computer system
- Management tools: Enterprise Resource Planning (ERP), round management software, Transport Management System (TMS), Warehouse Management System (WMS), transport software, Office pack, movement monitoring software

The inventory of ICTs used at these transport companies revealed the diversity of systems in place and the fact that several such systems were simultaneously operated at each company. Irrespective of their companies and jobs, all employees used a combination of ICTs, when performing their activity. During our observations, we chose to record the type of ICT used rather than its version, developer or supplier. Hence, only one EDI was counted when several different ones are used in a department. The average number of ICTs used by an employee was approximately four; this average generally comprised two communication tools and two management tools. Production tools were more specific to a job and their usage was therefore less general across the company.

The following observation was based on the fact that companies opt for certain ICTs, while others were imposed on them by their business contacts (customers, suppliers). There were many such business contacts. This resulted in multiple ICT combinations, which depended more on the business contacts than on the operation to be performed:

- Use of several "customer" EDIs to perform an operation (customer order validation), which then complement the company's in-house EDI (customer EDI and in-house company EDI both requiring data entry)
- Use of "parallel systems" depending on business contacts. Parallel systems included email, fax, conventional spreadsheet software, etc. for suppliers with no ERP or EDI

- Multiple procedures for the same external business contact; for example, order intake and validation using an EDI generating an email, which validates an order after customer EDI usage… and entry in the company in-house EDI.

All employees of the companies taking part were affected by these initial observations: superposition of different ICTs and plurality of ICTs for performing the same task. However, personnel performing some jobs were less affected: order preparers, forklift drivers and truck drivers. Their jobs usually involved the use of one or two production tools (RFID, on-board system, Voice Picking) and, to a lesser extent, one communication tool (usually a Smartphone). These workers appeared to be only indirectly affected by usage of ICTs imposed by company external contacts.

These general observations led to us refocus our initial question. The companies taking part in the study did not use a unique ICT category. We therefore retained the option of identifying work situation degradation factors based on the ICT category mainly implemented (communication, management or production tools). We compared the results for order preparers and forklift drivers and for other jobs in order to provide elements for understanding the relationship between degradation factors and usage diversity and intensity for the ICT types.

3.1 Work Intensification

The dimensions involved in work intensification are increase in interruptions, requests and acceleration in the pace or tempo of work [5]. The average time for most of the work operations was less than one minute in all the quantitative analyses. Operations by workers were performed at comparable and sustained rates at the companies taking part, despite their different nature (delivery round building, customer relations, data entry, handling, etc.). These operating rates were observed for both managers and first level operators. Two jobs represented exceptions to this: truck drivers and loading bay supervisors, whose average operation times were at least four to five times longer than those of other company workers. These two jobs are inconsistent in terms of ICT usage; the truck drivers used ICTs very little, while the loading bay supervisors used a combination of communication tools, WMS, traceability systems, etc. Moreover, the order preparers and forklift drivers, who had been previously identified as having ICT user profiles similar to those of truck drivers, performed operations lasting approximately one minute.

Beyond the sustained work rates observed, we need to show whether these increase when ICTs are implemented.

Frequent Interruptions Frequency of communications governs work tempo because it represents interruptions in the operations in progress. Communications were numerous (direct, telephone, email/messaging or on-board system) and 61 % of them were conducted through ICTs. The employee received them in 2/3^{rds} of cases. The split between received and emitted communications was similar in all the activities involved. Interruptions were noted in relation to the loading bay supervisors, the platform managers and the reception operators… these workers were interrupted via communication, management or production tools. Order preparers, forklift drivers and truck drivers were little affected by interruptions, but they could cause them to change an itinerary, add or remove a collection or a delivery, or perform a priority picking operation. These interruptions were therefore different to those observed to affect other workers. In these situations, the interruptions were mediated by communication or production tools.

Acceleration Mediated by ICTs Acceleration of the pace of work of order preparers was observed with a "prescriptive" ICT such as Voice Picking. It is not the Voice Picking system that directly imposes the order preparer's work rate; it is also its mode of operation: delivery of data such as the address or quantities of goods to be picked is broken down into elementary units, which are given to the preparer step by step. Each preparer reply triggers the subsequent Voice Picking data.... leading to a new reply from the preparer, who effectively self-accelerates. Comparison of the order preparation activity with and without Voice Picking revealed work rate acceleration and increased productivity of 15 % and 20 % respectively, when Voice Picking was implemented [6]. This increase in productivity and thus in the overall load handled led to an increase in the physical stresses to which these employees were subjected.

Increased Mental and Psychological Stresses Some companies transferred certain operations considered "outside their core business" to other company departments in order to optimise operation of departments subject to high demand (heavy workload, numerous communications, frequent interruptions, etc.). However, transferring operations "outside core business" leads to a paradox, namely an increase in work rate in both the departments taking on these additional operations and the department to be relieved of them. To illustrate this paradox, we offer the example of an operations department at a transport company taking part in the study. The operations department was a vital department that managed customer relations, located the goods, scheduled and monitored driver activity in real time, managed physical resources, etc. The company had transferred operations involving claims processing, physical accident management, vehicle pool control, driver work contract management, etc. to its accounting department. Processing these operations required information on the activities performed and traceability of work situation status, decisions taken, changes in schedule, etc. It was the operations department that provided these data. The accounting department therefore requested access to this information from the operations department and these new demands from the accounting department represented a 36 % increase in requests for transport operations department personnel.

Summary of Work Intensification Our results confirm work intensification. This affects all the jobs monitored, even those implementing a small number and variety of ICTs. Communication, production and management tools all contribute to work intensification.

The work intensification noted above for different jobs has consequences for other company workers; for example, acceleration in order preparers' work leads to higher procurement and shipping work rates. This acceleration has, at the very least, a "mechanical" effect on workers in upstream and downstream departments: forklift drivers, procurement and shipping personnel, drivers, etc.

3.2 Information Overload

Information overload comprises three dimensions [7]: (1) the excessive information volume, (2) the limit of individuals' cognitive capacities in processing information and (3) the communication component through dialogue multiplication mediated by ICTs.

During our interviews, the notion of information overload was not referred to directly and irrespective of the interview's job. Nevertheless, all those interviewed mentioned their need to concentrate, their recourse to information management strategies (Post-It stickers, intermediate monitoring chart, etc.), risks of errors and oversight in the event of interruptions and fatigue.

Our quantitative results show that, in 70 h of observation, the volume of information to be processing during communications (1956 oral or telephone communications) was accompanied by an even larger volume of information (3201), i.e. 46 data media/hour on average. These data were extracted from hardcopy or digital purchase orders, emails, job-related software, etc. These usages could take a few seconds or several minutes. They were often fragmented and could represent information acquisition, searching or building. They were performed under in contexts involving time-related pressure and as double tasks in some situations. Moreover, several different data could be "activated" in parallel for certain tasks such as building a delivery round, for example. Finally, there were many information media with different purposes. This multitude of media denoted multiple methods of structuring the information to be used, processed and also supplied. Furthermore, they were scattered about in different forms within the various ICT tools. The volume of information was therefore large. Conditions under which this information was used, such a double tasking, time-related pressure and interruptions in processing, are consumers of cognitive capacities and are all the more so when the information is scattered and mediated by a multitude of ICTs [8]. All three dimensions of information overload were therefore present.

For example, every type of tool was used by transport operations department personnel; their usage could be broken down into 39 % communication tools, 30 % production tools and 31 % management tools. Similar results were obtained for every job except for order preparers, forklift drivers and truck drivers. The latter employees in fact used fewer ICT tools, which were also used separately or independently of each other. Data were thus concentrated within just one operation-dedicated tool. In these three cases, the information volume was nevertheless large but it directly prescribed or dictated the activity, while such information tended to form a basis for interpretation in other jobs. Finally, communication tools were little used; truck drivers used such tools for an average of 3.5 h (14 h for transport operations department personnel) out of the 70 h monitored.

As before, the information overload was neither local nor dependent on just one work situation. It was produced and promoted by various workers both within and outside the company and it propagated.

3.3 Greater Activity Control

Greater activity control was referred to by all the interviewed workers. There were two types of control [9, 10]: direct control by a technology or "machine", control using traces provided by the "machine".

"Machine"Control This type of work control is implemented by production and management tools, which prescribe or dictate performance of an operation or activity. Hence, when an operation is not performed in the expected order or when the reply provided by the employee is not the reply expected by the control system, the latter stops the process until the "right" answer has been given. In the case of the order preparers, forklift drivers, loading bay and reception personnel, the tool imposed a sequence of operations or actions. For example, at a transport platform, ERP required that the goods received at the platform pass through 6 stages or "statuses" before being released for delivery preparation. Situations involving breaks in workflow were observed. In such situations, the relevant goods were at the platform, but they could not be delivered despite the urgency of the situation: The platform was temporarily saturated and the system could not allocate the goods to storage and picking location. Picking was rendered impossible by the system without this location. An impression of being subjected to the system, its pace and its constraints was widely felt and expressed. This machine-based control was also encountered in jobs involving customer relations and procurement management. In these jobs, we observed a forceful prescriptive process dictating activity performance, accompanied by frequently curtailed opportunities for action; for example, a customer manager could not delay a delivery date or modify a product reference, when an order error had been detected, even with the customer's agreement or at the customer's request. It was up to the customer to cancel a request through its EDI or ERP before editing a new order form. These restrictions led to not only customer dissatisfaction and sometimes tense relationships with the transport company's customer manager, but also to statements such as "the ERP controls everything! We're just pawns.... What about customer relations? Quality of work?"

"Trace" Control This type of control was referred to by all interviewees from the companies taking part in relation to communication, production and management tools. Such tools enable one to trace who has done what, at which moment and for how long. The first element quoted by all workers involved real-time identification of the user and, hence, of his/her responsibility for the actions taken. Identification was considered spying or mistrust by order preparers, forklift drivers and truck drivers. This control was implemented in relation to truck drivers, for example, when their delivery route did not correspond to the optimum itinerary in terms of kilometres travelled. It was also embodied by establishing a driver rating based on diesel consumption. Some workers were more guarded in their statements. They stressed the advantages of this control in dispute situations; it effectively provided an objective element, which often ensured healthier relations between workers in relation to disputes with customers. Workers also emphasised the benefit of this control when ensuring equity of treatment among employees; the tracing process was aimed at detecting "abnormal" events rather than strictly controlling a prescribed procedure. Finally, in view of the time-consuming aspect of trace usage, these workers insisted on the limits of its application under the conditions of time-related pressure prevailing at these companies.

Summary Introduction of ICTs has led to an evolution in work activity control, which applies to all employees independent of their level of responsibility at companies. All ICT tools are involved in work control except for communication tools, which appear to be unaffected by the "machine" control dimension. The feeling of the different workers taking part was lukewarm in relation to any type of tool or any specific job within their companies: for some, such controls caused deterioration in quality of work, time-related pressure and mistrust; while for others, they prompted healthier relations between personnel. Control had an effect on the areas of action of the various departments: it allowed identification of "who has to do what", albeit without guaranteeing the quality of action performed by a department or for a department intervening later in the processing system.

3.4 Weakening of Inter-personnel and Work Group Relationships

Under certain conditions, non-uniformity of ICT-paced or traced personal performance leads a work group to implement a mechanism that exerts pressure between co-workers, to strengthening the control exercised by the work group on individuals and to increasing competition between individuals or teams.

Co-worker Support No pressure between co-workers was observed or reported. On the other hand, co-worker support has disappeared. Assistance among order preparers had indeed been a common phenomenon, taking the form of help in handling heavy loads, when preparing an order on which the preparer had fallen behind or was suffering from tiredness, etc. This support decreased, when production tools (RFID or Voice Picking) were implemented. The same phenomenon was also observed for customer managers, when management tools were implemented. Co-worker support is prevented by the tool because customers are allocated by name to a manager, who becomes the only person permitted to take action on his/her portfolio of customers, unless his/her management intervenes.

Increasing Competition Between Individuals or Teams In some jobs, such as order preparation, the "values" of the preparer workforce had evolved from job recognition based on pallet quality criteria to prepared quantity criteria. A good preparer was not the one who had made up a "good" pallet, but the one who had made it up quickly. Furthermore, communications between co-workers had deteriorated: 84 % of preparers (120 preparers consulted) reported a decrease and deterioration in these communications.

With implementation of a management tool, creation of competition between truck drivers became established based on their performance ratings achieved in terms of diesel consumption. Competitive situations were also noted among the platform manager and the loading bay supervisor: under these conditions, each of them had to achieve targets "traced" by the tool by overriding consequences for the other team.

Summary Management and production tools were referred to as being causes of a weakening of relationships and work groups. Situations associated with this weakening and communication tools were not observed or mentioned. Here again, the phenomenon is independent of the jobs and tasks observed. Repercussions internal to a work situation were linked to repercussions in adjacent work situations.

3.5 Blurring of Boundaries Between Private and Work Spheres

All workers taking part in the study were unanimous, when confronted by the issue of blurring of private-work sphere boundaries: "There's no blurring… except in unusual situations, which would only involve managers". Nevertheless, interviews can be quoted as tempering this assertion. For example, order preparers using Voice Picking stated that they were subject to a number of language-related reflexes after leaving their shift: preparers used the word "OK" 400 to 500 times an hour in mass-market retailing activities. They reckoned it took approximately one hour after the end of their shift for this reflex to fade away. With regard to the transport operations department, its personnel contacted their colleagues to obtain a report on the situation a few hours before starting their shift. The platform manager took his work laptop computer home to monitor activity progress on days and nights with a heavy workload. Moreover, he would return to complement shift teams in the event of difficulties. The company manager took home files requiring time to avoid interruptions…These few interviews therefore indicated that the boundaries between private and work spheres were not as clear as those initially portrayed: So-called "unusual" situations occurred regularly and the populations involved were not limited only to managers, even though the nature of boundary blurring for the order preparers was different to that observed for other workers. Production, management and communication tools were implemented in the observed situations.

4   Health and Safety Consequences of Five Degradation Factors

The five degradation factors were frequently combined and interlinked. Several points were regularly repeated in relation to these degradation factors: reduction in physical and psychological recovery time, fatigue, stress, weakening in capacity for action, time-related pressure. Available knowledge of the health consequences of ICT usage are indirect; it requires assessment of degradation factors associated with health [3, 4, 10] and safety effects, such as increased risks of occupational accident, MSD and RPS. Acceleration of the pace of work and repetitive movements [11], efforts made to keep up the work rate are all embodied by a stiffening of movement, which raises the probability of injuring oneself or contracting a musculoskeletal disorder (MSD). Fatigue is nevertheless associated with increases in accident risks. With regard to time-related pressure, studies [12] have shown that employees protect themselves less and are exposed to an increase in accident risks when subject to such pressure.

5   Discussion – Conclusion

Information and communications technologies are widely used at transport and logistics companies. All jobs are affected by these tools even through the functions fulfilled are different. Most jobs use "packages" of ICTs rather than a single software programme, service or tool.

There are differences in some degradation factor dimensions for two ICT types, namely communication and production tools. In communication tools, the "activity control by machine" and "weakening of relations between personnel" dimensions were not observed or reported by the employees interviewed. This observation concerning "weakening of relations between personnel" was unexpected; multiple studies [2–4] insist on an explanation relationship between communication tools (forums, emails, social networks) and this factor. What hypotheses can be advanced for investigating this difference? Communication tools could represent a means for workers to deal with weakening of relations between themselves and between work groups rather than being the cause of such weakening. Investigation of this communication–weakening of relations relationship remains necessary.

With regard to production tools, the "interruption" dimension in relation to work intensification does not appear to be essential. This may be explained by the purpose of production tools, which effectively model tasks, rationalise them to accelerate the production process, to fluidify it. Interruption would therefore be an epiphenomenon to be avoided on a productive level.

Thus, considering all the conclusions of the present study, it is difficult to attribute specific degradation factors to types of tools or to attribute one factor to one tool independently of the other tools used in the work situation concerned.

Another contribution of this work is that it shows that the job-based transversality of these tools is accompanied by propagation of degradations to other work situations. Work intensification for order preparers guided by Voice Picking is effectively embodied by quicker movements, greater repetitiveness, higher loads handles, probably shorter recovery time, etc. The consequences for these employees are greater risk of MSD and stress [13, 14]. Occupational stress is linked to the pace of work imposed by the "machine" and results from high time-related pressure combined with little decision-making freedom. Work intensification propagated to procurement managers corresponded to more demands and thus frequent interruptions that curtailed their concentration capacity and gradually led to the feeling of not being capable of performed quality work or of even performing the job [3, 4]. This causes fatigue, irritation and more stress, when a high workload is combined with heavy time-related pressure [12]. Increased activity for procurement managers will itself induce greater activity for the reception department in terms of both the volume of information to be processed by this department and the volume of goods to be moved through the platform. This will also have a resounding effect and consequences on these employees' health and safety due to work intensification in their department. This example of propagation of a degradation factor from one work situation to another is only partial for it continues outside corporate boundaries to different departments at transport companies, suppliers, customers and every intermediary. Moreover, this propagation involves all the five degradation factors previously considered and accompanies both information and material flows.

What prevention approaches can be prompted to emerge from these conclusions? Two families of consequences can be distinguished: the first applies to analysis of a work situation involving the use of ICTs. In view of the variety and plurality of the ICTs present, consideration of a single user-ICT combination is increasingly inappropriate in an approach to understanding a work situation. The temptation is nevertheless strong since the user himself or herself often ascribes most of his or her ills to a specific ICT. Hence, an emailing or messaging system is frequently blamed for the increase in interruptions, time-related pressure, blurring of boundaries, depersonalisation, loss of meaning, etc. Our conclusions would tend towards envisaging more analysis of the combination of ICTs used in a work situation rather than just one isolated ICT.

The second consequence applies to the phenomenon of propagation of degradation factors from one work situation to another. Detection of a problematic work situation usually prompts analysis of the situation followed by proposal of prevention solutions appropriate to the situation. With integration of the propagation phenomenon into the approach, we consider that analysis of the problematic situation could incorporate factors relating to several work situations and could therefore enhance the efficiency of proposed solutions; the information and material flows convey degradation factors to work situations that act on one of these flows. Implementation of a suitable but targeted solution for a work situation does not prevent continued propagation of propagation factors. Consideration of the propagation phenomenon is therefore equivalent to consideration of the information flow and hence of its path between the various contact persons extending beyond a specific work situation. This leads us to envisage more global prevention solutions for workers acting on the flow.

In conclusion, this research should be pursued to test various hypotheses involving the relationships between these degradation factors and ICT types. This type of study should also be extended to other business sectors in order to verify whether the conclusions are specific to just one sector structured into networks of companies implementing information and material flows.

References

1. Eppler, M.J., Mengis, J.: The concept of information overload: a review of literature from Organization science, Accounting, Marketing, MIS and Related disciplines. Inf. Soc. **20**, 325–344 (2004)
2. Klein, T., Ratier, D.: L'impact des TIC sur les conditions de travail. Rapport et documents Centre d'Analyse Stratégique (2012)
3. DG Emploi. The Increasing Use of Portable Computing and Communication Devices and its Impact on the Health of EU Workers, Commission européenne, décembre 2009
4. Chesley, N.: Information and communication technology use, work intensification and employee strain and distress. Work Employ. Soc. **28**(4), 589–610 (2014)
5. Gollac, M., Volkoff, S.: Citius, altius, fortius [L'intensification du travail]. In: Actes de la recherche en sciences sociales, vol. 114, pp. 54–67. Les nouvelles formes de domination dans le travail, septembre 1996

6. Govaere, V.: La préparation de commande en logistique- mutations technologiques et évolutions des risques professionnels. Notes documentaires 2302 INRS, 214, 1–14 (2009)
7. Isaac, H., Campoy, E., Kalika, M.: Surcharge informationnelle, urgence et TIC. L'effet temporel des technologies de l'information. Manag. Avenir **3**(13), 149–168 (2007)
8. Bowman, L.L., Levine, L.E., Waite, B.M., Gendron, M.: Can students really multitask? An experimental study of instant messaging while reading. Comput. Educ. **54**(4), 927–931 (2010)
9. Levy, K.E.C.: The contexts of control: information, power, and truck-driving work. Inf. Soc. **31**(2), 160–174 (2015)
10. Joling, C., Kraan, K.: Use of technology and working conditions in european union, european foundation for improvement of living and working conditions, Luxembourg (2008)
11. Davezies, P.: Les coûts de l'intensification du travail. Santé et Travail, 57 (2006)
12. Sadeghniiat-Haghighi, K., Yazdi, Z.: Fatigue management in the workplace. Ind. Psychiatry J. **24**(1), 12–17 (2015)
13. Karasek, R.A.: Job demands, job decision latitude, and mental strain: implications for job redesign. Adm. Sci. Q. **24**, 285–308 (1979)
14. Chouanière, D., Cohidon, C., Edey Gamassou, C., Kittel, F., Lafferrerie, A., Langevin, V., Moisan, M.-P., Niedhammer, I., Weibel, L.: Expositions psychosociales et santé: état des connaissances épidémiologiques, Documents pour le médecin du travail, n° 127, INRS, 3e trimestre (2011)

Human-Robot Interaction Modelling for Recruitment and Retention of Employees

Rajiv Khosla$^{(\boxtimes)}$, Mei-Tai Chu, and Khanh Nguyen

Department of Management and Marketing, La Trobe Business School, La Trobe University,
Melbourne, VIC 3083, Australia
r.khosla@latrobe.edu.au

Abstract. The well-executed recruitment and retention of employees in organisations in a highly competitive global market has grown significantly in the last decade. The need for managers to be emotionally intelligent for better management and productivity to deal with employees from generation Y and Z is also in great demand. In this paper we presents a framework which embodies human computer interaction techniques like facial emotion recognition, speech recognition and synthesis in socially assistive robot with human-like communication modalities to capture, analyse, profile and benchmark verbal and non-verbal data during a real-time job interview for hiring salespersons. This research fundamentally changes how employers can leverage the data analysis to seek for the best job applicant and how they perceive the use of human computer interaction (HCI) techniques and information technology in human resource management practice. Existing approaches for recruitment primarily rely on selection criteria and/or psychometric techniques followed by face to face interviews by subjective judgements of human beings. For example, the high turnover of salespersons in the industry has shown limited success of these procedures. Additionally, existing approaches lack benchmarking analysis internally by comparing the profile of most cultural fit employees. Thus, this research incorporates behavioural psychology, data mining, image processing, HCI modelling and techniques to provide a more holistic recruitment application using emotionally aware social robot. The implications of this research not only apply into the hiring and benchmarking of employees, but also collecting big data (verbal and non-verbal) for decision-making, personalised profiling and training.

Keywords: Human-robot interaction · Job interview · Emotion recognition · Profiling and benchmarking · Verbal and non-verbal data analytics

1 Introduction

Recruiting the right type of employees such as salesperson who matches the organizational needs has a critical impact on the performance and sustainability of the sales force, sales manager, and the organization as a whole [1, 2]. High turnover and poor retention of salespersons in organizations is commonly seen and has exposed the limited success of existing hiring processes [1]. Emotionally aware social robots have hardly been used in human resource management. In this paper we report the use of

© Springer International Publishing Switzerland 2016
F.F.-H. Nah and C.-H. Tan (Eds.): HCIBGO 2016, Part II, LNCS 9752, pp. 302–312, 2016.
DOI: 10.1007/978-3-319-39399-5_29

emotionally aware robots to facilitate hiring and benchmarking of employees vis-a-vis existing employees based on their job related emotional and cultural or cognitive behaviour fitness.

In this paper we model a sales candidate's interview with an Emotionally Intelligent Robotic System (EIRS). EIRS is based on integration of psychology based selling behaviour model [3], artificial intelligence, image processing and soft computing techniques. Most existing approaches to salesperson's hiring rely primarily on the interview process and/or psychometric tests for selling behaviour evaluation [3]. Some of the limitations of the interview process include human factor and subjectivity, time constraints, and lack of uniformity [4].

Unlike general behavioural profiling systems like Myers-Briggs profile based on psychometric techniques (which rely on indirect questions related to a candidate's motivation, temperament, etc.) [5], EIRS is based on direct questions related to selling behaviour which are well understood by sales managers and sales candidates. Additionally, the indirect methods (e.g., Myer-Briggs) based on existing psychometric techniques for selling behaviour profiling has encountered with resistance from candidates as well as line/sales managers. Any measure of candidate's emotions (using psychometric technique driven emotional intelligence tests [6]) is again derived indirectly from the questions and is compared to an absolute value or number thus limiting their applicability in terms of developing organization specific benchmarks. In this paper we are proposing a direct and independent measure of a candidate's emotional state using physiological indicators like facial expressions.

A set of procedures are undertaken to correlate a sales candidate's emotional profile with their selling behaviour profile (based on their cognitive responses to selling behaviour questions) computed by the EIRS. The novelty and significance of the contribution include: (i) First novel robotic system for conducting job interviews - sustainable management of employees; (ii) Embodiment of interview in emotionally aware robot results in natural social interaction; (iii) Improving information quality for decision making in real time by including verbal and non-verbal data; (iv) Customisation of interviews based on correlation of verbal and non-verbal responses; (v) Cost effective candidate filtering for large and small organisations; and (vi) Innovative fundamental shift towards robot based social innovation and design of sustainable organisations of the future.

The structure of this paper is followed by the system architecture section. Section 3 demonstrates the research outcomes, and the last section concludes this paper.

2 System Architecture

This section describes the architecture (Fig. 1) of EIRS system and technical background utilised in each system component.

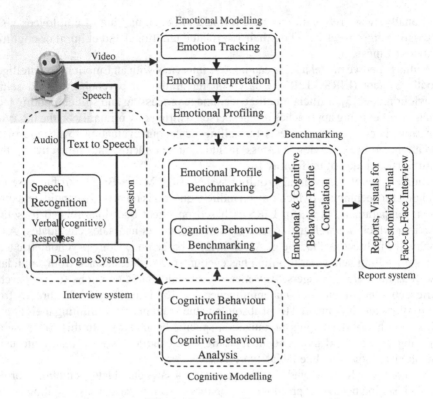

Fig. 1. System architecture

2.1 Interview System

The interview system is used for conducting job interview consisting of three main components: text-to-speech engine, speech recognition and dialogue system. The text-to-speech engine is responsible for vocalising the text questions to the candidate, while the speech recognition capture the audio responses of the candidate and convert them into text.

The dialogue system is responsible for managing the job interview dialogue with the candidate. Besides the human voice and speech recognition and emotion tracking capacities, the robot is interacting (interviewing) the candidate in a very interacting manner with rich human-like characteristics like gestures and emotive facial expressions.

During conducting the interview, video capturing and cognitive responses of the candidate will be input in the emotional profiling and cognitive profiling components for profiling and benchmarking.

2.2 Cognitive Behaviour Modelling

The behavioural model developed by Buzzotte, Lefton & Sherberg [7] has been used for predicting selling behaviour profiles of salespersons. The two dimensional behavioural model [3, p. 171] used for predicting four behavioural categories, namely, Dominant-Warm (DW), Dominant-Hostile (DH), Submissive-Warm (SW) and Submissive-Hostile (SH) is shown in Fig. 2. This model has been used based upon interactions with senior managers in the sales and human resources arena in the consumer and manufacturing industries in Australia [8].

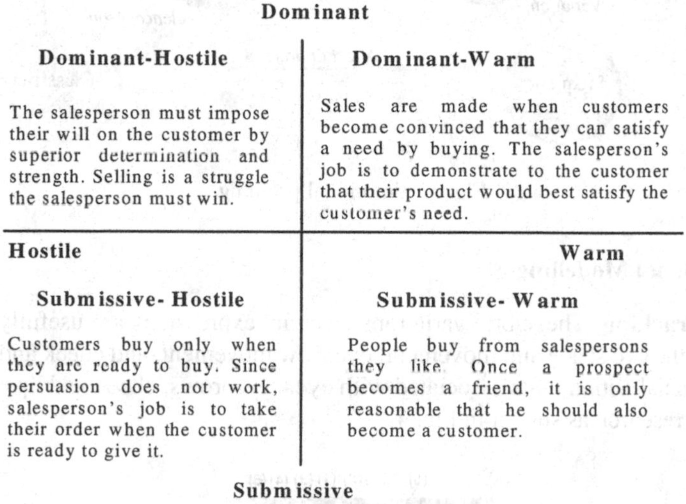

Dominant

Dominant-Hostile	**Dominant-Warm**
The salesperson must impose their will on the customer by superior determination and strength. Selling is a struggle the salesperson must win.	Sales are made when customers become convinced that they can satisfy a need by buying. The salesperson's job is to demonstrate to the customer that their product would best satisfy the customer's need.
Hostile	**Warm**
Submissive- Hostile	**Submissive- Warm**
Customers buy only when they are ready to buy. Since persuasion does not work, salesperson's job is to take their order when the customer is ready to give it.	People buy from salespersons they like. Once a prospect becomes a friend, it is only reasonable that he should also become a customer.

Submissive

Fig. 2. Salesperson behaviour profile [3, p. 171]

For analysing the selling behaviour profile of a salesperson 17 areas related to the model have been identified for evaluation of a sales candidate behaviour profile as selling as a profession of assertiveness, decisiveness, prospecting, product, customers, competition, success and failure, boss, peers, rules and regulations, expenses and reports, training, job satisfaction, view about people, relationship with non-selling departments, and general attitudes [8]. These areas have been identified after several brainstorming discussions with sales managers (domain experts) and knowledge available in the literature [9]. Weights have been assigned to 17 areas on a scale of 1 to 10 using AHP (Analytical Hierarchy Process) technique [10]. The selling behaviour attributes associated with the 17 areas are designed in the form of a questionnaire. The questionnaire consists of 76 questions with at least four questions corresponding to each area. The psychological inputs or answers provided by a sales candidate are used for determining the selling behavioural profile of the candidate. EIRS combines deep knowledge in the form of a selling behavioural model (and 76 questions related to it) and shallow knowledge in the form of behaviour categorization heuristics representing knowledge and experience of the sales managers (an Expert System).

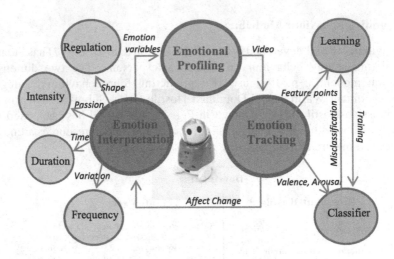

Fig. 3. Emotional profiling

2.3 Emotional Modelling

Emotion Tracking The subtle variations in facial expressions are usefully modelled by tracking the eye shape and movement, eyebrow movement, and cheek and lip movement. The facial action units associated with eyes, eyebrows, cheek and lips have been used in this research as shown in Fig. 4.

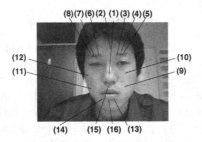

Fig. 4. Tracking feature points

In order to continuously monitor the changes between emotional states, the movement of 16 facial points (Fig. 4) are tracked and classified by LVQ (Linear Vector Quantization) [11] supervised classification algorithm into positive and negative emotional sates, modelled by Affect space model [12] (Fig. 5). The reason for selecting LVQ is that it can give a nonlinear separation of the sample space. This property of the LVQ algorithm becomes useful when dealing with complex class domains where a linear decision border is not sufficient (Fig. 3).

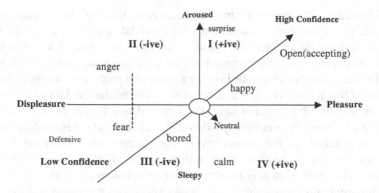

Fig. 5. Affect space model with positive and negative emotional

Emotion Interpretation The emotional responses of a sales candidate are interpreted by four emotion variables (intensity, duration, frequency and shape). Emotion intensity measures the strength of affect [13], and can be defined as the relative degree of displacement away from a neutral expression, of the pattern of muscle movements involved in emotional expressions of a given sort [14]. In our case, this degree of displacement corresponds to the displacement of tracking feature points. The displacements of these tracking points are used as input vector for Fuzzy inference to infer the emotion intensity. In this work, the intensity is divided by 3 degree (high, med and low). We select the sigmoidal function $f(x) = \dfrac{1}{1 + e^{-a(x-c)}}$ as the membership function for intensity (Fig. 6).

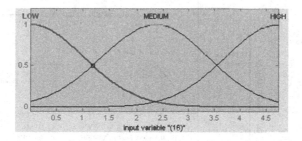

Fig. 6. Intensity membership function

The duration of emotion measures how long the emotion lasts and is recorded as the time when the emotion occurs (change from neutral to + iv/− iv) to the emotion disappears (change from + iv/− iv to neutral). To capture the duration of emotion, the locations of the tracking feature points at the frame before the emotion occurs (corresponding to neutral state) are stored as reference locations to measure feature movement for emotion tracking until the emotion ends (back to neutral state). The emotion frequency defines the number of emotion changes over a period of time [13]. Higher frequency of positive valence shows of acceptance and acknowledgement as well as readiness to take remedial action.

Emotion Profiling The system attempts to make use of the candidate's emotional state to determine the correlation or commitment the candidate has to the entered response. Rather than attempting to determine the absolute emotional state of a person or sales candidate i.e., exactly where their emotional state lies in the affect space model, we have modelled a change in emotional state in either a positive direction or a negative direction. It is proposed that a positive change in emotional state of the candidate that coincides with the answering of a question indicates a candidate's higher commitment to the answer given. Conversely a negative emotional state change indicates a reduced commitment of the candidate to the answer given. The psychologists point out that facial expression alone may not be an accurate indicator of the emotional state of a person but changes in facial expression may indicate a change in emotional state [11, 15]. In our case, the transient or temporal changes in facial expressions and emotional states as the sales candidate answers different questions are modelled.

2.4   Correlations and Benchmarking

Figure 7 is a graph of the candidate's answers to questions in the area of success and failure, affirmative and negative for each of the behaviour categories. The graph also shows his emotional state as detected by this system on the same axis. The continuous line represents answers and the dashed line is emotional state. There is a divergence with the question relating to the dominant-warm, (DW) behaviour category. This correlation indicates a conflict with the answer given by the candidates in the indicated area/behaviour category. This should translate, in practice, to a follow up in an interview if this system were to be used in a hiring situation.

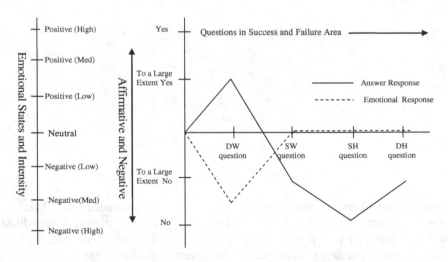

Fig. 7. Correlation of emotional profile and selling behaviour profile

For behavioural benchmarking, an existing sales person's behavioural category as predicted by the system is compared against sales manager's categorization of the salesperson based on their experience of working with them.

3   Implementation and Results

The SRBS system has been implemented for conducting the job interview with sales-persons. One of our social robots (i.e., Jack) was employed to conduct the interview with sales candidates (Fig. 8). During the interviews, the emotional responses of the candidates are tracked and profiled by the emotional component. Meanwhile, the cognitive responses are captured by the interview system are input into the cognitive profiling component.

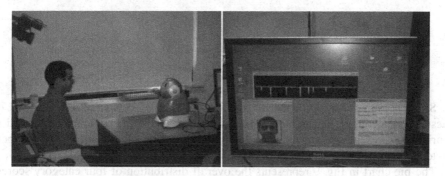

Fig. 8. The robot is conducting job interview with a candidate (left), and his emotional responses are profiling (right).

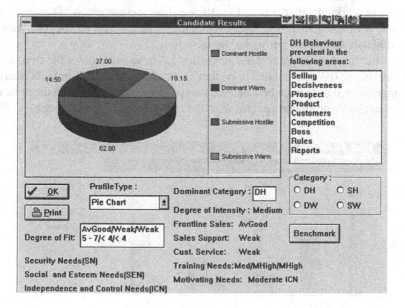

Fig. 9. Candidate result screen

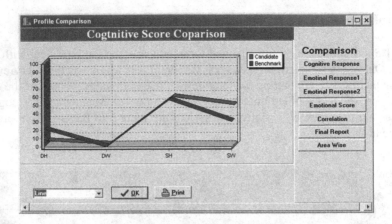

Fig. 10. Benchmarking based on cognitive responses

SRBS combines deep knowledge in the form of a selling behavioural model (and 76 questions related to it) and shallow knowledge in the form of behaviour categorization heuristics representing knowledge and experience of the sales managers (an Expert System). There are overall 400 rules in the system.

The pie chart in Fig. 9 represents the overall distribution of four category scores. That is, the upper right hand corner of the figure shows the area wise breakup of a candidate's selling behaviour as related to the Dominant-Hostile (DH) category.

The field tests compared an existing salesperson's behavioural category as predicted by the system against sales manager's categorization of the salesperson based on their experience of working with them. In Fig. 10, we show a comparison of the candidate's profile (one with low dominant hostile score) with the benchmark profile (one with high dominant hostile score) of a particular organization.

The hiring manager is particularly interested in the orientation of the two profiles. That is, are the two profiles parallel or do they cross each other. They are less interested in the magnitude of difference between the two profiles (which if required can be deciphered from the Y coordinate dimension of the comparison of profile graph).

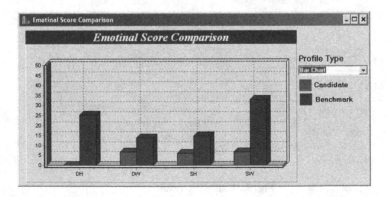

Fig. 11. Benchmarking based on emotional responses

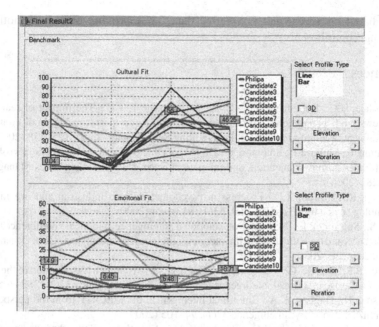

Fig. 12. Comparison of cognitive and emotion response between all candidates

The system the benchmarking of emotional and cognitive behaviour profiles of the candidate against the according selected benchmarking profiles (as shown in Figs. 10 and 11). The cognitive and emotional profiles of all candidates are also compared (Fig. 12).

These benchmarking data together with the reports can be used for conducting customized interviews and probing the candidate in areas or competencies where the emotional profile and behaviour profile based on cognitive inputs are not aligned with each other or are fairly divergent from each other.

4 Conclusion

This paper have presented human-robot interaction modelling for recruitment (named EIRS) involving verbal and non-verbal data modelling and benchmarking for improving information quality as well as quality of decision making. EIRS supports employers to analyse data about their employees through: (i) organization specific benchmarks by using emotional and cognitive behaviour profiles of job applicants with those of existing team of employees; (ii) creating an organisation wide repository of job related emotional and cognitive behaviour profiles based on verbal and non-verbal data for emotionally intelligent management and deployment of employees in various roles and teams; (iii) customisation of face to face interviews based on high information quality and profiles to save time and resources; and (iv) employing social robot for natural social interaction between employees and information technology compared to existing screen based technologies, and (v) developing a range of other root enabled personalised services based on verbal and non-verbal data for improving employee motivation, training and commitment.

References

1. Barksdale, H.C., Bellenger, D.N., Boles, J.S., Brashear, T.G.: The impact of realistic job previews and perceptions of training on sales force performance and continuance commitment: a longitudinal test. J. Pers. Selling Sales Manag. 23(2), 125–138 (2003)
2. Jaramillo, F., Mulki, J.P., Solomon, P.: The role of ethical climate on salesperson's role stress, job attitudes, turnover intention, and job performance. J. Pers. Selling Sales Manag. 26(3), 271–282 (2006)
3. Murphy, K.R., Shon, R.D.: Progress in psychometrics: can industrial and organizational psychology catch up? Pers. Psychol. 53(4), 913–924 (2000)
4. Fox, S., Spector, P.E.: Relations of emotional intelligence, practical intelligence, general intelligence, and trait affectivity with interview outcomes: it's not all just 'G'. J. Organ. Behav. 21(2), 203–220 (2000)
5. Palmer, B.R., Gignac, G., Manocha, R., Stough, C.: A psychometric evaluation of the Mayer–Salovey–Caruso emotional intelligence test version 2.0. Intelligence 33(3), 285–305 (2005)
6. Føllesdal, H., Hagtvet, K.A.: Emotional intelligence: the MSCEIT from the perspective of generalizability theory. Intelligence 37(1), 94–105 (2009)
7. Buzzotte, V.R., Lefton, R.E., Sherberg, M.: Effective selling through psychology: dimensional sales and sales management strategies. Psychological Associates, New York (1981)
8. Khosla, R., Goonesekera, T., Mitsukura, Y.: Knowledge engineering of intelligent sales-recruitment system using multi-layered agent methodology. In: Zhong, N., Raś, Z.W., Tsumoto, S., Suzuki, E. (eds.) ISMIS 2003. LNCS (LNAI), vol. 2871, pp. 646–651. Springer, Heidelberg (2003)
9. Szymanski, D.M.: Determinants of selling effectiveness: the importance of declarative knowledge to the personal selling concept. J. Mark. 52(1), 64–77 (1988)
10. Saaty, R.W.: The analytic hierarchy process—what it is and how it is used. Math. Modell. 9(3–5), 161–176 (1987)
11. Kohonen, T.: Learning vector quantization. In: Michael, A.A. (ed.): The Handbook of Brain Theory and Neural Networks, pp. 537–540. MIT Press, Cambridge (1998)
12. Lang, P.J.: The emotion probe. Studies of motivation and attention. Am. Psychol. 50(5), 372–385 (1995)
13. Diener, E., Larsen, R.J., Levine, S., Emmons, R.A.: Intensity and frequency: dimensions underlying positive and negative affect. J. Pers. Soc. Psychol. 48(5), 1253–1265 (1985)
14. Hess, U., Blairy, S., Kleck, R.: The intensity of emotional facial expressions and decoding accuracy. J. Nonverbal Behav. 21(4), 241–257 (1997)
15. Izard, C.E.: Facial expressions and the regulation of emotions. J. Pers. Soc. Psychol. 58(3), 487–498 (1990)

Operator Information Acquisition in Excavators – Insights from a Field Study Using Eye-Tracking

Markus Koppenborg[✉], Michael Huelke, Peter Nickel,
Andy Lungfiel, and Birgit Naber

Institute for Occupational Safety and Health of the German Social
Accident Insurance (IFA), Sankt Augustin, Germany
{markus.koppenborg,michael.huelke,peter.nickel,
andy.lungfiel}@dguv.de

Abstract. Poor operator direct sight can lead to collisions between excavators and humans, especially during reversing movements. Viewing aids, such as mirrors and camera monitor systems (CMS) are intended to compensate this. As empirical evidence on operators' visual information acquisition is scarce, this study investigated utilization of mirrors and CMS during regular work on construction sites by using eye-tracking and task observation. Results show that, during reversing movements, especially the left mirror and the CMS monitor were used. Implications of utilization and neglect are discussed with regard to safety and machinery design, such as configuration of viewing aids.

Keywords: Accident prevention · Earth-moving machinery · Viewing aids · Camera monitor systems · Closed-circuit television CCTV · Situation awareness

1 Introduction

Among earth-moving machinery, hydraulic excavators have accounted for the majority of registered accidents during the last years [1] and a considerable number of these were related to collisions between the machine and humans during reversing movements or rotating of the upper structure [2]. While tragic for all people involved, accidents cause delays in the work process, and can also imply investigations by law enforcement.

A plausible explanation for many collision accidents can be a lack of direct or indirect operator sight from the cabin to the surrounding area. The machine's counter-weight and the boom obstruct direct sight and thus make recognition of humans in the vicinity of the machine difficult for operators. Compensating this to some extent, operators can use different rearview mirrors, which are usually installed in varying number and configuration. Additionally, manufacturers and individual construction companies have begun to install camera monitor systems (CMS) displaying images of the rear area or the right side on a monitor in the cabin. Moreover, some parts around the machine, such as the left side, can be seen directly but require operators to turn their head. Thus, a number of different and partly redundant information sources exist, that can be useful to support operators' understanding of the surrounding for

© Springer International Publishing Switzerland 2016
F.F.-H. Nah and C.-H. Tan (Eds.): HCIBGO 2016, Part II, LNCS 9752, pp. 313–324, 2016.
DOI: 10.1007/978-3-319-39399-5_30

reversing and other movements. However, it remains largely unclear how excavator operators actually acquire visual information during regular work activity.

Therefore, the current study was initiated by the German Social Accident Insurance Institution for the Building Trade (BG BAU). As a first step, the aim was to find out whether and, if so, how operators use mirrors, CMS monitors and direct sight for reversing movements. In conjunction with subsequent studies, results can support future measures of prevention to further decrease accidents.

2   Related Work

2.1   Accident Prevention, Information Acquisition and Situation Awareness

Construction sites are highly dynamic workplaces where a variable number of workers and machines interact in a changing physical environment. Excavators add to the dynamic by their high movement variability, thus increasing the risk of collisions. Organizational measures of prevention have a long history on construction sites and relate to rules and procedures, such as traffic patterns, optimized material flow, restricted areas around the machine, stopping rules for the operator, or a banksman for maneuvering. Personal measures of prevention can include safety instructions, operator training, or protective equipment, such as warning wests or transponder systems (for German regulations see [3]). Although these are important additional measures to prevent collisions, priority has to be given to technical measures to enhance visibility, such as enlarged cabin windows, shorter machine tails, and additional viewing aids (i.e. mirrors or CMS).

With regard to the latter, excavators are usually equipped with a rearview mirror left of the cabin and one or more rearview mirrors right of the cabin, which display the lateral and rear areas of the machine. In some cases, right mirrors are arranged in such a way that, independent of the boom's position, at least one mirror can be seen from the cabin. Parabolic mirrors on the counterweight are used on older excavators to display the area immediately behind the machine, but require operators to turn their body and head. This can be avoided by using CMS that display the area directly behind the machine on a monitor in the cabin.

Working with excavators can place high demands on the operator in terms of visual information acquisition and processing. While performing their primary excavating tasks, operators need to be informed about the conditions of the machine (i.e. position, engine status) and that of loaded materials (i.e. stability), while being aware of the surrounding environment (i.e. humans or obstacles). Situation Awareness relates to this latter aspect, and states that the system shall inform the operator about the elements in the environment, their meaning and their status in the near future [4]. More specifically, the design of the system has to be in a way that facilitates the flow of information from the different technical elements to the operator and support his understanding of the situation [5, 6]. From this perspective, in order to facilitate operator awareness, excavator viewing aids need to be configured and designed in a way that optimally supports operator information acquisition. This applies to support for the primary excavating tasks (e.g. digging) and also for monitoring the surroundings to avoid collisions (e.g. during reversing or rotating movements).

2.2 Standards on Visibility and Viewing Aids in Excavators

According to Machinery Directive 2006/42/EC [7] with its binding character for machine manufacturers and distributers in the European Union, visibility conditions must be such that the operator can move the machine in complete safety for himself and exposed persons. Inadequate direct view must be compensated by appropriate devices providing the operator with indirect view on the surroundings of the machine. As explained by European Commission [8] this can be established by means of mirrors or CMS (i.e. closed circuit television, CCTV).

Further specification comes from EN ISO 474-1 [9] on general safety requirements for earth-moving machinery, which refers to ISO 5006 [10] on visibility performance criteria. This standard allows a total number of three to nine maskings (i.e. "blind spots") of varying width at a distance of 12 m around the machine. At a distance of 1 m, no masking of more than 300 mm in width is allowed. Where these requirements cannot be met, additional mirrors or CMS can be employed for which requirements are listed in ISO 14401 [11] and ISO 16001 [12], respectively. However, a recent decision by the European Commission [13] concluded that these performance criteria fail to meet the essential health and safety requirements provided by Machinery Directive 2006/42/EC. Consequently, a revised version of ISO 5006 is expected for publication in the near future.

2.3 Empirical Evidence on Information Acquisition in Mobile Machinery

Much work has been done with regard to ergonomics, occupational safety and health when working with construction machinery (e.g. cabin proportions, zones of comfort and reach, vibration and noise), of which body and head posture can be related to visual information acquisition. When operators turn their head or body to attain a more favorable viewing angle, awkward postures can result, a relationship that has been described with regard to mining vehicles [14], backhoes and excavators [15] and construction equipment in general [16]. However, awkward body posture can also result from factors other than poor visibility, such as position of seats or controls.

Methods for objectively assessing visibility from the cabin and obstructions by parts of the machine (i.e. "blind spots") have been applied to different types of mobile equipment, such as in mining machinery [17], and loaders and excavators [18]. To investigate how operators acquire visual information during regular and dynamic work activities in a real environment, Eger et al. [14], used eye-tracking in load-haul-dump vehicles in underground mining. The authors could show that, regardless of the direction of travelling (e.g. driving backward), glances were concentrated on a few relatively unobstructed areas around the machine, while other (important) areas were neglected. Similarly, Hella et al. [19] observed that operators of graders and other mobile machinery mostly attended their respective tool or equipment, even when appearance of pedestrians around the machine was quite frequent.

Fukaya et al. [20] investigated eye-movements of subjects in a simulated excavator task in virtual reality, but did not include viewing aids in their analysis. These authors found that glance duration on parts of the machine accounted for over 70 % of total dwell time, while glance duration on the surroundings was only 20 %. Similar results were obtained in a second study in which four experienced operators completed work cycles of loading a truck both in simulated virtual reality and with a real excavator in an outdoor environment [21]. Here, the authors reported more horizontal eye-movements during swinging as compared to other movements, such as loading the bucket, which could be related to visual information acquisition for prevention of collisions. Details on viewing aids (i.e. mirrors and CMS) and reversing movements were not reported.

However, to assess, develop and select suitable viewing aids and other technologies (e.g. person identification systems) that optimally support operators for critical maneuvers and thus prevent accidents, evidence on operator visual information acquisition is needed. Therefore, this study investigated operators' utilization of viewing aids and direct sight during excavator operation. This was accomplished by means of eye-tracking and observation during regular work on real construction sites. As a first step, utilization of mirrors, CMS monitors and direct sight was analyzed during reversing movements of the excavator.

3   Methods

3.1   Sample

Nine sites of five local civil engineering construction companies were visited, each with a different operator and excavator (see Table 1). Measurement duration was between 3 and 5.5 h (M = 4.2, SD = 0.8; Table 1), excluding regular breaks and all pauses related to setting up and calibrating of devices. Sites differed regarding their surrounding conditions, such as the amount of co-workers, machines, obstacles and passersby on or around the workspace.

The sample comprised crawler and wheeled excavators of different manufacturers with a length of 8.2 to 10.7 m and a mass of 17 to 32 tons. Only regular attachments (i.e. hoes and grabs) were used for typical work activities, such as trenching, grading, sloping, pipe-laying, object transport, and loading and spreading of material (including loading of trucks).

In all machines direct sight from the cabin to the rear area was obstructed by the counter weight and direct sight to the right side was partly obstructed by the boom. All machines were equipped with a CMS depicting the area directly behind the machine on a monitor in the cabin, one left rearview mirror and one, two or three right rearview mirrors. Four excavators had an additional camera displaying the right side of the machine on the monitor (with split screen). No excavator had mirrors installed on the counter weight of the machine. Configuration and adjustment of all mirrors and CMS were in accordance with regulations and corresponded to what operators were used to working with for at least one year.

Operator mean age was 41.5 years (SD = 13.1), reported professional experience with excavator operation was 17.3 years (SD = 8.8). Operators (all males) were road

Table 1. Characteristics of machinery, operators and work activities (abbreviations: LS = loading and spreading of material, G = grading, T = trenching, S = sloping, OT = object transport, PL = pipe-laying)

Site no.	Excavator type and attachment	Operator age and years of experience	Measurement duration (h)	Excavator operations
1	Crawler; trench cleaning bucket, hoe	47 (6)	4	LS, G
2	Wheeled; trench cleaning bucket, hoe	38 (3)	5	LS, T, OT
3	Wheeled; hoe, grab	56 (25)	5	LS, T, S, OT
4	Crawler; hoe	38 (12)	3.75	LS, G
5	Crawler; hoe	51 (27)	3	LS, T, PL
6	Wheeled; hoe, grab	58 (25)	5	LS, T, OT
7	Crawler; hoe	26 (11)	3	LS, G, T, OT
8	Wheeled; trench cleaning bucket, hoe	36 (22)	4.75	LS, G, S
9	Crawler; trench cleaning bucket	53 (25)	4	LS, G

builder, car or construction machinery mechanic, engine fitter or construction builder by formal training.

3.2 Apparatus

Eye-movements were measured using a head-mounted eye-tracker "Dikablis" (Ergoneers GmbH, Manching, Germany) with a sampling rate of 25 Hz, scene camera field of view of 120°, four point calibration, contrast pupil detection and D-Lab 3 (Ergoneers GmbH, Manching, Germany) as recording software. A laptop computer was stored behind the operator and connected to the eye-tracker in such a way that operator head and body movements were not limited. Exiting the cabin was possible at all times by disconnecting the eye-tracker, and data recording resumed after reconnection.

Simultaneous to eye-movement recording, excavator operations were observed and category coded using a tablet computer and a software tool with buttons for each category [22]. Additionally, operations were video recorded using a GoPro Hero 3® for subsequent correction of observational data, if necessary. Information on site and machine characteristics, as well as demographic data and operators' experience with viewing aids were gathered by guided interviews.

3.3 Procedure

All sites were visited on two consecutive days. During the first visit a trial measurement was conducted to let operators get accustomed to the measurement devices. Importantly, the purpose of the study was described in broader terms (i.e. to improve cabin design) so as to minimize behavioral adaption. Written informed consent was obtained from operators and all other involved personnel. Main measurements on the second visit started in the morning and lasted until the early afternoon or until the end of the shift. Eye-tracking and activity observation were done continuously, while battery change and recalibration of the eye-tracker were done at convenient moments so as to interrupt work processes as little as possible. After measurements operators were interviewed and were thanked with a small present.

3.4 Data Preprocessing and Analysis

When necessary, observational data were corrected manually and frame by frame by using video recordings of work activities and Noldus Observer® XT 12 (Wageningen, The Netherlands) coding software. As an excavator's upper structure can turn over 360°, direction of travelling can be ambiguous. Therefore, movements were regarded reversing movements when direction of the cabin was opposite to direction of travelling with a tolerance of ±45°. This criterion was applied for a period of 15 s before, until the end of the movement. For subsequent eye-movement preprocessing and analysis, reversing intervals were defined, each including one reversing movement of the excavator plus a period of 4 s previous to the start of the movement.

Eye-movement data was processed using D-Lab 3. During intervals, incorrect pupil position was corrected frame by frame and manually. Further, glances on four different areas of interest (AOI) were coded frame by frame and manually, and according to [23]. The first three AOI related to viewing aids for indirect sight, namely the CMS monitor, the left mirror, and the right mirror(s). The fourth AOI was defined as the area next to and behind the machine, which could be seen directly when operators rotated their head ("look over the shoulder", defined as all glances on surroundings for which combined operator head and eye movements exceeded a 90° turn to either side).

As a measure of utilization of AOIs, percentage of intervals with one, two, more than two, or no glances at all was calculated. As a second measure, percentage of intervals with glances on each AOI was calculated, both over the aggregated sample and individually for each construction site.

4 Results

4.1 Description of Reversing Movements and Glances on AOI

During measurements, a total number of 415 reversing movements were observed (M = 46.1, SD = 25.5). Movement duration was 5.4 s on average (SD = 6.2), with a skew to the right (i.e. there were more movements with shorter duration) and median of 4.0 s. Taken together, all movements summed up to 2236.3 s (37 min and 16.3 s).

During reversing intervals, a total of 1006 glances were counted on all four AOI (i.e. CMS monitor, left mirror, right mirror(s) and rear area by head rotation).

4.2   Percentage of Intervals with Glances on AOI

As a measure of utilization of different viewing aids, amount of attended AOI per reversing interval was counted. Figure 1 shows that in 12.3 % of all cases, there was no glance on any AOI, while in 37.1 %, glances on one AOI were found. In the majority of intervals (42.2 %), glances were found on two different AOI and in 8.4 % of all intervals glances on more than two different AOI were found.

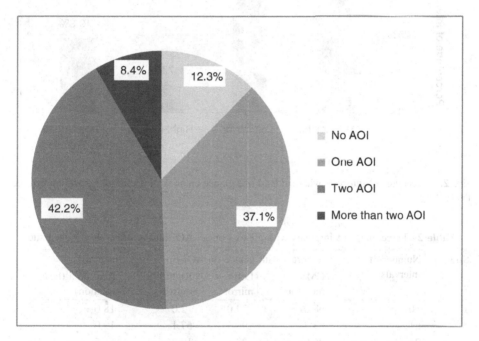

Fig. 1. Amount of AOI that were attended during intervals in percent

In a next step, percentages of reversing intervals with glances on each AOI were calculated. On an aggregate level, glances on the CMS monitor during intervals occurred in 56.9 % of all intervals. Similarly, glances on the left mirror occurred in 64.1 % of all intervals, while glances on the right mirror(s) were found in 7.2 %. Glances on the left and right rear areas by rotating the head (i.e. "look over the shoulder") were found in 19.3 % of all intervals (Fig. 2).

Similarly, glances were calculated for individual construction sites. Results revealed variations of the aggregated values as shown in Table 2. For instance, utilization of the CMS monitor varied between 10.4 % and 98.2 % (site No. 9 vs. No. 6). Similarly, utilization of the left mirror varied between 23.1 % and 100 % (site No. 3 vs. No. 6).

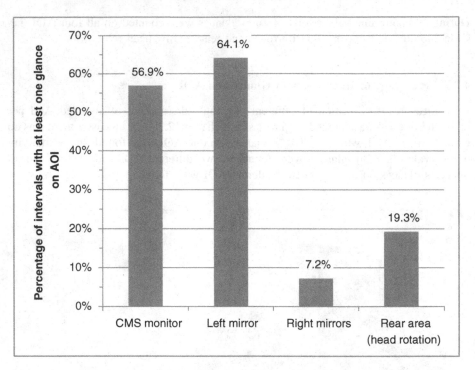

Fig. 2. Percentage of intervals where at least one glance on an AOI occurred. For variations, see Table 2.

Table 2. Percentages of intervals with glances on an AOI during intervals for each site

Site no.	Number of intervals	Intervals with glance on AOI (in % of all intervals)			
		CMS monitor	Left mirror	Right mirror(s)	Rear area (head rotation)
1	50	68.0	74.0	2.0	18.0
2	21	85.7	90.5	57.1	19.0
3	26	26.9	23.1	19.2	61.5
4	96	56.2	55.2	1.0	21.3
5	48	66.7	68.8	0	2.1
6	55	98.2	74.6	0	5.5
7	24	50.0	45.8	12.5	20.8
8	18	94.4	100	22.2	11.1
9	77	10.4	62.3	5.2	26.0

Glances on the right mirror varied between 0 % and 57.1 % (site No. 2) and those on the rear area varied between 2.1 % and 61.5 % (site No. 5 vs. No. 3).

5 Discussion

5.1 Summary and Implications

Many accidents with excavators are related to insufficient operator sight from the cabin to the areas around the machine, so that humans or objects in the vicinity cannot be seen properly. Mirrors and camera monitor systems are intended to support operators to gain an understanding of the surroundings. However, little is known about how operators acquire visual information during regular work, which is an important aspect for assessing, developing and selecting viewing aids and other technologies (e.g. person identification systems). Therefore, operator utilization of information sources for reversing movements was investigated under real conditions by means of eye-tracking in combination with observation of work activities. Results showed that operators engage in active search for information relevant for reversing. However, the finding that multiple sources were used for about half of all reversing movements suggest that utilization of only one information source may not always be sufficient. Eye-movement analysis on an aggregate level further showed that all viewing aids, especially the left mirror and the CMS monitor, were used for reversing. Analysis of individual construction sites revealed variations of these aggregate values. Results can be used to further develop methods for accident prevention on construction sites.

For reversing movements, especially the left mirror and the CMS monitor were used. This emphasizes their relevance for operators gaining an understanding of the rear areas and thus for prevention of accidents when reversing. Both viewing aids may also be important for achieving operator Situation Awareness as they can be helpful to identify elements in the environment (i.e. humans or objects), understand their meaning and predict their status in the near future. However, there are other modalities (i.e. auditory or haptic information) and other sources of information (i.e. short term and long term memory) that contribute to Situation Awareness. To fully explain how Situation Awareness is achieved for the operation of excavators a more in-depth investigation would be necessary.

Results showed that operators used the CMS monitor and mirrors and also turned their head to look directly at lateral and rear areas. This may point towards an information need that could not be met by using viewing aids only or direct view only. It is possible that information sources served different functions during reversing movements. As the CMS monitor displays the area directly behind the machine, it may have been attended primarily for checking for obstacles prior to the movement. Other information sources, like the mirrors or direct view may provide better information on relative distances between the machine and objects and may therefore be used for maneuvering during longer movements.

Although information sources (i.e. viewing aids and rear area) were used for many reversing movements, it should be interesting to analyze cases where these sources were neglected. Further analyses may reveal common characteristics of these cases, such as effects of personal preferences, habituation or training. Further, it can be assumed that the type of work activity (i.e. object transport vs. grading) influences information acquisition behavior. Similarly, situational factors, such as confined spaces or the amount of people and machines on site contribute to operators' utilization of viewing aids. However, situational factors could not be controlled in this study and thus varied across our measurements.

As another important factor, the design of viewing aids should be mentioned because this, too, influences how operators use mirrors and the CMS monitor. For example, viewing aids' display quality, position, size and field of vision can be regarded important as these can determine their relative distance to the operator and the size of displayed elements (e.g. a human). Improvements regarding these aspects may not only lead to increased utilization, but could also enhance perception and understanding of attended information and, finally, drive behavioral adaption that increases safety when moving with excavators.

It is important to note that eye-movement analysis can reveal central, but not peripheral visual information acquisition. However, it cannot be ruled out that peripheral vision plays a role in information acquisition when operating excavators. Furthermore, reversing intervals included a reversing movement and a period of four seconds before the start of the movement. It should be interesting to investigate periods preceding these intervals as they may contain information acquisition behavior that has yet to be analyzed.

It should further be noted that observation or the eye-tracker may have caused reactivity in operators. To avoid this, trial measurements were completed by all participants so as to get accustomed to the measurement devices. Further, the purpose of the study was not disclosed until the end of the measurements. Also, operators were assured that no evaluation of their work would take place and that all data would be analyzed anonymously. Finally, measurements lasted quite long, so that after some initial behavioral adaption operators may have returned to their every-day working style.

5.2   Conclusion

Eye-tracking and task observation were used in a field study to investigate whether, and how excavator operators used viewing aids for reversing. Operators actively engaged in search for relevant information for reversing movements. In many cases, one or more viewing aids were used, and especially the left mirror and the CMS monitor which emphasizes their importance for the safe operation of excavators. Cases of neglect of viewing aids may be explained by differing task demands or by situational factors, and can be useful for evaluation, selection and development of viewing suitable viewing aids. Improvements could eventually lead to higher levels of utilization, understanding and safer behavior, and may thus help reduce accidents with excavators.

Acknowledgements. We would like to thank Mara Kaufeld for her support and all machine operators for their kind participation. Further, we thank Reinhold Hartdegen, Kurt Hey and Horst Leisering for their cooperation.

References

1. Deutsche Gesetzliche Unfallversicherung DGUV: Accident Statistics with Earth-Moving Machinery, Reporting Years 2009–2013 (2015, Unpublished data)
2. Berufsgenossenschaft der Bauwirtschaft BG BAU: Accident Statistics with Excavators, Reporting Years 2013 – 2014 (2015, Unpublished data)
3. Deutsche Gesetzliche Unfallversicherung DGUV: DGUV Regel 100-500, Betreiben von Arbeitsmitteln. DGUV, Sankt Augustin (2008). [DGUV Rule 100-500, Operation of Work Equipment]
4. Endsley, M.: Toward a theory of situation awareness in dynamic systems. Hum. Factors **37** (1), 32–64 (1995)
5. Salmon, P.M., Walker, G.H., Stanton, N.A.: Broken components versus broken systems: why it is systems not people that lose situation awareness. Cogn. Technol. Work **17**, 179–183 (2015)
6. Stanton, N.A., Stewart, R., Harris, D., Houghton, R.J., Baber, C., McMaster, R., Salmon, P., Hoyle, G., Walker, G., Young, M.S., Linsell, M., Dymott, R., Green, D.: Distributed situation awareness in dynamic systems: theoretical development and application of an ergonomics methodology. Ergonomics **49**, 1288–1311 (2006)
7. European Commission: Directive 2006/42/EC (Machinery Directive). O. J. EU L, 157/24 (2006)
8. European Commission: Guide to Application of the Machinery Directive 2006/42/EC. European Commission, Brussels (2010)
9. EN ISO 474-1: Earth-Moving Machinery – Safety – Part 1: General Requirements. CEN, Brussels (2009)
10. ISO 5006: Earth-Moving Machinery – Operator's Field of View – Test Method and Performance Criteria. ISO, Geneva (2006)
11. ISO 14401: Earth-Moving Machinery – Field of Vision of Surveillance and Rear-View Mirrors – Part 2: Performance Criteria. ISO, Geneva (2009)
12. ISO 16001: Earth-Moving Machinery – Hazard Detection Systems and Visual Aids – Performance Requirements and Tests. ISO, Geneva (2008)
13. European Commission: Implementing Decision No. 2015/27 (Earth-Moving Machinery). O. J. EU L, 4/24 (2015)
14. Eger, T.R., Godwin, A.G., Henry, D.J., Grenier, S.G., Callaghan, J., Demerchant, A.: Why vehicle design matters: exploring the link between line-of-sight, driving posture and risk factors for injury. Work **35**(1), 27–37 (2010)
15. Kittusamy, N.K., Buchholz, B.: An ergonomic evaluation of excavating operations: a pilot study. Appl. Occup. Environ. Hyg. **16**(7), 723–726 (2001)
16. Kittusamy, N.K., Buchholz, B.: Whole-body vibration and postural stress among operators of construction equipment: a literature review. J. Saf. Res. **35**, 255–261 (2004)
17. Eger, T.R., Salmoni, A., Whissell, R.: Factors influencing load-haul-dump operator line of sight in underground mining. Appl. Ergon. **35**, 93–103 (2004)
18. Hoske, P., Gubsch, I., Kunze, G., Bürkle, K., Kamusella, C., Schmauder, M.: Prognose und Bewertung der Sicht für mobile Arbeitsmaschinen. Teil 4: Konzepte zur Visualisierung und Bewertung virtueller Sichtprozesse. Wissensportal baumaschine.de **2**, 1–5 (2010). [Prediction and Assessment of Visibility in Mobile Machinery]
19. Hella, F., Zoré, F., Payet, R.: Les Bonnes Pratiques pour Prévenir les Collisions Engins-Piétons. Ce Que Révèlent les Observations de Terrain. Hygiène et Sécurité du Travail **236**, 26–28 (2014). [Good Practices for Prevention of Collisions between Machines and Pedestrians. Revelations from Field Observations]

20. Fukaya, K., Nakamura, T., Umezaki, S, Lu, J., Egawa, Y.: Development of excavator simulator and characteristics of operator. In: Proceedings of 41st Society of Instrument and Control Engineers Annual Conference, vol. 5, pp. 2815–2819. IEEE Press, New York (2002)
21. Nakamura, T., Fukuya, K., Mannen, S.: Eye movement and useful field of view in the operations of an excavator. In: Gale, A.G. (ed.) Vision in Vehicles, vol. 10, pp. 159–167. Loughborough University, Leicestershire (2012)
22. Koppenborg, M., Lungfiel, A., Naber, B., Nickel, P., Huelke, M.: Ein flexibles Gerät zur Tätigkeitskodierung per Beobachtung – Anforderungen und Ergebnisse einer Erprobung. In: 61. Kongress der Gesellschaft für Arbeitswissenschaft, B.1.12, pp. 1–6. GfA-Press, Dortmund (2015). [A Flexible Device for Coding Work Activities by Observation - Requirements and Preliminary Results]
23. ISO 15007: Road Vehicles – Measurement of Driver Visual Behaviour with Respect to Transport Information and Control Systems – Part 1: Definitions and Parameters. ISO, Geneva (2002)

Extending the Effective Range of Prevention Through Design by OSH Applications in Virtual Reality

Peter Nickel[✉]

Institute for Occupational Safety and Health of the German Social Accident Insurance (IFA),
Sankt Augustin, Germany
peter.nickel@dguv.de

Abstract. Prevention through design (PtD) is presented as a concept for designing out risks early in design and across the life cycle. PtD is an internationally recognized initiative and it is a strategy linked to safety disciplines, to the hierarchy of controls, and to new technologies. With two research projects it has been demonstrated how to use VR as new technology for PtD modeling and simulation and as a means for improving OSH early in work systems design. Investigations of virtual reconstructions of virtual accidents supported course of events and root-cause analyses. Dynamic visualizations triggered discussions about safety and usability issues in design. Risk assessments of virtual river locks with standardized components facilitate measures for risk reduction to be fed back to machinery planning. Benefits and limitations of VR applications on PtD were discussed and suggestions for fostering endeavor of PtD were given.

Keywords: Prevention through design · Virtual reality · Risk assessment · Accident analysis · Usability · Occupational safety and health

1 Introduction

Prevention through Design (PtD) is a concept of relevance for all industry and services sectors by applying its principles in the design and redesign of work premises, tools, equipment, machinery, substances and work processes. Definitions about PtD may vary given the different views of what is covered by PtD and when and how to apply the concept. A common denominator for PtD, however, is that it is heading to prevention of occupational injuries, illnesses, and fatalities by including prevention considerations in all designs that impact workers [1]. PtD is interwoven with safety engineering, ergonomics and human factors applications aiming at adapting work systems design to human requirements [2, 3]. PtD effectively contributes to the hierarchy of controls for measures of hazard and risk reduction and for improving OSH at work [4–7]. PtD is an OSH strategy for designing out risks at source and by considering safety and health implications throughout the work systems life cycle [1]. PtD is also relevant for new technologies, processes and materials during their conception and before their introduction into the market [8].

© Springer International Publishing Switzerland 2016
F.F.-H. Nah and C.-H. Tan (Eds.): HCIBGO 2016, Part II, LNCS 9752, pp. 325–336, 2016.
DOI: 10.1007/978-3-319-39399-5_31

1.1 PtD and Ergonomics

Safety engineering as a rule factors human safety into the design process. Traditional links between concepts of PtD, human factors and ergonomics are related to an ergonomics approach for work system design with human-system interaction at the core and systems design aiming at optimizing human well-being, health and safety, and overall system performance. Similar to PtD, design principles in ergonomics call for adaptation of technical system components to foster safe and healthy human behavior at work [e.g. 2].

Early developments in industrial psychology [9] influenced perspectives on systems design and interdependencies of entities in psychotechnics were discussed [10]: While subject psychotechnics rather referred to an adaptation of operator's psychological traits and competencies to requirements and conditions of job and environment, object psychotechnics in contrast covered designs and procedures for optimal adaptation of technical and production factors to the operator's psychological nature. Though, nowadays interactions between technical, organizational and personal subsystems are taken into account in work systems design [3, 7], this early distinction already points out at least two perspectives for interventions, with the latter being preferred in PtD and assumed to be effective and sustainable.

1.2 PtD and the Hierarchy of Controls

Even though legal requirements for OSH and risk assessments may differ across countries, the hierarchy of controls remains fairly similar and provides some guidance for selecting effective measures for risk reduction and prevention in systems design. In Germany, a hierarchy of controls traditionally follows levels like (a) eliminating hazard (e.g. substitution), (b) technical measures (e.g. safeguard), (c) organizational measures (e.g. job rotation), (d) personal measures (e.g. personal protective equipment, PPE), and (e) instructional measures (e.g. warning sign). Albeit shorter, this hierarchy is similar to the ten level 'general principles of prevention' as listed in the EU OSH Framework Directive [4]. The hierarchy in OHSAS 18001 [6] also has five levels, however, with PPE listed lowest. Different perspectives on the hierarchy may also widen opportunities for interventions [7].

OSH legislation e.g. in Europe or Australia with directives and guidelines are regarded especially useful in facilitating PtD. Manufacturers are required to design safe machinery that meet a set of minimal health and safety requirement and employers are held responsible for providing safe work equipment to the employees [11]. As a consequence, technology for designing safe equipment is available across countries; however, business decision makers and purchasers may not always value or request for it or manufacturers may not create demand for it by promoting it on the market [12]. Despite differences in OSH legislation across countries, PtD principles are equally important everywhere. The concept of PtD is a guiding principle for priority consideration of high level measures to combat hazards and risks at the work across the life cycle from early on.

1.3 PtD as a Strategy and an OSH Initiative

Notwithstanding its long tradition, PtD has been re-launched by OSH organizations for promoting initiatives to achieve a cultural change so that preventing work related accidents and health problems and enhancing OSH is the norm. PtD has been risen to among the most important topics for improving OSH today [1, 13]. PtD is not only a concept; it is an OSH strategy with ambitious goals for designing safe and healthy work from early on that requires commitment and active involvement of management and workers.

PtD is an US national initiative, internationally recognized not only by OSH organizations. A strong impact on the initiative resulted from activities of the Institute for 'Safety through Design' calling for an integration of hazard analysis and risk assessment methods early in design, redesign, and engineering stages, and taking all actions necessary so that risks of injury or damage are at an acceptable level [14]. Reports on successful concept application, activities, case studies, success stories, challenges and overall progress could be gathered and documented at the Safety by Design workshop held by the New Technology and Work Network [15], at the NIOSH PtD workshop [e.g. 16], and at the NIOSH conference on 'PtD: A new way of doing business' [e.g. 17], to name but a few. Activities resulted in the development of a PtD plan for the US national initiative and in a progress report on the initiatives' state including mission statement, aggregated outcomes in research, education, practice, and policy as well as future objectives for 2015-2020 [1].

1.4 PtD and New Technologies

The prospect of increasing impact of information technologies and others on work organization, tasks, and processes calls for identification and assessing health and safety risks associated with new technologies and for integration of OSH principles in their development [8]. The potential of new technologies to change the nature of work and to affect the work environment may not only bring great opportunities but also health and safety risks. It is therefore helpful to draw on a PtD strategy in that it allows transfer of existing knowledge to new applications and work environments [e.g. 18], consideration of OSH and usability implications early in the design stage while anticipating the life cycle [e.g. 17], and use of technologies themselves for improving OSH in future work place design (e.g. simulating future work processes) [13].

Inclusion of all stakeholders (e.g. engineering, procurement, OSH officials) in the design loop is seen an important factor for conducting successful business [19]. Digital planning information in combination with simulation and visualization techniques assist in creation and progress of new designs, in analysis and assessment of design options and related hazards while being also able to outline future work situations and achievements [20, 21]. Across industry and services sectors activities should result in improved understanding and knowledge of new technologies as well as development of safe and usable design solutions while at the same time demonstrating good practice in PtD.

1.5 Virtual Reality in and for OSH

Simulation techniques such as virtual reality (VR) have been mentioned among new technologies to be addressed as those shaping the future nature of work. However, they also provide a means to analyze, assess and eliminate hazards and risks in applications of new technologies and to develop and apply PtD for new technologies early in design with a focus on usability across the life cycle [13].

Over the past decades, VR has matured into a simulation tool for humans to interact with dynamic, three-dimensional virtual environments and into a methodology for different areas of applications. In industry and services VR allows applied research in human-machine system analysis, design, and evaluation for training, for demonstration, and for visualisation purposes [22]. VR has the potential to better bridge gaps between experimental research and traditional investigations at the shop-floor level while using specific advantages of simulation research [23] and being careful with human, material and financial resources. In addition, VR enables creating scenarios not desirable or too dangerous to face in reality, or providing past, present and future systems in the context of use [24–28]; by that extending the effective range of interventions for PtD. This opened up new perspectives for applications on OSH principles and PtD by fostering prospective rather than corrective accident investigations and hazard and risk assessments early in design.

2 Prevention Through Design by Analysis of Accidents and Near-Misses from a VR Study on Usability of Safety Devices

Occupational accidents including near misses or incidents in industry and services are preventable by conducting effective investigations that identify causal factors and develop actions and that avoid similar events in the future. Conducting accident investigations is challenging and unfortunately, accidents or near misses are not always investigated [29]. This often is due to lack of information about potential causal relationships and knowledge gaps about how, when and what has happened under specific but unknown circumstances. Accident investigations rely on information, methods and procedures, but also draw on experience with similar situations as well as mental simulation and imagination of inspectors conducting assessments.

VR applications have already demonstrated its potential to support accident investigations. By visualizing and reconstructing post-accident scenarios VR provides vivid experiences for inspectors and may trigger reasoning about potential causes [e.g. 30]. Accidental situations were implemented in virtual training scenarios intended to support operators to cope with situations and to learn strategies preventing accidents in the future [e.g. 31]. Though applications of VR for systems design are mainly used to investigate design solutions [24, 32–34], they also provide a basis for generating training scenarios [35], and they may even result in virtually hazardous situations with accidents or near misses eventually going to happen.

In a VR study on the usability of an additional safety measure for mobile elevating work platforms (MEWP) 22 inexperienced and experienced drivers were asked to perform inspection tasks for about 2 h each in an industrial hall [34]. Work scenarios have been developed to allow for close to reality inspections while driving with a MEWP in an industrial hall. They have also be designed to deliberately provoke accidents and near misses by constricting access to work places, reducing illumination of working areas and adding obstacles in the environment. As a consequence, virtual accidents occurred as rare events and accidentally as in reality, i.e. collisions of the MEWP or its driver with objects in the working environment. Some collisions were similar to those already mentioned in accident reports from Germany [27, 36].

Whether and how VR may also be of benefit for investigations of those virtual accidents has been addressed in a subsequent study. In contrast to traditional accident investigations, it was possible to reconstruct and replay work sequences based on data logged during the VR study for events (i.e. collisions) and movements (i.e. controls, MEWP, driver) in the industrial setting. Dynamic visualizations in 3D as reconstructions of MEWP movements in the industrial hall provided insights about time and location of collisions including information about the course of events, directions and speed of the MEWP as well as driver activities. MEWP control movements could be displayed in parallel. As is possible in VR simulations, sequences with accidents could be observed from different points of view such as the MEWP driver or an observer at ground position.

Accident prone locations in the industrial hall have been identified and served further illustration. Among them was an inspection place in mid industrial hall. Once the driver arrived, his/her view was limited to the MEWP platform. Leaving this place with the platform being close to one of the walls (see Fig. 1) occasionally resulted in collisions of the telescopic MEWP or the driver. From an observers point of view it is recognizable that lowering the MEWP platform does not follow a vertical line but circular arc (i.e. downwards and backwards). In this situation for the drivers it is most probably not possible to acquire all information required about relative position, control options and trajectory of the MEWP beam. Imperfect or incomplete information acquisition resulted in erroneous decision making and action implementation. According to dynamic reconstructions of virtual accidents and near misses by VR simulations it has been reasonable to assume impairments of human information processing (e.g. limited perception, complex action implementation for simple trajectory of MEWP beam, task-MEWP misfit) [37, 38]. Additional circumstances such as impaired vision or obstacles may have also affected MEWP movements in this exemplary accident situation.

Simulating the course of events of accidents provided information about when (e.g. first half of a session performing inspection tasks), where (e.g. low inspection place at mid industrial hall), what happened (e.g. MEWP departure from constricted opening of inspection place) with what kind of consequences (e.g. back of the head collides with wall). Information available is advantageous to explore measures for reducing the risk of future accidents by referring to PtD principles. Overall results suggested that VR simulations in close to reality work scenarios can support accident investigations by improving insights into relevant processes and by providing potential explanations.

Fig. 1. Accident prone situation in dynamic reconstruction of VR work environment

3   Prevention Through Design by OSH Improvements in Standardisation of Machinery Components

Use and application of standardized components is very common in machinery development and design. Standardized components and elements for prospective tools and machines may for example refer to screws as described in international or national standards (e.g. ISO), bearings of manufacturers having a long reputation for their reliability and quality in engineering industries (e.g. manufacturer standard), and more complex units when giving electric drives priority over hydraulic drives due to application requirements (e.g. company standard). Benefits of standardized components are seen for all types of machinery including special purpose machinery manufacturing. It is no longer necessary to invent new designs and interfaces for these components, to manufacture them separately, to specifically propose procedures for testing functionality and safety requirements, and to develop specific procedures for maintenance. Finding a suitable balance between standardization and individualization, however, often remains a challenge in machinery design.

Recently, the German Federal Ministry of Transport and Digital Infrastructure has given high priority to standardization of machinery components in the context of the some 7,500 km German network of inland waterways. Among many facilities at waterways, river locks are special purpose machinery with several components from mechanical engineering (e.g. gates, inspection safety closings) and construction engineering (e.g. lock chamber, cavern for gate drive). Standardization of river lock components is seen important since it has the potential to simplify the planning process, to speed up the construction process, to draw upon spare capacity for increasing freight transport volumes, to decrease maintenance efforts, to improve OSH, and to reduce costs across the life cycle [39]. An expert group on standardization of river locks has therefore been appointed by the Federal Ministry to identify components yielding good practice in river lock design, operations and maintenance. Most relevant components have already been agreed upon [40] and several are already going to be used for future river lock construction [e.g. 41].

With the PtD perspective, improvements in OSH are seen most effective early in design, because once machinery is built, it should be in service for long and redesign due to safety issues would be resource-demanding, if not impossible, when river lock construction has already been completed. This is where a current research project takes up, aiming at improving OSH for standardized components preferably in the planning stage for a new river lock. Improving OSH has a life cycle perspective in that hazards and risks of standardized components not yet taken into account by the expert group should be assessed. Standardized components should be used for all future river locks in the German network of waterways. The endeavor is challenging because hazard and risk assessment of machinery components itself does not result in machinery safety; i.e. the whole is greater than the sum of the parts. In addition, the future river lock in its future context of use (i.e. life cycle) should be included in OSH assessments; even though it is not yet available.

Assessments for OSH improvements are guided along legal requirements relevant across the life cycle. Hazard and risk documentation requirements according to the EU Construction Site Directive [42] will be supported as it has an impact on machinery operation and maintenance activities. Risk assessments will be performed for the whole machinery according to the EU Machinery Directive [5]. Risk assessments according to the EU OSH Framework Directive [4] will be supported by developing procedures for maintenance activities.

It is possible to draw on experiences already gained in a feasibility study on whether and how to use VR modelling of a river lock extension for risk assessment support according to EU Machinery Directive [5, 43] (see Fig. 2). The current project, however, goes beyond in that it refers to standardized components, to a new river lock, to different types of risk assessments and operational stages as well as to procedure development and documentation support. For VR master planning model development an iterative multi-step procedure has been established and agreed upon [44] based on literature reviews and recommendations from studies in similar contexts [24, 32, 35, 45–48]:

- Clarify and specify purposes for setting up a VR model
- Understand and describe the context of use
- Define and select scenarios

- Select all relevant information and identify the source of information
- Design model components and specify level of detail
- Specify and develop tools for human-system interaction within scenarios
- Merge components, environments, dynamics and interactions into master model
- Evaluate the usability of the VR model
- Apply the VR model for risk assessment support

Fig. 2. VR model for risk assessments of a virtual river lock extension in a feasibility study

The procedure presented is specific, as it will result in a VR model for a future river lock with standardized components; however, it is also generic as it can easily be adapted for model development of any other machinery or work system.

The project refers to a new river lock currently under planning (i.e. Wanne-Eickel Nordschleuse) for barges up to 190 m long and 12.5 m wide, replacing an old and smaller one, and using standardized components. Standardized components that may not be included for this river lock under planning will be considered separately in specific versions of the VR master model. Scenarios for river lock operations have already been compiled and documented with further details about machinery components involved and dynamics required for simulation.

Among the most important scenarios are upstream and downstream locking of barges and draining of river lock for chamber and gate maintenance. This is because both scenarios refer to the machinery as a whole, integrate individual activities at different locations at the lock and integrate several other scenarios in the course of events. With a view to EU Machinery Directive [5] it was seen important to start with aft and head of the river lock and to cover mechanical and construction engineering parts of the machinery and their interactions. With a view to the EU OSH Framework Directive [4] it was seen important to focus on maintenance operations with several operators involved (e.g. draining of river lock and gate maintenance) and on safety issues with regard to the lock superstructure (e.g. guard railing, maintenance for lightning and camera systems). Information gathered from both types of risk assessments will also feed safety plan documentation requirements according to the EU Construction Site Directive [42]. With an emphasis on PtD at river locks it is advisable to take a complement approach with regard to risk assessments and design requirements from all EU Directives [4, 5, 42].

4   Discussion and Conclusion

PtD has a long tradition in systems design in industry and services as it is closely connected to safety engineering, ergonomics and human factors. The concept is interwoven with risk assessments and has high priority in the hierarchy of controls. PtD became an OSH initiative and has been established as a strategy for designing out hazards and risks associated with the entire life cycle [1].

Knowledge available and experiences gained by successful PtD should demonstrate how PtD can be achieved and what could be done to put PtD into practice. However, research into PtD is important to transfer and translate scientific findings into practice or to conduct applied research in settings relevant for practice. New modelling and simulation methods such as VR have been suggested when establishing and changing work tasks and processes as well as developing or adjusting related machinery, work equipment and materials [8, 13]. Two VR studies have been chosen to illustrate successful PtD in practical contexts.

In the study on virtual inspection task performance with MEWP it was possible to investigate virtual accidents and near misses that occurred as rare events and similar to those already documented in accident reports in reality. While accident investigations in reality often rely on observations of final consequences of unsafe design only, reconstructions of accidents in VR simulated applications enable insights into the course of events, human system interactions, and potential root causes of the accidents. Thereby, measures for hazard and risk reduction and usability issues can be addressed more specifically, effectively and early in design.

PtD in the VR study on risk assessments of machinery design and maintenance activities is based on original planning information for a future river lock using standardized components. The dynamic VR model in 1:1 scale provides common ground for easy comprehension, imagination and discussions among interdisciplinary inspection teams and supports risk assessments and design reviews by additional VR simulation features. Measures for risk reduction can be developed and fed back in the planning stage of the river lock including its standardized components. The assessments with the VR planning model cannot fully replace those in reality to be conducted when construction is finished or when maintenance activities are due. Assessments of virtual models will, however, ease those for standardized river locks in reality. Besides, some of the hazards and risks will then be already designed out so that they are of no more concern for future human system interaction; avoiding also some redesign and downtimes in future river lock operations.

In the studies presented, VR modeling and simulation has been used as both, new technologies as well as means to enhance safety and health at work, respectively. It could be demonstrated that VR applications are particularly useful when designing safe work-places and should be further developed [13]. Both applications designed in VR provided support for and illustrated the PtD concept and principles. In addition, by creating scenarios not or not yet available in reality, VR also extended the effective range of interventions for PtD. PtD has the potential to affect prevention culture in that it is proactive in contrast to more traditional and reactive risk management approaches. More PtD research is needed for safe development of technologies, processes and substances during their conception and before their introduction into the market [8].

Since simulations such as in the VR studies are based on modelling of reality with reduced complexity, care must be taken when results from VR simulation studies should be directly applied to practice. Benefits and limitations for successful PtD applications as identified in both VR projects, however, will also hold for other machinery and work systems in industry and services. This provides a sound basis for guiding similar projects along lessons learned and experiences gained in the studies presented.

Acknowledgements. It is a pleasant duty to acknowledge support for the VR accident study by the Sub-committee 'Goods Handling, Storage and Logistics' of the DGUV Expert-committee 'Trade and Logistics'. Also acknowledged is the support for the VR study on OSH for standardised components of machinery by the German Social Accident Insurance Institution of the Federal Government and for the Railway Services (UVB). The investigations are conducted in close cooperation with the Federal Waterways and Shipping Administration (WSV). The author is very grateful to the efforts of Andy Lungfiel for developing and discussing the VR scenarios.

References

1. NIOSH: The state of the national initiative on prevention through design. Progress report 2014, Department of Health and Human Services, CDC, Atlanta (2014)
2. EN ISO 6385: Ergonomic Principles in the Design of Work Systems. CEN, Brussels (2004)
3. Sanders, M.S., McCormick, E.J.: Human Factors in Engineering and Design. McGraw-Hill, New York (1993)
4. EU OSH Framework Directive 89/391/EEC of 12 June 1989 on the introduction of measures to encourage improvements in the safety and health of workers at work (with amendments 2008). Off. J. Eur. Union L **183**, 1–8, 29 June 1989
5. EU Machinery Directive 2006/42/EC of the European Parliament and the Council of 17 May 2006 on machinery, and amending Directive 95/16/EC (recast). Off. J. Eur. Union L **157**, 24–86, 09 July 2006
6. BS OHSAS 18001: Managing Safety the Systems Way. BSI, London (2007)
7. Lehto, M.R., Cook, B.T.: Occupational health and safety management. In: Salvendy, G. (ed.) Handbook of Human Factors and Ergonomics, pp. 701–733. Wiley, Hoboken (2012)
8. EASHW: Priorities for Occupational Safety and Health Research in Europe: 2013–2020. EU Publication Office, Luxembourg (2013)

9. Münsterberg, H.: Die Grundzüge der Psychotechnik. Barth, Leipzig (1914)
10. Giese, F.: Psychotechnik. Hirt, Breslau (1928)
11. Lin, M.-L.: Practice issues in prevention through design. J. Saf. Res. **39**, 157–159 (2008)
12. Schulte, P.A., Rinehart, R., Okun, A., Geraci, C.L., Heidel, D.S.: National prevention through design (PtD) initiative. J. Saf. Res. **39**, 115–121 (2008)
13. EASHW/PEROSH: Position Paper 2. Leadership in Enabling and Industrial Technologies: Prevention through Design. EASHW, Bilbao (2015)
14. Manuele, F.A.: Prevention through design (PtD): history and future. J. Saf. Res. **39**, 127–130 (2008)
15. Hale, A., Kriwan, B., Kjellen, U.: Safety by design based on a workshop of the new technology and work network. Editor. Saf. Sci. **45**(1–2), 3–9 (2007)
16. Howard, J.: Prevention through design – introduction. J. Saf. Res. **39**, 113 (2008)
17. Lamba, A.: Practice. Designing out hazards in the real world. Prof. Saf. **58**(1), 34–40 (2013)
18. Creaser, W.: Prevention through design (PtD). Safe design from an Australian perspective. J. Saf. Res. **39**, 131–134 (2008)
19. Zarges, T., Giles, B.: Prevention through design (PtD). J. Saf. Res. **39**, 123–126 (2008)
20. Gambatese, J.A.: Research issues in prevention trough design. J. Saf. Res. **39**, 153–156 (2008)
21. Gambatese, J.A.: Research. The power of collaboration. Prof. Saf. **58**(1), 48–54 (2013)
22. Hale, K.S., Stanney, K.M. (eds.): Handbook of Virtual Environments: Design, Implementation, and Applications. CRC Press, Boca Raton (2015)
23. Chapanis, A., van Cott, H.P.: Human engineering tests and evaluations. In: van Cott, H.P., Kinkade, R.G. (eds.) Human Engineering Guide to Equipment Design, pp. 701–728. AIR, Washington (1972)
24. Määttä, T.J.: Virtual environments in machinery safety analysis and participatory ergonomics. Hum. Factor Ergon. Man **17**(5), 435–443 (2007)
25. Miller, C., Nickel, P., Nocera, F., Mulder, B., Neerincx, M., Parasuraman, R., Whiteley, I.: Human-machine interface. In: Hockey, G.R.J. (ed.) THESEUS Cluster 2: Psychology and Human-Machine Systems – Report, pp. 22–38. Indigo, Strasbourg (2012)
26. Naber, B., Koppenburg, M., Nickel, P., Lungfiel, A., Huelke, M.: Effects of movement speed, movement predictability and distance in human-robot-collaboration. In: XX World Congress on Safety and Health at Work 2014 – Global Forum on Prevention, Poster Exhibition. ILO, ISSA, DGUV, Frankfurt (2014)
27. Nickel, P., Lungfiel, A., Nischalke-Fehn, G., Trabold, R.-J.: A virtual reality pilot study towards elevating work platform safety and usability in accident prevention. Saf. Sci. Monit. **17**(2), 1–10 (2013)
28. Wickens, C.D., Hollands, J.G., Banbury, S., Parasuraman, R.: Engineering Psychology and Human Performance. Pearson, Upper Saddle River (2013)
29. ILO: Investigation of Occupational Accidents and Diseases. A Practical Guide for Labour Inspectors. International Labour Office, Geneva (2015)
30. Mallet, L., Unger, R.: Virtual reality in mine training. In: SME Annual Meeting and Exhibition 2007, Ch. 07–031, pp. 1–4. SME, Englewood (2007)
31. Kalwasiński, D.: Simulation of the sense of touch with the use of a simulator. Zeszyty naukowe politechniki poznańskiej – organizacja I Zarzadzanie **65**, 31–42 (2015)
32. Helin, K., Evilä, T., Viitaniemi, J., Aromaa, S., Kilpeläinen, P., Rannanjärvi, L., Vähä, P., Kujala, T., Pakkanen, T., Raisamo, R., Salmenperä, P., Miettinen, J., Patel, H.: HumanICT. New Human-Centred Design Method and Virtual Environments in the Design of Vehicular Working Machine Interfaces. VTT, Tampere (2007)

33. Nickel, P., Pröger, E., Kergel, R., Lungfiel, A.: Development of a VR planning model of a river lock for risk assessment in the construction and machinery industry. In: Zachmann, G., Perret, J., Amditis, A. (eds.) Conference and Exhibition of the European Association of Virtual and Augmented Reality, pp. 7–10. The Eurographics Association, Geneva (2014)

34. Nickel, P., Lungfiel, A., Bömer, T., Koppenborg, M., Trabold, R.-J.: Wirksamkeit einer ergänzenden Schutzmaßnahme in virtueller Realität zur Unfallprävention bei Hubarbeitsbühnen. In: GfA (ed.) Gestaltung der Arbeitswelt der Zukunft, pp. 85–87. GfA-Press, Dortmund (2014)

35. Marc, J., Belkacem, N., Marsot, J.: Virtual reality: a design tool for enhanced consideration of usability 'validation elements'. Saf. Sci. **45**, 589–601 (2007)

36. Stocker, K., Deuchert, A., Zepp, C.: Hubarbeitsbühnen (Sicherheit und Gesundheit). BGHM-Aktuell **4**, 16–20 (2011)

37. Reason, J.: Human Error. CUP, Cambridge (1990)

38. EN ISO 10075-2: Ergonomic Principles Related to Mental Workload – Part 2: Design Principles. CEN, Brussels (2000)

39. BMVI: Verkehrsinvestitionsbericht für das Berichtsjahr 2012 [Report on traffic investments for 2012]. Deutscher Bundestag, Drucksache 18/580, 18 February 2014

40. Jander, A.: Aktuelle Situation der Standardisierung von Schleusen. In: Tagungsband BAW-Kolloquium 2012 Innovation mit Tradition: Hydraulischer Entwurf und Betrieb von Wasserbauwerken, pp. 33–38, BAW, Karlsruhe (2012)

41. Ebers-Ernst, J., Maßmann, B.: Ersatz von fünf Schleusen am Dortmund-Ems-Kanal. In: Tagungsband HTG-Kongress 2015, pp. 279–288. HTG, Hamburg (2015)

42. EU Construction Directive 92/57/EEC on the implementation of minimum safety and health requirements at temporary or mobile construction sites. Off. J. Eur. Union L **245**, 6–22, 28 August 1992

43. Nickel P., Pröger E., Lungfiel A., Kergel R.: Flexible, dynamic VR simulation of a future river lock facilitates prevention through design in occupational safety and health. In: IEEE VR 2015, Annual International Symposium on Virtual Reality, pp. 385–386. IEEE Digital Library (2015)

44. Nickel, P., Kergel, R., Wachholz, T., Pröger, E., Lungfiel, A.: Setting-up a virtual reality simulation for improving OSH in standardisation of river locks. In: Safety of Industrial Automated Systems, SIAS 2015, pp. 223–228. DGUV, Berlin (2015)

45. Bouchlaghem, D., Shang, H., Whyte, J., Ganah, A.: Visualisation in architecture, engineering and construction (ACE). Autom. Constr. **14**(3), 287–295 (2005)

46. Chun, C.K., Li, H., Skitmore, R.M.: The use of virtual prototyping for hazard identification in the early design stage. Constr. Innov. **12**(1), 29–42 (2012)

47. EN IEC 61160: Design Review. CEN, Brussels (2005)

48. Sacks, R., Whyte, J., Swissa, D., Raviv, G., Zhou, W., Shapira, A.: Safety by design: dialogues between designers and builders using virtual reality. Constr. Manag. Econ. **33**(1), 55–72 (2015)

Scoping Review on Human-Machine Interaction and Health and Safety at Work

Swantje Robelski[✉] and Sascha Wischniewski

Federal Institute for Occupational Safety and Health, Dortmund, Germany
{robelski.swantje,wischniewski.sascha}@baua.bund.de

Abstract. Continuous technological developments are ongoing challenges in the design of safe and healthy workplaces. Concepts of human-machine interaction (HMI) are an essential part of these developments which have to be examined constantly with regard to their influence on humane work. In order to map the existing knowledge on relations and design, a scoping review on human-machine interaction in production systems was conducted. Focussing on findings concerning physical and mental health as well as performance and job satisfaction, an extensive selection- and review-process led to the inclusion of 102 studies into the scoping review. The results were split content-based into three subcategories: function allocation, interface and interaction design as well as operation and supervision of machines and systems.

The results on function allocation stress the meaning of a task-oriented assignment of degrees and levels of automation, which both have an influence on workload and performance. Nevertheless, questions of trust and human involvement play an important role, too, and a global optimal balance of performance, workload and subjective feelings has not been found yet. Conclusions concerning the effects of human-machine interaction on mental health cannot be drawn from the studies of the scoping review. The studies dealing with interface and interaction design point to a confirmation of existing guidelines on ergonomic design. Yet, questions concerning mental health and work satisfaction remain broadly unanswered. A successful operation and supervision process is mainly determined by machine and system characteristics such as reliability. The concept of technological coupling may be used to describe the interaction of humans and machines. Studies using this framework indicate a tendency towards a poorer mental health and less intrinsic job satisfaction in cases of tight technological coupling.

Further research should address the relation between mental health and human-machine interaction. Additionally, existing knowledge and guidelines need to be revised with regard to the demands of new technologies and new ways of interaction such as human-robot collaboration.

Keywords: Human-machine interaction · Function allocation · Interface design · Safety and health at work

© Springer International Publishing Switzerland 2016
F.F.-H. Nah and C.-H. Tan (Eds.): HCIBGO 2016, Part II, LNCS 9752, pp. 337–347, 2016.
DOI: 10.1007/978-3-319-39399-5_32

1   Human-Machine Interaction in Future Production Work

Industrial work is an important economic factor in a high-wage country such as Germany. Statistics show that a considerable number of jobholders are working in the manufacturing sector which offers jobs for a quarter of the working population [1].

Furthermore, developments like industry 4.0 stress the integration of physical and computer-based processes into cyberphysical systems where new forms of interaction and knowledge demands hold challenges for the design of industrial working systems.

Past and present technological developments thus emphasize the meaning of human-machine interaction which is highly important for humane work. Human-machine interaction that is insufficiently designed can be seen as a risk factor: the increasing complexity of technologies, working processes and human-machine interfaces may in these cases increase emotional and mental stress for machine operators [2]. In order to investigate these assumptions, the presented scoping review was prepared.

The research question to be answered was whether human-machine interaction effects outcomes such as (mental) health, wellbeing, job satisfaction and performance considering the moderating influence of age and gender.

2   Method

2.1   Scoping Review as a Means to Prepare Reviews

A scoping review is a review method that aims towards a broad mapping of knowledge. In general, a scoping review does not exclude sources based on their origin, study design and quality, thus offering a broader scope for research questions. The scoping review may be used to disseminate and summarize research findings so that research gaps can be identified [3]. [4] find that scoping studies may set "the scene for a future research agenda" (p. 75). Additionally, a scoping review is used to assess whether further insights into the topic should be gained by the preparation of a systematic review [3].

[3] propose five steps for conducting a scoping review: (1) identification of the research question, (2) identification of relevant studies, (3) study selection, (4) charting of data, (5) collation, summary and report of the results.

Some critics of narrative review forms have been summarized by [4]. Critical aspects include insufficient quality of the texts, reasons for in- and exclusion of material are not discussed or contrary views are not reflected. To answer these critics the present scoping review included an extensive documentation of inclusion and exclusion criteria. Furthermore, the depiction of contrary and conflicting evidence on one topic was seen as an important aspiration leading to a holistic picture of the current state of research.

2.2   Study Selection Process

A complex search algorithm was developed and applied in the databases EBSCOhost and Pubmed. The search algorithm was composed of four parts: (a) a set of terms like human-machine interaction, man-machine systems and supervisory control was used to describe and capture aspects of human-machine interaction; (b) outcome variables of interest allocated to the categories (mental) health (e.g. depression, depressive symptoms, musculoskeletal diseases, pain), wellbeing (e.g. complaints, headache, well-being, happiness), job satisfaction (e.g. sick leave, absenteeism, intention to leave, work satisfaction) and performance-variables (e.g. organizational effectiveness, quality of service) which were completed HMI-specific terms such as error and accident; (c) terms such as production, conveyor belt and industry were intended to focus on industrial working systems; (d) the search algorithm was concluded by a Boolean Not-operation in order to exclude subject areas such as military, education and service industries.

In July 2014 the search algorithm was applied in the databases leading to 21.075 hits. In order to edit the hits a software program for reference management was used. There, a first reduction of hits could be accomplished by searching for not-suiting terms within titles and keywords. A lot of articles didn't address the targeted content, as keywords such as genome, pharmacology or protein show. Moreover, the titles of the references were analysed according to the search terms. This procedure led to the exclusion of 16.941 hits. The next step within the selection process was the analysis of the remaining 2086 articles based on their abstracts. Again, the main part of articles could be excluded (1.779) because the abstracts didn't address the aspects in question. Finally, 269 articles were chosen to be analysed fully.

In their article on the advancement of scoping reviews, [5] emphasize the iterative character of the study selection process (step 3 according to [3]) which should be as transparent as possible. In order to ensure both transparency and quality within the study selection process a second reviewer who accompanied the abstract review process was involved. Calculating the interrater-reliability according to [6] assured the quality of the selection process. Therefor a set of 50, randomly chosen abstracts was read by a second, independent rater, who was briefed according to the selection criteria. The computation of consensus between the two rater resulted in a coefficienct of concordance of $\kappa = .81$. Afterwards, there was a short feedback on the decisions and the criteria applied. Then another set of 50 randomly chosen abstracts was rated. The second rating generated a Cohen's Kappa of $\kappa = .89$. Both scores can be seen as highly concordant [7].

The next step of the selection process was the examination of full texts. Of the 269 firstly included studies another 167 were excluded. The reasons are manifold ranging from diverging contexts to an insufficient description of variables and methods. Finally, 102 studies were included into to the scoping review in order to be analysed in detail.

2.3 Study Characteristics

According to [3] a basic numerical analysis was performed prior to a content-based structuring. It includes study characteristics such as year of origin or the geographical distribution of the studies.

In order to gain a broad depiction of the studies no time limit had been set for the database search. The main part of the studies analysed originated from the years 2005 to 2015, as can be seen in Fig. 1.

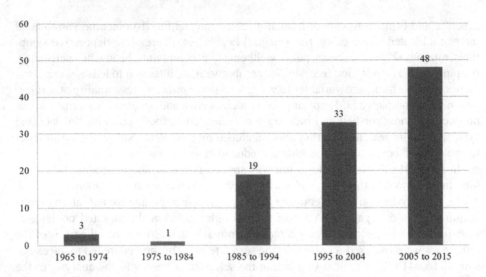

Fig. 1. Number of studies per decade

Furthermore, the countries of origin of the studies were considered. In Fig. 2, it can be seen that most of the studies were completed in Northern American countries.

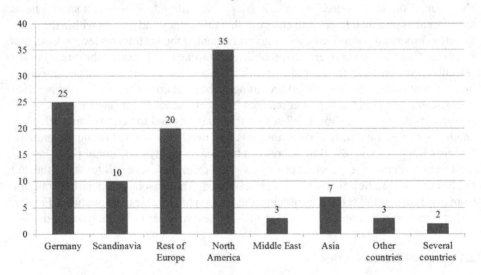

Fig. 2. Number of studies by country of origin

With 25 studies, Germany is the country that produced the second most contributions to the scoping review followed by other European countries (20 studies) and studies conducted in the Scandinavian region (10 studies).

2.4 Structuralizing the Studies

With respect to the manifold study focuses the material was assigned to three features of human-machine interaction namely function allocation, interface and interaction design as well as operation and supervision of machines and systems. The chosen classification is based on a theory-driven approach.

Function Allocation

The feature function allocation emphasizes the priority of working tasks that should determine the allocation of functions between humans and machines [8]. According to [9] function allocation plays an important role for the emergence of mental workload. A possible reason is described by [10] who state that function allocation influences cognitive functions.

Interface Design

Another important aspect to be considered when designing human-machine systems is the design of interfaces and interactions, which depicts the second feature of human-machine interaction within the scoping review. Aspects of interface design can be understood as input and output modalities of machines and systems [9]. This feature comprises depictions and displays, aspects of ergonomic design and forms of interaction. The latter was described by [11] as the regular exchange between human and (computerized) systems where different processes of feedback exist. An example of this interchange between human and systems are multiple forms and modalities of feedback.

Operation and Supervision of Machines and Systems

The last feature of human-machine interaction chosen for structuralizing the studies can be seen as the result of the prior features. Given a certain function allocation and interface design, employees have to work with machines considering certain machine and context characteristics. On an operational level cases of application are described.

3 Results

On a general level the scoping review shows that the main part of the studies was conducted within laboratorial settings. Laboratory studies often include characteristics of intervention studies meaning that there is a manipulation of conditions between two or more groups.

Considering the three features of human-machine interaction Fig. 3 shows that the main part of the analysed studies addresses aspects of interface design (41 studies). Studies dealing with operation and supervision of machines represent the second most observed content (33 studies). Within the scoping review studies covering function allocation are analysed the least (25 studies).

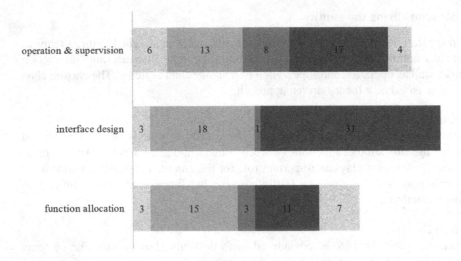

(mental) health ▪ wellbeing ▪ job satisfaction & motivation ▪ performance ▪ workplace characteristics

Fig. 3. Distribution of studies regarding features of human-machine interaction and outcome-categories

With regard to the set of dependent variables a strong focus on performance can be observed. Aspects of wellbeing which also include workload or user satisfaction have been examined frequently, too. Job satisfaction on a general level and aspects of work motivation didn't play a considerable role in the analysed studies. The same applies to (mental) health.

Since some studies describe changes in workplace that are related to the introduction of new machines and systems, workplace characteristics were identified as another set of independent variables. They include positive as well as negative perceived changes introduced by new technological facilities.

With the ongoing development of technologies a blend between human-machine interaction and human-computer interaction can be observed. Today, most machine control units are based on computer technology [12]. Since machines are endowed with computer-based processes, new challenges on human-machine interaction are imposed. Within this context [13] point out that computers and information systems connect humans and machines in manufacturing environments. In order to account for these similarities some results concerning human-computer interaction (HCI) are emphasized, too. The results concerning the three features of human-machine interaction are described in more detail within the next paragraphs.

3.1 Function Allocation

The study situation remains unclear for the relation between function allocation and (mental) health. Studies scatteredly touch this relation in very different contexts and with diverging methodological approaches, so that it seems difficult to come to verified conclusions. The relation between function allocation and aspects of job satisfaction or motivation remains unclear, too. As can be seen in Fig. 3, both areas of dependent variables were examined by three studies respectively.

Stronger evidence for possible effects of function allocation can be observed for aspects of wellbeing. Studies show that degree of automation as well as level of automation exert influence on workload. Subjective workload decreases, as degree and level of automation increase [14]. However, there are complex interactions with other states of wellbeing such as trust and the desire for (manual) control [15].

Computer-based adaptive automation can be distinguished between event-based, performance-based and psychophysiological-based approaches as well as modelling-based strategies [16]. Within this context [17] could show that there was no clear picture between an event-based, performance-based and adaptable automation with regard to performance variables. However, subjective state measures such as workload and strain could benefit from a performance-based approach while measures referring to self-confidence yield advantageous results for an adaptable automation. An example of a psychophysiological-based automation can be found in [18]. The authors show that both variations of automation mode (EEG-based and a yoked version of EEG data) result in comparable level 1 situation awareness. With regard to subjective workload, a self-initiated usage of the support system induces higher workload ratings than a computer-based initiation [18].

Furthermore, the scoping review includes studies showing that there is a need to differentiate between routine and non-routine situations with regard to performance and operator workload. As was underlined by the analysis of [19], advantages of higher degrees of automation on performance cannot be maintained in non-routine situations often.

With regard to workplace characteristics it can be stated that the introduction of new technologies may be related with positive outcomes such as skill enhancement [20]. But rather negative effects such as a limitation in authority may also occur.

In short, strategies of automation design and function allocation should consider different trade-offs between aspects of performance and states of wellbeing or workload. Moreover, principles of function allocation can be acting as stressors or resources in changing workplace characteristics and aspects of job control. For the investigation of adverse or beneficial effects of human-machine interaction job control can be seen as a connective element. With the current state of research conclusions concerning long-term effects on strain cannot be drawn.

3.2 Interface and Interaction Design

Since most machines are equipped with displays representing computer-based processes in the background, aspects of interface and interaction design play an important role in HMI and HCI.

Within this context feedback design is an important factor. As new technologies enable the usage of several feedback modalities, [21] recommend bimodal feedback which can be related to decreased workload. The authors conclude that of several multi-modal feedback variations, the most advantageous results could be obtained by the combination of haptic and visual feedback. [22] demonstrate differences between men and women regarding their reaction on negatively framed feedback. This study undermines the importance of aspects such as individualization which is also entrenched by the norm ISO 9241-110 [23].

With regard to the usage of modern technologies such as head-mounted displays (HMDs) studies indicate a short term occurrence of physical complaints like headaches [24]. [25], using a test duration of 2×4 h, show that the use of the HMD does not cause impairments on the visual system. However, an increased muscular activity in the neck region and an increase in subjective complaints in the time course are detected. Yet, it is not possible to deduce long-term effects based on the studies included within in the scoping review.

The cooperation of humans and robots can be seen as a special form of human-machine interaction. The studies included in the scoping review suggest that visual features as well as the intended work domain must be taken into account when designing human-robot interaction [26]. Outcome variables that seem to be influenced by human-robot interaction are aspects of workload, user satisfaction, performance or feelings of safety [27].

In general, the studies dealing with interface and interaction design confirm existing findings on the advantages of ergonomic design so far. Concerning the examined outcome variables, especially user satisfaction, workload and performance benefit of ergonomic design principles such as redundant information representation. Results on job satisfaction and motivation have been found rarely so that there is an insufficient data base for conclusions.

3.3   Operation and Supervision of Machines and Systems

The studies in this feature of human-machine interaction descend from broad areas of application. A concept that was introduced within the context of advanced manufacturing technologies – namely technological coupling – finds evidence for negative health outcomes related to the occurrence of tight technological coupling [28]. The author also shows that tight coupling exerts negative influence on job satisfaction [28]. These results could be confirmed in later works [29]. Moreover, the operation and supervision of machines and systems affects workplace characteristics indicating a strong connection to task-related factors such as decision latitude. [30] show a negative correlation between tight coupling and timing as well as method control.

Additionally, several studies indicate that system characteristics hold an important meaning for the operation and supervision of systems and machines. Especially aspects of wellbeing such as workload and performance are affected by system characteristics such as reliability and error rate. On a general level it can be seen that reliable systems are related with higher trust ratings [31] and decreased workload [32]. Concerning performance variables, [33] find in their literature review that low reliability of systems (≤ 0.7) erases possible performance benefits of the automated system.

Summarizing, the operation of systems is influenced by system characteristics and can change job structures as well as skills of jobholders which should be taken into account in the development of new systems. Situational (e.g. quantitative workload) and individual (e.g. age) factors influence the interaction of humans and machines. For the supervision of systems the scoping review does not yield clear conclusions.

4   Discussion

The Scoping Review on human-machine interaction can be seen as a comprehensive appraisal of the literature. Within the review process a heterogeneous picture could be drawn reflecting the manifold areas of application, design and concepts that are examined within the context of human-machine interaction.

With regard to the method chosen, the scoping review allows a broad collection of knowledge. Nevertheless, a topic as extensive as human-machine interaction may have benefitted from a stronger focus. Even studies that were grouped within the same feature of human-machine interaction showed great content-related differences. As a consequence, a detailed comparison of studies was not feasible. However, a major advantage offered by the broad overview of a scoping review is the possibility to identify research gaps. The scoping review on human-machine interaction shows that there is a great need to intensify research activities on the relation between human-machine interaction and aspects of (mental) health. Changes in workplace and task characteristics induced by technological systems may be seen as a connective element which stresses the meaning of a task-focus within human factors research. Further research questions refer to the applicability of current concepts and design options on advanced technologies. As for human-robot interaction, existing knowledge has to be verified and broadened in order to meet future challenges such as fenceless collaboration. From a methodological point of view the scoping review encourages to conduct field studies as well as studies with the targeted population of employees since many findings results from laboratory studies with student samples. Moreover, it can be seen that a differentiation between age groups and gender is pursued only rarely. With demographic change at hand these considerations should be taken into account more strongly, thus leading to age-differentiated design principles that enable safe and healthy work. Additionally, long-term effects should be focussed more strongly by longitudinal studies.

However, the literature on human-machine interaction shows an abundance of design principles. Principles such as the arrangement of displays according to gestalt-laws or advisories concerning the density of information can be found in German regulatory documents. On an international level, ISO norms like ISO 6385 [34] point to a human-centred design of machines and systems. With regard to the design of dialogues ISO 9241-110 [23] names aspects such as suitability for the task, self-descriptiveness, controllability, conformity with user expectations, error tolerance, suitability for individualisation, and suitability for learning that stem mainly from human-computer interaction research. The application of these principles is a starting point for ergonomic design.

In conclusion, 102 analysed studies on human-machine interaction point out that mainly wellbeing and performance are affected by features of human-machine interaction. Nevertheless, the design of working tasks plays an essential role, too, because it determines the interactions between humans and machines. As was already described by [10], a human-machine system is more than the sum of its parts. The design of future human-machine systems should account for the increasing complexity of machines and systems. Visions of industry 4.0 and cyberphysical systems contain new challenges for the design of human-machine interaction so that it becomes ever more central to ensure a transparent, comprehensible and ergonomic design of machines and systems. Therefore further research should focus on a detailed description of human-machine systems and outcome variables in order to gain a comprehensive understanding of their interactions. Thus, the identification of both detrimental and beneficial forms of human machine interaction can ensure safety and health at work.

References

1. Federal Statistical Office. https://www.destatis.de/DE/ZahlenFakten/Indikatoren/LangeReihen/Arbeitsmarkt/lrerw013.html
2. Flaspöler, E., Hauke, A., Pappachan, P., Reinert, D., Bleyer, T., Henke, N., Beeck, R.O.D.: The human-machine interface as an emerging risk. Office for Official Publications of the European Communities, Luxembourg (2009)
3. Arksey, H., O'Malley, L.: Scoping studies: towards a methodological framework. Int. J. Soc. Res. Methodol. **8**, 19–32 (2005)
4. Jesson, J., Matheson, L., Lacey, F.M.: Doing Your Literature Review: Traditional and Systematic Techniques. Sage, Los Angeles (2011)
5. Levac, D., Colquhoun, H., O'Brien, K.: Scoping studies: advancing the methodology. Implementation Sci. **5**, 1–9 (2010)
6. Cohen, J.A.: A coefficient of agreement for nominal scales. Educ. Psychol. Meas. **20**, 37–46 (1960)
7. Landis, J.R., Koch, G.G.: The measurement of observer agreement for categorical data. Biometrics **33**, 159–174 (1977)
8. Ulich, E.: Arbeitspsychologie. Schäffer-Poeschel, Stuttgart (2005)
9. Hacker, W., Sachse, P.: Allgemeine Arbeitspsychologie, 3rd compl. rev. edn. Hogrefe, Göttingen (2014)
10. Hollnagel, E., Woods, D.D.: Cognitive systems engineering: new wine in new bottles. Int. J. Man Mach. Stud. **18**, 583–600 (1983)
11. Heinecke, A.M.: Mensch-Computer-Interaktion, 2nd rev. edn. Springer, Heidelberg (2012)
12. Groover, M.P.: Automation, Production Systems, and Computer-Integrated Manufacturing. Pearson, London (2015)
13. Mehrabi, M.G., Ulsoy, A.G., Koren, Y.: Reconfigurable manufacturing systems: key to future manufacturing. J. Intell. Manuf. **11**, 403–419 (2000)
14. Lin, C.J., Yenn, T.-C., Yang, C.-W.: Evaluation of operators' performance for automation design in the fully digital control room of nuclear power plants. Hum. Factors Ergon. Manuf. Serv. Ind. **20**, 10–23 (2010)
15. Sauer, J., Nickel, P., Wastell, D.: Designing automation for complex work environments under different levels of stress. Appl. Ergon. **44**, 119–127 (2013)
16. Inagaki, T.: Adaptive automation: sharing and trading of control. In: Hollnagel, E. (ed.) Handbook of Cognitive Task Design, pp. 147–169. Lawrence Erlbaum Associates, Mahwah (2003)
17. Sauer, J., Kao, C.-S., Wastell, D.: A comparison of adaptive and adaptable automation under different levels of environmental stress. Ergonomics **55**, 840–853 (2012)

18. Bailey, N.R., Scerbo, M.W., Freeman, F.G., Mikulka, P.J., Scott, L.A.: Comparison of a brain-based adaptive system and a manual adaptable system for invoking automation. Hum. Factors J. Hum. Factors Ergon. Soc. **48**, 693–709 (2006)

19. Onnasch, L., Wickens, C.D., Li, H., Manzey, D.: Human performance consequences of stages and levels of automation: an integrated meta-analysis. Hum. Factors J. Hum. Factors Ergon. Soc. **56**, 476–488 (2014)

20. Balogh, I., Ohlsson, K., Hansson, G.-Å., Engström, T., Skerfving, S.: Increasing the degree of automation in a production system: consequences for the physical workload. Int. J. Ind. Ergon. **36**, 353–365 (2006)

21. Vitense, H.S., Jacko, J.A., Emery, V.K.: Multimodal feedback: an assessment of performance and mental workload. Ergonomics **46**, 68–87 (2003)

22. Djamasbi, S., Loiacono, E.T.: Do men and women use feedback provided by their decision support systems (DSS) differently? Decis. Support Syst. **44**, 854–869 (2008)

23. ISO 9241-110:2006. Ergonomics of human-system interaction – Part 110: Dialogue principles

24. Ames, S.L., Wolffsohn, J.S., McBrien, N.A.: The development of a symptom questionnaire for assessing virtual reality viewing using a head-mounted display. Optom. Vis. Sci. **82**, 168–176 (2005)

25. Grauel, B.M., Terhoeven, J.N., Wischniewski, S.: Beanspruchungsoptimaler Einsatz von Head-Mounted Displays als Arbeitsassistenz. Technische Sicherheit **5**, 39–42 (2015)

26. Kuchenbrandt, D., Häring, M., Eichberg, J., Eyssel, F.: Keep an eye on the task! How gender typicality of tasks influence human–robot interactions. In: Ge, S.S., Khatib, O., Cabibihan, J.-J., Simmons, R., Williams, M.-A. (eds.) ICSR 2012. LNCS, vol. 7621, pp. 448–457. Springer, Heidelberg (2012)

27. Bortot, D., Ding, H., Antonopolous, A., Bengler, K.: Human motion behavior while interacting with an industrial robot. Work **41**, 1699–1707 (2012)

28. Corbett, J.M.: A psychological study of advanced manufacturing technology: the concept of coupling. Behav. Inf. Technol. **6**(4), 441–453 (1987)

29. Corbett, J.M., Martin, R., Wall, T.D., Clegg, C.W.: Technological coupling as a predictor of intrinsic job satisfaction: a replication study. J. Organ. Behav. **10**, 91–95 (1989)

30. Dvash, A., Mannheim, B.: Technological coupling, job characteristics and operators' well-being as moderated by desirability of control. Behav. Inf. Technol. **20**, 225–236 (2001)

31. Bailey, N.R., Scerbo, M.W.: Automation-induced complacency for monitoring highly reliable systems: the role of task complexity, system experience, and operator trust. Theoret. Issues Ergon. Sci. **8**, 321–348 (2007)

32. McFadden, S.M., Vimalachandran, A., Blackmore, E.: Factors affecting performance on a target monitoring task employing an automatic tracker. Ergonomics **47**, 257–280 (2004)

33. Wickens, C.D., Dixon, S.R.: The benefits of imperfect diagnostic automation: a synthesis of the literature. Theoret. Issues Ergon. Sci. **8**, 201–212 (2007)

34. ISO 6385:2004. Ergonomic principles in the design of work systems

A Model Based Approach to Web Application Design for Older Adults Using MVC Design Pattern

Christopher Romanyk, Ryan McCallum, and Pejman Salehi(✉)

School of Applied Computing, Sheridan Institute of Technology
and Advanced Learning, Oakville, Canada
{christopher.romanyk, ryan.mccallum,
pejman.salehi}@sheridancollege.ca

Abstract. Recent studies show sixty percent of older adults access the internet at least once a week. However, poor website usability and design have been identified as two key factors which negatively impact internet usage among this demographic. Often the specific needs of this user group are not addressed properly by modern web application design, and this can hinder the usability and user experience of these applications and sites for older adults. To solve this issue, we have developed a universal design approach by introducing software-modeling constraints for the MVC design pattern to better address the needs of older adult users on the web.

Keywords: Model-based software development · Aging · HCI · OCL · Model view controller design pattern · Modern web application design

1 Introduction

The Model View Controller design pattern (MVC) is one of the most employed software design patterns currently in use [1]. It is versatile in nature, and benefits from significant horizontal implementation over multiple software systems. The pattern's popularity entails that software users of all ages and backgrounds are frequently exposed to applications based on MVC. This prevalence creates a unique opportunity to develop, design and manage standards that can impact a large web based audience.

In an MVC application the view (V) is what the user directly sees on the screen in front of them. It is the collection of components which represent the user interface elements such as text fields, buttons and images. The model on the other hand, represents the underlying, logical structure of data in a software application and the structure of the information needs to be presented to the user through view (V). In other words, the view is the reflection of the information stored in model elements.

The controller (C) manages the interaction between the model (M) and the View (V). For instance, in an online banking statement application, the controller asks the underlying subsystems to retrieve the necessary information for particular statement and populates the appropriate model (M) elements. Thereafter, the controller sends the model elements to the proper view (V) in order to represent the information to the user. Figure 1 shows the general components of the MVC design pattern.

© Springer International Publishing Switzerland 2016
F.F.-H. Nah and C.-H. Tan (Eds.): HCIBGO 2016, Part II, LNCS 9752, pp. 348–357, 2016.
DOI: 10.1007/978-3-319-39399-5_33

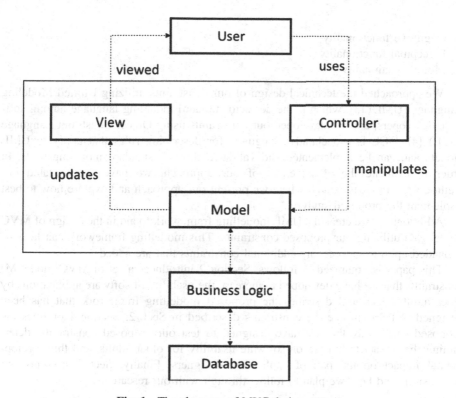

Fig. 1. The elements of MVC design pattern

As people age, various impairments begin to affect older adults more frequently [2]. Many of these impairments relate to HCI, with web usage for older adults being traditionally addressed through interface design. In order to address these difficulties, developers focus most of their efforts on the user interface's design, which is captured by the view (V) in MVC design pattern, and not on the model (M), which encapsulates the information to be represented to the user. To address these problems properly in MVC, the model (M) must also be designed appropriately, as MVC models (M) and views/interfaces (V) are directly related. Usability issues for older adults in MVC occur when a view/interface (V) is visually appropriate for older adults, but the logical processes in the model (M) have not been designed to meet the needs of these users. Logical design and processes in web applications can exercise a significantly positive effect on the usability of software for older adults.

To this end, we have developed a set of model-level constraints for the logical design component of MVC applications to increase usability among older adults. Before designing our constraints, we investigated specific web application and data elements that historically have caused poor usability for older adults, identifying several age-related impairments and areas of functional decline that affect the usability of the documented application elements. We observed that declining functionality in the following areas affects application components relating to the model (M) in MVC:

- Cognitive functionality
- Perceptual functionality
- Motor functionality

We approached the technical design of our constraints utilizing Unified Modeling Language (UML) [3], which is the de facto standard modeling language among software developers, and we developed our constraints using Object Constraint Language (OCL) [4]. OCL is a declarative language for describing rules that apply to UML models and can be implemented and validated through standard modeling tools. In order to evaluate the effectiveness of our approach, we have encapsulated our methodology in a case study, where we present our approach and explore how to best implement the proposed study.

Additionally, we created a UML modelling framework to aid in the design of MVC models(M) utilizing our proposed constraints. This modelling framework can later be expanded upon to enforce any additional constraints that are added.

This paper is organized as follows. Section 2 introduces a set of MVC model(M) constraints that we have developed to increase the usability of software applications by older adults. Section 3 describes the proposed modelling framework that has been designed to help enforce the constraints described in Sect. 2. Section 4 outlines the proposed case study that we have designed to test our proposed constraints, determining the impact they have on software usability for older adults, and the developmental impact on the part of application designers. Finally, Sect. 5 presents our conclusions and how we plan to follow through with our research.

2   Proposed Constraints

Limited Simultaneous Content: We propose a constraint that states the number of properties viewed by users should be limited to no more than five properties per model.

Several studies have explored how older adults process multiple pieces of information and have noted how this behavior differs from their younger counterparts. Results show that older adults incur cognitive decline relating to their attention and the processing of multiples pieces of information. Furthermore, this decline is more prominent when task switching occurs [2]. While there are various opinions as to why older adults may struggle with selective and divided attention, generally older adults are slower at processing information than their younger counterparts [5]. Recognizing that older adults show decreased performance when processing multiple pieces of information and acknowledging how their decreased processing speed relates to difficulties with selective and divided attention, we have decided to address these issues by ensuring that information viewed by users does not require the users to split their attention or process varied amounts of information simultaneously.

Limit the Number of Audiovisual Media Elements to Two: We propose a constraint limiting non text-based properties to two or less. Many older adult web application users are dealing with some form of perceptual difficulty relating to hearing and or visual impairments [6]. Current data suggests that over 40 percent of all older adults are dealing with some form of hearing impairment or hearing loss [7]. Links between ageing and the prevalent loss of visual acuity are also well documented in older adults [8]. Noting that a large percentage of older adults may have difficulty interacting with web applications that heavily feature audio and or image-based elements, we have designed a constraint that helps increase usability by maintaining that a large percentage of the information provided to users be of a textual nature.

Limited User Input Field Length to Two Hundred and Fifty Characters: We propose a constraint that suggests input fields for users should be limited to less than 250 characters. There is established research that shows a direct tradeoff between speed and accuracy when relating to older adult users and movement. Current literature shows that older adult users tend to have slower reaction and movement times compared to younger users [9]. Keeping in mind the fact the older adults often will attempt to increase their movement accuracy by performing actions more slowly, it is sensible to limit the amount of movement-based activities required by the user. Limiting activities that may require movement, such as typing, ensures that the web application's ease of use will remain high and expedient. As such, we propose that limiting the length of fields relating to user input will help amend these issues and maintain high levels of usability.

Two Types of Password Fields: We propose a constraint that suggests password credential field types be limited to text or image blurb types.

The current de facto standard for web application credentials and password management is a typed password often containing a combinations of mixed case letters, characters, numbers and symbols; often referenced as alphanumeric. Recent studies into the effective password and credential management of older adults have suggested that a viable alternative to the traditional password is the visual password, as older adult users can recognize images with an accuracy rating of nearly 99 percent [10]. Additionally, current research data relating to security suggests that visual passwords are far more secure than traditional alphanumeric passwords. A recent survey suggests that when logically implemented in a manner that is appropriate for older adults without visual perceptual issues, visual passwords are a welcome alternative to alphanumeric passwords, both as a means of ease of use and security. We have designed a constraint that guides and allows for the use of visual passwords in web applications.

Four-Character Length Minimum on User Passwords: We propose that password field length be a minimum of four characters for text password fields.

Significant amounts of literature suggest cognitive issues relating to working memory are prevalent with older adult users [2]. While remembering a password may appear to be a matter of recall or short term memory, password creation can be a function of working memory. Several elements relating to online credential management can include having to generate unique password combinations of varying complexity. When the user is forced to start manipulating alphanumeric characters on mass while creating passwords, the nature of the process changes from simple recall of common words or historical passwords to a working memory process in which unique passwords are created. A recent study examining credentials of application users stated that older adult's users showed a tendency to use shorter passwords than their younger counterparts [11]. While the study was inconclusive as to why older adult users generally utilized shorter passwords than their younger counterpart, the study hypothesized a potential link between the state of working memory for older adults and preferred password length. Understanding that certain elements of credential management can theoretically engage working memory helps to bolster the notion that length of passwords used by older adults could be related to declines in working memory. As such we have chosen to allow a shorter minimum length password for older adult users in line with the presented research.

3   Modeling Framework

In order to provide software designers with an effective tool to enforce the constraints and the guidelines specified in Sect. 2, we have developed a small modeling framework as an extension to the Unified Modeling Language (UML) through its profiling mechanism. More particularly, we identified different elements necessary to design the Model (M) layer of MVC for older adults and introduced the necessary stereotypes as new modeling elements for this purpose. Finally, we specified the constraints using Object Constraint Language (OCL), the standard language to capture constraints for UML models.

The final profile, called Older Adult Model Design Profile (OAMDP), is implemented using IBM Rational Software Architect (RSA) [12]. Figure 2 presents the implementation the profile class diagram. The OA_Model represents the model element of MVC, which is tailored for older adult users. This element is designed as an extension to the <<metaclass>> Class from UML metamodel. OA_UserInput and OA_Output are the stereotypes designed to represent the attributes of the OA_Model element as an extension to the <<metaclass>> property. OA_UserInput is further expanded into OA_TextInput and OA_NonTextInput to represent text-based and non-text-based input attributes respectively. Text password and non-text password are also specified to better capture different types of passwords.

After specifying the stereotypes in our profile, we defined the constraints using the OCL language which will be presented in the remainder of this Section.

Limited Simultaneous Content.

```
context OA_Model
inv:
self.getAllAttributes()->size() <= 5
```

Limit the Number of Media Elements to Two.

```
context OA_Model
inv:
self.getAllAttributes()
->select(p:Property | p.oclIsTypeOf
(OA_NonTextInput))->size() <=2
```

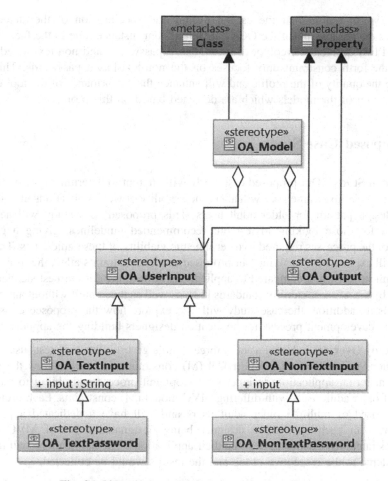

Fig. 2. Older adult model design profile class diagram

Limit User Input Field Length to Two Hundred and Fifty Characters.

```
context OA_TextInput
inv:
self.input.size()<250
```

Two Types of Password Fields.

```
context OA_NonTextPassword
inv:
self.input.oclIsTypeOf('Image')
```

Four-Character Length Minimum on User Passwords.

```
context OA_TextPassword
inv:
self.input.size()<5
```

It is worth noting that the careful design and specification of the stereotypes decreases the complexity of the OCL constraints. For instance, due to the fact that we specified two different stereotypes for text-based passwords and non-text-based passwords, the forth constraint only focuses on the non-text-based passwords. This will improve the quality of the profile and will enhance the performance of the tool during the validation of the models which are designed based on this profile.

4   Proposed Case Study

Purpose of Study: Our proposed case study will attempt to determine how our newly proposed modelling framework will affect the usability of web applications utilizing the MVC design pattern for older adult users. This proposed case study will act as a blueprint for those looking to test our recommended guidelines, giving a general outline of the processes required to determine the viability of these guidelines. The case study will explore how applying our proposed model constraints affect the usability of web applications when compared to applications built to the current best standards, as defined by the w3 accessibility standards [13], as well as those built without any formal standards. In addition, the case study will also explore how the proposed constraints affect the development process for application designers building the application.

Case Study Overview: Using a set of three sample groups, the study tests usability of applications using differing MVC model (M) constraints, as well as how these constraints affect an application designer's development process and ability to meet the needs of older adult users with differing MVC model (M) constraints. Each group will be comprised of multiple older adult users and will have a dedicated application designer, with each application designer being designated a set of MVC model (M) constraints with which to develop their applications. The applications will then be administered to the respective group and the results would be collected.

Application Designer: Three application designers will each be requested to develp a separate application for a specific group. Each application designer will be explicitly informed of their target demographic and will be provided with either our model constraints, current best practices, or no supplementary information.

The first application designer will be given no constraints, and will be requested to develop an application to the best of his/her ability. This application will be referred to as the baseline application and will act as the baseline to which the other applications will be compared.

The second application designer will be given a set of constraints based on the w3 accessibility standards. This application will be referred to as the standard application. The third application designer will be given a hybrid set of constraints. These constraints will be based on the w3 accessibility standards, but will also leverage our proposed constraints. This application will be referred to as the hybrid application.

Application Requirements: To ensure consistent results, it is imperative to give each application designer a set of development requirements that are within the same functional domain. This means that each application must have similar functionality, and cannot deviate in terms of its in intended use. It is suggested that these requirements include a technological stack.

Groups: The groups will be separated based on the MVC model (M) definitions of their application. Of the three groups, there will be a single control group, and two test groups. The control group would be given the control application and would act as the baseline, while the second and third groups will be given the standard application and the hybrid application, respectively.

Evaluation of Results: The case study sets out to evaluate the impact that our proposed constraints have on the usability of applications for older adults, as well as the developmental process for application designers.

To evaluate the effectiveness of the applications, it is suggested that the common functionalities of the applications be compiled and then delineated based on whether they were affected by the MVC model (M) constraints. A series of tasks would then be extracted from those functionalities that were affected. These tasks would then be given to the user groups as an evaluation for each group's respective application. The results of these tasks would be evaluated using the following criteria: (1) whether the task was successfully completed, (2) how intuitive the user found the process of interacting with the software, (3) whether there were any notable issues with the application that violated current best practices relating to ageing and HCI.

To determine the developmental impact on the application designers, the development time difference ($d_1 = s - b$) between the baseline application (b) and the standard application (s), and the difference ($d_2 = h - b$) between the baseline application (b) and hybrid application (h) will be compared. Positive numbers indicate that the baseline was completed more quickly than the compliment, where negative numbers indicate the opposite. The difference in time ($t = d_2 - d_1$) relative to the baseline will also be evaluated, with a positive result indicating that it took less time to complete the standard application, and a negative result would indicate that the hybrid application took less time to complete. Additional qualitative results will be gathered and analyzed relating to the process's difficulty, as experienced by the application developers.

While looking at creating a set of model constraints to help improve application usability for older adults, we chose to focus on the MVC model (M) due to the direct relation between the model (M) and view (V). In this relationship, the view (V) displays information to the user while the model (M) encapsulates the information that is displayed; the MVC model (M) represents the data's structure and the view (V) displays this structured data.

5   Conclusions and Future Works

Our research led us to find a number of areas in which the MVC model (M) design had a negative impact on application usability by users. Taking these areas into consideration, we designed a number of MVC model (M) constraints. These constraints included limiting simultaneous content such that MVC models (M) would have five or fewer properties, limiting the number of simultaneously-displayed media elements to two or fewer, limiting the length of input fields to two hundred and fifty characters or fewer, using either text-based or image blurb types as a form of password, and implementing a minimum length of text-passwords to four characters.

While the above constraints are a viable starting point in helping address the needs of older adult users using MVC applications, there were additional outcomes from designing our model constraints. We discovered that well-designed OCL model constraints not only affect the usability of web applications, but also serve as an effective method of communicating HCI best practices to software professionals. While our initial five constraints show that certain issues relating to ageing and HCI can be addressed at the model level, they also show the effectiveness of communicating these issues through OCL model constraints.

Additionally, we will by looking at a methodology of enabling the refactoring of existing models. This would allow user to automatically modify existing models to make them consistent with our constraints and modelling framework.

Finally, our proposed case study serves as a test framework for those who wish to attempt to verify the utility of our constraints. The study provides an outline of steps that can be followed to test the value of our proposed constraints, and how to determine their impact on the application design process.

References

1. Tichy, F.: A catalogue of general-purpose software design patterns. In: Proceedings of the Technology of Object-Oriented Languages and Systems, 1997, TOOLS 23 (1997)
2. Glisky, E.L.: Changes in cognitive function in human aging. In: Riddle, D.R. (ed.) Brain Aging: Models, Methods, and Mechanisms. CRC Press/Taylor & Francis, Boca Raton (2007)
3. Object Management Group, Unified Modeling Language (UML) superstructure, version 2.4.1, formal/2011-08-06. http://www.omg.org/spec/UML/2.4.1/Superstructure2012
4. Object Management Group, Object constraint language, version 2.2. http://omg.org/spec/OCL/2.4/PDF/
5. Kerchner, G.A., Racine, C.A., Hale, S., Wilheim, R., Laluz, V., Miller, B.L., Kramer, J.H.: Cognitive processing speed in older adults: relationship with white matter integrity (2012)
6. Vicki, L.H.: Age and web access: the next generation. In: W4A 2009 Proceedings of the 2009 International Cross-Disciplinary Conference on Web Accessibility (W4A), pp. 7–15 (2009)
7. Cruickshanks, C.J., Wiley, T.L., Tweed, T.S., Klein, B.E.K., Klein, R., Mares-Perfman, J. A., Nondahl, D.M.: Prevalence of hearing loss in older adults in Beaver Dam Wisconsin. Am. J. Epidemiol. **149**(9), 879–886 (1988)
8. West, S.K., Munoz, B., Rubin, G.S., Schein, O.D., Bandeen-Roche, K., Zeger, S., German, S., Fried, L.P.: Function and visual impairment in a population-based study of older adults. The SEE Project. Salisbury Eye Evaluation (1997)
9. Ketchman, C.J., Stelmach, G.E.: Movement control in the older adult. In: Pew, R.W., Van Hemel, S.B. (eds.) National Research Council Steering Committee for the Workshop on Technology for Adaptive Ageing (2004)

10. Nelson, D., Vu, K.L.: Effectiveness of image-based mnemonic techniques for enhancing the memorability and security of user-generated password. Comput. Hum. Behav. **26**, 705–715 (2010)
11. Pilar, D.R., Jaeger, A., Gomes, C.A., Stein, L.M.: Passwords usage and human memory limitations: a survey across age and educational backgrounds (2012)
12. Rational Software Architect, IBM Rational Software (2016). www-03.ibm.com/software/products/en/ratisoftarchfami
13. W3 Accessibility. https://www.w3.org/standards/webdesign/accessibility

Using Smart Glasses for the Inclusion of Hearing-Impaired Warehouse Workers into Their Working Environment

Antti Matthias vom Stein[✉] and Willibald A. Günthner

Institute for Materials Handling, Material Flow, Logistics,
Technische Universität München, Munich, Germany
{vomstein,guenthner}@fml.mw.tum.de

Abstract. Handicapped people have limited access to the job market. The research reported in this paper aims to remedy this deficiency for the target group of hearing-impaired workers in warehouses. We investigate the suitability of a technology called Pick-by-Vision to advance the inclusion of people with hearing disabilities. This technology visually assists an order picker at gathering relevant information to execute his working tasks through the usage of smart glasses, also known as data glasses or head-mounted displays. Apart from the goal of inclusion in working-specific processes, communication barriers between the hearing-impaired and their hearing coworkers should also be reduced to approach an inclusion in the whole working environment. The ongoing research project is application-oriented and therefore accompanied by industrial partners. One of these partners operates a warehouse and already employs several handicapped people that contribute to the research in stages of requirements analysis, system design and evaluation.

Keywords: Smart glasses · Inclusion · Order picking

1 Introduction

In the year 2008, the United Nations Convention on the Rights of Persons with Disabilities [1] came into force. One principle of the Convention is the 'Full and effective participation and inclusion in society' which results amongst others in Article 27 – Work and Employment. This article declares 'the right of persons with disabilities to work, on an equal basis with others'. But still, handicapped people have hindered access to the job market. For instance, in Germany nearly 33,500 mandatory workplaces for severely disabled people have not been filled in the year 2013 [2]. Companies would rather pay countervailing charges than employ handicapped people.

Therefore, workplaces for persons with disabilities have to be created and designed in such a way that these disabilities have diminished or no effect on productivity or just play no role with respect to the working process. We think that, in specific fields of work, appropriate technologies can empower the employment of handicapped workers without decreasing the productivity, being as beneficial as employment of non-impaired people.

In this paper, we focus on hearing-impaired order pickers in warehouses. Due to their hearing impairment, the receiving of auditory information is not possible. The loss of

© Springer International Publishing Switzerland 2016
F.F.-H. Nah and C.-H. Tan (Eds.): HCIBGO 2016, Part II, LNCS 9752, pp. 358–368, 2016.
DOI: 10.1007/978-3-319-39399-5_34

this information channel can impair the work and its quality and also jeopardizes safety when alarm sirens are not heard. As information is needed during order picking, the information must be provided over the visual system. Therefore, we apply a visual technology called Pick-by-Vision that deploys smart glasses. This technology has been introduced by our institute [3]. We now step forward from basic research to a real-life application and design an overall system with regard to inclusion.

2   Order Picking

Order picking is a fundamental process in intralogistics throughout the whole supply chain. It is the upstream process for the supply of customers or production facilities with ordered articles. It is defined as the collocation of specific subsets from a total assortment of goods based on an order [4] (Fig. 1).

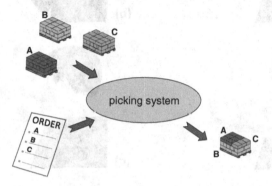

Fig. 1. Schematic representation of order picking

There are both manual and automated order picking systems. Manual order picking systems are very common due to their flexibility; no physical infrastructure has to be built up. Because of low investments, they often are the only alternative for small and medium-sized enterprises. The principle on which they work is called 'Man-to-goods picking', meaning that the order picker moves through the warehouse to each storage location of the ordered articles.

One main part of a manual order picking system is the information system responsible for providing the order information to the picker and vice versa for gathering the status of the order processing. It is mostly embedded in a Warehouse Management System (WMS), which collects the orders and prepares them for the picking process. The main information are the location label, the number of articles to pick and optionally an article designation.

The information system comprises the human-computer interface in order picking, which is realized by different implementations as discussed in the following subchapters.

2.1 Paper List

The simplest implementation of an order picking information system is the paper list (Fig. 2a). The order picker gets all the needed order information from a printed list he has to carry with him. He picks all items listed and usually confirms every pick by marking it off the list. This system is very convenient, as it doesn't use any additional equipment.

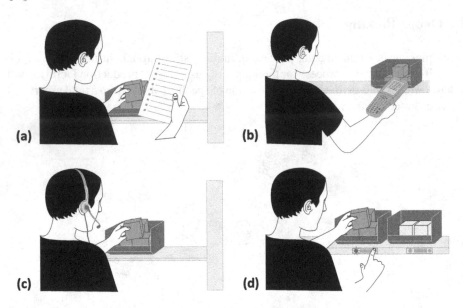

Fig. 2. Order picking information systems: (a) Paper list, (b) Mobile data terminal, (c) Voice picking, (d) Pick-by-Light

Due to human nature, this picking process is error-prone. Positions of an order are skipped or omitted. There is no automated verification if the correct article is picked. Furthermore, the order picker has to handle the list and a pen with the adverse effect that he doesn't have both hands free for the actual activity. Therefore, more sophisticated systems have been established called paperless order picking systems.

2.2 Common Paperless Order Picking

In contrast to the paper list, paperless order picking systems imply a direct interaction between the order picker and the information system. The order picker is directed through the order processing making it impossible to miss an order's position. Each order position or pick has to be confirmed, commonly by the automated identification of an article or its storage location. Identification is an essential operation in order picking and prevents one from picking the wrong article. The error rate is decreased and performance is increased in comparison with the paper list. The identification result also triggers the information system either to show the next order position or, in case of an incorrect pick, to initiate any error process. In addition, identification data enables the WMS to update the warehouse inventory in real-time for accurate inventory management.

There are several paperless order picking systems that differ in the human-computer interaction.

- **Mobile Data Terminal:** A mobile data terminal (MDT, Fig. 2b) contains a display, a code scanning unit and a keyboard. Order information is to be read on the display. The usage of MDTs is very flexible, but a main drawback is the form factor, which is very bulky. When articles are picked, the MDT must be put aside or into a belt holster, which results in a low performance.
- **Voice Picking:** In voice picking systems (Fig. 2c), information is transferred vocally. The order picker wears a headset and order instructions are provided by verbalized prompts. The order picker confirms picks by speaking pre-defined commands and specific confirmation codes of articles or storage locations. As a main advantage, the usage of voice picking systems is fully hands-free.
- **Pick-by-Light:** In Pick-by-Light systems (Fig. 2d) each storage location is equipped with a noticeable light, a button and, in most instances, with a numerical display. The worker picks articles from a highlighted storage location and confirms the pick by pushing its button. Due to the installation of equipment at each storage location, investment costs are very high, while the system offers low flexibility.

2.3 Pick-by-Vision

Pick-by-Vision also belongs to the paperless order picking technologies. Order information is provided by smart glasses in the pickers direct field of vision (Fig. 3). The modality of interaction for confirmation, identification and further data input is not determined. Either the smart glasses or additional devices can be used for interaction. The main benefit is the mobile, but hands-free provision of information. As an advantage over voice picking, the information is provided at once and not sequentially as it is in speech.

Fig. 3. Pick-by-Vision: Smart glasses provide order information in the pickers field of vision

The technology, Pick-by-Vision, has been introduced before by our institute, and various systems with different complexity have been investigated [5, 6]. In comparison with the paper list, order picking performance is increased while the error rate decreases. Mostly due to the oversized form factor of smart glasses so far, it has been rarely applied in industry. Now, smart glasses of the latest generation, along with Google Glass, have smaller dimensions, enabling Pick-by-Vision to be used realistically and productively.

We define Pick-by-Vision as an augmented reality technology in the broader sense because the user's perception of the real-world environment is augmented by computer-assisted information during his working process. It should be noted that the information presentation doesn't inevitably have to be an exact superposition of virtual objects over real-world objects as in other familiar augmented reality systems that we call systems with *congruent* information presentation [7]. In the case of a basic Pick-by-Vision system, order information is presented by texts or pictograms while still being an augmented reality application. In this case, we speak of a *context-sensitive* information presentation since the information is shown in the context of the current working process. There has been research about information systems with congruent information presentation as well [8].

3   Inclusion on the Example of Order Picking

The aim of our research is the inclusion of hearing-impaired workers into the warehouse working environment using the example of order picking. We are going to achieve that on the basis of a technological system. The logistics process, order picking, and the contrary process, replenishment, shape the main use case of our system. First of all, we need to select an appropriate order picking technology. In the next step, we define further use cases that should advantage inclusion.

3.1   Selection of an Order Picking System

The selection of an order picking system always depends on the individual case. In our case, we are looking for a manual order picking system with an appropriate human-computer interface for hearing-impaired workers. Nevertheless, we derive the selection as general as possible.

With respect to profitability, order picking using paper lists and mobile data terminals is quite inefficient. Pick-by-light systems have a high throughput, but can be discarded because of high investment costs and the systems' inflexibility. Especially in our case, the system must cope with a changing inventory structure of paper and office products. Voice picking turned out to be the most beneficial technology with regard to the properties error rate, throughput, investment and flexibility [9, 10]. However, hearing-impaired workers cannot use voice picking systems. That leads to the remaining technology Pick-by-Vision, which we apply in our research.

It should be mentioned that Pick-by-Vision hasn't been developed with the intention of inclusion, though it shows to be a very suitable option in the case of hearing-impaired order pickers. Furthermore, the technology dissolves the incriminating situation for hearing-impaired order pickers of being suspended from their field of activity by the progressing voice picking systems. In that way, Pick-by-Vision also contributes to the prevention of psychological stress. This can be seen in the strong motivation of the hearing-impaired order pickers employed by our industrial research partner.

3.2 Further Use Cases

Beside the pure execution of logistics processes, we expand the system with more functionality regarding inclusion. Two more use cases are defined.

The first relates to the communication between users of the system. A textual call function should be implemented so that a hearing-impaired worker is able to notify coworkers or supervisors even without visual contact. That will be useful when a worker resides in a remote location of the warehouse and needs support.

The second use case incorporates messages in general, related to work, safety and social topics. Work-related messages, for example, inform employees of meetings or disruptions in the materials handling system. Disruptions can also be reported by users to the system. To enhance safety, fire alarms, which cannot be heard by the hearing-impaired, are visualized on the smart glasses in addition to the statutory mounted caution lights. Regarding the third option, messages can also contain social news such as current birthdays, weddings or other events. Hearing-impaired workers told us in discussions that they often miss informal information or the office grapevine. Because workers should not be overloaded with too much information during the work activities, it is contemplated to just send a notification that informal messages have been sent. These messages can be read at a common location like the break room.

Messages are sent from a central instance to all users of the smart glasses. It is up to the internal organization of the company to supervise the messages.

4 System Requirements

We will focus on the main requirements in this paper. It should be considered that the system will be used by both hearing-impaired and non-hearing-impaired workers. The pilot application will be at our industrial research partner, a medium-sized mail order company, who operates a warehouse for all kinds of paper and office products.

4.1 Requirements Due to Hearing Impairment

We found out that there actually are just two major requirements that are caused by the hearing impairment.

- The first important requirement is to consider that the system does not distinguish distinctly between hearing-impaired and non-hearing-impaired users since that would reduce the degree of acceptance among the hearing-impaired.
- The second point regards the human-computer interface. Feedbacks of operating activities should at least be visual or haptic and not only acoustic. For instance,

barcode scanners beep if they have successfully read a code. This feedback could also be realized by a haptic vibration signal.

4.2 Smart Glasses

We concentrate on practical requirements regarding the implementation for a real-life application.

- Due to a strong demand for low costs in the field of logistics, we focus on consumer products rather than military solutions.
- The smart glasses must also be useable for spectacle wearers.
- There are further requirements on the optical properties. A clear view of the real-world environment should be ensured. This involves factors like the position and brightness of the virtual image, contrast of the display and also the size of the frame.
- As described above, the information presentation that we use is context-sensitive. Instructions and information are provided in a textual form or by pictograms. No augmented reality tracking for an accurate superposition of virtual objects over real-world objects is needed. Thus, sensors like a camera or inertial sensors as well as a powerful processor are not crucial.
- Battery should last for a shift.
- This requirement primarily affects the company organization. Investigations showed that prolonged work with smart glasses can have an effect on strain [11]. It is suggested to extend the duration of breaks.

4.3 Identification

The identification process is essential in guaranteeing high quality in order picking. In general, there is either the identification of articles or the identification of storage locations. The identification of articles could be realized with smart glasses since it is possible to hold articles in front of the smart glasses' camera.

Though in our case, many articles are too small for barcode imprints or just don't have a barcode so that their storage locations have to be identified. Imagine the order picker has to pick an article from a storage location at the ground-level of a shelf. The attached barcode of the storage location will also be at ground-level. It is hardly possible to identify this storage location by a smart glasses camera since the order picker cannot lead his head to the barcode without any contorted maneuver. It is much more ergonomic and also much faster to direct a scanning device to a barcode than his head. Furthermore, if there are multiple small storage locations there will also be many identification codes in the camera image, posing the question of which one to choose for identification. Yet another issue is lighting conditions. Smart glasses' camera systems do not emit light for the scanning procedure as it do scanning devices, which therefore deliver more robust results.

Nevertheless, we implemented a barcode scanning app in our smart glasses using the open source ZXing library [12]. We found out that orienting the smart glasses to a barcode by watching the camera's video stream in the smart glasses display is more difficult and time-consuming than just aiming a scanner's reticle to the barcode. The direct optical feedback on the barcode is easier to handle than the indirect video feedback.

In summary, an extra scanning device is indispensable in our case. That potentially seizes a free hand as a drawback. But it also brings the positive side effect that the smart glasses' battery capacity is saved since cameras and image processing algorithms would consume substantial energy.

4.4   Data Input for Special Cases

Only the input of identification data is necessary during the usual order picking process. But there are three situations that require further data input.

- Error handling in the order picking process
- Textual call function
- Notification of a disruption in the materials handling system

To avoid complexity, only predefined entries or requests can be selected. For instance, if the order picker wants to report a disruption, he should be able to choose from a list that enumerates several typical disruptions in the warehouse facilities. No text should be entered. Only in case of an article shortage is a numerical input required to update the virtual inventory of the WMS.

Because data input with smart glasses is often not practical, an additional device can be used. This must be aggregated with the scanning device.

5   System Design

Having set the fundamentals of the overall system, we turn towards the system design. Thereby we center on the hardware that we use for the application. First, we give a short overview of the system architecture.

5.1   System Architecture

The system architecture is illustrated in Fig. 4. The central component is the WMS. It has interfaces to the clients, the Pick-by-Vision system and control terminals, as well as to peripherals, like a fire detector.

5.2   Smart Glasses

We have been working with three different smart glasses so far. These are the well-known Google Glass, the Vuzix M100 and the Sony SmartEyeglass, each having advantages and drawbacks. They represent different types of head-mounted displays (HMD), monocular and binocular as well as optical see-through and non-see-through glasses. The Vuzix M100 embeds a very open Android platform that easily allows one to implement applications and connect external devices, while it wasn't possible to connect a barcode scanner via Bluetooth to the Google Glass. Sony's binocular display enables a

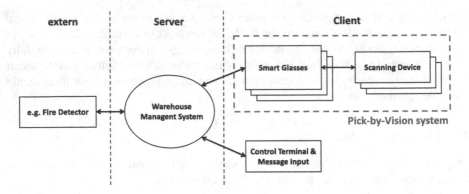

Fig. 4. Overall system architecture including the Pick-by-Vision system. The smart glasses communicate through Wi-Fi with the WMS and through Bluetooth to the scanning device.

very impressive spatial information presentation as if the order information were hovering in the warehouse surroundings.

In a preliminary mock-up, we presented the glasses to our research participants and actual order pickers, both hearing-impaired and non-hearing-impaired. Most of them would prefer the Sony SmartEyeglass. This result must be handled with caution. Actually, it is mostly based on the fact that the Sony glasses, which have a stable frame, are easier to put on. The other two, especially the Vuzix, require some adjustment to fit properly. There are extra frames available for both of them that should be used for practical usage and moreover allow the use of prescription lenses. That in turn isn't possible using the Sony smart glasses without a custom-made mounting that we constructed.

As we haven't found the perfect smart glasses that fulfill all our requirements yet, we will not commit to one choice. The system is openly designed to integrate upcoming smart glasses as well.

5.3 Identification Device

For the identification process, we had to find a way to comply with two opposite require-ments. The Pick-by-Vision system should be preferably hands-free. Otherwise, it is best that an identification device is directed by the users hand toward an identification code. We propose two alternatives, as shown in Fig. 5.

The first solution integrates a scanning device in a glove (Fig. 5a). Scanning is trig-gered by pressing a button at the forefinger with the thumb. Both hands can be used to pick articles. Though the scanning device on top of the glove can get stuck when the order picker grabs articles from narrow shelves. With the second alternative, a mini scanner is affixed to a cord reel that is attached to the order picker (Fig. 5b). This is possible since mini scanners don't weigh much.

Both scanning devices give a tactile feedback when a code has been scanned success-fully. We suggest using imaging scanners instead of laser scanners since they don't have to be directed vertically to codes, which protects the picker's wrist.

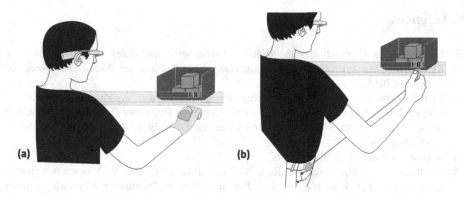

Fig. 5. Proposals for the identification process

To enable complex data input, we chose a mini scanner with four buttons. One button triggers the scan, the three others are programmable and are used to click through a menu (up, down, confirm). In case of the glove, these operations must be done with the smart glasses' interaction options as a third interaction device is not productive.

6   Conclusion and Outlook

We presented a system that allows the inclusion of the hearing-impaired in order picking processes. Pick-by-Vision, with the use of data eyewear, presents itself as a suitable technique for an order picking information system because it dispenses with the use of the auditory information channel. As a drawback, data input is limited with smart glasses, and identification as an essential process in order picking cannot be fulfilled. We give two proposals that enable this human-machine interaction and constrain hands-free working as little as possible.

Based on this system, we implemented additional functionality beside the order picking process that offers benefits to hearing-impaired workers. This will not only advance an inclusion in the specific working process of order picking, but also in the working environment.

In the next step of the project, the enhancement from a mockup to a productive system in cooperation with industrial partners is planned. In productive operation, the system will be analyzed and iteratively improved. Afterwards, the system will be deployed in another warehouse to achieve a more universal application in a heterogeneous application field.

Acknowledgments.   The research project 'Work-by-Inclusion' (01KM141207) is funded through the Project Management Agency DLR in the framework of grants from the equalization fund for inter-regional projects for participation of severely disabled people in working life from the German Federal Ministry of Labour and Social Affairs.

References

1. United Nations. Convention on the Rights of Persons with Disabilities. Web, 8 January 2016
2. REHADAT Statistik. Beschäftigungsstatistik schwerbehinderter Menschen. Web, 24 November 2015
3. Reif, R., Günthner, W.A.: Pick-by-vision: an augmented reality supported picking system. In: 17th International Conference in Central Europe on Computer Graphics, Visualization and Computer Vision, WSCG 2009 - In Co-operation with EUROGRAPHICS, Full Papers Proceedings, pp. 57–64
4. VDI. Richtlinie 3590 Blatt 1 (1994)
5. Günthner, W.A., Blomeyer, N., Reif, R., Schedlbauer, M.: Pick-by-Vision: Augmented Reality unterstützte Kommissionierung. Forschungsbericht, Institute for Materials Handling Material Flow Logistics, Technische Universität München, Garching (2009)
6. Günthner, W.A., Rammelmeier, T.: Vermeidung von Kommissionierfehlern mit Pick-by-Vision. Forschungsbericht. Institute for Materials Handling Material Flow Logistics, Technische Universität München, Garching (2012)
7. Günthner, W.A., Wölfle, M.: Papierlose Produktion und Logistik. Forschungsbericht. Institute for Materials Handling Material Flow Logistics, Technische Universität München, Garching (2011)
8. Schwerdtfeger, B.: Pick-by-vision: bringing hmd-based augmented reality into the warehouse. Dissertation, Technische Universität München (2010)
9. Günthner, W.A.; Lecture Notes. Materials handling and material flow technology. Institute for Materials Handling Material Flow Logistics, Technische Universität München (2015)
10. Arnold, D., Isermann, H., Kuhn, A., Tempelmeier, H., Furmans, K.: Handbuch Logistik. Springer, Berlin (2008)
11. Wille, M., Wischniewski, S., Adolph, L., Theis, S., Grauel, B., Alexander, T.: Prolonged work with head mounted displays. In: ISWC 2014 Adjunct, pp. 143–150 (2014)
12. Open source project ZXing, 25 January 2016. https://zxing.org

Biological, Biomimetic and Sociological Aspects of Human-Robot Interaction in Work Environments

Alexandra Weidemann[✉], Diego Compagna, Manuela Marquardt,
Mirco Martens, and Ivo Boblan

Technische Universität Berlin, Berlin, Germany
a.weidemann@tu-berlin.de

Abstract. Human-robot cooperation in work environments is an upcoming, but still crucial topic in the study of human-robot interaction (HRI). Aspects of work safety are substantial. In many areas where industrial robots are used in the production process, they are separated by security spaces from the workers. Nonetheless, there is an upcoming need for robots taking part in collaborative actions with human workers. For this purpose, the interaction with the robot has to be safe, as well as intuitive and unproblematic. The construction of interactive working robots can learn from different disciplines in order to achieve this goal of successful and convenient human-robot interaction. This article presents insights from biology, biomimetic robotics and sociology regarding perceptual, constructional and interactional issues. Biological aspects help understanding how humans work and allow the transfer of these insights to the construction of robots and human-robot interaction. Abstracting biological principles and transferring them to the construction of robots is the part of biomimetic robotics. A biomimetic approach unfolds a huge potential for the safety issue in HRI. Sociological insights may help evaluating human-robot interactions behind the foil of human-human interactions and contribute important social factors.

Keywords: Human-robot interaction · Physiology · Biomimetic · Sociology · Safety

1 Introduction

Before the 19th century, horses were used for heavy work. Horses have been carrying loads, drawn equipment and were indispensable as livestock in people's lives [2]. With the invention of machines everything changed. The machines could undertake the work of humans and horses gradually, resulting in the reduction of production costs and duration. Consequently, demands could be accomplished more quickly, easily, and cost-effective. In the beginning machines took over transport and handling tasks. With time, machines improved and could perform independent filigree work increasingly, the so-called robot [3, 9, 12, 16, 20, 34].

The history of the robot began with a fiction in a film like in many other technological developments. Nowadays they are becoming increasingly important and have become indispensable in many areas of the working environment. The first industrial robot is a product of the 1960s. Together with George Dovel, Joe Engelberger developed the first

© Springer International Publishing Switzerland 2016
F.F.-H. Nah and C.-H. Tan (Eds.): HCIBGO 2016, Part II, LNCS 9752, pp. 369–379, 2016.
DOI: 10.1007/978-3-319-39399-5_35

of these robots and produced it with the for this purpose especially established company *Unimation* [3, 9, 34]. A new phase of 'Advanced manufacturing' was introduced (in German also called 'Industrial revolution 4.0 [2, 10]). This process is divided into two phases: First, industrial robots were introduced; they were stationary and separated from humans. Now, there are autonomous mobile robots: stationary and mobile robots are working together with humans [21].

Since the 80s, industrial robots are used routinely in the automobile manufacturing. Robots enter everyday life and the world of work. Up to date already 176,000 robots are in use in Germany [10, 17].

Initially, the machines and robots were delimited by cages or other shelters from the human employees, making an interaction rarely possible. Today, machines and robots should be user-friendly and thus the research focuses on a human-centered interaction [16, 18, 20, 36].

The question arises, how a robot must be designed in order to realize a successful and compatible interaction – and to guarantee work safety at the same time.

In this respect, it is worthwhile to consult different disciplines to understand the biological/physiological, psychological and cognitive abilities of people and to take advantage of this knowledge to apply it to the construction of robots (1). In the second section, we will discuss the potential of biomimetic robotics for the issue of work safety (2). A sociologically informed approach may help to evaluate human-robot interactions in contrast to human-human interaction and focus on important social interactional aspects (3). We close the contributions with different disciplinary focuses with some concluding remarks (4).

2   Physiological Abilities of Humans

The window to our world is assisted and in the same time limited by the physiology of our senses. We need the feedback of our environment to discern and interact with it. Through our senses, information in a magnitude of 10^9 bit/s is received; whereas only 10^1–10^2 bit/s are added and processed consciously. The remaining information will be processed subconsciously or strained to be not used. As a comparison, by speaking and motor information, we produce about 10^7 bit/s [28].

Generally, we perceive our world with 5 senses, but concerning human-robot inter-action, vision, touch, and acoustics are especially considered to be important and should therefore be focused in the following. The stimuli of the environment affect the body in various forms of energy, mainly mechanical and electromagnetic waves. There are specific receptors in the sensory organs and each sensory cell has its adequate stimulus which effects a specific sensory impression. The different qualities of a stimulus within one sensory modality (acoustics, vision, touch) can be differenced by quantities like intensity and frequency, e.g. sound or light [11, 24–29].

The optical sense alone contributes about 80 % of the information of the surrounding and thus establishes most of our perception [11].

The light enters the eye on the retina, consisting of rods (10^8) and cones (5×10^6). These special cells convert the photons into electrical signals. These are then transferred via different cells in the retina next to the optic nerve (*Nervus Opticus*). The stimuli are transmitted to the thalamus, where the optic nerves of both eyes intersect, via the visual pathway (*Tractus Opticus*) to the primary cortex where they are processed. This is followed by two different ways, the "What-way" or the "Where-way". The "What-way" leads into the temporal lobe (temporal cortex) via the ventral-temporal brain path. Here, it is processed what the observed object looks like. The dorsal-parietal pathway is the "Where-way" which leads to the parietal lobe. Here is processed where the observed object is in space. The pathway from the eye to the brain requires about 250–350 ms [6, 11, 24–29].

Human have a very small spectrum of vision of 380–780 nm. When exceeding this color range it may result in cognitive impairment or even in an eye injury [11, 29].

In terms of vision, a proper and pleasant color choice is important for an easy interaction, in order to make the worker feel comfortable.

Haptic perception is generally performed via the largest human organ, the skin – and especially via the hands. Here mechanical stimuli are received by 4 different receptors. The receptors are located at different depths in the skin and perceive various types of haptic stimuli. The so-called Merkel cells record details of a touched object, for example a bottle, and the specific pressure, and Meissner's corpuscles are responsible for grip detection. These two receptor types are sporadically spread on the index and middle fingers, but also on the thumb, and irregularly distributed on the palm of the hand. The slightly deeper Ruffini corpuscles record the stretching of the skin and the penetration depth of objects on the skin. Ruffini's corpuscles are represented in the center of the hand and at a large area on the index, middle and ring fingers. For the perception of vibrations, the Pacinian corpuscles are responsible, which are the lowest in the skin. They are mainly located on the middle finger and on the outer palm [6, 11, 24–29].

The receptors of the skin pass the information via the spinal cord and the thalamus to the cerebrum. This area is specifically constructed. The various parts of the body are displayed differently in size on the somatosensory area. The higher the density of receptors of a body region, the more accurate and lager the part of the body is mapped in the brain. This is represented by the so-called homunculus [11, 25, 27]. There are two somatosensory gyri. The somatosensory region is mainly responsible for touch, pressure, joint position and reflects, and contains and processes four full maps of the body surface. The second somatosensory area receives bilateral information of the body and is important for the differentiation of size and nature of objects [29]. In addition, the region information transfers from one hand to the other. The reaction time is about 80–150 ms [11].

Haptics are important for human well-being and humans respond to tactile stimuli promptly. Therefore, handles, switches, and pads should be designed so that they, for example, appeal to the relevant hand areas. This should be in accordance with the appropriate receptors and thus give the human the required feedback from the robot.

In acoustic perception, sound waves pitch the ear cups, then are reflected repeatedly and pass through the external auditory canal to the eardrum. This is deflected and transfers the energy through the malleus, anvil and stapes to the inner ear. The sound signal arrives at the water-filled interior of the *Scala vestibuli*. About the oval window, the vibrations of the ossicles are transferred to the atrial transition. The movements of the perilymph are then passed over the Helicotrema to the *Scala tympani* and eventually to the round window. The entirety of these movements leads to deflection of the basilar membrane and the tectorial membrane. This causes the inclination of the stereovilli to the hair cells. This will open ion channels and the membrane voltage changes. The hair cells innervate fibers of the auditory nerve (*Nervus cochlearis*) which enters the CNS and passes to *Nuclei cochleares*. Over the thalamus, the information is transferred to the auditory cortex. The basilar membrane has special areas where it can perform best. Those special areas respond to certain sound frequencies. This structure is also found in the auditory cortex. Thus, certain frequencies are processed there easiest. The reaction time is about 100–150 ms. A human hears between 20 and 20,000 hertz [6, 11, 24–29]. If this threshold is exceeded there is a decrease in the ability to concentrate and also a feeling of uncertainty. Therefore, in order for a human to feel comfortable and sounds to be heard clearly, a suitable frequency and intensity of a tone should be selected.

The use of the comfort zones leads to the best recording and cognitive capabilities in humans and enables a simple and intuitive interaction with robots.

Perception is in principle indirect, meaning the stimulus information is passed to the appropriate areas of the brain via the thalamus as a hub, thus filtering the amount and distributing the information.

The specific regions decode the previously encoded information from the sensory organs, distinguish the information and communicate with each other. The composition and conscious reconstruction of information gives us an overall picture. A human being is confronted with a lot of information that cannot be recorded and processed. The selection of information passed is of utter importance and already begins in the sensory organs. Additionally, filtering processes occur in further certain regions of the brain [24, 25, 27, 29].

Remarkably, individual perception fractions can be shifted by brain on the timeline, which in turn collects perception performances and fills gaps in perception. The brain has to manipulate our perception of time in the performance for continuous, gapless perception. Perception is also a memorizing process, storing patterns of perception, and depends on our attention [11].

The question that rises is how can a human being, due to its biological and cognitive abilities, interact intuitively and modestly?

Given the biological role-model, and its failsafe operation, as an outline for biomimetic developments, it is necessary to consider the processes of perception and its application, to exploit the comfort zone of people for optimal interactions. Consequently, robotic developments are driven by the ideal of compatibility of human and robot perception. Robotic perception works with sensors that shall be able to receive the same information and to solve all the different tasks humans are able to perform. The information is then processed via adaptive artificial intelligence. The sensors absorb signals and transfer them to the robot's controller. Sensors are available for a variety of measurements in a variety of forms of changes in the environment [3, 20]. The sensors of the robot can principally detect even a wider range of stimuli than the physiological senses of nature. But they are restricted by the progress of artificial consciousness and processing. The "brain" of the robot would be faced with the task to reconstruct images from the jumble of lines, shadows, and flitting spots of colors that are documented by cameras and microphones [7, 19, 38]. A vast challenge is progressing robotic hands that handle a variety of tasks as human hands do, in terms of the tactile sense. The options for detection are much more complex than in the physiology of a human. In case of humans, millions of years of evolution and adaption led to a filtering process, which would remain to be solved by the engineers and programmers for the development of robot haptic [19, 34, 38].

Therefore, to follow a biomimetic approach, we should consider the following question: How can a robot act accordingly and adapt to a human being to achieve a simple and convenient interaction?

Biological models establish new application possibilities in the field of robotics, especially in the biomimetic robotics.

3   Biomimetic for Security at Work

Biomimetic is defined according to the VDI guidelines as follows:

"Biomimetic combine biology and technology with the goal of solving technical problems through the abstraction, transfer, and application of knowledge gained in interdisciplinary cooperation from biological models" [31 Part 1].

In the course of 3.8 billion years' biological structures have improved. There is a huge pool of ideas from biology that are available for the solution of technical problems [31, 32].

Biomimetic are technological developments inspired by nature. They usually pass through several stages of abstraction and the modification of biological starting points.

The knowledge about the analysis of living systems can be used to create new inventions and innovations and transfer them to technical systems.

The application of research and development approaches is of interest for technical applications [31].

Applying biomimetic aspects to the development of robots is advantageous. Biomimetic robots are "robots that possess an implementation of at least one dominant biological principle and are usually developed based on the biomimetic development process" [32 Part 1].

The source of the benefits gained from the use of biomimetic robots can come from inherent physical properties as well as from a biomimetic-based "behavior".

Biomimetic robot systems are powerful and fast. In the past, the development of robots was always lead by an increase of positioning accuracy and motion speed. To achieve these improvements, it was necessary to use heavy and stiff structures coupled with non-back-drivable transmission mechanisms. These robots were optimized to work fast, accurate and self-sufficient in a well-defined and constrained environment. In addition, all working steps have to be predefined and highly repeatable [30].

For fully automated work and production steps, these kinds of robots might be the best solution. But in fact the industry is now shifting towards automated production of small batch, customized and short-life-cycle products [31]. Therefore, industrial workspaces and tasks can change very fast and a human user becomes more and more important, because only humans are able to understand changing situations and problems correctly. Due to this, a collaboration of human workers and a robot is often the only solution [17, 22].

The upcoming need of a safe and human-friendly coexistence in a shared workspace of a human and a robot leads to a new set of requirements a robot has to fulfill. The robot should have an understanding of the unstructured environments, especially of human demands [1, 22].

However, they can only be used for human-robot interaction when implementing further measures.

In respect to the positive and useful aspects that a robot implicates, humans should still pay attention to the safety when dealing with robots. Above all, this is important because robots are now working increasingly without cages or other shelters, hence directly with the workers at a workstation [3, 17, 20, 34].

The reorganization and changes of properties of the robot would reduce the risk of a human-robot interaction without protective screens. This would come hand in hand with savings in terms of space, time, and investment costs [32]. Humans should have the opportunity to push the robot away in an instance and/or to be able to push a button to escape a dangerous situation.

The robot cannot judge how far his act endangers humans. Therefore, the consequences in case of errors are very high and it is not yet completely clarified who bears the fault on failures or accidents [17].

Important topics of today's robot research are features like light weight design and passive (inherent) and active (controlled) compliance [1].

The use of controlled dissipation would cause less injuries and damage during an impact than a comparable rigid system. In the case of bruises and anxiety, certain softness (passive flexibility or elasticity) in the kinematic chain (hand-arm system) would help to facilitate the self-liberation.

With the help of these properties, a biomimetic robot can be designed that is "safer" than a comparable rigid industrial robot [32].

The more biological principles are combined in a biometric robot, the more one can guess that the robot approaches its biological model in its properties and its behavior [32].

This shows that an intuitive use and an adaptive behavior of the robot are of high priority and are beneficial for further human-robot interactions. This could ensure that a human can interact simpler and by reflexes according to situation. Furthermore, the robot could judge a situation and the surroundings due to certain settings of the situation and thus interact and react adequately [17].

All persons involved in the operation, such as the operator, maintenance personnel, and programmers must be familiar with the operating and maintenance instructions of the machines and robots. This can be ensured through training. However, these may not contain all the safety measures in detail which are necessary for the protection of personnel in the workplace. The security can be considered only on a defined machine, a particular process and on an existing environment [17, 34].

The protection of personnel can be subdivided into the following categories [17]:

- Safety during construction and commissioning
- Safety during operation
- Safety during programming
- Safety during the monitoring and maintenance
- Safety in the handling of e.g. student projects

The more intuitive an interaction is performed, the more it will be regarded as successful by humans. Humans should keep their sense of sovereignty over the robot and should not subordinate [8, 17].

Furthermore, it should be noted that the working majority is afraid of losing their jobs by robots. But will robots replace us in all work matters? Absolutely not!

The world of work is changing and deforming as it already has changed the last few centuries. The market is dependent on many factors and all companies must remain economically competitive (worldwide) [3, 17]. Thus, it seems inevitable that humans work together with robots. It could be possible that some work will be completely over-taken by robots. But this re-opens new work fields, for example in the development and research of those robots which need to be re-occupied by humans. With the rapid process of technology, the demand for workers increases [16, 19, 21, 36].

4 Sociological Aspects for Human-Robot Interaction at Work

From a sociological point of view, it is of paramount importance to consider the basic patterns of interaction within human-human interaction (HHI) for the design of a safe human-robot interaction (HRI) in work environments. Several studies in the field of HRI are leading to the assumption that the gaze of the robot is crucial for the assess-ment of the interaction and has a significant impact on a positive process in performing a cooperative task [23, 37, 38]. Even if a "point of interaction" – embodied as a face with eyes – is completely irrelevant for the function of a robot within work environments, it could be nonetheless vital for a healthy, cognitive exon-erative and insofar in total safe HRI design. To understand the key factors, that are defining the HRI as sound and superior to developments focusing on mere function-ality, it is insightful to take the HHI as a reference. Even if the implementation of HRI deviates from the standards of HHI, we claim that the orientation towards HHI is the key for the design of a proper and human-centered configuration of HRI. To achieve these goals, we are proposing a conceptual framework based on some basic sociolog-ical assumptions in regard to the main factors that are characterizing interaction among humans. The framework should be able to identify the crucial features for a successful interaction and by doing so also increase the acceptance of the workers to willingly engage themselves in HRI.

The main focus of the proposed evaluation framework is to address two key questions related to a successful and pleasant interaction between humans and robots: First, which are the dominant factors that determine whether the interaction is fluid and smooth. Second, to which extent do humans prefer an interaction model with a strong orientation towards conventional interaction experiences among humans – or do they rather prefer an interaction experience similar to typical human-machine interactions? As we already stated in a recent published paper [40], a useful instrument to gain fruitful answers to these questions is the instrument "Breaching Experiments" which was developed by Garfinkel [12] to estimate the strategies that are adopted by humans to achieve a successful interaction between at least two humans. The main categories to describe the HRI at stake in all socially relevant dimensions are taken by a model introduced by

Burghart and Haeussling [5] and further developed by Burghart and Steinfeld [4]. They developed a HRI scheme operating on four levels that is built relying on basic aspects of interaction among humans, although further adapted for the study of HRI. The different levels include the Interaction Context, the Interaction/Co-operation, the Activity of Actors and non-verbal Actions and Emotions. While the scheme is just a systematically ordered pool of elementary criteria (from simple to complex, from mechanistic to cognitive elaborate, from functional to emotional) for analyzing and evaluating HRI, the presented method, which will be further elaborated in the upcoming months within the scope of a FabLab environment, is presenting instruments to empirically measure and determine the relevance of each criteria defined in the model.

Besides "Breaching Experiments" as the core instrument to study empirically the HRI by taking into consideration the scheme proposed by Burghardt and Häussling to estimate the quality of the interaction, the theoretical background is mainly defined by Erving Goffman's "Frame Analysis" [15] within his work on "Microstudies on Social Interaction" [13, 14]. The baseline is the assumption that every social interaction is depicted by situated (i.e. contextual dependent) expectations and the way how these expectations are held stable over a relatively long lasting period of time (relying on Goffman) and which mechanisms are used – resp. among the interacting entities commonly established as viable – to negotiate an alignment of the expected expectations on both sides (relying on Garfinkel).

In the past decade scholars dedicated to the study of social robots started to analyze the HRI from a holistic point of view, focusing more and more on the interaction experience [e.g. 35]. These insights should be transferred to HRI in work environments insofar as both the interface and the cooperation between worker and machines – resp. robots – are becoming significantly more interactive. Main overall outcomes of HRI focusing on the interaction experience are the insights, that the HRI situation is dominated far more by agency issues than anthropomorphism. Likewise, that the HRI is unique and could not be totally analogized with the interaction situation among humans, however it could be described using similar instruments resp. methods. Another main finding seems to be the relevance of the context and the situated perspectives of the entities involved in the HRI.

The mentioned insights could be in equal measure described and further analyzed adopting the proposed method based on Garfinkel's "Breaching Experiments" (in light of Goffman's "Frame Analysis"). The method is always taking into consideration the specific situatedness related to the successful performance of a social interaction between two entities, due to the fact that it is operating always within the culturally shaped margins of what is seen as a functioning interaction. When adopting the method to deliver fruitful findings related to the main criteria for a proper HRI in work environments – as a very specific socially shaped domain of Human-Machine cooperation – the relevance of the context and the situated perspective of the involved entities is always taken into consideration as an essential component of the basic assumptions the method is relying on. The aim of carrying out HRI experiments within the scope of sociological theories, concepts and methods is to analyze the interaction regardless of the peculiarity as a situation that is taking place within a social environment. The orientation towards the study and understandings of HHI is leading to a holistic assertion of the HRI, especially according to safety issues in work environments. Without considering the factors that are crucial for a successful inter-action respectively cooperation among humans, it will turn out impossible to design a safe interaction between humans and robots. Within the scope of very functional cooperation settings, without several interaction sequences, other factors may be of more importance and characteristics of HHI are less important and can be neglected. When developing robots for more intense exchange with humans, that in turn are making more negotiations between them indispensable, the – in part less by function-ality characterized – aspects that are defining HHI are becoming more important.

"Breaching Experiments" are highly suitable to determine what humans do expect from the robot while engaged in an interaction sequence with it, and to what extent they are willing to repair the breach – i.e. they are willing to give the robot a second chance even if its action does not fit the expectations. To conclude the remarks related to the relevance of a sociological perspective for the development of safe HRI in work envi-ronments – applied for instance to the above stated importance of the gaze of the robot as a socially expected key factor, one may induce breaching experiments to find out if the robot's gaze has a positive impact on the interaction compared to robots without a gaze. One may find out that the robot's gaze is beneficial for the cognitive load, the stress level and the overall assertion of the situation, even if the robot is not always working as expected. In this regard it is important to bear in mind that the more the situation between robots and humans could be described as a social interaction, the more it will be affected by expectation flaws and the execution of repairing strategies e.g. negotia-tions about how to deal with an unexpected course of the interaction or outcome.

5 Conclusion

To conclude, different disciplinary perspectives can contribute important aspects regarding the safety and intuitiveness of human-robot interaction in work environments. Knowing about the physiological constitution of the human may help designing human-robot interaction in work contexts, taking into account the specific strengths of humans (e.g. complex perception, response capacities, adaption and improvisation) and robots (e.g. strength, speed, consistency) in order to achieve a successful cooperation.

With the knowledge about the physiology and the comfort zones of the human, cognitive abilities can be optimally utilized and in the light of a biomimetic approach, these insights can be abstracted to technological parameters and implemented in the construction of biomimetic robots. For an intuitive interaction, social aspects become crucial. Robots working with humans should be able to adapt to the behaviour of the human and orientate themselves in complex working environments. For the acceptance of robots, understanding and using certain social cues may be of paramount importance. Sociological concepts may help evaluating the interaction of humans and robots in contrast to human-human interaction.

Acknowledgments. The Research presented in this paper was primarily supported by the German Ministry of Education and Research.

References

1. Albu-Schaffer, A., Eiberger, O., Grebenstein, M., Haddadin, S., Ott, C., Wimbock, T., Wolf, S., Hirzinger, F.: Soft robotics. IEEE Robot. Autom. Mag. 15(3), 20–30 (2008)
2. Ammann, T.: Industrie 4.0: von Menschen und Pferden, Stern, 10 September 2015, 14:26 Uhr (2015). http://www.stern.de/digital/thomas-ammann/wird-der-mensch-durch-die-industrie-4-0-als-arbeitskraft-ueberfluessig–6443432.html
3. Brooks, R.: Menschmaschinen-wie uns die Zukunftstechnologien neu erschaffen; campus, S. 85–105, 129–142, 151–164 (2002)
4. Burghart, C., Aaron, S.: Workshop on Metrics for Human-Robot Interaction. In: Workshop Proceedings, School of Computer Science - University of Hertfordshire, Amsterdam, 15 March 2008
5. Burghart, C., Roger, H.: Evaluation criteria for human robot interaction. In: Proceedings of the Symposium on Robot Companions: Hard Problems and Open Challenges in Robot-Human Interaction, pp. 23–31 (2005)
6. Carter, R., Aldridge, S., Page, M., Parker, S.: The Human Brain Book. Dorling Kindersley Limited, London (2009). s. 76–93, 100–102
7. Clausen, P., Korndörfer, V., Scharff, R.: Computer und Roboter, Was ist was? Band 37, 40–44 (1999)
8. De Greff, J., Belpaeme, T.: Why robots should be social: enhancing machine learning through social human-robot interaction. PLOS One 10, e0138061 (2015)
9. Flannigan, C.: Robots at Work-SwRi-developed technologies are guiding the future of automation in industry. Technical Today, pp. 14–17 (2013)
10. Franke, M.: Industrie 4.0- Mein Arbeitskollege, der Roboter, arbeits-abc.de (2015). http://arbeits-abc.de/industrie-4-0-mein-arbeitskollege-der-roboter/. Accessed Nov 2015
11. Frings und Müller: Biologie der Sinne-Vom Molekül zur Wahrnehmung, s. 4–6, 119–188, 190–226, 250–268, 281–326. Springer Spektrum, Heidelberg (2014)
12. Garfinkel, H.: Studies in Ethnomethodology. Polity Press, Cambridge (1967)
13. Goffman, E.: Interaction Ritual: Essays on Face-to-Face Behavior. Anchor Books, New York (1967)
14. Goffman, E.: Relations in Public: Microstudies of the Public Order. Basic Books, New York (1971)
15. Goffman, E.: Frame Analysis. Harper & Row, New York (1974)
16. Graetz, G.: Robots at Work (2015)
17. Hesse, S., Malisa, V., et al.: Robotik, Montage, Handhabung; Fachbuchverlag Leipzig im Carl Hanser Verlag, S. 13–15, 25–29, 229–241, 257–375 (2012)
18. Khatib, O., Yokoi, K., Brock, O., Chang, K., Casal, A.: Robots in human environments (2001)
19. Klempert, O.: Auch Roboter schärfen langsam ihre Wahrnehmung, Die Welt, 18 May 2009. http://www.welt.de/wirtschaft/webwelt/article3754869/Auch-Roboter-schaerfen-langsam-ihre-Wahrnehmung.html. Accessed Nov 2015
20. Knoll, A., Christaller, T.: Robotik. Fischer-Verlag, Frankfurt am Main (2004). S. 5–16, 31–33, 60–62
21. Missala, T.: Paradigms and safety requirements for a new generation of workplace equipment. Int. J. Occup. Saf. Ergon. (JOSE) 20(2), 249–256 (2014)
22. Mizanoor Rahman, S.M., Member, IEEE: A novel variable impedance compact compliant series elastic actuator for human-friendly soft robotics applications. In: IEEE RO-MAN: The 21st IEEE International Symposium on Robot and Human Interactive Communication, 9–13 September, Paris, France (2012)

23. Moon, A., Troniak, D.M., Gleeson, B., Pan, M.K.X.J., Zheng, M., Blumer, B.A., MacLean, K., Croft, E.A.: Meet me where I'm gazing: how shared attention gaze affects human-robot handover timing. In: Proceedings of the 2014 ACM/IEEE International Conference on Human-Robot Interaction, pp. 334–341. ACM (2014)

24. Richard, D., Chevalet, P., Soubaya, T.: Biologie in Farbtafeln. Springer Spektrum, Heidelberg (2013). s.155–164, 170–174

25. Schmidt, S.: Neuro- und Sinnesphysiologie, 5. Auflage. Springer, Heidelberg, S. 182–228, 243–311 (2006)

26. Schmidt, T., et al.: Einführung in die Physiologie des Menschen, 17. Auflage. Springer, Heidelberg, pp. 178–287 (1976)

27. Schmidt, T., Lang, F.: Physiologie des Menschen, 28. Auflage. Springer, Heidelberg, S. 273–294, 295–316, 334–356, 367–407 (2000)

28. Silbernagl und Despopoulos: Taschenatlas Physiologie, 7. Auflage, Thieme, S. 314–319, 350–377 (2007)

29. Thomson, R.F., et al.: Das Gehirn - Von der Nervenzelle zur Verhaltenssteuerung, 3. Auflage. Spektrum Verlag, s. 239–285 (2011)

30. Tsagarakis, N.G., Laffranchi, M., Vanderborght, B., Caldwell, D.G.: A compact soft actuator unit for small scale human friendly robots. In: Proceedings of 2009 IEEE International Conference on Robotics and Automation, pp.4356–4362 (2009)

31. VDI: VDI Guideline 6220, Part 1: Biomimetics – Conception and Strategy. Differences between Biomimetic and Conventional Methods/Products. Verein Deutscher Ingenieure e.V., Düsseldorf (2012)

32. VDI: VDI Guideline 6222, Part 1: Biomimetics – Biomimetic Robots. Verein Deutscher Ingenieure e.V., Düsseldorf (2013)

33. Wassink, M., Carloni, R., Stramigioli, S.: Port-Hamiltonian analysis of a novel robotic finger concept for minimal actuation variable impedance grasping. In: Proceedings of 2010 IEEE International Conference on Robotics and Automation, pp. 771–776 (2010)

34. Weymayr, C., Ritter, H.: Roboter-Was unsere Helfer von morgen heute schon können, Bloomsbury Kinderbücher&Jugendbücher, S. 37, 49–54, 64–99, 136–153 (2011)

35. Young, J.E., Sung, J.Y., Voida, A., Sharlin, E., Igarashi, T., Christensen, H.I., Grinter, R.E.: Evaluating human-robot interaction. Int. J. Soc. Rob. 3(1), 53–67 (2011)

36. Zanchettin, A.M., Bascetta, L., Rocco, P.: Acceptability of robotic manipulators in shared working environments through human-like redundancy resolution. Appl. Ergon. 44, 982–989 (2013)

37. Zheng, M., Moon, A., Gleeson, B., Troniak, D.M., Pan, M.K.X.J., Blumer, B.A., Meng, M.Q.H., Croft, E.A.: Human behavioural responses to robot head gaze during robot-to-human handovers. In: Proceedings of the 2014 IEEE International Conference on Robotics and Biomimetics. IEEE, Bali (2014)

38. Zheng, M., Moon, A., Croft, E.A., Meng, M.Q.-H.: Impacts of robot head gaze on robot-to-human handovers. Int. J. Soc. Robot. 7, 1–16 (2015)

39. Zielke, J., Neumayer, I.: Künstliche Intelligenz und Wahrnehmung, planet wissen, 23 July 2014. http://www.planet-wissen.de/technik/computer_und_roboter/kuenstliche_intelligenz/pwiekuenstlicheintelligenzundwahrnehmung100.html. Accessed November 2015

40. Compagna, D., Boblan, I.: Case-sensitive methods for evaluating HRI from a sociological point of view. In: Tapus, A., André, E., Martin, J.-C., Ferland, F., Ammi, M. (eds.) ICSR 2015. LNCS, vol. 9388, pp. 155–163. Springer, Heidelberg (2015). doi: 10.1007/978-3-319-25554-5_16

Where Is Siri? The Accessibility Design Challenges for Enterprise Touchscreen Interfaces

Shuang Xu[1(✉)], Chester Cornelio[1], and Marisa Gianfortune[2]

[1] Lexmark International, Inc., Lexington, KY, USA
{shxu, ccorneli}@lexmark.com
[2] Cornell University, Ithaca, NY, USA
mng35@cornell.edu

Abstract. Accessibility design on office products is essential to providing independence and equal employment for people with all abilities. In this paper, we reported findings from a usability evaluation with 12 blind users on the keyboard navigation and voice guidance designs on a Lexmark multifunctional printer. Results of this study indicated that visually impaired users were confused by a number of issues associated with the current design. They expected mature accessibility solutions such as VoiceOver and Siri on the touchscreen devices in workplaces. Design recommendations were proposed to address the usability concerns identified in this study. However, to improve accessibility designs on enterprise products, user experience designers still need to overcome challenges such as supporting users with different disabilities and to cope with constraints from development cost and schedules.

Keywords: Blind users · Smartphones · Touchscreens · Accessibility · Printers · Voice guidance · Keyboard navigation

1 Introduction

The inaccessibility of today's office equipment has been a main factor to the high unemployment rate among people who are visually impaired. With tactile controls being replaced by touchscreens on office devices such as printers, scanners, fax machines, phones, and more, it poses significant challenges for visually impaired employees to remain independent and efficient in their workplaces [1].

Research investigations in the last decade have developed various accessibility solutions for touchscreen mobile devices. For instance, VoiceOver on Apple iOS devices is a well adopted assistive tool for blind users to access information and stay connected. Americans with Disabilities Act provides policies to improve the support for accessibility accommodations in workplaces. Section 508 of the Rehabilitation Act requires that agencies must ensure that all members of the public access and use of the data and information developed, procured, maintained, by the Federal Government.

Despite these efforts, the percentage of workers with disabilities in the US has declined in recent years [2]. As some researchers point out, people with disabilities are often concerned of drawing negative social attention [3], therefore hesitate to request

© Springer International Publishing Switzerland 2016
F.F.-H. Nah and C.-H. Tan (Eds.): HCIBGO 2016, Part II, LNCS 9752, pp. 380–392, 2016.
DOI: 10.1007/978-3-319-39399-5_36

help in workplaces [1]. On the other hand, mainstream accessibility solutions can be costly and are less likely to be used on enterprise products. As Burton and Huffman concluded after their investigation of the accessibility of multifunctional printers, keeping office environment accessible for employees of all abilities is challenging.

In this paper, we report findings from a usability evaluation of the keyboard navigation and voice guidance designs on a high end multifunctional printer. The printer has a touchscreen display, running on an open-source User Interface (UI) infrastructure[1]. By attaching a QWERTY keyboard to the printer and following the voice guidance from the embedded speaker, visually impaired users can navigate and complete printing tasks on their own. The keyboard navigation also benefits users with motor disability, to whom gesture-based navigation is very difficult, if not impossible.

Twelve (12) participants were recruited via a local non-profit blind community for the usability evaluation. Each participant went through predefined task scenarios. Participants' performance data, subjective ratings, and their qualitative comments were gathered in this evaluation. Results from this study uncover a number of usability concerns of the current design, as discussed in Sect. 5. In the end of this paper, we pointed out the remaining challenges for designing assistive interactions on enterprise products. Accessible office devices and working environments are essential to provide equal employment opportunities and independence for people of disabilities. By sharing what was learned from this investigation, we hope to draw more attention to the inclusive designs on enterprise products.

2 Literature Review

In 2013, cell phone ownership in the United States reached 91 % in adults [4]. Approximately 69.6 % of legally blind participants in a WebAIM survey reported use of VoiceOver by Apple as their primary mobile screen reader [5]. VoiceOver features synthetic voice readouts of elements of a page that allow users to navigate interfaces by gesturing to select or move. Screen readers such as VoiceOver work primarily by treating graphical layouts as a linear interface [6]. A linear interface presents the elements on the screen as items in a list, and users can jump from one list to another to find items they are searching for. Gestures on VoiceOver work by allowing users to move up and down a list, select an item, or exit the current list [7]. With the addition of Siri to Apple devices, many blind users can talk to their devices without having to memorize gestures or steps. Apple's inclusive designs nicely match blind users' mental models, which makes them the leader in accessibility solutions on mobile devices.

In 2014, the blind community within the United States reached numbers of 7.3 million [8]. Employment rates for blind Americans remains staggeringly low, with only 40.2 % employed in 2013 [2]. With the number of employed being so small, the importance of making the workplace blind-accessible is apparent. This increase of screen-based technology in the office creates the most problems for disabled employees at a reported 42.6 % of total workplace problems [1]. Visually impaired workers often

---

[1] For legal reasons, Lexmark Inc. cannot reveal the name of the UI infrastructure provider.

require extra software, such as screen readers, to complete tasks. Screen reader software may create distractions, cost more, and have bugs [1].

For many offices, the multifunction printers are the most frequently used and important pieces of office equipment because of the great span of tasks they can accomplish [9]. In the past, copiers and printers were easily accessible to visually impaired users because of the tactile hard buttons that made up their interface [10]. With the passing of the 508 Accessibility Laws, many multi-function printers have become more accessible [11]. However, most accessibility solutions for enterprise products have had relied on open-source technological solutions, because up until the Fall of 2014, Apple had kept many of its products from other business development [12]. In 2015, Apple has increased its enterprise partners of 40 % [13].

Enterprise software has had some success in accessibility design for multi-function printers. For example, Canon's Voice Guidance Kit allows users to attach a speaker to the side of the machine for voice readouts. Even with these accessibility features on printers, many advanced functions remain inaccessible to the blind user. Computer software must often be combined with external screen readers to fill in for slow or undocumented parts of the accessibility software as in Samsung's SmarThru. Synthetic readouts may only cover certain functions or have missing graphical readouts [14]. Within an office setting, there are still numerous challenges for workers with disabilities even when accommodations are made [1].

3 Accessibility Design

3.1 Keyboard Navigation

To address these challenges, a team of interaction designers, usability researchers, and accessibility specialists embarked the accessibility design enhancement on Lexmark products. Keyboard navigation allows a user to move the focus on the screen to explore the available functions, with the TAB key or the four Arrow keys (up, down, left, right). TAB navigation follows a predefined sequential path, where a user can click on TAB key to move forward to the next item and click on TAB + SHIFT keys to go backwards. In our design, the TAB navigation was defined as a Z-path to match users' eye-flow, as shown in Fig. 1. The TAB navigation loops from the last stop to the first stop on the screen.

The navigation with Arrow keys followed the native open source UI behavior:

- UP: navigates to the closest UI component above the current focus,
- DOWN: navigates to the closest UI component below the current focus,
- LEFT: navigates to the closest UI component on the left, and
- RIGHT: navigates to the closest UI component on the right.

Enter key is used for selection once the target is in focus, while the ESC key is used to exit without saving changes or go back to the previous screen.

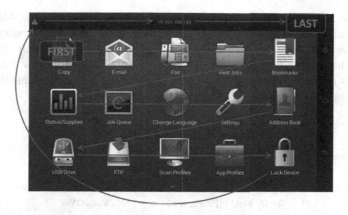

Fig. 1. TAB navigation on the Home screen

3.2   Voice Guidance

The voice guidance prompts (i.e., the instructions read when a component is in focus) followed the format defined by the native interface. Additional information was added to specify how to make a selection or change the value. Figure 2 lists some GUI components and their voice guidance designs.

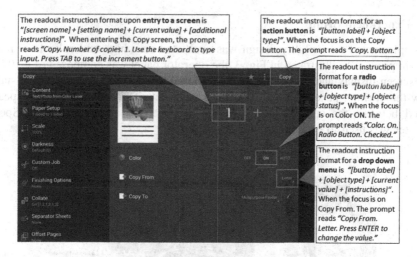

Fig. 2. Examples of voice guidance design on the copy landing screen

4   Usability Evaluation

4.1   Participants

Twelve 12 (6 legally blind and 6 totally blind) people participated in the evaluation. All participants were recruited from a non-profit organization in a Midwest city in the

United States. The recruitment had a controlled balance in participants' vision status ("totally blind" refers to *no vision* and "legally blind" refers to *a central visual acuity of 20/200 or less in the better eye with the best possible correction*). Participants were required to have some touchscreen experience, but not necessary to be familiar with certain types of touchscreen device. We were not able to find participants that did not use iOS mobile devices (see demographics info. in Table 1).

Table 1. Participant demographics.

Participant	Gender	Age	Vision status	Touchscreen experience	Assistive tools
P1	M	68	Totally blind	iPhone	VoiceOver, JAWS
P2	F	58	Legally blind	iPhone, iPad	ZOOM
P3	F	44	Totally blind	iPhone, iPad	VoiceOVer
P4	M	30	Totally blind	iPhone	VoiceOver, JAWS
P5	F	48	Legally blind	iPad	Portable CCTV
P6	F	68	Legally blind	iPhone, iPad	N/A
P7	F	57	Totally blind	iPhone	VoiceOver
P8	M	40	Totally blind	iPhone, iPad	VoiceOver(Mac), JAWS(PC)
P9	M	56	Legally blind	iPhone	VoiceOver, Ease of Access
P10	M	68	Legally blind	iPhone	VoiceOver, MagicLite
P11	F	48	Legally blind	iPhone, iPad	VoiceOver, Siri, ZoomText
P12	M	69	Totally blind	iPhone	VoiceOver, Siri, JAWS

4.2 Experiment Setup

The implemented accessibility design was evaluated on a high-end color laser multi-function printer. As illustrated in Fig. 3, the operator panel was composed of a 10 inch touchscreen display and a num-pad. An additional QWERTY keyboard was installed below the operator panel. The voice prompts were output from the embedded speaker located between the operator panel and the keyboard. A Nuance Text-To-Speech vocalizer was used to generate the voice readout.

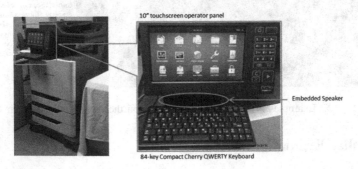

Fig. 3. Devices used in the evaluation

4.3   Procedure

In the beginning of each session, the participant was given a brief introduction of the purpose of this study. We then collected their feedback on the default settings.

Next, the participant was given a set of tasks that represented typical printer usage in workplaces. These task scenarios included:

- Look for functions and icons on the Home Screen
- Check current status of paper tray and toner cartridge
- Make a copy with required settings
- Log in with username and password
- Find details about an error message
- Change menu settings of the printer

The assigned tasks were arranged to let the participant navigate through multiple screens, experience different screen layouts, and interact with various GUI control components. Participants were encouraged to think out loud of their confusion or comments during each task to help us identify areas of success or usability concerns.

The following measures were gathered for each task to examine participant's performance and perception of the current design:

- *Task completion time.* (Measured in seconds.)
- *Task success rate.* (Success/failure ratio of all participants on one task.)
- *Ratings on ease of use.* (On a 7-point Likert Scale: 1 = Difficult, 7 = Easy.)
- *Ratings on satisfaction.* (On a 7-point Likert Scale: 1 = Dissatisfied, 7 = Satisfied)
- *Post-task comments.*

5   Results and Discussion

5.1   Findings

Table 2 reports the overall success rates across all tasks. Although most participants were able to complete the assigned tasks, many of them struggled when navigating on the Copy Screen to change settings, trying to locate the notification center on the Home Screen, and looking for detailed instructions of an error message.

Table 2. Task success rates

	Home screen	Status of supplies	Error message	Login screen	Copy screen	Menu settings
All	83.33 %	86.21 %	85.00 %	93.55 %	82.72 %	100.00 %
Totally Blind	83.33 %	85.71 %	75.00 %	100.00 %	68.29 %	100.00 %
Legally Blind	83.33 %	86.67 %	91.67 %	88.89 %	95.00 %	100.00 %

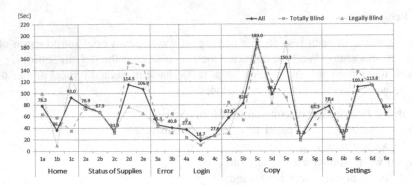

Fig. 4. Task completion time

To identify the paint points in each task, we examined the completion time of the sub-level scenarios (data of failed tasks was removed). Figure 4 shows that participants, especially the totally blind participants, had difficulties in the following areas:

- Task 5c (189 s) and Task 5e (150 s), where they were asked to navigate from the Copy landing screen to the left menu and find an option to change the copy setting.
- Task 2d (115 s) and Task 2e (106 s), where they were asked to find the tray settings in Status of Supplies and make changes to paper type and paper size.
- Task 6c (110 s) and Task 6d (114 s), where they were asked to change settings on a checkbox option list that was embedded in an accordion menu.

Participants' perception was collected after each task. Their subjective ratings on ease of use and satisfaction (see Table 3) confirmed the usability concerns mentioned above. In addition, participants reported low satisfaction on the error message design.

5.2   Discussions

Keyboard Navigation

Arrow Navigation. One of the major pain points in the navigation design was on the Copy Screen. As mentioned in Sect. 3.1, arrow navigation followed the native open source UI behavior. Users were allowed to use Arrow keys to go in or out of a setting

Table 3. Subjective ratings on Ease of Use and Satisfaction.

		Home screen	Status of supplies	Error message	Login screen	Copy Screen	Menu settings
Ease of Use 1: very difficult 7: very easy	All	5.33	4.75	5.50	6.36	4.92	5.50
	Totally blind	5.33	4.83	6.00	6.60	5.17	6.67
	Legally blind	5.33	4.67	5.17	6.17	4.67	4.80
Satisfaction 1: dissatisfied 7: satisfied	All	6.00	5.38	5.20	6.73	5.33	6.13
	Totally blind	6.00	5.17	6.00	6.80	5.67	7.00
	Legally blind	6.00	5.58	4.67	6.67	5.00	5.60

group freely, following the visual layout of the GUI components. Figure 5 shows the Arrow key behavior on the Copy screen. Totally blind participants were disoriented on this screen because "the arrow keys were jumpy". For example, clicking the DOWN arrow from the Copy Number took the user to Color Off button, but clicking the UP arrow from there took the user to the copy number Increment button. To make it more confusing, the left menu is a scrollable list, which means clicking LEFT arrow from the Copy From button or Copy To button could take the user to different options on the left menu depending on the current scroll position of the list. While this arrow navigation might help users with low vision or motor disability, totally blind users expected a hierarchical navigation where a setting that has multiple options is treated as one stop in the navigation flow.

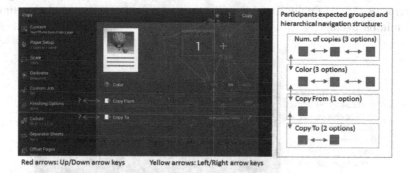

Red arrows: Up/Down arrow keys   Yellow arrows: Left/Right arrow keys

Fig. 5. ARROW navigation on the Copy screen vs. users' expectation

Unexpected Layout. Usability concerns also arose in areas where the standard GUI controls were customized for a better visualization. E.g., the Copy Scale presets were designed to make the 6 options more visible to sight users (see Fig. 6). When using the arrow keys to navigate these options, 6 of 12 participants were confused by this 2×3 layout as they expected a simple vertical or horizontal list of options.

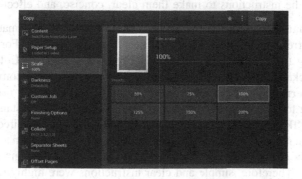

Fig. 6. Copy scale settings

Voice Guidance

Long and Unprioritized Prompts. In this evaluation, we noticed that most participants tended to decide whether they had found the target based on the first few words of the voice prompt. For examples, the voice prompt for Notification Center was "*10.199.108.143. Press Enter to open the Notification Center.*" As many participants did not understand what an IP address was, they navigated away before hearing the key information they were looking for. On the Copy Screen, the TAB navigation followed the numbered sequence as shown in Fig. 7. Because the native UI design did not support TAB navigation into the left menu, at the first menu option (stop #8) the user was expected to use the UP and DOWN arrow keys to browse other options. Most participants navigated away after they heard "*Content. Text/Photo from color laser.*" After missing the target multiple times and feeling stuck in a looped navigation, 7 participants (58 %) finally found the Copy settings, with a task completion time of over 3 min on average.

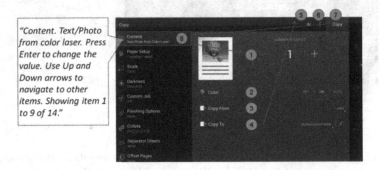

Fig. 7. TAB navigation on the Copy screen

Confusing Prompts. Confined by the native UI infrastructure, the voice prompt design followed a fixed syntax. This proved to be a main concern as it greatly limited how we could structure the instructions to make them clear, concise, and effective.

- **Fixed format.** The prompt of GUI controls used the format as "[setting name] + [current highlighted item] + [object type] + [status]". For example, the Color setting (OFF/ON/AUTO) shown in Fig. 7 was read as "Color. On. Radio button. Checked." Such syntax made voice prompts difficult to comprehend.
- **Technical terminology.** Some technical jargons and acronyms used in prompts were foreign to participants and therefore confused them. For instances, "Edit box (textbox)", "IP address", "Cyan", and "IR (Intervention Required)". Trying to memorize the navigation path and functions available on the screen at the same time is cognitively demanding, any additional workload could downgrade blind users' performance. Therefore, simple and clear instructions were highly desired.

Other Issues

Entry to Accessibility Mode was not intuitive. Based on their current touchscreen experiences, all 12 participants expected to use gestures to start the accessibility mode. It did not occur to anyone that they should long-press the hard button number 5 (which has a tactile cue for easy discovery), as required by the current design.

Reading is too slow. The Text-to-Speech speed was fixed at 160 words per minute. Participants would like to have the reading speed adjustable to satisfy their needs as first-time users, and as power users once they were familiar with the interface. This finding affirms what was reported in our previous accessibility research [15].

Inconsistent key behaviors. "Information Sent to Lexmark" setting was a checklist option menu embedded in an accordion menu (see Fig. 8). To go to the selections, the user clicks on ENTER to expand the collapsed menu, then TAB to navigate to the option, and use ENTER again to select the option. Participants found this confusing and suggested using a different key, such the Spacebar, for secondary selections. In the example of the Slider control, using LEFT/RIGHT keys will decrease/increase the setting value and also save it automatically. When interacting with the slider control, 8 participants were confused if they should press ENTER to confirm the selection as they did on other screens. A few legally blind participants were unsure how to go to the left menu after the value was set as pressing LEFT key would decrease the value.

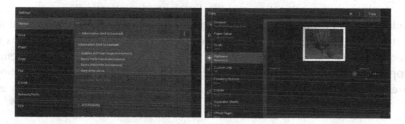

Fig. 8. Mixed use of TAB and ENTER keys (left) and slider control for Copy darkness (right)

Inconvenient Data Entry. Most participants had no problem in entering data. However, they did not realize that they had to erase the current value before keying in the new data. When the new entry was appended to the existing value and triggered an error message for "invalid entry", 4 participants were confused. Some suggested having a type-over design to avoid such confusion and inconvenience.

Need Details in Trouble-Shooting Instructions. Due to safety concerns, we did not want to encourage blind users to remove paper jams or replace supplies on their own. In this study, 5 participants expressed that they wanted more details than a generic error message of "Printer requires attention." Blind users preferred to be informed so that they could decide if they needed help or would fix simple errors on their own.

5.3   Design Recommendations

We recommended the following changes to enhance keyboard navigation and voice guidance designs on Lexmark enterprise printers.

- **Support gesture initiation of accessibility mode.** Entering accessibility mode via gestures better meets users' expectation.
- **Support replay/pause/resume of voice guidance.** First-time users may need to listen to the prompts more than once. It is necessary to provide dedicated keys to allow users to replay or pause/resume the prompt easily.
- **Support adjustable readout speed.** Depending on their levels of experience, working environments and preferences, users will have various needs for the readout speed. Screen readers should offer an easy way to adjust the readout speed.
- **Prioritize key information.** Keeping the important information in the beginning of the prompt will allow users to navigate more accurately and quickly.
- **Clarify submit actions.** Some actions are irreversible on shared enterprise printers, such as "Send email, Print, or Delete a file, etc." Indication of such actions needs to be clear in the prompt to allow blind users to make informed decisions.
- **Group options within the same setting.** Grouping options for each setting in voice guidance can help blind users understand the hierarchical relations of the GUI elements and keep a linear navigation path among different groups.
- **Ensure consistent navigation-selection paradigm.** Consistent controls can help blind users quickly develop skills to navigate and select. E.g., using the TAB/Arrow keys exclusively for navigation and the Enter key for selection.
- **Avoid overloading control keys.** Using the same control key to support different functions is confusing. Consider other keys for designated purposes. It helps users associate a function with a specific key and make it easy to learn and remember.
- **Support type-over for user entry**. When a soft num-pad or keyboard appears, the current value should be highlighted to allow it to be overridden by the new entry.

5.4   Remaining Challenges

While we are working with the development teams to address the usability concerns identified in this study, a few design challenges remain unresolved:

Firstly, iPhones and iPads have been the mainstream touchscreen mobile devices used by people with visual impairments. Linear navigation design via VoiceOver and gesture interaction is well accepted by blind users and becomes their expectation of accessibility design. But using these mass market solutions can greatly increase the cost of production. Thus, enterprise products often lack mature assistive technologies as compared to what is available on consumer products.

Secondly, to ensure that blind users are oriented when navigating on touchscreens, it is necessary to transform a planar layout of the Graphic User Interface (GUI) into a linear or hierarchical structure. The auditory representation of such structure should convey the logical relationship among the GUI elements. However, in development environment where resources are limited and schedules are pressing, it is difficult for product management to prioritize the additional efforts needed to overcome the technical limitations inherited from the native UI infrastructure.

Finally, office products are often shared by multiple users. It is very hard to design a "one size fit all" solution that supports users with different disabilities. E.g., in the current design, arrow keys navigation better facilitated users with low vision or motor disabilities but confused totally blind users as it was impossible to predict or memorize where the "jumpy" arrow keys would take them to. Log-in based personalization can be the future direction to support various preferences on enterprise products.

6 Conclusions

In this paper, we reported findings from a usability evaluation of the keyboard navigation and voice guidance designs on a Lexmark multifunctional printer. Our observation indicated that mainstream accessibility solutions on iOS touchscreen devices have been commonly adopted by visually impaired users. When interacting with enterprise products such as printers, users expected similar experience as how they used VoiceOver or Siri on their personal devices. It was frustrating for the first-time users to unlearn what they had been used to, and quickly adapt to a new accessibility tool.

We proposed a number of design recommendations to alleviate the usability concerns identified in this study. For inclusive designs on enterprise products, unfortunately, user experience researchers and interaction designers will continue facing challenges such as supporting users with different disabilities, as well as pressures from development cost and product release schedule.

Improving accessibility designs on office products is critical to ensure that people with disabilities can have equal access to employment and stay independent. By sharing what we have learned through this research journey, we hope to see future investment in this area for technological solutions to the challenges we confront today.

References

1. Branham, S., Kane, S.: The invisible work of accessibility: how blind employees manage accessibility in mixed-ability workplaces. In: ASSETS 2015, pp. 163–171. ACM Press, New York (2015)
2. Disability Status Report. https://www.disabilitystatistics.org
3. Jokisuu, E., McKenna, M., Smith, A.W., Day, P.: Improving touchscreen accessibility in self-service technology. In: Antona, M., Stephanidis, C. (eds.) UAHCI 2015. LNCS, vol. 9176, pp. 103–113. Springer, Heidelberg (2015)
4. Cellphone Ownership Hits 91 % of Adults. http://www.pewresearch.org/fact-tank/2013/06/06/cell-phone-ownership-hits-91-of-adults/
5. Screen Reader User Survey #6 Results. http://webaim.org/projects/screenreadersurvey6/
6. Kocieliński, D., Brzostek-Pawlowska, J.: Linear interface for graphical interface of touch-screen: a pilot study on improving accessibility of the android-based mobile devices. In: MobileHCI 2013, pp. 546–551. ACM Press, New York (2013)
7. Apple VoiceOver Guide. https://www.apple.com/voiceover/info/guide/

8. Blindness Statistics. https://nfb.org/blindness-statistics
9. Can You Make Me Some Copies, Please? https://www.afb.org/afbpress/pub.asp?DocID=aw070206
10. Huffman, L., Uslan, M., Burton, D., Eghtesadi, C.: A study of multifunctional document centers that are accessible to people who are visually impaired. J. Visual Impairment and Blindness **103**(4), 223–229 (2009)
11. Accessing the Machine: Two Solutions for Using Large Multifunctional Copy Machines. https://www.afb.org/afbpress/pub.asp?DocID=aw070408
12. Apple's Enterprise Push will Depend on More than Just Hardwar. http://www.zdnetcom/article/apples-enterprise-push-will-depend-on-more-than-just-hardware/
13. Tim Cook: Apple's Sales to businesses Grew 40 % this Year, to $25 Billion. http://www.businessinsider.com/apple-ceo-tim-cook-says-enterprise-is-a-major-growth-vector-2015-10
14. Man versus Machine: A Review of Multifunctional Desktop Copiers. https://www.afb.org/afbpress/pub.asp?DocID=aw070310
15. Xu, S.: Improving accessibility design on touchscreens. In: Antona, M., Stephanidis, C. (eds.) UAHCI 2015. LNCS, vol. 9176, pp. 161–173. Springer, Heidelberg (2015)

Mobile Applications and Services

Evaluation Approaches for HCI Related Aspects of Occupational Safety Regulations Exemplified by Mobile Hotel Booking Applications

Richard A. Bretschneider(✉)

Hotel Reservation Service, Cologne, Germany
richard.bretschneider@gmail.com

Abstract. The popularity of smartphones led to a rising and still increasing amount of mobile hotel bookings through applications like Booking.com, Expedia or HRS. Usually these kind of applications allow the users to book the amount of hotel rooms, the amount of nights and amenities needed for a stay in a hotel. Compared to classical travel bureaus or bookings made on stationary desktop computers, apps offer a higher degree of flexibility and personalization as they are not primary designed for the planning stage of a trip. Mobile apps also make it possible to change initial aspects of the booking on the trip or to give the traveler personal real-time information regarding the trip. Business travelers often are obliged to use certain applications their company defined in their travel regulations. Therefore this paper aims at defining the requirements of occupational safety regulations in this kind of applications.

Keywords: Occupational safety · User experience · Travel · Context · Hotel booking · Mobile

1 Introduction

Booking.com, Expedia or HRS are companies selling hotel rooms online. Usually these kind of applications allow the users to book the amount of hotel rooms, the amount of nights and amenities needed for a stay in a hotel. Compared to classical travel bureaus or bookings made on stationary desktop computers, apps offer a higher degree of flexibility and personalization as they are not solely used at the planning stage of a trip. Mobile apps make it possible to change initial aspects of the booking or to give the traveler personal real-time information regarding the trip. Business travelers often are obliged to use certain applications their company defined in their travel regulations. Therefore the question arises if these applications have to meet the requirements of occupational safety regulations like other business software does. In our research we focus on two aspects of occupational safety:

1. Human factors and ergonomics of mobile apps
2. Travel- and risk-management

F.F.-H. Nah and C.-H. Tan (Eds.): HCIBGO 2016, Part II, LNCS 9752, pp. 395–402, 2016.
DOI: 10.1007/978-3-319-39399-5_37

For the human factors and ergonomics part we analyze the typical tasks business travelers have to fulfill to achieve their trips and what role hotel booking apps play in these tasks. Furthermore we critically evaluate if current German health protection laws provide sufficient regulations to fulfill the needs of business travelers working with small screens (smartphones). In a second step we explore the main factors and categories of a companies occupational safety measures on business trips. The goal is to develop a set of evaluation approaches to pursue the question if hotel booking apps can (partly) be used as a substitute for classical travel- and risk-management in future research.

2   Human Factors and Ergonomics on Mobile Small Screen Devices

The German ordinance on occupational safety and health protection during work with visual displays (Bildschirmarbeitsverordnung - BildscharbV) [1] sets a juristic framework for workplaces and software used in occupational environments. Furthermore the BildscharbV regulates standards on stationary desktop work places but says little about aspects regarding mobile devices. As Kohn and Stamm [6] point out the BildscharbV still is valid on mobile working places except the following aspects:

- Inclinable Keyboard (limited)
- Variable arrangement of the work equipment (limited)
- Desk, chair, footrest, copy holder (not always possible)
- Sufficient space, light, windows, etc.

These aspects apply mostly to tasks done over a longer period of time whereas our scope of interest – hotel booking apps- usually are being used occasionally. Kohn and Bretschneider-Hagemes also mention that in todays environments of remote work (which also includes working with screens while on business trips) also psychological stress needs to take into consideration regarding a holistic view on occupational safety [3]. They also constitute the term 'mobile computer-assisted work' as any location-independent work assisted by computers. For software design that takes aspects of Human-Computer-Interaction into account especially four sections of the BildscharbV have to be considered:

21.1 The software must be adapted to the tasks to be done
21.2 The systems must give information about the dialogue flow to the user immediately or on request
21.3 The users must be able to influence the dialogue flow of the systems. Possible errors must be explained and the user needs to have the possibility to correct them with a limited amount of work.
21.4 It must be possible to adapt the software to the knowledge and experience of the users regarding to the tasks to be done.

In this paper, we present a study as part of a larger research agenda that aims at understanding the influence of mobile hotel booking applications on business travelers regarding aspects of occupational safety and how they influence the user experience. The aim is to analyze the users needs and the external influences in the various and changing usage contexts and to develop a set of evaluation approaches for mobile applications and devices respecting current regulations and norms.

3   Mobile Hotel Booking Apps

Mobile hotel booking apps are software products developed for smartphones, tablets and/or smartwatches that can access central reservation systems (CRS) to make transactions related to room bookings in hotels. A CRS for hotel bookings does typically include the following functionality:

- Check amount of rooms(-types) available
- Display rates for rooms in a dedicated time frame
- Allow the user to make a reservation
- Explain conditions
- Describe amenities and generic hotel information

Well known developers of such systems are for instance Booking.com, Expedia or HRS (Fig. 1).

Fig. 1. Examples of hotel booking apps Expedia, Booking.com and HRS

3.1   CRS System

Schulz describes that the hotel booking business as part of the tourism industry is a system that can be modeled by dividing it into three groups of actors [9] (Fig. 2):

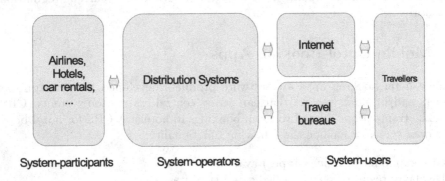

Fig. 2. Hotel business model by Schulz [9]

1. **System-participants.** These are mostly hotels, airlines or car rentals. Also tour operators, trains, buses etc. are part of this group. The participants hold the objects of interest (e.g. hotel rooms, flights, . . .) the users are interested in to obtain.
2. **System-operators.** Operators take over the communication part between participants and users. They have the task to distribute and inform about the various products of the different participants. Hotel booking app services are located in this group.
3. **System-users.** Users are travelers / end-customers on the one hand but also travel bureaus on the other hand.

Before the rising popularity of the internet it was more common to rely on intermediaries like travel bureaus or other services with access to system-operators. Through the emerging booking app offers travelers now have a lot of opportunities to reach out for system-operators or system-participants directly.

4   Occupational Safety on Business Trips

Workers on business trips need to have the ability to make short-term decisions, to plan under difficult circumstances and to orientate in a flexible way [10]. The German law obligates employers to take responsibility for a safe work environment that ensures the workers health and life at work [2]. This applies to work environments like offices or factories as well to security issues on business trips.

4.1 Travel- and Risk-management

Employers can conclude a travel insurance but this only reduces their risk of liability. Furthermore it is necessary to act preventative regarding their employee's safety. Therefore companies have to take care of travel- and risk-management which typically consists of the following tasks [4]:

– Document the current location (Hotel, conference venue, ...) of each employee on a business trip
– Save the employee's contact data (phone number, email, ...)
– Access to current risk profiles of the destinations for business trips / give the information to the travelers if needed
– React in case of emergency and crisis

Especially in large companies with a lot of business travelers in different countries this can become highly complex. The important information about the travel destination's security is multifaceted [4]:

– Security situation (climatic situation, crime, ...)
– Security organizations (police, military, ...)
– Up-coming events (elections, holidays, ...)
– Safety reports (traffic situation, rescue services, ...)

The companies have to ensure their employee's on business trips have access to these information. Especially when security situations change while on a business trip these recentnesses need to be communicated to the travelers who are concerned. Hotel booking apps usually save the travelers residence and the time of arrival and departure which is the main necessary contextual data needed to make statements about the current travel- and risk-situation. Our further research aims to answer the question if hotel booking apps therefore are an appropriate medium for two main cases:

1. For travelers informing themselves about current risks at their intended residence of their business trip
2. If this way of communicating the risks is sufficient to take responsibility for a safe work environment that ensures the workers health and life regarding §618 Bundesgesetzbuch (BGB)[1]

4.2 Phases of Business Trips

When Business trips typically can be divided into several phases:

– Planning stage before the trip
– On the way to the destination
– While the trip Preparing the return trip
– The return journey
– Post-trip

---
[1] Paragraph of the German statute book for the regulation of workers health and life.

A special focus has to be given the factor that situations might change and have an impact on the trip. For instance the plane/train to the destination might be delayed so that the traveler arrives after the latest possible check-in time. Another typical change to the initial travel plan while already on the trip is the amount of nights the traveler stays at the hotel. And also the traveler might get ill, neither able to continue to work nor able to start the back journey.

5   Evaluation of Occupational Safety Aspects in Mobile Hotel Booking Apps

Regarding BildscharbV 21.1 the term 'tasks to be done' in the context of hotel booking for business travel needs to be defined and clarified, taking the different contexts into account. The superordinate target 'book a hotel' needs to be narrowed down to several sub-requirements to make it possible to compare prices, distances or amenities and to meet individual regulations for travel expenses and invoices. BildscharbV 21.3 mentions 'possible errors' that need to be explained with the possibility to correct them. These errors can either be caused by the system, the environment or the user. It is to be defined which errors are important in the different context where travel apps are being used and how the quality of explanations and possible ways to correct them can be evaluated. As a consequence of the changing contexts and influences due to the mobility of smartphone usage scenarios, standards which have been developed for the regulation of stationary desktop work places are not sufficient anymore. Aspects like – to name only a few- ambient light, ambient noise or distance between worker and monitor can not be regulated and standardized in a mobile context as it is possible in an office with stationary hardware [6].

5.1   Evaluation Approaches for Software Products

We understand software as a term covering different communicative patterns [8]. In the study we examine which characteristics of those patterns are relevant to evaluation of occupational safety and health protection and the criteria by which they are assessed. The advantages and drawbacks of evaluation approaches from the disciplines of cognitive psychology, informatics and communication sciences need to be taken into account. Its also important to take the users reactions to the changing contexts into account which might lead e.g. to orientation change of the device, switching to a different device or choosing a different way of holding or positioning the device [5,7].

5.2   A Survey on Device Usage on Business Trips

We now have pointed out connections and intersections between standards in HCI, the German BildscharbV, characteristics of the usage of mobile handheld devices on business trips and employers travel- and risk-management. Also categories for the evaluation of occupational safety and mobile handheld devices have been discussed. To gain insights on the relationship of both topics our first step in a longer research agenda will be an online survey examining the behavior of business travelers regarding the usage of mobile hotel booking apps.

Scope of the Survey. This survey will investigate the usage of computational devices before and while business trips and occupational safety aspects that employees experienced on their trips. It is of high interest for our study to find possible correlations between job title / position, travel frequency and occupational safety concerns that already occurred. Also our goal is to investigate what typically causes business travelers to change their initial travel plans and how helpful computational devices, either stationary or mobile, were to solve these situations. Furthermore we set a focus on an overview on the employer's existing security tools and travel policies to gain knowledge how employee's use them and how much they know about them. The aim of this study is to gather a first set of insights to develop further research projects in the intersection of hotel booking apps and occupational safety. Regarding the use of mobile booking apps our main focus of interest is which devices are important for different types of business travelers at the various stages of their trips.

Survey Questions

1. Demographics
    (a) Age
    (b) Nationality
    (c) Gender
    (d) Education
2. Job
    (a) Job title / position
    (b) Organization type
    (c) Number of employees
3. Business travel
    (a) Travel frequency
    (b) Devices used at different stages of the trip
    (c) How often does the travel plan change?
    (d) Variation of travel destinations
    (e) Familiarity with travel destinations
4. Occupational safety
    (a) Concerns causing anxiety on business trips
    (b) Company's travel policy
    (c) Company's security tools
    (d) Security tools not offered by the company

Further Research. We expect that our survey will give us important hints on the context in which mobile hotel booking apps are being used. Furthermore it could be seen as a foundation for developing guidelines for hotel booking apps for business travelers based on the BildschArb. Also through the investigations about unplanned changes to the travel plans we will gain information about how employers can use this kind of apps to fulfill the requirements of the travel- and risk-management. Depending on our research outcomes further research could include usertests with existing applications and/or prototypes. This could lead towards more insights about the usefulness of hotel booking apps in special contexts such as specific concerns causing anxiety on business trips. Also it could deepen the knowledge about how these kind of applications could be optimized for the contexts and situations related to occupational safety.

References

1. Verordnung über sicherheit und gesundheitsschutz bei der arbeit an bildschirmgeräten (bildschirmarbeitsverordnung - bildscharbv) (1996)
2. Paragraph 618 pflicht zu schutzmaßnahmen bürgerliches gesetzbuch (bgb) (2008)
3. Bretschneider-Hagemes, M., Kohn, M.: Ganzheitlicher arbeitsschutz bei mobiler it-gestützter arbeit. Mobile Arbeit - Gute Arbeit? Arbeitsqualität und Gestaltungsansätze bei mobiler Arbeit, pp. 33–52 (2010)
4. Diedenhofen, T.: Fürsorgepflicht des arbeitgebers bei dienstreisen (2008). Accessed 17 February 2016
5. Hoober, S., Shank, P.: Making mlearning usable: how we use mobile devices (2014). Accessed 30 November 2015
6. Kohn, M., Stamm, R.: Ist die bildschirmarbeitsverordnung noch zeitgemäß? - ansätze zur einer regelung des betrieblichen arbeitsschutzes für mobile it-gestützte arbeitsformen. Arbeit, Beschäftigungsfähigkeit und Produktivität im 21. Jahrhundert. Bericht zum 55. Kongress der Gesellschaft für Arbeitswissenschaft, pp. 565–568 (2009)
7. Loi, D.: Do people want touch on laptop screens? (2012). Accessed 30 November 2015
8. Sandig, B.: Formen des Bewertens. Anabasis, Krakau (2003)
9. Schulz, A.: Informationsmanagement im Tourismus: E-Tourismus: Prozesse und Systeme (2010)
10. Vogl, G.: Mobile arbeit und dienstreisen. Mobile Arbeit - Gute Arbeit? Arbeitsqualität und Gestaltungsansätze bei mobiler Arbeit, pp. 135–146 (2010)

Distracted Driving: Scientific Basis for Risk Assessments of Driver's Workplaces

Benno Gross[✉], Sylwia Birska, Michael Bretschneider-Hagemes, and Endri Kerluku

Institute for Occupational Safety and Health, Sankt Augustin, Germany
benno.gross@dguv.de

Abstract. At professional driver's workplaces, mobile devices are used as telematics applications for information exchange between dispatchers and drivers. In addition to the wide-ranging benefits, it nevertheless emerges potential for new risks, such as distracting drivers. The present study is based on conditions encountered in an existing company in the passenger transport sector and is part of a consultation of the Institute for Occupational Safety and Health, Germany to support the implementation of a risk assessment regarding the applied telematics software. In order to analyze the impact on driving performance and visual processing of the used telematics application, the study employed two driving simulation sessions (LCT, rFactor 1) and one eye-tracking session. Results indicated that the examined application may be considered tolerable in terms of the AAM criteria for In-Vehicle Information and Communication Systems.

Keywords: Distraction · Risk assessment · Professional drivers · In-vehicle information systems

1 Introduction

Mobile information and communications technology is being used as equipment in many different areas in the work environment. Due to the comprehensive availability of mobile internet and the networking of information systems, the importance of traditional location-based activities is increasingly replaced by time-efficient, flexible and location-independent "mobile work".

In all fields of professional driver's workplaces such as road haulage or mobile services, telematics applications on mobile devices have become more or less the standard on German roads. Using these devices, dispatchers communicate their schedules and assignment plans, drivers process them on the move, queries are answered, and route changes are operated.

In addition to technical safety issues, e.g. crash safety and restricted visibility, particularly due to the widespread use of retrofitted devices, a new quality of risk has arisen due to the distraction of the driver while using mobile applications on the road. As professional driver's work is already marked by considerable deadline pressure and a high degree of flexibility, the operation of such devices on the road also entails considerable extra demand [1].

© Springer International Publishing Switzerland 2016
F.F.-H. Nah and C.-H. Tan (Eds.): HCIBGO 2016, Part II, LNCS 9752, pp. 403–411, 2016.
DOI: 10.1007/978-3-319-39399-5_38

2   Leading Question

Employers are obliged to ascertain the workplace-related hazard potential, to define the measures required to protect the health and safety of employees in a risk assessment and ensure the implementation of such measures. For the use of mobile information and communications technology as equipment at work employers have to provide optimal devices and usable software, have to adopt work organizational measures and appropriately train their personnel to exclude to potential hazards.

The present study is based on conditions encountered in an existing company and is part of a consultation to support the implementation of a risk assessment. As subject of investigation the telematics application from the passenger transport sector was chosen. The company operates a limousine service and uses an in-house developed software solution on a mobile device for communication between dispatchers, customers and drivers. In the framework of the consultation, the following aspects regarding the reduction of potential hazards were considered particularly relevant:

- Equipment inside the vehicle must comply with the standards of the ECE regulations R 21 [2]. Therefore, all devices must not create any additional risk due to their crash behavior. The devices must not have a sharp edge radius and shall not be positioned in the head area in the airbag inflation zones. Therefore, additional testing (e.g. crash test) by a certified vehicle inspection company is recommended.
- Equipment inside the vehicle must not cause visual obstruction within the meaning of §35b of the German Road Traffic Licensing Regulations (Straßenverkehrs-Zulassungs-Ordnung, StVZO) [3].
- The software must be designed according to the guidelines of the European Statement of Principles on the Design of Human-Machine Interaction (ESoP) [4]. Due to the effects of the interface design on the task load, additional testing is recommended.

In addition to the above issues, the aspect of distraction caused by using telematics on the road can become a major thread to the health and safety of professional drivers.

The operation of the used telematics application has a high degree of automation (automatic transfer of customer information, route guidance, etc.). Therefore, the only use while driving is a confirmation of incoming messages. All subsequent operations are carried out in the parked vehicle.

The purpose of the present study was to further explore whether the deployed telematics application used by the company (hereinafter referred to as test app) can be regarded as tolerable by the AAM criteria for In-Vehicle Information and Communication Systems [5].

3   Hypotheses

Hypothesis 1: The impact of the test app on driving performance is not higher than that of a scientifically recognized reference task.

Hypothesis 2: The test app meets the AAM criteria for In- Vehicle Information and Communication Systems regarding glance behavior.

4 Methods and Materials

For the combined assessment of cognitive, visual and motor distraction, two different driving simulation softwares (LCT, rFactor 1), each with two different groups of participants, were being employed.

In both sessions, the test persons were confronted while driving (primary task) with two distraction tasks (secondary tasks): Manual radio tuning (hereinafter referred to as radio app) and confirming a job assignment in the test app. According to the AAM criteria, radio channel changing may be regarded as a tolerable reference demand due to the use of telematics applications while driving. If the distraction demand of a typical telematics application task is evidently within this range, its use is currently considered acceptable.

In addition, the assessment of glances is conducted in a driving simulation setting with eye- tracking. The single glance durations, and total glance time required for task completion of the test app were analyzed based on absolute criteria by the AAM. Consequently, an application may be considered tolerable, if 85 % of the sample does not exceed a total glance time for task completion of 20 s and 85 % of single glance should not be longer than 2 s [6].

4.1 Driving Simulator

For all examinations, the driving simulator of the Institute for Occupational Safety and Health, Germany was employed, which is modeled on real conditions of a passenger car: Position-adjustable driver and passenger seats (type: Ford Mondeo) are mounted on a basic framework. A Logitech force-feedback game steering wheel with foot pedals is located at a height-adjustable center console in front of the driver's seat. In addition, the driving simulator has a manual transmission mounted between the front seat, which was not used during the sessions (control elements used were steering wheel, accelerator, brake). For the operation of secondary tasks, a standard mount for mobile devices was attached to the center console.

The simulation software was presented on a 27" Samsung flat screen monitor with a resolution of 168×1050 pixels (32 bit). Depending on the settings of the position-adjustable driver's seat, the eye to display distance varied from 85–100 cm.

Both, the technical structures and their arrangements were based on a maximum achievable level of realism regarding operational practice.

4.2 Eye-Tracker

Eye-movements were measured using a head-mounted eye-tracker "Ergoneers Dikablis" with a sampling rate of 25 Hz, scene camera field of view of 120°, four point calibration and contrast pupil detection. A laptop computer was stored behind the participant and connected to the eye-tracker in such a way that participant head and body movements were not limited.

4.3 Software

ISO 26022 [7] makes use of the lane change test (LCT). The LCT is a simulation-aided method for measuring reactions in a dual-task laboratory setting for simulating and quantifying the effects of defined parameters of driving performance due to the use of secondary tasks, such as telematics applications at the driver's workplace.

The LCT is a reduced driving task with a 3 km standardized three-lane track, 18 lane changes and a constant driving speed of 60 km/hour [8].

In addition to the simplified model of the LCT test environment, a more realistic driving simulator rFactor 1 was employed that enabled evaluation of further performance parameters (ability to stay in lane). The run simulated an approximately 3 min drive on a two lane highway with curves and traffic signs (speed zones: 30, 50, 70 km/hour) with no flow or oncoming traffic.

4.4 Tasks

Display and execution of secondary tasks were carried out on a Samsung Galaxy Note II mobile device, which was mounted on the center console of the driving simulator.

The secondary task consisted of an input message with information of a navigation destination on the test app. All tasks were indicated by an acoustic and a visual signal. During a run in the driving simulator, an identical task occurred 2 times and was carried out by the test person immediately after presentation. The displayed pop-up window ("job update received") had to be confirmed by clicking an "ok" button. The task was considered completed once the test person had read a single-line display of the navigation destination.

A standardized radio app was used as a reference task, whose functionality was based on an analogue radio without defined broadcast slots. The tuning was carried out via 2 arrow keys for increasing and decreasing search run. During a run in the driving simulator, participants were asked a total of 2 times to skip to the next interference-free channels.

4.5 Procedure

Before each session, participants were asked to provide demographic information. Then they started with practice trials of respective driving simulation until they felt comfortable with the handling. Following the test phase 1 baseline run was carried out. Thereafter both secondary tasks (test app, radio app) were introduced to the participants. This was followed by two runs with the secondary tasks in permuted task order.

The sessions in which the eye-tracker was used, were carried out as described before with additional instruction for the method used. All runs by the participants were made while wearing the eye tracker system.

Overall, one session lasted approximately 30 min.

4.6 Participants

19 participants took part in the LCT sessions. 3 had to be removed from the data set for being statistical outliers (mean values more than 2 SD different from group average). Among the participants were 5 female and eleven male participants aged 25 to 59 years (M = 39.7 (SD = 10.3)).

16 participants took part in the rFactor 1 sessions. 3 had to be removed from the data set for being statistical outliers (mean values more than 2 SD different from group average). Among the participants were 3 female and 13 male participants aged 18 to 61 years (M = 41.7 (SD = 12.5)).

5 participants (one female; four male) using the eye-tracker ranged in age from 20 to 40 years (M = 33 (SD = 9.1)). All participants used the LCT.

All participants were in possession of a driving license and had no previous experience with the simulation software used.

4.7 Calculated and Analyzed Data

In all sessions, different data were collected: In the sessions using a reference task (test app, radio app), the driving performance of the participants was detected while the eye tracker sessions focused on the visual processing of the participants.

The driving performance of the LCT was defined by the deviation of each entire individual run in reference to a standardized racing line (MDEV). In the rFactor 1 sessions, the deviation of the absolute numbers of excess from median strip and edge line was detected as driving performance.

The assessment of glances was conducted by analyzing the single glance durations and total glance time for task completion of the test app based on absolute criteria.

5 Results

5.1 Driving Performance

For the LCT sessions, MDEV values of runs operating the test app (LCT + test app) were displayed and set in reference to the runs using the radio app (LCT + radio app).

Figure 1 shows the average MDEV recorded from the participants employing the reference task radio app (MDEV = 0.48; SD = 0.11) and the runs while operating the test app (MDEV = 0.45; SD = 0.16).

Results indicated no significant effect (p > .05) between the two MDEV values of the reference task radio app and test app.

The analysis of driving performance in rFactor 1 was determined by the ability of lane keeping of the participants and is shown in Fig. 2. Performance data of the driving task was captured of runs operating the radio App (rFactor 1 + radio app) as well as data of runs with the test app (rFactor 1 + test app).

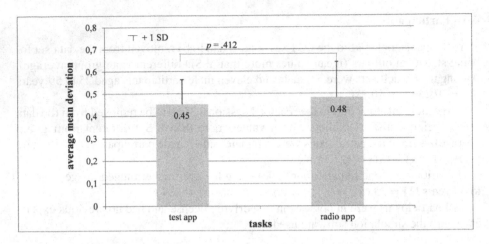

Fig. 1. Average mean deviation (LCT)

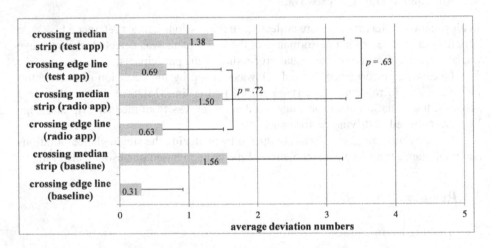

Fig. 2. Average deviation numbers (rFactor 1)

The average deviation number from the median strip in the secondary task test app was 1.38 (SD = 1.89) compared to driving with the reference radio app M = 1.5 (SD = 1.79). The average deviation number from the edge line using the test app was 0.69 (SD = 0.79) and for the reference task M = 0.63 (SD = 0.89).

The significance test showed no significant differences of exceeding both the median strip (p > .05) and the edge lines (p > .05) in the test app and the reference task radio app (see Fig. 2). In addition, Fig. 2 shows the respective deviation frequency in relation to the baseline drive without active processing of a secondary task (control condition).

5.2   Glance Behavior

The evaluation of participants' glances was carried out according to absolute criteria of AAM Guidelines. The results show that the total glance time for task completion was well below the defined limit of 20 s (see Fig. 3).

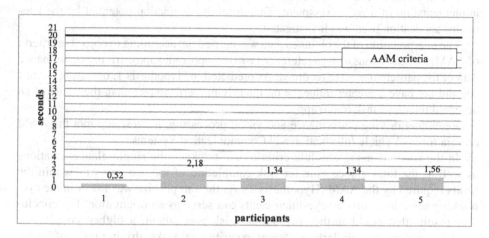

Fig. 3. Total glance time for task completion

Additionally, average single glance time was investigated as a criterion. Similarly to the total glance time, average single glance time remained below the limit of AAM guidelines of 2 s (see Fig. 4).

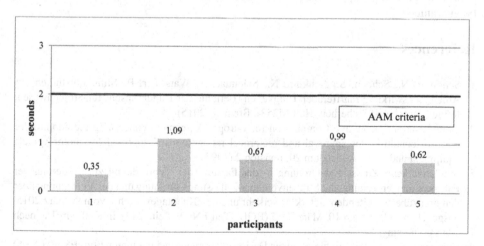

Fig. 4. Average single glance time

6 Discussion

The purpose of the present study was to find out whether the telematics application described (test app) can be considered tolerable in terms of causing distraction. Together with other factors, the issue of the distraction by telematics has high relevance for the implementation of a risk assessment. Therefore, the distraction potential by the telematics application used was investigated.

The interpretation of the obtained data was carried out according to objective criteria of AAM: In the sessions using a reference task (test app, radio app), driving performance data of the participants were recorded. As predicted in Hypothesis 1, operating the test app did not have a greater influence on the driving performance than the usage of an accepted reference task (radio app).

Regarding driving performance and visual processing, the test app met the AAM criteria for In- Vehicle Information and Communication Systems.

In the sessions using absolute criteria (eye-tracker), the single glance durations as well as the total glance time for task completion of the test app was within the limits required by the AAM (Hypothesis 2). As the sample size was lower in the eye-tracking session, results on eye-movements can serve as an orientation. For conclusive results that could further substantiate risk assessment, a higher sample size would be necessary. Similarly, different experimental tasks, driving tasks of longer duration or naturalistic driving studies under real conditions could help to corroborate the findings.

Results suggest that the use of the examined app may be considered to be a minor hazard. However, drivers should be informed of residual hazards and instructed in the appropriate use of the app, since a hazard-free use in any real driving conditions cannot be guaranteed.

References

1. Schömig, N., Schoch, S., Neukum, N., Schumacher, Wandtner, B: Simulatorstudien zur Ablenkungswirkung fahrfremder Tätigkeiten (Berichte der Bundesanstalt für Straßenwesen, Reihe Mensch und Sicherheit, Heft M253). Bremen (2015)
2. United Nations Economic Commission for Europe: Agreement concerning the adoption of uniform conditions of approval and reciprocal recognition of approval for motor vehicle equipment and parts. Addendum 20, revision 2 (1993)
3. Straßenverkehrs-Zulassungs-Ordnung in der Fassung der "Verordnung zur Änderung der Fahrpersonalverordnung, der Straßenverkehrs-Zulassungs-Ordnung und der Verordnung über den grenzüberschreitenden Güterkraftverkehr und den Kabotageverkehr" vom 9. März 2015, ausgegeben zu Bonn am 10. März 2015 (BGBl. Teil I Nr. 9, Seite 243), in Kraft am Tag nach der Verkündung
4. European Statement of Principles on the Design of Human Machine Interaction (ESoP) (2005)
5. Alliance of Automobile Manufacturers Driver Focus-Telematics Working Group: Statement of Principles, Criteria and Verification Procedures on Driver Interactions with Advanced In-Vehicle Information and Communication Systems–including 2006 updated sections. Washington, DC (2006)

6. Graf, S.: Interaktions- und Suchverfahren zur Integration mobiler Endgeräte in Fahrerinformationssysteme. München (2012)
7. ISO 26022: Road vehicles - Ergonomic aspects of transport information and control systems - Simulated lane change test to assess in-vehicle secondary task demand (2010)
8. Mattes, S.: The lane-change-task as a tool for driver distraction evaluation. In: Strasser, H., Kluth, K., Rausch, H., Bubb, H. (Eds.), Quality of Work and Products in Enterprises of the Future, pp. 57–60, Stuttgart (2003)

Patient Engagement in the Medical Facility Waiting Room Using Gamified Healthcare Information Delivery

Raheel Hassan[✉], Nathan W. Twyman, Fiona Fui-Hoon Nah,
and Keng Siau

Department of Business and Information Technology,
Missouri University of Science and Technology,
101 Fulton Hall, 301 W. 14th Street, Rolla, MO 65409, USA
{rshkvf,nathantwyman,nahf,siauk}@mst.edu

Abstract. This study explores the proposition that medical facility waiting rooms are an opportune setting to engage with and educate patients while they are waiting for care. In collaboration with emergency department (ED) personnel, we developed *ER Hero,* a tablet-based application for waiting rooms that introduces patients to ED professionals and operations through mini-games and story-like interaction. We evaluated this prototype with human participants to determine how well it performed when compared to paper-based information disclosure presenting the same information. Participants using the application exhibited increased ED knowledge, decreased nervousness, and increased interest. The gamified application outperformed a paper-based approach on some of these aspects. Quantitative and qualitative results of this study have helped identify key design factors necessary for effective engagement with patients in the medical facility waiting room, improved communication between patients and hospital personnel, and enhanced patient experience in the waiting room.

Keywords: Healthcare · Gamification · Human-computer interaction · User experience · Patient satisfaction · Patient self care · Patient relationship management

1 Introduction

Hospital visits are often stressful for both patients and their associates. The first experience and first impression of a hospital visit usually occur in a waiting room. Nearly 50 % of patients associate waiting rooms with boredom, anxiety, or both, even for patients who are visiting for chronic or routine health examinations [1]. Patients' waiting room experiences are a major concern for hospitals and healthcare facilities as patients arrive with certain expectations from the emergency department. These expectations are often influenced by individual specific, pre-encounter, and intra-encounter experiences [2]. Opportunities to engage with patients in a more meaningful and productive manner pre- and intra-encounter have presented themselves in the waiting room, with the average waiting time being 24 min nationally [3]. With the advent of technologies allowing development of gamified healthcare applications, a new opportunity has arisen

© Springer International Publishing Switzerland 2016
F.F.-H. Nah and C.-H. Tan (Eds.): HCIBGO 2016, Part II, LNCS 9752, pp. 412–423, 2016.
DOI: 10.1007/978-3-319-39399-5_39

which gives healthcare facilities a chance to have a more meaningful interaction with patients before they are seen by medical personnel. *Gamification*, or the use of "game thinking" and "game mechanics" in non-game environments [4–7] can be used as a tool to create more engaging and interactive healthcare applications. In this study, we explore the idea that a gamified informational application in a waiting room could help patients feel less anxious about and more prepared for their upcoming experience. We explore the possibility that a gamified system presenting general relevant medical health information can help decrease nervousness and strengthen future communication between the patient and their healthcare team.

This study progressed by first identifying and understanding the cognitive and affective changes that can be influenced by a gamified healthcare system. Through user research, testing, interviews, and follow up evaluations, key measures were assessed and used for data analysis. Additionally, through the interaction with and study of selected games, the process regarding how these games are designed and developed may be explored and further understood, allowing for identification of usability and user experience development techniques that may be applied to a new program catered specifically to patients in clinic waiting rooms. Ultimately, these findings would allow for the testing and research of gamified materials in hospital waiting rooms, with the purpose of understanding how the provision and dissemination of health information may benefit hospitals and clinics in their attempt to increase patient satisfaction, retention, and treatment experience.

2 Literature Review

Several studies have investigated the waiting room experience and its effects on patients. This body of research provides evidence that the medical waiting room can be a viable opportunity to engage with patients through educational means. Gamification research suggest potential for improved outcomes using a gamified approach.

2.1 Waiting Room Experience and Patient Satisfaction

Poor patient satisfaction ratings can be costly to the facility and its associated health care providers. Healthcare facilities invest heavily in the design of calming atmospheres in order to reduce the antagonistic effect that waiting rooms have on their occupants. To complicate matters, patients' fear and anxiety in the waiting room is often augmented by anticipation of painful procedures and misconceptions that may surround their medical conditions [8].

In medical emergency departments, the most important factors surrounding patient satisfaction include perceived and actual waiting times, frequency of updates regarding process and treatment, staff demeanor and attitude, environment, and perceived standards of technical care [9]. Waiting times can last up to 53 min before being seen by a healthcare provider [3], and can lead to the feeling that the increasing wait time is indeed time wasted and that care has been neglected [10]. Patient satisfaction factors can be improved significantly via greater communication among triage staff and patients, but often it is difficult to achieve optimal communication when ED waiting rooms are overburdened [11]. Limited human resources mitigate medical personnel's ability to sufficiently interact with patients to reduce the anxiety and agitation stemming from fear and unfamiliarity.

2.2 Patient Education and Engagement

Many healthcare facilities have equipped their waiting rooms with various toys, reading materials, and multimedia systems. Inclusion of these amenities can be an effective means of diverting patients' focus away from the time spent waiting and their immediate illness. Such amenities, however, are usually not informative in nature and do not address the upcoming interaction that is often the source for increased stress and anxiety. We suggest that a medium that informs patients about their visit has greater potential to decrease stress and anxiety. When an "informed, activated" patient interacts with a "prepared, proactive practice team," the management of both acute and chronic diseases is most effective [12].

Research has shown that patients' overall experience and recall of provided electronic health information improved when compared to physical and verbal instruction [13]. One study evaluated the benefits of an educational multimedia program explaining what patients should expect to encounter during their ED visit [14]. Ultimately, the research indicated that patient's satisfaction can be increased when they are introduced to the normal care plan and operations of the emergency room.

Educational multimedia used in the waiting room can provide familiarity for the patients as well as relevant information and knowledge. Patients responded to information provided positively, indicating they not only understood the content provided to them, but would confidently engage in conversations with their care providers during their treatment [15]. These outcomes may help to increase patient satisfaction, benefitting both the facility and its providers.

In studies regarding learning, the relationship between emotion and cognitive activity is quite strong. A user's affective state has a direct impact on both learning and emotional outcomes. For example, concentration and excitement can lead to increased learning and satisfaction, whereas frustration and boredom can lead to decreased motivation and effort [16]. For learning strategies, gamification is one method that has recently become a popular subject of study. Gamification has the potential to be applied to education as it engages and motivates users and actively adjusts their affect as they complete processes revolving around non-game contexts [4–6].

2.3 Application of Gamification in Healthcare Settings

Gamification refers to adding game-like elements to an otherwise utilitarian task [4]. Gamification can enhance user engagement and creation of positive patterns, including increasing user activity, social interaction, and quality and productivity of actions [17]. The incorporation of game-like features can increase motivation because the level of involvement and agency is increased for the task at hand.

While many have observed the benefits of gamification when it is successful, exactly how to leverage gamification to elicit a deep level of engagement is still unclear [18]. Exploring the application of gamification to healthcare information dissemination is an exciting opportunity that can provide valuable insight into how patients may find their waiting room experience different from the typical process. Incorporating information regarding healthcare facility visits can serve as a safe method to link with patients in the waiting room.

Patients in the waiting room are often anxious, bored, or uncomfortable. These feelings result not only from pain and discomfort brought about by their medical condition, but also by a lack of familiarity with the clinical environment. Further, patients may be afraid to ask questions due to overwhelming diagnostic results and terminology, lack of knowledge of the medical procedures they may potentially encounter, and sometimes an uninformed mistrust of their caretakers. The introduction of gamified health materials has presented an opportunity to address these drivers of fear and anxiety and engage with patients in a way that would develop a feeling of motivation, support, and inclusion in their treatment plans.

3   Methodology

To explore the potential of a gamified healthcare information education system in the waiting room, we first evaluated currently available games. Finding each option to be insufficient for this context, we developed an initial prototype in collaboration with medical professionals in a local ED. We evaluated this prototype in a quasi-experiment involving a simulated waiting room experience and online participation.

3.1   Preliminary Research

Health-focused applications on both tablets and mobile phones were assessed for educational content and interactivity. While many were very interactive, most did not provide any means of educational material beyond very basic medical care, such as placing bandages, ointment, and gauze. Other games, while educational, were geared towards practicing medical professionals, with specific diagnoses, interventions, procedures, lab results, and patient information in mind. These were deemed unsuitable for the general audience.

3.2   Prototype Development

Five ER nurses from a local hospital ED were interviewed to inform initial direction and requirements for the application. Follow-up sessions with some of these nurses and other professionals provided additional feedback as the prototyping process progressed. Table 1 outlines the design specifications that were established in the interviews.

Patients in the waiting room are informed primarily through verbal conversation or written pamphlets. Personnel are typically so busy they do not even have time to do more than the required paperwork with patients, leaving little or no time for further

Table 1. Initial design factors from nurse interviews

Design factor	Justification
Medical facility professionals and functions should be the main topics presented	Keeping information focused on the functions and operations of the ER promotes learning about the processes and people, instead of introducing uncertainty about possible diagnoses or conditions
Avoid mention of illnesses/medical conditions or specific diagnoses	Patients who are provided extraneous information about other illnesses may develop unwarranted or uninformed fears/concerns which can lead to anxiety and confusion
Keep textual content at an eighth-grade reading level	Simplified content caters to broad range of patients, reduce the likelihood of unknown, unexplained, or confusing terminology
No timers in the mini-games	Not showing a timer may prevent association with possibly a prolonged wait time
Factors specific to an emergency department	
Education of triage process, levels of acuity, and patient priority	These concepts are critical components of ER patient processing, yet are often poorly understood by patients, leading to frustration and misunderstanding
Education of pain medication approval and administration	Patients often ask for pain medication that is unwarranted. It is important for patients to understand that physicians must approve/oversee certain medication administration, especially narcotics. Patients should understand that techs, nurses, and other staff cannot simply provide pain medications to patients at any time
Help patients articulate their symptoms as well as employ a pain scale	Patients often have difficulty articulating their symptoms and describing their pain level. Providing patients with the descriptors and standards used by medical staff would aid communication
Description of patient arrivals (e.g., ambulance, ICU, personal vehicle)	Patients should be aware that the ER does not simply treat walk-ins or ambulance arrivals. Staff can often be called to other sections of the hospital to provide emergency care

interaction. The only other mentioned educational medium was informational guides provided at the end of a visit, which was said to be "vague with regards to diagnoses" and often overlooked by patients "due to the sheer amount of paperwork after treatment." The educational interventions that do occur in the waiting room are often met with frustration by patients who have performed web searches on their symptoms, resulting in varying or different information, leading to confusion and an early development of conflict.

Based on the interviews, it was determined that the application was to include educational information regarding the processes, professionals, and environment in the Emergency Room. Axure RP Pro was used to create the prototype of the game due to its iterative capabilities. The educational information included in the game was gathered from interviews of ER personnel and general ER practices of the local Emergency Department.

Figure 1 shows a sample image of an ER Hero mini-game.

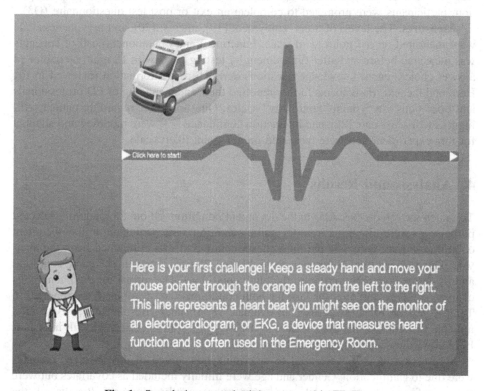

Fig. 1. Sample image and mini-game used in ER Hero

3.3 Experiment

As this research depends heavily on the function of the application, multiple iterations were required for its development. An experiment allows evaluation of the feasibility of the idea, as well as provides insight into important design factors. The experiment was designed to assess gamified prototype performance compared to a baseline that presents standard educational text.

Participants. Students (N = 104) from a midwestern university in the United States were recruited to participate in a quasi-experiment. While patients of all ages can be found in medical facility waiting rooms, focusing on a specific subset of the target population helped to make the project scope more manageable at this early stage.

Experimental Task. Participants were provided a preliminary questionnaire (Q1) when they signed up for participation. To begin participation, participants were prompted to complete a pre-test questionnaire (Q2). Half of participants were assigned to read an educational document, and the other half engaged with the ER Hero application. Both ER Hero and the educational document contained the same educational text. The application group was tested on a desktop computer. Participants were prompted to load the ER Hero game and complete the program. The baseline group was provided the document and also asked to complete the materials. Upon completion, participants were prompted to complete an exit or post-test questionnaire (Q3).

Measures. The levels of users' enjoyment [19], interest [20], and nervousness [21] were measured on a 7 point likert scale. Functional and operational recall of concepts was measured before and after engagement by testing users with 12 multiple choice (4 answer choices each) knowledge questions derived from information reviewed in ER Hero and the text. Participants further reported their understanding of ED professionals and operations via 5 point "familiarity" scales. Questionnaires regarding patient willingness to discuss care [22], and interaction confidence [23] were modified and adapted for this experiment and were measured on a 7 point likert scale.

4 Analysis and Results

To match the sample size (25) in the document condition, all but 25 randomly selected participants were discarded from the game condition. One participant in the document condition did not complete the final questionnaire and was eliminated from the analysis. This reduced total N for analysis to 49 (i.e., 25 participants in the game condition and 24 in the document or control/baseline condition). The means for the phenomena of interest before and after the task for both conditions (i.e., combined) are reported in Table 2. Paired t-tests were used to evaluate significance. Results of the evaluation indicate that educational engagement in the waiting room is correlated with increased ED knowledge, both objective and perceived.

Regression models were used to determine how much of the observed changes were due to gamification. Gender and age were initially included as covariates but were not significant in any model, and were subsequently removed. Results of the exploratory regression models are presented in Table 3. The results suggest that those who used the gamified application reported greater perceived knowledge compared to those who used plain text. Objective analysis, however, revealed no such advantage.

Both types of patient engagement (i.e., gamified application and standard text combined) were correlated with moderate increases in interaction confidence and willingness to discuss healthcare with medical professionals. The gamification in the current prototype did not outperform plain text presentation. In general, patient engagement was correlated with decreased enjoyment, with no apparent effect on nervousness or interest. However, there was no evidence that the drop in enjoyment was correlated with the gaming application, and those who used the gaming application reported significantly less nervousness and more interest.

Table 2. Outcomes of waiting room educational intervention (task)

Phenomena of interest	Pre-task estimate	Post-task estimate	Difference (95 % confidence interval)
Enjoyment	4.52	3.92	**−0.59*** (−0.33– − 0.85)
Nervousness	2.31	2.51	0.16 (−0.12–0.44)
Interest	4.34	4.57	0.24 (−0.09–0.58)
Functional recall	3.5	5.06	**1.56*** (1.15–1.97)
Professional recall	3.76	5.02	**1.22*** (0.80–1.65)
Understanding of ED functions	2.64	3.72	**1.08*** (0.79–1.37)
Understanding of ED professionals	2.38	3.68	**1.30*** (1.04–1.56)
Interaction confidence	4.82	5.33	**0.52*** (0.29–0.74)
Willingness to discuss healthcare	5.30	5.59	**0.30** (0.09–0.51)

Notes: ***$p < .001$; **$p < .01$; significant effects emphasized.

Table 3. Regression results for game (task) condition (vs. document).

Phenomena of interest	Intercept (Std. error)	Pre-task estimate (Std. error)	Game effect (Std. error)
Enjoyment	3.17*** (0.24)	0.16** (0.05)	0.08 (0.10)
Nervousness	2.04*** (0.42)	0.31* (0.15)	**−0.56*** (0.25)
Interest	2.62*** (0.68)	0.36* (0.15)	**0.79*** (0.27)
Functional recall	4.10*** (0.52)	0.25 (0.14)	0.17 (0.33)
Professional recall	3.63*** (0.56)	0.38* (0.15)	−0.09 (0.39)
Understanding of ED functions	2.58*** (0.36)	0.30* (0.12)	**0.69*** (0.21)
Understanding of ED professionals	2.18*** (0.29)	0.48*** (0.11)	**0.70*** (0.19)
Interaction confidence	2.49*** (0.52)	0.58*** (0.10)	0.11 (0.20)
Willingness to discuss healthcare	2.27*** (0.47)	0.62*** (0.08)	0.11 (0.17)

Notes: ***$p < .001$; **$p < .01$; *$p < .05$; significant game effects emphasized.

5 Discussion

As discussed in previous research related to ehealth [24–27], patients who are well informed are more likely to have a more positive experience. To support our gamified program as an effective medium for education, our analysis shows that perceived knowledge was significantly higher in those who used the application. This indicates that users who used the application recognized specific information readily and developed general confidence in their ability to understand their experiences and interactions in the ER. The visual and experiential memory formation that resulted from the use of ER Hero should allow the patients to apply their knowledge when engaging with ER professionals and experiencing medical testing such as having an imaging study performed. We hope to assess whether there is such improvement in future iterations of the application with real patients. We believe that when a user makes the associations between events and processes in the application with their real-time experience, the process becomes encoded and enters the patient's long term memory. These learning components that are built into the game augment the patient's real-life experience, as well as potential future experiences, making the entire healthcare process more relatable, and better understood and appreciated.

It was also shown that in both user groups, interaction confidence and willingness to discuss their health care issues increased. It is possible that the informative and inviting dialogue that developed between the characters within the game helped to lower these perceived communication barriers. We believe that the patient-caretaker relationship is another critical component of the patients' experience interaction. With our preliminary educational intervention, we are able to help users feel more comfortable in their interactions, which in turn makes the entire process more comfortable, and thus may have a positive effect with regard to overall satisfaction. Willingness to discuss healthcare issues is another barrier that is often not easily broken. In these results, however, the use of a gamified medium is effective in helping patients feel more confident. The resulting increased perceived knowledge and newfound confidence supports the gamified program as a viable method for patient development over a simple document.

In general, patient engagement was correlated with decreased enjoyment, with no apparent effect on nervousness or interest. The decreased enjoyment could be due to the text based nature of the application, as gamified components were intermittent amongst multiple dialogues presenting information in a story-like fashion. In our next iterations, we hope to expand the gamified nature of the application so that it is less linear in nature and is also text-heavy. With expansion of the gamified features, the next iteration should use the game aspects to bring the information to the user instead of having the game items embedded within the information. Overall, however, there was no evidence that the drop in enjoyment was correlated with the gaming application, and those who used the gaming application reported significantly less nervousness and significantly more interest.

This opposing valence in interest and nervousness brings us to believe that the gamified application creates an environment for the user to integrate themselves into. When reading a document one may find that they are still very much in the present.

We developed characters (doctors, nurses, techs, etc.) within the game who address the patient, draw them into the experience, and introduce challenges that the user invested themselves in (and in this process learned about the ED). We believe this relationship helps to create meaningful connections with the users who then become more at ease.

6   Limitations and Future Directions

This study was a preliminary test for future iterations and applications. We focused on our prototype that was deployed on desktop computers as opposed to the intended medium of a tablet. In the current study, the test subjects were not real patients and they were not situated in the hospital waiting room. They did not have a wound or ailment as a distraction. Instead, users were prompted to imagine they had an arm injury. Further, some users were tested in the controlled environment of the lab and others were tested on their own personal devices, which could have led to inconsistencies in results.

Future iterations will be designed for and tested on a tablet device. Future testing will also be conducted with real patients in order to avoid any influence of selection bias in the results. While it has been shown that an educational intervention does not improve patient satisfaction, this has not been tested with a gamified application [28], making future testing of this program essential to understanding its worth. In this study, nonetheless, the application has shown promise.

It would be beneficial to test subjects on their perceived waiting time (which is a major factor in patient satisfaction) while engaged with the application versus reading a document. Including timers within the application for mini-game segments is also an area of interest for this research project. Exploration into the measurement of time perception needs to be pursued solely in controlled conditions. Further, the application can be expanded to realms beyond the ER waiting room. Focuses such as vaccination and breastfeeding education are areas we are interested in exploring in future iterations. Once these areas are explored and the program is in real patients' hands, we will be able to understand the effect of this application on overall educational value and its effects on patient outcomes.

References

1. Gates, J.: An inquiry—aesthetics of art in hospitals. Aust. Fam. Physician 37(9), 761–763 (2008)
2. Soremekun, O., Takayesu, J., Bohan, S.: Framework for analyzing wait times and other factors that impact patient satisfaction in the emergency department. J. Emerg. Med. 41(6), 686–692 (2011)
3. Groeger, L.: ER Wait Watcher, 19 December 2014. https://projects.propublica.org/emergency/. Accessed 15 Jan 2015
4. Deterding, S., Sicart, D., Nacke, L., O'Hara, K., Dixon, D.: Gamification: using game-design elements in non-gaming contexts. In: Part 2 Proceedings of the 2011 Annual Conference Extended Abstracts on Human Factors in Computing Systems, pp. 2425–2428. ACM (2011)

5. Nah, F.F.-H., Telaprolu, V.R., Rallapalli, S., Venkata, P.R.: Gamification of education using computer games. In: Yamamoto, S. (ed.) HCI 2013, Part III. LNCS, vol. 8018, pp. 99–107. Springer, Heidelberg (2013)

6. Nah, F.F.-H., Zeng, Q., Telaprolu, V.R., Ayyappa, A.P., Eschenbrenner, B.: Gamification of education: a review of literature. In: Nah, F.F.-H. (ed.) HCIB 2014. LNCS, vol. 8527, pp. 401–409. Springer, Heidelberg (2014)

7. Nah, F., Eschenbrenner, B., Zeng, Q., Telaprolu, V., Sepehr, S.: Flow in gaming: literature synthesis and framework development. Int. J. Inf. Syst. Manag. 1(1/2), 83–124 (2014)

8. Ward, C.M., Brinkman, T., Slifer, K.J., Paranjape, S.M.: Using behavioral interventions to assist with routine procedures in children with cystic fibrosis. J. Cyst. Fibros. 9(2), 150–153 (2010)

9. Taylor, C., Benger, J.: Patient satisfaction in emergency medicine. J. Emerg. Med. 21(5), 528–532 (2004)

10. Sayah, A., Rogers, L., Devarajan, K., Kingsley-Rocker, L., Lobon, L.F.: Minimizing ED waiting times and improving patient flow and experience of care. Emerg. Med. Int. 2014, Article ID 981472, 1–8 (2014)

11. Nielsen, D.: Improving ED, patient satisfaction when triage nurses routinely communicate with patients as to reasons for waits: one rural hospital's experience. J. Emerg. Nurs. 30, 336–338 (2004)

12. Wagner, E.H., Austin, B.T., von Korff, M.: Organizing care for patients with chronic illness. Milbank Q. 74(4), 511–544 (1996)

13. Rhodes, K., Lauderdale, D., Stocking, C., Howes, D., Roizen, M., Levinson, W.: Better health while you wait: a controlled trial of a computer-based intervention for screening and health promotion in the emergency department. Ann. Emerg. Med. 37(3), 284–291 (2001)

14. Papa, L., Seaberg, D.C., Rees, E., Ferguson, K., Stair, R., Goldfeder, B., Meurer, D.: Does waiting room video about what to expect during an emergency department visit improve patient satisfaction? Can. J. Emerg. Med. 10(4), 347–354 (2008)

15. Moerenhout, T.: Patient health information materials in waiting rooms of family physicians: do patients care? Patient Prefer. Adherence 7, 487–497 (2013)

16. Sabourin, J., Lester, J.C.: Affect and engagement in game-based learning environments. IEEE Trans. Affect. Comput. 5(1), 45–56 (2014)

17. Hamari, J.: Transforming homo economicus into homo ludens: a field experiment on gamification in a utilitarian peer-to-peer trading service. Electron. Commer. Res. Appl. 12(4), 236–245 (2013)

18. Hamari, J., Koivisto, J., Sarsa, H.: Does gamification work? A literature review of empirical studies on gamification. In: Proceedings of the 47th Hawaii International Conference on System Sciences (2014)

19. Fu, F.L., Su, R.C., Yu, S.C.: EGameFlow: a scale to measure learners' enjoyment of e-learning games. Comput. Educ. 52, 101–112 (2009)

20. Renninger, K.A., Hidi, S.: The Power of Interest for Motivation and Engagement. Routledge, New York (2016)

21. Izard, C.E.: Patterns of Emotion: A New Analysis of Anxiety and Depression. Academic Press, New York (1972)

22. Maly, R.C., Frank, J.C., Marshall, G.N., DiMatteo, M.R., Reuben, D.B.: Perceived efficacy in patient–physician interactions (PEPPI): validation of an instrument in older persons. J. Am. Geriatr. Soc. 46, 889–894 (1998)

23. Potts, H.W., Wyatt, J.C.: Survey of doctors' experience of patients using the internet. J. Med. Internet Res. 4(1), e5 (2002)

24. Siau, K.: Health care informatics. IEEE Trans. Inf. Technol. Biomed. 7(1), 1–7 (2003)

25. Siau, K., Southard, P., Hong, S.: E-healthcare strategies and implementation. Int. J. Healthc. Technol. Manag. **4**(1&2), 118–131 (2002)
26. Siau, K., Kam, H.: E-healthcare in ABC county health department (ABCCHD) – trade-offs analysis and evaluation. J. Inf. Techno. **21**(1), 66–71 (2006)
27. Siau, K., Shen, Z.: Mobile healthcare informatics. Med. Inf. Internet Med. **31**(2), 89–99 (2006)
28. Sun, B., Morrissey, J., Rice, P., Stair, T.: A patient education intervention does not improve satisfaction with emergency care. Ann. Emerg. Med. **44**(4), 378–383 (2004)

Understanding User Experience Journeys
for a Smart Watch Device

Jay Lundell[1(✉)] and Corrie Bates[2]

[1] Intel Corporation, Hillsboro, OR, USA
jay.lundell@intel.com
[2] Thug Design, Portland, OR, USA
corrie.bates@thugdesign.com

Abstract. Although a great deal of work has been done in assessing User Experience, relatively little has been done in analyzing the course of User Experience over time. In a longitudinal study of the Apple Watch*, we tracked 90 people who had pre-purchased the watch for over four months of use. In this study, we identify three categories of user journeys for a smart watch, and describe users' most memorable episodes. We discuss how these user journeys and the memory of specific episodes relate to the overall assessment of the Apple Watch, and why some individuals stopped using their watch.

Keywords: User experience · Smart watch · Longitudinal study · Usability

1 Introduction

The term 'user experience' is often discussed in HCI literature, however, there are in fact many different definitions of user experience [1]. The origin of the term is usually attributed to Donald Norman, who sought to broaden the focus of usability research to encompass emotions, thoughts, and context in addition to the traditional focus on task performance. While some definitions refer to user experience as a specific episode, we prefer to consider user experience as an accumulation of a series of episodes. Thus, we prefer the UPA definition, "every aspect of the user's interaction with a product, service, or company that make up the user's perceptions of the whole." We consider User Experience as a journey that consists of numerous episodes in which the user interacts with technology or otherwise thinks about the technology or technology collateral.

Although this framework might be generally accepted by the HCI community, relatively little has been done to describe or understand how this journey unfolds. Our intent in this study is to examine the temporal aspect of user experience; how the user experience unfolds over time, and how individual episodes might contribute to an overall assessment of experience.

Another aspect of our research is to focus on the domain of wearable devices; specifically, smart watches. It is widely reported that smart watches and other wearables (such as fitness bands), have a high rate of abandonment. An often described scenario is that a user will acquire a wearable device, use it for a while, lose interest in using it, and put it away in a drawer. We are interested in determining why users do this. What

© Springer International Publishing Switzerland 2016
F.F.-H. Nah and C.-H. Tan (Eds.): HCIBGO 2016, Part II, LNCS 9752, pp. 424–433, 2016.
DOI: 10.1007/978-3-319-39399-5_40

is it about the user experience that leads a user to stop using it? What are the differences between users who continue to use a device, and those who stop? Presumably, people purchase a device with the expectation that they will use it. What experiences lead them to abandon the device? What are the differences between people who continue to use a smart watch and those who stop using it?

2 Background and Related Work

2.1 Theories of User Experience

Donald Norman proposed a three tier theory of user experience. In this framework, experience occurs at three levels: visceral, behavioral, and reflective [2]. The visceral level is the emotional reaction that the user experiences in the moment of interaction. It is the 'gut reaction' that users have, and can be elicited by the aesthetic design of a device, the touch and feel, animation, etc. Visceral reactions may be sub conscious and out of our control. The behavioral level constitutes the thoughts and behaviors we experience during interaction with the technology. At the behavioral level, it is the operations and conscious, intentional actions that affect our reactions to the experience. The reflective level occurs after the experience itself. Reflective experience is the combination of our memory of the experience and the interpretation and value judgments assigned to that memory. As pointed out by Norman and others, the reflective, remembered experience can be quite different than the in-the-moment experience [3–5].

2.2 User Experience Over Time

However, as we have already pointed out, user experience over a period of time is the culmination of many experiences. There have been relatively few studies that examined user experience over time. Kujala and Miron-Shatz [6] studied 27 mobile phone users, finding that the memory of emotions felt (both positive and negative) were overestimated, and that positive peak episodes were related to emotional responses and usability evaluation.

Karapanos et al. [7] proposed a framework of user experience over time, based on a study of 6 Apple iPhone* users over the period of one month. In analyzing respondents' daily diary entries, they proposed that three phases occur: Orientation, Incorporation, and Identification. In each of these phases, different forces are at play, and different product qualities assume more influence. In the Orientation phase, *Familiarity* is the driving force, while aspects of attractiveness and learnability play key roles in assessment of the experience. During Incorporation, *Functional Dependency* is the key driver, and usefulness and long-term usability are key to experience assessment. Finally, users enter the Identification phase, in which *Emotional Attachment* is the driving force, while personalization and social considerations assume more focus in evaluation.

Another recent study tracked smart watch usage in detail using wearable cameras to capture watch interactions of 12 participants [8]. The intent was to understand how smart watches are integrated into everyday life. This study found that the flood of messages that users received were generally seen as being brief enough that they did not take users out of the flow of most activities, and this aspect was seen as a positive by most user.

However, one question which is not addressed by any of the longitudinal studies is which types of users are likely to find longstanding value in the device, and which types of users do not. In this study, we attempt to find answers to this question.

3   Methods

3.1   Recruiting and Data Collection

We knew that even with a highly anticipated, well publicized release of a smart watch, it is a challenge to locate a large sample of users who actually would purchase the device and who would agree to participate in a long term study. Therefore, we used dscout*, a consumer research company to recruit from their panel of users people who had pre-purchased the Apple Watch prior to the release of the product. The only recruitment criteria was that they could prove that they had actually pre-purchased the watch, and that they agreed to answer the survey questions and perform certain 'missions[1]' throughout the length of the study. The initial recruit population consisted of 137 users. We wound up analyzing the data from 90 of those users who responded to all three of the detailed surveys at pre-purchase, 30 days, and 120+ days. A subset of 47 users also provided detailed, step by step data on their out-of-box experience within the first 24 h of receiving the watch, and 30 of those users also provided detailed videotaped and written evaluations of at least 12 features of the watch (a suggested list of features was supplied, but users were free to select their own features, as long as there were at least 12 selected).

We collected a wide variety of data through the four months of the study, including videotaped 'snippets' (performed by the participants using their cell phone) and on-line surveys. The surveys contained open ended questions as well as scale measures. Here are some examples of the open ended questions:

1. "In a couple of sentences, tell us why you decided to purchase the Apple Watch." (asked prior to receiving the watch)
2. "Tell us what's working or going well in this moment with the Apple Watch. Please be specific." (asked in the first 24 h of receiving the watch)
3. "Tell us what's NOT working or not going so well in this moment with the Apple Watch. Please be specific." (asked in the first 24 h of receiving the watch)
4. "In a few sentences, describe a specific experience with your Apple Watch that really stands out to you. What were you doing with the Watch? Where were you? This experience can be either a positive or a negative one, just as long as it's significant!" (asked after using the watch for about 30 days)

---

[1] A mission was an instruction to make a video and/or answer a survey at a particular time during the study. Some missions asked users to evaluate a specific aspect of the product, while others were open to any topic concerning their experience with the product.

In this paper, we will focus on a few measures: the Net Promoter Score [9], the most memorable experience, how often they wear the Apple Watch at 120+ days, and how well the watch has met initial expectations.

3.2 The Net Promoter Score

Our interest in following the user experience over time was to assess how the user experience affects the overall assessment of a smart watch. While we collected information about usability and usage, we also included the Net Promoter Score as one of our benchmark assessment methods. The Net Promoter Score (NPS) has been touted as a single score that can predict product success [9], and, while there is some controversy about its validity [10], it is generally accepted as a valuable measure. We used this because the success of smart watches as a product category is a major focus of our research, and because its definition and use is not explicitly tied to User Experience measurement, and can act as a more objective standard of product assessment. The NPS is an 11 point scale (0 to 10) in which the respondent is asked, "On a scale of 0 to 10, how likely are you to recommend this product (or brand) to a friend or family member?" We asked users to rate their Apple Watch on this scale at several points during the study.

3.3 Population

Of the 90 users, 27 were females and 63 were males. Subjects all resided in the US. Sixty subjects purchased the Sport Watch and 30 subjects purchased the more expensive Apple Watch. Subjects ranged in age from 18 to 58.

4 Results

4.1 Overall Experience Findings

At 30 days and 120+ days of owning their watch, subjects were asked to report whether they were wearing their watch more often, about the same, less often, or had stopping using the watch altogether. The data are shown in Table 1. Of the 90 subjects, 6 people reported that they had stopped using their watch versus 0 at 30 days, and 18 people reported using their watch less often than in the first week, versus 13 people at 30 days. This is a statistically significant difference (Chi Square, 8.12, $p = 0.044$).

Table 1. Frequency of using the Apple Watch at 30 days vs 120+ days

"About how often do you wear your Apple Watch NOW compared to your first week of owning it?"	30 days	120+ days
Stopped using	0	6
Less often	13	18
Same amount	62	50
More often	15	16

Table 2 shows the average Net Promoter Score for each of the categories of user. For those who stopped using the watch, the NPS average was 2.83 versus 8.62 for those who reported using the watch more often.

Table 2. Average Net Promoter Score by use of Apple Watch at 120+ days

"About how often do you wear your Apple Watch NOW compared to your first week of owning it?"	NPS avg.
Stopped using	2.83
Less often	5.50
Same amount	7.52
More often	8.63

Subjects were also asked an open ended question at 120+ days, "We know it's been a while, but after owning your Apple Watch for over 90 days, how does it stack up to your initial expectations? In a few sentences tell us - is it meeting them, exceeding them or falling short and WHY?" The 90 responses were analyzed in categorized in the following way. If the answer was unequivocal, such as "The Apple Watch has exceeded my expectations and the reason is ..", responses were categorized as such. There were two other types of responses: 1. Those who stated "exceeded", "met", or "did not exceed", but then went on to describe aspects that countered their claim, 2. Those who did not explicitly state whether expectations were met or not, but made other statements that required interpretation.

The authors conducted a session with three other HCI experts to code the responses. Dividing up the responses, two experts independently rated each response. Any disagreements were discussed between all of the experts and a unanimous decision was obtained. Table 3 shows the results.

Table 3. Apple Watch expectations assessment at 120+ days by number of responses and average Net Promoter Score.

"We know it's been a while, but after owning your Apple Watch for over 90 days, how does it stack up to your initial expectations?"	Number of responses	NPS avg.
Exceeded expectations	20	8.85
Met expectations	34	7.97
Below expectations	24	4.38
Mixed	12	6.42
Total	90	7.00

4.2 Types of User Experience Journeys

As we looked at the quantitative and qualitative data provided by the subjects, we began to see patterns in the types of journeys described. We conducted detailed user journey analyses on 30 subjects who had provided both detailed feedback on the first 24 h, and detailed feedback on at least 12 features of the Apple Watch, in addition to completing the surveys at pre-purchase, 30 days, and 120+ days. For these 30 subjects, we had a rich amount of quantitative scales, videotaped snippets of their experiences, and open ended responses to a variety of questions throughout the four months of use.

We identified three types of user journeys: 1. The Communicator, 2. The Tool Techie, and 3. The Detractor.

The Communicator. The communicator is best represented by Micah. Micah lives in Wisconsin, and previously used a Jawbone UP. Prior to receiving the Apple Watch, Micah expected to use his watch to help him stay connected to friends and family. He was a bit apprehensive about the battery life of the watch. After the first 24 h, Micah was delighted with the watch appearance, saying it was "sexy, sleek, and sophisticated." He had already tried Apple Pay* and Siri* voice recognition, and was impressed. However, his first 24 h were not without some frustration. He was disappointed that there was no sleep tracking (unlike his Jawbone), and some of the apps did not install correctly during setup. At 30 days, Micah's had changed his focus to the ability to stay connected via his watch. He reported that notifications filled him with excitement and delight, and phone calls made on the watch were clear and without distortion. The experience that most stood out to him was the episode in which he was able to share a digital "touch" with his mother, calling it a "magical moment."

With Micah and other "Communicators" like him, it was clear that the convenience of staying current with text and email, combined with new communication features such as digital touch, were what stood out to him and kept him engaged with his Apple Watch throughout the study. Micah's expectations were well met in providing him with a convenient method of staying connected, while his concerns about battery life and activity were alleviated. After four months, Micah still gave his Apple Watch a '10' on the Net Promoter Score.

The Tool Techie. The tool techie is best represented by Alex. Like Micah, he still uses his Apple Watch after four months, and gives it high ratings. However, the reasons why Alex loves his watch are quite different. Prior to receiving his watch, Alex expects the watch will be a convenient tool for easily accessing quick snippets of information. Unlike Micah, he does not list "staying connected" as one of the reasons for purchasing the watch. He expresses a bit of concern over lack of support for third party apps. For Alex, it is important that the watch provide a multitude of convenient tools and information.

In the first 24 h, Alex is impressed with the physical appearance of the watch, but most likes the Hue app that he installed, allowing him to change the light settings in his house, and the New York City public transit app, which allows him to see bus schedules from his watch. He is also excited about the activity tracking capabilities. He reports that "Everything works great, and it seems like I'm constantly finding new things I can do with it."

At 30 days, Alex cites Maps and Navigation and Siri as his 'top features', in addition to the Hue app. He feels that the remote control app for his Apple TV* is 'futuristic', but a little clumsy to use. He likes the text messaging for short messages, but reports that he winds up using his phone for most meaningful communication. Still later at

120+ days, Alex lists Fitness Tracking, Apple Pay*, and Passbook as his most important features.

One aspect we noticed with Tool Techie user types is that, although they usually wound up liking and continuing to use the watch, their reasons for purchasing the watch often did not line up with the reasons they wound up liking it. Alex, for example, did not have much in the way of clear expectations, but was simply anticipating lots of 'cool tools'.

The Detractor. The detractor is a person who is ultimately disappointed in the watch, and either stops using it or greatly reduces use of it. In all, about 27 % of users fell into this category. Tito represents a typical detractor. Prior to receiving the Apple Watch, he states that he hopes the Apple Watch is better than his Pebble* watch. Thus, unlike the communicator and the tool techie, his expectations are lower and have a bit of a negative slant.

In the first 24 h, Tito's reactions, however, are quite positive. He likes the packaging and finds it easy to put on and comfortable. He is also impressed with the accurate voice recognition of Siri. However, like many others, he is a bit disappointed by the length of time required to do the app update during setup. At 30 days, he has found few capabilities that he really likes or finds important. The feature he mentions as 'nice' is the ability to set a timer using Siri (voice). He finds value in receiving text messages, but sending them is 'tricky', and navigation via maps, in his opinion, 'sucks'. Most tellingly, his most memorable experience lacks any sort of interactivity:

> "I took my Apple Watch off for a day. Then, I kind of forgot about it. It ended up underneath the seat of my car when I found it a week later."

At four months, Tito had stopped using the watch.

For the most part, detractors all had different reasons for not liking their watch. All claimed that the watch had fallen short of their expectations, but initial expectations were often vague for these people. What is clear, however, is that all detractors failed to find a compelling usage for the watch that overrode the irritations and negative episodes. Their final assessments were not so much negative, but rueful:

> "(It is) Falling short (of my expectations). I haven't worn it for 2 months. I'm not heartbroken tho, it just seems like a flop to me. I'm perplexed. I bought the original iPhone immediately and loved it. Not the same here."

4.3   The Most Memorable Experience

After 30 days, we asked all 90 users the following question:

> "In a few sentences, describe a specific experience with your Apple Watch that really stands out to you. What were you doing with the watch? Where were you? This experience can be either a positive or a negative one, just as long as it's significant!"

We analyzed all 90 open ended responses and categorized them, looking for themes of the experience that most stood out to users. Our intention was not to identify the most liked or disliked features, but to identify themes that characterized the content of these stories. As a result, we have identified key value propositions for smart watches.

Micro Interactions. Micro interactions were often described by subjects as quick updates that appear on the watch that requires minimal attention and time. The quote below is typical of these types of episodes.

> *"Sometime in that first week of having the watch, I was doing dishes. I got a text message, I was able to look at it, used Siri to respond to it, and never actually had to stop what I was doing. The Apple Watch shines in these moments - small, quick interactions that would otherwise take me out of the moment."*

Clearly, a key aspect of the value of smart watches is that they allow for quick interactions that are prohibitive on smart phones. In a recent study, the average interaction time for smart phones was 38 s, while the average time for smart watches was 7 s [8]. One of the conclusions of that study was that smart watch interactions, unlike smart phone interactions, don't generally distract users from their current task because of the brevity of most interactions.

Unexpected Features. Many episodes were described in which the user discovered a feature that they either did not know about, or that appeared in a surprising way. For example:

> *"My real stand out experience was using the maps app. My girlfriend and I were traveling by car to a restaurant we had never been to before. I asked for directions on my iPhone and the maps app started to give me directions, however to my surprise my watch started tapping me on the wrist - it too was giving me directions even though I hadn't asked for them on my watch! I thought this was really clever and a good example of how the watch can help you in your daily life."*

Delightful Interactions. Delightful interactions were characterized by non-essential features that were nevertheless memorable in their novel interaction style. These interactions often appeared as novel effects or animations that enhanced an otherwise mundane experience (Fig. 1).

> *"I think my most significant experience with the Apple Watch was when I first opened it, turned it on, and paired it with my iPhone 6 Plus. I was wowed by the ability to pair the two devices via the camera. I was ready to go through a more tedious process."*

Social Status. Some people described experiences in which the watch features or functions were not central – rather, the experience was in the reactions users received from other people.

> *"The biggest thing that stands out to me was when I was walking in the mall with it on and some random guy walks up and asked if it was the new Apple Watch. When I said "yes" he started hollering and making a big scene about how awesome it looked. That was when I felt the best about making my decision to buy the watch."*

While some may argue that the Apple Watch in particular may be different in this regard because of the high publicity around the watch and the brand value of Apple*, we would argue that social status is an aspect of many new technologies, such as owning the latest large UHD TV or a new car.

Fig. 1. The pairing process for the Apple Watch involved 'capturing' a novel animation with the iPhone.

Discreet Updates. Discreet updates were similar to micro interactions, except the central aspect mentioned was that the interaction was not noticed by others, and the discretion afforded by the device was the central aspect of the watch.

"I was in class during a presentation and i also needed to communicate with my brother on a time sensitive matter, i was able to do it discretely with my watch without attracting the attention of my strict professor, that was when i knew i made the right purchase."

5 Discussion and Conclusion

While 27 % of the Apple Watch users reported using their watch less or not at all after 120 days, this may be in fact a very positive score for smart watches overall. To our knowledge, there have been no similar data reported on other smart watches or wearable devices. Anecdotally, the consensus seems to be that there is widespread abandonment of a variety of wearable devices – more than we have seen in this study.

The other way to look at it is that 73 % reported using the watch the same or more often than they initially used it. The most typical feeling expressed by these respondents is exemplified by the following response:

"…it's completely integrated into my life. It's lost the "wow" factor on me because I'm used to it by now, but that's not to say I'm not in love with it. I'm not as excited about it anymore because I'm accustomed to using it."

We found some evidence that supports the framework proposed by Karapanos et al. [7], that identification occurs, at least for those whose initial expectations were met. The contribution of this work is to point out some of the aspects in which technology fails in the incorporation phase. This occurs when users do not find compelling value that leads users to integrate the technology into their daily routines. Sometimes this was because an intended usage did not meet expectations, or because of an unforeseen barrier to usage arose. For example, some users reported ongoing connectivity problems or very slow responsiveness, things that were not expressed as concerns initially.

We identified three types of users and their user experience journey for the Apple Watch: Communicators, Tool Techies, and Detractors. Communicators bought the watch for the potential to enhance their ability to stay in touch, and were generally very satisfied with the value provided. Tool Techies weren't always so sure what they would find valuable in the watch, but found a variety of valuable features, from fitness tracking to payment, to IOT apps such as Hue. The Detractors were generally less enthusiastic than others before purchase, and several reported previous bad experiences with other technology. Detractors simply failed to find enough compelling value to want to use the watch on a daily basis.

We have only begun to touch on an understanding of the user experience journey for wearable devices, or for technology in general. The current study was in some ways unique given the unique nature of Apple products and the Apple enthusiasts who buy their products. Much more research into other brands and types of wearables needs to be done to generalize the findings here, but at least there is now a baseline against we can begin to compare with other products.

Acknowledgements. We wish to thank our colleagues Kahyun Kim, Anne McClard, and Cindy Merrill for their help in the qualitative analysis of the responses, and John R. Hayes for statistical analysis. Also, thanks to Paul Sorenson for his ongoing support of this project.

References

1. All About UX. http://www.allaboutux.org/ux-definitions
2. Norman, D.: Emotional Design. Basic Books, New York (2005). ISBN 0-465-05136-7
3. Norman, D.: Memory is more important than actuality. Interactions **16**(2), 24–26 (2009)
4. Bruun, A., Ahm, S.: Mind the gap! comparing retrospective and concurrent ratings of emotion in user experience evaluation. In: Abascal, J., Barbosa, S., Fetter, M., Gross, T., Palanque, P., Winckler, M. (eds.) INTERACT 2015. LNCS, vol. 9296, pp. 237–254. Springer, Heidelberg (2015)
5. Schwarz, N., Kahneman, D., Xu, J., Belli, R., Stafford, F., Alwin, D.: Global and episodic reports of hedonic experience. In: Using Calendar and Diary Methods in Life Events Research, pp. 157–174 (2009)
6. Kujala, S., Miron-Shatz, T.: Emotions, experiences and usability in real-life mobile phone use. In: Proceedings of ACM CHI 2013 Conference on Human Factors in Computing Systems, vol. 1, pp. 1061–1070, 27 April 2013
7. Karapanos, E., Zimmerman, J., Forlizzi, J., Martens, J.B.: User experience over time: an initial framework. In: Proceedings of ACM CHI 2009 Conference on Human Factors in Computing Systems, vol. 1, pp. 729–738 04 April 2009
8. Pizza, S., Brown, B., McMillan, D., Lampinen, A.: Smartwatch in vivo. In: Proceedings of CHI 2016, San José, CA, USA (2016)
9. Reichheld, F.F.: The one number you need to grow. Harvard Bus. Rev. **81**, 46–54 (2003)
10. Grisaffe, D.B.: Questions about the ultimate question: conceptual considerations in evaluating Reichheld's net promoter score (NPS). J. Consum. Satisf. Dissatisf. Complain. Behav. **20**, 36 (2007)

Designing and Evaluating Barrier-Free Travel Assistance Services

Wolfgang Narzt[1]([⊠]), Stefan Mayerhofer[1], Otto Weichselbaum[1], Gustav Pomberger[1], Astrid Tarkus[2], and Martin Schumann[2]

[1] Johannes Kepler University Linz, Altenberger Street 69, 4040 Linz, Austria
{wolfgang.narzt,stefan.mayerhofer,otto.weichselbaum,
gustav.pomberger}@jku.at
[2] evolaris next level GmbH, Hugo-Wolf Gasse 8/8a, 8010 Graz, Austria
{astrid.tarkus,martin.schumann}@evolaris.net

Abstract. Using public means of transport implies making travel arrangements. Passengers have to study route schedules and are required to obtain tickets. For these tasks (mobile) assistance services already enable travelers to comfortably compile their journeys online. Nevertheless, we consider these services inadequate providing complicated interfaces with proprietary handling concepts. People are supposed to operate technical systems and negotiate through a jungle of tariffs, although these tasks could be automated without requiring users' attention. The Be-In/Be-Out (BIBO) principle implements this consideration and enables hands-free interaction for all travelers (especially handicapped people) automatically obtaining their rights to use means of transport while boarding. The infrastructure in the vehicles detects the presence of passengers and initiates invoicing in the background. We have developed a prototypical BIBO system including elaborated privacy concepts for multimodal barrier-free transport and have been evaluating user acceptance against the background of the transparent passenger. As a result, users confirm simplification of service consumption, convenience of use, efficiency and time savings in contrast to their lack of trust.

Keywords: Be-In/Be-Out (BIBO) · Transparent passenger · User acceptance

1 Introduction

Users of public means of transport may access a manifold spectrum of ancillary (mobile) services (e.g., departure apps, delay monitors, vehicle position indicators, online ticket services, etc.) helping them to conquer necessary tasks during their journey. However, we question the appropriateness of these services: Do they really provide the support we actually need? Or are they tailored for distinguished user groups? Do we face too many complicated user interfaces? The past has revealed that many of our supporting services have a deep technical background. Because there is interconnectedness of traffic data, because there are smartphones, and because there are special sensors, technicians have developed systems for other technicians (casually expressed). Humans and their individual requirements have taken a back seat (if we consider complicated handlings at ticket

© Springer International Publishing Switzerland 2016
F.F.-H. Nah and C.-H. Tan (Eds.): HCIBGO 2016, Part II, LNCS 9752, pp. 434–445, 2016.
DOI: 10.1007/978-3-319-39399-5_41

printers, cumbersome input options at web-sites, a manifold of mobile apps that all implement different interaction paradigms, and the jungle of tariffs, in general [1, 2]).

Derived from these inadequacies, we have a vision of developing appropriate (intermodal) travel assistance services enabling self-determined and sustainable mobility. Human beings and their personal needs, their travel habits and problems – and not technical achievements – should be the main stimuli for designing supporting systems [14]. Travelers should not care about actively and consciously operating technical interfaces. They should be able to stay focused to their current activities without spending time for consuming fiddling, automatable services. Instead, the surrounding environment, equipped with unobtrusive embedded technology, should automatically and context-sensitively trigger processes "in the background", i.e. unnoticed by their users without bothering them to manually interact with complicated technical interfaces.

In the course of a national research project within the realm of the research initiative "Mobility of the Future", funded by the Austrian government from 2014 to 2016 with cooperating universities, public transportation companies and NGOs representing different person groups with special needs, we have developed new paradigms and technical systems for user guidance and conceived an emancipated mobility approach, serving people with disabilities as well as children, elderly people or humans with cognitive impairments. Our ambition was to simplify usage of public transport by new ideas and technological solutions. Users and their needs were put forward for designing innovative services that omit technology-focused interfaces and assist travelers seamlessly.

2   Be-In/Be-Out (BIBO)

For our investigations, we have picked the process of obtaining tickets as an exemplary service with immature accessibility concepts. The current process is time-consuming and complicated: Ticket printers and online platforms confuse travelers with pricing models, force them to study tariffs and require detailed route specifications for creating a ticket. They compel travelers to interrupt their journey in order to make demands on the service. Our approach for an appropriate (barrier-free) ticketing system is derived from the Be-In/Be-Out (BIBO) principle [9] enabling people to implicitly obtain tickets simply by entering and leaving public means of transport. The infrastructure in busses and trains detects the passengers' presence and issues tickets while boarding (referring to the exact routes passengers have taken). Thus, people are able to interact with a technical system while continuing their natural behavior – no need to glimpse at displays or to press buttons.

The legal prerequisites for BIBO systems are clear: A contract between transit company and passenger may come off without active acknowledgement by the passenger, so the boarding process on its own may initiate ticketing. However, the technical implementation is challenging: How can we design a system that declines operating technical interfaces? We could think of a pure infrastructure-based system, i.e. technical gadgets in the vehicles detect and identify boarding passengers with no prerequisites for travelers (whatever technology enables such a scenario – we believe that there is no mature one at present). Yet, we would not agree with direct personal identification as included in this process. It will be indispensable to have passengers carry electronic equipment identifying them, but offering encryption. This technical "companion" is supposed to be unobtrusive and should be some kind of commodity item a traveler is carrying anyway, e.g., his mobile phone. While the mobile phone is predestined due to its distribution and computing power, it must not be the exclusive gadget if we want to fulfill our demands in respect to self-determined mobility. Even if passengers are able to operate mobile phones, we should not force users to install apps and associate electronic tickets with their phone. We think of an alternative – a simple object like a key fob (equipped with transmission technology and a battery) that passengers keep in their pockets performing the equal procedure for ticket issuing as the mobile phone – and granting barrier-free service consumption quintessentially.

Considering these requirements, we chose Bluetooth Low Energy (BLE) for implementing a prototypical BIBO system [11]. BLE is available in all recent smartphone generations and is currently causing a hype in terms of autonomous identification with battery life times of more than two years (catchword: "iBeacons"). Whereas BIBO systems in their current test setups from Siemens [17], Trapeze [18] or Scheidt and Bachmann [15] are based on active Radio Frequency Identification (RFID), we are convinced that BLE is more powerful and offers better opportunities for distribution [13]. We have conducted a series of tests investigating technical feasibility and user acceptance. We have conceived a privacy concept counteracting the issue of the transparent passenger, who is wearing gadgets determining entry and exit points. In this paper, we try to quantify simplicity, manifest users' thoughts about service easement and respond to their concerns regarding privacy and misuse.

3   Economic Relevance

BIBO systems seem to have economic potential, as large producers have implemented and tested technological variants using active RFID. But how many users do BIBO systems actually address? We have put an eye on the potential target groups and tried to find out a figure characterizing the market size. The numbers of passengers using public means of transport in Vienna in 2013 give some insights (see Fig. 1.).

We do not address travelers using public means of transport on an annual basis. Annual season tickets (and also school season tickets, monthly or weekly tickets) already enable passengers to simply hop on and off arbitrarily without infrastructural technology (although, usage of such tickets is often limited to certain transit companies, and exact route payoffs are unavailable). We want to support passengers that use public means of transport every now and then (e.g., business travelers staying in a foreign town for just a day or two, or also tourists), i.e. people that obtain single tickets or short-time passes at on-site ticket printers.

The figures from our transport partner Vienna Public Transportation Systems (Wiener Linien) from 2013 classify 23.4 % of all passengers into this category (i.e. 13.9 % single tickets and 9.5 % short-time passes), so nearly ¼ of all passengers in Vienna. Considering the total passenger count of 900 Million people in 2013, we calculate a potential market size of nearly 600,000 passengers a day, just in Vienna. This means 600,000 printed tickets each day.

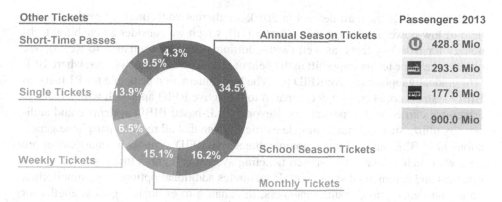

Fig. 1. Passenger Figures for Vienna (*Source: Wiener Linien, "Zahlen, Daten, Fakten", 2013, in German*)

4 State-of-the-Art

The technical basis for BIBO systems has been RFID with active tags carried by the passengers. A series of research projects use this technology for implementing prototypical and nearly market-ready BIBO systems: One of the first implementations was EasyRide [5] implemented by the Swiss Federal Railways Association, Transports Publics Genevois, Swatch, Siemens and Ascom, with comprehensive user tests (i.e. 900 participants) in Geneva and Basel. While the basic concept turned out to be applicable, the project was not pursued, as technology was immature in 2001. The project Calypso by RATP, Innovatron, ASK, Otlis, and Carris [9] ended with similar results (80 % detection rate). However, the interaction principles were promising and have been adopted in consecutive research projects, like Allfa [4] or FastTRACK [9]: Allfa is a BIBO system built by Siemens VDO, Fraunhofer, GWT and VVO and has been tested for half a year in Dresden, Germany, in busses, trams and trains with 2,000 users or about 120,000 trips, resulting in an overall acceptance rate of 68 % (20 % uncertain and 12 % rejecting). Current implementations based on (mature) active RFID enable passengers to utilize public transport systems on test routes in Switzerland or Germany with a small, battery-empowered RFID tag. The most familiar systems are Esprit from Scheidt and Bachmann with a small LED display on the tag [16], ComfoAccess from Trapeze in Switzerland [18] or the eTicket system from Siemens in Germany [17].

The BIBO concept comprises a contactless, mid-range radio-based identification and communication principle where passengers carry electronic tags. The mid-range aspect allows creating on-board architectures with a single communication unit in the center of a vehicle. Mid-range communication on the other hand is prone to uncertainty regarding reliable assignment of passenger and vehicle. This specific disadvantage can be compensated by virtual fences at the entrance doors (i.e. vicinity detectors) ensuring to unambiguously recognize boarding activities of passengers (Walk-In/Walk-Out, WIWO) [9]. Further variants are Check-In/Check-Out (CICO) systems, where users actively have to "show" their electronic tags at special entry- and exit gates, or Check-In/Be-Out (CIBO) systems as a combination of CICO and BIBO.

With the BLE standard defined in 2010, an alternative technology evolved in the field of low-power mid-range data transfer [10], which we consider an enabling technology for BIBO systems, as well (with additional benefits compared to RFID). We observe the same technology shift in the field of indoor positioning systems, where BLE [16] gradually replaces active RFID [6]. The basic interaction principle for BLE-based BIBO systems could be a copy compared to the active RFID approach with a battery-driven tag carried by the passengers. Beyond, BLE-based BIBO systems could additionally utilize smartphones as mobile entities. Given that all recent smartphone generations have BLE onboard while comparable active RFID systems in smartphones are rare, we conclude that a BLE-based ticketing system is highly attractive both from a practical and commercial standpoint. It facilitates additional options, e.g., monitoring, proprietary encryption, system openness, the chance to evaluate signal strengths for proximity determination, larger distribution channels, etc. Also the British Department for Transport considers BLE a future technology for BIBO [9] and confirms the pretended advantages in terms of hybrid applicability (both via tag or smartphone).

The BIBO approach is regarded proven (both conceptually and technologically by active RFID and also recently by BLE [11, 13]). Yet, it is unclear whether users would accept this new interaction paradigm considering the risk of becoming transparent to transportation providers. The tests in Dresden reveal that more than 30 % of the passengers reject BIBO or are uncertain about it [4]. While we do not know the reasons for denial, we assume that passengers (1) feared being traced and (2) refused to carry additional RFID tags (note that the service was unavailable on mobile phones then).

5   The Transparent Passenger

The issue of the transparent passenger addresses the technical possibility of transit companies to exactly trace customers on their routes. Hence, it is indispensable to provide an elaborated privacy concept along with BIBO systems preventing passengers from disclosing their personal data. Without that, we would create the next step towards a supervised society. Apart from the option of an anonymous prepaid version (which we do not favor, though, as it always comes along with the problem of too low balance), we present an accounting model that separates movement and personal data and therefore counteracts the transparent passenger. Figure 2 provides a closer look.

Previously we had two players: the passenger and the transit company. Now the bank enters as mediator. Passengers inform their bank that they want to use the BIBO system. The bank encodes their personal data and provides an encrypted key that authorizes passengers to use the new electronic ticket. For the transit companies, passengers are now anonymous numbers. Their movements via public transportation cannot be traced to them personally. At the end of each month the accrued costs are transferred to the bank, where the anonymous numbers are mapped back to real customers. As the bank receives no movement information, we have a clear separation of personal and dynamic data. The bank simply bills passengers for their fares. Thus, the passengers are the only persons who know where and when they traveled and how much they paid.

This principle follows the idea of Apple Pay[1] or Google Wallet[2], where the payment process is separated from the purchased wares. Payments in the US may already be carried out by this mechanism (or at least a similar version of it). Europe is supposed to adopt anonymous payments, which creates the future basis for our accounting model.

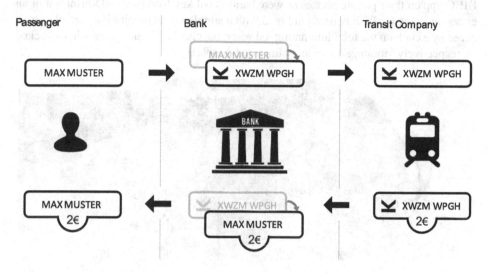

Fig. 2. Avoiding the transparent passenger

6 Research Methodology

While the basic concepts for our BIBO system were clear (i.e. hands-free interaction requiring no attention by its users, a pricing model referring to the exact routes passengers have taken, a privacy mechanism separating movement and personal data, and a technology choice including smartphones and arbitrary commodity items), we were facing two main research questions that had to be answered in the course of our research project eliminating uncertainness before the development of a product:

1. Does the proposed BIBO principle ease multimodal service consumption for users? Do passengers consider it an adequate interaction method in respect to barrier-free, emancipated and self-determined mobility?
2. Are passengers concerned about privacy? Are they worried about personal route recordings as BIBO ticketing is based on automatic technical detections, or what measures can be implemented in order to take passengers' fears?

In order to answer these questions, we have implemented a prototypical BIBO system based on BLE and installed it in busses of our transportation partners (for a detailed technical description of the system we refer to [7, 8, 11–13]). Therewith, we conducted a

---

[1] http://www.apple.com/apple-pay/.
[2] https://www.google.com/wallet/.

series of structured and application-oriented user acceptance tests in December 2015. We intended to "measure" the appropriateness of usability with persons from different target groups representing people with mobility handicaps (amongst them blind and cognitively impaired people from our NGO project partners). They could either participate using our BIBO app on their private phones or were handed out key fobs (see a 3D-print-out of an encasing frame for BLE beacons in Fig. 3 with a simple visual monitoring metaphor triggered by a click on the fob illuminating red when not checked in and green when checked in, respectively vibrating for visually impaired people).

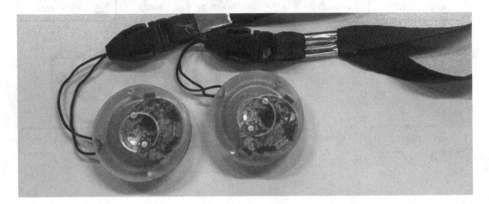

Fig. 3. Electronic key fobs

The test has been conducted with two technically equipped busses from our project partner Upper Austrian Regional Public Transportation Association on predefined routes in Linz (see an impression of the circular routes in Fig. 4 with a total distance of 12 km and 26 bus stops).

After a short oral briefing about the functions of our BIBO system the test persons were requested to hop on and off the two reversely driving busses and experience the BIBO interaction paradigm while riding (including random ticket verifications by special inspectors and live monitoring options for the passengers regarding their covered distances. In addition, they were requested to complete a questionnaire regarding simplicity of use and their confidence in such a system or their privacy concerns.

For this test we chose a small sample of test persons in order to gain first insights into usability and privacy concerns (note that the tests will be extended to a larger sample size in a second step in order to quantify the results in an acceptancy study).

We have used the System Usability Score (SUS) method [19, 20] for small sample sizes in order to deduct valid statements in terms of usable or unusable systems. The SUS method aggregates the answers of 10 standardized questions with one of five responses that range from *strongly agree* to *strongly disagree* and calculates a total score, the interpretation of which is depicted in Fig. 5: A value of 100 describes a perfect system without any usability problems. Values above 70 stand for good and excellent usability. Values between 50 and 70 may be interpreted as marginal, and anything below indicates severe problems.

Fig. 4. Test routes

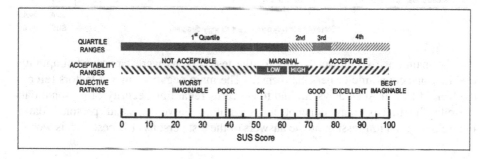

Fig. 5. System Usability Score (SUS)

7   Results

The test had been conducted with 16 test persons whereby 1 person was visually impaired and 1 person had cognitive limitations. The majority of the test persons were students aged 21 to 30 (8 persons), 4 persons were between 31 and 40 and 2 persons each were either below 20 or above 40 years. None of the test persons was older than 50 years. We had a balanced sample of persons regarding their attitude in terms of public means of transport: half of the persons enjoy using bus and train and the other half had a neutral attitude with just 1 person disliking public transport. 9 persons have not heard about the Be-In/Be-Out principle at all, 5 at least knew about smart card solutions (either CICO systems or multimodal city tickets, e.g., the Oyster Card in London) and only 2 were familiar with contactless and hands-free ticketing services. All of the test persons were technophile, i.e. they had no concerns using mobile technology. 10 persons even regarded themselves as early adopters, especially those with physical and mental impairments. Note that all of our NGO partners having disabilities (i.e. blind and visually handicapped people) exceedingly favor the use of smartphones as these devices enlarge their options for information and communication.

For these test persons we have calculated a SUS score, which is also valid for small samples. The overall SUS score for the test persons is 86.0, which attests excellent usability within the SUS scale (see Table 1).

Table 1. SUS Score

N°	SUS Question / Test Person	1	2	3	4	5	6	7	8	9	10	11	12	13	14	15	16	ø	Corr
1	would use system frequently	4	4	4	4	3	4	1	4	4	3	4	4	3	4	1	4	3,4	3,4
2	found system complex	0	1	0	1	0	1	0	0	0	1	0	0	1	0	0	0	0,3	3,7
3	thought system easy to use	4	4	4	4	4	-	3	4	4	4	4	4	4	3	4	4	3,9	3,9
4	need support of technical person	0	0	0	0	0	1	0	3	0	0	-	2	0	0	0	0	0,4	3,6
5	found functions well integrated	4	3	3	3	3	3	3	0	3	3	4	3	3	5	2	3	3,0	3,0
6	too much inconsistency	0	1	1	2	2	0	0	4	0	2	2	0	0	2	2	3	1,3	2,7
7	people would learn quickly	4	4	4	3	3	4	4	0	4	3	3	4	4	3	3	4	3,4	3,4
8	found system cumbersome	0	0	0	1	0	0	0	4	0	0	1	0	0	0	0	0	0,4	3,6
9	felt confident	1	3	3	3	2	4	4	4	4	3	4	4	3	3	2	3	3,1	3,1
10	needed to learn a lot before	0	0	0	0	0	0	0	0	0	1	0	0	0	0	0	0	0,1	3,9

Score (4 = strongly agree … 0 = strongly disagree)   Sum 34,4
                                                            SUS 86,0

The main positive impact factors for the test persons were: approved simplicity, usability and economic or personal benefit. The main negative impact factors refer to the lack of trust in such a system and to concerns regarding security of personal data (despite the transparency concept for separating movement and personal data). Figure 6 gives an impression on the answers of the test persons (1 is best … 5 is worst).

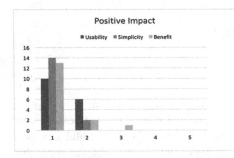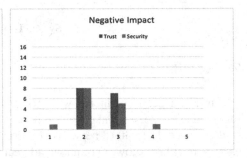

Fig. 6. Impact factors

These figures confirm simplification of service consumption (as assumed for research question 1). The test persons attested (in personal statements): simplicity, clearness, convenience of use, efficiency, time saving, the inclusion of various target groups with physical or cognitive impairments and the fact that people do not have to think about or cannot forget to obtain tickets, anymore. In contrast, the test persons were concerned about empty batteries, lost key fobs, special cases with cars or cyclists near the busses (i.e. within the signal range of BLE), still the transparent passenger (see research question 2) and monitoring live costs vs. Monthly accrued costs (including bonuses if applicable, e.g., for frequently taken routes). Some test persons also missed acoustic signals when boarding confirming the successful operation of the service.

As our testing sample was small we do not dare to compare active RFID-based vs. BLE-based BIBO systems in respect of usability and privacy. However, our investigations indicate that the majority of travelers prefer to use their mobile phones prior to beacons (10 out of 16 would use their smartphones, 3 the fobs and another 3 would not care), which implicates that our assumption in terms of required smartphone availability for BIBO systems is presumably correct, thus favoring the BLE-based version.

8 Conclusion and Future Work

Be-In/Be-Out systems are considered to represent one of the next steps towards barrier-free travel assistance services [14, 17, 18]. Their concepts are supposed to simplify utilization of public transport. As the major focus of our research, we have extended the scope of existing RFID-based BIBO systems by using an alternative, but potentially more powerful embedded state-of-the-art technology, BLE, and have developed privacy concepts counteracting the transparent passenger. Whereas the final tests for measuring the potentials of our system are still to come, we have a preliminary result with a small test group confirming simplicity and convenience of use. The users' confidence in BIBO systems is still not fully at hand inferring that special campaigns ought to eliminate people's concerns prior to commercial launch. Our attention was also called to special cases, e.g., dyschromatopsia (i.e. the disability to distinguish between red and green) hindering people to decode our monitoring metaphor on the key fobs.

Besides these deficiencies, we are also discussing options for multimodal and area-wide roll-outs, because many scientifically successful and economically valuable research projects fail because of lacking strategic or political concepts for commercial conversion. Our research project is built on a clear vision and on a solid basis concerning economic transfer from the very first:

The regulation (EC) No 1370/2007[3] [3] administers the assignment of public transport for European members. The main objectives of this regulation are *"[...] to guarantee safe, efficient and high- quality passenger transport services through regulated competition, guaranteeing also transparency and performance of public passenger transport services, having regard to social, environmental and regional development factors, or to offer specific tariff conditions to certain categories of traveler, such as pensioners, and to eliminate the disparities between transport undertakings from different Member States [...]."*

---

[3] Regulation (EC) No 1370/2007 of the European Parliament on public passenger transport services by rail and by road and repealing Council Regulations (EEC) Nos 1191/69 and 1107/70.

The translation of this regulation means that until 2021 every transit company in Europe has to acquire licenses from a central instance for operating selected routes. These licenses pre-scribe transportation frequencies, barrier-free appointments, and technical equipment for a networked integration. As the grantor of these licenses in Austria is a member of this research team, we are able to sustainably implement technical requirements for BIBO systems as part of future licenses, enabling us to roll out research results area-wide within a multimodal transportation environment.

References

1. Anderson, S., Riehle, T., Lichter, P., Brown, A., Panescu, D.: Smartphone-based system to improve transportation access for the cognitively impaired. In: 37th Annual International Conference of the IEEE Engineering in Medicine and Biology Society (EMBC), pp. 7760–7763, 25–29 August 2015
2. Carmien, S., Dawe, M., Fischer, G., Gorman, A., Kintsch, A., Sullivan, J., James, F.: Socio-technical environments supporting people with cognitive disabilities using public transportation. ACM Trans. Comput. Hum. Interact. **12**(2), 233–262 (2005)
3. European Commission: Regulation (EC) No 1370/2007 of he European Parliament and of the Council of 23 October 2007 Nos 1191/69 and 1107/70. Official Journal of the European Union, L315, pp. 1–13, October 2007
4. Gründel, T., Lorenz, H., Ringat, K.: The ALLFA Ticket in Dresden. Practical Experience of Fare Management Based on Be-In/Be-Out & Automatic Fare Calculation. In: IPTS Conference, Seoul (2006)
5. Gyger, T., Desjeux, O.: EasyRide: active transponders for a fare collection system. IEEE Micro Comp. Soc. **21**(6), 36–42 (2001)
6. Hähnel, D., Burgard, W., Fox, D., Fishkin, K., Philipose, M.: Mapping and localization with WID technology. In: IEEE International Conference on Robotics and Automation, New Orleans, USA, pp. 1015–1020 (2004)
7. Haselböck, S.: Automatische Fahrgelderhebung mit Bluetooth Low Energy im öffentlichen Personenverkehr. Master Thesis, Institut für Wirtschaftsinformatik/Software Engineering, JKU Linz, August 2015
8. Höfler, N.: Einsatz von Bluetooth Low Energy in Be-In/Be-Out Systemen - Evaluierung der Eignung zur Personenerfassung in öffentlichen Verkehrsmittel, Master Thesis, Institut für Wirtschaftsinformatik/Software Engineering, JKU Linz (2015)
9. Lorenz, H.: Be-In-Be-Out Payment Systems for Public Transport. Final Report, Dep. for Transport, UK, p. 160 (2009)
10. Mackensen, E., Lai, M., Wendt, T.: Bluetooth Low Energy based wireless sensors, pp. 1–4. IEEE Sensors, Taiwan (2012)
11. Narzt, W., Mayerhofer, S., Weichselbaum, O., Haselböck, S., Höfler, N.: Be-In/Be-Out with Bluetooth Low Energy: Implicit Ticketing for Public Transportation Systems. Intl. Conf. on Intelligent Transp, Systems (IEEE ITSC), Las Palmas (2015)
12. Narzt, W., Furtmüller, L.: Imitating near field communication with bluetooth low energy. In: Proceedings of the 13th International Conference on Advances in Mobile Computing & Multimedia (MoMM), Brussels, Belgium, December 2015
13. Narzt, W., Mayerhofer, S., Weichselbaum, O., Haselböck, S., Höfler, N.: Bluetooth Low Energy as Enabling Technology for Be-In/Be-Out Systems 13th Consumer Communications & Networking Conference (IEEE CNCC), Las Vegas (2016)

14. Riehle, T., Anderson, S., Lichter, P., Brown A., Hedin, D.: Public transportation assistant for the cognitively impaired. In: Annual International Conference of the IEEE on Engineering in Medicine and Biology Society, EMBC, pp.7585–7588 (2011)
15. Scheidt and Bachmann, ID-basiertes Be-in/Be-out Ticketing (BiBo): Die höchste Komfortstufe im Fahrgeldmanagements. INSIDER, pp. 1–4 (in German) (2014)
16. Schwarz, D., Schwarz, M., Stückler, J., Behnke, S.: Cosero, Find My Keys! Object Localization and Retrieval Using Bluetooth Low Energy Tags. In: Bianchi, R.A., Akin, H., Ramamoorthy, S., Sugiura, K. (eds.) RoboCup 2014. LNCS, vol. 8992, pp. 195–206. Springer, Heidelberg (2015)
17. Siemens: Integrated mobility with eTicketing, Answers for infrastructure and cities, Germany, pp. 1–12 (2012)
18. Zeller, R.: Trapeze renews LIO operations control system in Leipzig. Trapeze Comp. Mag., pp. 1–4 (2013)
19. Brooke, J.: SUS: a quick and dirty usability scale. In: Jordan, P.W., Thomas, B., Weerdmeester, B.A., McClelland, A.L. (eds.) Usability Evaluation in Industry. Taylor and Francis, London (1996)
20. Lewis, J.R., Sauro, J.: The factor structure of the system usability scale. In: Kurosu, M. (ed.) HCII 2009. LNCS, vol. 5619, pp. 94–103. Springer, Heidelberg (2009)

Wearable Technology in Hospitals: Overcoming Patient Concerns About Privacy

Ksenia Sergueeva[✉] and Norman Shaw

Ryerson University, Toronto, Canada
sergueeva.ksenia@ryerson.ca, norman.shaw@ryerson.ca

Abstract. Wristbands that record patients' details and track their location have recently been adopted by some Canadian hospitals. This new technology has the potential to save costs and enhance patient safety. However, there are risks that the data collected will be viewed by non-authorized users and that medical history will be exposed unnecessarily. Patients may therefore be reluctant to accept these wristbands. The purpose of this paper is to investigate factors associated with these patient concerns so that hospitals are able to overcome them and continue with the adoption of wearable technology. The Unified Theory of Acceptance and Use of Technology (UTAUT) is extended with Protection Motivation Theory (PMT) and perceived privacy risk. A qualitative empirical study, based on interviews with hospital staff, is planned to identify the themes that support this theoretical framework.

Keywords: Wearables · Hospitals · Technology adoption · Privacy

1 Introduction

Today's healthcare industry is confronted with a number of challenges, which include increasing costs [1], growing incidences of errors in medical files [2], inadequate staffing [3] and inefficient workflow [4]. Canada will have spent $215 billion on Healthcare in 2014 [1] and with the costs of healthcare continuing to grow, healthcare providers are under constant pressure to provide efficient services to a growing population using limited financial and human resources, while maximizing patients' safety [3].

Correct patient identification is one of the foundations of patient safety in any healthcare setting [5]. Misidentification of patients can occur in any location where healthcare is provided, such as hospital wards, laboratories, imaging departments and private healthcare clinics [6]. Some of the consequences of patient misidentification can result in wrong diagnosis and treatment, which could result in fatal consequences. The Institute of Medicine estimates that 98,000 deaths occur annually in US hospitals resulting from preventable medical errors including medication and diagnostic mistakes [5]. A study published in the Canadian Medical Association Journal reports that there are approximately 70,000 medical errors in Canada each year [7].

One of the proposed solutions is wristbands equipped with location based service capability ('LBS wristbands'), that help track the patient's location in healthcare facilities. LBS technology is an information system that uses real-time GPS data or Internet

© Springer International Publishing Switzerland 2016
F.F.-H. Nah and C.-H. Tan (Eds.): HCIBGO 2016, Part II, LNCS 9752, pp. 446–456, 2016.
DOI: 10.1007/978-3-319-39399-5_42

and wireless communications data to provide spatial and temporal information processing capability to end-users [8]. These LBS wristbands enable more than just the tracking of location; in addition, they can capture and record such measures as body temperature and heartbeat. These wristbands can improve patient safety and streamline patient data collection, thereby increasing patient satisfaction and reducing administrative costs for health care. The patient's wristband ID can be scanned together with the ID of the medical professional who is treating the patient. Vital indicators, including blood pressure, pulse, temperature and oxygen saturation are recorded electronically on a computer and instantly transferred into the patient's electronic medical record [9]. This technology reduces the opportunity for human error because manual entry is eliminated when the patient's data is entered directly into the computer. Medication history is stored centrally, allowing staff to access it simultaneously across multiple locations of the hospital [9]. The wristbands can also offer the unique function of alerting staff if a patient with dementia or a young child wanders away from the department [10].

One of the issues that arises with the use of this technological innovation within healthcare is the privacy concerns of the patient. If medical staff can locate the patient at any given time, then potentially non-medical staff are also able to track patient movement. Another concern is access to a patient's personal, medical information. The data on the wristband needs to be secure with only authorized access on a 'need to know' basis. LBS wristbands in a hospital setting have the potential to be a valuable addition, reducing costs and increasing patient safety, but hospitals must be cognizant of patients' concerns. Therefore, our research question is: How are hospitals able to overcome patient's' privacy concerns when implementing wristbands that track their location and store their medical information?

There have been limited studies of the acceptance of LBS wristbands in North America in the context of North American hospitals [11, 12]. We address this gap in the literature by combining the theoretical frameworks of technology acceptance [13] with protection motivation theory [14] and propose a qualitative study in a Canadian hospital. This paper is structured as follows. In the next section, we elaborate on the theoretical foundations of the research. In the following section, the propositions of this research are introduced. We then provide an overview of the proposed methodology, followed by the conclusion, which summarizes the benefits of our study.

2   Literature Review and Theoretical Background

2.1   Adoption of Location-Based Services (LBS)

Location-Based Services (LBS) refer to information systems (IS) that use real-time GPS data and cellular triangulation to identify the exact location of the user [8, 15]. LBS is used to detect the physical location, within a given perimeter, of an object that is carried or worn, thereby enabling customized services to be delivered [16]. Users may carry a smartphone with wireless capabilities or they may wear identifiable tags which can be detected by installed sensors within a defined physical space. The location can be pinpointed by an infrastructure, such as Bluetooth beacons or Wi-Fi access points.

Consumers volunteer to share their location with organizations in order to receive valued added services. For example, retailers are able to push promotional offers to those customers who have opted to provide information about themselves [17]. Sometimes it is simply the sharing of location, while at other times it is additional personal data, such as purchase preferences or, in the case of a hospital, medical information. With the growing concern about the security of shared data, consumers have to determine if the usefulness of sharing information is worth the risks of compromising personal privacy [18].

In the Technology Acceptance Model (TAM), Davis [19] posited that both perceived usefulness (PU) and perceived ease of use (PEOU) were the key variables that influence the intention to use an innovation. Many studies have shown that PU is more dominant than PEOU [20, 21] and Goodhue et al. [22] showed, with the theory of Task, Technology, Fit, that usefulness depends upon the task to be accomplished. In the context of healthcare, LBS wristbands are able to perform valuable tasks: for example, they can monitor patient conditions allowing data to be stored centrally so that medical services can be enhanced with increased safety for patients [23].

However, there are privacy concerns with LBS due to the risks of unauthorized access to personal information [12]. If data is inappropriately handled or disclosed to a third party, it poses a threat that could lead to the identification of users and their real-time location [24]. Consumers need to be assured that their data is secure; otherwise they will be unwilling to trade the usefulness of the added value provided by LBS for the risks of breach of privacy [25]. Several other researchers have examined LBS to better understand consumer attitudes toward user acceptance of the technology [12, 26, 27]. Xu & Gupta [26] examined the effect of privacy concerns and personal innovativeness and found that privacy concerns were greater when initially adopting LBS compared to concerns during continued usage. Zhou [12] suggested that service providers need to take into consideration consumers' perception of the privacy risk in order to increase the adoption of LBS.

Given that the LBS wristband is a new technology in healthcare, potential consumers may perceive a high level of privacy risk because the LBS wristband collects location and personal health data in real time.

2.2   Perceived Privacy Risks

Privacy concerns relate to the risk of unwanted disclosure of personal information [28, 29]. These concerns are relevant when studying users' intention to use LBS, as the user's location and personal information are automatically collected and shared with the provider and therefore potentially available to non-authorized parties.

Previous studies identified that privacy concerns directly affect behavioural intentions to adopt LBS [16, 26, 30]. Consumers are more willing to share information if they trust the other party, as they perceive their privacy risk to be less [27]. They are influenced by their perceived value of the services to be received when they give up some privacy, which Sutanto et al. [31] termed as the 'personalization-privacy paradox'. In addition, Dinev & Hart [32] suggested that individuals have lower privacy concerns if they perceive they have control over the use of their personal information.

Consumers judge that their medical and financial information is more sensitive than information about their demographics and shopping preferences [33]. In the context of healthcare, several researchers have proposed that privacy concerns have significant effects on the adoption of web-based healthcare services [34] and electronic health records [35]. In a study of health wearables, Gao et al. [11] determined that perceived privacy risk has a significant effect on an individual's behaviour intention.

We include the construct of perceived privacy risk in our theoretical framework as hospitals need to show patients that the value of the LBS wristbands overcomes the risks of data disclosure to non-authorized parties.

2.3 Unified Theory of Acceptance and Use of Technology (UTAUT)

There are other factors that influence technology acceptance. Venkatesh et al. [36] evaluated eight theories of acceptance, including TAM, and formulated the unified theory of acceptance and use of technology (UTAUT). In UTAUT, PU from TAM was replaced by Performance Expectancy, and PEOU was replaced by Effort Expectancy. In addition, UTAUT included social influence [37] and facilitating conditions [38] with age, gender, and experience as moderating factors. Previous tests of UTAUT have explained approximately 70 % of the differences in behavioural intention and 50 % in actual use of the technology [39].

UTAUT has been applied to the adoption of health information technologies (HIT). Examples include: the introduction of telemedicine [40, 41], the adoption of IIIT in clinics in Thailand [42], and the use of electronic medical records [43]. Kohnke et al. [44] have employed UTAUT as the theoretical foundation to understand the behavioural intention of patients and clinicians to use the eHome Health Care Telehealth equipment and found that when clinicians and patients have a higher confidence in the IT system and its support, they are more likely to accept the technology [44]. Furthermore, the study of Liang et al. [45] investigated the role of team climate in the acceptance of a computerized physician order entry (CPOE). They found that team climate influences facilitating conditions, which in turn influences the acceptance of the CPOE [45]. Hence, performance expectancy and facilitating conditions of UTAUT are important factors in studying behavioural intention to use technology in healthcare.

However, in a study of technology wearables in healthcare, UTAUT was used as the foundational theory and in addition privacy concerns and health behaviour theory were introduced to enrich this context [11]. This suggests that using UTAUT and privacy concerns alone to study health technology acceptance is not enough. Several studies of technology adoption in healthcare [11, 45, 46] have suggested that research on health technology acceptance should take both the technology acceptance theories and the health behaviour theories into account. One of the proposed health behaviour theories is Protection Motivation Theory (PMT).

2.4 Protection Motivation Theory

Because we are studying the acceptance of health information technology (HIT), we need to ensure that our framework is applicable in the context of healthcare [39].

Hence, we add Protection Motivation Theory (PMT), which is an accepted health behaviour theory [46].

PMT is a model that predicts the adoption of protective technologies and it has been applied in healthcare settings [47]. Patients are motivated to protect themselves from threats. According to PMT, there are two stages [48]. The first stage is the threat appraisal and the second stage is the coping appraisal. In the first stage, the user perceives they are vulnerable and they assess the perceived severity of the threat. For example, patients in a hospital may perceive that they are vulnerable to being mistaken for another patient. The perceived severity could be high if they fear they will be given the wrong treatment. The likelihood of adopting a protective technology increases when patients' perception of severity and vulnerability are high.

In the coping appraisal stage, users seek a means of coping with or avoiding the threat. The individual assesses the effectiveness of the technology (i.e. its response efficacy) and their perceived ability to use that technology (i.e. their self efficacy). The likelihood of adopting a protective technology increases as the levels of response efficacy and self efficacy increase. Patients need to determine that wearing an LBS wristband would be a means of overcoming the threat: they would judge that the wristband will function correctly (resource efficacy) and that they would have the ability to wear it (self efficacy). Because of perceived privacy risk, patients need to be assured that the response efficacy is not compromised by any leakage of information [48].

PMT is not exclusive to healthcare. Several research studies [49–51] have applied PMT to behavioural intention to use an innovation. Chenoweth et al. [51] identified that perceived vulnerability, perceived severity, and response efficacy are all significant influencers of user intention to adopt spyware technology. Although researchers have found that self-efficacy does not significantly influence user intention to adopt technology, they have suggested that self-efficacy would have a greater importance in health-related PMT research. Gao et al. [11] studied wearable technology and Sun et al. [46] evaluated mobile health services. Both of these studies combined PMT and UTAUT to explain adoption behaviour of health technologies. Gao et al. [11] found that medical wearable device users are more influenced by factors such as performance expectancy, effort expectancy, self-efficacy, and perceived severity in their decision to adopt a medical wearable device. In the context of our research, where we are investigating the acceptance of LBS wristbands by the patient, there is no skill required in wearing the bracelet and we therefore eliminate the construct of self-efficacy from our model.

Perceived vulnerability and perceived severity of the health-threat could influence patients: they would be more likely to accept the use of LBS technology if they perceived their health to be threatened. Patients may also be influenced by the constructs of facilitating conditions and social influence, both of which are included in UTAUT. Facilitating conditions refer to the infrastructure that supports the LBS wristband, enabling location and data to be securely collected and stored. In addition, patients are influenced positively when they see that other patients are wearing the wristbands and that medical staff expect compliance. By combining PMT with UTAUT, we are able to seek a richer explanation.

3 Research Propositions

Our research propositions take into consideration a technology acceptance theory (UTAUT) and a health behaviour theory (PMT). Our dependent variable is patients' willingness to accept LBS wristband technology. The influencing factors in our theoretical foundation are: performance expectancy, social influence, facilitating conditions, threat appraisals and perceived privacy risk. In this section we develop our propositions.

3.1 Theme 1: Performance Expectancy

LBS wristbands are an effective technology with the capability to save lives. Within our research context using LBS wristbands will increase efficiency by providing medical staff with the knowledge of where the patient is located. For example, if an infant goes missing, an alarm would sound and staff would be able to locate the missing child. Patients can be confident that they are correctly identified and will be given the correct treatment. Thus, if LBS hospital wristbands enable users to reduce threats to their health, they will be more likely to accept this technology. From previous studies on technology acceptance, most consumers tend to adopt technology on the basis of its usefulness [11]. This is supported by UTAUT, where studies have shown that performance expectancy positively influences intention to use [36]. Hence:

Proposition 1: Performance expectancy will positively influence patients' willingness to accept LBS wristbands.

3.2 Theme 2: Social Influence

Previous studies using UTAUT in LBS context, demonstrated that social influence is a significant factor to adoption intention [11]. Users conform to their peers' opinions when considering wearing an LBS wristband. Hence, if all of the patients are wearing the wristbands, individuals, who are more concerned about privacy, are more likely to accept the technology based on the actions of others. This is supported by the empirical results of UTAUT, which showed that social influence has an impact on intention to use [36]. Users comply with opinions of others who are important to them and when these others recommend the use of LBS wristbands, they will be influenced to accept the technology. Therefore:

Proposition 2: Social influence will influence patients' willingness to accept LBS wristbands.

3.3 Theme 3: Facilitating Conditions

Facilitating conditions have been referred to by Venketesh et al. [36] as the belief of an individual that the user system is supported by an organizational and technical infrastructure. In PMT, response efficacy refers to the ability of the resources to deal with the threat. In the case of LBS wristbands, the threat is the risk of a breakdown of privacy protection. Assurance for the patient that LBS wristbands work flawlessly depends on the technical infrastructure of the hospital. The patient must be confident that hospital staff are properly trained, that data is captured accurately and that it is stored securely. Medical personnel need to be trained to use the system and the resources must be in place to correct any malfunctions which may arise. From the patient's point of view, they must be assured that facilitating conditions are in place such that their identity is correctly captured and that information will not be shared with non-authorized personnel. They would then perceive that their vulnerability is low.

Proposition 3: Facilitating conditions influence patients' willingness to accept LBS wristbands.

3.4   Theme 4: Threat Appraisals

PMT's threat appraisals include perceived vulnerability and perceived severity as factors that influence the decision to accept a technology [48]. Perceived vulnerability refers to probability of the threat to their health and perceived severity refers to the degree of the harm that the consumer might endure [14]. In other words, health behaviour is influenced by responses to the threat appraisal. Sun et al. [46] showed users are more likely to adopt health technology when the threat is to their health. In our research context, we assume that users are more likely to use LBS wristbands in order to protect themselves from health-related risks. For example, if a patient has a serious health condition and they faint outside their hospital room, the staff will be able to locate them via their LBS wristband, and this, in turn, would lead to a safer outcome for their healthcare. In addition, by wearing the LBS wristband to identify themselves, patients can be more confident that threats to their health are reduced because they are matched to the correct treatment and medication.

Proposition 4: Threat appraisals influence patients' willingness to accept LBS wristbands.

3.5   Theme 5: Privacy Concerns

Individuals are willing to provide personal information for a value added service. In the context of hospital care, the value is increased hospital efficiency and enhanced patient care delivered in a safe manner. For example, the LBS wristband allows a patient to be located, but that also means that the patient may be restricted to where they can go and what they can do as they are under constant electronic observation. Patients need to be confident that the data will not be misused or accessed by non-authorized individuals. Because of the sensitive nature of health information, we propose:

Proposition 5: Privacy concerns will negatively influence patients' willingness to accept LBS wristbands.

4   Research Methodology

Our study will be based on a qualitative approach, which will involve interviews of medical staff at a local hospital. Interviews will be conducted with the aid of an interview protocol based on a semi-structured questionnaire. We plan to interview twenty medical staff to elicit their opinions on overcoming patients' privacy concerns with the use of LBS wristbands. In order to develop the interview protocol, we will be helped by subject matter experts at the local hospital. With the assistance of the hospital executives, we will recruit twenty medical staff, from different disciplines, to be interviewed. Before conducting the interviews, we will have a trial run where we will interview two individuals and solicit their feedback on the clarity of the interview questions and the protocol.

Each interview will be approximately one hour and will be recorded and subsequently transcribed. The transcriptions will be entered into NVivo, which will be used to identify themes. The analysis of the responses will then be compared to our propositions and will inform our theoretical approach.

5   Conclusion

Because patient safety is the main priority at healthcare facilities, it is important to identify the right patient. Medical errors will be decreased, costs reduced and patient satisfaction will be heightened. LBS wristbands have the potential to improve patient safety and they have just started to be implemented at some healthcare facilities in Canada. In addition to tracking patients, they can streamline patient data collection, thereby increasing patient satisfaction and reducing administrative costs for health care. However, LBS wristbands raise issues of privacy concerns about the security and confidentiality of personal medical information. The qualitative study proposed in this paper will empirically test our theoretical foundation in which we combine UTAUT and PMT with the addition of perceived privacy risks. The results will provide a more comprehensive understanding of a patient's acceptance of LBS wearable devices in a hospital setting, and provide a theoretical foundation for future healthcare technology adoption research. Hospital practitioners will benefit from a deeper understanding of the patients' concerns.

References

1. Information, C.I.f.H.: National health Expenditure Trends, pp. 1975–2014 (2014). [cited 2016 February 23]
2. Bhattacherjee, A., Hikmet, N.: Physicians' resistance toward healthcare information technology: a theoretical model and empirical test. Eur. J. Inf. Syst. **16**(6), 725–737 (2007)
3. Varshney, U.: Pervasive healthcare. Computer **36**(12), 138–140 (2003)
4. Lapointe, L., Rivard, S.: A triple take on information system implementation. Organ. Sci. **18**(1), 89–107 (2007)
5. Dhatt, G.S., et al.: Patient safety: patient identification wristband errors. Clin. Chem. Lab. Med. **49**(5), 927–929 (2011)

6. Lichtner, V., Galliers, J.R., Wilson, S.: A pragmatics' view of patient identification. Qual. Saf. in Health Care **19**(Suppl 3), i13–i19 (2010)
7. Baker, G.R., et al.: The Canadian adverse events study: the incidence of adverse events among hospital patients in Canada. CMAJ Can. Med. Assoc. j. j. de l'Association medicale canadienne **170**(11), 1678–1686 (2004)
8. Junglas, I.A., Watson, R.T.: National culture and electronic commerce: a comparative study of U.S. and German web sites. e-Service J. **3**(2), 3–34 (2004)
9. Standard, N.: Wristband idea helps keep patients safe (NEWS)(Brief article). Nurs. Stand. **26**(31), 10 (2012)
10. Stastna, K.: Is this the future of hospitals in Canada? CBC (2013). http://www.cbc.ca/news/health/is-this-the-future-of-hospitals-in-canada-1.1393280
11. Gao, Y., Li, H., Luo, Y.: An empirical study of wearable technology acceptance in healthcare. Ind. Manage. Data Syst. **115**(9), 1704–1723 (2015)
12. Zhou, T.: Examining location-based services usage form the perspective of unified theory of acceptance and use of technology and privacy risks. J. Electron. Commer. Res. **13**(2), 135–144 (2012)
13. Davis, F.D., Venkatesh, V.: A critical assessment of potential measurement biases in the technology acceptance model: three experiments. Int. J. Hum. Comput. Stud. **45**(1), 19–45 (1996)
14. Rogers, R.W.: A protection motivation theory of fear appeals and attitude change. J. Psychol. **91**(1), 93 (1975)
15. Dhar, S., Varshney, U.: Challenges and business models for mobile location-based services and advertising, pp. 121–128. ACM (2011)
16. Zhu, T., et al.: Toward context-aware location based services
17. Fard, H.K., Chen, Y., Son, K.K.: Indoor positioning of mobile devices with agile iBeacon deployment. IEEE
18. Chen, X., Pang, J.: Protecting query privacy in location-based services. GeoInformatica **18**(1), 95–133 (2014)
19. Davis, F.D.: Perceived usefulness, perceived ease of use, and user acceptance of information technology. MIS Q. **13**(3), 319–340 (1989)
20. Taylor, S., Todd, P.A.: Understanding information technology usage: a test of competing models. Inf. Syst. Res. **6**(2), 144 (1995)
21. Legris, P., Ingham, J., Collerette, P.: Why do people use information technology? a critical review of the technology acceptance model. Inf. Manag. **40**(3), 191–204 (2003)
22. Goodhue, D.L., Thompson, R.L.: Task-Technology Fit and Individual Performance. MIS Q. **19**(2), 213–236 (1995)
23. Coyle, L., et al.: Sensor Aggregation and Integration in Healthcare Location Based Services. IEEE
24. Eeckhoudt, L., Thomas, A., Treich, N.: Correlated risks and the value of information. J. Econ. **102**(1), 77–87 (2011)
25. Vicente, C.R., et al.: Location-related privacy in geo-social networks. IEEE Internet Comput. **15**(3), 20–27 (2011)
26. Xu, H., Gupta, S.: The effects of privacy concerns and personal innovativeness on potential and experienced customers' adoption of location-based services. Electron. Markets **19**(2/3), 137–149 (2009)
27. Xu, H., et al.: Effects of individual self-protection, industry self-regulation, and government regulation on privacy concerns: a study of location-based services. Inf. Syst. Res. **23**(4), 1342 (2012)

28. Li, Y.: Empirical studies on online information privacy concerns: literature review and an integrative framework. Commun. Assoc. Inf. Syst. **28**(1), 453–496 (2011)
29. Junglas, I.A., Spitzmuller, C.: A Research Model for Studying Privacy Concerns Pertaining to Location-Based Services. IEEE
30. Mao, E., Zhang, J.: The role of privacy in the adoption of location-based services. J. of Inf. Priv. Secur. **9**(2), 40–59 (2013)
31. Sutanto, J., et al.: Addressing the personalization-privacy paradox: an empirical assessment from a field experiment on smartphone users. MIS Q. **37**(4), 1141 (2013)
32. Dinev, T., Hart, P.: Internet privacy concerns and their antecedents - measurement validity and a regression model. Behav. Inf. Technol. **23**(6), 413–422 (2004)
33. Sheehan, K.B., Hoy, M.G.: Dimensions of privacy concern among online consumers. J. Public Policy Mark. **19**(1), 62–73 (2000)
34. Bansal, G., Zahedi, F.M., Gefen, D.: The impact of personal dispositions on information sensitivity, privacy concern and trust in disclosing health information online. Decis. Support Syst. **49**(2), 138–150 (2010)
35. Angst, C.M., Agarwal, R.: Adoption of electronic health records in the presence of privacy concerns: the elaboration likelihood model and individual persuasion. MIS Q. **33**(2), 339–370 (2009)
36. Venkatesh, V., et al.: User acceptance of information technology: toward a unified view. MIS Q. **27**(3), 425–478 (2003)
37. McKenna, B., Tuunanen, T., Gardner, L.: Exploration of location-based services adoption. In: 2011 44th Hawaii International Conference on 2011 System Sciences (HICSS). IEEE (2011)
38. Odeyinde, O.B.: An empirical investigation of the impact of privacy concerns and the unified theory of acceptance and use of technology on location-based services usage intention. ProQuest Dissertations Publishing (2014)
39. Holden, R.J., Karsh, B.-T.: The technology acceptance model: its past and its future in health care. J. Biomed. Inform. **43**(1), 159–172 (2010)
40. Wu, P.F.: A mixed methods approach to technology acceptance research. J. Assoc. Inf. Syst. **13**(3), 172 (2012)
41. Wu, P.F.: A mixed methods approach to technology acceptance research. J. Assoc. Inf. Syst. **13**(3), 172–187 (2012)
42. Kijsanayotin, B., Pannarunothai, S., Speedie, S.M.: Factors influencing health information technology adoption in Thailand's community health centers: applying the UTAUT model. Int. J. Med. Informatics **78**(6), 404–416 (2009)
43. Ken, T., et al.: Electronic medical records: TAM, UTAUT, and culture. Int. J. Healthc. Inf. Syst. Inform. (IJHISI) **4**(3), 55–68 (2009)
44. Kohnke, A., Cole, M.L., Bush, R.G.: Incorporating UTAUT predictors for understanding home care patients' and clinician's acceptance of healthcare telemedicine equipment. J. Technol. Manage. Innov. **9**(2), 29–41 (2014)
45. Liang, H., et al.: Understanding the influence of team climate on IT use. J. Assoc. Inf. Syst. **11**(8), 414 (2010)
46. Sun, Y., et al.: Understanding the acceptance of mobile health services: a comparison and integration of alternative models. J. Electron. Commer. Res. **14**(2), 183 (2013)
47. Prentice-Dunn, S., Rogers, R.W.: Protection motivation theory and preventive health: beyond the health belief model. Health Educ. Res. **1**(3), 153–161 (1986)
48. Floyd, D.L., Prentice-Dunn, S., Rogers, R.W.: A meta-analysis of research on protection motivation theory. J. Appl. Soc. Psychol. **30**(2), 407–429 (2000)

49. Lee, Y.: Understanding anti-plagiarism software adoption: An extended protection motivation theory perspective. Decis. Support Syst. **50**(2), 361–369 (2011)
50. Ifinedo, P.: Understanding information systems security policy compliance: An integration of the theory of planned behavior and the protection motivation theory. Comput. Secur. **31**(1), 83–95 (2012)
51. Chenoweth, T., Minch, R., Gattiker, T.: Application of protection motivation theory to adoption of protective technologies. In: Proceedings of the 42nd Hawaii Conference on System Sciences (2009)

Adoption of Smartphone Apps by Hotel Guests: The Roles of Trust and Word of Mouth

Norman Shaw$^{(\boxtimes)}$

Ryerson University, Toronto, Canada
norman.shaw@ryerson.ca

Abstract. With the growth of smartphones, organizations are increasingly engaging with their customers through mobile applications (apps). In the context of hotels, guests are able to receive enhanced services during their stay if they provide additional personal information. They learn about these applications through word of mouth and in order to adopt the apps, they must have a degree of trust in the hotel that their data is safe. In order to guide practitioners in their app development, this research empirically tests the influence of trust and word of mouth. The research model is based on extending the Technology Acceptance Model, focusing on guests' use of smartphone apps during their hotel stay. Analysis of the responses from US guests indicates that consumers learn about new applications by word of mouth and are influenced by perceived usefulness, which is mediated by trust.

Keywords: Technology acceptance · Trust · Word of mouth · Hotel smartphone apps · PLS

1 Introduction

Smartphones are 'smart' because they can be connected to the Internet and can run software applications (apps) that allow the owner to interact with other actors without geographical limitations [1]. Their penetration of the cell phone market is continuing to grow: at the end of 2014, it was estimated that 14 % of the 7 billion mobile phone subscribers owned smartphones [2, 3] while in North America, the penetration was considerably higher at 60 %. Hotel companies are recognizing that many of their guests are smartphone owners who want apps that add convenience and comfort while being reliable and secure [4]. As an example, guests are now booking online through their mobile phones and tablets [5] and, at an estimated compound growth rate of 32 %, mobile travel sales in the US will be $65 billion by 2018 [6].

The most common hotel related apps found in the app stores of iTunes and Google Play are those that support hotel and travel sales [7]. Goh *et al.* [8] sorted them into five groups: travel planning, transportation, reservations, portals/search engines, health & safety information and context-aware services. However, none of these groupings addressed the use of the apps when the guests were 'on property'. Our research addresses this gap in the literature by focusing on apps that would be used by guests during their stay. Our research question is 'what factors influence guests' adoption of mobile apps that enhance their stay while on property'.

© Springer International Publishing Switzerland 2016
F.F.-H. Nah and C.-H. Tan (Eds.): HCIBGO 2016, Part II, LNCS 9752, pp. 457–468, 2016.
DOI: 10.1007/978-3-319-39399-5_43

There are numerous apps that hotel operators and software providers could develop, such as setting the room temperature, controlling the TV, pre-ordering dinner, managing loyalty points, checking-in/checking-out and substituting as a room key [9]. The objective of our research is to guide the investment choice of those organizations that are developing and implementing apps for hotels. Our foundation is the Technology Acceptance Model (TAM) [10]. Because these hotel apps involve the exchange of personal and financial data, we add the construct of Trust [11, 12]. Furthermore, because smartphone users need to learn that an app exists and understand how it might be useful, we add the construct of Word of Mouth to the research model [13].

This paper is organized as follows. Section 2 is the literature review, where we develop our hypotheses and illustrate them with our research model. Section 3 is the research methods where we provide more background on each construct and introduce the scales by which they will be measured. Section 4 is the analysis of the results. In Sect. 5 we discus the results and include the limitations of the current research and offer suggestions for future research. We present our conclusions in Sect. 6.

2   Literature Review and Development of Hypotheses

2.1   Technology Acceptance

Our foundational theory is the Technology Acceptance Model, TAM, [10] which posits that individuals will adopt a technology if it is both useful and easy to use. [14, 15]. The model is parsimonious with two independent variables that predict intention to use: perceived usefulness (PU) and perceived ease of use (PEOU) [10]. It has been applied in many areas, including mobile commerce [16], reserving a room with the help of a mobile app [17] and using a self-serve kiosk to check-in [18]. As a well-established theory that explains an individual's adoption of a technological innovation, we have selected TAM to be the core theoretical framework of our research.

While on property, potential uses of the smartphone would be the control of room temperature, acting as a remote for the TV, ordering room service, paying for hotel services or managing loyalty points [19]. We theorize that these apps will motivate hotel guests to use their smartphones to make their stay more comfortable and we propose the following hypothesis.

- *Hypothesis 1: Perceived usefulness positively influences intention to use specialized apps at a hotel.*

Given that smartphone users are familiar with downloading apps and utilizing them, there should be no difficulty in guests learning to use new apps. Therefore, our second hypothesis is:

- *Hypothesis 2: Perceived ease of use positively influences intention to use specialized apps at a hotel.*

2.2   The Role of Trust

In an e-commerce context, McKnight *et al.* [20] defined trust as the confidence in the other party's competence, integrity and benevolence. Some of the transactions at a hotel involve exchanging personal information as well as payment data, such as credit card or loyalty membership number. Guests expect that the data exchanged for a hotel product or service will be performed in a dependable manner with minimal risk [11]. Consumers are concerned about the safety of their data when sharing personal data during their hotel stay [21]. In a qualitative study of attitudes towards mobile payments, Dahlberg *et al.* [22] found that trust was a concern and they recommended that future researchers add the concept to TAM. We therefore add trust to our model:

- *Hypothesis 3: Trust positively influences intention to use specialized apps at a hotel.*

2.3   Word of Mouth

When a new innovation becomes available, consumers need to be made aware of it. For online applications, word of mouth (WOM) is a major source of information [23]. Owners of smartphones are able to find out about new apps through word of mouth [24, 25]: personal word of mouth (PWOM) refers to the personal interaction with friends, family and colleagues; virtual word of mouth (VWOM) refers to consumers learning via the virtual world, such as postings on websites; and written word of mouth (WWOM) refers to the gathering of information via articles published in magazines and newspapers. WOM has been substituted for subjective norms [25]. Similarly for services in the hospitality industry, word of mouth is an important information source for prospective guests [26]. We add word of mouth to our model, defining it as a second order construct, comprised of PWOM, VWOM and WWOM as the first order constructs. We hypothesize:

- *Hypothesis 4: Word of mouth positively influences intention to use specialized apps at a hotel.*

2.4   Trust as a Mediating Variable

Consumers become aware of how they might use their smartphone at hotels through word of mouth. They may be persuaded that the apps will be useful at their next stay, but those who have less trust in the providers of the apps may be less open to adopting them. We hypothesize that trust is a mediating variable, mediating the effect of perceived usefulness on intention to use.

- *Hypothesis 5: Trust mediates the influence of perceived usefulness on intention to use specialized apps at a hotel.*

2.5   Research Model

The research model is shown in Fig. 1.

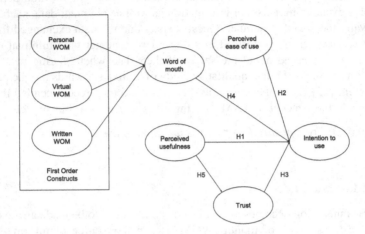

Fig. 1. Research Model for Acceptance of Smartphone Usage at Hotels

3   Research Methods

Design. With the assistance of subject matter experts, an online survey was designed to operationalize the research model. Scales were adopted from the literature. We used the services of a company that specializes in recruiting individuals who are willing to respond to surveys and be engaged with research. The final number of valid responses for further analysis by Partial Least Squares (PLS) was 597 (45 % of the surveys sent). The high response rate received in a short timeframe was due to the recruitment and retention expertise of the company that we used to manage the survey data collection and we recognize that this is a potential limitation of the study (See *Limitations*).

Data Analysis. The data collected was analyzed with PLS, which enables both the validity of the indicators and the relationships between the constructs to be evaluated. PLS was selected because it is suitable for predictive applications and theory building [27].

The first step in the analysis was the evaluation of the measurement model [28]. Internal consistency was tested by calculating Cronbach's alpha and evaluating composite reliability. The convergence of indicators on their constructs was tested by calculating the average variance extracted. In addition, the Fornell-Larcker criterion was used to test the discriminant validity of all the constructs in the model. The second step in the analysis was the evaluation of the structural model [28]. In order to include the second order constructs in SmartPLS, we adopted the repeated indicators approach [29]. To test the role of trust as a mediating variable between perceived usefulness and intention to use, we calculated the Variance Accounted For (VAF) factor, following Preacher's method of multiplying the indirect effects [30].

4 Results

4.1 Descriptive Statistics

In the sample, there were 296 males (49.6 %) and 301 females (50.4 %). Almost half the sample (48 %) was between 18 and 40 years of age and the remaining 52 % was 41 and above, with the oldest participant being 75. The age distribution is shown in Table 1. Age groups of sample.

Table 1. Age groups of sample

Ages	Number	%	Cum %
18 to 25	58	10	10
26 to 30	81	14	23
31 to 40	149	25	48
41 to 50	156	26	74
51 to 60	105	18	92
61 to 70	41	7	99
Over 70	7	1	100
Totals	**597**		**100 %**

The median length of ownership for those who possessed a smartphone was 3.5 years with 50 % having owned a smartphone for three years or more.

4.2 The Measurement Model

The cross loadings of the measurement model were calculated by the SmartPLS software and the indicators were shown to be collinear. All correlation coefficients were greater than the threshold value of 0.708 [31].

By running a Bootstrap within SmartPLS with 5,000 samples using the replacement method, the t statistic for each cross loading was calculated and in every case, the significance was $p < 0.001$.

The internal consistency of each construct was assessed via Cronbach's alpha [32], where values above 0.8 indicate reliability. The Average Variance Extracted (AVE) for each construct further confirmed the reliability of the model, where the AVE was above the guideline of 0.5 with the exception of the higher order construct, word of mouth. In addition, the Composite Reliability was above the guideline of 0.6 [31].

Discriminant validity was tested using the Fornell-Larcker score, where the AVE must be greater than the square of the correlations [33]. The results satisfied these criteria, with the exception of word of mouth due to it being a higher order construct. Table 2 compares the correlations with the square root of AVE (shown in italic bold along the diagonal).

Table 2. Values for Fornell Larcker test

Construct	Intention to use	Perceived ease of use	Perceived usefulness	Personal WOM	Trust	Virtual WOM	Word of mouth	Written WOM
Intention to use	*0.932*							
Perceived ease of use	0.634	*0.854*						
Perceived usefulness	0.736	0.714	*0.886*					
Personal WOM	0.398	0.386	0.39	*0.871*				
Trust	0.718	0.654	0.73	0.335	*0.937*			
Virtual WOM	0.434	0.43	0.444	0.466	0.384	*0.833*		
Word of mouth	0.486	0.491	0.499	0.736	0.436	0.885	*0.714*	
Written WOM	0.376	0.404	0.404	0.442	0.363	0.676	0.859	*0.879*

Note: the bold value along the diagonal is the square root of the AVE.

4.3   The Structural Model

The SmartPLS algorithm calculated the R^2 measures for each endogenous variable and the path coefficients for each path within the model. R^2 for intention to use was 0.511, which is considered moderate [34]. The significance of each path coefficient was calculated by bootstrapping with 5,000 samples using the replacement method. All hypotheses were supported with $p < 0.001$, with the exception of hypothesis 2. Results are shown in Fig. 2.

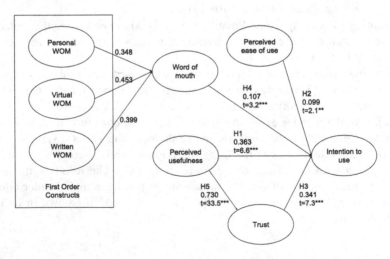

Fig. 2. Results of analysis of structural model

The effect size was calculated in a series of steps, where each exogenous variable was removed from the model in turn and the new R squared calculated. The effect size of Trust and PU were medium.

4.4   Intention to Use

In the questionnaire, participants were asked about their intention to use specific services at a hotel that would be enabled by the smartphone. See Table 3.

Table 3. Intention to use specific hotel services enabled by smartphone apps

Service enabled by smartphone	Avge score
Tracking balance of loyalty points	63
Paying with loyalty points	61
Booking hotel facilities (e.g. spa or restaurant)	60
Receiving hotel invoice digitally	59
Receiving e-coupons	58
As a room key	53
Receiving promotional messages while at hotel	51
Using the room TV to show movies and photos stored in your smartphone	45

These results provide more details about the features that guests perceive as beneficial. Participants indicated their preference to use their smartphone to save money through using loyalty points or receiving e-coupons. Although the room key is available at some properties, this service was less important to guests.

4.5   Trust as a Mediator

We ran the bootstrap with 597 observations per sub-sample and 5,000 samples with no sign changes. First the model was run without trust, and then it was run with trust. The total effect, c, without trust, was significant as was the direct effect, c'. Further, the indirect effect was calculated as the product of a and b [30].

All paths in Fig. 3 were significant at p < 0.001, leading to the support of the hypothesis that trust is a mediator. We then calculated the Variance Accounted For (VAF) factor, as follows:

$$VAF = a*b/(a*b + c')$$
$$= 41\%$$

VAF can have values from 0 % to 100 %, where 100 % represents full mediation. A value of 41 % is a moderate VAF level [28, 35]. Our conclusion is that trust as a mediator has a moderate effect on perceived ease of use, accounting for 41 % of the variance.

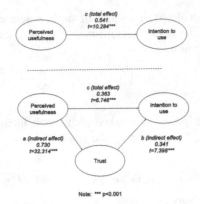

Fig. 3. Path Model for trust as a Mediator

4.6   Support of Hypotheses

Table 4.

Table 4. Support of hypotheses

1	Perceived usefulness positively influences intention to use specialized apps at a hotel	Supported (p < 0.001)
2	Perceived ease of use positively influences intention to use specialized apps at a hotel	Supported (p < 0.01)
3	Trust positively influences intention to use specialized apps at a hotel	Supported (p < 0.001)
4	Word of mouth positively influences intention to use specialized apps at a hotel	Supported (p < 0.001)
5	Trust mediates the influence of perceived usefulness on intention to use specialized apps at a hotel	Supported (p < 0.001)

5   Discussion

The main influencing factor was PU, which had a medium effect on intention to use. This is consistent with other studies of TAM [36, 37]. Individuals use systems because of the promise to deliver a desired outcome. For example, in the case of smartphone apps at a hotel, guests have indicated that they would value the tracking of loyalty points and the receipt of e-coupons.

Prior to using an IT artefact, the individual must be made aware of it. With the introduction of smartphones and their promise of simplicity, applications are being developed continuously. With limited time available to learn 'what's new', individuals learn through word of mouth by reading, listening and observing others. In our study, word of mouth was significant. Guests are made aware of hotel apps through their interaction with friends, reading articles in print and surfing the Internet for reviews.

In the analysis of our results, trust influenced intention to use, confirming the findings of Duane et al. [38]. Trust represents the consumers' confidence that their data is secure, their privacy assured and that their personal information will be safe. In addition, trust mediated the effect of perceived usefulness on intention to use. A guest may determine that there are significant benefits to using a specific functionality on their smartphone, such as using loyalty points to pay for their stay, but those guests who lacked trust would be less inclined to use such an app.

5.1 Theoretical Contribution

TAM has been the theoretical foundation of a number of studies of mobile commerce [39], which is defined as the use of mobile devices to share personal information in order to conduct an array of business services, such as location based marketing, booking a hotel room, mobile ticketing and mobile banking [39]. Secure apps at the hotel are focused on optimizing the guest experience through sharing personal information, including payment-oriented data such as credit card details and loyalty membership points. Past studies have focused on guests' use of mobile apps to access the Internet to book reservations and seek specific information about a hotel prior to their stay [40], but there have been limited studies of the acceptance of smartphone apps that add functionality and convenience for use by guests at hotels during their stay.

Our theoretical contribution is the extension of TAM to the context of guest acceptance of the use of their smartphone to enhance their experience during their stay at hotels. Smartphone users become aware of the many apps available to them through word of mouth: they see their friends using the app (an example of personal word of mouth, PWOM), they read a review from a trusted source (an example of virtual word of mouth, VWOM) or a written source (written word of mouth, WWOM). We combine the first order constructs of PWOM, VWOM and WWOM into a higher order construct, word of mouth. Although trust has been incorporated into models of TAM [11, 22], we evaluate its moderating influence on perceived usefulness where the exchange of sensitive information is involved.

A further contribution to theory is the comparison of the influence of PU to that of PEOU. Meta-analysis of the TAM literature has indicated that PU has a stronger influence than PEOU [36]. In our study we confirm these findings and agree with Gefen and Straub, who proposed that PEOU relates to the 'intrinsic characteristics of the IT artefact...whilst PU is a response to user assessment of its extrinsic outcomes' [41]. These results suggest that if the IT artefact is simple to use and its use is similar to current actions, PEOU has a minor influence on intention to use.

5.2 Limitations and Future Research

Our sample of respondents was provided by a professional organization experienced in conducting surveys with selected audiences. The participants have voluntarily offered their services and receive some form of compensation for taking a survey. Only participants who owned a smartphone were asked to complete the survey. Therefore the results reflect the responses of a population that is willing to respond to surveys and that owns a smartphone. Results may not be generalizable to the population as a whole.

A further limitation is that the research was conducted with residents of the USA, and the findings may not be applicable to other geographical or cultural groupings.

Our theoretical contribution lays the groundwork for future researchers. The model can be tested across a broader cross section of the general population. The data can be segmented to determine whether age and income are moderating factors. Further analysis could evaluate the differences between guests who stay at different types of hotels, who are more frequent travellers and who are members of a hotel's loyalty club. Recognizing that guests have a choice of where to stay and which apps to use, researchers could evaluate the perceptions of trust for apps from different providers.

6 Conclusion

Today, smartphones are smart enough to perform many transactions when connected to the Internet or a wi-fi network. Specialized apps can offer greater convenience for guests when they stay at hotels. The development of these apps depends upon providers investing further in the software and the infrastructure, and their decision to invest depends upon the acceptance by guests of this new technology. In order to understand the factors that influence guests, we have applied the Technology Acceptance Model, which is a seminal theory for an individual's acceptance of a new IT artefact. As in most exchanges of personal information, the acceptance of smartphone apps is influenced by trust. Our theoretical contribution is the extension of TAM to the context of guests' intention to use apps to enhance their experience during their stay. We have included the construct of trust and added the construct of word of mouth to explore how consumers become aware of the benefits of new technologies through word of mouth.

Many hotels have on-line websites and mobile apps that promote the brand and enable prospective guests to plan their trips and make reservations prior to their stay. Some hotels are now starting to offer their guests mobile apps to enhance their stay while on property [42, 43]. Guests are able to use their smartphones to retrieve their loyalty point balance, to pay with their points, and to receive e-receipts to keep track of their folio charges. They can check-in, open their room, control their TV and set the room temperature all from their smartphone.

The implication for hotels and their app developers is that they should focus on apps that are useful to guests during their stay. Our results show that guests are motivated to use these apps so long as they recognize their utilitarian value. In addition, as part of the design, the hotel should ensure that the app is clearly identified with their brand, in order to engender trust. Our results show that when an app requests the input of personal information, trust is an important factor.

A further contribution of this paper is that guests learn about new apps from others through word of mouth. The implication for hotels is that they should encourage this sharing of information through the hotel website, Facebook page or Twitter handle. As smartphone usage continues to grow, together with the ability of apps to offer more options, guests can look forward to improved services during their hotel stays.

References

1. Carayannis, E.G., Clark, S.C., Valvi, D.E.: Smartphone affordance: achieving better business through innovation. J. Knowl. Econ. **4**(4), 444–472 (2013)
2. IDC: Despite a Strong 2013, Worldwide Smartphone Growth Expected to Slow to Single Digits by 2017, According to IDC (2014). http://www.idc.com/getdoc.jsp?containerId=prUS24701614
3. Berkus, D.: Ride the prevailing winds… Hotel Yearbook 2014 Special Editon on Technology (2013). 76
4. Shea, T.: Unlocking opportunities…and the door to your hotel room. Hotel Yearbook 2014 Special Edition on Technology (2013). 76
5. Kucukusta, D., et al.: Re-examining perceived usefulness and ease of use in online booking: The case of Hong Kong online users. Int. J. Contemp. Hospitality Manage. **27**(2), 185–198 (2015)
6. eMarketer US Mobile Travel Sales to Increase 60 % in 2014. eMarketer (2014)
7. Chen, M.-M., Knecht, S., Murphy, H.C.: An Investigation of Features and Functions of Smartphone Applications for Hotel Chains (2014)
8. Goh, D.H., et al.: Determining services for the mobile tourist. J. Comput. Inf. Syst. **51**(1), 31 (2010)
9. Nancy Trejos, n., Hotels' mobile apps act as concierge, butler for guests, in Gannett News Service McLean (2013)
10. Davis, F.D.: Perceived usefulness, perceived ease of use, and user acceptance. MIS Q. **13**(3), 319–340 (1989)
11. Gefen, D., Karahanna, E., Straub, D.W.: Trust and TAM in online shopping: An integrated model. MIS Q. **27**(1), 51 (2003)
12. Lee, J.-H., Song, C.-H.: Effects of trust and perceived risk on user acceptance of a new technology service. Soc. Behav. Pers. Int. J. **41**(4), 587–597 (2013)
13. Jalilvand, M.R., Samiei, N.: The impact of electronic word of mouth on a tourism destination choice: Testing the theory of planned behavior (TPB). Internet Res. **22**(5), 591–612 (2012)
14. King, W.R., He, J.: A meta-analysis of the technology acceptance model. Inf. Manage. **43**(6), 740–755 (2006)
15. Ma, Q., Liu, L.: The technology acceptance model: A meta-analysis of empirical findings. J. Organ. End User Comput. (JOEUC) **16**(1), 59–72 (2004)
16. Wu, J.-H., Wang, S.-C.: What drives mobile commerce? An empirical evaluation of the revised technology acceptance model. Inf. Manage. **42**(5), 719 (2005)
17. Kwon, M.J., Bae, J., Blum, S.C.: Mobile applications in the hospitality industry. J. Hospitality Tourism Technol. **4**(1), 81–92 (2013)
18. Kim, M., Qu, H.: Travelers' behavioral intention toward hotel self-service kiosks usage. Int. J. Contemp. Hospitality Manage. **26**(2), 225–245 (2014)
19. Kim, J., Connolly, D.J., Blum, S.: Mobile technology: an exploratory study of hotel managers. Int. J. Hospitality Tourism Adm. **15**(4), 417–446 (2014)
20. McKnight, D.H., Choudhury, V., Kacmar, C.: Developing and validating trust measures for e-commerce: An integrative typology. Inf. Syst. Res. **13**(3), 334–359 (2002)
21. Wang, L., et al.: Impact of hotel website quality on online booking intentions: eTrust as a mediator. Int. J. Hospitality Manage. **47**, 108–115 (2015)
22. Dahlberg, T., Mallat, N., Öörni, A.: Trust enhanced technology acceptance model - consumer acceptance of mobile payment solutions tentative evidence. Stockholm Mobility Roundtable. Citeseer (2003)

23. Ulmanen, H.: Antecedents of and their effect on trust in online word-of-mouth: case Finnish discussion forums (2011)
24. Cheung, C.M., Xiao, B., Liu, I.L.: The impact of observational learning and electronic word of mouth on consumer purchase decisions: the moderating role of consumer expertise and consumer involvement. In: System Science (HICSS), 2012 45th Hawaii International Conference on System Sciences. IEEE (2012)
25. Parry, M.E., Kawakami, T., Kishiya, K.: The effect of personal and virtual word-of-mouth on technology acceptance. J. Product Innov. Manage. 29(6), 952–966 (2012)
26. Litvin, S.W., Goldsmith, R.E., Pan, B.: Electronic word-of-mouth in hospitality and tourism management. Tourism Manage. 29(3), 458–468 (2008)
27. Gefen, D., Straub, D.W., Boudreau, M.C.: Structural equation modeling and regression: guidelines for research practice. Commun. AIS 4(7), 1–77 (2000)
28. Hair, J.F., et al.: A Primer on Partial Least Squares Structural Equations Modeling (PLS-SEM). SAGE Publications, Thousand Oaks (2014)
29. Wetzels, M., Odekerken-Schröder, G., Van Oppen, C.: Using PLS path modeling for assessing hierarchical construct models: guidelines and empirical illustration. MIS Q. 33(1), 177–195 (2009)
30. Preacher, K.J., Hayes, A.F.: SPSS and SAS procedures for estimating indirect effects in simple mediation models. Behav. Res. Methods Instr. Comput. 36(4), 717–731 (2004)
31. Henseler, J., Ringle, C.M., Sinkovics, R.R.: The use of partial least squares path modeling in international marketing. Adv. Int. Mark. 20, 277–319 (2009)
32. Cronbach, L.J., Meehl, P.E.: Construct validity in psychological tests. Psychol. Bull. 52(4), 281–302 (1955)
33. Fornell, C., Larcker, D.F.: Evaluating structural equation models with unobservable variables and measurement error. J. Mark. Res. 18, 39–50 (1981)
34. Hair, J.F., Ringle, C.M., Sarstedt, M.: PLS-SEM: Indeed a silver bullet. J. Mark. Theory Pract. 19(2), 139–152 (2011)
35. Shrout, P.E., Bolger, N.: Mediation in experimental and nonexperimental studies: new procedures and recommendations. Psychol. Methods 7(4), 422 (2002)
36. Legris, P., Ingham, J., Collerette, P.: Why do people use information technology? A critical review of the technology acceptance model. Inf. Manage. 40(3), 191–204 (2003)
37. Turner, M., et al.: Does the technology acceptance model predict actual use? A systematic literature review. Inf. Softw. Technol. 52(5), 463–479 (2010)
38. Duane, A., O'Reilly, P., Andreev, P.: Realising M-Payments: modelling consumers' willingness to M-pay using Smart Phones. Behav. Inf. Technol. 33(4), 318–334 (2012)
39. Zhang, L., Zhu, J., Liu, Q.: A meta-analysis of mobile commerce adoption and the moderating effect of culture. Comput. Hum. Behav. 28(5), 1902–1911 (2012)
40. Kim, D.Y., Park, J., Morrison, A.M.: A model of traveller acceptance of mobile technology. Int. J. Tour. Res. 10(5), 393–407 (2008)
41. Gefen, D., Straub, D.W.: The relative importance of perceived ease of use in IS adoption: a study of e-commerce adoption. JAIS 1, 1–30 (2000)
42. Null, C.: Best Hotel Apps. In: Travel & Leisure (2014)
43. NewsRX: Intelity; Intelity Releases Mobile Hotel Platform for 21st-Century Travelers. J. Eng. 737 (2014)

Author Index

Printed in the United States
By Bookmasters